SECOND EDITION

STUDENT LEARNING IN PHYSICAL EDUCATION

Applying Research to Enhance Instruction

STEPHEN J. SILVERMAN, EdD
TEACHERS COLLEGE, COLUMBIA UNIVERSITY

CATHERINE D. ENNIS, PhD
UNIVERSITY OF MARYLAND

Editors

HUMAN KINETICS

Library of Congress Cataloging-in-Publication Data

Student learning in physical education : applying research to enhance
instruction / Stephen J. Silverman, Catherine D. Ennis, editors.-- 2nd
ed.
     p. cm.
Includes bibliographical references and index.
  ISBN 0-7360-4275-X (Hard Cover)
  1. Physical education and training--Study and teaching. 2. Learning.
I. Silverman, Stephen J. II. Ennis, Catherine D.
  GV361 .E65 2003
  796'.07--dc21

                                        2002154303

ISBN-10: 0-7360-4275-X
ISBN-13: 978-0-7360-4275-8

Acquisitions Editor: Bonnie Pettifor; **Managing Editor:** Melissa Feld; **Assistant Editor:** Susan C. Hagan; **Copyeditor:** Bob Replinger; **Proofreader:** Anne Meyer Byler; **Indexers:** Stephen J. Silverman and Catherine D. Ennis; **Permission Manager:** Dalene Reeder; **Graphic Designer:** Robert Reuther; **Graphic Artist:** Denise Lowry; **Photo Manager:** Dan Wendt; **Cover Designer:** Fred Starbird; **Art Manager:** Kelly Hendren; **Illustrator:** Accurate Art; **Printer:** Sheridan Books

Printed in the United States of America   10   9   8   7   6   5   4   3

Human Kinetics
Web site: www.HumanKinetics.com

United States: Human Kinetics
P.O. Box 5076, Champaign, IL 61825-5076
800-747-4457
e-mail: humank@hkusa.com

Canada: Human Kinetics
475 Devonshire Road Unit 100, Windsor, ON N8Y 2L5
800-465-7301 (in Canada only)
e-mail: info@hkcanada.com

Europe: Human Kinetics
107 Bradford Road, Stanningley, Leeds LS28 6AT, United Kingdom
+44 (0) 113 255 5665
e-mail: hk@hkeurope.com

Australia: Human Kinetics
57A Price Avenue, Lower Mitcham, South Australia 5062
08 8372 0999
e-mail: info@hkaustralia.com

New Zealand: Human Kinetics
Division of Sports Distributors NZ Ltd.
P.O. Box 300 226 Albany, North Shore City, Auckland
0064 9 448 1207
e-mail: info@humankinetics.co.nz

CONTENTS

Preface v

PART I OVERVIEW OF THE FIELD

Chapter 1 *Enhancing Learning: An Introduction* 3
Stephen J. Silverman and Catherine D. Ennis

Chapter 2 *How the Field Evolved* 9
Amelia M. Lee

Chapter 3 *Research: What It Is and How We Can Learn From It* . 27
Stephen J. Silverman

PART II ADDRESSING THE NEEDS OF DIVERSE STUDENTS

Chapter 4 *Context of Schools* 43
LeaAnn Tyson Martin

Chapter 5 *Student Learning and the Social Construction of Gender in Sport and Physical Education* 67
David Kirk

Chapter 6 *Students With Disabilities in Physical Education* 83
E. William Vogler

PART III PROMOTING STUDENT LEARNING

Chapter 7 *Using Curriculum to Enhance Student Learning* 109
Catherine D. Ennis

Chapter 8 *Standards-Based Program Design: Creating a Congruent Guide for Student Learning* . . 129
Leslie T. Lambert

Chapter 9 *Student Issues in Physical Education Classes: Attitudes, Cognition, and Motivation* 147
Melinda A. Solmon

Chapter 10   *Effective Instruction in Physical Education* 165
                Judith E. Rink

Chapter 11   *Assessment in Physical Education: The Future Is Now!* 187
                Terry M. Wood

PART IV   PROMOTING VALUED OUTCOMES
AND ATTITUDES

Chapter 12   *Health-Related Physical Education:*
                Physical Activity, Fitness, and Wellness 207
                Thomas L. McKenzie

Chapter 13   *Teaching Sport Within Physical Education* 227
                Peter A. Hastie

Chapter 14   *Teaching Personal and Social Responsibility*
                in Physical Education 241
                Don Hellison

Chapter 15   *Interdisciplinary Curriculum in Physical Education:*
                Possibilities and Problems 255
                Judith H. Placek

PART V   LEARNING TO TEACH:
AN ONGOING PROCESS

Chapter 16   *Learning to Teach Physical Education* 275
                Mary O'Sullivan

Chapter 17   *Teachers' Knowledge Construction* 295
                Inez Rovegno

Chapter 18   *Organizational Socialization:*
                Factors Affecting Beginning Teachers 311
                Sandra A. Stroot and Christine E. Whipple

Chapter 19   *Enhancing Learning: An Epilogue* 329
                Catherine D. Ennis and Stephen J. Silverman

Author Index   331   •   *Subject Index*   337

About the Editors   345   •   *About the Contributors*   347

PREFACE

Those who teach, serve as instructional supervisors, develop curricula, work as teacher educators, or study physical education are engaged in an enterprise that has the goal of helping students become physically educated. When students develop the skill, knowledge, and attitude that help them participate in physical activity, we are doing what our national organizations and most of us as individuals promote as the goals for physical education. Student learning—in a variety of domains—is the key to effective physical education. In turn, the accumulated body of research helps us understand the factors that may influence and enhance learning.

This book describes the research base about teaching, curriculum development, and teacher education. Although these three areas may appear distinct when reading about them in a textbook or research journal, we know that they intersect in multiple ways to provide a rich teaching and learning environment for students in physical education. A large body of research about physical education is now available to provide information for both practitioners and researchers. We think it is important to synthesize this information and provide it in a practical, readable format for students, practitioners, and researchers. We are convinced that physical educators can immediately apply some of these findings to their classes and that other information can help reflective practitioners refocus their thinking, gradually and purposefully enhancing the learning environment for their students. To this end, we have asked leading scholars in the field to explain and summarize the research findings in the chapters that follow. These chapters address many issues—some provide background about our field, schools, and research, and many directly address teaching and learning in physical education and physical education teacher education.

This book is directed to graduate students who need a comprehensive introduction to the area, physical education teachers, physical education supervisors, and teacher educators. We believe that interested practitioners can understand research when it is written with practical purposes in mind. The authors of each of the chapters wrote with that goal in mind—to summarize what we know and address what the results mean for practice. In this edition of the book we have extended this emphasis, asking authors to end each chapter with a section that provides implications for practice that highlight major conclusions. We hope these will reinforce the focus in each chapter and, perhaps, serve as a springboard for discussions of issues in physical education practice and research.

We have organized the book in five parts. **Part I** provides an overview of the field. In chapter 1 we provide definitions and frame the discussion that occurs in the rest of the book. Chapter 2, by Amelia Lee, and chapter 3, by Steve Silverman, focus on the history of the subdiscipline and on obtaining and using research, respectively. These chapters provide a foundation for reading the remainder of the book.

Part II deals with issues related to diversity in school settings. We believe that every school is different and that diversity, while sometimes a challenge, is manageable. Diversity clearly is an important consideration in educational decision making. Chapter 4, by LeaAnn Tyson Martin, addresses the context of schools in our society. Chapter 5, by David Kirk, and chapter 6, by Bill Vogler, address the specific issues of gender and students with disabilities in physical education. These chapters seek to enhance instructional sensitivity and improve teachers' abilities to individualize content and instruction as necessary for each student.

Part III deals with promoting student learning. In chapter 7, Cathy Ennis discusses ways that context and values influence curriculum development. Chapter 8, by Leslie Lambert, addresses the process of curriculum development and standards-based program design. Melinda Solmon, in chapter 9, discusses student cognition, motivation, and attitude and how physical education addresses these issues. In chapter 10 Judy Rink summarizes what we know about effective teaching of motor skill. In the final chapter in this section Terry Wood discusses the use of assessment in promoting learning. Unfortunately, we have found that the assessment process is often divorced from the learning process. We believe that need not be the case. The chapters in this section provide a great deal of information about what promotes student learning in physical education.

Part IV presents programmatic approaches to physical education that have proven track records. The authors of these chapters are scholars with extensive practical experience in teaching various aspects of physical education. Fitness and physical activity have received much attention in recent years. Thom McKenzie focuses on the rationale and design of health-related approaches to physical education in chapter 12. Peter Hastie discusses the several innovative models associated with the teaching of sport in chapter 13. In chapter 14, Don Hellison discusses teaching of self- and social responsibility. Don's extensive experience in inner-city school and recreational programs brings to his chapter a special sense of what can be accomplished through physical activity. Judy Placek, in the last chapter in this section, examines several strategies for integrating physical education with other curricular areas.

Part V deals with teacher training and development. As the title ("Learning to Teach: An Ongoing Process") suggests, we view this as a continuing and fluid process. Mary O'Sullivan, in the first chapter in the section, discusses the challenges and possibilities inherent in preservice teacher education. This is followed, in chapter 17, by Inez Rovegno's discussion of how teachers construct knowledge and understanding about their professional practice. In chapter 18, Sandy Stroot and Christine Whipple discuss the literature on socialization into teaching, or how students learn to think of themselves as professional physical educators. We hope that this research can help beginning teachers and future teacher educators understand the induction experience. The final chapter is a short epilogue that pulls together the major constructs of complexity, connection, and diversity that serve to organize and integrate the pedagogical areas of curriculum, teaching, and teacher education.

The contributors to this volume are the leading scholars in these three fields. We greatly appreciate their willingness to contribute to this book and their work in helping us finish this edition. We hope you find their work as interesting as we do and that you will use the information to enhance student learning in physical education.

PART I

OVERVIEW OF THE FIELD

CHAPTER ONE

ENHANCING LEARNING: AN INTRODUCTION

Stephen J. Silverman • *Catherine D. Ennis*

Physical education is an integral part of the curriculum in most schools. Although state-mandated requirements differ (National Association for Sport and Physical Education [NASPE], 2001), many resources are devoted to physical education. In an age of accountability and educational reform, we want all students enrolled in physical education courses to receive quality instruction throughout a well-designed curriculum taught by dedicated professional physical educators. Although some may view this goal as unattainable, we believe that communication between professionals in physical education can influence the quality of physical education programs. This edition of this book continues our efforts to integrate and synthesize the research on teaching, curriculum, and teacher education in physical education. The volume of research continues to grow and provides information that can help teachers and teacher educators make informed decisions.

The field of research in physical education pedagogy, sometimes called sport pedagogy in the international community, has made great strides over the past few decades. Thirty years ago, few specialists were trained to do research on physical education pedagogy. The field was characterized by a lack of research that could be used by teachers, teacher educators, or curriculum developers. At that time, Locke (1977, p. 2) concluded, "the profession has no cumulative body of knowledge about teaching motor skills or any of the cognitive and affective learnings which are adjunct to skill acquisition." Although Locke was bemoaning the progress the field had made, he saw a future: The title of his paper was "Research on Teaching Physical Education: New Hope for a Dismal Science."

We have, in large part, realized much of that hope. As evidenced by the contributors to this book, many well-trained researchers now work in the field of physical education pedagogy. Although there once were few focused research efforts, many scholars now specialize in a specific subarea within the field. As this book makes clear, the amount and quality of research has grown substantially. In the first edition of this book, we cited Piéron and Graham (1984), who said that the area was in its adolescence in the 1980s and that in the 1990s we thought the field had reached young adulthood. The growth of physical education pedagogy since then suggests that the field could now be characterized as firmly into adulthood. A great deal of maturing is yet to come, but we've made substantial progress and have cause for celebration of the combined efforts of our field.

While we celebrate growth we must be mindful that we still have much to learn. The database is not complete, and the research synthesized here tells us what we know now.

In some instances we know a great deal; in others the available information is less well known. As the years pass we will know more. As with all research in the social sciences, the field continues to evolve—we will never know all that we want to know. But that does not mean we should not use the research now available to make informed decisions.

To help readers get the most out of this book, we introduce some concepts and definitions in this chapter. In the first section we provide an overview of the areas within physical education pedagogy. In the second section we briefly discuss some issues in using research to inform the educational process and enhance learning.

THE FIELD OF PHYSICAL EDUCATION PEDAGOGY

As the number of research specialists in physical education pedagogy has grown, we have seen an increased specialization within the field. No longer can we think of the field as a single area. You will note when you read the chapters that follow that each specialization includes many research subareas.

We can think of the field of physical education pedagogy as having three subareas: teacher education, curriculum, and teaching. Although these areas are distinct, they overlap to some degree. As figure 1.1 suggests, the research in all three subareas may even come together as one. Some research easily falls into one of these categories, but other research is not so easily categorized. Nevertheless, the three areas provide a general framework for understanding the subareas within our field.

Before discussing each of the subareas of pedagogy, we should note that each area has both a research side and an applied side. Some people conduct research on teaching physical education, and others teach physical education. The same can be said of teacher education and curriculum. Often, those doing research also may be involved in teacher education and curriculum development; they may teach physical education activity courses as part of their assignment at a college or university. Likewise, teachers enrolled in graduate school may conduct research in one of the subareas while simultaneously teaching physical education. In addition, collaborative research, in which teachers and researchers work together, can be designed to merge theoretical and practical information. Both the researcher and practitioner are strong players in the field.

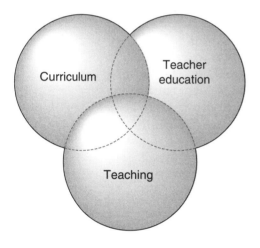

FIGURE 1.1   Subareas in physical education pedagogy.

Research on *teacher education* focuses on teacher training and development. This kind of investigation may ask teacher candidates why they entered the field, how they developed and learned to be teachers, and what factors promoted or inhibited subsequent growth while they were employed as teachers. Research may also address how teachers are trained and which methods seem to be the most beneficial in reaching the goals of a teacher education program. The chapters in part V by Mary O'Sullivan (chapter 16), Inez Rovegno (chapter 17), and Sandy Stroot and Christine Whipple (chapter 18) concentrate on these issues.

Although once focusing exclusively on what is taught in physical education, research in *curriculum* now explores other issues as well. Curriculum researchers study what is taught, why teachers select content for their classes, how teachers' values influence curriculum selection and implementation, and the process by which curriculum is designed. This area deals with the subject matter of physical education and how we determine what should be taught. The chapters by Cathy Ennis (chapter 7) and Leslie Lambert (chapter 8) in part III review research on curriculum issues.

Research on *teaching* physical education concentrates on teaching effectiveness from the perspectives of teachers and students. This research addresses such issues as the relationships between student and teacher behaviors and student learning, how students mediate the intended instruction from the teacher, and how teaching methods influence learning. Research on teaching physical education has focused mostly on motor-skill learning but in recent years has addressed other goals related to knowledge, affect, or social development. The chapters by Melinda Solmon (chapter 9) and Judy Rink (chapter 10) in part III provide an overview of this research.

As we noted earlier, the three subareas may overlap. For instance, issues in teaching and curriculum may combine in research on student learning. Curriculum and teacher-training issues overlap in studies that focus on teacher-training curriculum and its development. Likewise, the areas of teaching and teacher education intersect when we consider the best ways to train prospective physical education teachers or when teaching appraisal is the research focus. Although the three-way combination complicates things further, it is less likely that all areas will overlap in one research paper.

Often, such overlap occurs when curriculum is developed and teaching methods are suggested for reaching the curricular goals. In application, teaching and curriculum go hand in hand. The chapters in part IV by Thom McKenzie (chapter 12), Peter Hastie (chapter 13), Don Hellison (chapter 14), and Judy Placek (chapter 15) show how research and scholarship on teaching and curriculum interact to influence what and how subject matter is taught in physical education.

USING RESEARCH TO ENHANCE LEARNING

Research is the basis for much of the decision making in Western society. Although research is often presented in the news, reporters usually present only the conclusions and implications, ignoring the researchers' caveats. Yet these caveats are important. For instance, when considering whether the results of a medical study have implications for us, we need to know if the subjects were older or younger than ourselves, had preexisting medical problems, lived in an environment different from our own, or exhibited certain behaviors. The information can change our lives if we are afflicted with a disease or have no effect if we are not. The details influence the utility of the research.

The situation in physical education is similar. Some research will be helpful, whereas other research will not. The authors of the chapters that follow have tried to make distinctions and address the topics most important for physical educators. Each author has put a great deal of work into his or her chapter; thoughtful contemplation is necessary to make the information useful to you. All research is situation specific. It occurs at a certain time and place that likely is different, in some ways, from most other situations. Research tells much about the situation being studied, but it might not be applicable to other situations—or then again, it might. A single study gives us some insight into the problem, but we may not understand how the phenomenon being studied functions in other situations. This is one difficulty in applying research directly to other classes, grade levels, or situations.

How do you know if the research can be helpful in providing solutions to questions about professional practice? You should consider two important points when examining research. First is the quality of the research. A good research question followed by a poorly designed or executed study will tell us little. No matter how good the question and how much we want to know the answer, poor research cannot answer the question. Fortunately, the dramatic rise in the number of physical education researchers over the last few decades has helped improve the overall quality of investigation. Publication outlets have become more rigorous, and many manuscripts undergo review by multiple reviewers and an editor. Most research published in refereed journals has undergone a review that warrants some confidence in the results.

The second thing to consider is whether the situation is similar to yours. If you are teaching physical education and want to apply certain research, you should ask yourself the following: Is the grade level similar to those I teach? Are the students similar? Are my resources (particularly instructional time, facilities, supplies, and personnel) similar? Can I do what I need to do to implement what I have learned? Do I want to use what I have learned? All these questions are important. The chapters that follow provide much information about physical education; your answers to the above questions will help you decide whether it will be useful in your situation.

No single study, of course, will provide all the answers. Selecting a specific situation (e.g., schools in a certain area) and sample (e.g., middle school students) for a study is one of the trade-offs that investigators must make to assure good research. Personnel and financial resources dictate that large, universal studies are rarely possible. Researchers make decisions that influence these trade-offs, and without them, they could conduct no research. A small, well-designed study provides valuable information to both researchers and practitioners. The results of these studies can be used for future research. Replication in a variety of environments is beneficial and allows better interpretation of results. As Judy Rink discusses later, in the case of student practice, multiple studies with similar results permit stronger conclusions than those we can draw from a single study.

We believe that a database is available for making educated decisions about physical education teaching, teacher education, and curriculum development. The research is robust—and provides insight for making decisions. As Gage (1978, 1985) noted in discussing classroom research, no one result can be implemented in isolation from other teaching variables or from the personality and capabilities of the teacher. Other research in physical education (Silverman, Subramaniam, & Woods, 1998; Silverman, Woods, & Subramaniam, 1999) confirms that many variables interact for learning to occur. Helping students to learn is an interactive process, and each new situation and student requires using the available information to the best of our ability. Researchers and teachers make educated decisions and must combine their knowledge and experience to produce sound results.

SUMMARY AND PRELUDE

We assume that you, as a reader of this book, are interested in studying the results of research so that you can enhance student learning in physical education. It would be easy to dismiss the utility of research without thoroughly examining it. We urge you to be creative as you read and think about the chapters that follow. Trying to implement a new idea and finding that it doesn't work is OK and, in our opinion, preferable to not trying.

As you explore the chapters that follow you will note that some common themes emerge. Among the many theses are that it takes time for students to learn, that if students do not feel successful and competent they may not learn what we intended them to learn, and that the teaching is a two-way street in which students influence teachers as much as teachers influence students. Often the research suggests that alternatives to traditional practice have the potential to improve student learning and help teachers reach their goals. The research also provides insight that may extend this learning so that today's students become tomorrow's physically active adults.

For change to occur, as Inez Rovegno notes in chapter 17, those implementing change need time to develop a knowledge base and then extend it to their professional practice. A number of years ago cognitive scientists Rumelhart and Norman (1978) suggested that there were three ways for knowledge to become ingrained in memory for easy use. Their model states that the more complex the knowledge, the more complex the task of getting it to memory and using it easily. They believed—as do we—that it takes time and effort for change to occur. We hope that as you read the chapters that follow you use the information from research to help you make decisions about your professional practice. Reading and understanding the ideas in this book is only the first step in using the information to enhance student learning in physical education.

IMPLICATIONS FOR PRACTICE

1. The field of physical education pedagogy has grown greatly over the past 30 years.
2. Physical education pedagogy includes three subareas: teacher education, curriculum, and teaching.
3. Each of the three subareas of physical education pedagogy can be focused on research or on practice.
4. Research can provide physical educators with information to make informed decisions about their practice.
5. Teaching and learning in physical education is a complex process, and any single research result must be considered in light of other research and the teaching environment in which it may be implemented.
6. Change takes time and effort!

REFERENCES

Gage, N.L. (1978). *The scientific basis of the art of teaching.* New York: Teachers College Press.

Gage, N.L. (1985). *Hard gains in the soft sciences: The case of pedagogy.* Bloomington, IN: Phi Delta Kappa.

Locke, L.F. (1977). Research on teaching physical education: New hope for a dismal science. *Quest, 28,* 2-16.

National Association for Sport and Physical Education (NASPE). (2001). *Shape of the nation: A survey of state physical education requirements.* Reston, VA: Author.

Piéron, M., & Graham, G. (Eds.). (1984). *Sport pedagogy* (The Olympic Scientific Congress proceedings, volume 6). Champaign, IL: Human Kinetics.

Rumelhart, D.E., & Norman, D.A. (1978). Accretion, tuning, and restructuring: Three modes of learning. In J.W. Cotton & R.L. Klatzky (Eds.), *Semantic factors in cognition* (pp. 37-53). Hillsdale, NJ: Lawrence Erlbaum.

Silverman, S., Subramaniam, P.R., & Woods, A.M. (1998). Task structures, student practice, and student skill level in physical education. *Journal of Educational Research, 91,* 298-306.

Silverman, S., Woods, A.M., & Subramaniam, P.R. (1999). Feedback and practice in physical education: Interrelationships with task structures and student skill level. *Journal of Human Movement Studies, 36,* 203-224.

CHAPTER TWO

HOW THE FIELD EVOLVED

Amelia M. Lee

The history of research in physical education pedagogy reflects a gradual change in the conceptualization of effective teaching and teacher education. This evolution has largely determined the nature of the research conducted and the extent to which the findings have been deemed useful for informing practice. The goal of this chapter is to describe the variety of ways researchers have gone about studying teaching, teacher education, and curriculum in physical education. The alternative forms of research will be described from a historical perspective, with a description of the relationships between practitioners and researchers along the way. In general, researchers have taken two perspectives, and these can be explained by describing an observer with a pair of binoculars. At times we focus our binoculars on a particular component of the teaching-learning setting and try to identify characteristics of teaching that will lead to greater learning. We look at capacities and actions of teachers and learners, seeking to discover relationships and differences. The earlier research represents examples of such attempts to meticulously analyze the teaching-learning process with the hope of providing recipes for practitioners.

Because of dissatisfaction with the earlier narrow lens for studying teaching and learning, researchers offered a broader conceptualization, focusing more on perspectives of the participants, their backgrounds, and the social context. The goals, thoughts, feelings, expectations, and attitudes of teachers, teacher educators, and students are accepted as important data for the research process of later years. These researchers use a wider angle to view the learning environment and study the significance of social, cultural, and political influences. In recent years the broader view (wide angle) has given attention to questions of social justice and power relations of gender and race embedded in the learning endeavor.

For years research has been used to gain a theoretical and practical understanding of teaching, teacher education, and curriculum in our field. Researchers formulate questions to help us understand more about what good teaching is and how to prepare teachers who can implement quality instructional programs in schools and gymnasiums. This chapter will serve as an introduction to the various approaches that researchers have used to seek answers to pedagogical questions in our field.

EVOLVING CURRICULUM AND EARLY RESEARCH EFFORTS

To understand the contributions of groups of scholars and the types of influences serving to guide their research efforts, it is informative to look briefly at how the curriculum in physical education has evolved over the years. The history of physical education reflects the cultural, economic, social, and political forces of the times. Understanding the curriculum from a historical perspective can assist in the interpretation of research findings.

First Programs

Physical education programs in the United States appeared in the early 1800s and were primarily therapeutic exercises. At the turn of the 20th century a shift in focus occurred, and the concern for individual development brought about new aims and objectives for physical education programs (Jewett, Bain, & Ennis, 1995). The programs of the early 1900s replaced rigid exercises with natural play and recreational activities, an approach that became known as "education through the physical." Although physical education struggled to survive the educational crisis during the depression of the 1930s, the new program continued to gain support, and the concept of total development through physical activities shaped the program of activities until the 1960s. During the 1940s and 1950s the concerns brought about by World War II and the perceived need to promote physical well-being resulted in increased attention to fitness programs in our schools. Even with the emphasis on physical fitness, sport was the dominant curricular offering.

Research Efforts

Pedagogical research began in the 1940s with attempts to find teacher characteristics or presage variables that would correlate highly with teacher effectiveness or product variables. The criteria of teacher effectiveness in this early model were typically teacher ratings by administrative personnel or by students. These researchers tried to identify personal traits of teachers such as appearance or enthusiasm that were thought to be linked to good teaching. Another form of early classroom research compared the measured achievement of classes taught by one method with that of classes taught by another (Brophy & Good, 1986). These approaches failed to produce relevant and consistent findings about what effective teaching is. According to Medley (1979) the early research using the teacher rating scales produced no evidence to show that teachers possessing certain characteristics were more effective in promoting student achievement or any of the goals of education. The methods studies were inconclusive because the differences in the methods were not sufficient to show differences in student achievement (Medley, 1979).

Research on Motor-Skill Acquisition

At the time that classroom pedagogical researchers were interested in defining teachers as possessors of desirable traits and users of effective methods (Medley, 1979), researchers in physical education were concerned with identifying ways that teachers could facilitate the acquisition of motor skills. Physical educators specializing in the area of motor learning produced most of the research activity during this time. Before 1960 physical education was defined only as a teaching field, so the student population was limited to those preparing to be teachers. Thus, researchers in motor learning, as well as those specializing in other areas within the field of physical education, were concerned with directing their research findings to practicing or prospective teachers. The review paper by Nixon and Locke (1973), entitled "Research on Teaching Physical Education," published in the *Second Handbook of Research on Teaching*, described studies of schedule patterns (e.g., three days a week versus two days a week for skill practice), class size, the usefulness of mechanical learning aids, and the effects of different ways to present and analyze the practice task. A typical methods study in physical education, for example, compared two methods of teaching beginning basketball (Whilden, 1956).

Nixon and Locke's (1973) review focused on the research in physical education that was most concerned with teaching as a means of facilitating the acquisition of motor skills, but they warned that knowing how students learn and knowing how to help them learn are two different kinds of knowledge. These authors concluded that because of a host of methodological difficulties, including the general absence of theory as a tool in designing the research, the findings did not provide any information that would improve teaching practice in physical education. They also called for more descriptive analytic research in motor-skill learning, in which methods for the systematic recording of events and behaviors could be devised and tested. During the next decade interest in systematic observation of teachers and events in the gymnasium led to the development of a number of instruments to collect and describe quantitative data about teaching, and this helped to define the process-product research programs of the 1970s.

MAJOR CHANGES IN PROGRAMS

Several happenings in the 1960s changed the conceptualization of the field of physical education. The article by Franklin Henry in 1964 described physical education as an academic discipline. We became interested in defining a body of knowledge for our field and offering undergraduate majors for students seeking careers outside of teaching (Bain, 1990). Signaling a concern for establishing a scientific knowledge base for the discipline, many groups began to rename their programs to reflect an academic major rather than a teaching field. These changes led to some confusion about the subject matter of our field as well as the range of goals that researchers, curriculum designers, and teachers are expected to accomplish.

Proponents of a movement approach to teaching physical education challenged the traditional sport and fitness emphasis in the 1960s, recommending that a Laban-based movement education framework be used to structure content in games, dance, and gymnastics (Barrett, 1985). Movement education, borrowed from British curricular models, emphasized an understanding of movement concepts through problem solving and discovery, and for several years this approach offered legitimate competition for the dominant sport curriculum. Critics were concerned, however, that research efforts had not provided support for the approach. Although the movement approach had an effect on some elementary school programs in the country, the subject matter of physical education, for the most part, continued to be sport and fitness.

Subsequent growth of the subdisciplinary areas and the various definitions of goals resulted in a lack of agreement about what the nature of the physical education curriculum should be. The curricular focus has changed throughout history according to national and personal priorities related to social, economic, and political concerns (Jewett et al., 1995). From the 1960s to the present there have been numerous views and resulting generic curricular models described (e.g., fitness model, conceptual model). Although these changes made the researcher's job more complex, the resulting growth of pedagogy research specialists in the field was positive. Although some viewed the research role of the subdiscipline specialist to be more prestigious than that of the pedagogical specialist, the development of more sophisticated research methodology has resulted in increased pedagogical research productivity (Silverman & Skonie, 1997). Efforts after the major changes of the '60s have produced a sophisticated knowledge base related to teaching and teacher education in physical education. The time frames for the categories of research that follow overlap and cannot be presented in chronological order.

RESEARCH PROGRESS

The 1960s were followed by other research that focused on teaching in physical education. Research in this period began as descriptions and grew into research examining relationships among teacher and student variables. Research on teaching in physical education grew substantially and became more focused.

Descriptions of Teachers and Classes

By the 1970s pedagogical researchers were ready to give up on the methods focus of the '50s and '60s and eager to consider the use of observational instruments that classroom researchers had collected. Physical educators began to focus on the development and standardization of valid and reliable instruments for recording and analyzing teacher and student behaviors in the gymnasium. Anderson and his colleagues (Anderson & Barrette, 1978) took the lead when they described the behaviors of teachers and students in physical education classes in a monograph entitled *What's Going On in Gym*. Other work by Cheffers (1973) adapted the Flanders Interaction Analysis (CAFIAS) for use in physical education. At Ohio State University, Siedentop and his colleagues (Siedentop & Hughley, 1975) developed the OSU Teacher Behavior Instrument, used originally with student teachers but later with cooperating teachers as well as in-service teachers. These initial efforts led to the development of other instruments, which were eventually compiled and published (Darst, Zakrajsek, & Mancini, 1989). Although pedagogical researchers have used many different types of observation systems, the academic learning time-physical education (ALT-PE) (Siedentop, Tousignant, & Parker, 1982) instruments have probably been used most often. After a series of ALT-PE studies, which extended through the 1980s (Aufderheide, 1983; Godbout, Burnelle, & Tousignant, 1983; Metzler, 1980; Piéron & Haan, 1979; Placek, Silverman, Shute, Dodds, & Rife, 1982; Silverman, Dodds, Placek, Shute, & Rife, 1984; Metzler, 1989), it was concluded that students spend a small proportion of time engaged in motor activities related to motor-skill achievement. Another example of an observation system is the "Qualitative Measures of Teaching Performance Scale" (QMTPS) developed by Rink and Werner (1989). This instrument uses a qualitative technique to identify characteristics of task presentation, such as teacher demonstration and use of cues. McKenzie, Sallis, and Nader (1991) developed the System for Observing Fitness Instruction Time (SOFIT) to obtain information on student activity levels during health-related physical activity classes. The SOFIT estimates energy expenditure using a coding system.

Teacher Behavior Research

Following the development of instruments for systematic observation, researchers became involved in a whole line of teacher effectiveness studies. This approach was an improvement over earlier attempts that relied on high-inference scales of teacher effectiveness, but the results were mixed and thus disappointing to both researchers and teacher educators. One popular technique was a correlational design in which various teacher behaviors (process) were correlated with student achievement (product). The process-product model was based on the premise that rule-following teaching, which means exhibiting the teacher actions identified by research, would improve student learning. Although the early process-product studies (Oliver, 1980; Taylor, 1976; Yerg, 1981a; 1981b; Yerg & Twardy, 1982) helped to define physical education pedagogy as an important focus for research, the research evidence provided conflicting conclusions about the links between teacher behavior and variations in student learning. The work on teacher feedback, for example, was studied vigorously, based on a strong belief in its value and the assumption that feedback was a process necessary for motor-skill learning. After years of research (Godbout, Brunelle, & Tousignant, 1987; Salter & Graham, 1985; Silverman, Tyson, & Krampitz, 1992) with conflicting results it was concluded that feedback may not be as essential for motor-skill learning as once believed (Lee, Keh, & Magill, 1993; Silverman, 1994).

Changing Teacher Behavior

Taking into consideration the picture of the typical physical education class presented by the observational research evidence, many physical educators set out to determine the behaviors of good teachers, define those behaviors, and teach them to novices. Believing that higher frequencies of certain teacher behaviors would result in greater student learning, researchers trained students to change the type and quality of information delivered to students. Using applied behavior analysis, researchers concluded that teachers can be trained to increase their level of enthusiasm (e.g., Carlisle & Phillips, 1984; Rolider, Siedentop, & Van Houten, 1984) and modify their feedback behavior (e.g., Cusimano, 1987; Hawkins, Wiegand, & Landin, 1985; Landin, Hawkins, & Wiegand, 1986; van der Mars, 1987). These studies showed that behavioral analytic techniques and systematic feedback can change teacher behavior, and this finding had great appeal to researchers asking questions about teacher effectiveness. Others began to question whether focusing on a single "best way to teach" was productive for teacher education, and in the research programs that follow scholars and teacher educators take a different approach. It has become increasingly important for researchers to explain their findings, and although the research describing relationships between what teachers do in physical education classes and what their students learn did not produce consistent results, the methodology was promising. A major weakness was that the findings failed to provide any insight into how the selected teacher actions affected student learning. Little information explained how the designated teacher behaviors translated to good teaching. This approach was a step forward, however, from the earlier focus on comparison of teaching methods, and it led the way to a more mature, respected area of inquiry for those interested in the study of teaching and teacher education.

Focus on Time

Just as the process-product research program got underway, critics began to direct attention to its weaknesses. First, although some teacher behaviors might be associated with student achievement, the correlations were usually low and not always significant. A more serious concern seemed to be the difficulty in explaining the reasons for the relationships between teacher behavior and achievement (Brophy & Good, 1986). Thus, just as the teacher behavior research was gaining momentum in the late '70s and early '80s, a student-mediating paradigm was offered as an alternative. Based on a belief that attention to the immediate responses of students would provide better estimates of the effects of teaching (Shulman, 1986), the observable activities of the learners during class became viewed as mediators of instruction. Using concepts from the work of Carroll and Bloom (Carroll, 1963; Bloom, 1974) student-engaged time became the variable of interest. Initial research efforts using time as a student-mediating variable in pedagogical research were found in the Beginning Teacher Evaluation Study (BTES) (Fisher et al., 1978). These researchers theorized that the amount of time a student was engaged with the subject at an appropriate difficulty level was the crucial variable underlying successful teaching. Thus, within this modified process-product framework the variable identified as academic learning time (ALT) was accepted as the process variable linking measures of teacher behavior to student learning. Although Doyle (1977) advocated the study of a broader range of student-mediating processes that govern learning, ALT emerged as the quantitative measure used in research for the next several years.

Contributions of ALT-PE Research

With the availability of the revised ALT-PE Instrument (Siedentop et al., 1982), research relating student-engaged time to achievement was the next logical step. After the series of studies describing how time is spent in physical education classes, researchers shifted the emphasis toward process-product designs using student-engaged time as the process variable. The first attempts by physical educators to demonstrate a relationship between ALT-PE and student achievement were not successful (Godbout et al., 1987; Silverman, 1983; Yerg, 1983; Yerg & Twardy, 1982), probably because task difficulty and the quality of student practice were difficult to determine. Later research, which considered the context in which instruction occurs and the nature of the task being taught, revealed that engaged time is related to achievement. For example, Silverman, Tyson, and Morford (1988) found that when students spent time practicing and received feedback from the teacher, they achieved more, but results also indicated that the type of practice was important. A number of studies supported the notion that practice in class using correct technique would influence student achievement, and with this measure of practice researchers were able to connect engagement and learning outcomes consistently (Ashy, Lee, & Landin, 1988; Buck, Harrison, & Bryce, 1991; Dugas, 1984; Silverman, 1985, 1990). It became clear that the quality rather than the total amount of practice is more important to student learning (Ashy et al., 1988; Silverman, 1990).

UNDERSTANDING MORE ABOUT TEACHER DEVELOPMENT

At the same time that some researchers were interested in quantifying desirable teacher actions, others were interested in determining why teachers behave as they do in the gymnasium. This approach recommended taking a broader view and emphasized the need to move beyond the detailed analysis of one or two aspects of teacher behavior. In a viewpoint first set forth by Lortie (1975), an individual's biography, rather than a teacher education program, is viewed as the primary determinant of how effective a teacher will be. In this perspective, personal dispositions, educational experiences as a student, early role models, and the school environment serve as socializing agents for teachers and are difficult to offset in teacher education. Another perspective found in the literature of the 1970s was that prospective teachers enter the educational system without any opinions or impressions and are passive recipients in the social structure of the system.

Some early evidence supported the notion that the educational social structure washed out the effects of teacher education programs (Templin, 1979). In the 1980s it became apparent that both of the early approaches overlooked the interaction between the teacher's personal perspectives and the social structure. Another early study by Templin (1981) indicated that students serve as socializing agents. Thus, from an interactive viewpoint socializing agents can include the numerous forces that influence the development of teachers. Teachers react to both student and classroom influences, and the reciprocal nature of this process shapes teacher behavior in significant ways.

Although no early program of research was comparable to the teacher effectiveness efforts (Bain, 1990), much was written about the salient influences in the process of teacher socialization. Physical education scholars in this tradition have played a critical role in alerting other professionals to question the value of available research for guiding the practice of teachers. As Sandy Stroot notes in chapter 18, the most recognized spokesperson for this research focus is Lawson (1983a, 1983b, 1986, 1988, 1990), whose work emphasized the importance of understanding the roles that various socializing agents play in the development of effective physical education teachers. The socialization process, according to Lawson (1983a), is a lifelong process, not beginning with a teacher education program but instead beginning early in life and continuing throughout the educational career.

Templin and Schempp (1989) delineated an interactive view of teacher socialization that views the prospective teacher as an active agent in his or her own socialization process, controlling the direction of both biography and social structure. These authors put together a volume of essays that summarized the major influences in the process of teacher socialization in physical education. In a monograph edited by Stroot (1993) various authors summarized research using the occupational socialization model defined by Lawson (1986). The research reported examined recruitment into physical education (e.g., Dodds et al., 1992), the socialization process during teacher preparation (e.g., Graber, 1991), and experiences of teachers as they enter the school setting (e.g., O'Sullivan, 1989). Research (Schempp, 1989) has identified the individual's biography as the fundamental base for teacher socialization, advancing the notion that primary influences on the socialization process occur before teacher education. Other researchers (Graber, 1989; Solmon, Worthy, Lee, & Carter, 1991; Solmon, Worthy, & Carter, 1993) have studied the interaction between the teacher's personal perspective and the social structure of the educational system. Findings from these studies support the view of the teacher as an active agent in controlling the direction of biography and social structure in the socialization process. Other recent work has used the life history approach (Templin, Sparkes, & Schempp, 1991) to gather in-depth information about the lives of teachers and influences of the socialization process.

Ample research suggests that the physical education context in today's schools serves as a constraint to teacher development. A number of studies have identified influential contextual factors in the workplace, and much of this research has focused on obstacles that teachers encounter as they try to develop professionally. Unfortunately, both beginning and experienced teachers often report physical education as being marginalized (O'Sullivan, 1989; Pissanos, 1995; Smyth, 1995) and lacking support, adequate funding, and a plan for scheduling to allow for enhanced learning (e.g., Macdonald, 1995; Solmon et al., 1993). Some recent studies have focused on the positive effects of the school context that might promote teacher knowledge and program development (Anderson, 1994; Rovegno, 1993; Rovegno & Bandhauer, 1997). Taken together, the findings from this line of research support the view that teaching is a complex endeavor and that the context of teaching can influence professional development in both positive and negative ways. Available research clearly indicates that some teachers can facilitate their own development and change a school culture to one that promotes quality physical education programs (Hebert & Worthy, 2001; Rovegno & Bandhauer, 1997)

CHANGING CONCEPTIONS OF TEACHING AND LEARNING

As the research literature was increasing during the 1980s, the focus broadened to include the mental processes of teachers and students as well as their behavior. Scholars in this tradition (Clark & Peterson, 1986; Wittrock, 1986) brought attention to the need for researchers to go beyond describing what teachers and students do in classes, relating what teachers do to student behavior, and planning intervention programs to change the behavior of teachers. The study of cognitive processes represents an approach to research based on the assumption that what teachers and students think and believe affects what they do.

Based on research in cognitive psychology, which describes the thinking and actions of experts and novices in a variety of fields (Chi, Glaser, & Rees, 1982), many researchers have investigated the cognitive components of teaching expertise. Several studies have examined expertise in observational skill, finding that experts differ from novices in diagnosing movement skills (Dodds, 1994) and can more easily select and prioritize salient cues for a motor task (Pinheiro & Simon, 1992). On the other hand, although novice teachers have difficulty extracting the salient cues from the teaching environment, they can learn observational skills during field experiences (Barrett, Allison, & Bell, 1987; Bell, Barrett, & Allison, 1985). Other studies have demonstrated that training can improve the movement analysis capabilities of novices (Beveridge & Gangstead, 1988). Researchers (Sharpe, 1997; Sharpe & Hawkins, 1992) have also been successful in showing that when compared to novices, expert physical education teachers have higher levels of subject matter and pedagogical knowledge.

Using different forms of cognitive mapping techniques, researchers have studied the knowledge bases of expert and novice teachers (Ennis, Mueller, & Zhu, 1991; Housner, Gomez, & Griffey, 1993; Rink, French, Lee, Solmon, & Lynn, 1994), finding that experts have more complex knowledge structures about teaching and the curriculum. Using field systems analysis other researchers (Sharpe & Hawkins, 1992) have been successful in showing that when compared to novices expert physical education teachers have higher levels of subject matter and pedagogical knowledge. Although researchers have made some successful attempts to explore and characterize knowledge about teaching, none of the studies have traced this knowledge to actual teaching processes. The expert-novice research is limited and does not at this point contribute significantly to the advancement of teaching.

Teacher Beliefs and Decision Making

The chapter "Teachers' Thought Processes" (Clark & Peterson, 1986) in the *Third Handbook of Research on Teaching* was helpful in conceptualizing the domain of teachers' thought processes into the categories of preactive planning, interactive decision making, and teacher theories and beliefs. The first two categories represent a temporal distinction between teacher thought processes occurring before teaching (preactive) or during teaching (interactive). The third category examines the influence of teachers' theories and beliefs on planning and decision making. As the research focus shifted to a study of the mental lives of teachers, researchers began to examine teacher thoughts during planning and actual instruction. Most of the planning studies (e.g., Byra & Sherman, 1993; Griffey & Housner, 1991; Housner & Griffey, 1985; Placek, 1984; Stroot & Morton, 1989; Solmon & Lee, 1991; Twardy & Yerg, 1987) compared the planning decisions of expert and novice teachers using think aloud techniques, analysis of lesson plans, interviews, and observation to collect data. Findings from these studies suggest that more and less experienced teachers differ in their thinking and decision making during preactive planning. When compared with inexperienced teachers, more experienced teachers request more information about the teaching situation, plan in more detail, and make more decisions concerning strategies for implementing instructional tasks.

On a smaller scale this line of research was extended to an investigation of the interactive thoughts of teachers during actual instruction (Byra & Sherman, 1993; Housner & Griffey, 1985; Walkwitz & Lee, 1992). Although data collection techniques vary, teachers generally viewed a videotape of a lesson recently completed and answered a series of questions regarding their thoughts and decisions during the lesson. Findings from the studies comparing experienced and inexperienced teachers (Byra & Sherman, 1993; Housner & Griffey, 1985) indicated that experienced teachers are more likely to implement new teaching routines when they perceive that lessons are not progressing as planned. Inexperienced teachers, on the other hand, tend to continue according to their plan, even when they perceive that the lesson is not progressing as planned. The studies of teachers' preactive and interactive thoughts have produced little information that can guide research or inform teaching. The planning studies asked teachers to verbalize their thoughts during planning, and the researchers analyzed and categorized those thoughts to determine the type of planning decisions made. The interactive studies have been criticized for using frequency counts of thoughts and feelings that were believed to precede behavior (Shulman, 1986). This approach to analysis is similar to the early process-product work and probably lacked the complexity needed to answer important questions about teaching. The researchers assumed frequency counts of teacher choices during planning and teaching activities would influence student learning. The limitations to this approach were recognized in the early 1990s, and the emphasis shifted to research designed to gain an understanding of relationships between teacher beliefs and decisions they make about instruction.

The teacher-thinking research in physical education that has focused on beliefs is based on the assumption that teachers base their decisions and actual behaviors on what they believe. Ennis and her colleagues (Ennis, Mueller, & Hooper, 1990; Ennis, Ross, & Chen, 1992; Ennis & Zhu, 1991) have clearly shown that teachers' belief systems influence their decisions about selection of content, teaching strategies, and tasks in physical education. Ennis (1994) provides evidence that individuals may choose to resist knowledge that conflicts with their belief systems (e.g., Faucette, 1987). Consistent with these findings is Veal's (1988, 1992) research on teachers' beliefs about assessment. This work indicates that teachers and teacher educators differ in their beliefs about assessment and what teachers actually do is not always consistent with their self-reports. A recent study has investigated the relationships between belief systems and actions. Kulinna, Silverman, and Keating (2000) reported that teachers may have a strong belief in physical activity and fitness but this did not translate into sound programs. Other recent research has examined the extent to which beliefs about teaching physical education can be changed (Xiang, Lowy, & McBride, 2001). Although many questions are still unanswered, the incorporation of teacher beliefs into studies with multiple data sources can contribute to future understanding of how to improve education.

Student Mediation

The recognition of student-mediating processes as important variables has led researchers to study the cognitive, affective, and motivational components of student thinking. This line of research, as Melinda Solmon indicates in chapter 9, is grounded in a belief that teachers do not directly influence achievement but rather influence students to think and behave in certain ways (Lee & Solmon, 1992). Researchers are paying more attention to the role that students play in their own learning. This work has identified background variables that influence the extent to which students choose to participate in tasks defined by the teacher (Greenockle, Lee, & Lomax, 1990), and it has analyzed how the thoughts and feelings of students as they practice a motor skill mediate the instruction provided by the teacher (Lee, Landin, & Carter, 1992). Other research has studied student perception of teacher behavior (Martinek, 1988), described how students perceive and give meaning to teachers' instructional behaviors in different ways (Hanke, 1987), and explained student attitude and perceptions toward physical education (Silverman & Subramaniam, 1999; Subramaniam & Silverman, 2000).

Research has demonstrated that students' entry characteristics, as well as their motivational beliefs and use of learning strategies, play an important role in their actual participation patterns during instruction. Solmon and Lee (1996) found that students who had adequate skill and positive feelings about their competence were more engaged, better at detecting and correcting errors during practice, and reported more positive affective thoughts and higher levels of motivation. In subsequent years other researchers (Xiang & Lee, 1998; Xiang, Lee, & Williamson, 2001) have sought to understand more thoroughly the mediating role of competence beliefs in achievement cognition. Other lines of related work have included the construct of student goal perspective (Solmon & Boone, 1993) and interest (Chen & Darst, 2001) to understand achievement motivation in motor-skill settings. These research programs have served to demonstrate clearly that teachers do not directly influence student learning regardless of whether the outcomes are skill related, motivational, or affective.

An extension of the student-mediating paradigm has included research on student understanding of domain-specific knowledge (Griffin & Placek, 2001). These researchers investigated students' conceptions of fitness and invasion games and analyzed how these interact with other aspects of learner cognitions. Although the integration of social and cognitive mediational constructs has helped to explain some complex dimensions of student achievement motivation and learning, the researchers, thus far, have paid little attention to the variations among teachers and how subject matter and context interact with motivational and cognitive beliefs of students (Shulman, 1986). With the exception of the Griffin and Placek (2001) study, we still know little about how student understanding of the content mediates instruction.

INTEGRATED APPROACH

Rather than focusing on one or two aspects of a teaching-learning environment and analyzing thoughts and actions in great detail, researchers in the last decade have provided evidence to complete the picture of teachers as facilitators in the learning environment and students as active participants playing a bigger role. This line of thinking is consistent with constructivist approaches to teaching and learning. The viewpoint assumes that individuals actively construct knowledge based on their interpretations of their experiences in the situation and that existing knowledge and expectations influence these interpretations. Although the thoughts and feelings of the participants are important in this research, the approach places more emphasis on how teachers and students interact in the context of the learning environment. The setting in which the research is conducted is believed to be a key in determining reasons for teacher and student thoughts and actions in physical education. From an integrated perspective, teaching and learning are viewed as more dependent on the social and historical context. Some researchers have provided a more holistic picture of how students learn from teaching by grounding their work in both teaching and learning orientations (Griffin & Placek, 2001). This work has supported a path for understanding the complex relationships among students, learning, instruction, and subject matter. One assumption of an integrated approach is that students' learning processes are not exclusively cognitive in nature and motor patterns can emerge through law-based interactions within the environment. Recent studies (Barrett & Collie, 1996; Sweeting & Rink, 1999) have investigated how teachers can manipulate the physical surrounding and the task constraints in ways that motor patterns will emerge naturally. Attention to students as active participants in learning has led researchers to analyze other ways in which teaching and learning are connected. Studies by Ennis and her colleagues (Ennis et al., 1997; see chapter 7) have provided a framework for understanding how students and the social context influence teaching and the curricular goals.

New assumptions brought about by the integrated perspective and expanded conceptions have directed research toward studies that identify ways students can learn motor skills that will influence their ability to create solutions in new situations. Several recent studies have offered views on the value of a games-for-understanding approach for maximizing student learning (e.g. Hastie, 1996; Turner & Martinek, 1995; see chapter 13 by Peter Hastie). These findings tend to direct attention away from the traditional direct teaching styles to more indirect approaches (Mosston & Ashworth, 2002). Researchers have explored critical thinking (McBride, 1991) as a framework to help students develop holistically and gain a deeper understanding of the content (e.g., McBride & Cleland, 1998). Other studies (Rukavina, Lee, & Solmon, 2000) are beginning to focus on indirect approaches to teaching as a way to present content more holistically that will lead to more problem solving and critical thinking. Rink (2001) argues that rather than showing one particular kind of teaching to be better than another, researchers should seek to understand what is taking place in the learning process. Consistent with this recommendation, at least one recent study (Chen, 2001) has explored how one teacher engaged students in critical thinking to promote conceptual understanding.

CONCERN FOR BROADER SOCIAL ISSUES

During the brief history of pedagogical research in physical education there have been different and sometimes conflicting conceptions of what good research is and how useful it is for improving practice. Many researchers have set out to show school physical education as it really is today and describe situations and practices that place limits on some groups based on gender, ethnicity, or social class. Some focus on unwritten rules, or hidden curriculum, that might define activities and behaviors that are appropriate and expected for the various subgroups in the class. These expected patterns of behavior or the roles defined for different students in the class are believed to be constructed by interactions in the specific context. These researchers were not interested in studying the effectiveness of the teacher in terms of student movement outcomes. Rather, the purpose is to describe how the structure of a typical physical education class failed to serve the needs of some student subgroups.

Researchers have made a strong move to uncover the actions and language of teachers that prohibit all students from taking advantage of the instructional activities (e.g., Bain, 1985; Griffin, 1985; Fernandez-Balboa, 1997; Kirk, 1986). These researchers have described the hidden curriculum as disturbing and unacceptable because the dominant groups seem to gain from the practices. In recent years a number of studies have highlighted the lower participation of girls in physical activity and have rejected the equity approach, or simply providing equal opportunities, as a way to bring about changes (e.g., Wright, 1996). In search for a broader view, feminist theoretical perspectives question gender discrimination and offer historical, cultural, and ideological tools of analysis to understand gender differences in physical education classrooms. A social feminist perspective views females as oppressed by patriarchal consciousness, dominated by boys, and often labeled as inferior to males. Patriarchal oppression in physical education classrooms denies equal opportunity to female students and produces gender injustice (e.g., Satina, Solmon, Cothran, Loftus, & Stockin-Davidson, 1998).

CONCERN FOR BROADER HEALTH ISSUES

In light of the recognized health benefits of physical activity for the health and well-being of children and youth, public health officials and researchers are currently targeting school physical education as a place to promote more physical activity. McKenzie and his colleagues (e.g., McKenzie, Marshall, Sallis, & Conway, 2000) report that students in today's physical education classes do not participate in adequate amounts of moderate to vigorous physical activity and have provided evidence (McKenzie, Sallis, Faucette, Roby, & Kolody, 1993) that with intervention teachers can succeed in increasing the amount of time students are physically active. These researchers are recognizing that a critical step might be to study and understand how teachers can provide quality instruction in such a way that students will choose to be physically active after school and develop lifelong healthy lifestyles. As Thom McKenzie explains in chapter 12, this challenge will require an integrated approach to research and collaborative efforts among researchers, teacher educators, and practitioners.

SUMMARY

This chapter began with a discussion of two contrasting forms of research on teaching and teacher education and described a gradual shift from a narrow to a broader focus. Much of the early research was likened to an observer with a pair of binoculars searching for particular behaviors and techniques that might lead to a better understanding of what good teaching is. Research describing the minute details of teacher and student behavior and defining relationships between teaching processes and desirable student outcomes dominated the efforts of many researchers during the 1970s and 1980s.

Researchers who advocated a broader lens for the study of teaching and teacher education argued that the process-product research did not provide theoretical explanations for why certain behaviors and processes were related to student outcomes. Using a wider angle they directed attention away from counting events and behaviors toward a study of teaching-learning processes from the perspective of students and teachers. These approaches are concerned with explanations of thoughts as well as actions and consider prior knowledge, attitudes, goals, and feelings as mediating variables. Those using a wider angle are more concerned with the interactions between teachers and contexts, and they fear that using a narrow lens will result in a list of rules for teachers to follow. This approach makes them uneasy because they believe that a specific set of competencies reflects a technological rather than a reflective orientation.

The past two decades have been productive for pedagogical researchers in physical education with findings leading to a greater understanding of how learning occurs from teaching in the gymnasium. Researchers have used a range of perspectives, and efforts to refine the earlier models that used a narrower lens provided opportunities for professional dialogue and debate. Discussion of theoretical and conceptual research issues is a healthy sign, and the future for the field looks promising. During the next decade researchers will uncover additional problems and identify new methods for conducting research.

IMPLICATIONS FOR PRACTICE

1. A number of changes have occurred in the way researchers in physical education have gone about studying teaching, learning, and the educational experience in schools.
2. Some of the most significant changes in research on teaching over the past four decades stem from different views about the nature of the subject matter for physical education and the goals of researchers.
3. Research in the '70s and '80s looked for connections between teaching and student learning and sought to train teachers to use the research-based actions in the classroom.

4. At the time some researchers were studying links between teaching and learning, others examined the background characteristics of teachers that might influence their teaching.

5. By 1990 the complex nature of the relationship between teaching and learning was clear, and this understanding led to a broader focus for research.

6. The new conceptions brought about more concern for the thought processes of both teachers and students.

7. It soon became clear that teachers make decisions and take actions in class based on what they think and believe.

8. The student-mediating paradigm established that cognitive variables, such as attention and motivational levels, affect student engagement, effort, and achievement in physical education.

9. Researchers in the last decade have used constructivist approaches to develop a more complete picture of teachers as facilitators and students as active players in the teaching and learning environment.

10. In recent years research has expanded to include the examination of broader social and health issues.

REFERENCES

Anderson, W.G. (Ed.). (1994). Building and maintaining outstanding physical education programs: Key factors. *Journal of Physical Education, Recreation and Dance, 65*(7), 22-57.

Anderson, W.G., & Barrette, G.T. (Eds.). (1978). What's going on in gym: Descriptive studies of physical education classes. *Motor skills: Theory into practice* [Monograph 1].

Ashy, M.H., Lee, A.M., & Landin, D.K. (1988). Relationship of practice using correct technique to achievement in a motor skill. *Journal of Teaching in Physical Education, 7*, 115-120.

Aufderheide, S. (1983). ALT PE in mainstreamed physical education classes. *Journal of Teaching in Physical Education* [Monograph 1], 22-26.

Bain, L.L. (1985). A naturalistic study of students' responses to an exercise class. *Journal of Teaching in Physical Education, 5*, 2-12.

Bain, L.L. (1990). Physical education teacher education. In W.R. Houston (Ed.), *Handbook of research on teacher education* (pp. 758-781). New York: Macmillan.

Barrett, K.R. (1985). The content of an elementary school physical education program and its impact on teacher preparation. In H.A. Hoffman & J.E. Rink (Eds.), *Physical education preparation: Insight and foresight* (pp. 9-25). Reston, VA: American Alliance for Health, Physical Education, Recreation and Dance.

Barrett, K., Allison, P., & Bell, R. (1987). What preservice physical education teachers see in an unguided field experience: A follow-up study. *Journal of Teaching in Physical Education, 7*, 12-21.

Barrett, K.R., & Collie, S. (1996). Children learning lacrosse from teachers learning to teach it: The discovery of pedagogical content knowledge by observing children's movement. *Research Quarterly for Exercise and Sport, 67*, 297-309.

Bell, R., Barrett, K., & Allison, P. (1985). What preservice physical education teachers see in an unguided, early field experience. *Journal of Teaching in Physical Education, 4*, 81-90.

Beveridge, S., & Gangstead, S. (1988). Teaching experience and training in sport skill analysis. *Journal of Teaching in Physical Education, 7*, 103-114.

Bloom, B.S. (1974, September). Time and learning. *American Psychologist, 29*, 682-688.

Brophy, J., & Good, T.L. (1986). Teacher behavior and student achievement. In M.C. Wittrock, (Ed.), *Handbook of Research on Teaching* (3rd ed., pp. 328-375). New York: Macmillan.

Buck, M., Harrison, J.M., & Bryce, G.R. (1991). An analysis of learning trials and their relationship to achievement in volleyball. *Journal of Teaching in Physical Education, 10*, 134-152.

Byra, M., & Sherman, M.A. (1993). Preactive and interactive decision-making tendencies of less and more experienced preservice teachers. *Research Quarterly for Exercise and Sport, 64*, 46-55.

Carlisle, C., & Phillips, D. (1984). The effects of enthusiasm training on selected teacher and student behaviors in preservice physical education teachers. *Journal of Teaching in Physical Education, 4*, 64-75.

Carroll, J.B. (1963). A model of school learning. *Teachers College Record, 64*, 723-733.

Cheffers, J., (1973). *The validation of an instrument designed to expand the Flanders System of Interaction Analysis to describe nonverbal interaction, different varieties of teacher behavior and pupil responses.* Unpublished doctoral dissertation, Temple University, Philadelphia.

Chen, A., & Darst, P.W. (2001). Situational interest in physical education: A function of learning task design. *Research Quarterly for Exercise and Sport, 72,* 150-164.

Chen, W. (2001). Description of an expert teacher's constructivist-oriented teaching: Engaging students' critical thinking in learning creative dance. *Research Quarterly for Exercise and Sport, 72,* 366-375.

Chi, M., Glaser, R., & Rees, E. (1982). Expertise in problem solving. In R.J. Sternberg (Ed.), *Advances in the psychology of human intelligence* (pp. 7-75). Hillsdale, NJ: Erlbaum.

Clark, C., & Peterson, P.L. (1986). Teachers' thought processes. In M.C. Wittrock (Ed.), *Handbook of research on teaching* (3rd ed., pp. 255-296). New York: Macmillan.

Cusimano, B.E. (1987). Effects of self-assessment and goal setting on verbal behavior of elementary physical education teachers. *Journal of Teaching in Physical Education, 6,* 166-173.

Darst, P., Zakrajsek, D., & Mancini, V. (1989). *Analyzing physical education and sport instruction* (2nd ed.). Champaign, IL: Human Kinetics.

Dodds, P. (1994). Cognitive and behavioral components of expertise in teaching in physical education. *Quest, 46,* 153-163.

Dodds, P., Placek, J.H., Doolittle, S., Pinkham, K.M., Ratliffe, T.A., & Portman, P.A. (1992). Teacher/coach recruits: Background profiles, occupational decisional factors, and comparisons with recruits into other physical education occupations. *Journal of Teaching in Physical Education, 11,* 161-176.

Doyle, W. (1977). Paradigms for research on teacher effectiveness. In L.S. Shulman (Ed.), *Review of research in education* (Vol. 5, pp. 163-198). Itasca, IL: Peacock.

Dugas, D.M. (1984). Relationships among process and product variables in an experimental teaching unit. *Dissertation Abstracts International, 44,* 2709A. (University Microfilms No. 84-00, 193)

Ennis, C.D. (1994). Knowledge and beliefs underlying curricular expertise. *Quest, 46,* 164-175.

Ennis, C.D., Cothran, D.J., Davidson, K.S., Loftus, S.J., Owens, L., Swanson, L., & Hopsicker, P. (1997). Implementing curriculum within a context of fear and disengagement. *Journal of Teaching in Physical Education, 17,* 58-72.

Ennis, C.D., Mueller, L.K., & Hooper, L.M. (1990). The influence of teacher value orientations on curriculum planning within the parameters of a theoretical framework. *Research Quarterly for Exercise and Sport, 61,* 360-368.

Ennis, C., Mueller, L., & Zhu, W. (1991). Description of knowledge structures within a concept-based curriculum framework. *Research Quarterly for Exercise and Sport, 62,* 309-318.

Ennis, C.D., Ross, J., & Chen, A. (1992). The role of value orientation in curricular decision making: A rationale for teachers' goals and expectations. *Research Quarterly for Exercise and Sport, 63,* 38-47.

Ennis, C.D., & Zhu, W. (1991). Value orientations: A description of teacher's goals for student learning. *Research Quarterly for Exercise and Sport, 62,* 33-40.

Faucette, N. (1987). Teachers' concerns and participation styles during in-service education. *Journal of Teaching in Physical Education, 6,* 425-440.

Fernandez-Balboa, J.M. (1997). Introduction: The human movement profession: From modernism to postmodernism. In Fernandez-Balboa, J.M. (Ed.), *Critical postmodernism in human movement, physical education and sport* (pp. 3-10). Albany, NY: SUNY Press.

Fisher, C.W., Filby, N.N., Marliave, R., Cahen, L.S., Dishaw, M.M., Moore, J.E., & Berliner, D.C. (1978) *Teaching behaviors, academic learning time and student achievement: Final report of Phase IIIB, Beginning Teacher Evaluation Study* (Technical Report V-1). San Francisco: Far West Laboratory.

Godbout, P., Burnelle, J., & Tousignant, M. (1983). Academic learning time in elementary and secondary physical education classes. *Research Quarterly for Exercise and Sport, 57,* 11-19.

Godbout, P., Burnelle, J., & Tousignant, M. (1987). Who benefits from passing through the program? In G.T. Barrette, R.S. Feingold, C.R. Rees, & M. Piéron (Eds.), *Myths, models and methods in sport pedagogy* (pp. 183-197). Champaign, IL: Human Kinetics.

Graber, K.C. (1989). Teaching tomorrow's teachers: Professional preparation as an agent of socialization. In T. Templin & P. Schempp (Eds.), *Socialization into physical education: Learning to teach* (pp. 59-80). Indianapolis: Benchmark Press.

Graber, K.C. (1991). Studentship in preservice teacher education: A qualitative study of undergraduates in physical education. *Research Quarterly for Exercise and Sport, 62,* 41-51.

Greenockle, K., Lee, A., & Lomax, R. (1990). The relationship between selected student characteristics and activity patterns in a required high school physical education class. *Research Quarterly for Exercise and Sport, 61,* 59-69.

Griffey, D., & Housner, L.D. (1991). Planning, behavior and organization climate differences of experienced and inexperienced teachers. *Research Quarterly for Exercise and Sport, 62,* 196-204.

Griffin, L.L., & Placek, J.H. (Eds.). (2001). The understanding and development of learners' domain-specific knowledge [Monograph]. *Journal of Teaching in Physical Education.*

Griffin, P.S. (1985). Boys' participation styles in a middle school physical education sports unit. *Journal of Teaching in Physical Education, 4,* 100-110.

Hanke, U. (1987). Cognitive aspects of interaction in physical education. In G.T. Barrette, R.S. Feingold, C.R. Rees, & M. Piéron (Eds.), *Myths, models, and methods in sport pedagogy* (pp. 135-141). Champaign, IL: Human Kinetics.

Hastie, P. (1996). Student role involvement during a unit of sport education. *Journal of Teaching in Physical Education, 16,* 88-103.

Hawkins, A., Wiegand, R., & Landin, D.K. (1985). Cataloguing the collective wisdom of teacher educators. *Journal of Teaching in Physical Education, 4*, 241-255.

Hebert, E., & Worthy, T. (2001). Does the first year of teaching have to be a bad one? A case study of success. *Teaching and Teacher Education, 17*, 897-911.

Henry, F.M. (1964). Physical education: An academic discipline. *Journal of Health, Physical Education, and Recreation, 35*, 32-39, 69.

Housner, L.D., Gomez, R.L., & Griffey, D.C. (1993). Pedagogical knowledge structures in prospective teachers: Relationships to performance in a teaching methodology class. *Research Quarterly for Exercise and Sport, 64*, 167-177.

Housner, L., & Griffey, D. (1985). Teacher cognition: Differences in planning and interactive decision-making between experienced and inexperienced teachers. *Research Quarterly for Exercise and Sport, 56*, 45-53.

Jewett, A., Bain, L.L., & Ennis, C.D. (1995). *The curriculum process in physical education* (2nd ed.). Dubuque, IA: Brown.

Kirk, D. (1986). A critical pedagogy for teacher education: Toward an inquiry-oriented approach. *Journal of Teaching in Physical Education, 4*, 230-246.

Kulinna, P.H., Silverman, S., & Keating, S.D., (2000). Relationship between teachers' belief systems and actions toward teaching physical activity and fitness. *Journal of Teaching in Physical Education, 19*, 206-221.

Landin, D.K., Hawkins, A., & Wiegand, R. (1986). Validating the collective wisdom of teacher educators. *Journal of Teaching in Physical Education, 5*, 252-271.

Lawson, H. (1983a). Toward a model of teacher socialization in physical education: The subjective warrant, recruitment, and teacher education (Part 1). *Journal of Teaching in Physical Education, 2*, 3-16.

Lawson, H. (1983b). Toward a model of teacher socialization in physical education: Entry into schools, teacher's role orientations, and longevity in teaching (Part 2). *Journal of Teaching in Physical Education, 3*, 3-15.

Lawson, H. (1986). Occupational socialization and the design of teacher education programs. *Journal of Teaching in Physical Education, 5*, 107-116.

Lawson, H. (1988). Occupational socialization, cultural studies, and the physical education curriculum. *Journal of Teaching in Physical Education, 7*, 265-288.

Lawson, H. (1990). Sport pedagogy research: From information-gathering to useful knowledge. *Journal of Teaching in Physical Education, 10*, 1-20.

Lee, A., Keh, N., & Magill, R. (1993). Instructional effects of teacher feedback in physical education. *Journal of Teaching in Physical Education, 12*, 228-243.

Lee, A., Landin, D., & Carter, J. (1992). Student thoughts during tennis instruction. *Journal of Teaching in Physical Education, 11*, 256-267.

Lee, A., & Solmon, M. (1992). Cognitive conceptions of teaching and learning motor skills. *Quest, 42*, 57-71.

Lortie, D. (1975). *Schoolteacher: A sociological study*. Chicago: University of Chicago Press.

Macdonald, D. (1995). The role of proletarianization in physical education attrition. *Research Quarterly for Exercise and Sport, 66*, 129-141.

Martinek, T.J. (1988). Confirmation of a teacher expectancy model: Student perceptions and causal attributions of teaching behaviors. *Research Quarterly for Exercise and Sport, 59*, 118-126.

McBride, R.E. (1991). Critical thinking: An overview with implications for physical education. *Journal of Teaching in Physical Education, 11*, 112-125.

McBride, R.E., & Cleland, F. (1998). Critical thinking in physical education. *Journal of Physical Education, Recreation and Dance, 69*(7), 42-47.

McKenzie, T.L., Marshall, S., Sallis, J.F., & Conway, T.L. (2000). Student activity levels, lesson context, and teacher behavior during middle school physical education. *Research Quarterly for Exercise and Sport, 71*, 249-259.

McKenzie, T.L., Sallis, J.F., Faucette, N., Roby, J., & Kolody, B. (1993). Effects of a curriculum and inservice program on the quantity and quality of elementary physical education classes. *Research Quarterly for Exercise and Sport, 64*, 178-187.

McKenzie, T.L., Sallis, J.F., & Nader, P.R. (1991). SOFIT: System for observing fitness instruction time. *Journal of Teaching in Physical Education, 11*, 195-205.

Medley, D. (1979). The effectiveness of teachers. In P. Peterson and H. Walberg (Eds.), *Research on teaching: Concepts, findings, and implications* (pp. 11-27). Berkeley, CA: McCutchan.

Metzler, M.W. (1980). The measurement of academic learning time in physical education. *Dissertation Abstracts International, 40*, 5365A. (University Microfilms No. 80-90,314)

Metzler, M.W. (1989). A review of research on time in sport pedagogy. *Journal of Teaching in Physical Education, 8*, 87-103.

Mosston, M., & Ashworth, S. (2002). *Teaching physical education* (5th ed). San Francisco: Benjamin Cummings.

Nixon, J.E., & Locke, L. (1973). Research on teaching in physical education. In M.W. Travers (Ed.), *Second handbook of research on teaching* (pp. 1210-1242). Chicago: Rand McNally.

Oliver, B. (1980, April). *Process-outcome relationships and motor skills learning*. Paper presented at the annual meeting of the American Educational Research Association, Boston.

O'Sullivan, M. (1989). Failing gym is like failing lunch or recess: Two beginning teachers' struggle for legitimacy. *Journal of Teaching in Physical Education, 8*, 227-242.

Piéron, M., & Haan, J. (1979, July). *Interactions between teacher and students in a physical education setting: Observation of student behaviors*. Paper presented at the International Council of Health, Physical Education, and Recreation Congress, Kiel, Germany.

Pinheiro, V., & Simon, H. (1992). An operational model of motor skill diagnosis. *Journal of Teaching in Physical Education, 11*, 288-302.

Pissanos, B.W. (1995). Providers of continued professional education: Constructed perceptions of four elementary school physical education teachers. *Journal of Teaching in Physical Education, 14,* 215-230.

Placek, J. (1984). A multi-case study of teacher planning in physical education. *Journal of Teaching in Physical Education, 4,* 39-49.

Placek, J., Silverman, S., Dodds, P., Shute, S., & Rife, F. (1982). Active learning time in a traditional elementary physical education setting: A descriptive analysis. *Journal of Classroom Interaction, 17*(2), 41-47.

Rink, J. (2001). Investigating the assumptions of pedagogy. *Journal of Teaching in Physical Education, 20,* 112-128.

Rink, J., French, K., Lee, A., Solmon, M., & Lynn, S. (1994). A comparison of pedagogical knowledge structures of preservice students and teacher educators in two institutions. *Journal of Teaching in Physical Education, 13,* 140-162.

Rink, J., & Werner, P. (1989). Qualitative measures of teaching performance scale (QMTPS). In P. Darst, D. Zakrajsek, & V. Mancini (Eds.), *Analyzing physical education and sport instruction* (2nd ed.). Champaign, IL: Human Kinetics.

Rolider, A., Siedentop, D., & Van Houten, R. (1984). Effects of enthusiasm training on subsequent teacher enthusiastic behavior. *Journal of Teaching in Physical Education, 3,* 47-59.

Rovegno, I. (1993). Content knowledge acquisition during undergraduate teacher education: Overcoming cultural templates and learning through practice. *American Educational Research Journal, 30,* 611-642.

Rovegno, I., & Bandhauer, D. (1997). Norms of the school culture that facilitated teacher adoption and learning of a constructivist approach to physical education. *Journal of Teaching in Physical Education, 16,* 401-425.

Rukavina, P.B., Lee, A.M., & Solmon, M.A. (2000). Maximizing student learning: A comparison of task communication strategies. *Journal of Sport Pedagogy, 7,* 61-75.

Salter, W.B., & Graham, G. (1985). The effects of three disparate instructional approaches on skill attempts and student learning in an experimental teaching unit. *Journal of Teaching in Physical Education, 4,* 212-218.

Satina, B., Solmon, M.A., Cothran, D.J., Loftus, S.J., & Stockin-Davidson, K. (1998). Patriarchal consciousness: Middle school students' and teachers' perspectives of motivational practices. *Sport, Education and Society, 3,* 181-200.

Schempp, P. (1989, April). *A case study of one physical education teacher's knowledge for work.* Paper presented at the annual meeting of the AERA, San Francisco.

Sharpe, T. (1997). Research note: An introduction to sequential behavior analysis and what it offers physical education teacher education researchers. *Journal of Teaching in Physical Education, 16,* 368-375.

Sharpe, T., & Hawkins, A. (1992). Study III expert and novice elementary specialists: A comparative analysis.

In A. Hawkins & T. Sharpe (Eds.), *Journal of Teaching in Physical Education* [Monograph] *12,* 55-75.

Shulman, L. (1986). Paradigms and research programs in the study of teaching: A contemporary perspective. In M.C. Wittrock (Ed.), *Handbook of research on teaching* (pp. 3-36). New York: Macmillan.

Siedentop, D., & Hughley, C. (1975). OSU teacher behavior rating scale. *Journal of Physical Education and Recreation, 46,* 45.

Siedentop, D., Tousignant, M., & Parker, M. (1982). *Academic learning time-physical education coding manual.* Columbus, OH: Ohio State University.

Silverman, S. (1983). The student as the unit of analysis: Effect on descriptive data and process-outcome relationships in physical education. In T. Templin & J. Olson (Eds.), *Teaching in physical education* (pp. 277-285). Champaign, IL: Human Kinetics.

Silverman, S. (1985). Relationship of engagement and practice trials to student achievement. *Journal of Teaching in Physical Education, 5,* 13-21.

Silverman, S. (1990). Linear and curvilinear relationships between student practice and achievement in physical education. *Teaching and Teacher Education, 6,* 305-314.

Silverman, S. (1994). Communication and motor skill learning: What we learn from research in the gymnasium. *Quest, 46,* 345-355.

Silverman, S., Dodds, P., Placek, J., Shute, S., & Rife, F. (1984). Academic learning time in elementary physical education (ALT-PE) for student subgroups and instructional activity units. *Research Quarterly for Exercise and Sport, 55,* 365-370.

Silverman, S., & Skonie, R. (1997). Research on teaching in physical education: An analysis of published research. *Journal of Teaching in Physical Education, 16,* 300-311.

Silverman, S., & Subramaniam, P.R. (1999). Student attitude toward physical education and physical activity: A review of measurement issues and outcomes. *Journal of Teaching in Physical Education, 19,* 97-125.

Silverman, S., Tyson, L.A., & Krampitz, J. (1992). Teacher feedback and achievement in physical education: Interaction with student practice. *Teaching and Teacher Education, 8,* 333-344.

Silverman, S., Tyson, L.A., & Morford, L.M. (1988). Relationships of organization, time, and student achievement in physical education. *Teaching and Teacher Education, 4,* 247-257.

Smyth, D.M. (1995). First-year physical education teachers' perception of their work place. *Journal of Teaching in Physical Education, 14,* 198-216.

Solmon, M.A., & Boone, J. (1993). The impact of student goal orientation in physical education classes. *Research Quarterly for Exercise and Sport, 64,* 418-424.

Solmon, M.A., & Lee, A.M. (1991). A contrast of planning behaviors between expert and novice adapted physical education teachers. *Adapted Physical Activity Quarterly, 8,* 115-127.

Solmon, M.A., & Lee, A.M. (1996). Entry characteristics, practice variables, and cognition: Student mediation of instruction. *Journal of Teaching in Physical Education 15*, 136-150.

Solmon, M.A., Worthy, T., & Carter, J.A. (1993). Interaction of school context and role identity of first year teachers. *Journal of Teaching in Physical Education, 12*, 313-328.

Solmon, M.A., Worthy, T., Lee, A., & Carter, J. (1991). Teacher role identity of student teachers in physical education: An interactive analysis. *Journal of Teaching in Physical Education, 10*, 188-209.

Stroot, S. (Ed.). (1993). Socialization into physical education. *Journal of Teaching in Physical Education* [Summer Monograph].

Stroot, S., & Morton, P. (1989). Blueprints for learning. *Journal of Teaching in Physical Education, 8*, 213-222.

Subramaniam, P.R., & Silverman, S. (2000). Validation of scores from an instrument assessing student attitude toward physical education. *Measurement in Physical Education and Exercise Science, 4*, 29-43.

Sweeting, T., & Rink, J.E. (1999). Effects of direct instruction and environmentally designed instruction on the process and product characteristics of a fundamental skill. *Journal of Teaching in Physical Education, 18*, 216-233.

Taylor, J.L. (1976). Development and use of the physical education observation instrument for rating patterns of teacher behaviors in relationship to student achievement. *Dissertation Abstracts International, 37*, 2615A (University Microfilms No. 76-26,009).

Templin, T. (1979). Occupational socialization and the physical education student teacher. *Research Quarterly, 50*, 482-493.

Templin, T. (1981). Student as socializing agent. *Journal of Teaching in Physical Education, Introductory Issue*, 71-79.

Templin, T., & Schempp, P. (Eds.) (1989). *Socialization into physical education: Learning to teach*. West Palm Beach, FL: Benchmark Press.

Templin, T., Sparks, A., & Schempp, P. (1991). The professional life cycle of a retired physical education teacher: A tale of bitter disengagement. *Physical Education Review, 14*, 143-156.

Turner, A.P., & Martinek, T.J. (1995). Teaching for understanding: A model for improving decision making during game play. *Quest, 47*, 44-63.

Twardy, B.M., & Yerg, B.J. (1987). The impact of planning on inclass interactive behaviors of preservice teachers. *Journal of Teaching in Physical Education, 6*, 136-148.

van der Mars, H. (1987). Effects of audio cueing on teacher verbal praise of students' managerial and transitional task performance. *Journal of Teaching in Physical Education, 6*, 157-165.

Veal, M. (1988). Pupil assessment practices and perceptions of secondary teachers. *Journal of Teaching in Physical Education, 7*, 327-342.

Veal, M. (1992). Pupil-based theories of pupil assessment: A case study. *Research Quarterly for Exercise and Sport, 63*, 48-59.

Walkwitz, E., & Lee, A. (1992). The role of knowledge in elementary physical education: An exploratory study. *Research Quarterly for Exercise and Sport, 63*, 179-185.

Whilden, P. (1956). Comparison of two methods of teaching beginning basketball. *Research Quarterly, 27*, 235-242.

Wittrock, M.C. (1986). Students' thought processes. In M.C. Wittrock (Ed.), *Handbook of research on teaching* (3rd ed., pp. 297-314). New York: Macmillan.

Wright, J. (1996). Mapping the discourses of physical education: Articulating a female tradition. *Curriculum Studies, 28*, 331-351.

Xiang, P., & Lee, A.M. (1998). The development of self-perceptions of ability and achievement goals and their relations in physical education. *Research Quarterly for Exercise and Sport, 69*, 231-241.

Xiang, P., Lee, A.M., & Williamson, L. (2001). Conceptions of ability in physical education: Children and adolescents. *Journal of Teaching in Physical Education, 20*, 282-294.

Xiang, P., Lowy, S., & McBride, R. (2002). The impact of a field-based elementary physical education methods course on preservice classroom teachers' beliefs. *Journal of Teaching in Physical Education, 21*, 145-161.

Yerg, B.J. (1981a). Reflections on the use of the RTE model in physical education. *Research Quarterly for Exercise and Sport, 52*, 38-47.

Yerg, B.J. (1981b). The impact of selected presage and process behaviors on the refinement of a motor skill. *Journal of Teaching in Physical Education, 1*, 38-46.

Yerg, B.J. (1983). Re-examining the process-product paradigm for research on teaching effectiveness in physical education. In T. Templin & J. Olson (Eds.), *Teaching in physical education* (pp. 310-317). Champaign IL: Human Kinetics.

Yerg B.J., & Twardy, B.M. (1982). Relationship of specified instructional teacher behaviors to pupil gain on a motor skill task. In M. Piéron & J. Cheffers (Eds.), *Studying the teaching in physical education* (pp. 61-68). Liege, Belgium: Association Internationale des Superieures d'Education Physique.

CHAPTER THREE

RESEARCH: WHAT IT IS AND HOW WE CAN LEARN FROM IT

Stephen J. Silverman

As professionals we hope we continue to learn throughout our careers. Getting new information, evaluating whether the information might help us perform our job better, and perhaps trying it out and evaluating its efficacy is something that professionals do. In fact, many states have amended certification guidelines so that teachers learn how to find and evaluate new information (e.g., New York State Education Department, Office of Teaching and Learning, 2002a) and have proposed codes of ethics that require teachers to seek further knowledge that has the potential to improve their practice (e.g., New York State Education Department, Office of Teaching and Learning, 2002b). Finding professional resources and research is the first step in using new information.

Because you are reading this book you probably are interested in getting new knowledge related to physical education. The chapters that follow provide a comprehensive, up-to-date review of the research on teaching, curriculum, and teacher education in physical education. This chapter will focus on finding additional resources and provide information to help you read research. The next section will discuss ways to find resources. The sections that follow discuss why we do research, how to use the results of research, and an introduction to the types of research found in physical education.

FINDING RESOURCES TO SUPPORT YOUR WORK

When the first edition of this book was published in 1996, far fewer resources were available to physical educators—and getting them required more work and time. Both professional resources and research reports are now readily available for those interested in physical education. Geography or the lack of colleagues no longer limits us—a global electronic community can provide professional ideas and colleagues willing to discuss those ideas. Physical educators now have access to an overwhelming variety of information.

Educational Materials and the Internet

The Internet is the easiest and most cost effective place to find professional resources for teaching physical education. As I was writing this chapter I did searches on Google of

Internet resources for teachers and then those just for physical education teachers. The result was nearly two million Web sites providing information for all teachers and just about half a million for physical education teachers. The physical education resources ranged from curriculum guides to lesson plans to information about promoting physical education to obtaining resources—and many other topics. I spent hours looking at various pages and would never be able to sift through all the information available.

Given how the World Wide Web has changed in the last decade (to get a perspective from just a few years ago see Finkenberg, 1997 and Silverman, 1997), much of the advice on finding resources I would give today may be outdated when you are reading this. But some general ideas will help physical educators make good use of the Internet. First, make use of comprehensive sites. A site such as PE Central (www.pe.central.vt.edu/), run by George Graham and his students, provides incredible resources to aid physical education teachers. Using sites that have many ideas and many teachers sharing their thoughts and best practices is an efficient way to use the Web.

Second, look at what is available on professional association Web sites. The American Alliance for Health, Physical Education, Recreation and Dance (AAHPERD) site (www.aapherd.org) and many of the state affiliates provide information that is helpful in promoting programs, finding information, and knowing what changes are occurring in the field. In particular, state association Web sites often provide information on statewide initiatives that are important to program planning and the role of physical education in schools.

Finally, you may want to participate in an electronic list server that permits you to eavesdrop or participate in a conversation with other professionals. NASPE-L is a national list server that is sponsored by the National Association of Sport and Physical Education (NASPE). You can join thousands of other physical educators by subscribing from their Web site (www.aahperd.org/naspe/template.cfm). In addition, many state associations and local physical education groups maintain electronic distribution lists that can connect you quickly to those who can provide resources—or where you can help others. Using electronic resources can keep you connected to up-to-date information quickly and for little cost.

Finding Research

Reading research that addresses questions in physical education that may be related to your teaching is another way to stay up-to-date on what is happening. The most efficient way to get that information is by reading research reviews in which others have synthesized the literature and drawn conclusions about what it says. Recent studies are published as research reports. These often provide background on the area in which you might be interested and offer an in-depth presentation of one attempt to find more information about the topic. Locke, Silverman, and Spirduso (1998) provide a discussion of what each type of paper contains and how professionals can best use them. Whether you are interested in finding research reviews or research reports, you must find them before you can read the papers.

The best way to find research reviews and research reports is by learning to use electronic retrieval systems specifically designed for this purpose. Many readers will be familiar with ERIC, the Educational Resources Information Clearinghouse, which is maintained by the United States government. ERIC indexes most of the journals in education, including physical education, and provides access to unpublished material through microfiche and now through Acrobat files that are immediately downloadable. ERIC is clearly the first stop for physical educators seeking research information. In addition, many university and public libraries have other tools that also can be helpful to physical educators, such as the Web of Science, Education Index, and ProQuest. Each of these provides slightly different databases. Searching more than one can be helpful in finding resources.

As you use electronic retrieval systems one thing will become immediately clear—learning how to use the system will save you lots of time. Each system works in different ways, which may change from time to time. Time you spend reading about how to use the system or attending a workshop on electronic retrieval will be time well spent. Reference librarians and experienced users can provide helpful hints, but nothing beats using a system for developing proficiency in finding information on your own. Once you can find resources, many libraries permit you to access them electronically, and you can read the papers on your screen or print them for future reference.

RESEARCH IN PHYSICAL EDUCATION

To make the task of reading the chapters that follow a little easier and to help readers when they read original research articles, the remainder of this chapter presents an overview of how to read research and the basics of different research types likely to be found in the physical education literature. Because researchers often provide conclusions that can improve the educational process, practitioners will benefit by being able to understand the investigative process and perhaps read some of the original research. To evaluate its applicability, they need to know a little about the mechanics of research. Practitioners must be able to decide if researchers' suggestions are appropriate for the situation in which they are working or whether the results warrant the conclusions presented.

The research process sometimes seems mystical. An individual or a group collects data, writes a report, and publishes it. Often these research papers are difficult for non-researchers to read, even if they are practitioners in the same field. As with any skill, understanding and applying research requires learning and practice.

This chapter will not duplicate the work of those references that can help you get a more complete view of research methods (e.g., Denzin & Lincoln, 2000; Gall, Borg, & Gall, 2003; Locke, Spirduso, & Silverman, 2000; Thomas, 1993; Thomas & Nelson, 2001) or how to read research (Locke et al., 1998). Rather, it will provide a foundation for reading the chapters that follow. I will first discuss why we do research in physical education and present a way of thinking about the research process. Next, I will discuss how we can use the results of research in physical education. Then I discuss a couple of issues that are important to consider before we look at research methods. In the final section I will present an overview of the methods used for research on teaching, teacher education, and curriculum in physical education. This discussion will focus on the concepts that will help you understand later chapters in this book and will provide a framework for reading research reports.

Why Do We Do Research and Why Does It Matter?

As noted earlier, the research process often seems mystical and difficult. I remember reading the preface of a statistics textbook a few years ago in which the author noted that the best way to have people avoid you at a cocktail party is to tell them that you teach statistics and research methods. This suggests that many people either don't understand research or view researchers and what they do in a less-than-positive light. Kerlinger (1973) notes that we often think of the researcher as a nerd in a lab jacket desperately seeking facts in an attempt to expand some arcane theory or find a cure for cancer that is many years away.

In actuality, the research process is dynamic and enjoyable. Researchers develop ideas based on their experiences and on previous research. They have many false starts and some satisfying conclusions to their efforts. They try out their ideas and the interpretation of results with others—colleagues, graduate students, teachers—who may provide different and valuable insights. They worry as they progress, hoping all goes well until the data are ready for a research report. Once a researcher submits a paper for publication, anxiety may occur every time he or she checks the mail, wondering if the paper will be accepted and published. The research process, particularly in an area like physical education in which research often is conducted in schools, is a human enterprise. Sometimes it's enjoyable and goes well; sometimes it isn't fun and doesn't work out.

Why Do Researchers Persist?

When research doesn't go well or the initial experience of doing research is not satisfying, why do researchers persist? People conduct research for many reasons. Sometimes a research project is required for a graduate degree, or it may be that a faculty member is conducting research and publishing to keep his or her job and earn tenure. Those of us who have made a career in which research and scholarship play a major role originally may have conducted research for those reasons. I believe, however, that the motivation for continuing research is different. Most of the reasons for conducting research in physical education fall into two categories: (a) providing information to improve physical education and (b) contributing to the theoretical bases of physical education.

As the distinguished researcher Nathanial Gage (1966) noted a number of years ago, many people study educational issues because they want to improve teaching. They see issues in instructional settings and design research they believe will lead to informed improvement of their field. Much research has the goal of improving the way professionals conduct business. Most researchers hope their work will be valuable sometime to someone practicing in their field, even if that is a distant prospect or never happens.

Extending theory, or as Doyle (1978) suggested, understanding educational processes, is another reason for conducting research. Understanding why things happen in some situations and why they don't happen in others provides a theoretical base for a field. Knowing something works is one thing; knowing why it works provides different information and can result in deeper understanding of the field. Some claim that only research that immediately extends theory is valuable (see Gage, 1994 and Garrison & Macmillan, 1994 for a discussion of this issue in teaching research), but I believe that it takes a focused research program conducted over a number of years to provide greater understanding of the phenomenon being studied.

Some people believe that research practitioners cannot readily use is merely an academic exercise; others insist that research with ambiguous theoretical implications is fluff. These positions, however, polarize the issue. In the best situation, the researcher has both practical and theoretical reasons for conducting physical education research. Sometimes one motivation or the other dominates. The knowledge obtained from research often occurs progressively, in small increments, until eventually everything comes together and the whole makes more sense.

Whether the goal of research is improvement or understanding—or both—we can think of the research process as problem solving. We all do research in our everyday lives. We encounter problems and try to find answers. Sometimes we use trial and error, and other times we know a little more and have strategies for finding a solution. Research is just a sophisticated and formalized version of problem solving.

Informal and Formal Research

We all are familiar with the ways in which teachers solve problems, even if we don't think of it as research. For example, a teacher may note that many students are misbehaving. She asks herself why and notices that the misbehavior mostly occurs near the end of a practice session. She decides to switch activities so that students don't become bored, and she notices much less misbehavior. In effect, the teacher has asked a question, proposed a solution, and observed the results.

A similar situation occurs in research that is more formal. The researcher may ask "what if" questions (Locke et al., 2000) that have theoretical or practical implications. The researcher refines the question being asked, devises a method that answers the question, and then collects data to answer the question. He or she has posed a question and provided an answer. This answer may not be of immediate value for others who are in different situations or who believe that more evidence is needed through replication, but it provides one insight into the question. As you will note in the other chapters in this book, when studies are combined we have information that can influence both theory and practice.

Using the Results of Research

If we view research as problem solving, then when reading research we need to determine whether it applies to problems that occur in our particular situation. Alternatively, if you identify a problem or want to examine other ideas, you may want to turn to the literature and see if someone has investigated the topic. You will often find helpful research reviews. The other chapters in this book provide a review and summary of a rich literature on physical education.

Quick Guide to Reading Research

If you decide to read an original research paper to follow up on ideas learned here or for any other reason, you can use a variety of ways to ease your task and make the most of the information (for a detailed discussion see Locke et al., 1998). My first recommendation is to read the abstract to see if the information is interesting or helpful to you. Next, skim the article and evaluate again whether it seems applicable. Ask yourself whether the situation seems similar to your own. Is it close enough that you might get something useful out of the paper? If, at this point, you think the paper is worth pursuing, read it to figure out what the researcher did and what implications the information may have for you.

Normally, research papers have four sections: (a) introduction, (b) method, (c) results, and (d) discussion. The introduction sets the stage and explains the importance of the research. The question or purpose of the research usually appears near the end of this section. This section is usually placed in the context of previous research, and it may or may not discuss practical issues. The method section explains what the researcher did to answer the question. The participants and setting are especially important in determining whether the paper is applicable to your situation. For instance, if you work in an urban public school and the research was conducted in a private preparatory school, you may decide that the situations are so different that no comparison is possible. Or, if the research occurred in a setting with a small group of students, the suggestions may not work for the 30 students you teach in each class. (Note, however, that research papers may provide valuable information even in contexts that are quite different.) The results section presents the author's findings based on the questions that were asked. This section may have tables, statistical symbols, narratives, or other ways of presenting information. Finally, the discussion section interprets the results for theory or application or both. The section may include conclusions for practice or future research.

Many people, as noted earlier, find research reports difficult to read. Some papers are easier to read than others. Some will be of greater interest and will therefore sustain greater effort. The use of system language (terms that have specific meaning to researchers), jargon, statistical terms, and other peculiarities of the research report contribute to the difficulty. Researchers and journal editors strive to make their work clear, but even the best written research paper may be difficult for those without a background in research.

When reading research papers you should concentrate on what you need from the paper, not everything the author wrote. A friend of mine, a long-time public school teacher, reads the introduction to find the purpose of the study. She next reads the method section to determine if the setting, students, and intervention, if any, are relevant to her situation. When reading the results, she looks for summary statements and ignores the technical discussion. For example, she may read the topic sentence describing the result and then forego the statistical discussion that follows.

Finally, she reads the discussion to see if the conclusions or suggestions can be helpful and provide her with greater insight. Her strategy allows her to read information of interest without getting bogged down in the parts that have little relevance to the problems she faces. My friend doesn't get every detail from the paper, but she does get a lot of help.

Additional Tips for Reading Research

Two other things might be of value in reading and understanding research. First, you must not give up too easily. Ask for help, from faculty members at universities, curriculum directors with research training, and others. A discussion with someone else also may help. Second, if you have had a graduate research-methods course or have experience reading research, you can learn by helping others. We all benefit when we discuss with others or help them. Some of the most interesting discussions I've had with colleagues occurred when the topic was their research. You may find the same.

When seeking information from research, your main concern is whether the paper will help you. Researchers read many papers they will never cite. This reading helps provide a base for understanding the broad field (Locke et al., 2000). The same goes for practitioners. You should not expect every paper to be helpful. Some will help you understand what won't work or may not be applicable to your situation. Others will apply directly. The more you explore the literature, the easier it will be to select among papers.

One concern often expressed about educational research is that the results are obvious and that any reasonably intelligent person would come to a similar conclusion. Gage (1991, 1994) strongly states that this isn't the case, for several reasons:

- Understanding occurs only in hindsight and not before research is conducted.
- Research provides specificity for more complete understanding by answering questions like "how much?" and "how often?"
- By examining different contexts, research shows where results are not applicable.

Research provides information that you cannot obtain in any other way.

Prelude to Methods of Research in Physical Education

Research is conducted using a variety of methods guided by different types of questions. Research in physical education may focus on teaching, teacher education, or curriculum. To understand research and follow the discussion in this book, you should have a basic understanding of the various research paradigms, or models, used in physical education, and their characteristic methods. In this section, I will discuss the importance of defining questions as a preliminary step in research and why researchers use different approaches.

Importance of Defining Questions

If we take the view that research is a form of problem solving, then the problem is the key to research. If the researcher doesn't have at least a general idea of the problem, it's difficult to conduct good research. A good problem, stated as a question or hypothesis, guides research and makes a research paper easier to comprehend.

We can ask different types of questions about physical education. For instance, we may want to know how teachers develop and implement curriculum, how student teachers mature and gain pedagogical content knowledge, or how feedback and learning relate to each other in physical education. Each question has a different focus and may require a different paradigm, or approach, to answer the question being posed. As Amelia Lee noted in the previous chapter, researchers have addressed many different questions in physical education, and the questions have evolved over the years. Research paradigms and methods have expanded, and many tools are available to do research.

Merits of Different Paradigms

Debate has persisted over whether one research paradigm is superior to another (e.g., O'Sullivan, Siedentop, & Locke, 1992; Schempp, 1987, 1988; Siedentop, 1987). At times this debate has been acrimonious. My position is similar to that of Guba (1985, p. 87), who states, "no single paradigm provides more than a partial picture." We must have research in a variety of subareas and by a variety of approaches to attain fuller understanding of our field. As you will surely note as you read the chapters that follow, researchers use many methods, each providing information necessary for a broad picture of physical education.

The various paradigms often present research in different ways and require different criteria for writing the research report and communicating information (Bruce & Greendorfer, 1994; Creswell, 1994, 1998; Locke et al., 1998). This diversity, in my mind, is valuable. You will see some of this diversity in this book, as the contributors refer to individual research papers. Although methods vary, note that much of the research conducted across paradigms occurs in natural settings with real teachers, students, student teachers, and teacher educators. This common factor has been important to the advancement of knowledge in physical education.

Methods of Research

Many discussions of research paradigms or methods begin with a presentation of the philosophical underpinnings of each paradigm. That discussion is beyond the concern of this chapter, because we can read research and get an idea of its value without detailed discussion of these issues. If you are interested in pursuing philosophical issues, you can find a basic introduction in the first chapter of Creswell (1994). Here I will discuss the research paradigms that have been widely used in physical education research or are emerging in the field, along with their characteristic methods. I will provide an overview of each method and a few references as places to start to get more information. In addition, I will cite literature using the method so, if you wish, you can read an example of the research method in an actual physical education study. Although we can categorize research in different ways, research paradigms can be broadly classified as qualitative or quantitative. These two classifications can be further broken down. Figure 3.1 provides a diagram of the major research paradigms and subparadigms that researchers use in physical education and that I will discuss in this chapter.

Each of the paradigms and subparadigms has different names in different literature and uses research methods that may or may not be used in a closely related research paradigm. Devotees of one method may think alternative methods are very different, whereas others may think they are similar. In this chapter I will discuss four quantitative methods: (a) description; (b) correlation and prediction; (c) experiment and quasi-experiment; and (d) applied behavior analysis or single-subject research. For the sake of simplicity and to aid in understanding I have classified qualitative research into three broad categories: (a) ethnography-like interpretive research; (b) phenomenology-like interpretive research; and (c) critical theory.

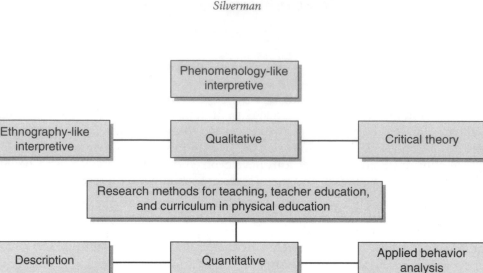

FIGURE 3.1   Common research methods in teaching, teacher education, and curriculum in physical education.

Quantitative Research

The general aim of quantitative research is the description, prediction, and explanation of the situation being studied. Most research-methods books (e.g., Gall et al., 2003; Thomas & Nelson, 2001) provide a good overview of these methods. As the name implies, quantitative research conveys data using numbers and statistics. As Lee discussed in her chapter, physical education includes a long history of various types of quantitative research. Each of the groupings presented below can be conducted in isolation. Or, as Rosenshine and Furst (1973) suggested, the various methods can be combined in programmatic research.

A common aspect of much of the quantitative research in physical education over the past two decades, particularly teaching research, is the use of observation of teacher and student behavior (Silverman, 1991). As Locke (1977) discussed in an early paper on physical education research, the use of observation was a requirement for improving the research at that time. Early research did not collect direct data on physical education (Nixon & Locke, 1973), and the results were not particularly helpful to practitioners or researchers.

Description.   The general goal of descriptive studies is to find out what is occurring in a situation. "How do students spend time in physical education classes?" "What kind and how much feedback do teachers give students in physical education?" and "What goals do teachers have for their classes?" are typical of the questions that guide descriptive research. Researchers do not attempt to describe relationships or measure the effectiveness of an intervention. Providing a description of what occurred in the group being studied and in various subgroups is the focus. Means and standard deviations, bar charts, and tables often represent the data.

The best example of a large-scale descriptive project in physical education is the work of Bill Anderson and his students at Teachers College, Columbia University (Anderson & Barrette, 1978). The research group videotaped many physical education classes, designed instruments to analyze and describe what was on the tapes, and presented a multidimensional view of physical education. This research program influenced many who subsequently engaged in physical education research.

Correlation and Prediction. Correlation and prediction studies use similar techniques to understand the relationships between two variables or among a number of variables. Questions such as "Is there a positive relationship between student time on-task and student achievement?" and "Is there a relationship between teachers' control ideology and their goals for physical education?" examine the relationship between two variables. A more complex study might ask, "What are the interrelationships of student and teacher variables in predicting student achievement in physical education?" Such a study may measure many variables and use them in combination. Papers using this methodology report simple and multiple correlation coefficients, provide percent variation of the criterion variable (student achievement in the last question above) accounted for by the other variables (usually reported as an R^2), or may report complex models of the interrelations among variables (often presented as a structural equation model).

The work that I have done with valuable assistance from students and colleagues represents this type of research (e.g., Silverman, 1990, 1993; Silverman, Kulinna, & Crull, 1995; Silverman & Tyson, 1994; Silverman, Tyson, & Krampitz, 1992; Silverman, Tyson, & Morford, 1988). We pretested and posttested a large group of students and provided them with instruction between the tests. We videotaped the instruction and collected process data (e.g., amount of time spent in various categories, the amount and type of student practice, and teacher feedback to students) from the videotapes. The process data obtained by observation were correlated with student achievement in the individual studies cited above. Finally, we combined the data from all the studies to examine the interrelationships of the variables in predicting student achievement.

Experiment and Quasi-Experiment Research. Experiment and quasi-experiment research involve the analysis of differences between groups. Some research in this category may compare students randomly assigned to treatments versus those in a control group (experiments). Other research may use existing, intact groups and compare differences in a dependent variable (quasi-experiments). The difference between randomly assigned groups and intact groups determines, to a degree, what kind of conclusions one can make about a treatment. Although many would suggest that experiments yield the best knowledge (see Campbell & Stanley, 1963, for the classic discussion), it is difficult to do good experiments in natural settings (Cook & Campbell, 1979; Silverman, 1985; Silverman & Solmon, 1998). Randomization is just not possible in many school settings.

A study using an experiment or quasi-experiment design might ask questions such as "Do high-skilled students receive more teacher feedback than low-skilled students?" "Does the reciprocal style result in greater motor-skill learning than the command style?" or "What is the difference in the amount of physical activity between fitness and skill-based curricula?" Again, the purpose is to determine group differences in means on one or more variables. Group differences are established by various statistical techniques, and papers using this paradigm report means and standard deviations and the results of *t*-tests, analysis of variance, or multiple analysis of variance.

The work of Mike Goldberger and his students (Goldberger, 1983; Goldberger & Gerney, 1986, 1990) is a good example of experiment research in physical education. They have conducted a systematic examination of Mosston's spectrum of teaching styles (Mosston & Ashworth, 2002), comparing the effect of various teaching styles on student achievement in motor skills and other common goals of physical education. Students in these studies were pretested on the dependent variables, randomly assigned to treatments (teaching style) where they received instruction, and then posttested. In addition, the researchers observed and collected data during instruction to verify that the teaching style was being implemented as intended.

Applied Behavior Analysis. Applied behavior analysis or single-subject research uses a small number of subjects to determine if an intervention can change the behavior of a subject. Gall et al. (2003) discuss this category of research design in the context of behavior modification. Questions that researchers might pose using this paradigm are "Will the use of students' names reduce off-task behavior?" "Will student teachers who view videotapes with focused observation use gym space more efficiently?" or "Will a reward system increase student physical activity outside of physical education classes?" In single-subject research, at the basic level, baseline data on the behavior of interest are collected, the intervention is implemented, and then the intervention is stopped. Data collection continues through the intervention and for a period afterward. The researcher plots the data to see if the desired effect occurs during the intervention and if removing the intervention reduces the behavior back to the baseline. The researcher visually inspects the data to make conclusions about the effectiveness of the intervention.

A good example of single-subject research is a study by Joel Schuldheisz and Hans van der Mars (2001) in which they were interested in seeing if active teacher class supervision increased the amount of moderate to vigorous physical activity (MVPA) children engaged in during fitness instruction. They collected observational data to establish a baseline (passive supervision by the teacher) and continued data collection throughout the study, alternating between active and passive supervision conditions to chart the effect of active supervision on student MVPA.

Qualitative Research

The use of qualitative research has grown greatly in the past two decades. In particular, interpretive research methods have flourished, and studies using those methods appear frequently in the physical education literature (Byra & Goc Karp, 2000). Many good references now exist for all forms of qualitative research. Denzin and Lincoln (2000) provide a comprehensive discussion of qualitative research. You may find, however, that the discussion in Creswell (1998) or Locke et al. (1998) is a good place to start for interpretive research. Thomas (1993) is a readable text on critical methods.

Many different names and categorizations are used for different traditions within qualitative research (e.g., see Creswell, 1998; Green, 2000). I have chosen to use the term *interpretive research* as a broader term to reflect two types of research you may encounter. Many related forms of research have similar goals, and most readers need not make the distinctions to read the research and get information for professional practice. Readers who study the research more closely will certainly want to understand the different traditions and associated differences in what they are called. Among the names applied to related studies are biography or life story, narrative, ethnography, interview, grounded theory, case study, phenomenology, and others. Although the distinctions are important, commonalities among the research forms make reading research reports similar.

Published papers of interpretive research describe themes found during data collection. Quotations, vignettes, and detailed descriptions support these themes. The data presentation is in prose, and a results section may read like a newspaper story (i.e., here's what I found and why).

Ethnography-Like Interpretive Research.   The term *ethnography* may be used in different ways in different contexts. For this discussion, researchers using this approach work to provide a rich description and understanding of a situation from the perspective of those being studied. The researcher wants to go beyond mere description and provide in-depth understanding of what is occurring and how the participants view the situation. Questions that the researcher might ask in an interpretive research study are "What is the relationship between student teachers and their supervisors during student teaching?" "How do teachers adapt and adjust during the first three years of teaching?" and "How do teacher educators work to revise their curriculum when state mandate imposes restrictions?" Among the methods interpretive researchers use are interviews, analysis of materials such as lesson plans and curriculum guides, and intense observation. This type of observation is different from that used in quantitative research, discussed earlier. Ethnography-like interpretive researchers may observe a wide range of activities and use field notes to record information.

Nell Faucette and her colleagues (Faucette, Nugent, Sallis, & McKenzie, 2002) completed a study that examined classroom teachers' responses to teaching physical education. These teachers were part of the Sports, Play, and Active Recreation for Kids (SPARK) project that Thom McKenzie discusses in chapter 12. Teachers participated in professional development and implemented the Project SPARK curriculum. The researchers interviewed the teachers in depth to get their perceptions about Project SPARK, and they combined the interview data with other data to provide the teachers' perspectives on the intervention and on teaching physical education.

Phenomenology-Like Interpretive Research.   The term *phenomenology* generally suggests studies that focus on personal meaning and how experiences come together to form a view of the participants' world (Creswell, 1998; Marshall & Rossman, 1999). This form of research often has an interpersonal aspect in data collection and in the research report (Creswell, 1998). These studies address personal meaning and may focus on topics with emotional aspects to both the researcher and the study participants. Phenomenology-like interpretive research may ask questions like "How does a physical educator understand his career?" and "How do lesbian physical educators experience their role of teacher and coach?" Besides making use of the data-collection techniques used for ethnography-like studies, researchers employ in-depth and personal interviews, longer narratives, and life histories to examine the questions they ask.

An interesting example of a phenomenology-like study is one by Kim Oliver (1999) that examined how adolescent girls construct meaning about their bodies. The girls participated in a number of interviews over a long period. In addition, they kept journals, wrote stories, and prepared personal biographies. Oliver analyzed the data and presented the way in which the girls constructed the meaning of their bodies.

Critical Theory.   Critical theory researchers approach their task from a different perspective. The critical theorist views research as a way to analyze power inequities in a situation or in society. An alternative form of critical research seeks to document the empowerment of individuals through interventions, counseling, or group activities. Critical research has no pretense of objectivity. Many critical researchers approach their work as a political enterprise with the goal of influencing change. Critical researchers may ask questions such as "Does participation in physical activity utilizing tools for self-responsibility empower the participants to take control of their lives?" and "How does the use of traditional teaching strategies affect the teacher-student relationship in physical education?" The first question relates to documenting empowerment activities, and the second pertains to examining power in a relationship.

The critical theorist researcher may use observation, field notes, and interviews. In addition, the researcher examining power may analyze textual material, television programs, movies, or other cultural phenomena. Reports examining power relationships present the question and the viewpoint of the author and then provide detailed support for the contention. As noted earlier, the paper may take a position from the start. Empowerment documentation papers may read like a combination of the other critical papers and interpretive research reports.

The work of Don Hellison (see chapter 14) is among the few focusing on empowerment in physical education. He has implemented a program, outside school hours, in inner-city Chicago that focuses on using physical activity as the instructional medium for developing social and self-responsibility of students. The goal is not acquiring motor skills or fitness but becoming responsible adults. The use of notes and interviews documents the progress of children in this program.

David Kirk's (1989) examination of the research-practice gap in physical education is a good example of a critical paper that examines power. He argues that the dominant approaches to research on teaching physical education have not resulted in curriculum changes. He discusses strategy, power, and politicization as he analyzes what he calls the "orthodox view" (p. 124) and concludes by providing an alternative view.

BECOMING A RESEARCH CONSUMER

Research in physical education has made great advances over the past quarter century. The quality and quantity of research has improved and, as will be noted throughout this book, the information available is impressive. A significant, positive development in physical education research is that trained researchers are now using a variety of research methods. Physical educators—researchers and practitioners alike—should appreciate the progress and encourage this diversity in the future.

Finding information to improve practice—or just to get ideas about teaching in physical education—is important to staying current and doing a good job in most professions. Information is available on the Internet, in research reviews, and in research reports. Becoming an informed research consumer will permit you to learn more and grow as a physical educator. Taking advantage of the many opportunities to learn more about research has the potential to make each of our careers more exciting and stimulating.

IMPLICATIONS FOR PRACTICE

1. Many states now require teachers to know how to find information to improve practice and consider keeping up-to-date an ethical responsibility.
2. Many sources of information about physical education are available. The Internet is a particularly efficient place to find information.
3. Research reports answer questions in systematic ways that can have both practical and theoretical implications for physical education.
4. Research reviews, like those in this book, are a good place to start learning more about a topic.
5. Computerized indexes can help you find both research reviews and research reports. Learning one or more indexes will be invaluable in retrieving research information.
6. You don't have to understand everything in a research paper to get something from it. Take what you need and don't worry about the parts for which you need more information.
7. Questions guide research, and in well-designed research the questions are formulated before the methods are completed.
8. Research can be done in a variety of ways. One is not better than another—different methods are more appropriate for answering different types of questions.
9. Staying current can help you become an informed consumer and grow as a professional educator.

REFERENCES

Anderson, W.G., & Barrette, G.T. (Eds.). (1978). What's going on in gym: Descriptive studies of physical education classes. *Motor skills: Theory into practice* (Monograph 1).

Bruce, T., & Greendorfer, S.L. (1994). Post modern challenges: Recognizing multiple standards for social science research. *Journal of Sport and Social Issues, 18,* 258-268.

Byra, M., & Goc Karp, G. (2000). Data collection techniques employed in qualitative research in physical education teacher education. *Journal of Teaching in Physical Education, 19,* 246-266.

Campbell, D.T., & Stanley, J.C. (1963). *Experimental and quasi experimental designs for research.* New York: Rand-McNally.

Cook, T.H., & Campbell, D.T. (1979). *Quasi-experimentation: Design and analysis issues from field settings.* Chicago: Rand-McNally.

Creswell, J.W. (1994). *Research design: Qualitative and quantitative approaches.* Thousand Oaks, CA: Sage.

Creswell, J.W. (1998). *Qualitative inquiry and research design: Choosing among five traditions.* Thousand Oaks, CA: Sage.

Denzin, N., & Lincoln, Y.S. (Eds.). (2000). *Handbook of qualitative research* (2nd ed.). Thousand Oaks, CA: Sage.

Doyle, W. (1978, April). *Research on the realities of the classroom: Who needs it?* Paper presented at the annual meeting of the American Educational Research Association, Toronto, Canada.

Faucette, N., Nugent, P., Sallis, J.F., & McKenzie, T.L. (2002). "I'd rather chew on aluminum foil." Overcoming classroom teachers' resistance to teaching physical education. *Journal of Teaching in Physical Education, 21,* 287-308.

Finkenberg, M.E. (1997). The Internet in kinesiology and physical education. *Quest, 49,* 327-332.

Gage, N.L. (1966). Research on cognitive aspects of teaching. In Association for Supervision and Curriculum Development and National Education Association, *The way teaching is* (pp. 29-44). Washington, DC: Author.

Gage, N.L. (1991). The obviousness of social and educational research results. *Educational Researcher, 20*(1), 10-16.

Gage, N.L. (1994). The scientific status of research on teaching. *Educational Theory, 44,* 371-383.

Gall, M.D., Borg, W.R., & Gall, J. (2003). *Educational research: An introduction* (7th ed.). New York: Longman.

Garrison, J.W., & Macmillan, C.J.B. (1994). Process-product research on teaching: Ten years later. *Educational Theory, 44,* 385-397.

Goldberger, M. (1983). Direct styles of teaching and psychomotor performance. In T. Templin & J. Olson (Eds.), *Teaching in physical education: Big Ten body of knowledge symposium series, volume 14,* (pp. 211-223). Champaign, IL: Human Kinetics.

Goldberger, M., & Gerney, P. (1986). The effects of direct teaching styles on motor skill acquisition of fifth grade children. *Research Quarterly for Exercise and Sport, 57,* 215-219.

Goldberger, M., & Gerney, P. (1990). Effects of learner use of practice time on skill acquisition of fifth grade children. *Journal of Teaching in Physical Education, 10,* 84-95.

Green, J.C. (2000). Understanding social programs through evaluation. In N.K. Denzin & Y.S. Lincoln (Eds.), *Handbook of qualitative research* (2nd ed., pp. 981-999). Thousand Oaks, CA: Sage.

Guba, E.G. (1985). The context of emergent paradigm research. In Y.S. Lincoln (Ed.), *Organizational theory and inquiry: The paradigm resolution* (pp. 79-104). Beverly Hills, CA: Sage.

Kerlinger, F.N. (1973). *Foundations of behavioral research* (2nd ed.). New York: Holt, Rinehart and Winston.

Kirk, D. (1989). The orthodoxy in RT-PE and the research/practice gap: A critique and an alternative view. *Journal of Teaching in Physical Education, 8,* 123-130.

Locke, L.F. (1977). Research on teaching physical education: New hope for a dismal science. *Quest, 28,* 2-16.

Locke, L.F., Silverman, S.J., & Spirduso, W.W. (1998) *Reading and understanding research.* Thousand Oaks, CA: Sage.

Locke, L.F., Spirduso, W.W., & Silverman, S.J. (2000). *Proposals that work: A guide for planning dissertations and grant proposals* (4th ed.). Thousand Oaks, CA: Sage.

Marshall, C., & Rossman, G.B. (1999). *Designing qualitative research* (3rd ed.). Thousand Oaks, CA: Sage.

Mosston, M., & Ashworth, S. (2002). *Teaching physical education* (5th ed.). San Francisco: Benjamin Cummings.

New York State Education Department, Office of Teaching and Learning. (2002a). *Adopted Part 80 of the commissioner's regulations, requirements for teachers' certificates and practices.* Retrieved March 18, 2002, from www.highered.nysed.gov/tcert/part80.html

New York State Education Department, Office of Teaching and Learning. (2002b). *Draft code of ethics and response form.* Retrieved March 18, 2002, from www.highered.nysed.gov/tcert/draft_code_ethics.htm

Nixon, J.E., & Locke, L.F. (1973). Research on teaching in physical education. In M.W. Travers (Ed.), *Second handbook of research on teaching* (pp. 1210-1242). Chicago: Rand-McNally.

Oliver, K.L. (1999). Adolescent girls' body narratives: Learning to desire and create a "fashionable" image. *Teachers College Record, 101,* 220-246.

O'Sullivan, M., Siedentop, D., & Locke, L. (1992). Toward collegiality: Competing viewpoints among teacher educators. *Quest, 44,* 266-280.

Rosenshine, B., & Furst, N. (1973). The use of direct observation to study teaching. In M.W. Travers (Ed.), *Second handbook of research on teaching* (pp. 122-183). Chicago: Rand McNally.

Schempp, P.G. (1987). Research on teaching in physical education: Beyond the limits of natural science. *Journal of Teaching in Physical Education, 6,* 109-110.

Schempp, P.G. (1988). Exorcist II: Reply to Siedentop. *Journal of Teaching in Physical Education, 7,* 79-81.

Schuldheisz, J.M., & van der Mars, H. (2001). Active supervision and students' physical activity in middle school physical education. *Journal of Teaching in Physical Education, 21,* 75-90.

Siedentop, D. (1987). Dialogue or exorcism? A rejoinder to Schempp. *Journal of Teaching in Physical Education, 6,* 373-376.

Silverman, S. (1985). Critical considerations in the design and analysis of teacher effectiveness research in physical education. *International Journal of Physical Education, 22*(4), 17-24.

Silverman, S. (1990). Linear and curvilinear relationships between student practice and achievement in physical education. *Teaching and Teacher Education, 6,* 305-314.

Silverman, S. (1991). Research on teaching in physical education. *Research Quarterly for Exercise and Sport, 62,* 352-364.

Silverman, S. (1993). Student characteristics, practice and achievement in physical education. *Journal of Educational Research, 87,* 54-61.

Silverman, S. (1997). Technology and physical education: Present, possibilities, and potential problems. *Quest, 49,* 306-314.

Silverman, S., Kulinna, P., & Crull, G. (1995). Skill-related task structures, explicitness, and accountability: Relationships with student achievement. *Research Quarterly for Exercise and Sport, 66,* 32-40.

Silverman, S., & Solmon, M. (1998). The unit of analysis in field research: Issues and approaches to design and data analysis. *Journal of Teaching in Physical Education, 17,* 270-284.

Silverman, S., & Tyson, L. (1994, April). *Modeling the teaching-learning process in physical education.* Paper presented at the annual meeting of the American Educational Research Association, New Orleans, LA.

Silverman, S., Tyson, L., & Krampitz, J. (1992). Teacher feedback and achievement in physical education: Interaction with student practice. *Teaching and Teacher Education, 8,* 333-344.

Silverman, S., Tyson, L., & Morford, L.M. (1988). Relationships of organization, time, and student achievement in physical education. *Teaching and Teacher Education, 4,* 247-257.

Thomas, J. (1993). *Doing critical ethnography.* Newbury Park, CA: Sage.

Thomas, J.R., & Nelson, J.K. (2001). *Research methods in physical activity* (4th ed.). Champaign, IL: Human Kinetics.

PART II

ADDRESSING THE NEEDS OF DIVERSE STUDENTS

CHAPTER FOUR

CONTEXT OF SCHOOLS

LeaAnn Tyson Martin

A school is generally considered an institution for teaching, a place of learning, or even a group of individuals who share common influences or beliefs. Rarely, if ever, is it defined as a workplace for teachers. How teachers perceive and interpret conditions of their workplace influences how they teach, how they interact, and in some cases, how they thrive or survive. A school and its teachers, however, do not function in isolation. Conditions that affect the nation, education, and students create the context of schools. Examining these conditions, or contextual factors, helps us understand the teachers' work environment and how teachers interpret their roles, which in turn affects students and what they learn.

The many contextual factors include characteristics of the community, the physical setting of the school, its organization and culture, and the students and colleagues within (Dreeban, 1973; Feiman-Nemser & Floden, 1986; Good & Brophy, 1986; Howarth, 2000; Lawson, 1989; Lippman, Burns, & McArthur, 1996; Malen, 1999; Oakes, Quartz, Ryan, & Lipton, 2000; Sandholtz, 1990). Although these factors are interrelated and intertwined, they each contribute separately to the teaching and the learning environment. The fact that teaching is "uniquely human" only adds to the complexity of context (Clark & Peterson, 1986).

Contextual factors can help teachers perform their work and increase student opportunities to learn effectively by creating positive conditions. In other situations they can hinder and constrain, creating dissatisfaction (Dreeban, 1973). In some cases teachers have the power to influence and change their workplace, making it a more satisfying and rewarding place to teach and learn. In other cases the ability to alter the context and culture of the school belongs to others (Good & Brophy, 1986).

Much research in education and physical education, particularly process-product investigations, has examined teaching and learning without considering context (Lawson, 1993; Talbert & McLaughlin, 1992), yet aspects of context certainly influence a teacher's work and the students' learning (Lippman et al., 1996; Ward, Doutis, & Evans, 1999). Considering the diversity of school districts, schools, and individuals within schools, it is logical to explore the variety of settings and conditions under which physical educators work (Lawson, 1993). Examination of how teachers respond to these settings and conditions is just as important. These investigations can provide greater insight about why teachers and students do what they do, why they feel as they do, and how they make sense of their work.

This chapter presents an overview of what we know about the school environment and how it might influence a teacher's work and a student's learning. A global examination of changes that have occurred and current conditions in education, schools, and students is presented first, followed by a discussion of contextual factors that specifically affect the physical education learning environment. Lastly, suggestions for physical education are offered.

NATIONAL ISSUES AND CONDITIONS

Changes that occur throughout the nation (and world) ultimately affect schools. Some of the most salient influences include increased cultural diversity, advances in technology and health care, and ongoing poverty. In a multitude of ways, these issues affect schools in how they operate, teachers in how they function, and ultimately, students in how they learn.

Increased Cultural Diversity

Many cultures influence society today. Early immigration into the United States was primarily from Europe (Graham, 1993). Over time more immigrants arrived from other parts of the world, creating awareness of ethnic diversity and issues of inequality (Woods, 1992). Assimilation, and later accommodation, of cultures became the norm. Ethnic minority populations are now the fastest growing groups, and projections are that in some areas the minority population will soon have an adult majority. Today, a pluralistic view is dominant, and individuals work to maintain separate, yet contributing, identities. America is truly a multicultural society (Trilling & Hood, 1999), with a myriad of cultures, languages, and customs in the schools. This circumstance presents challenges to educators as they work to meet the needs of a changing student population.

Advancements in Technology

Advancements in technology have influenced our culture and way of living more than any other change. Unlimited information is available to anyone who has the skills to access it. Consequently, the economy is creating new jobs and careers, which demand new skills to accommodate the needs and advances of the information society. Additionally, these skills are now common in the teacher's workplace, because educators use many features of technology on a daily basis. Technological literacy is necessary, yet many teachers find themselves less competent than their students in this regard.

The advancements in technology, however, have not occurred without associated problems. People can use many aspects of technology (such as electronic mail, videogames, online purchasing, information searching on the World Wide Web) in total isolation. Individuals may cocoon themselves by limiting their human interaction (Coelho, 1999; Trilling & Hood, 1999). Cyber addiction is an increasing problem (Hill & McLean, 1999), which may not be surprising considering that most computer resources are available and open 24 hours a day. Personal data available or provided online can be exploited, resulting in "technotheft" (Hill & McLean, 1999). Each day we learn more about how computer viruses and hackers can cause chaos in an increasingly technology-dependent society (Hill & McLean, 1999). These problems can be greater in educational settings because many schools have computers readily available.

Poverty

Poverty continues to be a concern. Although the number of persons falling below the poverty level has declined from 1959 to 1998 (National Center for Education Statistics

[NCES], 2001), the numbers of youngsters living in poverty is alarming. In 1998 17.8% of children who were 5 to 17 years old were in poverty. Of families living below the poverty level that same year, the percentage was higher for Hispanic and African American ethnic groups (NCES, 2001). Thus, the country is becoming increasingly diverse in both ethnicity and socioeconomic status. The gap is widening between the poor who are technologically illiterate and those who are literate (Trilling & Hood, 1999). Lower-income individuals will continue to be the have-nots, and those in middle- and upper-income populations will have increasing access to information and technology (Silverman, 1997). The "technology rich" will get richer.

Advances in Health Care

Along with advancements in technology, discoveries in bioengineering, biotechnology, molecular medicine, and genetic science will continue to affect health and longevity (Lambert, 1999). Ongoing research will generate better treatments for conditions associated with diseases and will even eliminate some of the diseases themselves. Advancements will occur in hormonal, vitamin, and mineral therapies, and the science of antiaging will evolve. One's lifespan may be rethought of as "healthspan" (Lambert, 1999). As a result, there are and will be more older people in the workforce. Some members of this population may require more health services, possibly competing for the same resources as their younger counterparts, increasing health care concerns.

Despite the medically supported recognition that physical activity is a means to prevent disease and prolong lifespan, the percentage of children who are obese or overweight has more than doubled in the last 20 years (Centers of Disease Control and Prevention [CDCP], 1997). Interestingly, over two-thirds of Americans with children believe their children are physically fit, with just under 30% viewing their children as extremely fit (National Association for Sport and Physical Education [NASPE], 2000). Nearly 7 of 10 adults do not get regular exercise, and 4 of 10 adults are not physically active at all. Advances in medicine will not compensate for unhealthy lifestyles. Moreover, it is a common belief that schools and teachers, not parents, are responsible for developing healthy children. Clearly, the role of the physical and health educator will become increasingly important.

Although these are certainly not all the issues that exist in a changing nation (and additional information will be presented in discussions to follow), they do have a great effect on education, schools, teachers, and students. Educational trends and schools are a reflection of and response to developments in the nation and the world. Conversely, schools work to influence and reshape the state of the nation and the world.

EDUCATIONAL CHANGES AND REFORM EFFORTS

The American people have a high regard for education (NCES, 2001). Some argue that education and schools have been slow to respond to a changing world, while others suggest that the role of education and the school has changed significantly during the last century. Initially, when families immigrated to this country, schools worked to assimilate children in attempts to form a more homogeneous society. As the country developed and prospered, schools assisted children in adjusting to modern life and preparing them for adult life. Attempts to assimilate increasingly diverse students and prepare them for a nation and world that were changing rapidly were not adequate. The role of the school then became that of accommodation and accessibility. Schools began to offer expanded and equitable opportunities for education including dropout prevention programs, college education assistance, "reentry" tools such as Veterans' Educational Assistance, alternative schools, general equivalency diploma (GED) credentials, and programs for nontraditional learners. Even if education today tends to focus on access, little effect occurs without connecting talk and action.

More recently, however, the role of education has been to ensure learning, and having this goal has placed American education under scrutiny by policy makers, parents, community members, and students. Many education initiatives have focused on improving the quality of education for all students, with the intent to close the gap between advantaged and disadvantaged students (Alexander, Heaviside, & Farris, 1999; Finley, 2000; Gallego, Hollingsworth, & Whitenack, 2001; Paige, 2001; Schevrich, Skrla, & Johnson, 2000). Education reform initiatives have a generations-long history in American education. A perceived problem, blamed on the failure of the educational system, generally triggers these initiatives (Finley, 2000; Ward & Doutis, 1999).

Accountability and Assessment

Key to most reform efforts is the application of higher standards for student achievement (Alexander et al., 1999; Orlich, 2000; Paige, 2001). These reform initiatives have to do with standardized testing, results-based education, and outcome-based education (Malen, 1999). The use of standardized tests offers avenues to assess accountability, and some argue that they bring clarity and alignment to a curriculum, as well as facilitate goal and standard setting (Meadows & Karr-Kidwell, 2001; Skrla, 2001). The accountability systems among and within the states, however, are diverse in terms of the tests used, grades tested, methods of reporting, levels of performance required, and assistance given to low-performing schools (California State Postsecondary Education Commission [CSPEC], 2001; Schevrich et al., 2000).

When standardized test scores are used for incentives, the testing is often referred to as high-stakes testing. In some cases, schools that perform well receive incentives funding and those that score poorly become labeled as "low performing" (CSPEC, 2001). When test results produce rewards and consequences (Jones, Jones, & Hardin, 1999), there are concerns that teachers spend a significant amount of time "teaching to the test," that school-based reward systems may pressure teachers (Jones et al., 1999; Malen, 1999), that students feel anxiety (Jones et al., 1999), and that the tests may not be appropriate for elementary children (Meadows & Karr-Kidwell, 2001).

Additionally, if incentive systems seem to reward the strongest performers, which might already be the highest funded schools, how can low-performing schools get aid and assistance to improve (Malen, 1999)? Questions remain about whether the standards and accountability initiatives have raised the scores of students, particularly students of color or low-income students (Schevrich et al., 2000). What is clear, though, is that teachers need to become "assessment literate" to administer tests, interpret tests, and develop goal-setting skills and strategies to improve student achievement (Fullan, 2000). For content areas traditionally not tested, such as physical education, the competition for time and resources will increase, as these areas will be seen as a lower priority without documented assessment.

School Choice and Educational Alternatives

American education currently includes more alternatives than ever. Until recently the most common choices for parents were public and private schools (Poetter & Knight-Abowitz, 2001). Now the choices include charter schools, home schooling, private schools, voucher use, magnet schools, schools within schools, and others. Despite the evolution of so many options, school choice continues to be a political issue (Poetter & Knight-Abowitz, 2001).

Charter Schools

One of the most successful and fastest growing choice alternatives has been charter schools (Ericson, Silverman, Berman, Nelson, & Solomon, 2001; Hill et al., 2001; Rose & Gallup, 2000). Charter schools are public schools of choice, open to all students (Donahoo, 2001; Hill et al., 2001). They are quasi-independent public schools that receive public state and local funds per pupil, yet they are free from many of the regulations and mandates of traditional public schools (Donahoo, 2001; Hill et al., 2001; Podgursky & Ballou, 2001; Poetter & Knight-Abowitz, 2001; Rose & Gallup, 2000; Short & Greer, 2002). Local school boards, colleges and universities, state departments of education, or other state agencies (Hill et al., 2001; Podgursky & Ballou, 2001) grant charters to the schools. The schools must meet learning standards, and the granting agency can close them if they do not demonstrate student learning (Hill et al., 2001). Yet the additional freedom to make budget, curricular, and personnel decisions can be appealing (Hill et al., 2001; Rose & Gallup, 2000). Because of the relative newness of this initiative, most charter schools are less than three years old. By the school year 2000–01 an estimated 1,735 to 1,790 charter schools were operating, enrolling approximately 430,000 students (Hill et al., 2001). Concerns about charter schools include the loss of revenues to traditional public schools, the stability of the charter schools (because they can be closed for lack of performance), and whether they can adequately serve students with special needs (Donahoo, 2001).

Home Schooling

Another rapidly growing alternative is home schooling, as a greater number of parents are exercising the option to educate their own children (Pawlas, 2001). Most parents who choose this option do so because of religious reasons, disenchantment with public schools, or concern about discipline and class size in public schools (Bauman, 2001; Bielick, Chandler, & Broughman, 2001; Pawlas, 2001). Until a few years ago parents who chose to home school their children generally did so during the child's elementary years, and they would later send the child to public secondary schools (Pawlas, 2001). But with information access made significantly easier with technological advances (Web sites for home schooling, online high schools, distance education), parents find it easier to home school youngsters at the secondary level as well. Estimates of the number of home-schooled children range from 850,000 to 1.7 million (Bielick et al., 2001; Poetter & Knight-Abowitz, 2001). The latter figure represents about 1.7% of students in the United States (Bielick et al., 2001), and the numbers are growing.

Other Educational Alternatives

Besides charter schools and home schooling, several other educational alternatives are available. Magnet schools are public schools that focus on specific academic subjects, such as science, so that they can recruit students who demonstrate some proficiency in the subject (Poetter & Knight-Abowitz, 2001). Career academies are similar, typically in the form of schools within schools, where students participate in an integrated curriculum around a career theme (Maxwell & Rubin, 2000). The intent of these academies, along with "school-to-work" reform efforts, is to prepare students better for the workforce (Maxwell & Rubin, 2000). Alternative schools meet the needs of specific students, such as those with behavior problems. These schools tend to have more flexible schedules, smaller student-teacher ratios, and have modified curriculum. Alternative schools are often the option of the parents, not the students (Poetter & Knight-Abowitz, 2001). Vouchers (currently a highly political issue) allow parents to use state funds of specific amounts to pay for their children to attend a private or public school of choice (McCarthy, 2000; Poetter & Knight-Abowitz, 2001). Although participating parents appreciate the choice involved, questions arise about the appropriateness of using government funds for children to attend private, sectarian schools (McCarthy, 2000; Poetter & Knight-Abowitz, 2001).

Public schools and teachers have felt the effect of the educational alternatives. As charter schools reduce financial resources to public schools, competition for resources increases. For content areas viewed as outside the core (such as physical education), resources may dwindle. Home-schooled students, although they receive the bulk of their academic education from parents, may participate in specialized public school programs or services (such as athletic teams, speech therapy, advanced courses), or they may attend public schools on a part-time basis (Bauman, 2001; Pawlas, 2001). Additionally, as more families and students exercise choices and options, families may not politically support school funding, which will affect programs and content areas (Bauman, 2001).

Alternative Scheduling

In recent years another strategy of reform has been for schools to move away from the traditional time schedule of classes and experiment with alternative forms of instructional time use. Block scheduling has been the most common form of this initiative. The intent of block scheduling is to provide longer segments of time for learning by increasing the length of the traditional secondary class period to anywhere from 80 to 110 minutes (Hackman, Hecht, Harmston, Pliska, & Ziomek, 2001). By the mid-1990s more than a third of high schools had implemented block scheduling (Visher, Teitelbaum, & Emanuel, 1999). The most common forms of block scheduling involve the "four-by-four" semester approach, in which students take four classes per semester, totaling eight classes each year, and the "eight-block alternating day" approach, in which students attend four classes on one day, alternating with a four-class schedule the next day (Hackman et al., 2001; Stader, 2001). Proponents of this scheduling claim that it can improve school climate, make it easier for teachers to incorporate technology, decrease fragmentation in the curriculum, and allow teachers to use innovative teaching strategies (Brake, 2000; Peterson, Schmidt, Flottmeyer, & Weincke, 2000; Stader, 2001). Those who oppose it say that it decreases time in instruction when examining the entire school year, that students spend too much time in electives at the expense of core subjects (which can benefit physical education), and that teachers and students do not concentrate as much with the extended time (Brake, 2000).

Parent Involvement

Because student achievement and parent involvement are linked (Desimone, 1999), it is not surprising that reform efforts recommend engaging parents in their children's learning (Hansen & Gentry, 2001; Nelso & Karr-Kidwell, 2001; Visher et al., 1999). Recent research, however, has suggested that ethnicity, income level, and type of parent involvement may make a difference in a child's achievement (Desimone, 1999), and that a father's participation has a positive effect on school success of the child (Wirt et al., 1999).

Many parents are involved in their children's education and school activities. In 1996 84% of students had parents who attended a meeting scheduled with a teacher, and 80% of students had parents who attended a general school meeting (Wirt et al., 1999). The majority of Gallup poll respondents said that parents had the greatest effect on student learning (Rose & Gallup, 2000).

Recommendations to involve parents include making the school a parent-friendly place. These efforts can involve having school individuals available who speak home languages, creating parent centers (equipped with phones and computers), providing child care for visiting parents, providing transportation for parents to and from school, and hosting educational workshops for parent involvement (Desimone, 1999; Nelso & Karr-Kidwell, 2001). Teachers must be creative in exploring ways to involve parents. Parents may be an untapped resource for many physical educators, because they have traditionally involved parents on a smaller scale than have classroom teachers.

Teacher Development

Teachers influence the work and learning of students. Thus, in many reform initiatives, increasing the quality of teaching is an objective (Finley, 2000; Paige, 2001). Most recommendations call for ongoing professional development for teachers. With so many reforms in the past couple of decades, teacher in-service is essential to prepare teachers adequately to implement the initiatives. Although generally thought of as beneficial, traditional professional development activities have been disjointed, have lacked teacher input and follow-up, and may not affect a teacher's behavior in the classroom (Visher et al., 1999).

Many teachers report feeling unprepared to meet some of the new initiative demands (e.g., performance standards, technology, helping students with special needs succeed, state and district curricula), but they feel more prepared after participating in professional growth activities on those topics ("Teachers' Feelings," 2000; Wirt et al., 1999). Alexander et al. (1999) surveyed teachers to determine their understanding and implementation of standards-based reform. Teachers who reported having implemented more reform initiatives in their classrooms were more likely to have attended professional development activities, and areas that the teachers were not implementing (such as "using innovative technologies") were the areas in which they indicated they needed the most instruction. Other research indicates that teachers report feeling the least prepared in areas such as integrating technology and addressing the needs of diverse students, the same topics they report receiving the least amount of professional development in the last 12 months ("Teachers' Feelings," 2000).

Clearly, teachers need to be provided with professional development activities, and teachers should have voices and input regarding their needs and interests (Visher et al., 1999). Many teachers, such as physical educators, have specific content area needs for professional development. Success of educational reforms depends on the implementation of the reforms by teachers, and teachers can only do so by learning (Finley, 2000).

Many educational reforms suggest collaboration as a measure to enhance communication, feedback, learning, and information gathering. Teachers and schools can engage in many types of collaborative relationships, some of which will be discussed later in this chapter. Collaborative partnerships between schools and universities are becoming more common. Numerous calls for reform have included recommendations for teachers and universities to work together to create more effective learning environments for students in public schools and universities (Aldrich, 2001; Bacharach & Hasslen, 2001; Gallego et al., 2001; Reed, Kochan, Ross, & Kunkel, 2001). Professional development schools, also referred to as PDSs, are cooperative endeavors between colleges or universities (involved in teacher preparation) and schools, in which teacher education candidates train with practitioners and university personnel in a school setting (Bacharach & Hasslen, 2001). This concept is not new—it took the form of laboratory schools and clinical schools in the 1960s (Aldrich, 2001). More than 600 PDSs currently operate in at least 47 states (Bacharach & Hasslen, 2001; Reed et al., 2001).

Future Literacy

Although there are strong recommendations to prepare students for the current workforce, and some reform movements are specifically intended to do that, little is known about whether the educational system effectively prepares future workers (Bailey & Gribovskaya, 1999). Technology has revolutionized the world and the education system more than any other event or development. Students in today's knowledge-based society need a vastly different skill and knowledge set than students of only a few years ago did. Consequently, students in the coming years will have even greater (or at least different) demands, not only to promote their success in school but also to facilitate their success in life.

Many needed skills and competencies are easily recognized. Clearly, technology skills are already essential. Surveys of American adults, however, indicated that only about half believed that online skills were very important (Associated Press, 2001). The use of technology, the Internet in particular, has increased concerns regarding authenticity of information and plagiarism (Associated Press, 2001; Tichenor, 2001). Thus, besides needing technology skills to access information, students will need skills to evaluate the quality of the information they receive and the appropriate use of that information. Trilling and Hood (1999) suggest that skills needed now, besides computing skills, include critical thinking and doing, creativity, collaboration, communication, cross-cultural understanding, and self-reliance. Short and Greer (2002) described "empowered students" as those who are articulate, self-assessors, decision makers, planners, organized, self-disciplined, adaptable, compassionate, independent, and responsible. Additionally, these empowered students have mastery of basic skills, a cooperative spirit, social skills, and strong self-esteem. Predictions would be that these students would succeed in tomorrow's world. Although new skills and competencies are generally not questioned, the most significant issue is whether the educational system is addressing them (Trilling & Hood, 1999), for its students and its teachers.

Summary of Educational Reform Initiatives

Many view educational reform efforts with skepticism. Most reform efforts are top down, meaning that those at the national, state, or district level initiate them (Howarth, 2000; Orlich, 2000; Trilling & Hood, 1999). Many such efforts suffer from lack of time or sustained funding. This lack of support for educational innovations and initiatives causes failure, and changes in student performance are not likely to occur (Carpenter, 2000). Additionally, many reform efforts tend to ignore the political and cultural contexts in which the students and teachers must work, despite recommendations that initiatives should consider context (Gallego et al., 2001; Kannapel, 2000; Oakes et al., 2000; Ward & Doutis, 1999).

Piecemeal approaches to education reform have been the norm (Education Commission of the States [ECS], 1999). Yet single strategies rarely make a significant difference (Visher et al., 1999). Therefore, some have suggested comprehensive or systemic reform, involving all aspects of the school, including instruction, curriculum, teacher professional development and training, administration and management, assessment, and parent and community involvement (ECS, 1999; Finley, 2000; Visher et al., 1999). But if teachers are struggling to implement rapidly generated reforms, they will probably be unable to participate fully in a multitude of reforms simultaneously.

Carpenter (2000) reported that an examination of the journal *Phi Delta Kappan* from 1987 to 1997 identified 361 "good ideas" or "silver bullets," including cooperative learning, charter schools, outcomes-based education, character education, and so on. Reform initiatives can confuse and frustrate teachers because teachers are unsure about which to implement and which to ignore (Finley, 2000). With any initiative a variety of measures can be used to evaluate effectiveness (drop-out rate, school climate, and so on), but unfortunately limited evaluative data (such as effect on student outcomes) are available about the effectiveness of most initiatives (Aldrich, 2001; Brake, 2000; Carpenter, 2000; Finley, 2000; Reed et al., 2001; Stader, 2001). Some reforms have produced limited gains, but not as much as would be hoped for or expected (Carpenter, 2000). Regardless, reform efforts appear to be continuing at a frantic pace (Finley, 2000).

The role of education has changed throughout the decades. Actual and expected changes in the world and nation create change in education. Today's teachers must prepare all students to function and succeed in tomorrow's world. Currently, the focus of education is on accountability—accountability of teachers to produce learning and accountability of students to demonstrate outcomes. The education reform initiatives presented here are not all inclusive, but they are the most visible, most implemented, and most politically charged, and they seem to have the greatest effect on public school education and teachers. The following sections will discuss other initiatives.

CHANGING SCHOOLS AND STUDENTS

The school is a reflection of the community—economically, socially, and culturally. Hence, community issues and problems become school issues and problems. Society has given schools a tremendous amount of responsibility in the last couple of decades, and schools may not be equipped (with personnel, curriculum, or facilities) to meet all the needs of all students.

How does the public perceive today's schools? In a recent Gallup poll, respondents indicated a high level of satisfaction with local schools (Rose & Gallup, 2000). Of public school parents in 2000, 62% would assign a grade of A or B to public schools nationally (Rose & Gallup, 2000). Only 20% of the polled public report that they have very little confidence in public education, and 36% report that they have a great deal or quite a lot of confidence (NCES, 2001). Contrary to popular belief, public opinion of schools has not declined and, in fact, is approaching an all-time high.

Today's School

Overall, the number of public schools is declining. In 1930 there were more than 262,000 schools, whereas in 2001 there were approximately 91,000 (NCES, 2001). Of schools that exist today, 28% were built before 1950 (Rowand, 1999). Because of burgeoning enrollments caused by the baby boom, the construction of schools increased between 1950 and 1969. Approximately 45% of American schools were built during this time (Rowand, 1999). These facts suggest that many schools in the United States are aging and in need of repair. Over 73% of public schools have undergone at least one major renovation (Rowand, 1999). Older schools have unique challenges because they may have more difficulty incorporating the needed support for technology tools, despite renovation. Additionally, the oldest schools in America also have higher proportions of children in poverty (Rowand, 1999). Thus, those students who have less access to technology at home are more than likely to have less access at school.

At the same time that school buildings are aging, the number of students they serve is increasing. From the 1988–89 to 1998–99 school year, the average elementary enrollment went from 433 to 478 students (NCES, 2001). Similarly, average enrollment at secondary schools grew from 689 to 707 students (NCES, 2001). Approximately one in four secondary schools has over 1,000 students, and enrollments of 2,000 to 3,000 are no longer rare (Weiss, 1999). Evidence is, however, that students from smaller schools have fewer discipline problems, lower dropout rates, and better attendance, creating the call for smaller schools (Weiss, 1999).

In the future, schools will be educating more children. After rapid growth in student enrollment in the 1950s and 1960s, elementary and secondary enrollment declined in the 1970s and early 1980s (NCES, 2001). Since 1985 the number of students has grown, particularly at the elementary level. From 1990 to 2000, enrollment in kindergarten through eighth grade increased from 29.9 million students to 33.5 million students, and upper-grades enrollment rose from 11.3 million to 13.5 million in the same period. Although elementary enrollment is expected to stabilize through 2010, the increased number of students now in elementary schools will produce a corresponding increase (approximately 4%) in secondary enrollment during the next decade (NCES, 2001). Total enrollment for elementary and secondary schools is predicted to be approximately 54.5 million students by the year 2006, and most increases will occur in the western states (Gerald & Hussar, 1999). Competition for resources is bound to increase.

Dropout rates remain a concern for the schools, although the dropout rate decreased from 14% in 1977 to 11% in 1999 (NCES, 2001). The improvement in the rate of dropout has not affected all students in all ethnic groups. High school completion rates for African American students have increased, closing the gap with white students, but students of Hispanic origin continue to have the highest dropout rates (NCES, 2001). An encouraging development is that 17 states have achieved a 90% high school completion rate (National Education Goals Panel, 2000).

In fall 2000 there were approximately 3.3 million elementary and secondary teachers, representing an increase of 18% from 1990 (NCES, 2001). The number of public school teachers has increased at a somewhat faster rate than the number of students, contributing to declining pupil-teacher ratios. The number of students per teacher decreased from 17.2 in 1990 to 16.2 in 1999 (NCES, 2001). The number of teachers is expected to increase in the future (Gerald & Hussar, 1999).

Approximately 68 million people were enrolled in schools and colleges in the fall of 2000 (NCES, 2001). The corresponding number of teachers in schools and colleges was 4 million. Support staff, administrators, and other education professionals numbered approximately 4.4 million. Taken together, approximately 76 million persons were providing or receiving education. Of the national population, one in four individuals was involved in education (NCES, 2001). This fact speaks to how decisions and changes regarding education affect many people in a variety of ways. Education continues to be of foremost importance in the future of the county.

The Teacher's Workplace

Work conditions and environments affect teachers' lives and, ultimately, the students they teach. External environmental factors can include central administration of the school district and the community, as well as state and national mandates or influences (Dreeban, 1973). Prominent factors of the internal work environment can include class size, facilities, collegial relationships, student characteristics, parental support, curricular materials, noninstructional duties, workload, curricular programs offered, opportunities for professional growth, planning time, school leadership, salary, histories of attempts at educational reform, and so forth (Good & Brophy, 1986; Malen, 1999; Pinkham, 1994; Sandholtz, 1990; Smyth, 1995). Each of these workplace factors and aspects of school culture can create positive and nurturing environments for teachers, or they can constrain and hinder teachers in their efforts. In some cases workplace conditions are changeable, whereas in other situations they are not.

In the variety of workplaces, teachers face different challenges. As discussed earlier, education reform efforts can frustrate teachers in their efforts to maintain implementation at the pace of their introduction. Some of the recommended reforms are not used. For example, few argue the merits of collegial relationships for teachers, yet many teachers work in isolation (Feiman-Nemser & Floden, 1986; Good & Brophy, 1986). With rewards of teaching numbered, teachers choose to negotiate changes, reduce their effort, or even leave the profession because the demands create an imbalance (Sandholtz, 1990).

Despite the challenges, most teachers report relatively high satisfaction with their jobs. A study in 1996 reported that 62.6% of teachers said they certainly or probably would teach again, and only 20.1% said they probably would not or certainly would not teach again (NCES, 2001).

Rewards can take a variety of forms, including salary, work schedule, status, student learning, and collegial relationships (Feiman-Nemser & Floden, 1986; Sandholtz, 1990). Malen (1999) suggests that even smaller classes, more instructional assistants, resources, exemptions from noninstructional duties (e.g., cafeteria duty), and additional planning time are rewards that are not often considered, because merit systems tend to focus only on merit pay. The same things that can serve as rewards and motivators for teachers if provided can be seen as challenges and demotivators if missing.

Despite some similar characteristics, schools in different locations may be distinctly different. For example, urban schools can pose unique challenges (Ennis et al., 1999; Lippman et al., 1996; Wirt et al., 1999). These schools tend to have higher enrollments and are more likely to serve lower-income students and have fewer resources available to serve them (Lippman et al., 1996). Principals in urban schools reported having more difficulty recruiting teachers and as a result were more likely to employ teachers who did not hold certifications in the subjects they taught (Lippman et al., 1996). Students at high-poverty schools were more likely to be taught one or more of their core subjects by teachers who had not majored or minored in the content area (Wirt et al., 1999). Examining differences in schools according to local context has been a beneficial addition to the literature in recent years.

Challenges in the Schools

The public's perceptions of schools are important because public financial support is necessary for schools to improve. In a Gallup poll conducted in 2000, 18% of the respondents cited lack of financial support as the biggest problem facing public schools, 15% perceived discipline as the major problem, 12% cited overcrowded schools, and 11% indicated that fighting, violence, or gangs were the major problem issues (Rose & Gallup, 2000). All other categories (including drug use, crime and vandalism, concern about standards and quality, low pay for teachers, difficulty getting good teachers, and so on) received less than 10% of the responses (Rose & Gallup, 2000).

The issue of school violence and crime has received a great deal of attention in recent years. Highly visible events have created the perception that violence has increased tremendously in the schools. In 1996–97 approximately 57% of the public schools reported criminal incidents, which could include serious violent crimes and lesser crimes such as vandalism, to the police (NCES, 2001). Of those reports, 10% were serious violent crimes, including rape, physical fights or fights with weapons, and robbery. In 1997 38% of schools reported acts of vandalism (NCES, 2001). In 1997, of high school seniors in large metropolitan areas, 38.9% reported having something stolen, 24.9% said they had property deliberately damaged, 21% had been threatened without a weapon, 10.6% had been threatened with a weapon, 11.8% were injured without a weapon, and only 4.3% had been injured with a weapon. Interestingly, in nonmetropolitan areas the percentages were higher for having had something stolen, had property damaged, been injured with a weapon, and been injured without a weapon (Wirt et al., 1999).

Urban schools tend to have higher concentrations of low-income students, transient students, students with risk-taking behaviors, students with less access to medical care, single-parent families, and students who have greater difficulty speaking English (Lippman et al., 1996). These schools appear to have more student absenteeism, greater problems with discipline, and more incidences of weapons possession and teen pregnancy (Lippman et al., 1996).

Current efforts to reduce school violence and crimes include the use of metal detectors, police or school guards, conflict resolution training, student identification cards, cameras, alarm systems, restricted access, and more visible identification of visitors. Many schools have adopted zero-tolerance policies to deter violence and crime. A study by Burgeson, Wechsler, Brener, Young, and Spain (2001) showed that 99.1% of school districts had policies prohibiting weapon possession or use, 97.1% had policies prohibiting fighting, but only 62.5% had policies prohibiting gang activities. Other recommendations include promoting smaller schools to decrease violence and even class disruptions (National Education Goals Panel, 2000; Weiss, 1999). An additional trend has been to limit the use of school facilities after hours, despite recommendations that schools should become more available to the community (Amstutz, Beglau, Whitson, Naumann, & Sherritt, 1992; Gallego et al., 2001; Hansen & Gentry, 2001).

Each year specific events may affect schools. Incidents of tremendous violence (e.g., Columbine shootings) changed the way many schools looked at weapons policies, how they handled student threats, and how they trained students to respond. On September 11, 2001, terrorism devastated the entire nation, an event that had immeasurable effects on children. Students became concerned about safety issues and terrorism. More than ever, the teaching of cultural understanding became important, and more discussions centered on topics such as hate crimes, stereotypes, bias, and racism (C-Span, 2001).

Changing Concept of School

Along with suggestions to make schools more parent friendly are reform efforts to make schools more community friendly (Oakes et al., 2000). Because local beliefs and cultures shape schools, it is logical that schools become more community-responsive. Methods of working within the community include offering extended-day programs, in which parents can attend classes (e.g., English as a Second Language [ESL] or computer classes) before and after the normal school day; providing health clinics at the school where families can visit; creating community centers that are open after hours and on weekends for recreational activities for youth and older adults; opening school libraries for public use; and providing summer programs for the community (Amstutz et al., 1992; Gallego et al., 2001; Hansen & Gentry, 2001). Already, many schools are open for community-sponsored activities. In a recent survey (Burgeson et al., 2001) 66.3% of schools reported that the athletic or physical activity facilities of the school were being used for community sports teams, open gym or free play, and community-sponsored physical activity classes or lessons.

In these circumstances the community is more involved in schools and the students are more involved in the community for learning experiences. The school expands to include a variety of learning spaces that may well not exist within the walls of the school building (Lambert, 1999; Trilling & Hood, 1999). Clearly, the concept of school is changing.

Changing Families and Students

Few would argue with the notion that students of today are different from students of generations past. Examining and understanding characteristics of the changing student body help school districts and teachers address the needs of youngsters in today's schools, and teacher education programs prepare teachers to educate tomorrow's students. Previous sections have addressed many aspects of student population and characteristics.

As indicated in figure 4.1, on any given day children face many challenges. Besides being responsible for educating children, schools have had to expand their curricula, health, and social services to provide essentials that many parents and families cannot.

Every Day in America

- 1 young person under 25 dies from HIV infection.
- 5 children and youth under 20 commit suicide.
- 9 children and youth under 20 are homicide victims.
- 9 children and youth under 20 die from firearms.
- 34 children and youth under 20 die from accidents.
- 77 babies die.
- 157 babies are born at very low birth weight (less than 3 pounds, 4 ounces).
- 180 children are arrested for violent crimes.
- 367 children are arrested for drug abuse.
- 401 babies are born to mothers who had late or no prenatal care.
- 825 babies are born at low birth weight (less than 5 pounds, 8 ounces).
- 1,310 babies are born without health insurance.
- 1,329 babies are born to teen mothers.
- 2,019 babies are born into poverty.
- 2,319 babies are born to mothers who are not high school graduates.
- 2,861 high school students drop out.*
- 3,585 babies are born to unmarried mothers.
- 4,248 children are arrested.
- 7,883 children are reported abused or neglected.
- 17,297 students are suspended from school.*

FIGURE 4.1   Various challenges faced by children. *Based on calculations per school day (180 days of 7 hours each).

The State of America's Children Yearbook, Children's Defense Fund, 2002.

In schools and classrooms, circumstances sometimes occur when achieving academic goals becomes secondary to improving a child's nurturing and life conditions. As a result, teachers have expanded their profession from educating to include "educaring." And, as students become more diverse, so too do their needs.

Family Structure and Roles

Diversity in family structure and characteristics has contributed to the changing student body. Single-parent and blended families are growing more numerous; families considered traditional, less so ("Family Characteristics," 2000; NCES, 2001). The percentage of children age 6 to 12 in two-parent households has decreased from about 90% in 1972 to approximately 70% in 1997 ("Family Characteristics," 2000). Schools must accommodate diverse family structures by offering additional services and being more flexible in scheduling parent programs or conferences.

As family structure changes, family roles may also be changing, as evidenced by increasing participation of mothers in the workforce. From 1972 to 1997 the percentage of children whose fathers were employed decreased slightly from 93.1% to 91.2% ("Family Characteristics," 2000). At the same time, however, the percentage of children whose mothers were employed increased from 38.5% to 66.4% ("Family Characteristics," 2000). The overall increase in education levels of mothers is part of the cause of this increase. In 1972 the percentage of children age 6 to 12 with mothers who had attained a bachelor's degree or higher was 7.2%, and just under 11% had some college education

("Family Characteristics," 2000). In 1997, however, the percentages increased to 20.5% with bachelor's degrees or higher and 28.8% with some college ("Family Characteristics," 2000).

Culturally Diverse Students

As previously mentioned, the student population is also becoming more culturally diverse. Many of the largest school districts in the country already have majority minorities. Many teachers and programs appear ill prepared to handle diverse students ("Teachers' Feelings," 2000). Besides speaking different languages, people of different cultures might also have different child-rearing practices and sex-role socialization norms that affect the students' educational experiences and how teachers do their work.

Ethnic minority students also appear to have different educational opportunities at home. Among students in grades 1 through 6, 21.7% of white students reported using a computer at home for word processing, whereas only 15.2% of Hispanic students and 11.2% of African American students reported doing so. For grades 7 through 12 the percentages were 50.1% for white students, 37.6% for Hispanic students, and 31.7% for African American students (Wirt et al., 1999). Although two-thirds of teens reported using the Internet as their major resource when doing a project for school (Associated Press, 2001), only 12.8% of African American students and 16.6% of Hispanic students in grades 7 through 12 indicated that they used the Internet on a computer at home (Wirt et al., 1999).

Student achievement measures are showing mixed results (NCES, 2001). Overall, math scores have increased from 1973 to 1996, but no significant changes have occurred since 1994 (NCES, 2001; Wirt et al., 1999). In the area of science some generally positive changes in scores have occurred in the last decade, but science performance of 17-year-olds was lower in 1999 than it was in 1970. In younger age groups, science performance was relatively unchanged from 1990 to 1999 (NCES, 2001). In reading, little change occurred between 1971 and 1999 (NCES, 2001; Wirt et al., 1999). Thus, despite the multitude of educational reform efforts, few changes have occurred in student achievement.

Student Drug Use

Although the majority of students do not use drugs or alcohol, the usage rate among students is disturbing. Overall, use of drugs and alcohol increased from 1991 to 1998. In 1998 the percentages of 8th grade students who reported using (within the last 30 days) alcohol was 23%, marijuana or hashish 9.7%, stimulants 3.3%, LSD 1.1%, cocaine 1.4%, tranquilizers 1.2%, cigarettes 19.1%, and inhalants 4.8% (Wirt et al., 1999). For 12th graders the percentages were alcohol 52%, marijuana or hashish 22.8%, stimulants 4.6%, LSD 3.2%, cocaine 2.4%, tranquilizers 2.4%, cigarettes 35.1%, and inhalants 2.3% (Wirt et al., 1999). Alcohol appears to be the most used, with about 74% of high school seniors reporting drinking alcohol, 37.8% reporting smoking marijuana or hashish, and 6.2% reporting using cocaine (NCES, 2001).

Availability of drugs is also an issue. In 1998 90.4% of 12th graders, 77.9% of 10th graders, and 50.6% of 8th graders reported it would be very easy or fairly easy to get marijuana (Wirt et al., 1999). For cocaine the percentages were 45.7%, 36.8%, and 25.7%, respectively (Wirt et al., 1999). For 8th graders the least available drug was heroin, but 18% reported it would be very easy or fairly easy to access. For 12th graders heroin was also the least available, but 35.6% said it was very easy or fairly easy to get. In 1999 30.2% of high school students were offered, given, or sold an illegal drug while on school property (NCES, 2001). Obviously, the availability of alcohol and cigarettes is even greater.

Students' Opinions About School

What do students think about school? In 1992 when 12th graders were administered a Likert-type scale that included statements about school climate (NCES, 2001), the statement receiving the highest percentage (80.2%) of "strongly agree" or "agree" responses was "Teaching is good." More than 66% of the 12th grade students gave the "strongly agree" or "agree" response to the following additional statements: "Teachers are interested in students," "Students are graded fairly," "There is real school spirit," and "Discipline is fair." The statements receiving the lowest percentages (less than 20%) of "strongly agree" or "agree" responses were "There are many gangs in school" and "I don't feel safe at this school." The combined results indicate that, overall, students were positive about school climate.

As communities change, schools and students change. Students are becoming more diverse and have different needs. Because teachers work in a complex environment with many variables, meeting the learning needs and interests of all students is challenging.

ISSUES AND CONDITIONS THAT AFFECT PHYSICAL EDUCATION

Most changes in the nation, education, schools, and students affect physical education. The profession is not immune to everything going on around it, and in some cases the effects (negative and positive) are greater in the physical education setting. Clearly, the workplace for physical educators and the learning environment for physical education students need examination.

As early as 1975 Locke described the physical educator's work. He identified positive aspects, such as long vacations and close association with sports, that serve to attract and (it is to be hoped) retain physical education teachers. He also described the realities of the job—lack of collegial interactions, large class sizes, lack of rewards—that physical educators deal with daily. Locke's (1975) work opened the door to the workplace of the physical educator.

Since 1975 much has been written to assist in understanding the context in which physical educators teach and physical education students learn. Many researchers have recognized the importance of examining factors that may influence whether the teacher thrives or barely survives (Lawson, 1989; Macdonald, 1999; O'Sullivan & Dyson, 1994; O'Sullivan, Siedentop, & Tannehill, 1994; Pinkham, 1994; Smyth, 1992, 1995; Solmon, Worthy, & Carter, 1993; Sparkes, Templin, & Schempp, 1990, 1993; Templin, 1989; Ward & Doutis, 1999; Ward et al., 1999). Whatever affects teachers will influence their teaching, and subsequently their students' learning.

Status of Physical Education

No federal law mandates the teaching of physical education, although the vast majority of schools (96.4%) require students to take physical education (Burgeson et al., 2001; NASPE, 2002). The requirements, however, differ according to grade level. Approximately 40% of elementary schools have a kindergarten physical education requirement, as do about half of schools with grades 1 through 5 (Burgeson et al., 2001). As students grow older, requirements decrease. Of the schools that have a requirement, few provide daily physical education for the entire school year (Burgeson et al., 2001; NASPE, 2002). Only about 25% of elementary schools (not including kindergarten), 18% of middle or junior high schools, and 6.9% of senior high schools provide at least three days a week of physical education (or its equivalent) for the duration of the school year (Burgeson et al., 2001). The majority of adults (81%) and teens (71%) believe that daily physical education should be mandated in schools (NASPE, 2002).

At the elementary level, state requirements for physical education vary, from 30 minutes per week to 150 minutes per week (NASPE, 2002). For middle or junior high schools, time requirements range from 80 to 275 minutes per week. Most students in high schools enroll in physical education for only one year, and the required time ranges from "none specified" to 225 minutes per week (NASPE, 2002). These differences create tremendous variation in programs.

Burgeson et al. (2001) report that 14.8% of districts have a maximum allowable pupil-teacher ratio in elementary physical education, with the average being 27:1 in those districts that have a policy. At the middle or junior high level 16.9% of districts have a maximum allowable pupil-teacher ratio, with an average of 32:1, and 19% of districts have a policy regarding high school pupil-teacher ratio, with the average being 32:1. Especially at the middle or junior high level and senior high level, class size appears to be greater than the national averages reported previously, affecting the physical educator's workload.

Approximately 70% of the states have someone who serves as a coordinator or someone who oversees physical education, and just over 60% of districts have someone responsible for coordinating physical education (Burgeson et al., 2001). This person, ideally, would provide leadership, support, representation, and coordination of programs, especially when reform initiatives are mandated.

Effect of Educational Reform and Technology

The challenge for reform has not been limited to education in general. In the past decade there has been a call to think differently about physical education, to redefine its role and the way in which it is delivered, particularly at the secondary level (Lawson, 1993, 1998; Locke, 1992; Macdonald & Brooker, 1997; O'Sullivan et al., 1994; Rink, 1993; Saffici, 1999; Siedentop, 1993; Siedentop & Locke, 1997; Stroot , Collier, O'Sullivan, & England, 1994; Tinning & Fitzclarence, 1992; Ward, 1999; Ward & Doutis, 1999; Ward et al., 1999). The irrelevance to students of many current physical education programs has created part of the need for change (Carlson, 1995; Cothran & Ennis, 1999; Macdonald & Brooker, 1997; Penney & Chandler, 2000). Increased attention to health care, recognition of the role that activity plays in disease prevention, and examination of current, often inadequate programs have no doubt also contributed to this attention.

Accountability and Assessment

Education reform efforts now focus on accountability. These reform efforts have or will include physical education, although core subjects such as math and reading have taken priority (NASPE, 2002). Teachers must get away from the "busy, happy, and good" syndrome (Placek, 1983) and the "participation means an A" mentality. The profession will continue to have marginal status if physical educators are not accountable for learning (Lawson, 1989; NASPE, 2002). If a student does not receive any learning from physical education, the requirement will receive little support. Subjects not required are often eliminated.

With the development of national standards, it is now easier to establish learning goals and be accountable for the achievement of those goals in physical education (NASPE, 1995). Of the states that have physical education standards, more than 80% report that national standards form the basis of state standards. Many states indicate that they have or are developing state standards for physical education or health and physical education (NASPE, 2002).

Most districts have adopted physical education goals and expected student outcomes (Burgeson et al., 2001). About 74% of districts have their own physical education curricula for elementary schools, about 81% have adopted their own for middle or junior high schools, and just over 78% have done so for senior high schools (Burgeson et al., 2001).

The assessment of the student outcomes, however, varies. Some states are generating assessments for physical education (NASPE, 2002). Written tests in physical education are required for elementary schools in 7.4% of districts, for middle or junior high schools in 13.6% of districts, and for senior high schools in 21.2% of districts. Physical performance (skill) tests are required in elementary schools of 15.9% of districts, in middle or junior high schools of 19.3% of districts, and in senior high schools of 21.6% of districts (Burgeson et al., 2001). As with general education reform, exploration of alternative methods of assessment and "authentic" assessment is occurring in physical education. Generally, the creation of methods and instruments for assessment follows the development of standards. Content that is not assessed is lower in priority, influencing administrative decisions that affect physical education (NASPE, 2002).

Technology

Advances in technology have been slower in acceptance and use, but physical educators have not ignored them. Recommendations for technology implementation for practitioners are appearing with much greater frequency in professional journals. These how-to articles suggest the use of a variety of tools to enhance teaching, including using computers to analyze movement and using digital cameras, software, heart rate monitors, personal digital assistants, and video cameras (Anderson, Mikat, & Martinez, 2001; Bolt, 2000; Darden, 1999; Juniu, 2002; Mendon & Van Blom, 1999; Mohnsen, 2001; Ryan, Marzilli, & Martindale, 2001). This technology can facilitate the teaching of physical education by providing interactive learning activities, assisting in assessment, providing demonstrations, monitoring learning and physical activity, and making activities and content more personalized for students (Lambert, 1999; Silverman, 1997). Advances in technology will also enable more students with special needs to participate in physical education activities (Hill & McLean, 1999). Yet the appropriate use of technology remains a consistent recommendation. For example, technology should not replace physical activity, and the fact remains that weak teachers will not become significantly better because they have computers (Coelho, 1999; Silverman, 1997).

The Physical Educator's Workplace

Many conditions and issues influence physical education as a learning and teaching environment. One of the most salient issues is the low status of physical education. Researchers have often studied and documented this aspect (Fejgin & Hanegby, 1999; Macdonald & Brooker, 1997; O'Sullivan, 1989; O'Sullivan et al., 1994; Sharpe & Templin, 1997; Smyth, 1995; Sparkes et al., 1990, 1993; Stroot et al., 1994; Stroot, Faucette, & Schwager, 1993; Templin, 1989; Templin, Sparkes, Grant, & Schempp, 1994; Ward & Doutis, 1999). The low status of physical education can be reflected in many ways—lack of general support for the physical education program, lack of administrative support, lack of parent support, lack of support from colleagues, and even lack of support from students themselves (O'Sullivan, 1989; O'Sullivan et al., 1994; Solmon et al., 1993; Sparkes et al., 1990; Stroot et al., 1994; Templin, 1989). Low status and lack of support can create job inhibitors, resulting in larger class sizes (as compared with other academic areas), limited access to facilities, limited equipment and resources, and lack of professional development opportunities (Lambdin, 1993; O'Sullivan, 1989; O'Sullivan & Dyson, 1994; Rovegno, 1994; Smyth, 1995; Solmon et al., 1993; Stroot et al., 1994;

Templin, 1989). With more schools adopting site-based management and with administrators, teachers, and parents making more decisions, low status can have tremendous budget implications because funding priority will go to content areas with higher recognition and greater perceived importance. Already, Fejgin and Hanegby (1999) suggest that physical educators have limited involvement in decision making, although teachers indicate they would like to have more input in issues such as scheduling (Lambdin, 1993; Stroot et al., 1994).

Marginalization

The effects of lack of facilities, time, and resources are obvious. For many elementary physical educators the teaching facility is a "cafegymnatorium," used as a cafeteria, gymnasium, and auditorium for any large gathering or large space need. With inadequate facilities or limited access to facilities, physical educators are unlikely to support recommendations to make these facilities available to the community and parents (Lawson, 1998).

Marginalization can contribute to feelings of isolation, and being isolated can contribute to feelings of marginality. Physical educators are often physically isolated, with the gymnasium not centrally located within the school or disconnected from the school building entirely. This physical isolation decreases opportunities for interactions with other teachers and contributes to feelings of professional isolation. A substantial amount of literature reports isolation of physical education teachers (Doutis & Ward, 1999; Pinkham, 1994; Sharpe & Templin, 1997; Smyth, 1995; Stroot et al., 1993; Templin, 1988, 1989; Templin et al., 1994). This separation can affect many areas of a teacher's workplace—involvement in decision making, collegial interaction and stimulation, perception of control, recognition, and so forth. It is not surprising that physical educators feel invisible (Doutis & Ward, 1999). Reform initiatives that recommend collaboration are even more salient for the physical educator.

Other duties and responsibilities associated with teaching offer another challenge to physical educators. For many teachers, nonteaching duties such as lunchroom duty, monitoring study hall, supervising open gym, and sponsoring student groups (such as safety patrol) contribute to workload issues (O'Sullivan, 1989; Pinkham, 1994; Smyth, 1992). Marginalization may contribute to the assignment of these duties, because these responsibilities may be given to teachers perceived as having easier teaching. In addition, many physical educators have coaching responsibilities, and secondary teachers are often expected to perform those tasks. Coaching demands affect time devoted to teaching and can create overloads and conflict (Lawson, 1989; Stroot et al., 1993, 1994; Templin, 1989; Templin et al., 1994). Given the visibility of athletics, it is not surprising that teacher-coaches receive more support and attention for their coaching (Stroot et al., 1993; Templin et al., 1994). When Lindholm (1997) examined job satisfaction of secondary physical education teachers, those who were teacher-coaches were not significantly more satisfied with their jobs than those who did not coach.

Low Status of Physical Education

The teaching profession is not plentiful in extrinsic rewards such at salary, power, and status. Physical educators report that students and interactions with them were the most important compensation or the sources from which they received the greatest reward (O'Sullivan, 1989; O'Sullivan et al., 1994; Stroot et al., 1994). Visible student learning also offers reward for physical educators. If a teacher monitors instead of teaches, student learning is less likely to occur. Keeping students "busy, happy and good" (Placek, 1983) provides little opportunity to view learning. And if assessment of student learning does not occur, student progress is less likely to be seen. If teachers hold students accountable for learning, the rewards of student progress are greater (Doutis & Ward, 1999). Given the priority of content areas that are subject to state-mandated testing, physical education can lose even more ground without documented accountability.

Unfortunately, although teachers derive rewards from teaching, they receive limited feedback or praise from administrators regarding their teaching (Lindholm, 1997; Templin, 1989). Only 40% of secondary physical educators indicated that they regularly received information about the quality of their teaching (Lindholm, 1997). Lindholm (1997) states that only 26% of secondary physical education teachers felt that they were "fairly rewarded" and "received sufficient pay" for the work they were performing. Less than half reported that they were "successful" at what they did. But 96% of secondary physical education teachers indicated that they were doing work they enjoyed, liked the people they worked with, and were comfortable with their job security (Lindholm, 1997).

The education literature has documented the benefits of collaboration and collegial relationships among teachers, and those elements remain components of reform measures. In physical education the need and value of collaboration and collegiality has also been recognized (Doutis & Ward, 1999; Rovegno & Bandhauer, 1998; Sharpe, Lounsbery, Golden, & Deibler, 1999; Stroot et al., 1994; Templin, 1989). Physical education teachers find it difficult both to establish collegial relationships with other teachers in the school and to find time to plan lessons and programs with their peers (Doutis & Ward, 1999). Cooperative relationships with colleagues and teamwork are viewed as job enhancers, and increased collegiality decreases isolation (Doutis & Ward, 1999; Stroot et al., 1994). Physical education teachers working collaboratively with universities, often in the form of professional development schools, report that they are rejuvenated, empowered, and have opportunities to participate in shared leadership (Rovegno & Bandhauer, 1998; Sharpe et al., 1999; Sharpe & Templin, 1997). Physical educators can engage in many collaborative relationships. Burgeson et al. (2001) reported that physical education teachers collaborated in physical education activities with health education staff (51.8% of schools), school health services staff (40.7%), mental health and social services staff (26.4%), food service staff (15.6%), health organizations such as the American Heart Association (50%), local youth organizations (29.2%), colleges and universities (29.4%), local businesses (17%), local health departments (16.2%), local hospitals (11.2%), and local fitness clubs (93%). Collegial relationships with parents are no less important, because negative parent involvement in physical education can detract from the work environment (Penney & Chandler, 2000; Smyth, 1995; Templin, 1989).

Many education reform initiatives recognize the necessity of professional development for physical educators. Professional development activities may not be provided or encouraged in physical education, or those that are offered may not seem relevant to the physical educator's work (Macdonald & Brooker, 1997; O'Sullivan, 1989; Smyth, 1992; Templin, 1989). During a two-year period, over half of states provided in-service on topics related to physical education, including injury prevention, teaching movement skills and concepts, teaching individual and dual sports, and teaching group and team activities (Burgeson et al., 2001). Teachers, however, indicate interest in staff development on topics such as assessment and evaluation, developing and using student portfolios in physical education, assisting students with developing individual fitness plans, teaching students with special needs, and using technology in physical education (Burgeson et al., 2001).

The work and learning environment in physical education includes many other prominent aspects. Readers may wish to refer to Bill Vogler's chapter (chapter 6) on students with disabilities, Leslie Lambert's chapter (chapter 8) on standards-based program design, Melinda Solmon's chapter (chapter 9) on student attitudes, cognition, and motivation, Terry Wood's chapter (chapter 11) on assessment, and Sandy Stroot and Christine Whipple's chapter (chapter 18) on socialization.

SUMMARY

The contextual factors of schools and physical education are worth examining. This research sheds light on the complexity of teaching, learning, and the school, but it also exposes what must be improved. The context of the teacher's and student's world is the result of external factors, such as national trends and mandates and locally determined and manipulated factors. Through joint efforts, districts, policy makers, administrators, and others can implement some changes. In other instances only teachers can create change. In these situations, teachers should initiate and take responsibility for creating a better place to teach and learn—for themselves and their students.

IMPLICATIONS FOR PRACTICE

1. Many of the recommendations for physical education parallel existing suggestions in educational reform. Some of these recommendations are not new, but the need for them continues.

2. Those affiliated with physical education should seek ways to connect with educational reform efforts (Ward & Doutis, 1999). Physical education is already greatly affected by these initiatives, but physical educators should validate the unique contribution that physical education can play in the education of today's child who will be tomorrow's contributing citizen (Penney & Chandler, 2000; Ward & Doutis, 1999). Working toward that goal involves examining the purpose of physical education and looking for ways to develop "movement and physical literacy" in learners (Penney & Chandler, 2000).

3. Physical educators should begin to view their roles as facilitators, using creative and innovative strategies to motivate and engage students and make physical education personally relevant and meaningful to them (Lambert, 1999; Macdonald & Brooker, 1997).

4. Physical educators should continue to explore ways to use technology to enhance student learning (Lambert, 1999).

5. Physical educators should continue to address in a multitude of ways the needs of diverse learners (Lawson, 1998; Macdonald & Brooker, 1997).

6. Physical educators should focus on accountability, student learning, and assessment and seek ways to better align curricula to address student outcomes (Burgeson et al., 2001; Macdonald & Brooker, 1997).

7. Physical education programs should seek ways to create more partnerships with individuals and groups in the community (Lawson, 1998).

8. Physical educators should continue to promote physical activity and physical education, especially by generating more allotted instructional time for physical education (Burgeson et al., 2001).

9. Physical educators should seek and be provided opportunities for professional growth (Burgeson et al., 2001). Staff development activities should focus on what teachers want and need, such as working with an increasingly diverse student population and integrating technology into the gymnasium.

REFERENCES

Aldrich, J.E. (2001, August). *Professional development schools: Listening to teachers' and teacher candidates' voices*. Paper presented at the annual meeting of the Association of Teacher Educators, Portland. (ERIC Document Reproduction Service No. ED457158)

Alexander, D., Heaviside, S., & Farris, E. (1999). Status of education reform in public elementary and secondary schools: Teachers' perspectives. *Education Statistics Quarterly, 1*(1), 50-52.

Amstutz, D., Beglau, M., Whitson, D., Naumann, D., & Sherritt, C. (1992). *Community involvement in school improvement*. Laramie, WY: Wyoming Center for Educational Research. (ERIC Document Reproduction Service No. ED352732)

Anderson, M., Mikat, R.P., & Martinez, R. (2001). Digital video production in physical education and athletics. *Journal of Physical Education, Recreation and Dance, 72*(6), 19-21.

Associated Press. (2001, August 21). Online homework involves blessings, pitfalls. *Bellingham Herald*, p. A1.

Bacharach, N., & Hasslen, R. (2001). *Creating a professional development school.* Bloomington, IN: Phi Delta Kappa Educational Foundation. (ERIC Document Reproduction Service No. ED457132)

Bailey, T., & Gribovskaya, A. (1999). *Reassessing a decade of reform. Workforce development and the changing economy.* Berkeley, CA: National Center for Research in Vocational Education. (ERIC Document Reproduction Service No. ED436643)

Bauman, K.J. (2001). *Home schooling in the United States: Trends and characteristics.* Suitland, MD: Bureau of the Census. (ERIC Document Reproduction Service No. ED456019)

Bielick, S., Chandler, K., & Broughman, S.P. (2001). *Homeschooling in the United States: 1999.* Washington, DC: National Center for Education Statistics. (ERIC Document Reproduction Service No. ED455926)

Bolt, B.R. (2000). Using computers for qualitative analysis of movement. *Journal of Physical Education, Recreation and Dance, 71*(3), 15-18.

Brake, N.L. (2000, November). *Student course taking delivered through a high school block schedule: The relationship between the academic core and student achievement.* Paper presented at the annual meeting of the Mid-South Educational Research Association, Bowling Green, KY. (ERIC Document Reproduction Service No. ED448194)

Burgeson, C.R., Wechsler, H., Brener, N.D., Young, J.C., & Spain, C.G. (2001). Physical education and activity: Results for the school health policies and programs study 2000. *Journal of School Health, 71,* 279-293.

California State Postsecondary Education Commission [CSPEC]. (2001). *Assessment and change: The role of student testing in California education. Higher education update.* Sacramento, CA: Author. (ERIC Document Reproduction Service No. ED452218)

Carlson, T. (1995). We hate gym: Student alienation from physical education. *Journal of Teaching in Physical Education, 14,* 467-477.

Carpenter, W.A. (2000). Ten years of silver bullets. Dissenting thoughts on education reform. *Phi Delta Kappan, 81,* 383-389.

Centers for Disease Control and Prevention [CDCP]. (1997). *Guidelines for school and community programs: Promoting lifelong physical activity.* Atlanta, GA: U.S. Department of Health and Human Services.

Clark, C.M., & Peterson, P.L. (1986). Teachers' thought processes. In M.C. Wittrock (Ed.), *Handbook of research on teaching* (3rd ed., pp. 255-296). New York: Macmillan.

Coelho, J.D. (1999). Physical education in the 21st century. *Teaching Elementary Physical Education, 10*(6), 29-30.

Cothran, D.J., & Ennis, C.D. (1999). Alone in a crowd: Meeting students' needs for relevance and connection in urban high school physical education. *Journal of Teaching in Physical Education, 18,* 234-247.

C-Span. (2001). *Teaching about September 11th and its aftermath.* Washington, DC: Author. (ERIC Document Reproduction Service No. ED457108)

Darden, G.F. (1999). Videotape feedback for student learning and performance. *Journal of Physical Education, Recreation and Dance, 70*(9), 40-45, 62.

Desimone, L. (1999). Linking parent involvement with student achievement: Do race and income matter? *Journal of Educational Research, 93,* 11-30.

Donahoo, S. (2001). *Perspectives on charter schools: A review for parents.* Washington, DC: Office of Educational Research and Improvement. (ERIC Document Reproduction Service No. ED455973)

Doutis, P., & Ward, P. (1999). Teachers' and administrators' perceptions of the Saber-Tooth project reform and their changing workplace conditions. *Journal of Teaching in Physical Education, 18,* 417-427.

Dreeban, R. (1973). The school as a workplace. In R.M.W. Travers (Ed.), *Second handbook of research on teaching* (pp. 456-473). Chicago: Rand McNally.

Education Commission of the States. (1999). *Comprehensive school reform: Five lessons from the field.* Denver: Author. (ERIC Document Reproduction Service No. ED439514)

Ennis, C.D., Solmon, M.A., Satina, B., Loftus, S.L., Mensch, J., & McCauley, M.T. (1999). Creating a sense of family in urban schools using the "Sport for Peace" curriculum. *Research Quarterly for Exercise and Sport, 70,* 273-285.

Ericson, J., Silverman, D., Berman, P., Nelson, B., & Solomon, D. (2001). *Challenge and opportunity: The impact of charter schools on school districts. A report of the national study of charter schools.* Washington, DC: Office of Educational Research and Improvement. (ERIC Document Reproduction Service No. ED455578)

Family characteristics of 6- to 12-year-olds. (2000). *Education Statistics Quarterly, 2*(1), 48-50.

Feiman-Nemser, S., & Floden, R.E. (1986). The cultures of teaching. In M.C. Wittrock (Ed.), *Handbook of research on teaching* (3rd ed., pp. 505-526). New York: Macmillan.

Fejgin, N., & Hanegby, R. (1999). Physical educators' participation in decision-making processes in dynamic schools. *Journal of Teaching in Physical Education, 18,* 141-158.

Finley, S.J. (2000). *Instructional coherence: The changing role of the teacher.* Austin, TX: Southwest Educational Development Lab. (ERIC Document Reproduction Service No. ED450110)

Fullan, M. (2000). The three stories of education reform. *Phi Delta Kappan, 81,* 581-584.

Gallego, M.A., Hollingsworth, S., & Whitenack, D.A. (2001). Relational knowing in the reform of educational cultures. *Teachers College Record, 103,* 240-266.

Gerald, D.E., & Hussar, W.J. (1999). *Projections of education statistics to 2009.* Washington, DC: U.S. Department of Education, National Center for Education Statistics.

Good, T.L., & Brophy, J.E. (1986). School effects. In M.C. Wittrock (Ed.), *Handbook of research on teaching* (3rd ed., pp. 570-602). New York: Macmillan.

Graham, P. (1993). Antiquarianism and American education: Assimilation, adjustment, access. In D. Ravitch & M. Vinovskis (Eds.), *Historical perspectives on the current educational reforms* (pp. 16-55). Washington, DC: Office of Educational Research and Improvement. (ERIC Document Reproduction Service No. ED359623)

Hackman, D.G., Hecht, J.E., Harmston, M.T., Pliska, A.M., & Ziomek, R.L. (2001, April). *Secondary school scheduling models: How do types of models compare to ACT scores?* Poster session presented at the annual meeting of the American Educational Research Association, Seattle. (ERIC Document Reproduction Service No. ED452230)

Hansen, J.M., & Gentry, R. (2001). Options within the new schoolhouse. *Kappa Delta Pi Record, 37,* 78-81.

Hill, J., & McLean, D.C. (1999). Introduction: Possible, probable, or preferable future? *Journal of Physical Education, Recreation and Dance, 70*(9), 15-17.

Hill, P., Lake, R., Celio, M.B., Campbell, C., Herdman, P., & Bulkley, K. (2001). *A study of charter school accountability.* Washington, DC: U.S. Department of Education, Office of Educational Research and Improvement.

Howarth, K. (2000). Context as a factor in teachers' perceptions of the teaching of thinking skills in physical education. *Journal of Teaching in Physical Education, 19,* 270-286.

Jones, M.G., Jones, B.D., & Hardin, B. (1999). The impact of high-stakes testing on teachers and students in North Carolina. *Phi Delta Kappan, 81,* 199-203.

Juniu, S. (2002). Implementing handheld computing technology in physical education. *Journal of Physical Education, Recreation and Dance, 73*(3), 43-48.

Kannapel, P.J. (2000). *Standards-based reform and rural school improvement: Similarities, differences, prospects for the future.* Washington, DC: Office of Educational Research and Improvement. (ERIC Document Reproduction Service No. ED448956)

Lambdin, D.D. (1993). Elementary school teachers' lives and careers: An interview study of physical education specialists, other subject specialists, and classroom teachers (Doctoral dissertation, University of Massachusetts, 1992). *Dissertation Abstracts International, 53,* 3441A.

Lambert, L.T. (1999). The future in plain sight. Dreaming but not hallucinating. *Teaching Elementary Physical Education, 10*(6), 6-10.

Lawson, H.A. (1989). From rookie to veteran: Workplace conditions in physical education and induction into the profession. In T.J. Templin & P.G. Schempp (Eds.), *Socialization into physical education: Learning to teach* (pp. 145-164). Indianapolis: Benchmark Press.

Lawson, H.A. (1993). Teachers' uses of research in practice: A literature review. *Journal of Teaching in Physical Education, 12,* 366-374.

Lawson, H.A. (1998). Rejuvenating, reconstituting, and transforming physical education to meet the needs of vulnerable children, youth, and families. *Journal of Teaching in Physical Education, 18,* 2-25.

Lindholm, J.A. (1997). Secondary school physical education motivation: An application of personal investment theory. *Journal of Teaching in Physical Education, 16,* 426-439.

Lippman, L., Burns, S., & McArthur, E. (1996). *Urban schools: The challenge of location and poverty.* Washington, DC: U.S. Department of Education.

Locke, L.F. (1975). The ecology of the gymnasium: What the tourists never see. *Proceedings of SAPECW* (pp. 38-50). (ERIC Document Reproduction Service No. ED104823)

Locke, L.F. (1992). Changing secondary school physical education. *Quest, 44,* 361-372.

Macdonald, D. (1999). The "professional" work of experienced physical education teachers. *Research Quarterly for Exercise and Sport, 70,* 41-54.

Macdonald, D., & Brooker, R. (1997). Moving beyond the crisis in secondary physical education: An Australian initiative. *Journal of Teaching in Physical Education, 16,* 155-175.

Malen, B. (1999). On rewards, punishments, and possibilities: Teacher compensation as an instrument for education reform. *Journal of Personnel Evaluation in Education, 12,* 387-394.

Maxwell, N.L., & Rubin, V. (2000). *High school career academies: A pathway to educational reform in urban school districts?* Kalamazoo, MI: Upjohn Institute for Employment Research. (ERIC Document Reproduction Service No. ED455266)

McCarthy, M.M. (2000). What is the verdict on school vouchers? *Phi Delta Kappan, 81,* 371-378.

Meadows, S., & Karr-Kidwell, P.J. (2001). *The role of standardized tests as a means of assessment of young children: A review of related literature and recommendations of alternative assessments for administrators and teachers.* Unpublished manuscript, Texas Woman's University. (ERIC Document Reproduction Service No. ED456134)

Mendon, K., & Van Blom, J. (1999). Using technology to enhance fitness. *Teaching Elementary Physical Education, 10*(3), 20, 30.

Mohnsen, B. (2001). Using instructional software to meet national physical education standards. *Journal of Physical Education, Recreation and Dance, 72*(3), 19-22.

National Association for Sport and Physical Education [NASPE]. (1995). *Moving into the future: National standards for physical education.* Reston, VA: American Alliance for Health, Physical Education, Recreation and Dance.

National Association for Sport and Physical Education [NASPE]. (2000). *Public attitudes toward physical education. Are schools providing what the public wants?* Reston, VA: American Alliance for Health, Physical Education, Recreation and Dance.

National Association for Sport and Physical Education [NASPE]. (2002). *2001 Shape of the nation report: Status of physical education in the USA.* Reston, VA: American Alliance for Health, Physical Education, Recreation and Dance.

National Center for Education Statistics [NCES]. (2001). *Digest of education statistics, 2000.* Washington, DC: U.S. Department of Education.

National Education Goals Panel. (2000). *Promising practices: Progress toward the goals 2000.* Washington, DC: Author.

Nelso, J., & Karr-Kidwell, P.J. (2001). *Soliciting support for the American public school: A guide to inform administration and educate parents.* Unpublished manuscript, Texas Woman's University. (ERIC Document Reproduction Service No. ED456529)

Oakes, J., Quartz, K.H., Ryan, S., & Lipton, M. (2000). Becoming good American schools. The struggle for civic virtue in education reform. *Phi Delta Kappan, 81,* 568-575.

Orlich, D.C. (2000). Education reform and its limits to student achievement. *Phi Delta Kappan, 81,* 468-472.

O'Sullivan, M. (1989). Failing gym is like failing lunch or recess: Two beginning teachers' struggle for legitimacy. *Journal of Teaching in Physical Education, 8,* 227-242.

O'Sullivan, M., & Dyson, B. (1994). Rules, routines, and expectations of 11 high school physical education teachers. *Journal of Teaching in Physical Education, 13,* 361-374.

O'Sullivan, M., Siedentop, D., & Tannehill, D. (1994). Breaking out: Codependency of high school physical education. *Journal of Teaching in Physical Education, 13,* 421-428.

Paige, R. (2001). *"No child left behind": A blueprint for education reform.* Washington, DC: Department of Education. (ERIC Document Reproduction Service No. ED452569)

Pawlas, G.E. (2001). Clearing the air about home schooling. *Kappa Delta Pi Record, 37,* 63-66.

Penney, D., & Chandler, T. (2000). Physical education: What future(s)? *Sport, Education and Society, 5,* 71-87.

Peterson, D.W., Schmidt, C., Flottmeyer, E., & Weinke, S. (2000, November). *Block scheduling: Successful strategies for middle schools.* Paper presented at the annual National Middle School Association Conference, St. Louis. (ERIC Document Reproduction Service No. ED448862)

Pinkham, K.M. (1994). Perspectives of secondary school physical educators on the school as a workplace. *Proceedings of the Special Interest Group Research on Learning and Instruction in Physical Education of the American Educational Research Association,* 17-19.

Placek, J.H. (1983). Conceptions of success in teaching: Busy, happy and good? In T.J. Templin & J.K. Olson, (Eds.), *Teaching in physical education* (pp. 46-56). Champaign, IL: Human Kinetics.

Podgursky, M., & Ballou, D. (2001). *Personnel policy in charter schools.* Washington, DC: Thomas B. Fordham Foundation. (ERIC Document Reproduction Service No. ED456567)

Poetter, T.S., & Knight-Abowitz, K. (2001). Possibilities and problems of school choice. *Kappa Delta Pi Record, 37,* 58-62.

Reed, C.J., Kochan, F.K., Ross, M.E., & Kunkel, R.C. (2001). Designing evaluation systems to reform, inform, and transform professional development schools. *Journal of Curriculum and Supervision, 16,* 188-205.

Rink, J.E. (1993). What's so critical? In J.E. Rink (Ed.), *Critical crossroads: Middle and secondary school physical education* (pp. 1-6). Reston, VA: National Association for Sport and Physical Education.

Rose, L., & Gallup, A. (2000). The 32nd annual Phi Delta Kappa/Gallup poll of the public's attitudes toward the public schools. *Phi Delta Kappan, 82,* 41-58.

Rovegno, I. (1994). Teaching within a curricular zone of safety: School culture and the situated nature of student teachers' pedagogical content knowledge. *Research Quarterly for Exercise and Sport, 65,* 269-279.

Rovegno, I., & Bandhauer, D. (1998). A study of the collaborative research process: Shared privilege and shared empowerment. *Journal of Teaching in Physical Education, 17,* 357-375.

Rowand, C. (1999). How old are America's public schools? *Education Statistics Quarterly 1(1),* 53-56.

Ryan, S., Marzilli, S., & Martindale, T. (2001). Using digital cameras to assess motor learning. *Journal of Physical Education, Recreation and Dance, 72(8),* 13-16, 18.

Saffici, C. (1999). The perceived relevance of physical education. *Physical Educator, 56,* 138-142.

Sandholtz, J.H. (1990). *Demands, rewards, and effort: A balancing act for teachers.* Stanford, CA: Center for Research on the Context of Secondary School Teaching, Stanford University, School of Education. (ERIC Document Reproduction Service No. ED338591)

Schevrich, J.J., Skrla, L., & Johnson, J.F. (2000). Thinking carefully about equity and accountability. *Phi Delta Kappan, 82,* 293-299.

Sharpe, T., Lounsbery, M.F., Golden, C., & Deibler, C. (1999). Analysis of an ongoing, district-wide collaborative approach to teacher education. *Journal of Teaching in Physical Education, 19,* 79-96.

Sharpe, T., & Templin, T. (1997). Implementing collaborative teams: A strategy for school based professionals. *Journal of Physical Education, Recreation and Dance, 68(6),* 50-55.

Short, P.M., & Greer, J.T. (2002). *Leadership in empowered schools. Themes from innovative efforts.* Upper Saddle River, NJ: Merrill Prentice Hall.

Siedentop, D. (1993). Thinking differently about secondary physical education. In J.E. Rink (Ed.), *Critical crossroads: Middle and secondary school physical education* (pp. 7-10). Reston, VA: National Association for Sport and Physical Education.

Siedentop, D., & Locke, L. (1997). Making a difference for physical education. What professors and practitioners must build together. *Journal of Physical Education, Recreation and Dance, 68(4)*, 25-33.

Silverman, S. (1997). Technology and physical education: Present, possibilities, and potential problems. *Quest, 49*, 306-314.

Skrla, L. (2001). Accountability, equity, and complexity. *Educational Researcher, 30(4)*, 15-21.

Smyth, D.M. (1992, April). *The kids just love him: A first year teacher's perceptions of how the workplace has affected his teaching.* Paper presented at the annual meeting of the American Educational Research Association, San Francisco. (ERIC Document Reproduction Service No. ED355177)

Smyth, D.M. (1995). First-year physical education teachers' perceptions of their workplace. *Journal of Teaching in Physical Education, 14*, 198-214.

Solmon, M.A., Worthy, T., & Carter, J.A. (1993). The interaction of school context and role identity of first-year teachers. *Journal of Teaching in Physical Education, 12*, 313-328.

Sparkes, A.C., Templin, T.J., & Schempp, P.G. (1990). The problematic nature of a career in a marginal subject: Some implications for teacher education programmes. *Journal of Education for Teaching, 16(1)*, 3-28.

Sparkes, A.C., Templin, T.J., & Schempp, P.G. (1993). Exploring dimensions of marginality: Reflecting on the life histories of physical education teachers. Journal of *Teaching in Physical Education, 12*, 386-398.

Stader, D.L. (2001). Block scheduling in small high schools: Perceptions from the field. *Rural Educator, 22(3)*, 37-41.

Stroot, S.A., Collier, C., O'Sullivan, M., & England, K. (1994). Contextual hoops and hurdles: Workplace conditions in secondary physical education. *Journal of Teaching in Physical Education, 13*, 342-360.

Stroot, S.A., Faucette, N., & Schwager, S. (1993). In the beginning: The induction of physical educators. *Journal of Teaching in Physical Education, 12*, 375-385.

Talbert, J.E., & McLaughlin, M.W. (1992). *Understanding teaching in context.* Stanford, CA: Center for Research on the Context of Secondary School Teaching, Stanford University, School of Education. (ERIC Document Reproduction Service No. ED342756)

Teachers' feelings of preparedness. (2000). *Education Statistics Quarterly, 2(1)*, 51-52.

Templin, T.J. (1988). Teacher isolation: A concern for the collegial development of physical educators. *Journal of Teaching in Physical Education, 7*, 197-205.

Templin, T.J. (1989). Running on ice: A case study of the influence of workplace conditions on a secondary school physical educator. In T.J. Templin & P.G. Schempp (Eds.), *Socialization into physical education: Learning to teach* (pp. 165-197). Indianapolis: Benchmark Press.

Templin, T.J., Sparkes, A., Grant, B., & Schempp, P. (1994). Matching the self: The paradoxical case and life history of a late career teacher/coach. *Journal of Teaching in Physical Education, 13*, 274-294.

Tichenor, S. (2001, May). *Cutting edge technology: Inspiration or irritation?* Paper presented at the annual meeting of the National Institute for Staff and Organizational Development, Austin. (ERIC Document Reproduction Service No. ED454928)

Tinning, R., & Fitzclarence, L. (1992). Postmodern youth culture and the crisis in Australian secondary school physical education. *Quest, 44*, 287-303.

Trilling, B., & Hood, P. (1999). Learning, technology, and education reform in the knowledge age, or "we're wired, webbed, and windowed, now what?" *Educational Technology, 39(3)*, 5-18.

Visher, M.G., Teitelbaum, P., & Emanuel, D. (1999). *Key high school reform strategies: An overview of research findings.* Washington, DC: U.S. Department of Education. (ERIC Document Reproduction Service No. ED430271)

Ward, P. (1999). An introduction to the Saber-Tooth project. *Journal of Teaching in Physical Education, 18*, 379-381.

Ward, P., & Doutis, P. (1999). Toward a consolidation of the knowledge base for reform in physical education. *Journal of Teaching in Physical Education, 18*, 382-402.

Ward, P., Doutis, P., & Evans, S.A. (1999). Lessons, conclusions, and implications of the Saber-Tooth project. *Journal of Teaching in Physical Education, 18*, 455-463.

Weiss, S. (1999). *Youth violence: The progress of education reform 1999–2001.* Denver: Education Commission of the States. (ERIC Document Reproduction Service No. ED433619)

Wirt, J., Choy, S.P., Bae, Y., Sable, J., Gruner, A., Stennett, J., et al. (1999). *The Coalition of Education 1999.* Washington, DC: U.S. Department of Education, National Center for Education Statistics.

Woods, L.A. (1992). Development of an inventory to assess multicultural education attitudes, competencies, and knowledge of physical education professionals (Doctoral dissertation, University of Georgia, 1992). *Dissertation Abstracts International, 53*, 2295A.

CHAPTER FIVE

STUDENT LEARNING AND THE SOCIAL CONSTRUCTION OF GENDER IN SPORT AND PHYSICAL EDUCATION

David Kirk

Many people who grew to adulthood during the 1980s and 1990s believe that society has moved a long way during their lifetimes to resolve gender issues in sport and physical education. Look, they say, at women marathon runners, women rugby players, women who play the serve-and-volley game in tennis, women pole vaulters. Look at girls and boys playing together in sports such as field hockey and football. Look at coeducational physical education classes. We even have men in countries like Australia playing traditionally female sports such as netball! Isn't this proof that we now have equality between the sexes when it comes to sport and physical education?

Some less sanguine members of the public point out in response that girls remain more likely to drop out of sport than boys. They comment that even at the elite level of sport performance, women do not earn the same rewards as men for performances that may be as good or better. Some suggest that to make sport played by women more acceptable to the sporting public, women have had either to play like men or to look sexier and more glamorous.

The people on the optimistic side of the debate are inclined to suggest that the barriers to girls' and women's full participation in physical education and sport have now been removed, and that whether and how they participate is the choice of the individual. Perhaps, they concede, more could be done to motivate disaffected and inactive girls. But the problem, if one still exists, is down to individual choice and enthusiasm rather than structural barriers.

The optimists may have a point; some progress has indeed occurred. But to believe a gender agenda in physical education and sport no longer exists is to underestimate the enormity and complexity of the issues and to overestimate what has been achieved. What the optimists perhaps don't realize is that physical education as an activity in the school curriculum has been gendered since its first appearance in the modern era, which dates from the mid- to late 1800s and the beginning of mass compulsory schooling. For well over one hundred years, then, the practices that make up physical education have been strongly associated with girls being feminine and boys being masculine. This gendered history has strongly influenced what we now regard as legitimate knowledge in physical education.

This influence is all the more profound when we note that there are many optimists in our midst, among the general public and the teaching profession, who are unable (or sometimes unwilling) to recognize these gender dimensions of physical education and who assume that the subject is gender neutral. The consequences of this inability to recognize the lasting influence of the gendered history of physical education are serious. Many girls and more boys than is often acknowledged fail to receive appropriate physical education in the present because of the ongoing influence of the past.

Even the pessimists often assume that when gender is raised as an issue in physical education, we are referring mainly to the "problem" of girls and their alleged low motivation and high levels of dropout from sport. Over the last decade and a half, however, we can no longer make this assumption because there has been a spectacular increase in interest in boys' experiences and the social construction of masculinity in physical education and sport. As a result of feminists' persistent critique of the dominant, or "hegemonic," form of masculinity and its celebration in sport, men have been forced to carry out serious studies into sport and masculinity. They have discovered that it is no longer safe to assume, and indeed never was, that current and past forms of physical education meet boys' needs.

This chapter begins with an attempt to define the words *sex* and *gender* because they are fundamental to our topic. In this context we consider the place of the gendered body in relation to the social construction of femininities and masculinities. We then turn to consider the emergence of gendered sport since the mid-1800s and how the influence of history has persisted to the present day. We look next at research about school physical education, particularly what we have learned about girls' and boys' experiences. The concept of the functional curriculum is introduced as a means to identify how young people learn gender in physical education classes. The chapter concludes with a brief consideration of the actions researchers and others have begun to take based on what we now know about the social construction of gender and physical education.

DEFINING SEX AND GENDER: GENDER AS A SOCIAL CONSTRUCT

The literature and everyday professional discourse of physical education and sport often use the terms *sex* and *gender* interchangeably. During the 1980s social theorists began to prefer the term *gender* to *sex* because doing so permitted them to move debates about women's and men's participation in physical activities beyond biology to include psychological, social, and cultural issues. As Hall (1990) noted, however, this psychosocial notion of gender was often used in direct contrast to the idea that the term *sex* refers to fixed biological categories of female and male. This was a problem for a number of reasons, and one that we will return to shortly.

The term in most common use today is *gender*. But despite these theoretical advances in sociology, commonsense assumptions that biology primarily explains differences between women and men in physical activities such as sport persist. Ironically, in the everyday professional discourse of teachers and coaches, the term *gender* has increasingly replaced *sex* as a way of referring to biological differences. This replacement of *sex* with *gender* and equation of gender with biology not only reinforces the notion that biology determines individuals' abilities to participate in physical activities but also risks losing the valuable notion that gender is socially constructed. Instead of accepting this messy and confusing use of words, it is worth retaining both terms, *sex* and *gender*, but defining carefully how we might best use them.

We can retain the word *sex* to refer to biological characteristics of femaleness and maleness. At the same time, we cannot assume that biology is either natural or fixed. Experiments with the genome and cloning provide ample evidence to show that biology is no longer beyond human manipulation. But even without such developments, men and women have for many years been using forms of training to alter their body shapes and sizes. Surgery can also intervene to change the femaleness and maleness of human bodies, the most obvious example being the so-called sex change. Forms of dress and cosmetics can affect the surface appearance of bodies to alter the degrees of femaleness and maleness. Most telling of all, however, is the existence of hermaphrodites, people born with both female and male sexual organs, or with indeterminate sexual organs.

Each of these examples suggests that we can use the term *sex* to refer to biology, but that we must do so by treating femaleness and maleness as relational concepts rather than as separate and fixed categories. So, it is possible for individuals with male reproductive organs to have one or more parts of their bodies that have a shape or size conventionally characterized as female, such as narrow shoulders and broad hips. Individuals with female reproductive organs may have broad shoulders and narrow hips, conventionally a male shape. When we use the term *sex* to refer to the biological characteristics of femaleness and maleness, we do so in the understanding that differences are matters of degree and that biological characteristics of femaleness only make sense in relation to (rather than in isolation from) maleness.

With this definition of *sex* in mind, we can now use the word *gender* to refer to a socially constructed pattern of behavior recognized as feminine or masculine. Because gender is socially constructed, it is dynamic, responding to social change. Gender is also constructed in relation to an individual's ethnic identity and social class. For example, Connell (1995) refers to various forms of masculinity including working class and "protest" masculinities, while Oliver and Lalik (2000) explore with adolescent girls the subtleties of skin color and hair texture in relation to Black and White femininities.

How gender is constructed changes over time and differs from one society to another and across social classes, ethnic groups, and cultural groups within the same society. Examples of such differences are commonplace in anthropological research (e.g., Reich, 1971). This literature shows that beyond the act of procreation, there are no "natural" male and female behaviors across societies. Indeed, to emphasize the point, anthropology shows that the act of procreation itself takes place in ways that in some societies would be counter to dominant forms of femininity or masculinity in others. Acknowledgement of the fluidity of gender has lead many social theorists, such as Connell (1995), to use these terms in the plural rather than the singular, to talk about femininities and masculinities both across cultures and within cultures.

The words *femininity* and *masculinity* therefore do not refer to the same things as femaleness and maleness, although femininity and masculinity incorporate the biological characteristics of sex. Gender is constructed through the interaction of biology with social and cultural values, which in turn are central to the formation of individuals' gendered identities. Just as femaleness and maleness must be viewed as relational rather than categorical concepts, so too must femininity and masculinity.

THE GENDERED BODY

A better way to understand this definition of gender may be to consider the body itself and the ways in which it is incorporated into the social construction of gender. This idea is particularly important in the field of physical education because the moving body is of central interest and concern.

Until recently, social scientists have neglected the human body. Many social theorists had acknowledged the individual within society, but relatively few had extended their analyses to include the part bodies play in producing and reproducing social practices. Part of the reason for this neglect was the success of the biological sciences in providing explanations of the structure and function of the body. We tend to take for granted that bodies are flesh, blood, and bones. The relevance of biological explanations of the body seems self-evident. The success of biological science has contributed to a naturalistic view of the body, a view that sees the body as a mainly biological phenomenon.

On the occasions when social theorists have turned their attention to the body, their theories have tended to reflect this naturalistic view (see Shilling, 1993). This view has lead, for example, to claims that biological factors such as strength ("men are stronger") and psychological factors such as motivation ("men are more aggressive") can wholly explain differences in sport performance between females and males. The naturalistic view is deterministic. An example of determinism would be the belief that a social behavior, such as being "masculine," is dependent on and determined by biological factors such as muscularity and physical size.

Recent work by sociologists, historians, and cultural theorists has challenged this naturalistic view of the body. Many of these researchers have argued that the society in which people live develops their understanding of their bodies. They claim that bodies are social at the same time that they are biological. To put this another way, the body is in nature and in culture simultaneously (Kirk, 1993).

The issue of gendering the body emerges as crucial to a discussion of the social construction of gender because it confronts directly the nature-culture dichotomy. As the examples of homosexuality and transvestism reveal, biologically male or female bodies do not, necessarily, denote culturally masculine or feminine people. The body is not merely the measure or manifestation of a sexed self; it is a shaper of gendered identity and is shaped by dominant notions of femininity and masculinity. Sexuality, like the body, is socially constructed, but biology sets limits on the extent to which degrees of femininity and masculinity are possible for any individual. In other words, a meshing of biological and cultural forces occurs around the construction of the gendered body.

The gendering of the body is a cultural process that appropriates the biological body as its raw material. To say this does not mean assigning priority to either realm, but it does state the relative contributions of each to the process of gendering the body. The body's surfaces may be the script in which an individual's femininity and masculinity is written and which others read. Physical appearance alone, however, does not provide a complete account either of sex, gender, sexuality, or self-identity. More accurately, the interaction of biology and culture produces gendered bodies, rather than cultural inscription or biology by themselves. The subtle shades of physical size, the occupation of space, the embodiment of force, varieties of physical shape, and the social values and meanings attached to them contribute to the relative femininity and masculinity of individuals.

Summarizing the question of definition, we can retain the word *sex* to refer to the femaleness and maleness of individuals while accepting that biology is neither fixed nor categorical. The word *gender* refers to femininity and masculinity, involving the meshing of biology, psychology, and culture. According to these definitions, gender is socially constructed, and so different forms of femininity and masculinity can be considered socially appropriate both across societies and within societies. As we will see, physical education and sport have been criticized by social theorists not because they are sites that contribute to the social construction of gender, but because in Western societies such as the United States and elsewhere they contribute to the construction of a particular, dominant form of masculinity that, as Bryson (1990) among others has noted, depends on domination and the positioning of "others" (i.e., those who do not practice the dominant form of masculinity) as inferior.

EMERGENCE OF GENDERED SPORT

Historical research has demonstrated conclusively that the activities we now recognize as modern sports, including the various codes of football, cricket, and baseball, were developed in the second half of the 19th century in schools serving boys from the middle and upper classes, at first in Britain but soon afterward in North America and elsewhere. These sports were developed from folk versions of the activities but owed their modern forms, including standardized rules, playing field dimensions, uniforms and so on, to these schools.

The schools serving the social elite of the emerging industrial capitalist nations of the 19th century did more than simply formalize folk activities. They also developed an educational ideology surrounding games that eminent historian J.A. Mangan (1981) has labeled the "games ethic." The games ethic provided sports with their educational rationale in the elite schools. This rationale aimed to instill in boys qualities of leadership, a sense of class, and, later, national superiority, controlled aggression, perseverance, deferred gratification, and loyalty to the team. The use of games to develop these characteristics of masculinity became so attractive to schools and so widespread that the use of games was, by the beginning of the First World War in 1914, a key indicator of the status of a school and its continuing success. In short, men originally developed modern sports for boys and men. Theberge (1985) has accurately described sport as a "male preserve."

This is not to deny women's early involvement in sport for similar reasons. As schools for girls of the middle and upper classes were established toward the end of the 19th century, many head teachers sought to emulate the example of the schools for boys (McCrone, 1988). But just as sport in the boys' schools aimed to develop a class-specific form of masculinity, so the sports for girls sought to develop a specific form of femininity approved by elite society. Netball, a sport that continues to be popular in Britain and its former colonies and is played mostly by women and girls, was developed in the 1890s as a modification of basketball. Indeed, netball in Australia and New Zealand was for many years known as women's basketball until women began to play the male version of basketball, thus forcing the name to be changed. Middle-class women developed the rules and styles of play in netball at the end of the 19th century in Australia, Britain, New Zealand, and North America. Rules such as the absolute prohibition of physical contact clearly demonstrate their ideas about appropriate behavior for "young ladies."

Even though sport in the schools for girls grew in popularity, it never matched the heights of devotion witnessed in boys' schools. And it did so in the face of staunch opposition from a wide cross-section of society in the late 19th and early 20th centuries. For example, the man behind the modern Olympic games and first president of the International Olympic Committee, Baron Pierre de Coubertin, stated that "women's sport is against the laws of nature and is the most unaesthetic sight human eyes could contemplate" (in Hargreaves, 1994). P.C. McIntosh, a historian of physical education in England, quoted a letter published in *The Lancet* medical journal in 1922 from a Miss Cowdroy, a high school headmistress, in which she stated that it was well known that

> eighty percent of gymnastics teachers had breakdowns, that playing strenuous games developed a flat figure with underdeveloped breasts, that athletic women suffered from nerves, heart trouble, rheumatism, suppressed menstruation and displacements, that they decried marriage, that their confinements were always difficult, that their children were often inferior, and that most athletic women seemed to have stifled what is finest in women—love, sympathy, tact and intuitive understanding (McIntosh, 1968, p.201).

So it is important to note that as the team games that remain major sports in contemporary Western societies like North America, Britain, and western Europe were emerging in the late 19th century, they were firmly and explicitly designed to emphasize the social characteristics of femininity and masculinity valued at that time. Although a section of the boys' elite school community always felt that the emphasis placed on sport was inappropriate because it was a potential distraction for boys from academic studies, they were a minority, even when the games ethic lost some of its momentum after the First World War. An even larger group opposed girls' participation in sport, but for a different reason, which was that sport undermined appropriately feminine behavior in girls and young women. But the key point to note is that throughout its modern history, since the mid-1800s, sport has been an important means of stressing differences between men and women, of maintaining those differences, and of celebrating the superiority of hegemonic masculinity over other forms of masculinity and femininity.

GENDERED SPORTS TODAY

In contemporary societies, girls and women now participate in increasingly large numbers in a growing range of sports. Moreover, some women now play sports that have traditionally been associated with men, such as various versions of football, and some men play sports formerly played only by women, such as netball. Does this mean that we have made progress and eliminated gender as a factor in the conduct of sport?

The fact that increasing numbers of girls and women now play "male" sports and some men now play "female" sports owes much to women's long struggle and perseverance in the face of extreme hostility from male organizers and administrators of sport. Even so, women cannot be full members of golf clubs in many parts of Britain, Australia, and the United States. In addition, the best women performers in sports such as soccer, running, golf, swimming, and tennis are not allowed to compete in the same competitions as men and thus cannot gain access to the same levels of prize money. Nor do they receive the same media attention as men and benefits that accompany this, such as sponsorship. Sport does not exist outside society but instead actively contributes to the social construction of gender in other spheres of life. So the inequalities and injustices between women and men that sport demonstrates are also present to a greater or lesser extent in society more generally.

At the same time, as many feminist researchers have pointed out, sport is a key site that celebrates a particular, dominant form of masculinity. Bryson (1990) among others has shown that this form of masculinity depends on physical and psychological domination. It is also exclusionary. To play sport, she argues, one must practice what Connell (1995) describes as hegemonic masculinity or else be treated as "other." In the case of men, to be other to the hegemonic form of masculinity is to be "unmanly," to risk being labeled a "wimp" or a "sissy," or to be accused of being gay. In the case of women, to be other to hegemonic masculinity is to be treated as inferior to men, as unable to compete with them on equal terms, even though women's femininity remains intact.

But as Bryson (1990) points out, women who challenge this position of other and who choose to play like men face further risks. In this case, their femininity *is* questioned, and women who develop "masculine" physiques, attitudes, and styles of play risk being labeled as "butch" or accused of being lesbian. So women are caught in a double-bind in sport. If they conform to dominant forms of femininity, they are unlikely to play sports at all or, if they do, they are likely to participate in traditionally "female" activities. The risk is that while their femininity remains unquestioned, some men (and other women) regard sporting women as inferior players. If, on the other hand, they choose to play in a manner traditionally viewed as masculine, sporting women risk having their femininity and their sexuality scrutinized and questioned.

Bryson (1990) also notes that particular sports are, in a sense, the flagships for the celebration of hegemonic masculinity. In Australian and British societies she identifies these as the various codes of football and cricket. In North America the equivalent sports might be, in addition to the football codes, baseball, basketball, and ice hockey. Boxing is an obvious example that she does not mention. Each sport celebrates and rewards physical violence, size, and aggression. Cheating and substance abuse is the norm even if officially prohibited, and the risk of serious injury is high and ever present.

This insightful point raised by Bryson (1990) prompts us to regard the term *sport* in a more discriminating way than much social theorizing on sport does. Not all sports, not even those played predominantly by men, require or condone physical violence and aggression. Nor is it appropriate to take professional sports as proof of the ways in which sport is practiced in other spheres, such as recreational sports and youth sports. What this insight does is raise questions about the extent to which the dominant form of masculinity is a requirement for playing sport.

Even Bryson (1990) appears to take the view that sports that require high levels of physical contact such as rugby necessarily involve physical domination and violence, a view that seems to be widely held in the feminist literature (see Skelton, 2000). But this may not be the case necessarily. Played within the rules as they currently exist, any contact that may cause harm to another player is prohibited. A need may exist for such physical contact among men in Western societies where heterosexuality is assumed the norm and touching among men is in most contexts regarded with suspicion (Connell, 1995). Although some level of physical contact in such sports is required, this contact must be controlled. Evidence of the growing popularity of sports such as rugby among younger children in Australia, New Zealand, and Britain, including girls, suggests that these young people may enjoy appropriate physical contact (Gard & Meyenn, 2000).

This proposition does not deny that sports such as football have symbolic properties that represent hegemonic masculinity. Connell correctly states that sports such as football require two key properties closely associated with hegemonic masculinity—"the irresistible occupation of space (and) the ability to operate on space or the objects in it" (Connell, 1983, p.18). We can see how participants can practice these properties of force and skill in an extreme way that causes harm to another person. An example of an extreme case would be warfare. Another example, less extreme, might be professional sports such as football. We might infer how force and skill then come to be used symbolically to represent hegemonic masculinity in ways that suggest they are exclusive to this form of masculinity.

But making this inference would be a mistake. It would be a mistake, for example, to assume that the practices of professional football represent the practice of all football playing, never mind all sports participation. Yet when force and skill as they are practiced in an extreme way in professional football become symbols of hegemonic masculinity, there is great temptation to assume that the practice of force and skill within any sport context means that an individual is practicing or seeking to emulate hegemonic masculinity. Abundant evidence suggests that young people use professional sports practices as models for the practice of sport (Hickey & Fitzclarence, 1999; Siedentop, 2002). Even so, this does not mean that participants can only practice sport in a form identical to that used in professional sports or in a form consistent with hegemonic masculinity.

GENDER AND SCHOOL PHYSICAL EDUCATION

As we have noted, modern sports emerged from schools serving socially and economically elite boys from the second half of the 19th century. A form of physical education also existed in government-funded schools following the introduction of compulsory elementary education in the late 1800s. This form of physical education had little to do with sport, however, and it was based instead on systems of freestanding gymnastics exercises. The most popular system in Britain and Australia was Swedish gymnastics or the Ling system, known in the United States as calisthenics. Marching and other maneuvers adapted from military training handbooks formed part of these physical training lessons (Mangan & Park, 1987).

Elementary school boys and girls were expected to participate in this form of physical training. Where girls took classes separate from boys, the gymnastics exercises were sometimes adapted to fit the dominant cultural stereotypes of femininity at the time. But most often boys and girls took classes together, as they did for most other aspects of the elementary school curriculum, and the exercises and marching routines were unambiguously masculine. At the same time, the various syllabuses and handbooks of physical training from the late 1800s to the 1940s tended to treat children not as female and male, but as androgynous (Kirk, 2000). This practice was possible because most children, even at the higher end of the elementary school, would have been in their early teens and most would have been prepubescent. But as compulsory mass secondary education was implemented in the middle of the 20th century, older and more physically mature boys and girls could no longer be treated indiscriminately, as somehow gender neutral.

Although sport was available to children attending government schools from the late 19th century, they did not form part of the official curriculum. Only a handful of children talented enough to be selected for competitive teams would have played sports. With the introduction of compulsory secondary education a sport-based form of school physical education became available for all children rather than only the social elite. As this form of physical education began to become widespread in schools, it adopted the already established separatist approach to sport for boys only and sport for girls only. Physical educators simply accepted without question that a sport-based form of physical education needed to cater to boys and girls differently.

TITLE IX: EQUALITY OF OPPORTUNITY FOR GIRLS?

Although the sex-segregated form of physical education continues to be the norm in countries such as Britain, it survived in government-funded schools in the United States only until the early 1970s. During the 1960s feminists in the United States began to question why girls did not have access to the sports available to boys, and they began to form the view that girls' physical education experiences within the sex-segregated model was unnecessarily restricted and possibly inferior to boys' experiences. Feminists argued that the prohibition on girls' participation in the same sports as boys was based on an outmoded, 19th century view of females as frail and weak (Mangan & Park, 1987). They pointed to the growing number of examples of women's achievements in sport and used these as evidence to suggest that girls could do anything in sport that boys could do. The notion of equality of opportunity, that girls had the same rights as boys in physical education, formed the basis of the liberal feminist position. Some radical feminists have described this liberal approach as "me-too" feminism.

As an outcome of lobbying in a range of spheres of life for equal opportunities for women, the United States Congress approved Title IX of the Education Amendments in 1972. Title IX stated that "No person . . . shall, on the basis of sex, be excluded from participation in, be denied the benefits of, or be subjected to discrimination under any education program or activity receiving Federal financial assistance." Guidelines for physical education released three years later specified that physical education must be the same for females and males and that all classes must be coeducational. The exception to this is classes in sex education and those involving contact sports, though separation here is optional rather than mandatory. Boys and girls must be treated equally in classes.

Subsequent research on the effects of Title IX suggests that this legislation did not have the effect many feminists had hoped for. Far from empowering girls by providing them with access to the same activities as boys, the already masculine-defined curriculum further reinforced girls' marginalization. For instance, some 15 years or more after the implementation of Title IX, Nilges's (1998) study of a fourth-grade physical education class suggested that equal access to a common curriculum does not eliminate disadvantage to girls, when they are positioned as physically inferior to boys by a curriculum form and pedagogical practices that are patriarchal.

Earlier, Vertinsky (1992) had noted that coeducational physical education did not provide a solution to gender inequity in physical education. She cited critics (e.g., Evans, 1989) who had shown that the invitation to girls to participate alongside boys in a curriculum that continued to be strongly gendered was even more detrimental to girls' experiences. Without challenging the social and cultural ideologies surrounding gender and physical education, Vertinsky argued that the provision of equal opportunities to participate in physical activities is doomed to disadvantage girls.

Single-sex physical education has fared no better than coeducational physical education in the years following the implementation of Title IX. In Britain, where sex-segregated physical education continues to be the norm in most secondary schools, Williams & Bedward (1999) noted that girls' participation in physical activity on their own time outside of the school often occurred in spite of their experience in physical education rather than because of it. A large number of other studies in Britain confirm the view that although physical education is conducted in single-sex classes, it has a negative effect on girls' interest in leading an active and healthy lifestyle.

The reasons why are well known to researchers. In many physical education classes in Britain, the range of activities available to girls is restricted to traditional female sports such as netball and field hockey, even though girls may demonstrate a strong interest in traditionally male sports such as football. Girls continue to be required to wear the traditional sports uniform, often consisting of short skirts and tight tops. Female teachers appear to be unwilling to take notice of girls' preferences, even at age 14 and above. Researchers propose that a generational and cultural gap exists between many of these teachers—who tend to be from middle-class backgrounds, to be talented in sport, and to have been educated in monocultural, single-sex schools—and their working-class students from multicultural backgrounds (Flintoff & Scraton, 2001; Williams & Bedward, 2001). Studies have also drawn attention to the requirement that girls alter their dress and appearance for physical education classes. As researchers have noted, this requirement, including wearing a sports uniform, removing jewelry, tying back hair, and so on, often conflicts with girls' emerging sense of their femininity. These studies have also noted a mismatch between the prevailing view of female bodies as decorative and passive and the requirement of sport-based physical education that they be active and functional (Kay, 1995; Wright, 1997).

This research suggests that merely choosing between single-sex or coeducational classes in physical education does not produce equity. If both options are ineffective and inappropriate for girls, then perhaps we have been asking the wrong question. Whether boys and girls should be in the same class is clearly an important issue, but the more significant point may be that the grouping of students needs to be accompanied by an explicit pedagogy that is antisexist and that actively promotes equity.

Deam and Gilroy (1998) consolidate much of the most recent thinking about girls' experiences of school physical education and seek to extend this thinking by looking beyond the school. They suggest that physical educators need to recognize how women understand physical activity in relation to domestic and paid labor, leisure, relationships, and other conditions that facilitate or constrain participation. They make the point that many girls and women consider sport in its traditional form unattractive. For many women sport is also inaccessible, according to Deam and Gilroy (1998), because of gender relations within families, particularly relationships to fathers and husbands, and to constructions of heterosexual femininity that disallow sport as a legitimate pursuit. They claim that girls' and women's engagement in physical activity can have positive effects, including increased assertiveness and confidence. This leads them to recommend the dismantlement of sport-based physical education and its replacement with a physical activity-based curriculum that may include sport and a range of noncompetitive activities.

WHAT ABOUT THE BOYS?

Although the literature reporting girls' generally unsatisfactory experiences of sport-based physical education has continued to grow since the 1970s, boys' experiences have until recently been largely ignored. This was partly because researchers assumed that if sport-based physical education is a male preserve, then boys' experiences must be positive. Men were also reluctant to accept that they may need to engage in a searching analysis of masculinity and sport. This situation has begun to change, and since the mid-1980s the literature on masculinity and sport has burgeoned (e.g., Messner & Sabo, 1990).

As this interest in masculinity and sport has developed, increasingly researchers have been drawn to concerns that boys, not girls, are the underperforming group in schools and the most likely group of young people to be at risk and marginalized in society (Connell, 1996). Although researchers such as Connell show convincingly that men as a group continue to be socially and economically privileged over women, the question "What about the boys?" has generated important educational issues for schools as well as much emotive reaction.

Some policy initiatives have been based on the notion that if sport is "where the boys are," then this is where community workers should start in their attempts to develop more tolerant and responsible forms of masculinity (Hickey & Fitzclarence, 1999). But for such approaches to be effective, they need to break some of the commonplace and deeply felt associations between sports such as football and the traits of dominant masculinity, including violence and homophobia (Skelton, 2000).

Other research around the issue of masculinity and sport has also begun to raise searching questions about boys' and men's physical and emotional experiences of sport, such as their experiences of both pain and pleasure through physical contact with other males (Gard & Meyenn, 2000; Light & Kirk, 2000). Such issues are potentially controversial in a school context in particular because they touch on topics that have until now been taboo. As researchers continue to conduct studies about boys' experience of physical education and its contribution to the social construction of masculinity, physical educators will likely feel increasing pressure to address issues of pleasure, sexuality, power, and related topics (Beckett, 1998).

HIDDEN CURRICULUM AND LEARNING GENDER

By the time children arrive at school, the gender process is already well under way. By the age of five or six, most children will have learned what their parents and peers think is appropriate behavior for boys and girls. Children may not be aware of this process, and the process may not be complete. But even in the early years of compulsory schooling, teachers will face children who have a (sometimes strong) sense of their gendered selves.

Learning gender goes on all the time, right through the period of compulsory schooling, even though this is not usually a topic on the official curriculum of most schools. The ways children learn femininity and masculinity is through what is commonly called the hidden curriculum. Because teachers and the educational literature use the term widely, its meaning has become notoriously flexible and ambiguous.

Dodds (1985) developed the notion of the "functional curriculum" to overcome this ambiguity and provide a more precise sense of the kinds of powerful but unofficial learning that goes on in schools of such things as gender. Dodds suggests that four levels of curriculum operate simultaneously within any physical education program. Taken together, these four levels of learning constitute what she calls the functional curriculum—the full, dynamic display from which students learn.

The first level she identifies is the explicit curriculum, which refers to "those publicly stated and shared items that teachers want students to acquire" (Dodds, 1985, p.93). This is the level of curriculum that appears in school programs, syllabuses, and policy documents, and teachers consciously pursue it. In countries such as Britain, boys and girls still commonly experience different activities as part of their physical education programs and participate in single-sex classes. Such practices send explicit messages to young people about gender-appropriate activities.

On a second level is a covert curriculum, which Dodds (1985, p. 93) claims refers to teachers' "unspoken, nonpublic agendas." The covert curriculum refers to those qualities that school documents or lesson plans rarely, if ever, acknowledge (such as "students responding quickly and quietly to instructions" or "students trying hard") but that teachers would readily agree they consciously and intentionally communicate to students in implementing the explicit curriculum. For example, teachers might covertly but intentionally condone some student behaviors, such as rough play by boys, because they believe that "boys will be boys."

A third level, the null curriculum, refers to ideas, concepts, and values that could be included in the explicit and covert levels of curriculum but are either intentionally or unintentionally and unknowingly left out. What is missing from a curriculum is significant, because as Dodds (1985, p.93) says, "Ignorance is not neutral; it is a void in the lives of our children. What is *not* there in physical education classes interacts somehow with what *is* there." For example, teachers could include explicit affirmative statements in their teaching that girls and boys should value each others' contributions to a game, but they may not do so.

Finally, Dodds's scheme uses the fourth level, the hidden curriculum, in a more restricted sense than the way other studies have commonly used it. In her scheme the hidden curriculum refers to the reflexive aspects of what teachers say and do in organizing programs, writing lesson plans, and teaching classes. For instance, the use of gestures or a particular tone of voice often does more than simply accompany the substance of what someone is saying. The way in which a teacher says something or moves while speaking is often crucial in conveying the meaning of the spoken words.

Wright (2000) has shown how this reflexive process works in terms of Dodds's definition of hidden curriculum. Her studies reveal that teachers' choices of language in physical education lessons often convey to girls that they are "weaker, less enthusiastic, (and) less skilled in those activities which are generally valued—that is, traditional team games" than boys (Wright, 2000, p.41). Teachers do not say these things explicitly and indeed are rarely conscious of using language that might have such an effect on girls. Close analysis of transcripts of teachers' talk during lessons, however, reveals that both female and male teachers use different language in their interactions with girls than they do with boys. A common if now stereotypical example would be when a teacher asks a class of boys and girls if she can have "four strong boys to help put the equipment away." The students themselves may not be conscious of the use of such language, but the effects nevertheless can be real.

In combination, these four levels of learning within the functional curriculum send powerful messages to young people about gender in physical education settings. Although some aspects of the official curriculum, such as different activities for boys and girls, convey explicitly that the school believes they should treat boys and girls differently, such actions are also the easiest to challenge because they are explicit. Potentially, the less explicit levels are more powerful because they communicate messages to young people about gender that are taken for granted, and in so doing they confirm and reproduce already existing gendered practices in physical education and sport and in society more generally.

FROM ADVOCACY TO ACTION: STRATEGIES TO ADDRESS THE GENDER AGENDA

When learning gender takes place in such complex ways, it is easy to see why what we have learned from research is not easily translated into strategies for action. Even when research does inform interventions intended to reform physical education, the outcomes of such actions are never assured. Researching and criticizing inequitable forms of physical education is not enough, even if the ways in which young people learn gender is complex and subtle. Increasingly, researchers and their colleagues are shifting their work from advocacy for change to action to create change.

Many continue to advocate change. For example, in relation to girls' experiences, Flintoff and Scraton (2001) note that their data suggest that

> PE programmes offer curricula activities and pedagogy built on out-dated gendered relations and identities, and which take insufficient account of the changing nature of young women's lives . . . even those who enjoyed physical activity still dismissed a lot of PE and questioned its purpose. (Flintoff & Scraton, 2001, p.18)

On the basis of evidence such as this, researchers Flintoff and Scraton propose that there needs to be a broadening of activities beyond traditional competitive sports, greater choice for girls about how they dress and what they do in physical education, and more emphasis on issues that interest girls such as health-related exercise. Williams and Bedward (2001) support these suggestions and claim that the need is for more flexibility and choice for girls before age 14 if school practice is to be consistent with the inclusive curriculum policy of the British government. Some of these proposals for action to reform physical education for girls may imply that sport should be eliminated from programs altogether.

One alternative form of physical education investigated by Humberstone (1990) did just this because it took place at an outdoor adventure center in Britain. Boys and girls in small coeducational groups attended the center with their teachers for one week. The curriculum involved land- and water-based activities that included considerable physical challenges, high dependency on teamwork, and some risk taking. Humberstone reported that the boys and girls developed a more sensitive understanding of themselves and each other following their outdoor-adventure experiences. In particular, these nonsport activities provided the boys with opportunities to rethink their views of girls' physical competence.

Although Williams and Bedward (2001) support the kind of alternative curriculum described by Humberstone, they argue against removing sport from physical education programs, citing evidence from their research that many girls in England would like to play boys-only sports such as football but are not permitted to do so. In the United States Ennis (1999) also rejects this implication that sport should be removed from physical education. Although she believes that alternatives to sport must be available to girls, she suggests that girls can gain valuable educational experiences using sport as a medium. But to do so, the dominant curriculum model in physical education needs to change.

Ennis (1999) criticizes what she calls the multiactivity model of physical education. She characterizes this model as follows: short units of activity; minimal opportunities for sustained instruction; little accountability for learning; weak or nonexistent transfer of learning across lessons, units, and year levels; few policies to equalize participation between boys and girls (in coed classes) and high- and low-skilled players; and a student social system that undermines teacher authority. In place of the multiactivity model Ennis (1999) examined Sport for Peace, an adaptation of Siedentop's (1994) Sport Education model combined with Peace Education (see chapter 13 by Peter Hastie for more detail). She reported that the model transformed the sport experience for girls, boys, and teachers and included enhanced student ownership, authentic cooperative environments, second chances to learn, and more tolerant attitudes of boys toward girls. These changes helped develop more positive conceptions of self and others, better social relationships, and different ways of understanding sport.

Oliver and Lalik (2001) used a different kind of intervention that integrated physical education and critical literacy to begin to understand how girls experience their bodies and to find ways to help girls learn to critique and resist cultural messages of the body that threaten their health and well-being. Their work suggested that to create curricula that supports girls' critique requires that teachers tap girls' interests, listen actively and respectfully to what girls say, use a variety of strategic questions aimed at helping girls elaborate or challenge their views, create safe spaces for girls to express their views, and support girls in the process of imagining alternative and preferred worlds. Their research also suggests that girls enjoy and appreciate having opportunities in school to study issues of the body they find meaningful. Oliver and Lalik's (2001) work has also explored ethnicity and social class as important dimensions of girls' gendered identities.

These are just a few of an increasing number of interventions that have begun to seek forms of physical education that are, in Vertinsky's (1992) words, "gender sensitive." Although Vertinsky noted that coeducational physical education had not addressed girls' physical education needs, she proposed that coeducational rather than single-sex programs may have greater potential to begin to challenge the cultural values, gender-identity development, and gender stereotypes associated with sport. To move toward gender-sensitive physical education, Vertinsky argues that teachers must place issues of gender center stage and teach explicitly about the social construction of gender to achieve greater gender equity.

Connell (1996) has also made this point in relation to developing strategies for educating boys. He argued that

> masculinities and femininities are actively constructed, not simply received. Society, school and peer milieu make boys an offer of a place in the gender order; boys determine how they will take it up. (Connell, 1996, p.220)

For boys to take up a place in the gender order that actively challenges hegemonic masculinity, Connell suggests that "gender-relevant" programs of instruction be required that target precisely the institutional practices of society and of schools that sustain hegemonic masculinity. According to this argument, few other subjects in the school curriculum require reform as radical as physical education because physical education is so strongly linked to the reproduction of the gender order and to the celebration of hegemonic masculinity in particular. Along with Vertinsky (1992), Connell (1996) proposes that teachers at all levels of the functional curriculum need to address the topic of gender.

SUMMARY

The purpose of this chapter was to explore the social construction of gender in sport and physical education. Definitions of the terms *sex* and *gender* were established. Notions of femaleness and maleness associated with sex and femininities and masculinities associated with gender need to be viewed as relational concepts. The chapter described the emergence of gendered forms of sport from the private schools serving socially elite males and females in the mid-19th century and the continuing influence on the gendered nature of sport in contemporary societies. From these beginnings, sport has remained a key site for the celebration of hegemonic masculinity and for the subordination of femininities and other masculinities. School physical education has also been gendered and has been shown to make inadequate provision for many girls and more boys than is usually supposed. The functional curriculum is a term used to demonstrate how young people learn gender in physical education. Finally, the chapter describes a shift from advocacy to action and provides three brief examples of interventions intended to challenge conventional processes of constructing gender in physical education.

IMPLICATIONS FOR PRACTICE

1. The term gender refers to a socially constructed pattern of behavior recognized as feminine or masculine, and sex refers to the biological markers of femaleness and maleness.
2. Physical education and sport programs are key sites for the social construction of gender.
3. Gendered forms of sport emerged from the private schools serving socially elite males and females in the mid-19th century.
4. From these beginnings, sport has remained a key site for the celebration of hegemonic masculinity and for the subordination of femininities and other masculinities.
5. School physical education has also been gendered and has been shown to make inadequate provision for many girls and more boys than is usually supposed.
6. Young people learn gender in physical education through a complex process that cuts across the explicit, covert, null, and reflexive levels of the curriculum.
7. A shift from advocacy to action in relation to gender and physical education has recently occurred, and examples of interventions that seek to challenge conventional processes of constructing gender in physical education are available.

REFERENCES

Beckett, L. (Ed.). (1998). *Everyone is special! A handbook for teachers on sexuality education.* Sandgate, Queensland, Australia: Association of Women Teachers.

Bryson, L. (1990). Challenges to male hegemony in sport. In M.A. Messner & D.F. Sabo (Eds.), *Sport, men and the gender order: Critical feminist perspectives* (pp. 173-184). Champaign, IL: Human Kinetics.

Connell, R.W. (1983). *Which way is up? Essays on class, sex and culture.* Sydney: Allen & Unwin.

Connell, R.W. (1995) *Masculinities.* Sydney: Allen & Unwin.

Connell, R.W. (1996) Teaching the boys: New research on

masculinity, and gender strategies for schools. *Teachers College Record, 98*, 206-235.

Deam, R., & Gilroy, S. (1998). Physical activity, life-long learning and empowerment—situating sport in women's leisure. *Sport, Education and Society, 3*, 89-104.

Dodds, P. (1985). Are hunters of the functional curriculum seeking quarks or snarks? *Journal of Teaching in Physical Education, 4*, 91-99.

Ennis, C.D. (1999). Creating a culturally relevant curriculum for disengaged girls. *Sport, Education and Society, 4*, 31-50.

Evans, J. (1989). Equality and opportunity in the physical education curriculum. *ACHPER National Journal, 123*, 8-11.

Flintoff, A., & Scraton, S. (2001). Stepping into active leisure? Young women's perceptions of active lifestyles and their experiences of school physical education. *Sport, Education and Society, 6*, 5-22.

Gard, M., & Meyenn, R. (2000). Boys, bodies, pleasure and pain: Interrogating contact sports in schools. *Sport, Education and Society, 5*, 19-34.

Hall, M.A. (1990). How should we theorize gender in the context of sport? In M.A. Messner & D.F. Sabo (Eds.), *Sport, men and the gender order: Critical feminist perspectives* (pp. 223-240). Champaign, IL: Human Kinetics.

Hargreaves, J. (1994). *Sporting females: Critical issues in the history and sociology of women's sports.* London: Routledge.

Hickey, C., & Fitzclarence, L. (1999) Educating boys in sport and physical education: Using narrative methods to develop pedagogies of responsibility. *Sport, Education and Society, 4*, 51-62.

Humberstone, B. (1990). Warriors or wimps? Creating alternative forms of physical education. In M.A. Messner & D.F Sabo (Eds.) *Sport, men and the gender order: Critical feminist perspectives* (pp. 201-210). Champaign, IL: Human Kinetics.

Kay, T. (1995). *Women and sport—a review of research.* London: Sports Council.

Kirk, D. (1993). *The body, schooling and culture.* Geelong, Victoria, Australia: Deakin University Press.

Kirk, D. (2000). Gender associations: Sport, state schools and Australian culture. *International Journal of Sport History, 17*(2/3), 49-64.

Light, R., & Kirk, D. (2000). High school rugby, the body and the reproduction of hegemonic masculinity. *Sport, Education and Society, 5*, 163-176.

Mangan, J.A. (1981) *Athleticism in Victorian and Edwardian public schools.* Cambridge, UK: Cambridge University Press.

Mangan, J.A., & Park, R.J. (Eds.). (1987). *From 'fair sex' to feminism: Sport and the socialisation of women in the industrial and post-industrial eras.* London: Frank Cass.

McCrone, K.E. (1988). *Sport and the physical emancipation of English women.* London: Routledge.

McIntosh, P.C. (1968). *PE in England since 1800* (2nd ed.). London: Bell.

Messner, M.A., & Sabo, D.F. (Eds.). (1990). *Sport, men and the gender order: Critical feminist perspectives.* Champaign, IL: Human Kinetics.

Nilges, L. (1998). I thought only fairy tales had supernatural power: A radical feminist analysis of Title IX in physical education. *Journal of Teaching in Physical Education, 17*, 172-194.

Oliver, K.L., & Lalik, R. (2000). *Bodily knowledge: Learning about equity and justice with adolescent girls.* New York: Peter Lang.

Oliver, K.L., & Lalik, R. (2001). The body as curriculum: Learning with adolescent girls. *Journal of Curriculum Studies, 33*, 303-333.

Reich, W. (1971). *The invasion of compulsory sex-morality.* Harmondsworth, UK: Penguin.

Shilling, C. (1993). *The body and social theory.* London: Sage.

Siedentop, D. (1994). *Sport education: Quality PE through positive sport experiences.* Champaign, IL: Human Kinetics.

Siedentop, D. (2002). Junior sport and the evolution of sport cultures. *Journal of Teaching in Physical Education, 21*, 392-401.

Skelton, C. (2000). "A passion for football": Dominant masculinities and primary schooling. *Sport, Education and Society 5*, 5-18.

Theberge, N. (1985). Towards a feminist alternative to sport as a male preserve. *Quest, 37*, 193-202.

Vertinsky, P. (1992). Reclaiming space, revisioning the body: The quest for gender-sensitive physical education. *Quest, 44*, 373-396.

Williams, E.A., & Bedward, J. (1999). *Games for the girls—the impact of recent policy on the provision of physical education and sporting opportunities for female adolescents—a report of a study funded by the Nuffield Foundation.* Winchester, UK: Winchester King Alfred's College.

Williams, A., & Bedward, J. (2001). Gender, culture and the generation gap: Student and teacher perceptions of aspects of National Curriculum Physical Education. *Sport, Education and Society, 6*, 53-66.

Wright, J. (1997). The construction of gendered contexts in single-sex and co-educational physical education lessons. *Sport, Education and Society, 2*(1), 55-72.

Wright, J. (2000). Bodies, meanings and movement: A comparison of the language of a physical education lesson and a Feldenkrais movement class. *Sport, Education and Society, 5*(1), 35-50.

CHAPTER SIX

STUDENTS WITH DISABILITIES IN PHYSICAL EDUCATION

E. William Vogler

World cultures have become more accepting of participation of individuals with disabilities in all walks of life, particularly in education. Evidence of this trend includes the placement of more children with disabilities into regular classrooms and recommendations from professional associations such as the National Council for the Accreditation of Teacher Education (NCATE) for schools to be more inclusive of individuals.

Physical education offers no exception to these changes, and worldwide events supporting this move have prompted physical educators at all levels. For example, conferences in the late 1990s, such as the World Health Organization's Conference for Active Living, Moving Toward Inclusion, the World Summit on Physical Education, the Paralympic Games, and the Foundation of Olympic and Sport Education, have had a central theme of physical activity for all and progressive inclusion and acceptance of individuals with disabilities in physical education. Specifically, at the World Summit on Physical Education, cosponsored by the International Council on Sport Science and Physical Education, UNESCO, the International Olympic Committee, and the World Health Organization, it was proposed that professional preparation programs better prepare physical educators for inclusive physical education worldwide (DePauw & Doll-Tepper, 2000). The problem is that little is known in the profession about the function of teaching children with disabilities in physical education.

The research on teacher education and teaching children with disabilities in physical education literature can be characterized as a mile wide and an inch deep. That is, a substantial amount of research has been conducted over the years in the field of adapted physical education, but no topic has been covered in much depth (Block & Vogler, 1994; Vogler, DePaepe, & Martinek, 1990; Vogler, Kudlacek, O'Connor, & Wiseman, 2000).

A bibliometric analysis between 1988 and 1998 revealed that 1,720 authors contributed to scholarly articles in adapted physical education pedagogy (O'Connor, French, Sherrill, & Babcock, 2001). Only 11 of those authors contributed four or more articles, and most contributed only one article, revealing the limitations of adapted physical education as a scholarly discipline. Furthermore, most of the research over the past 20 years has been largely descriptive and atheoretical (Vogler et al., 2000). Thus, we know little about the knowledge, skills, and experiences needed to become an effective physical education teacher in schools that now contain children with diverse disabilities in the regular classroom. We know less about the important teaching functions required if children with disabilities are to have a positive experience in physical education.

The purpose of this chapter is to address how teachers can provide instruction for children with disabilities in view of guidelines established by federal law and the research on teaching and teacher education in physical education. Teaching function will be discussed in relation to the research in the field. Implications for the practitioner will follow. Rink (2002) has characterized teaching function as all daily activities involved with the preparation and conduct of teaching. This topic is a focus of the chapter. Because litigation and legislation has greatly influenced teaching function of children with disabilities, I will first present a summary of these significant events.

SUMMARY OF LITIGATION AND LEGISLATION INFLUENCING TEACHING

Children with disabilities are now active participants in regular physical education (Sherrill, 1998). Before the late 1970s, however, children with disabilities were largely isolated in either institutions or separate schools, where they received little or no physical education. Unfortunately, when activity was present in their lives, it was often in the form of therapy or simply recess. A series of both litigation and legislation, notably in the 1970s, has led to more normalized participation for these children (Block, 1996).

One of the first landmark events (in 1954) influencing the educational lives of children with disabilities was the case of Brown versus the Board of Education (Topeka, Kansas). The outcome indicated that separate schooling for children of color was unequal on constitutional grounds. This result forced widespread change in policy and practice formally characterized by segregation. Using the same logic and principle, the Pennsylvania Association for Retarded Citizens (PARC) filed a similar suit against the Commonwealth of Pennsylvania in 1972. Similarly, it was found that separate was not equal and that schooling of children with retardation was the responsibility of school boards, just as it was their responsibility to educate children without disabilities.

In still another similar case (Mills versus Washington, DC, 1972), it was found that this reasoning applied to all children with disabilities, not just those with retardation. One of the interesting implications of the Mills case was that education was defined as more than just the three Rs (reading, writing, and arithmetic)—that it involved all activities of learning including learning to speak, dress, and simply to move or walk. The implications of these cases were staggering for school districts, in that education for children with disabilities was considered to be the domain of school boards, conducted by certified teachers, not by therapists, psychologists, and uncertified caregivers. Further, teachers were now responsible for implementing curriculum with which they were not familiar.

In physical education a variety of things would have to change. Adapted physical educators would have to be trained to provide real instruction and not therapy for students. Regular physical educators with mainstreamed children with mild disabilities in their classes had to learn modifications and adaptations to traditional activity. Physical educators whose classes included children with severe disabilities had to learn unfamiliar models for inclusion. They also would have to learn to work with Individual Educational Plan (IEP) teams, therapists, paraprofessionals, aides, parents, or in some cases adapted physical educators. Physical education teaching would move from what Berliner (personal communication, 1992) termed "the second most private thing you do" to a public activity in which one had to work with a team and be responsible to many voices.

These changes in teaching function were not based on research but on legal and moral imperatives for what was considered right and just (Stainback & Stainback, 1991). The transformation would be "putting the cart before the horse."

To prevent a scenario of massive litigation in the wake of the PARC and Mills cases, in 1975 the United States Congress passed the Education for All Handicapped Children Act (PL 94-142) (reauthorized and currently called Individuals with Disabilities Education Act or IDEA, PL 105-17), which has profoundly changed and guided the teaching of children with disabilities (*Federal Register,* 1977, 1992). This law pronounced a free and appropriate education, which translated into the following four rights for students with disabilities:

1. Nondiscriminatory testing, evaluation, and placement procedures
2. Individualized instruction
3. Education in the least restrictive environment (LRE)
4. Procedural due process of the law

Nondiscriminatory Testing, Evaluation, and Placement Procedures

As a result of PL 94-142 physical education teachers of children with disabilities are required to use a variety of assessment tools to help identify the need for adapted, regular, or some other type of physical education. These would include normative, criterion referenced, and subjective assessments in fitness, motor development, dance, sport, games, and so on. In addition, they have to use these assessments in a way that does not discriminate against students because of their disabilities. For example, a physical education teacher should not fail a hearing-impaired child because the teacher cannot use sign language to provide test instructions. Also, a teacher should not score a student in a wheelchair as having limited fitness because the student cannot perform the running portion of a fitness assessment. Clearly, the responsibilities and competencies of physical education teachers of children with disabilities need to be different from those teaching children without disabilities. New knowledge bases, techniques, and strategies are expected on the part of any physical education teacher involved in any aspect of the testing, evaluation, or placement process. For example, teachers should know more about the nature of disabilities, become proficient in techniques of handling students in wheelchairs, and be prepared to implement new models for inclusive physical education such as peer teaching. Given that the move toward inclusion is becoming common, all teachers need competencies and experiences previously thought needed only by adapted physical education teachers.

Individualized Instruction

A second right for students with disabilities in physical education involves individualized instruction or development of what is referred to as the Individualized Educational Plan (IEP). Any student in physical education who school district personnel have classified as having a disability must by law have an IEP that guides the entire educational process for that child throughout the school year. Physical education teachers whose classes contain any child with disabilities must be involved in the IEP process. An IEP team comprises a variety of personnel who have a stake in this process, including all of the child's teachers, a member of the local educational agency, the parents, and even the child when necessary. The physical educator on the team develops an IEP, which must include each of the following components:

1. A statement of the child's present level of educational performance, including an account of how the child's disability affects the child's involvement and progress in the general curriculum. A physical education teacher should assess physical and motor fitness, motor development, and development in other areas such as dance and sport skills to determine the present level of performance. The need to provide information in such a broad range of development offers a daunting time and competency challenge to physical education teachers.

2. A statement of measurable goals and objectives. Once assessment is completed and the present level of performance is determined, annual goals and behavioral objectives are written in an IEP to guide the educational process for the year. All members of the IEP team understand and agree on these objectives.

3. A statement about any special education and needed related services. Although no additional services may be needed, the IEP meeting is a good time to request and specify these services, such as therapeutic recreation, physical therapy, or occupational therapy. These services could be useful in conducting a physical education class when normal participation is not possible because of a disability. For example, a physical educator may determine that a student with cerebral palsy needs some degree of physical therapy for stretching and increasing range of motion to participate in the normal activity of the day. Or it may be necessary to have a paraprofessional or hearing-impaired translator in the class to assist in physical support or communication.

4. Other statements describe (a) the extent to which the child will participate with nondisabled children, (b) the projected date for the beginning of services, (c) how progress toward annual goals will be measured, (d) how parents will be regularly informed, and (e) the need for any assistive technology devices and services. These provide a standard way to monitor a variety of important aspects of the child's education such as the extent to which a child is included into the least restrictive environment.

Although any effective teacher might intuitively meet these IEP requirements, law mandates them. Schools are liable for legal redress should any portion of them be omitted.

IDEA calls for other plans besides the IEP. These are termed the Individual Family Service Plan (IFSP) and the Individual Transition Plan (ITP). The IFSP is a plan similar to the IEP for preschoolers with disabilities. Like the IEP, the IFSP involves a multidisciplinary approach to develop activities for preschoolers with disabilities, recognizing that early intervention is key to healthy development in all domains. Similar to the IEP and IFSP is the ITP, which is a plan to guide the student with disabilities into lifelong community roles. Although the law does not specifically mention physical education, participation by physical educators in the development of these plans is implied given the inherent relationship between physical and motor fitness and most lifelong leisure and employment activities.

Education in the Least Restrictive Environment (LRE)

A third right for students with disabilities is that they be educated in an environment that best meets their needs as specified in the IEP. To this end school districts must be prepared to offer a continuum of services that range from the most restrictive and least normal (one-on-one physical education with an adapted physical education teacher) to the least restrictive and most normal (regular physical education with no special resources or services). The initial assumption is that all children with disabilities will be included with students without disabilities in regular physical education unless the IEP team determines that an alternative placement is needed. There is major disagreement about this "right" as specified in IDEA. Those whom Block (1999a) has termed "inclusionists" believe that all children with disabilities belong in the regular classroom by right, irrespective of any circumstance. They believe that all "arrangements" at whatever cost need to be made to ensure inclusion. Currently, however, the law is not interpreted that way. The notion of LRE, as specified by law, is grounded in the idea that some children absolutely cannot learn the same curriculum, at the same rate, and in the same environment as others. Further, this provision recognizes that some children without disabilities cannot learn in the presence of some children with disabilities, for example, those who may exhibit aggressive and dangerous behavior. LRE simply recognizes that conditions of disability may require a variety of educational options.

Procedural Due Process of the Law

The final right specified by law for students with disabilities is that they and their parents should have due process if they want to question the educational process that educators plan to implement. According to IDEA, state and local educational agencies should be prepared to convene a hearing panel of experts who can sift facts and circumstances and make final binding judgments regarding challenges made to the educational process. For example, if not pleased with the result of an evaluation that portrays their child with disabilities in ways that clearly contradict the parents' experience, the parents can seek redress. Redress may take the form of a call for further or independent evaluation and changes in the IEP. The point of this right is that teachers or educational administrators cannot simply develop an educational process for the sake of convenience; they must do so in partnership with parents and others and recognize the right for parents to disagree and have opportunity for due process.

IDEA and Physical Education

Physical education had been deemed so important to the development of lives of children with disabilities that it is the only major curricular area mentioned specifically in IDEA. Accordingly, it has been defined so as not to confuse it with therapy or recess. The term *physical education* means the development of

- physical and motor fitness;
- fundamental motor skills and patterns; and
- skills in aquatics, dance, and individual and group games and sports (including intramural and lifetime sports).

The term includes special physical education, adaptive physical education, movement education, and motor development (*Federal Register*, 1977, 1992). The implications for physical educators are that curriculum development should begin with this definition (see figure 6.1).

FUNCTION OF TEACHING CHILDREN WITH DISABILITIES IN PHYSICAL EDUCATION

The function of teaching has remained remarkably similar over a period of many years. Dunkin and Biddle (1974) described a series of instantly recognizable classroom processes that still ring true today. For example, students largely matriculate with same-age peers in self-contained groups. Students have their own desks, listen to brief lectures or demonstrations, and then perform some individual or small-group project. Teachers typically plan, teach, and evaluate by themselves with only occasional support from an aide. In physical education Rink (2002) has described some of the ways in which a

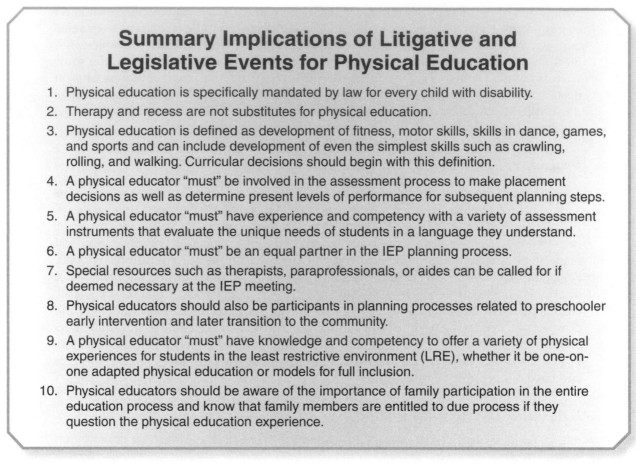

Summary Implications of Litigative and Legislative Events for Physical Education

1. Physical education is specifically mandated by law for every child with disability.
2. Therapy and recess are not substitutes for physical education.
3. Physical education is defined as development of fitness, motor skills, skills in dance, games, and sports and can include development of even the simplest skills such as crawling, rolling, and walking. Curricular decisions should begin with this definition.
4. A physical educator "must" be involved in the assessment process to make placement decisions as well as determine present levels of performance for subsequent planning steps.
5. A physical educator "must" have experience and competency with a variety of assessment instruments that evaluate the unique needs of students in a language they understand.
6. A physical educator "must" be an equal partner in the IEP planning process.
7. Special resources such as therapists, paraprofessionals, or aides can be called for if deemed necessary at the IEP meeting.
8. Physical educators should also be participants in planning processes related to preschooler early intervention and later transition to the community.
9. A physical educator "must" have knowledge and competency to offer a variety of physical experiences for students in the least restrictive environment (LRE), whether it be one-on-one adapted physical education or models for full inclusion.
10. Physical educators should be aware of the importance of family participation in the entire education process and know that family members are entitled to due process if they question the physical education experience.

FIGURE 6.1   Summary implications of litigative and legislative events for physical education.

teacher functions in performing a particular teaching act in a particular setting. Accordingly, teachers need to do the following in any one day of teaching:

1. Identify intended outcomes for learning
2. Plan learning experiences to accomplish those outcomes
3. Present tasks to learners
4. Develop the content

The purpose of this portion of the chapter is to discuss the teaching functions outlined by Rink (2002) in relation to research in the field of adapted physical education. For each function this is followed by implications for the practitioner who works with students with disabilities. Although the list of teaching functions is designed to indicate the steps a teacher should take in any one day, these functions will also be discussed in a broader context of how a teacher must function in events leading up to any one day of teaching. Thus, discussion of teaching function might include yearly as well as daily examples of assessment and curricular planning.

Function 1: Identify Intended Outcomes for Learning

One can argue that the first functions of teaching children with disabilities involve assessment to determine present level of performance and placement into the least restrictive environment (LRE). Intended outcomes cannot be identified without initial assessment. These determinations are federally mandated and are based on the following paraphrased statements found in the *Federal Register* (1977, 1992):

1. Tests must be provided in the child's native language or by other mode of communication and must be administered by trained personnel.
2. Test results should reflect aptitude or achievement and not be biased by a child's impairment.
3. No single procedure is used as the sole criterion for determining an appropriate educational program.
4. A multidisciplinary team makes the evaluation.
5. The child is assessed in all areas related to the disability in all domains including motor ability.

The federal mandates present a daunting task to physical educators. One could logically assume that physical educators would need a breadth of knowledge, experience, and competency unique to children with disabilities.

Research on Assessment Competencies Needed of Teachers of Children With Disabilities in Physical Education

The National Consortium for Physical Education and Recreation for Individuals With Disability (1995) published a series of competencies needed to provide appropriate teaching service to children with disabilities. The competencies were gleaned from surveys of physical educators who worked with children with disabilities and teacher educators at institutions of higher education. These competencies were linked to a particular job function and encompassed philosophy, attitudes, knowledge, and skills needed. Specifically mentioned was a need for an attitude of commitment, knowledge of instruments and protocols, knowledge of scientific and psychosocial foundations (e.g., biomechanics and motor learning), and skills in assessment. These particular skills were listed concerning (a) using and interpreting various types of assessment, (b) decision making, and (c) making referrals. Teachers acquire these competencies primarily at the preservice level, and they reinforce or enhance them at the in-service level or with further graduate education.

Research suggests that current preservice teacher-training programs are lacking in the preparation of these competencies. Several studies on needs assessment have produced evidence that those providing physical education services do not feel adequately prepared to assess or teach students with disabilities (Bird & Gansneder, 1979; Churton, 1986; Davis & Dummer, 1987; Dempsey, 1986; Melograno & Loovis, 1991; Sherrill & Megginson, 1984). Specifically, these studies have shown that the attitudes, perceived ability, and training or staff development services for teachers were inadequate.

In a more recent study Kelly and Gansneder (1998) surveyed 293 adapted physical education teachers. They reported that the teachers still had great need for training in teaching, motor development, and continuing education. Concerning assessment competency, these teachers reported a disparity in the amount of preservice training they received compared with what they now perceived was necessary to do the job adequately.

A major constraint in the development of competency required for assessment of children with disabilities is the diverse nature of disability itself (Sherrill, 1998). A physical education teacher has to contend with abnormalities of body structure and subsequent limitations of functional ability. In addition, one has to contend with "short stature, obesity, posture problems, deviant sizes and shapes of body parts, amputations, and abnormalities of muscle tone" (Sherrill, 1998, p. 283). Teachers are highly unlikely to develop a generalized competency or have sufficient experience to encounter all possible combinations of disabilities. The research on good form, mechanical efficiency, and developmental levels of movement for all children with specific disabilities related to assessment is noticeably absent. Research, however, shows that those assessing students with disabilities can expect to encounter some of the following known limitations in student abilities, performances, or behaviors:

• Students with mild to severe disabilities exhibit less academic learning time in physical education (ALT-PE) than their peers without disabilities (Aufderheide, 1983; Gagnon, Tousignant, & Martel, 1989; Shute, Dodds, Placek, Rife, & Silverman, 1982; Silverman, Dodds, Placek, Shute, & Rife, 1984; Temple, & Walkley, 1999; Vogler, Koranda, & Romance, 2000; Vogler, van der Mars, Cusimano, & Darst, 1990, 1992, 1998).

• Students with Down's syndrome have cardiac, skeletal, hypotonia, obesity, visual, hearing, kinesthetic, and timing problems (Block, 1991).

• Students with general movement difficulties were less vigorously active, played less with large playground equipment, and had less positive social interactions with peers (Bouffard, Watkinson, Thompson, Dunn, & Romanow, 1996). Further, students with movement difficulties have lower perceived physical or athletic competence (Cantell, Smyth, & Ahonen, 1994; Ninot, Bilard, Delignieres, & Sokolowski, 2000; Rose, Larkin, & Berger, 1997; Schoemaker & Kalverboer, 1994). Still further, students with movement difficulties have lower self-esteem (Henderson, May, & Umney, 1989) and are more motivated by mastery of task than by ego-oriented activities (Dunn, 2000).

• Mentally retarded individuals, regardless of age, possess cardiovascular fitness levels 20 to 40% below those of their nonretarded peers (Fernhall, Tymeson, & Webster, 1988).

• Hearing-impaired children were more similar than dissimilar in psychomotor behavior to their hearing peers with the exception of balance (Goodman & Hopper, 1992). Fitness levels were similar between these groups (Winnick & Short, 1986). Self-concepts of hearing-impaired children, however, were generally lower (Hopper, 1988).

• Self-concepts and psychomotor behavior of elementary-level children with mild disability were lower than those of children without disabilities (Martinek & Karper, 1982).

• The perception of students with physical disabilities of physical education was positively or negatively influenced as a function of their interaction with peers (Goodwin, 2001). Attitudes of children with physical disabilities toward physical education were poor compared with their peers without disabilities. Attitude was more favorable when students participated in physical activity outside school (Seaman, 1970).

• Students with emotional disturbance are more off-task, have poorer attitudes toward physical education, and have lower self-concept than their peers without disabilities do (Jeltma & Vogler, 1985; Politino & Smith, 1989; Vogler & French, 1983).

• Gross motor development in preschool children with learning disabilities is limited (Rimmer & Kelly, 1989).

• Students with visual impairment have lower fitness and more delayed motor development patterns than their counterparts without disabilities do (Winnick, 1985).

• Attitudes of students without disabilities toward their peers with disabilities are not clear, but some studies have shown that they can be positive when support services are available (adapted physical educator) and structured programs exist (Block & Zeman, 1996; Slininger, Sherrill, & Jankowski, 2000; Stewart, 1988; Vogler, 2000; Vogler et al., 2001). Additionally, researchers have found that females tend to have a more positive attitude toward their peers with disabilities than males do.

Another constraint in the development of competencies required to assess children with disabilities in physical education involves the rapidity with which changes occur in the assessment field. For example, the emphasis of assessment of physical fitness in the schools has shifted from performance to more health-related aspects (Sherrill, 1998). Consequently, a series of new instruments has been created to accommodate these changes, offering new opportunities to assess and accommodate students with disabilities. The FITNESSGRAM assessment (Cooper Institute for Aerobics Research, 1999) has replaced the older AAHPERD Health Related Fitness Assessment, and the test manual includes a special chapter on modifications for special populations. Students who cannot be accommodated with the modified FITNESSGRAM may be able to be assessed using a new personalized fitness testing approach, the Brockport Physical Fitness Test (Winnick & Short, 1999). This fitness assessment approach offers a heath-related fitness conceptual framework that is philosophically consistent with fitness curricula available to students with disabilities.

Summary Implications of Research Findings

- Teachers should expect to find a variety of limitations and uniqueness in student abilities, performances, and behaviors associated with students with disabilities, which may alter the expected or intended outcomes.
- To assess children with disabilities, teachers should develop a unique set of competencies not normally found in undergraduate teacher-training experiences.
- Teachers need to be aware of school and cultural shifts in emphasis away from strictly performance to more health-related fitness assessment of students with disabilities.

Function 2: Plan Learning Experiences to Accomplish Those Outcomes

A second important teaching function in teaching physical education to children with disabilities involves planning. A teacher of children with disabilities plans in different ways than a regular physical education teacher does. Recall that federal mandates require multidisciplinary planning by an Individual Educational Plan (IEP) team that includes

a. parents and sometimes the student with disabilities,
b. a special educator,
c. the regular teacher or teachers,
d. an agent from the local educational agency,
e. the physical educator or educators, and
f. others deemed necessary.

The physical educator must have completed all the appropriate physical and motor assessments of the child with disabilities and come to the IEP meeting prepared to identify intended educational outcomes in the least restrictive environment (LRE). In physical education a variety of LRE models offer variations on a theme of a continuum of placement (e.g., Aufsesser, 1991; Block, 1992). The Aufsesser (1991) model, presented here, included the greatest number of alternatives:

- Full-time regular physical education (mainstreamed) with or without consultation, and supplemental aids and equipment
- Integrated physical education with cross-age tutors, peer-age tutors, and reverse

mainstreaming (peers without disabilities coming to the environment of the student with disabilities)

- Community-based instruction (integrated or segregated)
- Split placement: adapted and regular physical education on either a fixed or a rotating schedule
- Regular school with either full-time adapted physical education or modified physical education
- Special-school placement with either adapted or modified physical education

Criticisms of the LRE approach have included concerns that this principle (a) legitimates restrictive environments, (b) makes it difficult to provide highly specialized services in a regular class (e.g., sign language for hearing impaired), and (c) forces students to have to "earn" the right to graduate to a LRE.

Inclusion and Mild Disabilities

The widespread research evidence that supports inclusion as an educational policy in the regular classroom has generally centered on the social and academic achievement of children. The research on inclusion of children with mild disabilities into the regular classroom is generally supportive of the policy. An educational review by Semmel, Gottlieb, and Robinson (1979) concluded that academic achievement and social adjustment of children with mild disabilities was just as likely to take place in mainstreamed classrooms as it is in self-contained classes. The authors noted that classroom management difficulties in inclusive settings were no greater than those in classes without children with disabilities. In another review Madden and Slavin (1983) observed that inclusive programs were more successful when specially designed to accommodate children with mild disabilities by including features such as cooperative learning, individualized instruction, and periodic resource rooms. These programs resulted in greater self-esteem, emotional adjustment, academic achievement, and greater acceptance by nondisabled classmates. Wang and Baker (1986) solidified previous review findings by conducting a metanalysis of the research base. They found that when only well-controlled studies were considered, inclusive programs were advantageous for children with mild disabilities with regard to academic and social adjustment. More current research and thinking on inclusion generally considers these findings valid (Baker, Wang, & Walberg, 1995).

Inclusion and Severe Disabilities

Educational research on inclusion of children with severe disabilities has become more frequent and conclusive in recent years. Some studies that have supported inclusion have focused on social acceptance, peer interaction, meaningful outcomes, and other variables that may predict successful transition from the school to the workplace (e.g., Chadsey-Rusch, 1990). One noteworthy qualitative study by Schnorr (1990) implied that it was important to include children with severe disabilities from early on in the elementary grades. The defining moment of school for students with disabilities centered on "where you belong," "what you do," and "with whom you play." Children without disabilities were more willing to include children with severe disabilities and considered them "one of us" as opposed to "one of them" if they were class members from the start and not pulled from class for physical education. The study stressed the importance of play between children with and without disabilities for social development of both groups.

Another important consideration in inclusive education has been its effect on the education of children without disabilities. In a review of a variety of outcomes for nondisabled students, Staub and Peck (1995) addressed various common concerns of parents, teachers, and advocates with inclusion. They concluded that the research on the nondisabled showed (a) no deceleration in academic progress, (b) no loss of teacher time allotted to or teacher attention given to the nondisabled child, and (c) no transference of undesirable behavior from students with disabilities to those without disabilities. These studies, in general, provide evidence that inclusion of children with severe disabilities can work.

Physical Education and Mild Disabilities

The research on inclusion and physical education has been limited to children with mild disabilities (Block & Vogler, 1994). Some studies have focused on comparisons of teacher and student behaviors in mainstreamed and other settings (e.g., Heikinaro-Johansson, 1992; Silverman et al., 1984; Temple & Walkley, 1999; Vogler et al., 1990, 1992, 1998). These studies have consistently reported that children both with and without mild disabilities had appropriate percentages of academic learning time (ALT) while participating together. Further, teacher behaviors such as the amount of time devoted to instruction, practice, classroom management, and transition were similar to their behaviors in classes of children without disabilities. Thus, inclusive environments can be effective places both for children to learn and for teachers to teach.

Appropriateness of inclusion has also been determined from other perspectives. For example, Beuter (1983) and Karper and Martinek (1983) found that students with disabilities developed self-concept and motor performance better in inclusive settings. Block (1995) and Rizzo (1984) found that attitudes of both teachers and students were favorable toward inclusion, although teachers were more favorable toward students with learning disabilities compared with students with severe disabilities. Further, teachers with previous hands-on experiences with disabilities were more likely to accept these children (Rizzo, Vispoel, & Walter, 1991).

What Do Students With Disabilities Say?

Most studies have viewed disabilities from a perspective of teachers and students without disabilities. A study by Goodwin and Watkinson (2000), however, listened to the experiences of children with disabilities in inclusive physical education. A group of 10- to 12-year-olds with varying degrees of disability expressed many of the same feelings about physical education as their peers without disabilities did. They wanted to belong, become more healthy and fit, become more skillful, and know more about sport and games. When they had bad days, their problems largely centered on their poor sense of body image, poor playing surfaces, and general lack of movement confidence. Students preferred being with classmates in the regular physical education program rather than a segregated one.

Physical Education and Severe Disabilities

Support for inclusion of children with severe disabilities is based more on notions of appropriateness and social justice than on what is known from research (Stainback & Stainback, 1990). In physical education, research on inclusion of children with severe disabilities into regular physical education is sparse. Block and Zeman (1996), Murata and Jansma (1997) and LaMaster, Gail, Kinchin, and Siedentop (1998) are the major sources of this research.

Block and Zeman (1996) (elementary level) and Murata and Jansma (1997) (secondary level) found that inclusive arrangements that used teacher assistants and peer teachers facilitated motor engagement, sport skill performance, and attitude toward disability for children both with and without disabilities. Block and Zeman (1996), specifically, noted that achievement and attitude in inclusive settings were not better than they were in experimentally controlled arrangements containing only children without disabilities. Murata and Jansma (1997) found that achievement was only marginally better than it was in experimentally controlled arrangements without added teacher resources. Because they observed no negative effects of inclusion, authors of both studies argued that their findings supported inclusion of children with severe disabilities.

LaMaster, Gail, Kinchin, and Siedentop (1998), however, reported that highly effective elementary-level teachers, without the support of an adapted physical education teacher, expressed frustration at the time-management conflicts that existed when they were constantly attending to children with severe disabilities. These otherwise highly effective teachers became relatively ineffective despite experimentation with many different teaching styles such as (a) individualized instruction, (b) peer teaching, (c) direct instruction, and (d) modification of lesson plans and equipment. They expressed guilt, described a sense of inadequacy, and cited a lack of human resource support and incomplete preservice training for inclusion.

Models for Successful Inclusion

In a review of classroom research Madden and Slavin (1983) judged that inclusive programs were more likely to be successful when specially designed, such as when cooperative learning, individualized instruction, and periodic resource rooms were a part of instruction. Specially designed models for inclusion have been grouped into three major categories: (a) curricular adaptations (changing what is taught), (b) instructional modifications (changing how we teach), and (c) human or people resources (changing who teaches) (Block, 1994; Block & Vogler, 1994; Vogler & Block, 1994). For example, a curricular adaptation (changing what is taught) might mean having a student with severe disabilities perform a similar task at a different level (e.g., pass, dribble, or shoot toward a modified target while peers use a standard-sized one). An instructional modification (how we teach) might mean taking a traditional game or activity and helping students modify the rules or structure so that students with disabilities can participate. For example, in softball a fielded ground ball must be thrown and caught by every fielder before a slower student in a wheelchair could be called out when attempting to reach first base. A human or people-resource modification (who teaches) might involve the use of a variety of individuals to provide instructional, managerial, and behavioral support to a physical education specialist. These could include peers, teacher aides, parents, retirees, grandparents, or even certified adapted physical education specialists. The question is whether this holds true in physical education.

Models in Physical Education.   Webster (1987) studied the effectiveness of a people resource in physical education from the perspective of peer tutoring. Untrained and then trained nondisabled peers provided physical education to three students of different ages (elementary, junior high, and high school levels) with moderate to severe mental retardation and other disabilities. Although not clearly reported, training details involved learning how to present tutors with "preferred practices for teaching handicapped (disabled) learners" (Webster, 1987, p. 396). Webster determined that academic learning time in physical education (ALT-PE) percentages more than doubled when trained peers worked directly with these students. DePaepe (1985) also studied the effectiveness of peer resources with children with moderate disabilities in a one-on-one setting and compared this with other teaching contexts (self-contained and mainstreamed classes). ALT-PE percentages of children with disabilities were highest with peer tutors (57%). The percentages with self-contained classes and mainstreamed classes were 33% and 20%, respectively. Vogler et al. (2000) studied the presence of a full-time adapted physical educator to work one-on-one in the regular kindergarten class with a student with severe disabilities. Results indicated that inclusion classes were highly effective in time engagement and management, and there was widespread social acceptance and successful motor participation. The authors concluded that the use of an adapted physical educator resource model was a highly effective educational practice. Teachers believed that potentially mediating factors for program effectiveness included (a) point of educational entry, (b) type and age appropriateness of class activity, (c) personality of the students, and (d) the training and experience of the human resource.

Additional Factors Important for Successful Inclusion.   Besides the factors previously cited are those that Block elaborated on (1999a, 1999b) in a two-part series on inclusion. His review revealed that the following factors were important to successful inclusion in physical education:

- Positive attitude committed to change (e.g., see Duchanne & French, 1998; Rizzo & Wright, 1988)

- Honoring individual differences—a commitment by physical educators to make modifications to their curricula

- Helping children feel they belong (e.g., see descriptions of reciprocal and peer tutoring by Mosston & Ashworth, 2002; Houston-Wilson, Dunn, van der Mars, & McCubbin, 1997)

- Collaborative planning (e.g., general, regular, and adapted physical educators getting together for continuous planning during the school year; see Stanton & Colvin, 1996 for examples)

- Administrative support and resources (e.g., see Janney, Snell, Beers, & Raynes, 1995, for examples in regular education)

- Release time and flexible scheduling (e.g., an adapted physical education consultant may need to spend a few days with the regular physical education teacher at the beginning of the school year to demonstrate suggestions for modifications in activity)

- Access to training (e.g., an administrator allows teachers of children with disabilities to attend in-service training programs)

- Providing necessary personnel and adapted equipment (e.g., providing trained paraprofessionals for physical educators; see Vogler, French, & Bishop, 1989; consultation services; see Heikinaro-Johansson, Sherrill, French, & Huuhka, 1995; and providing enough special equipment items such as beep balls, ramps, and railings)

Summary Implications of Research Findings

- Teachers should be aware of the federal law (Individuals with Disability Education Act) and implications of the least restrictive environment (LRE) concept with respect to alternative physical education models, particularly full inclusion.

- Inclusion can result in positive social, emotional, and physical benefits for children both with and without disabilities. This can be true even when children with severe disabilities are included.

- Teacher and student behavior in inclusive classes are consistent with those in classes without children with disabilities.

- Children both with and without disabilities prefer inclusive physical education especially if inclusion begins in the earliest grades.

- Attitudes of teachers and children both with and without disabilities are more positive when they have had previous exposure to disabilities.

- Inclusion classes for younger children using movement education activities may be effective because activities can be individualized.

- Inclusion classes for older children using sports and team games that require co-operation or teamwork may pose problems for teachers with children who do not want to use modifications for children with disabilities.

- Inclusion works best with nontraditional instructional models such as (a) curricular adaptations (changing what is taught), (b) instructional modifications (changing how we teach), and (c) human or people resources (changing who teaches, e.g., using peers and adapted physical education teachers). Class as usual will not work!

- When teaching children with severe disabilities, trained helpers contribute to successful experience.

- Adapted physical education teachers are the preferred model because of their experience and knowledge.

- Necessary factors for successful inclusion are (a) attitude and commitment to change, (b) honoring individual differences, (c) collaborative planning, and (d) administrative support.

Function 3: Present Tasks to Learners

A third important teaching function to teaching physical education to children with disabilities involves task presentation. A teacher of children with disabilities needs to present clear tasks in a way that motivates students to learn (Rink, 2002). Teachers must be good communicators when they first introduce a task. Some qualities of good task presentation include (Rink, 2002) (a) getting learner attention, (b) sequencing the content and organizational aspects of tasks, and (c) presenting the task clearly. These elements have unique implications in the teaching of children with disabilities.

Getting Learner Attention

A large proportion of students with disabilities often have associative conditions of disability that make attending behavior in class difficult. They often display short attention span, distractibility, hyperactivity, and other associative conditions that negatively influence their attending behavior (Sherrill, 1998). Rink (2002) suggested that teachers develop signals and other creative management procedures to enhance the attention of students. This is particularly important for children with disabilities who often do not respond to a traditional classroom management structure of rules, routines, and consequences that should ensure attentiveness among students without disabilities (Walker, 1979). Rather, some unique behavioral strategies are needed to motivate students with disabilities to stay on task. Behavioral strategies such as the consistent and systematic use of free-time activity as a reinforcer have long been shown to be effective in physical education environments to manage attending and other behaviors (Sherrill, 1998).

Research on Behavioral Techniques to Enhance Attending and Other Behaviors. A modest amount of behavioral research in physical education has focused on enhancing attending and other behaviors (Block & Vogler, 1994). For example, systematic reinforcement-punishment operant techniques have been used to enhance exercise maintenance (Allen & Iwata, 1980), exercise behavior, and fitness (Bennett, Eisenman, French, Henderson, & Shultz, 1989; Ellis, Cress, & Spellman, 1993; French, Silliman, Ben-Ezra, & Landrieu-Seiter, 1992; Rogers-Wallgren, French, & Ben-Ezra, 1992; Taylor, French, Kinnison, & O'Brien, 1998), motor performance (Hsu & Dunn, 1984), socially inappropriate behavior (Jansma, 1978), attending and on-task behavior (Bishop & French, 1982; Jeltma & Vogler, 1985; Vogler & French, 1983), physical performance (Lavay & French, 1986), fundamental skill (Silliman & French, 1993), and compliant behavior (Silliman, French, & Tynan, 1992).

These studies have compared a baseline behavioral state before and after an operant intervention. Baseline states have revealed woeful attending behavior in naturally occurring conditions, often making it impossible for learning to occur. Almost without exception, systematic and consistent behavioral interventions guided by operant conditioning principles have enhanced attending and other behaviors to appropriate levels for learning. For example, Vogler and French (1983) used a group contingency game called "Good Behavior Game" to enhance on-task behavior of elementary-level behaviorally disordered students from unacceptable (more than 20%) to better than average (more than 90%) levels. These students did not participate in any type of physical education because teachers did not have the skills or training to include them effectively in class activities. The group contingency operant strategies relied on peer pressure to behave for students to earn group free-activity time at the end of class and week. The proper implementation of this unique strategy resulted in behavior deemed better than what was typically seen in an average class (i.e., 70%) (Walker, 1979).

The implication of these studies for physical education is that teachers cannot rely on traditional management of rules, routines, and consequences to get students with disabilities to be attentive in the classroom. Rather, they must develop some planned instructional supplement to ensure their participation.

Sequencing the Content and Organizational Aspects of Tasks

When presenting a new learning task, a teacher must give instructions first on how students are to get into a position to learn (organizational aspect) and second on the learning task itself (content). Effective teachers provide separate instruction and opportunity for each without any overlap between the two tasks lest children become confused by having to process too much information. Because children process information more slowly than adults do and children with disabilities process information more slowly still, an effective instructor will allow more time for these presented tasks (Das, 1986; Thomas, 1980; Winther & Thomas, 1981).

Vogler et al. (1990) reported that expert physical education teachers of inclusive classes had shorter transition times between presented tasks in a lesson (21% of class time) compared with nonexperts (28%). Although corresponding motor-engaged percentages were not that different in teaching children without disabilities (30% for nonexperts to 33% for experts), the percentages were moderately different in teaching children with disabilities (18% for nonexperts to 25% for experts). The implication is that longer transition times may have a greater effect on children with disabilities, perhaps making them more vulnerable to ineffective teaching. Teachers should separate content from the organizational aspects, which should have the effect of shortening the transition times between the two tasks and making it easier for all children to process the tasks.

Task Clarity and Choosing a Way to Communicate

Another quality of task presentation is task clarity, or the clearness of instructions a teacher provides, and the way in which a teacher chooses to communicate (e.g., verbal instructions versus demonstration). Some suggestions for improving the clarity of communication include (Rink, 2002)

a. orienting the learner through a set induction (letting students know in advance what they are doing),

b. sequencing the presentation in logical order,

c. repeating things difficult to understand,

d. checking for understanding (asking students questions or to demonstrate), and

e. modeling or demonstration.

Children typically have clear channels of communication available to them with respect to seeing, hearing, and feeling unless, because of some disability, they have visual, auditory, or tactile difficulties preventing them from clearly obtaining information. Children with sensory visual or hearing impairments and those with some form of physical paralysis need to receive instruction by alternative modes of communication. The literature includes many physical and motor descriptions of these children and provides intuitive teaching suggestions based on their communication difficulties, but the pedagogical implications are not well researched (Sherrill, 1998; Winnick, 2002). For example, we know that visually impaired children are delayed motorically (e.g., Skaggs & Hopper, 1996) and that teachers should therefore present tasks by physical prompts and some type of auditory cueing to improve the students' skill levels. The physical education teaching literature, however, is still only in the description stage with regard to children with these disabilities.

The physical education literature on children with "soft" communication difficulties such as mild receptive and expressive problems (i.e., hearing, speaking, feeling) associated with learning disabilities (LD) provides a little more information. For example, Kowalski and Sherrill (1992) found that a verbal rehearsal strategy, "self-talk," by boys with learning disabilities helped clarify a presented task, resulting in improved motor performance on locomotor skills. Theoretically, self-talk in conjunction with the movement itself helped these boys process the presented information into memory more efficiently. Another facet of this study involved the effects of modeling when the presented model was either silent or verbal. The LD boys became significantly more proficient in motor skill when presented with a verbal model compared with no model or a silent model.

Presenting a physical or motor task by modeling is one of the most powerful forms of communication, and physical education teachers and coaches regularly employ it (McCullagh, Weiss, & Ross, 1989). An underlying basis for modeling is that somehow watching a task makes it easier to perform. Researchers have demonstrated that the effectiveness of a presented model depends on the status and skill level of the model (Magill, 1997). This finding has some interesting implications for children with disabilities. For example, children typically respond to a high-status (i.e., someone more popular) and high-skilled (e.g., someone better skilled) model (McCullagh, 1987). Teachers may have a dilemma in finding the right model combination for children with disabilities, who respond well to same-status but poorly skilled models. Some experimentation may be necessary to find the kind of model who is both motivating and properly skilled.

Feltz (1980) studied the effects of a good model combination (same status, a student with mental retardation, yet with high skill level) on the learning of a high-avoidance motor task (diving into a pool from a springboard). The same-status yet highly skilled model first demonstrated and then physically prompted the peer to shape the ultimate diving behavior in just four sessions. This was a remarkable accomplishment because the teacher working alone had spent a year just to get the student to jump feet first into the pool from the board.

Summary Implications of Research Findings

- Teachers should realize that students with disabilities may have more difficulty attending to presentation of instructional tasks than other students do. In these cases, nontraditional measures such as behavior modification, for example, the "Good Behavior Game," may be useful to enhance attending behaviors.

- Teachers should also be aware that children with disabilities may also need more time to process a normally presented instructional task. Therefore, teachers should make extra efforts to separate the presentation of an organizational task from an activity task so as not to confuse these students.

- Teachers should heed Rink's (2002) suggestion to clarify the presentation of tasks by using alternative modes of communication (e.g., presenting tasks in written form or with a model when the student has a hearing impairment). In addition, strategies such as self-talk and using models of same and higher status have been effective in clarifying task requirements for students with disabilities.

Function 4: Develop the Content

The final teaching function presented is content development, which Rink (2002 and in chapter 10 in this book) characterizes as the process of informing a class of a task activity and then refining, extending, or applying it. For example, when learning to shoot a basketball, a teacher would first inform the student or students how to perform it in an entry-level way. Practice trials to refine it (e.g., alter the fingers), extend it (e.g., try it at different distances), and apply it (e.g., try it in a game) would follow.

Rink (2002) believes that novice teachers tend to develop the content of a lesson without the necessary refinement and extension phases, thus depriving students of important practice opportunities. A comparative study of elementary physical education teachers by Sullivan, Vogler, Coleman, and Jones (2002) reinforced this notion. They found during the practice portion of a 30-minute lesson that expert teachers made 14 refinements while novices made only 3. Because children with disabilities are often developmentally delayed and need more practice trials than other children, they may be more vulnerable to novice teachers.

Variability of Practice

In essence, issues of content development are issues of "practice" concepts and the "progressions" a teacher develops to find a challenge that is neither too hard nor too easy when teaching a task. One of the single most demonstrated practice concepts in motor-skill learning is the notion of variability of practice as proposed by Schmidt (1975) and supported by Shea & Morgan (1979) in the motor domain. For example, when learning to shoot a basketball, a teacher should extend the task by having the student practice at variable distances rather than at progressively longer distances, a procedure guided by a conceptually less sound behavioral approach frequently used in special education (Skinner, 1953). One could also build variability into practice by altering the context of practice, such as hitting a tennis ball in differing wind or sun conditions in addition to different distances. Magill (1997) suggested that teachers of all children should build variability into a practice session when refining and extending learning physical education tasks.

One study addressing issues of practice variability versus constant practice in adapted physical education involved acquisition of fundamental skills by 11- to 15-year-old children with autism (Weber & Thorpe, 1992). These children practiced ball bouncing, kicking, ball rolling, jumping, and sliding until they learned some criterion. Results showed that the task variation condition produced significantly better skill acquisition than the constant condition. Unfortunately, the study did not assess retention and transfer of these practiced tasks, but the acquisition outcome falls in line with existing literature supporting content development under conditions of variability.

Ecological Task Analysis

Germane to any discussion of practice and the development of progressions of motor skill is the theory of dynamical or ecological task analysis systems (Davis & Burton, 1991). This theory poses that motor-skill acquisition depends on the relationship between the skill learner, the unique requirements of a task, and the environmental practice context. In essence, no single biomechanical movement is optimal (Gelinas & Reid,

2000). Thus, all skill progressions may not be necessary, particularly for students with disabilities whose body shape and size may be unique for the style of learning. This approach contrasts with "stage" theories suggesting that learners practice skills in a specific predetermined and progressive order.

To demonstrate ecological task analysis theory, Gelinas and Reid (2000) had children with physical disabilities practice swimming technique under two conditions, traditional progressive and nontraditional out-of-sequence order. The results showed that up to 80% of children using the nontraditional, out-of-sequence progressions learned the appropriate swimming technique, thus indicating that stage theory approaches may not be the best guiding approach for certain children with disabilities. Rather, when developing the content for children with disabilities, teachers should match the content to an outcome based on the unique biomechanical requirements of each child.

Summary Implications of Research Findings

- When developing the content of a lesson, teachers should not simply inform a student of a task before practice but make efforts to refine, extend, and apply the task as well. Students with disabilities and developmental delay who need extra practice trials may be particularly vulnerable to novice teachers, who typically omit refinement and extension phases of content development.

- Teachers should build variability of practice into the development of lesson content and avoid older models of constant practice.

- Teachers should recognize that because of unique biomechanical limitations, some children with physical disabilities may not need traditional progressions to develop skillful behavior. Teachers should match the content to an outcome based on the unique biomechanical requirements of each child.

SUMMARY

The research suggests that it is possible to integrate children with disabilities into physical education classes and that all children can learn and develop positive attitudes. For this to occur, teachers need to be familiar with the legislation that affects physical education, and they must work to provide meaningful educational experiences for each student. Although this may be difficult and require additional work, the research I have reviewed in this chapter provides insights for approaches that have the potential to help every student develop to the best of his or her potential.

IMPLICATIONS FOR PRACTICE

1. Federal law specifically mandates physical education for every child with disabilities.
2. Teachers should be aware of the federal law (Individuals with Disability Education Act) and implications of the least restrictive environment (LRE) concept with respect to alternative physical education models and particularly full inclusion.
3. Full inclusion of children with disabilities into regular physical education is more likely to work if teachers

   - have a positive attitude committed toward change,
   - honor individual differences,
   - help children feel they belong,

- plan collaboratively,
- have administrative support,
- have release time and flexible scheduling,
- have access to training, and
- have necessary personnel and adapted equipment.

4. Teachers should expect to find a variety of limitations and uniqueness in student abilities, performances, and behaviors associated with students with disabilities that may alter the expected or intended outcomes.

5. To assess children with disabilities, teachers should develop a unique set of competencies not normally found in undergraduate teacher-training experiences. Additional training may be indicated.

6. Teachers of children with disabilities must apply the same teaching functions that teachers would apply in any situation:
- Identify intended outcomes for learning.
- Plan learning experiences to accomplish those outcomes.
- Present tasks to learners.
- Develop the content.

REFERENCES

Allen, L.D., & Iwata, B.A. (1980). Reinforcing exercise maintenance. *Behavior Modification, 4*, 337-354.

Aufderheide, S. (1983). ALT-PE in mainstreamed physical education classes. *Journal of Teaching in Physical Education, 1*[Summer Monograph], 22-26.

Aufsesser, P.M. (1991). Mainstreaming and the least restrictive environment: How do they differ? *Palaestra, 7*(2), 31-34.

Baker, E.T., Wang, M.C., & Walberg, H.J. (1995). The effects of inclusion on learning. *Educational Leadership, 52*(4), 33-35.

Bennett, F., Eisenman, P., French, R., Henderson, H., & Shultz, B. (1989). The effect of a token economy on the exercise behavior of individuals with Down's Syndrome. *Adapted Physical Activity Quarterly, 6*, 230-246.

Beuter, A. (1983). Effects of mainstreaming on motor performances of intellectually normal and trainable mentally retarded students. *American Corrective Therapy Journal, 37*(2), 48-52.

Bird, P.J., & Gansneder, B.M. (1979). Preparation of physical education teachers as required under PL 94-142. *Exceptional Children, 45*, 464-466.

Bishop, P., & French, R. (1982). Effects of reinforcers on attending behavior of severely handicapped boys in physical education. *Journal for Special Educators, 18*(4), 48-58.

Block, M. (1994). *Including children with disabilities in physical education*. Baltimore: Paul H. Brookes.

Block, M. (1995). Development and validation of the children's attitudes toward integrated physical education-revised (CAIPE-R) inventory. *Adapted Physical Activity Quarterly, 12*, 60-77.

Block, M.E. (1991). Motor development in children with Down syndrome: A review of the literature. *Adapted Physical Activity Quarterly, 8*, 179-209.

Block, M.E. (1992). What is the appropriate physical education for students with profound disabilities? *Adapted Physical Activity Quarterly, 9*, 197-213.

Block, M.E. (1996). Implications of U.S. federal law and court cases for physical education placement of students with disabilities. *Adapted Physical Activity Quarterly, 13*, 127-152.

Block, M.E. (1999a). Did we jump on the wrong bandwagon? Problems with inclusion in physical education. *Palaestra, 15*(3), 30-36, 55-56.

Block, M.E. (1999b). Did we jump on the wrong bandwagon? Making general physical education placement work. *Palaestra, 15*(4), 34-42.

Block, M.E., & Vogler, E.W. (1994). Inclusion in regular physical education: The research base. *Journal of Physical Education, Recreation and Dance, 65*(1), 40-44.

Block, M.E., & Zeman, R. (1996). Including students with disabilities in regular physical education: Effects on nondisabled children. *Adapted Physical Activity Quarterly, 13*, 38-49.

Bouffard, M., Watkinson, E.J., Thompson, L.P., Dunn, J.L.C., Romanow, S.K.E. (1996). A test of the activity deficit hypothesis with children with movement difficulties. *Adapted Physical Activity Quarterly, 13*, 61-73.

Cantell, M.H., Smyth, M.M., & Ahonen, T.P. (1994). Clumsiness in adolescence: Educational, motor, and social outcomes of motor delay detected at 5 years. *Adapted Physical Activity Quarterly, 11,* 115-129.

Chadsey-Rusch, J. (1990). Social interactions of secondary-aged students with severe handicaps: Implications for facilitating the transition from school to work. *Journal of the Association for Persons with Severe Handicaps, 15,* 69-78.

Churton, M. (1986). Addressing personnel preparation needs to meet the challenge of the future. *Adapted Physical Activity Quarterly, 3,* 118-123.

Cooper Institute for Aerobics Research. (1999). *FITNESS-GRAM: Test administration manual (2ⁿᵈ ed.).* Dallas: Author.

Das, J. (1986). Information processing and motivation as determinants of performance in children with learning disabilities. In H. Whiting and M. Wade (Eds.), *Themes in motor development* (pp. 127-142). Hingham, MA: Kluwer-Academic.

Davis, K.T., & Dummer, G.M. (1987). Adapted physical education service delivery in Indiana. *Indiana Association of Health, Physical Education and Dance Journal, 16,* 8-11.

Davis, W.E., & Burton, A.W. (1991). Ecological task analysis: Translating movement behavior theory into practice. *Adapted Physical Activity Quarterly, 8,* 154-177.

Dempsey, S.D. (1986). *A comparison of college/university professors and specialists in adapted physical education in their perceptions of the importance of a specified set of professional competencies.* Unpublished doctoral dissertation, Oregon State University, Corvallis.

DePaepe, J. (1985). The influence of three least restrictive environments on the content motor-ALT and performance of moderately mentally retarded students. *Journal of Teaching in Physical Education, 5,* 34-41.

DePauw, K.P., & Doll-Tepper, G. (2000). Toward progressive inclusion and acceptance: Myth or reality? The inclusion debate and bandwagon discourse. *Adapted Physical Activity Quarterly, 17,* 135-143.

Duchanne, K.A., & French, R. (1998). Attitudes and grading practices of secondary physical educators in regular settings. *Adapted Physical Activity Quarterly, 15,* 370-380.

Dunkin, M.J., & Biddle, B.J. (1974). *The study of teaching.* New York: Holt, Rinehart & Winston.

Dunn, J.C. (2000). Goal orientations, perceptions of the motivational climate, and perceived competence of children with movement difficulties. *Adapted Physical Activity Quarterly, 17,* 1-19.

Ellis, D.N., & Cress, P.J., & Spellman, C.R. (1993). Training students with mental retardation to self-pace while exercising. *Adapted Physical Activity Quarterly, 10,* 104-124.

Federal Register, August 23, 1977, PL 94-142, the Education for All Handicapped Children Act.

Federal Register, September 29, 1992, Vol. 57, No. 189, the Individuals with Disabilities Education Act.

Feltz, D.L. (1980). Teaching a high-avoidance motor task to a retarded child through participant modeling. *Education and Training of the Mentally Retarded, 15,* 152-155.

Fernhall, B., Tymeson, G.T., & Webster, G.E. (1988). Cardiovascular fitness of mentally retarded individuals. *Adapted Physical Activity Quarterly, 5,* 12-28.

French, R., Silliman, L.M., Ben-Ezra, V., & Landrieu-Seiter, M. (1992). Influence of selected reinforcers on the cardiorespiratory exercise behavior of profoundly mentally retarded youth. *Perceptual and Motor Skills, 74,* 584-586.

Gagnon, J., Tousignant, M., & Martel, D. (1989). Academic learning time in physical education classes for mentally handicapped students. *Adapted Physical Activity Quarterly, 6,* 280-289.

Gelinas, J.E., & Reid, G. (2000). The developmental validity of traditional learn-to-swim progressions for children with physical disabilities. *Adapted Physical Activity Quarterly, 17,* 269-285.

Goodman, J., & Hopper, C. (1992). Hearing impaired children and youth: A review of psychomotor behavior. *Adapted Physical Activity Quarterly, 9,* 214-236.

Goodwin, D.L. (2001). The meaning of help in PE: Perceptions of students with physical disabilities. *Adapted Physical Activity Quarterly, 18,* 289-303.

Goodwin, D.L., & Watkinson, E.J. (2000). Inclusive physical education from the perspective of students with physical disabilities. *Adapted Physical Activity Quarterly, 17,* 144-160.

Heikinaro-Johansson, P. (1992). Mildly handicapped and non-handicapped pupils' physical activity and learning behavior in physical education classes. In T. Williams, L. Almond, & A. Sparkes (Eds.), *Sport and physical activity, moving toward excellence* (pp. 260-265). London: Spon.

Heikinaro-Johansson, P., Sherrill, C., French, R., & Huuhka, H. (1995). Adapted physical education consultant service model to facilitate inclusion. *Adapted Physical Activity Quarterly, 12,* 12-33.

Henderson, S.E., May, D.S., & Umney, M. (1989). An exploratory study of goal-setting behaviour, self-concept and locus of control in children with movement difficulties. *European Journal of Special Needs Education, 4,* 1-15.

Hopper, C. (1988). Self-concept and motor performance of hearing impaired boys and girls. *Adapted Physical Activity Quarterly, 5,* 293-304.

Houston-Wilson, C., Dunn, J.M., van der Mars, H., & McCubbin, J. (1997). The effect of peer tutors on the motor performance in integrated physical education classes. *Adapted Physical Activity Quarterly, 14,* 298-313.

Hsu, P.Y., & Dunn, J.M. (1984). Comparing reverse and forward chaining instructional methods on a motor task with moderately mentally retarded individuals. *Adapted Physical Activity Quarterly, 1,* 240-246.

Janney, R.F., Snell, M.E., Beers, M.K., & Raynes, M. (1995). Integrating students with moderate and severe disabilities into general education classes. *Exceptional Children, 61,* 425-439.

Jansma, P. (1978). Operant conditioning principles applied to disturbed male adolescents by a physical educator. *American Corrective Therapy Journal, 32*(3), 71-78.

Jeltma, K., & Vogler, E.W. (1985). Effects of an individual contingency on behaviorally disordered students in physical education. *Adapted Physical Activity Quarterly, 2*, 127-135.

Karper, W.B., & Martinek, T.J. (1983). Motor performance and self-concepts of handicapped and nonhandicapped children in integrated physical education classes. *American Corrective Therapy Journal, 37*(3), 91-95.

Kelly, L.E., & Gansneder, B. (1998). Preparation and job demographics of adapted physical educators in the United States. *Adapted Physical Activity Quarterly, 15*, 141-154.

Kowalski, E.M., & Sherrill, C. (1992). Motor sequencing of boys with learning disabilities: Modeling and verbal rehearsal strategies. *Adapted Physical Activity Quarterly, 9*, 261-272.

LaMaster, K., Gail, K., Kinchin, G., & Siedentop, D. (1998). Inclusion practices of effective elementary specialists. *Adapted Physical Activity Quarterly, 15*, 64-81.

Lavay, B., & French, R. (1986). The effect of different reinforcers on the physical performance of trainable mentally handicapped students. *American Corrective Therapy Journal, 40*(3), 58-61.

Madden, N.M., & Slavin, R.E. (1983). Mainstreaming students with mild handicaps: Academic and social outcomes. *Review of Educational Research, 53*, 519-569.

Magill, R.A. (1997). *Motor learning: Concepts and applications* (5th ed.). Dubuque, IA: Brown.

Martinek, T.J., & Karper, W.B. (1982). Entry-level motor performance and self-concepts of handicapped and non-handicapped children in mainstreamed physical education classes: A preliminary study. *Perceptual and Motor Skills, 55*, 1002.

McCullagh, P. (1987). Model similarity effects on motor performance. *Journal of Sport Psychology, 9*, 249-260.

McCullagh, P., Weiss, M.R., & Ross, D. (1989). Modeling considerations in motor skill acquisition and performance: An integrated approach. *Exercise and Sport Science Review, 17*, 475-517.

Melograno, V.J., & Loovis, E.M. (1991). Status of physical education for handicapped students: A comparative analysis of teachers in 1980 and 1988. *Adapted Physical Activity Quarterly, 8*, 28-42.

Mosston, M., & Ashworth, S. (2002). *Teaching physical education* (5th ed.). San Francisco: Benjamin Cummings.

Murata, N.M., & Jansma, P. (1997). Influence of support personnel on students with and without disabilities in general physical education. *Clinical Kinesiology, 51*(2), 37-46.

National Consortium for Physical Education and Recreation for Individuals With Disability. (1995). *Adapted physical education standards.* Champaign, IL: Human Kinetics.

Ninot, G., Bilard, J., Delignieres, D., Sokolowski, M. (2000). Effects of integrated sport participation on perceived competence for adolescents with mental retardation. *Adapted Physical Activity Quarterly, 17*, 208-221.

O'Connor, J., French, R., Sherrill, C., & Babcock, G. (2001). Scholarly productivity in adapted physical activity pedagogy: A bibliometric analysis. *Adapted Physical Activity Quarterly, 18*, 434-450.

Politino, V., & Smith, S.L. (1989). Attitude toward physical activity and self-concept of emotionally disturbed and normal children. *Adapted Physical Activity Quarterly, 6*, 371-378.

Rimmer, J.H., & Kelly, L.E. (1989). Gross motor development in preschool children with learning disabilities. *Adapted Physical Activity Quarterly, 6*, 268-279.

Rink, J.E. (2002). *Teaching physical education for learning.* (4th ed.). Boston: WCB McGraw Hill.

Rizzo, T.L. (1984). Attitudes of physical educators toward teaching handicapped pupils. *Adapted Physical Activity Quarterly, 1*, 267-274.

Rizzo, T.L., Vispoel, T.L., & Walter, P. (1991). Physical educators' attributes and attitudes toward teaching students with handicaps. *Adapted Physical Activity Quarterly, 8*, 4-11.

Rizzo, T.L., & Wright, R.G. (1988). Selected attributes related to physical educators' attitudes towards teaching students with handicaps. *Mental Retardation, 26*, 307-309.

Rogers-Wallgren, J.L., French, R., & Ben-Ezra, V. (1992). Use of reinforcement to increase independence in physical fitness performance of profoundly mentally retarded youth. *Perceptual and Motor Skills, 75*, 975-982.

Rose, B., Larkin, D., & Berger, G.G. (1997). Coordination and gender influences on the perceived competence of children. *Adapted Physical Activity Quarterly, 14*, 210-221.

Schmidt, R.A. (1975). A schema theory of discrete motor skill learning. *Psychological Review, 82*, 225-260.

Schnorr, R.F. (1990). "Peter? He comes and goes . . .": First graders' perspectives on a part-time mainstream student. *Journal for the Association of Persons with Severe Handicaps, 15*, 231-240.

Schoemaker, M.M., & Kalverboer, A.F. (1994). Social and affective problems of children who are clumsy: How early do they begin? *Adapted Physical Activity Quarterly, 11*, 130-140.

Seaman, J.A. (1970). Attitudes of physically handicapped children towards physical education. *Research Quarterly, 41*, 439-445.

Semmel, M.I., Gottlieb, J., & Robinson, N.M. (1979). Mainstreaming: Perspectives on educating handicapped children in the public school. *Review of Research in Education, 7*, 223-279.

Shea, J.B., & Morgan, R.L. (1979). Contextual interference effects on the acquisition, retention, and transfer of a motor skill. *Journal of Experimental Psychological: Human Learning and Memory, 5*, 179-187.

Sherrill, C. (1998). *Adapted physical activity, recreation, and sport* (5th ed). Boston: WCB McGraw-Hill.

Sherrill, C., & Megginson, N. (1984). A needs assessment instrument for local use in adapted physical education. *Adapted Physical Activity Quarterly, 1,* 147-157.

Shute, S., Dodds, P., Placek, J., Rife, F., & Silverman, S. (1982). Academic learning time in elementary school movement education: A descriptive analytic study. *Journal of Teaching in Physical Education, 1*(2), 3-14.

Silliman, L.M., & French, R. (1993). Use of selected reinforcers to improve the ball kicking of youths with profound mental retardation. *Adapted Physical Activity Quarterly, 10,* 52-69.

Silliman, L.M., French, R., & Tynan, D. (1992). Use of sensory reinforcement to increase compliant behavior of a child who is blind and profoundly mentally retarded. *Clinical Kinesiology, 46*(3), 3-9.

Silverman, S., Dodds, P., Placek, J., Shute, S., & Rife, F. (1984). Academic learning time in elementary school physical education (ALT-PE) for student subgroups and instructional activity units. *Research Quarterly for Exercise and Sport, 55,* 365-370.

Skaggs, S., & Hopper, C. (1996). Individuals with visual impairments: A review of psychomotor behavior. *Adapted Physical Activity Quarterly, 13,* 16-26.

Skinner, B.F. (1953). *Science and human behavior.* New York: Macmillan.

Slininger, D., Sherrill, C., & Jankowski, C.M. (2000). Children's attitudes toward peers with severe disabilities: Revisiting contact theory. *Adapted Physical Activity Quarterly, 17,* 176-196.

Stainback, S., & Stainback, W. (1991). A rationale for integration and restructuring: A synopsis. In J.W. Lloyd, N.N. Singh, & A.C. Repp (Eds.), *The regular education initiative: Alternative perspectives on concepts, issues, and models* (pp. 225-239). Sycamore, IL: Sycamore.

Stainback, W., & Stainback, S. (1990). *Support networks for inclusive schooling: Interdependent integrated education.* Baltimore: Paul H. Brookes.

Stanton, K., & Colvin, A. (1996). The physical educator's role in inclusion. *Strategies, 9*(4), 13-15.

Staub, D., & Peck, C.A. (1995). What are the outcomes for nondisabled students. *Educational Leadership, 1,* 36-40.

Stewart, C.C. (1988). Modifications of student attitudes toward disabled peers. *Adapted Physical Activity Quarterly, 5,* 44-48.

Sullivan, D., Vogler, E.W., Coleman, M., & Jones, D. (2002). The evaluation of expertise in elementary physical education teachers, *Journal of Sport Pedagogy, 8(2),* 38-52.

Taylor, J., French, R., Kinnison, L., & O'Brien, T. (1998). Primary and secondary reinforcers in performance of a 1.0-mile walk/jog by adolescents with moderate mental retardation. *Perceptual and Motor Skills, 87,* 1265-1266.

Temple, V.A., & Walkley, J.W. (1999). Academic learning time-physical education (ALT-PE) of students with mild intellectual disabilities in regular Victorian schools. *Adapted Physical Activity Quarterly, 16,* 64-74.

Thomas, J. (1980). Acquisition of motor skills: Information processing differences between children and adults. *Research Quarterly, 51,* 158-173.

Vogler, B., & Block, M. (1994). Models for full inclusion which work. *Teaching Elementary Physical Education, 5,* 20-22.

Vogler, E.W. (2000, June). *A review of inclusive physical education research.* Paper presented at the 2000 International Adapted Physical Education Conference, "Quality Adapted Physical Education for the 21st Century," National Taiwan Normal University. Taipei, Republic of China.

Vogler, E.W., Coleman, M., Howard, B., Kinchin, G., Koranda, P., & Block, M. (2001). Including a child with severe cerebral palsy in physical education: A longitudinal case study—year two. *Journal of Sport Pedagogy, 7*(1), 38-60.

Vogler, E.W., DePaepe, J., & Martinek, T. (1990). Effective teaching in adapted physical education. In Doll-Tepper, G., Dahms, C., Doll, B., von Selzam, H. (Eds.), *Adapted physical activity: An interdisciplinary approach* (pp. 245-250). Heidelberg: Springer.

Vogler, E.W., & French, R.F. (1983). The effects of a group contingency strategy on behaviorally disordered students in physical education. *Research Quarterly for Exercise and Sport, 54,* 273-277.

Vogler, E.W., French, R., & Bishop, P. (1989). Paraprofessionals: Implications for adapted physical education. *Physical Educator, 46,* 69-76.

Vogler, E.W., Koranda, P., & Romance, T. (2000). Including a child with severe cerebral palsy in physical education: A case study. *Adapted Physical Activity Quarterly, 17,* 161-175.

Vogler, E.W., Kudlacek, M., O'Connor, J., & Wiseman, R. (November, 2000). *Synthesis review of pedagogical research in physical education for students with disability.* North American Federation of Adapted Physical Activity Symposium, New Orleans.

Vogler, E.W., van der Mars, H., Cusimano, B., & Darst, P. (1990). Relationship of presage, context, and process variables to ALT-PE of elementary level mainstreamed students. *Adapted Physical Activity Quarterly, 7,* 298-313.

Vogler, E.W., van der Mars, H., Cusimano, B., & Darst, P. (1992). Experience, expertise and teaching effectiveness with mainstreamed and nonmainstreamed children. *Adapted Physical Activity Quarterly, 9,* 316-329.

Vogler, E.W., van der Mars, H., Cusimano, B., & Darst, P. (1998). Analysis of student/teacher behaviours in junior high physical education classes including children with mild disability. *Journal of Sport Pedagogy, 4*(2), 43-57.

Walker, H.M. (1979). *The acting-out child: Coping with classroom disruption.* Boston: Allyn and Bacon.

Wang, M.C., & Baker, E.T. (1986). Mainstreaming programs: Design features and effects. *Journal of Special Education, 19,* 503-521.

Weber, R.C., & Thorpe, J. (1992). Teaching children with autism through task variation in physical education. *Exceptional Children, 59*(1), 77-86.

Webster, G. (1987). Influence of peer tutors upon academic learning time-physical education of mentally handicapped students. *Journal of Teaching in Physical Education, 6,* 1987.

Winnick, J. (1985). The performance of visually impaired youngsters in physical education activities: Implications for mainstreaming. *Adapted Physical Activity Quarterly, 2,* 292-299.

Winnick, J.P. (2002). *Adapted physical education and sport* (3rd ed.). Champaign, IL: Human Kinetics.

Winnick, J.P., & Short, F.X. (1986). Physical fitness of adolescents with auditory impairments. *Adapted Physical Activity Quarterly, 3,* 58-66.

Winnick, J.P., & Short, F.X. (1999). *The Brockport physical fitness test manual.* Champaign, IL: Human Kinetics.

Winther, K., & Thomas, J. (1981). Developmental differences in children's labeling of movement. *Journal of Motor Behavior, 13,* 77-90.

PART III

PROMOTING STUDENT LEARNING

CHAPTER SEVEN

USING CURRICULUM TO ENHANCE STUDENT LEARNING

Catherine D. Ennis

Educators use the term *curriculum* to describe a range of educational experiences associated with student learning. A curriculum can refer to the content to be taught in a subject area, such as physical education, the courses and research experiences in a graduate curriculum, or the topics covered in one lesson or one course. For the purposes of this chapter I will define a *curriculum* simply as the learning experiences that occur within the school. This broad, inclusive definition includes both the planned and unplanned experiences that contribute to student learning. The term *curriculum* is derived from the Latin verb *currere*, to run the course, and in fact many students feel like they are running from class to class or grade to grade as they maneuver through a school curriculum. Usually a curriculum consists of topics, concepts, themes, or ideas that describe the scope, or content, to be taught or experienced. Once the scope of a curriculum is decided, teachers then arrange the topics into a sequence that is developmentally appropriate and consistent with educational expectations for learning.

Content scope in most subject areas includes numerous topics that reflect the richness of the knowledge base of that discipline. When designing a course or a program, curriculum developers must answer the key curriculum question "What knowledge is of most worth?" (Broudy, 1982; Schubert, 1990). In other words, they are really asking "What content is most important for these students to learn in this course at this time in their lives?" In physical education, answers to these questions are critical and reflect developmentally appropriate content and sequences consistent with the expectations of students, parents, and educators. Answering the question "correctly" for your students in your physical education program often can make the difference between student success or failure, enjoyment or disengagement, and perhaps even lifetime activity or a sedentary lifestyle (Cothran & Ennis, 1998). Because decisions about scope and sequence reflect the teachers' or curriculum developer's expertise and beliefs about best practice, we also can say that a curriculum reflects an educational philosophy. When an educational philosophy forms the foundation for curricular scope and sequence, the philosophy, at times, can become hidden in the daily details of teaching. The educational philosophy may be abstract and difficult for individuals who are not professional educators to understand.

WHAT AND HOW SHOULD STUDENTS LEARN?

Herbert Kliebard (1972) proposed that abstract educational philosophies, beliefs, and decisions could be made more concrete and accessible by using curriculum metaphors. His analysis of educational philosophies led him to propose three educational metaphors that reflect the belief systems of many curriculum developers, administrators, and teachers. Kliebard's metaphors use commonly understood concepts such as a factory, a garden, and a journey to emphasize the roles and expectations of educators and students within particular educational philosophies. Because we already understand the concrete activities, events, and context of a factory or a journey, we can use a metaphor as a tool to better envision a curricular structure with those characteristics (Ormell, 1996). As you read the following metaphors, compare your educational beliefs with the curricular focus and teachers' and students' roles in these metaphors to identify those most consistent with your perspective.

Curriculum as a Factory

When a curriculum is structured as a factory, students are viewed as raw materials brought to the factory to be shaped and molded into finished products. The teacher as the factory worker treats each student in exactly the same way using highly defined tools and standards. Careful attention to detail is essential if each student is to meet the narrowly defined criteria for a successful or acceptable product. The purpose of the factory curriculum is to use predetermined standards to produce student products of consistently acceptable quality.

Curriculum as a Garden

When the curriculum is envisioned as a garden, the many types of plants represent diverse students, each with specific needs and attributes. In this metaphor, the teacher is the gardener who carefully tends each plant, providing appropriate amounts of light, water, soil, and nutrients required for successful growth. The purpose of the curriculum is to provide a unique, nurturing environment centered on the needs of each flower, vegetable, and tree and to protect all plants from harm. Because of this care, each plant grows to its full potential with no two plants alike. Plants represent a range of sizes, fragrances, textures, and colors, providing infinite variety and opportunity for enjoyment in the garden.

Curriculum as a Journey

When the curriculum is designed as a journey, students represent the travelers who embark on an adventure to discover and explore new places and ideas. The teacher is the tour guide who plans the general itinerary, selecting accommodations and routes that all travelers experience. As in the most appealing tour packages, the tour guide also provides numerous opportunities for student travelers to venture out independently or in small groups on side trips or excursions to explore points of interest. The tour guide makes reservations, enlists the help of local experts and guides, and generally sees to the travelers' comfort and well-being. The purpose of the journey curriculum is to provide interesting and stimulating information that will be meaningful and useful to the student. Because of this curricular itinerary, travelers complete the journey having experienced a wide range of cultural and content knowledge. Many may choose to return later to favorite locations, deepening their knowledge of fascinating places or continuing their exploration alone or under the guidance of another knowledgeable guide.

Decisions of Most Worth

In each metaphor, the curriculum, student, and teacher take on particular roles and responsibilities leading to an "educated person." As within any curriculum, decisions are made either for or by the students that lead to the inclusion or exclusion of certain experiences considered worthwhile. Historically, curriculum developers assumed that, as in the factory metaphor, there was only one correct answer to the question "What knowledge is of most worth?" A narrow set of topics was considered essential for all students, and every successful student developed competence or proficiency in the knowledge and skills deemed of most worth to society. For example, most would agree that reading, writing, and calculating are essential skills for a productive life. Are there knowledge and skills that all students should learn in physical education to be considered physically educated? Are there essential skills, knowledge, and attitudes that students need to participate in physical activity for a lifetime? Leaders affiliated with the National Association for Sport and Physical Education (NASPE) have developed seven standards that professionals agree are the knowledge of most worth for physical education. School districts across the country are currently revising their curricula to reflect these standards (see chapter 8 by Leslie Lambert for a listing of the standards) In this chapter I will examine more deeply the research on values, beliefs, and contexts that inform the complex decision-making processes in physical education curriculum. I also will identify characteristics of curriculum coherence that enhance teaching and learning.

VALUE ORIENTATIONS IN CURRICULAR DECISION MAKING

In each of the preceding metaphors, teachers tried to create classroom environments to facilitate educational goals and enhance student learning. Value orientations reflect teachers' educational beliefs about what students should learn, how they should engage in the learning process, and how learning should be assessed (Eisner, 1992; Ennis, 1992, 1994a, 1994b; Jewett, Bain, & Ennis, 1995). Because teachers work in complex school environments, numerous contextual factors facilitate or constrain their ability to teach in a manner consistent with their value perspectives. Ennis (1995, 1996b) found that although most teachers believed they had the knowledge necessary to be effective in their jobs, barriers in the school context limited their ability to reach their curricular goals. Such barriers may include student disengagement, lack of administrative support, large class sizes, or inadequate equipment (Graham, Hopple, Manross, & Sitzman, 1993; Solmon, Worthy, & Carter, 1993; Talbert, McLaughlin, & Rowan, 1993). In this section I will describe five educational beliefs or value orientations—disciplinary mastery, learning process, self-actualization, social responsibility and justice, and ecological integration—and provide examples to demonstrate how contextual factors influence physical educators' ability to teach within each orientation.

Disciplinary Mastery

Disciplinary mastery (DM) educators focus on knowledge and skills as essential curricular elements (Schrag, 1992). They would answer the question "What knowledge is of most worth?" by pointing out that students should learn human movement patterns, skills, and skill themes. These basic movements and concepts lead to more complex movements, such as those used in dance, swimming, gymnastics, team sports, and fitness activities (Allison, Pissanos, Turner, & Law, 2000; Griffin & Placek, 2001). They would argue that students should meet specific performance and knowledge criteria and be able to demonstrate their knowledge in complex games. They might also advocate for a health-related fitness curriculum in which students learn components and principles associated with moderate to vigorous physical activity and the value of a healthy-active lifestyle (Corbin & Lindsey, 2002). An essential aspect of effective DM programs is the consistent and appropriate use of valid student assessments to measure students' progress toward clearly stated goals (Lambert, 1999).

DM teachers are most effective when they have access to instructional time, facilities, and equipment needed to enhance student performance. Students who are interested in learning about movement, sport, and exercise gain the greatest benefits from DM teachers. Although teachers always have difficulty working with poor facilities and equipment, limited instructional time, large class sizes, or disruptive or unmotivated students, DM teachers face particular difficulties (Hastie, Sanders, & Rowland, 1999). In these instances, even effective class managers report that they spend more time keeping children on task than they do providing instruction or giving specific, corrective feedback (Ennis, 1992).

Learning Process

Learning process (LP) teachers agree with their DM colleagues that students need the ability to perform and knowledge about performance to be physically educated persons. They believe, however, that students must not only perform skillfully but also know how to make decisions and solve problems about movement, sport, and exercise (Kirk, Burgess-Limerick, Kiss, Lahey, & Penney, 1999). For example, instead of explaining or demonstrating a set play for a throw-in in soccer, LP teachers might challenge students to create their own plays, using the soccer skills and strategies they have learned. Students in a physical education class might create five or more different solutions to this problem and then teach others these strategies, taking content ownership. They synthesize knowledge about the throw-in with an understanding of offensive and defensive strategies to create their own solutions (Griffin, Mitchell, & Oslin, 1997; Kirk & MacPhail, 2002). LP teachers encourage students to use knowledge to solve problems and to focus on the process of solving the problem as well as the product, or solution, itself (Ennis, 1992).

LP teachers create effective environments or contexts for learning by challenging their students to think about how and why certain movement or fitness activities lead to particular results. In other words, they teach students how to use knowledge to analyze a situation and how to alter or adjust their own behavior to be successful. These teachers are most successful when they work in a school with cross-disciplinary goals that focus on critical thinking or problem solving (Donnelly, Helion, & Fry, 1999; Ennis, 1990; Polman, 2000; Roberts & Östman, 1998). Students come to physical education already expecting to work independently and cooperatively to solve problems. They are receptive to applying knowledge, such as that associated with biomechanics or physiology, to their motor performance (Mohnson, 1998). LP teachers have special difficulties creating a learning environment in a situation in which students are not open to learning novel content using a variety of learning strategies. These students may not value the educational experiences or may have learning problems that limit their ability to work independently or focus on the problem (Ennis, 1996b, 1998b).

Self-Actualization

The self-actualization (SA) orientation (from Maslow, 1979) places the students' needs and interests at the center of the curriculum (Noddings, 1992). Like the gardeners in the metaphor, SA teachers attempt to match their curriculum to students' interests and motivational levels. A self-actualization curriculum orientation uses movement, sport, and exercise content as a means to help students develop positive self-esteem and a sense of efficacy or an "I can" attitude. Curricula developed from this perspective encourage students to try activities they think are difficult. Teachers help them move from dependence on external rewards to a more self-fulfilling, intrinsic reward system (Hellison et al., 2000). SA teachers focus on helping students develop a positive self-concept and to set and meet relevant personal goals. This approach requires students to persist or give effort, even when the task may be difficult. SA teachers are personally interested in their students' lives and work to incorporate knowledge that students believe is important into their physical education programs. SA teachers design curricula that are flexible and responsive to student diversity. These teachers have particular difficulty teaching in situations where the school administrators or other teachers require strict adherence to a rigid set of school policies, rules, standardized tests, goals, or objectives. These teachers prefer a loosely structured approach that honors students' voices in the selection of goals, learning activities, and evaluation procedures. SA teachers need the flexibility to shape a curriculum that entices uninterested, unmotivated, or disruptive students to engage in physical activity (Ennis, 1994a, 1994b; Martinek & Griffith, 1994).

Social Responsibility and Justice

Teachers who advocate social responsibility and justice (SRJ) are most concerned about helping students developing positive interpersonal relationships in an environment that emphasizes equity and social justice (Banks, 1993; Nilges, 1998). They use movement, sport, and fitness content to provide opportunities for students to work with others and to examine tasks and their own behavior to identify injustices (Napper-Owens, Kovar, Ermler, & Mehrhof, 1999). They focus on teaching students how to cooperate and accept personal responsibility for their roles in game play or group problem solving (Rønholt, 2002). They encourage students to develop leadership ability and make responsible, responsive decisions as they develop definitions of fairness, equity, empowerment, and agency.

SRJ teachers focus on interpersonal relationships among students in their classes. Issues of gender, race, and class equity are central to the curriculum (Treanor, Graber, Housner, & Wiegand, 1998). Students routinely make decisions evaluating fair play, equal opportunity, and perceptions of gender roles that are influential in student lives. They design situations in which students must work cooperatively to achieve success in physically and morally challenging situations. These teachers are sensitive to the needs, hopes, and desires of students who are searching for fairness and voice within the school environment. The focus of SRJ lessons is on developing thoughtful and reflective personal and social behaviors to respond effectively in a variety of situations. Students learn patience, negotiation, equity, and self-control (Hellison et al., 2000). The instructional plan includes a series of small social progressions leading to increased levels of social responsibility and justice. Like SA teachers, SRJ teachers have most difficulty when required to follow rigid approaches to performance-based physical education. For example, the requirement to administer individually oriented fitness tests may be inconsistent with their focus on cooperative goals or the need to have students examine and modify the testing environment consistent with goals of personal and social agency and empowerment (Ennis, 1994b).

Ecological Integration

Teachers who advocate ecological integration (EI; Jewett & Ennis, 1990) emphasize that the knowledge base, the learner, and the social setting blend to balance and enhance the learning environment. They point out to students the benefits of acquiring knowledge to solve personal or group challenges, leading to a socially just and equitable environment. EI teachers help students learn a range of physical activities and personal and social skills so that they can participate successfully in future group activities (Jewett & Mullan, 1977). Students learn that personal needs, at times, should give way to group concerns. Similarly, the group learns that sometimes it must be sensitive to an individual's needs and interests. EI teachers attempt to balance within the curriculum the influence of the knowledge base, the learners' needs and interests, and community expectations. They help students learn how knowledge connects meaningfully to life today and in the future (Jewett & Mullan, 1977).

EI teachers see the physical education program as an ecosystem. Events that happen in one part of the program affect future decisions in every other part. By emphasizing the inherent connectedness between content and life experience, EI teachers help students seek relationships between knowledge learned in science and mathematics class, for example, with concepts and principles learned in the gym (Kirk et al., 1999; Mohnson, 1998, Polman, 2000; Roberts & Östman, 1998). Students are successful when they use knowledge to make personal and social decisions that are in the schools' or their classmates' best interest. EI teachers find it especially difficult to teach effectively when teaching time is limited (because of either scheduling restrictions or large class sizes). In these situations, they have difficulty finding adequate instructional time to help students examine knowledge and responsibility issues while simultaneously participating in activities that contribute to the development of personal goals (Ennis, 1992; Hastie et al., 1999).

Setting Realistic Curriculum Goals

As you have read these descriptions of value orientations, you may have identified one or more orientations as consistent with your personal value perspective. Certainly, they each represent valid goals that are important for all students in physical education. So why can't we teach them all? Why can't the physical education curriculum include all these goals? In fact, most teachers' scores on the Value Orientation Inventory (Ennis & Chen, 1993) reflect several orientations that blend to form their value profile. Follow-up ethnographic research (Ennis, 1992) conducted in many physical education teachers' classrooms suggests that contextual factors enhance or constrain their efforts to teach and implement curriculum consistent with their desired value profile. In the next section I will present a model describing the influence of values and context on student learning.

INFLUENCE OF VALUES AND CONTEXT ON STUDENT LEARNING

Many contextual factors shape teachers' values and expectations for student learning and behavior within the school context. A model can help us understand how these influences affect student learning. Models provide a visual organization of relevant factors by describing the relationships among factors and explaining how each factor influences and is influenced by others. The values-context model, shown in figure 7.1, provides a framework for thinking about curricular decision making. The model can describe factors directly affecting what, how, and how much students learn in physical education. The values-context model treats teacher beliefs as an outcome of their personal and professional experience and as a predictor of at least some decisions teachers make about contents and methods in their programs.

The values-context model uses a series of concentric circles to depict influences in the educational environment. Each circle reflects social and cultural influences on physical

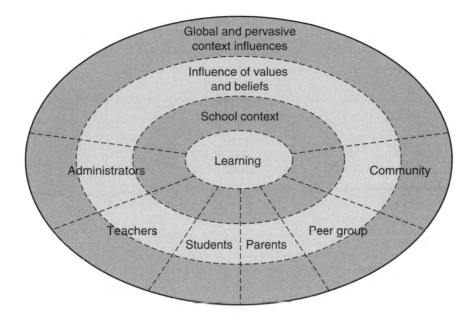

FIGURE 7.1   Values-context model.

education, shaping each level or layer of the teaching-learning process. A two-dimensional model such as this cannot entirely portray the dynamic interactions among the layers that influence the school environment. The model should be examined from both the inside out and the outside in, because each factor expands or contracts under the influence of ever-present contextual conditions. The influences described in the outer circle represent global and pervasive context variables. They affect every aspect of school experience and include the unique characteristics of students, families, neighborhoods, teachers, and schools that create the climate of expectations and performance within the school and the physical education setting. The second circle includes specific beliefs held by particular families, teachers and administrators, peer groups, and students that appear to directly influence the teaching learning process. These, in turn, influence the curriculum plan, teacher practices, and student decisions and behaviors. The inner circles focus on a range of student responses to curriculum and teaching. Educational decisions made in response to context and values directly influence learning by shaping the teachers' choice of content, methods, and evaluation strategies, enhancing or constraining student responses. The next sections will describe each circle in figure 7.1 in more detail.

Global and Pervasive Context Influences (Outer Circle)

This circle describes the context factors in the school setting. The variables are defined broadly to encompass the variety of circumstances that indirectly influence student learning. The school social system is composed of historical, cultural, economic, and political factors that affect characteristics of the community, school, family, teacher, and student. Each influences and responds to the effect of the others, creating a complex web of contextual expectations.

Community Influences

The community is part of a large social system that influences curricular values and choices (Banks, 1993). Most school populations include administrators, teachers, and students from several different neighborhoods and many cultural backgrounds. Cohesive groups of students from a particular neighborhood, ethnic group, or language group provide a social support structure to ease entry and facilitate functioning within the school. Belonging to one of these cultural or social groups gives individuals confidence and increases their comfort level with the school environment. Cultural and social groups function within set norms that are explicitly or tacitly valued by the group and shape community expectations (Eccles & Harold, 1993; Halas, 2001; Kantor & Brenzel, 1992). Although neighborhood groups can contribute to cohesion, they may also act negatively as social controls to limit group members' individuality. In the extreme, negative codes of social behavior held by gangs require individuals to become involved in illegal activities to maintain or increase their status within the group (Talbert et al., 1993).

Most teachers and administrators are aware of neighborhood cultural or social group structures and their negative influences on adolescents within the community (Wehlage, Rutter, Smith, Lesko, & Fernandez, 1989). Some students look to cliques or gangs for the social support that they may not be receiving at home or at school. To win status and approval from peers, sometimes these students are disruptive or verbally or physically aggressive. Teachers often attempt to work with these students in support groups or conflict-resolution teams to defuse aggressive behavior (Ennis et al., 1997; Ennis et al., 1999). They try to provide opportunities for students to receive rewards for positive, socially appropriate behaviors (National School Boards Association, 1993). Teachers' perceptions of neighborhood, community, or peer influences often affect activities they choose to offer in physical education class (Ennis, 1994a, 1994b). At times they may avoid content that is controversial, or they may include specific content, such as lessons on social responsibility and justice in an attempt to improve the class environment (Ennis, 1995, 1996b).

School Influences

Schools are more than buildings or athletic fields that serve as work places for teachers and students (Wehlage et al., 1998). They also encompass the values and beliefs of educational participants. Communities fund schools to transmit certain basic knowledge and appropriate behaviors to young people. Thus, they have a social mandate to provide opportunities for learning to take place (Lawson, 1998). To implement this mandate, principals and teachers develop rules, policies, and guidelines to protect students and provide for uniform delivery of diverse programs. In school districts that incorporate school-based management, teachers are involved in the daily school operation. They influence decisions involving individual students and funding for each subject area. Schools differ in size and climate (Cothran & Ennis, 1999). Students enrolled in large high schools, for example, comment that they sometimes become lost in the masses of people who crowd the halls and facilities. Although large schools are more economical for the community to finance, they often require administrators to develop creative organizational structures to help students feel welcome and involved. Administrators can divide students into teams with teachers and facilities assigned specifically to meet their needs. Physical education classes also may be large, forcing teachers to find innovative ways to provide corrective feedback and individualized instruction. Both large and small schools can develop climates that are warm and inviting to students. School climate reflects many tangible and intangible qualities that assist students in bonding with the school and its staff. Students are more likely to become engaged in schools when they perceive a warm, welcoming climate (Treasure & Roberts, 2001).

Family Influences

Family involvement in schools is one factor that contributes to a warm climate. Family involvement is the extent to which parents participate with their children in school activities (Eccles & Midgley, 1990; Lawson, 1998). Parents often help schools develop special programs that provide enriched educational opportunities for students. Historically, we have viewed the student as an isolated individual who comes to school for the primary purpose of learning. More recently, greater consideration has been given to the influence of students' backgrounds and family environments on their interest in and readiness to learn in school settings. Goals, attitudes, and interests held by family members, in turn, influence students' interests and levels of motivation to participate in certain activities. Family interests often reflect prior experiences with sports and recreational activities that enhance students' openness to new physical education activities.

Other influential factors include family culture and ethnic heritage that shape and support students' identity and pride in themselves. Likewise, parents' educational level and their expectations, willingness, and ability to nurture academic success are critical factors in academic achievement. Family characteristics appear to be major factors in students' readiness for school and their interest and motivation to be successful in educational settings. Family members' desire to engage with the teacher in an academic partnership often directly influences student learning.

Teachers' Influences

Teachers' background, experience, and level of teaching skills influence many aspects of their teaching, including their expectations for student behavior and learning. For example, students learn more when teachers hold high expectations for students and focus their energy, motivation, and enthusiasm on the instructional process (Kulinna, Silverman, & Keating, 2000). Teachers can solidify the parent-teacher educational partnership when they make an effort to understand the interests and concerns of students, community influences and groups, and family values and beliefs. This effort appears essential to maintaining a positive class climate. Further, teachers' mastery of a variety of class management, disciplinary, and teaching strategies contributes to their ability to enhance student learning. Years of experience at different teaching levels (e.g., elementary, middle, high school, university) and with different kinds of students (e.g., ethnicity, gender, urban or rural) also influence the nature and quality of the teachers' curricular decisions (Chen, 1999; Cothran & Ennis, 1998; Rovegno & Bandhauer, 1997; Tannehill, Romar, O'Sullivan, England, & Rosenberg, 1994). These experiences help them understand their students' goals, expectations, and needs, further enhancing the learning environment.

Students' Influences

The personal characteristics of students also contribute to or detract from learning. Students' age, maturity (Malina & Bouchard, 1990), gender (Nilges, 1998; Rønholt, 2002), and ethnicity (Peshkin & White, 1990) play a powerful role in their ability to respond positively to school settings, teachers, and learning environments (Eccles & Midgley, 1990; Wentzel, 1991). In addition, students' past performances also influence their future opportunities and the extent to which they appreciate or are prepared to learn new information. Students bring with them school records and test scores that document their aptitudes, talents, and interests. In physical education, many teachers keep extensive records of student performance in a variety of activities. Students also become well known for their personality or temperament (Ennis, 1995, 1996b). These factors influence adult expectations about what and how much students can learn (Ennis, 1998b). Oakes (1992) and Martinek and Griffith (1994) documented positive and negative consequences of adult expectations on student learning.

Influence of Values and Beliefs (Second Circle)

The school social system consists of complex interactions among many people who have a variety of goals and expectations for education (Pajares, 1992). Beliefs about the importance of the physical education experience in the total school curriculum affect resource allocations to the physical education program (Solmon et al., 1993). They influence decisions about content, teaching strategies, and evaluation (Schubert, 1990). Beliefs may focus on the physical education program or be specific to a particular child or group of children. The components in this part of the model represent the beliefs of key individuals and groups, such as families, teachers and administrators, peer groups, and students, who ultimately determine the success of the physical education program in enhancing student learning.

Family Beliefs

Family beliefs about the importance of physical education appear to play an influential role in some adolescents' interest in and willingness to participate in physical education. Families with school-age children are usually most involved in schools and most concerned with the quality of the educational experience (Eccles & Harold, 1993). The support of parents for the physical education program and their understanding of its benefits for their children, both now and across the life span, are critical. Parents' experiences in physical education often frame their expectations for their children's physical education program. Some parents may have been involved in quality physical education and athletic experiences and need little encouragement to support the program. Others may not remember much about physical education or may have had a negative experience during their school years. These parents may question the value of physical education in the school curriculum. Teachers may need to make an extra effort to convince these parents of the value of physical education.

Parents may also have beliefs or expectations specific to their own children. They may have preconceived perceptions of their children's abilities and interests that influence their expectations for achievement. They may have differing beliefs about what content is most important for their children to learn. Although some parents value physical education as a way to enhance their children's athletic ability, others may value physical education because of its socialization goals, and they may see it as an avenue for the development of interpersonal relationships (Wentzel, 1991). Parents whose children are more successful in physical education than they are in other school subjects may value physical education because it enhances their children's self-esteem.

Administrators' Beliefs

Administrators' beliefs about physical education are instrumental in their philosophical and financial support of physical education programs. Teachers rely on the support of administrators to create strong programs and maintain class control. When administrators value physical education highly, physical education teachers are encouraged to set goals leading to student learning. Even the most energetic, effective, and motivated teachers can quickly become disillusioned when administrators do not facilitate their efforts to teach an educationally sound physical education curriculum. Administrators should protect the instructional time allocated to physical education and intervene to limit the distractions that can occur when the gymnasium is used for after-school recreation, school picture days, and commencement rehearsals. Administrators are more likely to view the physical education program as essential when teachers construct a curriculum that contributes to the school's academic mission through cross-disciplinary themes and facilitates the health and well-being of students through quality instruction in developmentally appropriate physical activity.

Physical Education Teachers' Beliefs

Physical education teachers must believe in the value of physical education to sustain enthusiasm and motivation throughout their careers. The five value orientations, described earlier in this chapter, influence teachers' decisions about content in physical education. Teachers also have beliefs or a sense of efficacy about their own competence and the value of their work (Tannehill et al., 1994). Their sense of self-efficacy may include their ability to teach particular activities, work with certain types of students, or teach using different strategies. Teachers also have specific beliefs or expectations for students. They may direct these expectations toward particular students or toward groups of students, such as neighborhood groups. Teachers may have expectations for student achievement that are helpful in structuring interesting and challenging activities (Ennis, 1999). They also may under- or overestimate a student's potential, perhaps because of his or her size (e.g., too short, overweight), limiting that student's opportunity to be successful.

Peer Group Beliefs

Peer group beliefs about physical education may directly affect students' comfort level and willingness to participate in physical activity. Adolescent students are particularly concerned about being accepted by their peer group. Peer groups can form subcultures or cliques that have their own understandings, dress, and language (Wentzel, 1991). Teachers and coaches often address this need for affiliation by organizing teams and clubs (Siedentop, 1994). Students also are motivated to enhance their performance so that they can join the jump-rope team or the soccer club. Although teams and clubs provide a positive opportunity for students to affiliate with others, other group situations may not be socially positive or productive. The values of the groups may be inconsistent with the goals and activities of the physical education class. In extreme cases, students' disruptive behavior influences classroom climate, negating the positive aspects of the program (Wehlage et al., 1989).

Peer group pressures affect students in unique ways. Friends or rivals may influence students positively with creative ideas or negatively through verbal or physical intimidation (Ennis, 1996b). Many students find it almost impossible to ignore peer demands. They feel that they must comply with the group's wishes or be isolated from peer group support. Teachers may be unwilling or unable to convince students to participate in an activity when the group has decided that the activity is not interesting (Ennis, 1994b).

Students' Beliefs

Students also have strong beliefs about and expectations for physical education (Tannehill & Zakrajsek, 1993). They may enter the class with prior experiences that influence their willingness to engage physically and cognitively in the activities (see Stinson, 1993, for examples from high school dance education). They also have their own expectations for performance. Some students believe that they are physically talented and cannot wait to demonstrate their skills. Others feel that they are not skilled or cannot learn skills, and they hesitate or even refuse to participate in physical activity (Martinek & Griffith, 1994). Students also value some skills more than they do others. Valued skills are usually those that they feel successful performing or those that their peer or ethnic group values. Students have beliefs about the physical educator's role in structuring recreational or educational experiences. They may simply want to play the game and avoid instructional drills. Others hope that instruction can help them be better performers, enhancing their status in the peer group.

School Contexts (Inner Circle)

The two outside circles in this model apply to the role of context (outside circle) and values (second circle) in the curriculum decision-making process. Of course, these two constructs continuously and dynamically interact, shaping and reshaping each other.

The curriculum plan represents a blueprint of school district and teacher beliefs with activities planned to facilitate student learning within a particular school and class context. Teachers often base their teaching practices on what works successfully within specific classes. The belief that a unit or lesson must "work" (Richardson, 1992) within a context to be considered successful reflects the influence of context on teachers' efforts to plan and implement lessons. A key ingredient in lesson success is student responses to the content and the extent to which they are willing to participate. The inner circle of the values-context model demonstrates the compounded influences of the outer circles on the pedagogical elements in the curriculum plan, teacher practices, and student decisions within physical education.

Curricular Plans

Effective curricular plans are sensitive to community, school, family, teacher, and student values and characteristics. Although school districts are making concerted efforts to align curriculum plans with national, state, and local standards and outcomes, specific decisions regarding instructional tasks are still determined by teachers and reflect the opportunities and limitations found within the school. Curriculum developers and teachers can enhance the ability of the curriculum to facilitate and promote a warm climate by demonstrating sensitivity to students' needs and interests. The curriculum may include plans for an entire program, a year in that program, or units, themes, or lessons. The goals and activities within effective plans build progressively across lessons, units, and years, systematically enhancing student achievement. Curricular plans may vary considerably across school districts and individual schools based on the context and the participants' beliefs, influencing the curricular decision-making process.

Teacher Practices

Teacher practices including management, discipline, and teaching strategies may vary based on the teachers' value orientation, the content to be taught, and the students in their classes. Some content (e.g., weight training, wrestling, rock climbing, etc.) can be dangerous, and teachers should instruct in a direct, controlled manner to minimize injuries. This method also helps the teacher know immediately which students understand and can perform effectively. With other types of content (e.g., fitness, sport, or dance), creative thinking, cooperation, and leadership can be taught using methods that let students have more control over curricular and instructional decisions.

Richardson (1992) points out that a critical factor in teachers' decisions to select a particular curriculum approach or teaching strategy is the extent to which the plan or strategy "works." To work, a curriculum should fit within the context and the teachers' value orientation. It must also be acceptable to students, who may embrace or reject a program based on the extent to which it meets their expectations for physical education (Ennis, 1995, 1996b). The curriculum should fulfill their need for knowledge about movement, sport, and exercise, and it must be sensitive to them as individuals and be socially acceptable to their peer group. If students do not believe that they can participate successfully in a curriculum, some will respond by simply choosing not to take part (Ennis, 1994a). In other classes, students may feel that the program is enjoyable and exciting and be quite willing to respond positively. Often, an interesting, well-sequenced curriculum is a teacher' best management tool, ensuring student on-task behavior in activities they find meaningful.

Students' Responses

Students' responses to situations or issues are often the catalyst for teacher-initiated change in the curriculum plan and teaching strategies (Chen, 1996; Ennis & McCauley,

2002; Erickson & Shultz, 1992). For example, as students become more aware of the importance of healthy lifestyles, they are more interested in content about fitness and nutrition. They are more willing to engage in vigorous activities and to set and meet personal fitness and nutrition goals. Students also are constantly responding to the social context in schools and in physical education (Carlson & Hastie, 1997). When other students confront them, they often feel they must defend themselves to avoid future problems (Ennis et al., 1997). Teachers who monitor the level of student conflict in their classes can detect rising feelings of aggressiveness resulting, for example, in verbal harassment of low-skilled students. Teachers may choose to make changes in their curriculum that require students to work together positively to be successful (Ennis et al., 1999; Siedentop, 1994). Teachers and students can measure achievement as a group score, for example, focusing on the teams' ability to work cooperatively. Teachers respond daily to changes in the context and students' responses to school situations. They should continue to monitor the changing environment and modify their program to match students' constantly changing needs and interests (Chen, 1996).

Learning (Center Circle)

Student learning is the focus of the curriculum planning and teaching process. All participants in the school have a direct responsibility to contribute to the learning process. Each circle presented in the model represents critical components necessary for learning. Administrative and parental support is critical when creating a positive environment for student learning. They can encourage students and peer groups to take responsibility for mentally and physically preparing themselves to learn. Students can actively influence the learning process and facilitate effective teaching through responsive behavior.

Although some students learn because they are interested and excited about the subject matter of physical education, other students need help to value physical activity (Chen, 1998; Ennis, 1998a). Teachers can encourage student learning by selecting content that is interesting and meaningful to them and can help students make connections between the content and their lives. For example, some students may not realize how crucial physical activity is for a healthy life. Teachers can help them understand how activity promotes health and can promote learning by presenting content using teaching styles that involve students actively and directly in the learning process. This approach helps students organize the content and use it immediately in their lives. Teachers also promote learning by controlling or managing the instructional setting so that every student has the opportunity to participate. Teachers further foster learning by monitoring student progress on important content goals. Students need to understand what they are expected to learn, and they should be held accountable for learning. When teachers grade students solely on dress and participation, they trivialize the knowledge base of physical education. Students are more likely to value physical education when teachers hold them accountable for learning content that *they* believe is valuable and meaningful in their lives.

The complexity in the educational environment demonstrated in the values-context model is a major issue when designing the curricular scope and sequence. Context, values, and beliefs interact dynamically, placing demands on curriculum developers for both sensitivity and order. Historically, physical education curriculum has reflected a series of isolated activities and tasks that involved physical moving, but it may not have helped students understand and value the importance of physical activity. Current efforts to design educational physical education programs focus on achieving a sense of coherence that resonates meaningfully within the lives of students.

STRIVING FOR COHERENCE

Teachers' and administrators' educational beliefs and goals for student learning and students' diverse interests often work at cross-purposes, negatively affecting student learning. Designing a curriculum that students perceive to be meaningful and that is consistent with the educational goals of educators and the community is a challenging but not impossible task. James Beane (1995) defines a coherent curriculum as "one that holds together, that makes sense as a whole; and its parts, whatever they are, are unified and connected by the sense of the whole" (p. 3). Coherence or a sense of interconnectedness is an essential element of an effective and worthwhile curriculum. Connection is achieved when content is selected (scope) and sequenced consistently to reflect the local context and participants' values. This connectedness is evident both internally among physical education content components and externally through disciplinary connections to the academic content and mission of the school. Similarly, student and community perceptions of curricular relevance and connection to practical lived experience also shape evaluation of coherence. In a coherent curriculum, topics flow smoothly from one to the next with current knowledge serving as a foundation for the understanding of new, more complex information. In a coherent curriculum, students understand why the content is useful, interesting, and immediately relevant in their lives.

Of course, no one would purposely set out to design an incoherent curriculum! Unfortunately, when content is not connected internally and sequenced cumulatively, it cannot help students build new knowledge on previously learned knowledge in educational sequences essential for student learning. No one would purposely teach content that does not build progressively to provide breadth and depth of student learning. And surely no teacher would purposefully select content that some students find irrelevant, meaningless, and alien to their interests. . . . Or would they?

How Content Is Selected for Physical Education Programs

Think for a moment about content taught in many physical education programs in the United States. Do these programs include ill-advised content such as low-organized games (e.g., dodgeball, kickball) and unmodified team sports (e.g., soccer, volleyball, basketball) that are selected based on the season of the year, the availability of facilities, or the teacher's interest and enjoyment (Ennis, 1996a)? How likely is it in a secondary physical education curriculum that students will begin in the fall with soccer, flag football, or ultimate Frisbee. As the weather turns cooler, classes move inside for basketball, floor hockey, volleyball, or team handball. Later come the "spring" sports of tennis, lacrosse, and softball. Are these sports selected because they present the "knowledge of most worth," enabling students to participate in physical activity for a lifetime? Are these sports sequenced educationally to add advanced knowledge to foundational knowledge and skills learned in previous units (Ennis, 1999)?

If our educational goal is to build new knowledge on current knowledge, what sport unit should be taught following the soccer unit? What sport best prepares students to be successful and skilled at the complex game of volleyball? Currently, many secondary (and upper elementary) physical education programs require students to lurch from sport to sport with little emphasis on cumulatively building knowledge and skills for deep learning. How skillful do students become in mathematics if they are required to jump from fractions to geometry, to algebra, to statistics every three weeks? In subject areas that are educationally sequenced, teachers plan lessons so that students develop a strong foundation of skills and knowledge, progressively building new information on this foundation leading to success. In physical education, once students have completed the volleyball unit, they are now ready to build on those skills to be successful in . . . what? Unfortunately, limited facilities in many public schools designed to accommodate athletic teams and sport seasons make it difficult for teachers to sequence sports from an educational rather than a seasonal or facility standpoint.

Do students notice? Do they recognize the inherent incoherence in many elementary and secondary physical education curricula? Interviews with students (Cothran & Ennis, 1999; Graham et al., 1993) in a number of schools in the United States and internationally provide clear evidence that students do not find physical education coherent, relevant, or meaningful. Further, administrators, teachers, parents, and students perceive little value for physical education programs and criticize physical education for failing to contribute to the academic mission of the school.

What Makes a Coherent Curriculum

Beane (1995) proposed that a coherent curriculum includes a sense of reason and connectedness. Specifically, he suggested four factors that contribute to curricular coherence:

- Creating and maintaining visible connections between purposes and everyday learning experiences so that students and others who come in contact with the curriculum can readily acknowledge its current relevance and worth
- Creating contexts that organize and connect learning experiences so that students can understand how knowledge accumulates and deepens as they learn
- Striving to select and design curricula based on topics and issues that enhance the sense of content purpose and meaning for young people
- Including extensive opportunities for students to explore fully how they and others make sense of experiences (p. 7-9)

Coherence is probably an ideal that a curriculum never fully achieves. More likely it is a goal that teachers as curriculum developers move toward within the process of designing and implementing courses and programs that students eagerly seek and willingly participate in. Clearly, the issue of coherence is multilayered, involving the experiences of many diverse learners, teachers, and administrators within the school, parents and siblings within families, and supportive individuals within the community.

Developing Curricular Coherence

Note that the concept of curricular coherence conveys more than simple consistency or alignment with standards or objectives. Instead, a coherent curriculum seeks unity not only with other content but also with those who will experience it (Beane, 1995). Coherence is thus both a philosophical and a methodological issue that is of great relevance in the quest to enhance the value and relevance of physical activity for all students.

One way that physical educators are enhancing program coherence is through the design and implementation of curricular models that facilitate the development of content topics and themes (e.g., Griffin et al., 1997; Hellison et al., 2000; Siedentop, 1994). Models can help students understand both the rationale for physical activity tasks (why questions) and help teachers master pedagogical skills necessary to convey this information effectively to learners. Curricular models represent efforts to design coherent programs based on a specific theme or content. In chapters 11 through 13 of this text, curriculum developers discuss the major assumptions, goals, teaching strategies, and contributions of their models. Before selecting a particular model as the curriculum for physical education, administrators and teachers should examine the model developer's philosophy carefully to evaluate its coherence and applicability for students. The content of the model should reflect the knowledge that the community perceives to be of most worth for students within that grade or age group. The assumptions about the content and teaching should be consistent with the community's collective beliefs about what and how students should learn. From an instructional standpoint the model should present a clear plan for how the content should be sequenced and presented to students to facilitate learning.

Developers of coherent curriculum begin with a careful analysis of the knowledge of most worth to their students in specific locations or contexts. Context considerations are crucial to curricular success because the context in which students live shapes their interests, abilities, and attitudes. Teachers' selection of content topics, themes, and concepts should be consistent with the disciplinary knowledge base. Teachers can then sequence topics to provide a firm foundation of terminology, basic concepts, principles, and performance skills essential for learning and students' perceptions of success. Once students understand the knowledge foundation, teachers can use it as a solid platform on which to build and deepen skills and knowledge. A coherent curriculum appears connected both on paper and in the eyes of students. It includes clear transitions from topic to topic and directly teaches students how topics, skills, concepts, and principles are related. Coherence is essential to ensure the educational integrity of physical education and enhance the value of physical education and physical activity to diverse students nationwide.

IMPLICATIONS FOR PRACTICE

1. Although a curriculum can take many forms, it traditionally consists of topics, described as a scope arranged in a specific educational sequence designed to enhance learning.

2. The key question that curriculum developers should ask is "What knowledge is of most worth to my students in this setting?"

3. Educational metaphors can make philosophically abstract constructs, such as curriculum, comprehensible, thus facilitating understanding and support by students, parents, and community members.

4. Value orientations are educational belief systems that guide educators' decisions about content, instruction, and evaluation.

5. The educational context includes diverse participants' beliefs and perceptions, the physical structure of the setting, and the unique characteristics of the local community.

6. The educational context significantly influences educational decisions, facilitating or constraining student learning.

7. The educational context and participants' educational beliefs directly affect curricular complexity.

8. Curriculum coherence describes the extent to which content topics are perceived to build progressively from simple to complex understanding and performance.

9. The concept of curricular coherence goes beyond alignment with standards to include (a) disciplinary connectedness within the subject area, (b) interdisciplinary connectedness to other subject areas, and (c) student perceptions of content relevance and connectedness to significant aspects of their lives.

REFERENCES

Allison, P.C., Pissanos, B.W., Turner, A.P., & Law, D.R. (2000). Preservice physical educators' epistemologies of skillfulness. *Journal of Teaching in Physical Education, 19*, 141-161.

Banks, J.A. (1993). Multicultural education: Characteristics and goals. In J.A. Banks & C.A.M. Banks (Eds.), *Multicultural understanding* (pp. 1-28). Boston: Allyn & Bacon.

Beane, J.A. (1995). Introduction: What is a coherent curriculum? In J.A. Bean (Ed.), *Toward a coherent curriculum* (pp. 1-15). Alexandria, VA: Association for Supervision and Curriculum Development.

Broudy, H.S. (1982). What knowledge is of most worth? *Educational Leadership, 39*, 574-578.

Carlson, T.B., & Hastie, P.A. (1997). The student social system within sport education. *Journal of Teaching in Physical Education, 16*, 176-195.

Chen, A. (1996). Student interest in activities in a secondary physical education curriculum: An analysis of student subjectivity. *Research Quarterly for Exercise and Sport, 67*, 424-432.

Chen, A. (1998). Meaningfulness in physical education: A description of high school students' conceptions. *Journal of Teaching in Physical Education, 17*, 285-306.

Chen, A. (1999). The impact of social change on inner-city high school physical education: An analysis of a teacher's experiential account. *Journal of Teaching in Physical Education, 18*, 312-335.

Corbin, C.B., & Lindsey, R. (2002). *Fitness for life* (Updated 4th ed.). Champaign, IL: Human Kinetics.

Cothran, D.J., & Ennis, C.D. (1998). Curricula of mutual worth: Comparisons of students' and teachers' curricular goals. *Journal of Teaching in Physical Education, 17*, 307-326.

Cothran, D.J., & Ennis, C.D. (1999). Alone in a crowd: Meeting students' needs for relevance and connection in urban high school physical education. *Journal of Teaching in Physical Education, 18*, 234-247.

Donnelly, F.C., Helion, J., & Fry, F. (1999). Modifying teacher behavior to promote critical thinking in K–12 physical education. *Journal of Teaching in Physical Education, 18*, 199-215.

Eccles, J.S., & Harold, R.D. (1993). Parent-school involvement during the adolescent years. *Teachers College Record, 94*, 568-587.

Eccles, J.S., & Midgley, C. (1990). Changes in academic motivation and self perception during early adolescence. In R. Montemayor, G.R. Adams, & T.P. Gullotta (Eds.), *From childhood to adolescence: A transitional period?* (pp.134-155). Newbury Park, CA: Sage.

Eisner, E.W. (1992). Curriculum ideologies. In P.W. Jackson (Ed.), *Handbook of research on curriculum* (pp. 302-326). New York: Macmillan.

Ennis, C.D. (1990). Discrete thinking skills in two teachers' physical education classes. *Elementary School Journal, 91*, 473-487.

Ennis, C.D. (1992). Curriculum theory as practiced: Case studies of operationalized value orientations. *Journal of Teaching in Physical Education, 11*, 358-375.

Ennis, C.D. (1994a). Urban secondary teachers' value orientations: Social goals for teaching. *Teaching and Teacher Education, 10*, 109-120.

Ennis, C.D. (1994b). Urban secondary teachers' value orientations: Delineating curricular goals for social responsibility. *Journal of Teaching in Physical Education, 13*, 163-179.

Ennis, C.D. (1995). Teachers' responses to noncompliant students: The realities and consequences of a negotiated curriculum. *Teaching and Teacher Education, 11*, 445-460.

Ennis, C.D. (1996a). Students' experiences in sport-based physical education: [More than] apologies are necessary. *Quest, 48*, 453-456.

Ennis, C.D. (1996b). When avoiding confrontation leads to avoiding content: Disruptive students' impact on curriculum. *Journal of Curriculum and Supervision, 10*, 145-162.

Ennis, C.D. (1998a). The context of a culturally unresponsive curriculum: Constructing ethnicity and gender within a contested terrain. *Teaching and Teacher Education, 14*, 749-760.

Ennis, C.D. (1998b). Shared expectations: Creating a joint vision for urban schools. In J. Brophy (Ed.), *Advances in Research on Teaching, 7*, 151-182.

Ennis, C.D. (1999). Creating a culturally relevant curriculum for disengaged girls. *Sport, Education, and Society, 4*, 31-50.

Ennis, C.D., & Chen, A. (1993). Domain specifications and content representativeness of the revised Value Orientation Inventory. *Research Quarterly for Exercise and Sport, 64*, 436-446.

Ennis, C.D., Cothran, D.J., Davidson, K.S., Loftus, S.J., Owens, L., Swanson, L., & Hopsicker, P. (1997). Implementing curriculum within a context of fear and disengagement, *Journal of Teaching in Physical Education, 17*, 52-71.

Ennis, C.D., & McCauley, M.T. (2002). Creating urban classrooms communities worthy of trust. *Journal of Curriculum Studies, 34*, 149-172.

Ennis, C.D., Solmon, M.A., Satina, B., Loftus, S.J., Mensch, J., & McCauley, M.T. (1999). Creating a sense of family in urban schools using the "Sport for Peace" curriculum. *Research Quarterly for Exercise and Sport, 70*, 273-285.

Erickson, F., & Shultz, J. (1992). Students' experience of the curriculum. In P.W. Jackson (Ed.), *Handbook of research on curriculum* (pp. 465-485). New York: Macmillan.

Graham, G., Hopple, C., Manross, M., & Sitzman, T. (1993). Novice and experienced children's physical education teachers: Insights into their situational decision making. *Journal of Teaching in Physical Education, 12,* 197-214.

Griffin, L.L, Mitchell, S., & Oslin, J. (1997). *Teaching tactics in games and sports.* Champaign, IL: Human Kinetics.

Griffin, L.L., & Placek, J.H. (2001). The understanding and development of learners' domain-specific knowledge: Introduction. In L.L. Griffin & J.H. Placek (Eds.), [Monograph], *Journal of Teaching in Physical Education, 20,* 299-301.

Halas, J. (2001). Engaging alienated youth in physical education: An alternative program with lessons for the traditional class. *Journal of Teaching in Physical Education, 21,* 267-286.

Hastie, P.A., Sanders, S.W., & Rowland, R.S. (1999). Where good intentions meet harsh realities: Teaching large classes in physical education, *Journal of Teaching in Physical Education, 18,* 227-289.

Hellison, D., Cutforth, N., Kallusky, J., Martinek, T., Parker, M., & Stiehl, J. (2000). *Youth development and physical activity: Linking universities and communities.* Champaign, IL: Human Kinetics.

Jewett, A.E., Bain, L.L., & Ennis, C.D. (1995). *The curriculum process in physical education.* Madison, WI: Brown and Benchmark.

Jewett, A.E., & Ennis, C.D. (1990). Ecological integration as a value orientation for curricular decision making. *Journal of Curriculum and Supervision, 5,* 120-131.

Jewett, A.E., & Mullan, M.R. (1977). *Curriculum design: Purposes and processes in physical education teaching and learning.* Reston, VA: American Alliance for Health, Physical Education, and Recreation.

Kantor, H., & Brenzel, B. (1992). Urban education and the "truly disadvantaged": The historical roots of the contemporary crisis, 1945–1990. *Teachers College Record, 94,* 278-314.

Kirk, D., Burgess-Limerick, R., Kiss, M., Lahey, J., & Penney, D. (1999). *Senior physical education: An integrated approach.* Champaign, IL: Human-Kinetics.

Kirk, D., & MacPhail, A, (2002). Teaching games for understanding and situated learning: Rethinking the Bunker-Thorpe Model. *Journal of Teaching in Physical Education, 21,* 177-192.

Kliebard, H.M. (1972). Metaphorical roots of curriculum design. *Teachers College Record, 73,* 403-404.

Kullina, P.H., Silverman, S., & Keating, X.D. (2000). Relationship between teachers' belief systems and actions toward teaching physical activity and fitness. *Journal of Teaching in Physical Education, 19,* 206-221.

Lambert, L.T. (1999). *Standards-based assessment of student learning: A comprehensive approach.* Reston, VA: National Association for Sport and Physical Education.

Lawson, H. (1998). Rejuvenating, reconstituting and transforming physical education to meet the needs of vulnerable children, youth and families. *Journal of Teaching in Physical Education, 18,* 2-25.

Malina, R.M., & Bouchard, C. (1990). *Growth and physical activity.* Champaign, IL: Human Kinetics.

Martinek, T.J., & Griffith, J.B. (1994). Learned helplessness in physical education: A developmental study of causal attributions and task persistence. *Journal of Teaching in Physical Education, 13,* 108-122.

Maslow, A.H. (1979). Humanistic education. *Journal of Humanistic Psychology, 19,* 13-27.

Mohnson, B. (1998). *Concepts of physical education: What every student needs to know.* Reston, VA: National Association for Sport and Physical Education.

Napper-Owens, G.E., Kovar, S.K., Ermler, K.L., & Mehrhof, J.H. (1999). Curricula equity in required ninth-grade physical education, *Journal of Teaching in Physical Education, 19,* 2-21.

National School Boards Association. (1993). *Violence in the schools.* Alexandria, VA: Author.

Nilges, L.M. (1998). I thought only fairy tales had supernatural power: A radical feminist analysis of Title IX in physical education. *Journal of Teaching in Physical Education, 17,* 172-194.

Noddings, N. (1992). *The challenge to care in schools: An alternative approach to education.* New York: Teachers College Press.

Oakes, J. (1992). Can tracking research inform practice? Technical, normative, and political considerations. *Educational Researcher, 21*(4), 12-21.

Ormell, C. (1996). Eight metaphors of education, *Educational Research, 38,* 67-75.

Pajares, M.F. (1992). Teachers' beliefs and educational research: Cleaning up a messy construct. *Review of Educational Research, 62,* 307-332.

Peshkin, A., & White, C.J. (1990). Four Black American students: Coming of age in a multiethnic high school. *Teachers College Record, 92,* 21-38.

Polman, J.L. (2000). *Designing project-based science: Connecting learners through guided inquiry.* New York: Teachers College Press.

Richardson, V. (1992). Significant and worthwhile change in teaching practice. *Educational Researcher, 19*(7), 10-18.

Roberts, D.A., & Östman, L. (Eds.). (1998). *Problems of meaning in science curriculum.* New York: Teacher's College Press.

Rønholt, H. (2002). "It's only the sissies . . .": Analysis of teaching and learning processes in physical education: A contribution to the hidden curriculum. *Sport, Education and Society, 7,* 25-36.

Rovegno, I., & Bandhauer, D. (1997). Psychological dispositions that facilitated and sustained the development of knowledge of a constructivist approach to physical education. *Journal of Teaching in Physical Education, 16,* 136-154.

Schrag, F. (1992). Conceptions of knowledge. In P.W. Jackson (Ed.), *Handbook of research on curriculum* (pp. 268-301). New York: Macmillan.

Schubert, W.H. (1990). The questions of worth as central to curricular empowerment. In J.T. Sears & J.D. Marshall (Eds.), *Teaching and thinking about curriculum: Critical inquiries* (pp. 211-227). New York: Teachers College Press.

Siedentop, D. (Ed.). (1994). *Sport education: Quality PE through positive sport experiences.* Champaign, IL: Human Kinetics.

Solmon, M.A., Worthy, T., & Carter, J.A. (1993). The interaction of school context and role identity of first-year teachers. *Journal of Teaching in Physical Education, 12,* 313-328.

Stinson, S.W. (1993). Meaning and value: Reflections on what students say about school. *Journal of Curriculum and Supervision, 8,* 216-238.

Talbert, J.E., McLauglin, M.W., & Rowan, B. (1993). Understanding context effects on secondary school teaching. *Teachers College Record, 95,* 45-68.

Tannehill, D., Romar, J.E., O'Sullivan, M., England, K., & Rosenberg, D. (1994). Attitudes toward physical education: Their impact on how physical education teachers make sense of their work. *Journal of Teaching in Physical Education, 13,* 407-421.

Tannehill, D., & Zakrajsek, D. (1993). Student attitudes toward physical education: A multicultural study. *Journal of Teaching in Physical Education, 13,* 78-84.

Treanor, L., Graber, K., Housner, L., & Wiegand, R. (1998). Middle school students' perceptions of coeducational and same-sex physical education classes. *Journal of Teaching in Physical Education, 18,* 43-56.

Treasure, D.C., & Roberts, G.C. (2001). Students' perceptions of the motivational climate, achievement beliefs, and satisfaction in physical education. *Research Quarterly for Exercise and Sport, 72,* 165-175.

Wehlage, G.G., Rutter, R.A., Smith, G.A., Lesko, N., & Fernandez, T.R. (1989). *Reducing the risk: Schools as communities of support.* New York: Falmer Press.

Wentzel, K. (1991). Social competence at school: Relation between social responsibility and academic achievement. *Review of Educational Research, 61,* 1-24.

CHAPTER EIGHT

STANDARDS-BASED PROGRAM DESIGN: CREATING A CONGRUENT GUIDE FOR STUDENT LEARNING

Leslie T. Lambert

The educational standards movement is on center stage. A cast of relentless and vociferous champions and critics tout the relative merits and evils of standards as an organizing framework for educational programs. From external agency accreditation processes to politically motivated debates, standards are passed around boardrooms and statehouses like footballs spiraling toward one goal line or the other—one, the latest elixir to cure education's woes; the other, the surefire demise of public education. The fact is that standards themselves are rather inert. How their use is conceptualized and used as a blueprint in the program design process, however, is not.

Standards can become a stable fulcrum for program design that serves to guide the creation of a powerful, synergistic educational framework that can result in demonstrable student learning; likewise, standards can be used egregiously in program design and grossly miss the mark. So, standards themselves are not at all the issue; rather, the manner in which they are used (or not used) in a well-conceived design process is what is key.

In this chapter I will focus on the creation of standards-based program design in education. I will offer a view of important theoretical and applied perspectives about the use of standards in designing educational programs aimed toward creating a functional framework to guide a cohesive and coherent process leading toward student learning. In the first edition of this book the focus of this chapter was on goals and outcomes as the epicenter of curriculum design. In this revision my intent is to provide a wider-angled lens. Certainly, goals and outcomes will have their place, but a perspective for standards-based program design, with learners and learning being the nucleus, is the focus of this current edition. As we specifically consider physical education program design, we will use the Standards for Physical Education of the National Association for Sport and Physical Education (NASPE) (1995).

SEEKING CONGRUENCE AND UNDERSTANDING OF THE STANDARDS-BASED DESIGN PROCESS

Standards in education are nothing new (Eisner, 1995), but the current iteration of educational standards, unfolding and gaining momentum for over 15 years, is different in important ways. Now, a more holistic, organic conception guides the use of standards as the grounding point for a powerful lever of program design. This lever—the process of integrating and merging learning goals, curriculum design, instructional design, and assessment design components into a singular, confluent whole—is what I term the *standards-based program design process.* Though standards themselves have been part of educational processes for quite a while, the conceptualization of a sound, congruent standards-based program design has not—and that is the focus of this chapter.

Thinking About Standards-Based Program Design: Building on Solid Ground

Standards-based design is like any other form of program architecture. It can yield coherent and thoughtful educational programs or haphazard and superficial ones. Standards-based program design processes can either be facilitative and transformative in providing direction for powerful program design, or stifling, ineffective, and benign, yielding no positive effects on student learning. Done well and with a keen eye to sound, conceptual program development, the process can provide a coherence and continuity of program purpose unique among other forms of program design. Done poorly, it can be notably rigid and awkward, particularly if used in a mechanistic manner to focus programs on singular learning targets for all students or reduced to a hollow, drill-and-practice, "teach to the test" attempt for creating educational programs.

For many of us, the thought of an organic, holistic way of creating programs does not come naturally because we have learned to plan and implement educational programs in linear ways. Our operational, day-to-day practice of program design is often limited to rote and scripted creation of units of particular types of content (e.g., a sport, dance form, personal fitness pursuit). We organize a series of lessons focused on the content and then effect a transition (often a hasty transition, at that!) to the "real" activity. Following this ubiquitous and mechanical progression, we sometimes, but probably less often than we realize, administer an assessment of sorts—a skill test, a written test, or a student project. We naturally conform to the normative process of putting content for content's sake first in our thinking and planning, not student learning. We assume that learning is occurring, but alas, often it isn't. Indeed, one needs merely to cast a casual eye to the pedagogical literature that guides "best practices" to discover that we have researched and conceptualized the act of teaching far better than we have the act of learning!

Therein lies a deep, often subliminal, and unconscious compulsion to focus only on what we do as teachers without regard to true teaching effectiveness—the results (or lack thereof) of student learning. As long as our focus is primarily upon what we teach (content) and on what we as teachers do (methods) and not on student learning, we will continue to focus our lens, in large measure, on the wrong thing. Don't misinterpret this to say that best practices of teaching do not matter; quite the contrary. The "best" best practice should be the primacy of viewing all our teaching practices and decisions through the lens of effecting the greatest depth and breadth of student learning possible. Our ultimate aim should be to determine what content and pedagogical strategies would be most helpful in enhancing students' understanding and ability to act with and demonstrate their understanding.

Despite attempts to think differently, we tend to fall into the unconscious instrumentality of creating and then "covering the curriculum," and we do not conceive of teaching and learning as a fluid, flowing process that is necessarily nonlinear, nonscripted, contextual, and often idiosyncratic. Simultaneously, we lack a sense that the history of the educational pattern just described has repeated itself over and over for well over a century (Tyack & Cuban, 1995). This practice has left us with a legacy of good intentions, nice curriculum guides, nifty activities that are "fun" but often have little or no connection to students' learning important things. As we reflect on the countless numbers of workshops and conferences we have attended and educational materials we have perused for new ideas, has our goal been to motivate learning or to motivate interest in the activity so students will have fun? Although we certainly want students to enjoy what they are doing—why else would they be motivated to try or persist?—our primary goal should be that they enjoy and engage in something worth learning.

Standards-Based Program Design: What It Is and What It Isn't

The term *standards-based program design* is used comprehensively and subsumes all educational programming components—goal setting, curriculum design, instructional design, assessment design, and student learning outcomes. Standards-based program design can help delineate and give energy to focused, compelling, generative, and meaningful learning experiences for students.

What Standards-Based Program Design Is

Standards-based program design is a process for designing educational programs toward the end of student learning—what I like to think of as "truly important learning". Good design transcends the trivial and focuses on the major ideas and issues we must face as individuals and as a civilization. An effective design process clarifies, integrates, and activates the components of educational program planning:

1. The establishment of meaningful student learning goals to guide the selection of salient content that, when arrayed developmentally, will aid students and teachers in accomplishing the learning goals (curriculum design)
2. The creation of assessments that will be used at strategic points in the learning cycle to engage students and require them to demonstrate what they know and can do with what they know (assessment design) (Lambert, 1999)
3. The thoughtful consideration and crafting of decisions about instructional methods and strategies that are congruent with the desired learning goals and that facilitate students' individual and nuanced performance related to the goals (instructional design)

In essence, standards-based program design aims to set compelling student learning goals and content aimed at the realization of the goals, to develop myriad ways of engaging students developmentally in the process of learning (instruction), and to design ways to help stimulate and capture what students have learned through real and relevant demonstrations of what they know and can do with what they know and understand.

Done well, a standards-based program design process can yield a confluent, learning-focused articulation of all these program components. Student learning goals and curriculum design are framed by and lift up to valued content and process standards. Assessments are conceived of and designed to allow the student to demonstrate his or her understanding of concepts and principles and what he or she can do to apply these concepts and principles to valued and real life situations. Further, assessment is used not as an "I gotcha!" strategy but as a way to help students find learning targets (e.g., gaining useful knowledge, skills, and abilities and being able to apply them in real ways), continue to improve, and be responsible for their own learning. Instructional design is created with an eye toward both progression and congruence with what students will need to demonstrate during performance-based assessment and application of concepts. Instructional strategies aim to motivate and engage learners in ways that are active and interactive with the content, the instructional environment, and with fellow learners.

What Standards-Based Program Design Isn't

First, standards-based program design is not a prescriptive methodology requiring all students to learn at the same time, in the same way, or even at the same depth. It is not the process of being stuck in the mud of narrow and instrumental thinking (Gardner, 1991), focusing on mechanical and shallow notions of what learning is instead of rich and compelling ones. Done poorly, standards-based design processes can be ineffectual and stifling of true learning and deep understanding (Wiggins & McTighe, 1998). When standards-based design processes are used in rote and mechanical ways (Gardner, 1991, 1999) or as the "big stick" of high-stakes testing (Kohn, 1999), such use is fraught with misconceptions and problems. Indeed, this understanding and use of standards leads to monolithic programs that are rigid, one-size-fits-all attempts to "standardize" the learning process—an oxymoron of enormous proportion! At state and federal levels, we note numerous examples in which standards are nothing more than another iteration of the efficiency model of education that has long hindered our progress in education (Cremin, 1961, 1990). In far too many cases, standards-based design has been used to homogenize and standardize what is, by nature, idiosyncratic, contextual, and personal—the phenomenon of learning.

As educational leaders we need to understand what constitutes good programs that focus on learning and how to put in action and communicate the use of standards-based design as a transformative tool that can make a difference for our students and for us as teachers. We need congruent and carefully crafted designs that can empower learning and learners; we do not need the cookie cutter, high-stakes "ball and chain" of standardization that piles on more content instead of inspiring learning. Let's take a look at a single standard and a couple of learning experiences that might illustrate what may result in either event.

Assume, for a moment, that we are discussing one of the NASPE (1995) physical education standards, say standard #4: "The physically educated person will achieve and maintain a health enhancing level of physical fitness." (Caveat: Please don't assume that program design proceeds from a single standard; good design does not. For simplicity and to illustrate this point, however, we will look at only one standard.) Based on this standard, what do students need to learn? In what period of time? At what depth? Knowing that students are different and that their needs and goals are different, how do we avoid a monolithic approach to assessment? How will students have options in demonstrating their abilities and understanding relative to this standard? How best could instructional design align with the learning goals and the content array created for this learning experience?

If I am a teacher in this situation, I have a number of options; in this example, we will explore just two. One option is to administer a standard physical fitness test to determine the relative performance of students based on the criteria. Either students achieve the criteria or they don't. Another option (and the one to which I subscribe) is to focus on the main student learning (not performance) goal: that students demonstrate their understanding of what health-enhancing physical activity is for them personally; that they understand and can apply important, age-appropriate content and concepts; that they apply the concepts to their personal improvement; that they demonstrate their understanding of how to use any personal fitness data point to learn about and understand the fitness component or concept and to self-assess their ability; that they can safely and intelligently lead a physically active lifestyle; and that they understand that scores and measures are *not* important but that persisting across their lives in daily, moderate physical activity *is* important. For teachers, our gestalt occurs when we truly understand and use the standards-based program design process as a powerful guide in structuring engaging learning experiences and not as a monolithic process for aiming students toward homogenous learning results.

THEORETICAL BASES FOR EDUCATIONAL PROGRAM DESIGN

Will the proverbial "Model T" of efficiency (Callahan, 1964), the prevailing and resilient model of education that emanates from behavioral foundations and beliefs about learning continue to define and dictate educational structure and function? What do I mean? We continue to tangle with the dominant model of a centralized, bureaucratic system of education, circa the late 19th and early 20th centuries, and it appears to be as robust and resilient as ever. Its direction was established—in fact, legalized!—and its staying power has transported it into the beginning decade of the 21st century. More often than not, our de facto purposes in most educational settings are efficiency and control, not learning. Yes, we talk about learning, but we usually structure our programs on an antiquated programmatic architecture (often on content-based, disciplinary mastery [Jewett, Bain, & Ennis, 1995]). Examining the theoretical bases for educational program design will help illuminate this point.

What do we know about the theoretical bases for creating educational programs focused on student learning? Let's start by defining learning. The literature offers many definitions of learning, but Shuell's (1986) view remains the most compelling for me. To synthesize and expand a bit on his definition, I like to think of learning as a process that leads to an enduring change in an individual's knowledge, skill, or behavior resulting from practice or experience. So, learning is a process that leads to a change in one's ability or abilities. What, then, do we know about creating educational programs that lead to learning? Two theoretical foundations for eliciting learning are firmly ensconced in the learning theory literature—the behavioral foundation that has been the resilient, normative model of education for well over a century, and the cognitive foundation of learning.

Behavioral Theory as a Foundation of Learning

Historically and to date, the study of learning has had a decidedly behavioral bent (Ebbinghaus, 1913). Rising from the late 1800s and continuing well into the 1900s (through the mid-1960s), the dominant view of education processes and structures emulated those of industry that had resulted from the writings of Frederick Taylor (1911/1967) on the theory of scientific management. The factory metaphor (e.g., production of a product)—see chapter 7 by Cathy Ennis for more on this topic—reigned mighty, and the model of control and efficiency was superimposed on the process of education with barely a blink. In this model, top-level administrators controlled middle-level administrators who controlled teachers who controlled students. The study of learning focused on the memorization of simple and rote elements and on the behavior of the learner. The learner was seen, metaphorically, as a machine, and the learner "produced" responses (e.g., learning) to stimuli (e.g., teaching).

This view of learning focuses on the learner as a rather passive responder to externally imposed factors. This theoretical lens views students as recipients and accumulators of knowledge, able to "learn" by listening to lectures, by reading, or by rote drill and practice of isolated, decontextualized skills. Rarely does the eye genuinely focus on learning. Instead, it stares intently and singularly toward the obsession with content ("I covered it yesterday. If you didn't get it, then something is wrong with you.") Progress and achievement are measured by the ability of students to repeat what they have heard or read or practiced. As a result, students develop fragmented, decontextualized, naive, and simplistic knowledge and abilities that lead to misconceptions, stereotypes, and oversimplification of complex and subtle phenomena (Gardner, 1991, 1999; Wiggins & McTighe, 1998).

As mentioned earlier, the behavioral conception of learning was in its heyday during the late 1800s through the mid-1900s. It gave rise to the elemental, objectives-based approach to curriculum design that led to homogenous instructional experiences and convergent learning expectations. All students were expected to be on the same page of a book, working on the same skill or skill component in the gym, and they were compared one to the other without regard for previous learning and ability or level of understanding. The program design process focused on technical questions of procedure and specificity, not on larger, desired student learning outcomes and on what was most valuable to learn (Apple, 1982). Results of this view of learning include programs based on tangible bits and pieces of content; skills demonstrated in isolation, repeated in isolation, and tested in isolation; instructional strategies not aligned with larger learning goals; and curricula structured elementally and linearly—piece by piece, unit by unit, grade by grade, subject by subject.

You may be thinking, "Well, that's how it is in X and Y schools today and they are using standards from NASPE and from their state framework!" and you would be right. Although standards and their use are now ubiquitous and persuasive, their formidable presence belies the incomplete understanding of how they can and should be used to change the teaching-learning dynamic. Often, when we really examine our practices, we find ourselves forcing old wine into new skins (Lambert, 2000). We go to workshops or conferences, or our school systems launch new initiatives aimed toward best practices. The new knowledge, skills, and best practices make sense, are grounded in solid theory, and appear to have worked to motivate student learning. We become excited, try the new ideas, and in short order, they "don't work with my kids." We have taken the new idea (say, using standards to design curriculum and instruction) as our new skins, and we have placed our old conceptions and practices and beliefs right in the middle (the proverbial old wine). We struggle to gain deeper perspective and to transform the teaching-learning equation, but the struggle is in vain, and the deeper perspective is elusive because of our shallow understanding. The ironfisted hold that the behavioral conception of learning has on education and educators should not be underestimated. This idea has been incredibly pervasive and resilient to change (despite compelling evidence that it is incomplete and ineffective as a single model of how learning occurs), and it has been perpetuated by the "you teach as you were taught" notion of pedagogy and by tenacious and often vested parties who attempt to maintain a (failing) monolithic, bureaucratic notion of educational structure and function. This model has deep, doggedly persistent roots, and despite reasonable, well-grounded attempts to forge a new direction of best practices, it prevails.

Another view of learning, however, gives rise to the powerful standards-based program design process. Although the behavioral foundation of learning was front and center in the early 1900s, another view of learning, the cognitive foundation of learning, was rearing its small but noticeable head. John Dewey's (1899/1990) ideas and theories during the early 1900s foreshadowed this emerging school of thought and led the way toward using a more complete, whole, and nuanced lens on why and how we learn. Dewey's protestations against the prevailing paradigm of "efficiency" that Frederick Taylor (1911/1967) and his disciples had applied to every conceivable human activity during the early 1900s had a remarkable staying power of its own (Callahan, 1964). Although his ideas were marginalized at the time and deemed unworthy of deep and lasting consideration at the acme of the scientific, reductionist era of efficiency, Dewey did not allow the dominant school of thought to go unchallenged; his ideas were grist for the mill and in time, about 50 years later, emerged triumphant. Dewey's (1916/1966) beliefs about the individual, about the formation of human intelligence, about democracy, and about learning began to be seen as a provocative and compelling construct. His viewpoint nudged educational thought away from the stifling, prescriptive industrial ideal that has subordinated the individual and personal learning to the product and the machine toward a more holistic, active, and organic view of learning. His ideal—the worth of the individual in a democratic society—found its way to the mainstream of educational thought.

Cognitive Theory as a Foundation of Learning

From the 1960s interest grew in the cognitive paradigm for studying the phenomenon of learning. Dewey's ideas finally gained recognition, and theorists began to question the validity of simple stimulus response, efficiency metaphors of learning, and the absurd belief in the relative passivity of the learner while learning (Bruner, 1957; Miller, Galanter, & Pribram, 1960). Conceptions of learning began to be seen as systematic, involving "mental processes and knowledge structures that can be inferred from behavioral indices" (Shuell, 1986, p. 414). Alas, the process of learning and the organic framework within which learning occurred became the focus of study, not just the behaviors that resulted from the interaction between the process and the organism.

Dewey's ideas and Piaget's work in the 1950s and 1960s are often cited as the major catalysts to a new conceptual genre of learning theory—that of the engaged learner and of higher-order cognitive functioning. Various applications of this school of thought were debated and shaped during what was termed the "progressive era" in education. The cognitive foundation of learning moved the focus of how to study learning away from monitoring the learner's behavior following a single instructional intervention toward seeking to understand the mind and how it functions. Scholars pursuing this avenue of research and thought were more interested in comprehension and understanding than in rote memorization, more attuned to interrelationships between and among elements than to single, fragmented elements, and less intrigued with the resultant behaviors of the learner than with the organic and intricate processes that resulted in learning. Not until the 1990s did a discernable shift occur toward applying and validating the cognitive foundation of learning in education. Now, in the first decade of the 21st century, we are just beginning to witness a long awaited sea change in the way educators are thinking about and designing educational programs and learning experiences for students. The process, however, is just beginning.

TILTING TOWARD CHANGE: SEEKING A CONFLUENT WHOLE

No doubt, this conception of learning is having a transformative effect as we witness the recent past and current episodes of educational reform. Although some are critical of the fleeting waves of educational reform, I see it differently. E.O. Wilson (1998), Jared

Diamond (1999), and Robert Wright (2000) have helped me gain a different lens. Wilson's ideas about the organic patterns and processes of nature and the wisdom of integrating knowledge toward the end of deep understanding—of consilience—has helped shape my thinking and practice relative to my constant reinvention and attempt to improve education (as I create and synthesize and imagine better ways to engage learners and to engage myself as a learner). The merging of ideas and concepts into wider patterns and frameworks for thinking, doing, and believing is what learning is all about, whether it be individual learning or an organization or other system attempting to learn and improve itself. Diamond's (1999) broad palate of interdisciplinary understanding and synthesis brought to bear on the providence of human societies and the circumstance of the human condition and Wright's (2000) sweeping thesis on the pattern and flow of human destiny have further enriched and broadened my thinking in this area.

Barriers to Change

In the last edition of this chapter in this book, I challenged Shuell's (1986) conclusion that those embracing a cognitive view of learning were in the mainstream of educational thinking. Perhaps now I can accede to his assessment—at least to the fact that it is gaining steam. This view undergirds the "true" standards-based design process. I am quick to add, however, that far too many remain who espouse a constructivist view in philosophy yet continue to practice a reductionist form of education. I am reminded in my own work how vigilant I must remain to avoid falling back to the seemingly innate. The patterns in which I was steeped die hard, but at least I feel I am in good company because most of us are in this place together! We have changed our minds and our rhetoric, but we are at various places in our journeys toward transforming our practice. Some of this is because of the natural lag between how we have learned to teach (most current teachers learned in the behavioral paradigm) and create programs based on "what we will teach" and not necessarily for "what students will learn." Another culprit for this paradox comes from the misused and misunderstood "untrue" standards-based processes that lead schools, school districts, and entire states toward the mechanistic, routinized travesty of "teaching to the test," often the high-stakes test. A third barrier to full realization of the cognitive foundation of learning is that for it to work in practice, a commitment must be made to overcome deeply ingrained beliefs, habits, and ways of doing things. Many of our educational structures (e.g., buildings, schedules, traditional curriculum) are not designed for or necessarily facilitative to good practice and pedagogy. Said another way, what we may understand and resonate with in theory is difficult to realize in practice because we must be aware of, rid ourselves of, and transcend some of the prevailing operational (and often unconscious) beliefs and practices.

As we continue to gain a deeper understanding of standards-based program design, we are realizing the key tenets on which the process is based. Figure 8.1 provides some of these tenets. Over a decade ago Ted Sizer (1991) stated it well, and it still applies today in far too many learning environments.

> Today, most of the teachers, rather than the students, "do the work." We present material and expect merely that students will display back to us that to which they have been exposed. Not surprisingly, the kids forget much of what they learned in a matter of months. They were not engaged. They did not have to invent on their own. They saw little meaning to their work. So, . . . we must change the curriculum from display-of-content to questions-that-ultimately-provoke-content. Press the kids to do their work, to solve the problems presented. The cost? It takes longer to provoke kids to learn for themselves than it does to deliver the content to them. (p. 33)

Emerging Conceptions of Learning

1. Students learn best when actively engaged, not when passively receiving information.

   Implications: Goals and outcomes need to be dynamic and confluent—full of energy. Goals and outcomes need to lead to students doing, not just receiving.

2. Students learn best and take responsibility for their learning when they have choices about how they learn and how they ultimately demonstrate their learning.

   Implications: Goals and outcomes need to be strong, clear guides for learning. After the goals and outcomes are set, however, students should have control of choices that lead to the accomplishment of the outcomes. Different students are motivated and learn best from different kinds of learning experiences. Demonstrations of learning should be seen as divergent, not convergent.

3. Students learn best when prior knowledge is connected to new learning. Learners find meaning as new knowledge intersects with prior knowledge.

   Implications: Learning experiences should build connections between previous learning and new learning.

4. Students learn best when learning experiences are relevant and situated in social and cultural contexts.

   Implications: Goals and outcomes need to reflect a "living laboratory" approach. Tasks should connect with home, community, workplace, and real life.

5. "Less is more."

   Implications: The Bauhaus notion should guide the creation of goals and outcomes. Less time and energy spent on a single element of learning gives way to more time for seeking the connections between and among elements.

6. The teacher is seen as an ally, a partner in learning (facilitator, "guide on the side," coach).

   Implications: Goals and outcomes should help set the tone for the learning environment and foster new, more powerful learning relationships among teachers and students.

FIGURE 8.1   Emerging conceptions of learning: implications for the development of goals and outcomes.

Learning in Context

As educators we need to cease our focus on facts and simplistic, isolated skills as learning outcomes. Please understand my point here. Facts are important, as is using proper progressions in skills. They are not enough, however, because they are not what is truly worth learning; they are not whole, meaningful manifestations of the knowledge, skills, and practices important to deeper understanding and persistence. The better we understand the power of a concept and the principles that relate to the concept, the better we will be at helping our students situate facts and skills in a context. Without a context within which the fact can reside and relate, it is easily forgotten and useless unless grounded in meaning (Tomlinson, 1995, 1999). The same is true for an isolated skill. A skill performed in a rote manner, out of its more complex context, is relatively useless unless it is a closed skill. Furthermore, facts and isolated skills rarely motivate and engage students. Real, relevant, complex applications and performances do. Theory, facts, and skills merge when there is a real world problem to which we can apply them. Devoid of such a context, the learning event is benign, pat, and lacks any memorable qualities. Although we need progressions of learning from simple to complex, the confluence of knowledge, skills, and practices in applied settings leads to true learning.

Take, for example, a particular event in the Olympic Games. How would you teach your students about the progressive physical training necessary for an athlete to excel at a world-class level in this event? You could tell them and show them through lecture and visual demonstrations about genetics and performance; about energy production in both anaerobic and aerobic metabolism; about muscle fiber types; about nutrition; about motor control; about the specifics of the biomechanical principles of velocity, trajectory, center of gravity; about sport psychology principles; and on and on. The knowledge base for these fields is vast. You could teach until you felt that you "covered" enough content. Students could take notes, ask questions, watch a video or two, try out their event, and then take a test (written or skill-related) at the end of the series of lessons. But you could take another course of action.

As the teacher, you could begin with a simple question to yourself: What's really worth learning here? When students forget everything else, what is important to understand and be able to do? What concepts? What principles? What facts? What abilities? What principles of training? How the athlete acquires skills and abilities and becomes among the best in the world at that set of skills and abilities? What types of sport psychology techniques might be helpful in such highly stressful situations? Whatever your question or questions, they may lead to allowing students to select one Olympic event and to consider and analyze the event based on whatever questions are most important—questions about skill development, sport psychology applications, and physical fitness development components the specific athlete might need to understand and apply in order to improve.

In the first example of the preceding discussion we see a "cover the content" style of teaching, and the students are relatively passive. This method is typical of much teaching, and we can easily liken it to the behaviorist conception of how we learn—we listen, we watch, and we repeat back and do what we heard and saw. In the second example students are much more engaged. They generate problems and solve them. Learning unfolds from the questions and emerges as the students seek solutions and understanding. The second approach is more typical of the types of teaching and learning that can emerge from the understanding one gains from a constructivist conception of learning—we interact, we pose questions, we experiment. Content and facts follow concepts and principles. We move from the question or the issue or the problem to the knowledge, skills, and abilities we need to find an answer, a response, or a solution or to learn a skill.

EDUCATIONAL PROGRAM DESIGN: THE PIECES OR THE WHOLE?

The two conceptions of learning previously discussed have had an effect on how we design educational programs. The first, objectives-based program design, emanated from behavioral theory as a foundation of learning, whereas the second, the standards-based program design process, derived from cognitive theory as a foundation of learning. Naturally, all program components (goals, curriculum, instructional methods, assessment methods) were seen as part of the larger conceptual framework—bits and pieces versus compelling wholes, measurable objectives versus performance and demonstration of learning. Let's delve briefly into each approach.

Objectives-Based Approach to Program Design

The objectives-based approach to program design has shaped our thinking about planning and implementing educational programs for quite some time. From policy setting to practice, behavioral assumptions have guided mainstream thought about teaching and learning. Historically, curriculum studies emerged from a need to create a systematic process for selecting and ordering educational experiences (Bobbitt, 1918; Tyler, 1949). Program design became a technical enterprise resulting in goals and objectives that led to rather narrow and homogeneous learning expectations. Tyler's work is often touted as a prototype of this genre.

Tyler's (1949) process entailed devising a systematic plan for creating content-derived educational experiences through written objectives indicating the behavior that the student would develop. Tyler's work is seminal because it led to the dominant curriculum design process of forward mapping of curriculum, designing educational programs from the bottom up (K–12). Kirk's (1993, p. 251) analysis of the objectives-based approach to program design helps elucidate key limitations of the process: (a) objectives lead to "compartmentalization, marginalization, trivialization" of qualitative, subjective, and humanistic experiences, and (b) this approach has led to the assumption that motor learning can be easily assessed and measured because of its overt, performance nature and that other forms of learning are not as important.

The graphic in figure 8.2 provides the perspective of a program design process that begins at the entry year (kindergarten) and builds in complexity through the exit year (grade 12). This depiction shows the traditional objectives-based design process that derives from the behaviorist foundation of learning. This design process has dominated educational program design for well over a century and has shaped so much of what we think of and engage in when we consider the creation of curriculum, instruction, and assessment. Traditionally, programs evolve from bottom up—grade by grade, adding forward from the most basic, elemental components at the lower grades to more complex applications at the higher grades. Elemental components are most typically conceptualized and taught in isolation from other elements. At the height of the behavioral objectives movement (Bloom, 1956), goals and objectives took the form of intricate, specific, discrete elements that led to assessment of intricate, specific, discrete

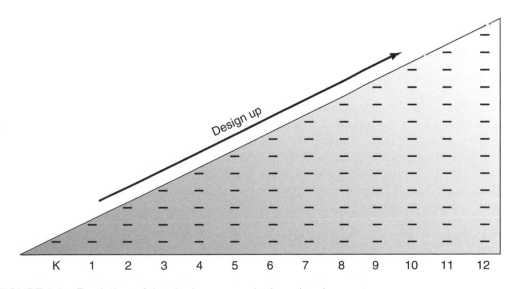

FIGURE 8.2   Depiction of the design-up curriculum development process.

elements of knowledge and skill. Program design processes, as a result, focused more on the elements (the pieces that teachers need to teach) than on the learning results we wish students to attain.

Standards-Based Approach to Program Design

The graphic in figure 8.3 depicts a different design perspective. It shows that the design process works from the end to the beginning, from grade 12 to kindergarten. Note, too, that this model has fewer components than the one in figure 8.2 and that the components are connected across the program. Further, the components should represent the "big ideas," the concepts and principles, not just facts and single elements, as is more typical of the objectives approach. This perspective emphasizes what students should know and be able to do with what they know when they exit high school (Lambert, 1999). Beginning with the ultimate learning outcome clearly leads program designers down a different conceptual path.

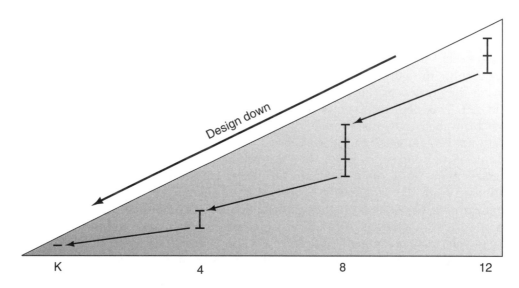

FIGURE 8.3   Depiction of the design-down curriculum process.

Since the late 1980s state departments of education and local education agencies have forged their first- and second-generation curriculum framework designs based on this approach. The "outputs"-oriented design process, the standards-based program design process (e.g., design focused on learning and on demonstration, in some measure, of learner outcomes) is often termed "backward design" or "reverse mapping" because the process leads to programs that are designed from the end back toward the beginning. Learner outcomes, most often based on disciplinary content and process standards (but certainly not limited to these), and assessments that require application of understanding and demonstration of learning are indigenous to the process of standards-based design.

"DOING" STANDARDS-BASED PROGRAM DESIGN

NASPE sponsored the creation of the National Content Standards for Physical Education (1995). Likewise, all other disciplines have their own set or sets of national content standards. The NASPE standards are written as all standards are written—as exit or culminating learning targets for which students are expected to demonstrate their understanding and abilities by the time they complete the pre-K–12 educational progression. The standards provide a general template or framework for each state or school district to use as they craft relevant programs of study (curriculum) for their students. Figure 8.4 lists the NASPE Standards. The book *Moving Into the Future: National Standards for Physical Education* (NASPE, 1995) provides a thorough review of each standard as well as selected grade-level benchmarks and suggestions for assessment to help guide teachers and students.

Content Standards in Physical Education

A physically educated person

1. demonstrates competency in many movement forms and proficiency in a few movement forms,
2. applies movement concepts and principles to the learning and development of motor skills,
3. exhibits a physically active lifestyle,
4. achieves and maintains a health-enhancing level of physical fitness,
5. demonstrates responsible personal and social behavior in physical activity settings,
6. demonstrates understanding and respect for differences among people in physical activity settings, and
7. understands that physical activity provides opportunities for enjoyment, challenge, self-expression, and social interaction.

FIGURE 8.4   NASPE Standards for Physical Education. These seven standards can provide a guide to states as they conceptualize their curriculum and standards-based frameworks that, in turn, can guide local district and school curriculum and assessment planning processes and products.

Reprinted from *Moving Into the Future: National Standards for Physical Education* (1995) with permission from the National Association for Sport and Physical Education (NASPE), 1900 Association Drive, Reston, VA 20191-1599.

Insights into the Process of Standards-Based Design

In the book *Standards-Based Assessment of Student Learning* (Lambert, 1999) I offer a view of the process of standards-based design from an assessment lens. Here, I will tilt the scope more in the direction one would have from the perspective of standards. First, it is helpful to conceptualize and develop standards-based design in a consilient way. What do I mean? Instead of taking things piece by piece, the power of this design comes when it is clear not only that all components intersect in meaningful ways but also that their very intersection creates a metabolism, a synthesis of its own. Goals flow into creative parameters for personalized assessment, which in turn provide a meaningful pathway for guiding instructional design. Individual learning becomes the shared and purposeful destination for all parties—students, teachers, administrators, and parents. The "jumping together" of knowledge and ideas, as Wilson (1998) offered as an explanation of consilience, has been a powerful gestalt on my own journey to think about, do, and communicate to others about standards-based design. I have used organic metaphors—ecosystems, species, genes, or DNA as a systemic communicator to all cells in the body to communicate wholistically. As mentioned earlier, the way we teach and have learned to teach is remarkably durable despite the enormous body of research that sheds a discouraging light on the few notable benefits of the behavioral paradigm.

So, here goes. Although the process may appear somewhat stepwise because of se-quencing of each logical chunk below, it is not; indeed, it is far messier than that! The flow of the process involves a sense of to and fro, and I'll explain as we go along. In truth, one could begin at various spots within this framework because order is not sanctimo-nious. Rather, one must think of the process as a whole, confluent one, from which no part can be omitted.

Using Standards as a Guide

A critical point must be reiterated here: we are aiming toward learning in this process, not focusing on teaching. Solid program design aimed toward student learning should begin with a clear notion about the depth of learning toward which one is aiming. As always, a taxonomy like Bloom's (1956) or Wiggins and McTighe's (1998), offers a use-ful framework as we consider different phases and different intentions about learning. We have often used these to structure curriculum. Their use is instructive as we scaffold toward and structure learning. Although a content standard or a confluence of standards may shape and guide (*guide* is the operative word!) learning, there should never be a monolithic, singular prescriptive demonstration of what's learned. That result would be especially naive and presumptuous because learning, by its very nature, is idiosyncratic. If I were a middle school teacher, my colleagues and I might be focusing on skill (stan-dard #1), concept attainment (standard #2), fitness (standard #4), and responsibility (standard #5) as our guiding standards. Perhaps we would also include standards from other content areas. Our content would array within and around those guideposts—per-haps individual sports and activities. The content would be the means to the end; the standards would guide the way toward appropriate individual learning related to those standards. Again, standards guide, they do not—indeed, should not—create perfor-mance conformity and cookie-cutter expectations of student demonstrations of their ultimate abilities.

Preventing Assessment from Becoming the Learning Goal

As standards begin to flow together to create depth and breath in student learning, individual standards coalesce to form a bigger, more macro guide. Ideas for how stu-dents might choose to demonstrate what they understand and can do with what they understand begin to emerge as well. As teachers pull up to the creative table of program design, particularly across disciplines, many ideas come together. Once the content array begins to take form, a second array begins to take shape around the question of assessment—the creation of ideas as to how students will ultimately, or at selected points along the way (e.g., benchmarks), demonstrate their learning. Teachers must take great care to avoid allowing the assessment to become the de facto learning goal. We should be forewarned that the measure or assessment itself may increase behaviors that subordinate learning to it. We have all seen this happen. Students want to know how they are going to be "graded," and then they perform to achieve the assessment and do not focus on what they need to understand and learn. In addition, we need to avoid viewing assessment as something done after the content is taught. Assessments must be conceptualized and communicated in a progressive, multidimensional way that guides students toward expressing what they have learned and what remains for them to learn.

Importance of Instructional Design

We have focused on thinking about the relative types and levels of learning desired and ways that will elicit rich and multifactorial demonstrations of ability and understanding, as we have looked briefly at content and assessment. The next step is to create a congruent and rich instructional design. One of the unfortunate casualties of the assessment emphasis of the past 5 to 10 years has been the lessened vigilance to instructional design. Instructional design is important, and in many cases it is the missing link in creating compelling and effective design processes. Instructional design is just that—thoughtful, careful, intentional, and congruent design of instructional patterns and modalities that put the engine of learning in motion. At the risk of being redundant, if not hyperbolic, the importance of the word *design* cannot be overstated. Standards create the parameters of a blueprint that become a frame of the design to guide learning. Assessments are derived from the standards, and they elicit student demonstrations of improved skills, practices, and understanding. Instructional patterns, then, coalesce with the other components of the design.

Summary of Insights Into the Process of Standards-Based Design

It is just this simple—and just this profoundly difficult. Done well, standards-based design is just as tedious as it is compelling relative to the fundamental internal consistency that must be present, just as dastardly frustrating as it is logical in the wholeness it affords, and just as confusing as it is clear as we try to loosen our white knuckles that cling to past practices.

So, with content arrayed around standards as guides, assessments created and communicated, and with a congruent and multimodal instructional design, it is time to teach.

BEYOND STANDARDS-BASED DESIGN: IMPLICATIONS FOR PRACTICE

After numerous years of thinking about and working with others to wade into the waters of standards-based design, I offer several closing points that I believe are vitally important in creating useful, learning focused, and transformative programs.

Think about the content standards in an interconnected pattern. Conceptualizing them singularly causes us to tread water and maintain the status quo in program design. Such conceptualization does not lead the way toward making progress and transforming our programs. Think about the standards as a confluent whole, leading toward a single and compelling outcome: each student finding his or her way toward a personal and demonstrable understanding of how to lead a healthy, physically active life beginning from where he or she is right now and going forward. We need to push past the expectation that each student learn the same things in the same ways (despite their many differences and varying interests) as they try to understand how to lead active, healthy lives. Let me clarify. I do believe that students need to learn a progression of skills and knowledge. They need to learn to combine skills in ever more complex ways as they learn to apply their knowledge and abilities to sport, dance, and recreational forms. They need to understand and demonstrate their ability to design and implement a goal-defined direction for leading a physically active lifestyle. I do not believe, however, that every student should learn basketball or football or tennis or golf or jazz dance or inline skating or whatever, although some will choose one or more of these as their interest areas. I believe that our goal is to help students find one or more physical activity forms that they can engage in and enjoy at least at a recreational level for the rest of their lives. The activity, however, is *not* the end goal. Each activity is the means to the end of a learning goal, not the end in itself! This is an important distinction. Our role as teachers is to create safe, sound educational opportunities, rich and viable learning choices, and personalized guidance toward learning to be physically active for a lifetime—and, yes, it necessarily might look quite different for each student. Clearly, our challenge as teachers is not to continue to add more activities to the curriculum. Instead, we must think differently about how to motivate learning and its achievement, about how to differentiate opportunities for learning so that more of our students learn, and about how to create coherent and engaging instructional connections to the content so that students can find success and enjoyment with their physical activity experiences when they are under our tutelage (and when they are not).

• Avoid the lure of the smorgasbord program—the implementation of single-day or short-term units of instruction aimed at exposing students to as many activities as possible. Although this type of program might register high on the novelty meter, it does next to nothing to enhance learning. Instead of the relentless pursuit of finding more things to add to the bag of tricks, we would spend our energies far more productively by creating a focused program based on a careful plan for learning. This plan should include more depth, more consideration of how to engage student learning through differentiation and personalization, and more thought about how to create compelling and rich assessments that provide interesting learning challenges that inspire student motivation to learn and persist.

• If you are devoted to trying to focus your teaching on the real test of program and teaching effectiveness—student learning—then continue to learn all you can about what that means. Surely, student learning is related to teaching effectiveness, but incompletely so. To me, a scenario like the following characterizes the truest measure of quality teaching: (a) Your students faced unexpected learning challenges in your lesson; (b) With your guidance your students were able to think about and understand the challenges; (c) They were able to determine what things they needed to ask, learn, and practice next in order to improve and overcome the challenges; (d) Then they set out to do so.

• Learning is not only about repeating what we have been told or shown; it is about understanding how learning occurs and how we each need to be engaged in the process of creating new understanding and new abilities so that true and lasting learning can occur.

• Learning is messy. Learning is intrinsic. Students will learn not because someone "makes them" but because they choose to. If learning is to occur, as teachers we must be reflective and conscious of what we are doing, why we are doing it, and how we are practicing our craft. The teaching and learning process should not be left to chance. Our job is to understand the best practices of our field that are guided by theory and scholarship and to use our professional wisdom in putting them to work toward the goal of student learning.

• It's hard. To move ourselves and our programs in this direction takes an uncommon investment in thinking differently and doing our work differently. Often, we have to overcome the ways we have always done things. It takes time, it takes trial and error, and it takes a commitment to constant professional learning, reflection on our craft, and dialog with others on a similar journey toward transforming educational programs. The bottom line is that each of us must choose our path. How you choose will determine your success as a professional and, in turn, the success of your students in finding their way toward leading physically active, healthy lives.

IMPLICATIONS FOR PRACTICE

1. The focus of standards-based design processes in education should be on creating quality programs of education that engage students, motivate learning, and lead progressively toward deep, meaningful learning experiences focusing on important concepts and issues (e.g., concepts and issues of the human condition, of improving our world).

2. Our educational programs should abandon trivia and superficial coverage of content and skills and focus on helping students develop greater depth of knowledge and ability. This focus applies to all content areas, including physical education.

3. The National Association for Sport and Physical Education has developed a set of standards to guide the development of physical education programs of study in K–12 schools.

4. The standards-based program design process can, at once, be a guide for program creation and a catalyst for thinking differently about more congruent and compelling learning structures and processes.

5. Educational program design is evolving from an objectives-based process to one based on standards or student learning outcomes. Objectives-based design is predicated upon a behavioral perspective of how people learn, whereas standards-based design is derived from a constructivist perspective. These two paradigms of learning are dissimilar in both theory and practice. As educational organizations continue the evolutionary process from one set of theoretical tenets and practices to the other, they must resolve competing or incongruent curriculum, instruction, and assessment processes and practices.

6. Standards and accountability are not new concepts in education. The current iteration and emphasis on standards, however, has taken a decidedly technical turn toward what, to many people, seems like standardization. This is problematic because such an approach can quickly lead to monolithic, one-size-fits-all notions of curriculum, instruction, assessment, and student learning outcomes. Some of which we are witnessing today.

7. The current focus on standards seems to subvert, if not prevent, the very things it sets out to address: educational programs focused on facilitating the process of every student's learning and development; and teachers, students, and parents/guardians joining together in responsibility to and responsibility for creating strong academic programs that lead to student learning.

8. The standards-based program design process is organic, generative, and holistic. It is based on the fundamental premise that significant and meaningful student learning is the outcome and that teaching is a means to that end. The standards-based program design process also assumes that learning is by nature idiosyncratic and individual. In such a process, the congruence of curriculum, instructional methods, and assessment processes is paramount.

9. The design process is not a template or process for creating nifty ideas that are quick ends in themselves, fun to do, and activity oriented. Instead, the process is about creating engaging, meaningful programs that result in demonstrable student learning.

10. A well-conceived design process should attend the important question "What's worth learning?" and it should include many and diverse voices. The question "Who decides what's worth learning?" is equally important.

REFERENCES

Apple, M. (1982). Curricular form and the logic of technical control: Building the possessive individual. In M. Apple & L. Weiss (Eds.), *Cultural and economic reproduction of education* (pp. 247-270). New York: Routledge & Kegan Paul.

Bloom, B. (1956). *Taxonomy of educational objectives. Handbook I: The cognitive domain.* New York: David McKat.

Bobbitt, F. (1918). *The curriculum.* Boston: Houghton Mifflin.

Bruner, J. (1957). Going beyond the information given. In J.S. Bruner, E. Brunswick, L. Festinger, F. Heider, K. Muenzinger, C. Osgood, & D. Rapport (Eds.), *Contemporary approaches to cognition* (pp. 41-69). Cambridge, MA: Harvard University Press.

Callahan, R.E. (1964). *Education and the cult of efficiency.* Chicago: University of Chicago Press.

Cremin, L. (1961). *The transformation of the school: Progressivism in American education: 1876–1957.* New York: Knopf.

Cremin, L. (1990). *Popular education.* New York: Harper & Row.

Dewey, J. (1990). *School and society and the child and the curriculum.* Chicago: University of Chicago Press. (Original work published in 1899)

Dewey, J. (1966). *Democracy and education.* New York: Free Press. (Original work published in 1916)

Diamond, J. (1999). *Guns, germs and steel: The fate of human societies.* New York: Norton.

Ebbinghaus, H. (1913). *Memory.* (H.A. Rugert & C.E. Bussenius, Trans.). New York: Teachers College Press. (Original work published in 1885)

Eisner, E. (1995). Standards for American schools: Help or hindrance? *Phi Delta Kappan, 76*(10), 758-764.

Gardner, H. (1991). *The unschooled mind: How children think and how schools should teach.* New York: Basic Books.

Gardner, H. (1999). *The disciplined mind.* New York: Simon & Schuster.

Jewett, A.E., Bain L.L., & Ennis, C.D. (1995). *The curriculum process in physical education.* Dubuque, IA: Brown & Benchmark.

Kirk, D. (1993). Curriculum work in physical education: Beyond the objectives approach? *Journal of Teaching in Physical Education, 12,* 244-265.

Kohn, A. (1999). *The schools our children deserve.* Boston: Houghton Mifflin.

Lambert, L.T. (1999). *Standards-based assessment of student learning: A comprehensive approach.* Reston, VA: NASPE.

Lambert, L.T. (March, 2000). The new physical education. *Educational Leadership, 57*(6), 34-39.

Miller, G.A., Galanter, E., & Pribram, K.L. (1960). *Plans and the structure of behavior.* New York: Hold, Rinehart, & Winston.

National Association for Sport and Physical Education. (1995). *Moving into the future: National physical education standards: A guide to content and assessment.* Reston, VA: American Alliance for Health, Physical Education, Recreation and Dance.

Shuell, T.J. (1986). Cognitive conceptions of learning. *Review of Educational Research, 56,* 411-436.

Sizer, T.R. (1991). No pain, no gain. *Educational Leadership, 48*(8), 32-34.

Taylor, F.W. (1967). *The principles of scientific management.* New York: Norton. (Original work published in 1911)

Tomlinson, C.A. (1995). *How to differentiate instruction in mixed ability classrooms.* Alexandria, VA: ASCD.

Tomlinson, C.A. (1999). *The differentiated classroom: Responding to the needs of all learners.* Alexandria, VA: ASCD.

Tyack, D., & Cuban, L. (1995). *Tinkering toward Utopia: A century of public school reform.* Cambridge, MA: Harvard University Press.

Tyler, R.W. (1949). *Basic principles of curriculum and instruction.* Chicago: University of Chicago Press.

Wiggins, G., & McTighe, J. (1998). *Understanding by design.* Alexandria, VA: ASCD.

Wilson, E.O. (1998). *Consilience: The unity of knowledge.* New York: Vintage.

Wright, R. (2000). *Nonzero: The logic of human destiny.* New York: Pantheon.

CHAPTER NINE

STUDENT ISSUES IN PHYSICAL EDUCATION CLASSES: ATTITUDES, COGNITION, AND MOTIVATION

Melinda A. Solmon

Early educational research tended to focus on teaching, while learning and learners received comparatively little attention. As the field has evolved, this focus on teaching and teachers has shifted to include a broader view that recognizes the influence that students have in the teaching and learning process. Peterson (1988), as she examined the first two editions of the *Handbook of Research on Teaching* (Gage, 1963; Travers, 1973), observed that the words *student, learner,* or *learning* appeared in none of the chapter titles in the first edition and the only mention of any of these terms in the second edition occurred in a chapter entitled "Skill Learning." The words *teaching* or *teacher,* however, dominated titles in the first and second editions. According to Peterson (1988), a shift was evident by 1986, when the third edition of the *Handbook of Research on Teaching* (Wittrock, 1986a) was published. That edition included a separate chapter on students' thought processes, and the words *student, learning,* or *learner* appeared in 8 of the 35 chapter titles. An emphasis on teachers and teaching was still evident, but researchers were beginning to acknowledge the importance of including student issues in educational research.

In the fourth edition of the *Handbook of Research on Teaching* (Richardson, 2001), although the words *student, learner,* or *learning* appear in only 5 of 51 chapter titles, "The Learner" is one of eight major sections of the handbook, and student issues are addressed throughout many of the chapters. Examination of this newest edition supports the idea that student issues have become an important concern in educational research. In research on teaching and learning in physical education, an emphasis on student issues is also apparent, as two recent *Journal of Teaching in Physical Education* monographs have focused specifically on learners (Graham, 1995; Griffin & Placek, 2001).

Why is it important to consider student issues? Although it may seem obvious that complete understanding of how teachers can be most effective must include a view from the students' perspective, sometimes, in practice, teaching is viewed in isolation from learners and learning. An incident that I recall from a professional meeting illustrates this phenomenon. While serving with several colleagues on a university committee charged with the responsibility of revising procedures for the evaluation of teaching, the use of measurable student outcomes in the process of evaluating teaching was considered. A tenured full professor with an established reputation as an outstanding teacher recoiled at that prospect, exclaiming, "I know that I am an effective teacher. I can't help it if the students do not learn. Their learning is their responsibility, not mine. What they learn is not a reflection of how I teach!" The individual failed to see the irony in that statement. If students are not learning, how can the teaching be effective? Teaching and learning are interactive processes. One could argue that individuals can learn independently or in the absence of teaching, but the reverse argument is more difficult to support. If we are to increase our understanding of how teachers can be more effective in physical education, we must consider the role that students play in their learning and ultimately their influence on the teaching-learning process.

Amelia Lee clearly outlined in chapter 2 the evolution of research on teaching in physical education, so there is no need to repeat her review of that process, but I refer to it to demonstrate how and why researchers' interest in student issues emerged. The process-product paradigm dominated educational research before and through the 1970s and into the 1980s. This paradigm assumes a direct link between teachers' actions and student learning. Typically, teacher behaviors were coded using observational systems in an attempt to identify teaching behaviors that led to student achievement, as measured by scores on standardized achievement tests. Although this body of research made a valuable contribution to the literature by providing a basis for the investigation of effective teaching behaviors, it became apparent that this unidirectional view of teaching and learning (i.e., teaching behavior directly causes student achievement) was too simplistic to explain this complex process. Explanations of the need to extend the process-product paradigm are clearly evident in the literature (Doyle, 1977; Lee & Solmon, 1992; Shulman, 1986). In summary, researchers have recognized several faulty assumptions inherent in the process-product approach that contends the link between teacher behavior and student achievement is direct:

a. There is one right way to teach (i.e., we can identify the "right" way to teach by linking observable teacher behaviors to student achievement).

b. All individuals learn in the same way (learners are uniformly affected by instruction).

c. The relationship between teacher behavior and student achievement is linear (more of a specific behavior is better, rather than recognizing an "optimal" level).

d. The relationship between teacher behavior and student achievement is unidirectional (teachers affect students, but students do not affect the instruction process).

In consideration of these and other criticisms of the process-product paradigm, educational research agendas have expanded to encompass the influential role that students have in the instructional process. Social cognitive paradigms that extend the process-product paradigm by including cognitive mediational components between the process (teacher behavior) and the product (student achievement) have dominated recent educational research. The focus of this chapter is to integrate the findings from these studies about student issues that are influential in teaching and learning in physical education classes.

About the same time that researchers began to extend the process-product paradigm by including a focus on learners, contextual factors within our society and schools also increased the emphasis on student issues. LeaAnn Tyson Martin in chapter 4 describes the contextual factors that have had and will continue to have a profound effect on schools in our society. As she clearly describes, conditions in our society that affect schools have changed dramatically over the past decades. The relevant issues here are changes in the ways that students and parents conceptualize schools. When I was a student I do not believe that my teachers were even remotely concerned about whether or not I "valued" the content or if it had personal meaning to me. They assumed (correctly) that my parents valued the schooling process and that whatever they (the teachers) said that I had to learn, I would. Perhaps in that context, the process-product model was more tenable, but this is no longer the case. Children do not come to school assuming that they have to learn whatever it is the teacher says they have to learn.

Part of teaching in the 21st century, and in my view perhaps the most important aspect of teaching, is to understand students from a variety of backgrounds and the societal issues that affect their educational processes. Designing programs that will meet students' needs and convincing them that what we are teaching has meaning to them and can enhance their quality of life has become an essential teaching skill. When I was a student I felt I was a powerless pawn who had to do whatever was required, but as Ennis and her colleagues (Cothran & Ennis, 1997; Ennis et al., 1997) described, students today exert a powerful influence on curricular issues and instructional practices in physical education classrooms. You may believe that the "old system" was better and yearn for the "good old days," but those days are gone. We must move forward according to the conditions of the times and consider student issues if we are to enhance instruction in physical education classes.

My intent in this chapter is to present information about student issues in an effort to synthesize research about student issues that has application for practitioners. To achieve that goal, I have organized themes around three key student issues: attitudes, cognition, and motivation. I begin by defining these three constructs and then provide a brief overview of theoretical perspectives that enable researchers and practitioners to explain, interpret, and give meaning to student issues as they apply to physical education classrooms. The theoretical overview is followed by a discussion of specific issues about student attitudes, cognitions, and motivation. I conclude with implications for research and practice about structuring the environment in physical education classrooms to maximize student engagement.

DEFINING ATTITUDES, COGNITION, AND MOTIVATION

When I began my teaching career in an inner-city school, I encountered the expression "He's (or she's) got an attitude." My first reaction was that I thought everyone had an attitude, and it could be good or bad. I quickly realized that, generally speaking, "having an attitude" was not a good thing, given that the expression usually inferred that she or he had a bad attitude. Attitudes are powerful influences on decisions we make concerning many aspects of our lives, and attitudes toward physical education and physical activity are certainly determining factors in whether individuals choose to engage in an activity. According to Silverman and Subramaniam (1999) attitude permeates everything we do. They acknowledge that although the term *attitude* is commonly used in our society, its meaning from a psychometric perspective has not been clearly delineated. Salient beliefs determine how an attitude is formed (Ajzen, 1988, 1993). Those beliefs, and consequently the attitudes that result from them, can range from positive to negative and can vary in intensity. Strong positive attitudes should be associated with positive affect and adaptive patterns of behavior, whereas negative attitudes are likely to evoke negative affect and avoidance behaviors.

Webster's Seventh New Collegiate Dictionary (Merriam-Webster, 1969) defines *cognition* as "the act or process of knowing including both awareness and judgment," but in educational research literature the term *cognition* is generally used interchangeably with thought processes (Peterson, 1988; Wittrock, 1986b). Cognitive approaches assume that thought governs action (Roberts, 1992), and individuals are believed to engage in a wide array of cognitions or thought processes in achievement settings, including perceiving the environment, attending to and concentrating on cues, and making decisions concerning the nature of their interactions in class. From a cognitive perspective, teachers must consider what students are thinking in order to understand what and how they are learning.

According to Roberts (2001), "motivation refers to dispositions, social variables, and/ or cognitions that come into play when a person undertakes a task at which he or she is evaluated, or enters into competition with others, or attempts to attain some standard of excellence" (p. 6). He argues that theories that investigate motivation and how it affects achievement must address three aspects: the energization, direction, and regulation of behavior. A comprehensive view of motivation, then, deals not only with the initiation of a behavior but also the maintenance of that behavior over time. Motivation is a complex, multifaceted construct that has been the focus of a large body of research in general education, physical education, sport, and exercise settings. As Roberts points out, there are at least 32 clearly identified theories of motivation, so it is not possible to present a complete review of that work in this chapter. I will present major constructs in physical education research that have applicability to student learning.

Attitudes, cognition, and motivation are interrelated, interdependent factors rather than isolated constructs. In fact, attitudes and motivation are often included under the broad umbrella of cognitions. I have chosen to present them in a linear fashion, beginning with attitudes as a basis for cognitions, cognitions that may vary as a function of those attitudes, and finally motivation as a way to optimize attitudes and cognitions. As represented in figure 9.1, however, these three constructs do not operate in isolation. Rather, student attitudes, cognitions, and motivation nest within a framework of factors such as the school context, teachers' actions and values, students' entry characteristics, and the motivational climate in the class. Depicted as an interactive triad in the figure, these factors interrelate in complex ways to affect ultimate student learning.

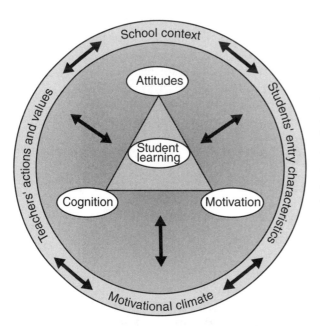

FIGURE 9.1   A model of the influence of attitudes, cognition, and motivation on student learning.

FRAMEWORKS FOR UNDERSTANDING STUDENT ISSUES

Having established the relevance of considering student issues such as attitudes, cognition, and motivation in physical education classes, we then need a framework to help us organize and understand those issues. Researchers have used several theoretical approaches to interpret or explain student issues in their attempts to extend our understanding of the teaching and learning process. My intent is not to provide an in-depth discussion of these frameworks but instead to present a brief explanation. I have provided references for those who wish to explore these theoretical perspectives further.

Cognitive Mediation

When it became apparent that the two-factor structure of the process-product paradigm lacked sufficient complexity to provide a framework for the study of the teaching-learning process, educational researchers began to modify or extend the paradigm by inserting a third factor into the model between the process and the product, allowing for inclusion of mediating elements (Doyle, 1977; Lee & Solmon, 1992; Shulman, 1986). That is, researchers recognized that what students do in classes is an important step, or mediating factor, between what teachers do and what students learn. This approach also recognized that what students do in classes, besides being a bridge between teacher behavior and student achievement, affects not only what students learn but also what teachers do. Traffic on the bridge goes both ways. Although this modification seems simple, it is a powerful reconceptualization of the role of the teacher. Rather than directly causing learning, as inferred in the process-product paradigm, the teacher from this perspective has the job of structuring the learning environment in a way that encourages students to think and act in ways that will, in turn, enable them to learn. Learners are viewed as active and controlling agents in their own learning. Initially, researchers using the mediating paradigm relied on overt, observable, or objective measures such as numbers of practice trials or time on task, but Doyle (1977) was critical of this method and encouraged researchers to investigate implicit processes such as affective, cognitive, and motivational aspects of student thinking during learning.

Constructivism

Like the cognitive mediation paradigm, a constructivist approach (von Glasersfeld, 1987) views students as active agents in their learning. Constructivism emphasizes that students bring with them to an educational setting prior knowledge and experiences from which they interpret and give meaning to their present experience. From a constructivist perspective, knowledge is not something transmitted from the teacher to the learner. Rather, the learner constructs knowledge through her or his interpretation of events from the framework of prior experience, in effect, building or constructing knowledge that has individual meaning. Cognitive mediation and constructivism are parallel frameworks that researchers have used in the study of teaching and learning in physical education. Both frameworks recognize that learning does not occur spontaneously from teaching but instead is a dynamic, constructive operation that depends on the learner's effortful involvement.

STUDENT ATTITUDES

Students enter achievement settings with attitudes formed from their beliefs about that setting (Ajzen, 1988, 1993). The beliefs may originate from a variety of sources, such as family influences, prior experiences, and peer influences, but students' attitudes clearly play an influential role in physical education. From the cognitive mediational perspective, we can see how student attitudes function as mediators between teachers' actions and student learning. Students with positive attitudes about the content are more likely to attend to instruction, exert effort, and consequently achieve, whereas students in the same class receiving the same instruction with negative attitudes are more likely to ignore or reject the instruction, withdraw effort, avoid challenge, and consequently fail to achieve.

Silverman and Subramaniam (1999), in their review of measurement and outcome issues on student attitude toward physical education and physical activity, indicate that we need more research to understand the attitude-achievement relationship in physical education, because as they point out, research to date on student attitude has produced mixed results. Despite the confusion evident when results of studies of attitude in physical education are compared, a few generalizations can be made based on the research thus far. Two broad categories of influence on student attitude are characteristics of the physical education program and characteristics of students.

Program Characteristics

In studying attitude as a function of characteristics of the physical education program, several researchers have found evidence that contextual factors do affect how students feel about the subject matter (Silverman & Subramaniam, 1999). The influence of the teacher, the curriculum, and the perceived importance of physical education content, as Cathy Ennis discusses in chapter 7, have been identified as contextual factors that affect students' feelings about physical education.

Studies that have examined the influence of the teacher on student attitudes have provided evidence that students' levels of enjoyment of the class are linked to their feelings about the teacher (Carlson, 1995; Martin, 2000; Sanders & Graham, 1995; Solmon & Carter, 1995; Tjeerdsma, Rink, & Graham, 1996). Teachers have proved to be strong determinants of both positive (Figley, 1985) and negative (Luke & Sinclair, 1991) attitudes. In their psychometric analysis used in the development of an instrument to assess student attitudes in physical education, Subramaniam and Silverman (2000) provide additional evidence that the teacher is a powerful influence on student attitudes. Although whether students' feelings about the teacher are more salient in positive or negative attitudes has not been determined, it is clear that teachers play an important role in the formation of students' attitudes toward the class.

The physical education curriculum is also an important determinant of student attitudes. Enjoyment and perceived usefulness of the curriculum, as well as a sense of belongingness, emerged as important aspects of student attitudes that differentiated high- and low-attitude students (Subramaniam & Silverman, 2002). Studies with young children indicate that curricula that focus on a variety of enjoyable activities within a flexible structure had a positive influence on student attitudes (Martin, 2000; Sanders & Graham, 1995; Solmon & Carter, 1995). McKenzie, Alcaraz, & Sallis (1994) found that children's feelings about activities within the curriculum differed. Although children's attitudes toward physical education activities were positive, they expressed a stronger preference for skill-related activities as compared with activities related to health. In the study by Luke and Sinclair (1991), curriculum content was the most important determinant of attitudes.

Just as some aspects of the curriculum have been identified as positive influences on attitudes, several curricular characteristics are linked to negative attitudes. Researchers have identified dissatisfaction with the content offered, particularly at the secondary level, as a major factor in students' discontent in physical education (Figley, 1985; Luke & Sinclair, 1995; Solmon, in review). Students have identified repetition of the same activities and sports year after year with no modifications to address their concerns as a major source of their negative feelings about their physical education experiences (Carlson, 1995). An overemphasis on competition in the physical education curriculum that leads to negative experiences can also be a factor in students' developing an intense dislike for physical education (Carlson, 1995; Ennis, 1996). Another curriculum factor associated with negative attitudes toward physical education is the marginal status of physical education in the school curriculum. Over 50% of 10th and 11th grade participants in a study by Tannehill, Romar, O'Sullivan, England, and Rosenberg (1994) rated physical education as the least important subject in the curriculum. When students view a subject as unimportant, it is understandable that their attitudes are not positive.

Student Characteristics

Although student attitudes undoubtedly vary a great deal, we can identify some trends related to student characteristics. Many of the studies that report positive student attitudes about physical education were conducted in elementary schools (Martin, 2000; McKenzie et al., 1994; Sanders & Graham, 1995; Solmon & Carter, 1995). Conversely, discussion of student discontent with physical education tends to focus on students' experiences in secondary physical education (Luke & Sinclair, 1991; Solmon, in review), although certainly some secondary students do report positive attitudes (Rice, 1988). Sufficient evidence is available to conclude that attitudes toward physical education decline as children progress through their schooling (Silverman & Subramaniam, 1999), but some students still maintain positive attitudes. An important research goal is to learn more about how to foster positive attitudes as students enter secondary settings.

Researchers have also studied gender as a factor in student attitude. In their review of studies that have examined attitudes as a function of gender, Silverman and Subramaniam (1999) present evidence that girls may have attitudes that are less positive than those of boys, especially at high school ages. They conclude, however, that some of the differences that appear to be gender related may be a function of methodologies and that evidence does not support firm conclusions about gender and attitude.

Student attitudes also vary as a function of skill level. We know that low-skill students have different experiences in physical education than skillful students (Silverman, 1993; Solmon & Lee, 1996). According to Harter's (1978) competence motivation theory, children will engage and persist in activities in which they feel competent and are at risk to withdraw from activities in which they have low perceptions of ability. We can logically predict that highly skilled students would display attitudes toward physical education that are more positive, whereas students of low skill levels would be at risk for negative affect. Evidence supports that notion with children who are old enough to make social comparisons (Carlson, 1995; Portman, 1995). Attitudes of young children, who have not yet developed the ability to evaluate their performance in reference to others, do not seem to vary as a function of skill. For example, Martin (2000) reports that all second graders in her study had positive attitudes about physical education, regardless of skill level, although there were subtle differences in ways that high- and low-skilled children described why they liked the class. Although higher skill levels have generally been associated with attitudes that are more positive, a link between attitudes and student learning in physical education classes has not been established (Silverman & Subramaniam, 1999).

Can Attitudes Be Changed?

If attitudes are influential factors that affect student engagement in physical education classes, then two issues are important to consider from a practitioner's point of view: maintaining the positive attitudes that elementary school children have as they progress through their schooling and changing negative attitudes to positive ones. No long-term studies have addressed how positive attitudes can be maintained, but some evidence suggests that attitudes are changeable (Brodie & Britwistle, 1990; Zimbardo & Leippe, 1991). Silverman and Subramaniam (1999) concluded in their review that more research was needed concerning student attitudes in physical education, and they have developed and validated an instrument to measure student attitude that will be a valuable tool in future investigation of the topic (Subramaniam & Silverman, 2000). Certainly, though, sufficient evidence is available to conclude that student attitudes are important issues for teachers and researchers to consider. Attitudes can lay the foundation for the kinds of cognitions in which students choose to engage during instruction in physical education, and they ultimately affect what students learn.

STUDENT COGNITION

A cognitive approach, based on the assumption that thought governs action (Roberts, 1992), explores student learning by examining the ways that teachers influence student thinking, which, in turn, affects student achievement. As can be seen in overviews of the research on student thinking in classrooms (Wittrock, 1986b, 1987) and physical education (Lee, 1997; Lee & Solmon, 1992), investigating student thinking is a complex endeavor. Student cognition is a multifaceted process that encompasses a wide array of thought processes, and it is not possible in this chapter to address all of them. I will focus on three phases of student cognitions that demonstrate how student thinking affects what students learn: (a) student perceptions, (b) attention and concentration, and (c) student decision making.

Student Perceptions

Based on the lens of prior knowledge and experience, students enter classrooms with baggage, including attitudes, that affects how they interpret classroom events or the meanings that they give them. Perhaps you have had the experience of hearing someone describe a conversation that you were involved in and thought, "That's not how I remember it." Or possibly you have had the experience of clearly explaining instructions to your students only to discover when they begin to execute a task that your instructions may not have been all that clear. These scenarios demonstrate how individual interpretations of an event, filtered through existing attitudes and knowledge, can vary. Students in the same class can interpret things in different ways, and students often interpret information differently than the teacher intends (Wittrock, 1986b).

Considering students' perceptions of teacher expectations illustrates how students perceive teacher behaviors differently. Martinek (1988) examined the perceptions of high- and low-expectation students about teacher feedback and compared their perceptions to objective coding of the teachers' behavior. High-expectation students actually received more corrective behavior feedback and less praise, but those students indicated that they received more praise. Low-expectation students received more praise than corrective behavior feedback, and their perceptions of the teacher's behavior were accurate. High-expectation students tended to attribute corrective feedback to teacher characteristics, such as the teacher's being in a bad mood, whereas low-expectation students attributed that behavior to personal causes or something they (the students) had done. In this case, students mediated the teacher feedback in different ways. High-expectation students were able to dismiss corrective feedback, and low-expectation students tended to take it personally.

Students actively interpret and give meaning to instructional behaviors and are able to discern subtle differences in teachers' actions. Solmon and Carter (1995) investigated kindergarten and first-grade children's definitions of physical education using a constructivist perspective. When asked what the teacher wanted them to learn in physical education, girls expressed the belief that the teacher wanted them to learn how to follow the rules, whereas boys said the teacher wanted them to learn skills. The teacher in this study did not intend to send different messages to boys and girls about her priorities for them, but she unintentionally did so by praising the girls for their behavior and the boys for their skill. When confronted with the evidence of this, the teacher reflected on her own beliefs and values and realized that she did have higher skill expectations for boys than for girls. In her efforts to provide an equitable, safe environment and provide positive feedback for everyone, students interpreted her actions differently than she had intended.

The Solmon and Carter (1995) study examined implicit values or messages (Bain, 1989), but studies that are more recent have examined students' perceptions of explicit teaching behaviors with the goal of learning how students construct their knowledge (Griffin, Dodds, Placek, & Tremino, 2001; Nevett, Rovegno, & Babiarz, 2001; Placek et al., 2001). Students' misconceptions have also been studied, and it is clear that misconceptions that develop about the content are linked to the nature of the instruction (Hare & Graber, 2000). These and other studies of student perceptions that document disparities between what teachers intend and what students perceive (Lee, Landin, & Carter, 1992; Tjeerdsma, 1997; Tjeerdsma, et al., 1996) demonstrate that to understand how students learn from teaching, we must consider how students give meaning to instructional behaviors and classroom events.

Attention and Concentration

Based on their perceptions of the environment and the meanings they assign to their experiences, students direct their attention and concentration within the environment. How they concentrate and what they pay attention to are important considerations in their thought processes. When compared with observer estimates of time on task, students' self-reports of their attention levels are more accurate predictors of student achievement (Wittrock, 1987), so it appears that students are aware of their cognitions with regard to their attention and concentration levels, and can accurately report them. Knowing what students are paying attention to and then being able to direct their attention in ways that will help them learn is an important aspect of student cognition.

By asking students what they were thinking about during instruction and practice, we discover how their attention levels relate to achievement. Langley (1995) described students' thoughts during practices as task focused and reflecting a concern about making errors. Students who are successful in practice are those who tend to be able to focus their attention on elements of the skill, whereas those who struggle tend to have negative affective thoughts reflecting worry about the ability to perform (Lee et al., 1992; Solmon & Lee, 1996). Students of differing skill levels seem to pay attention to different things. In the Solmon and Lee study (1996), skillful students appeared to be inattentive during instruction and self-reported relatively lower levels of attention as compared with unskilled students during instruction by the teacher. During practice, however, they were able to attend more effectively to detecting errors and correcting them, whereas unskilled students were not able to do this. These studies suggest that learning more about how students attend to instruction and concentrate during practice can help teachers structure the environment to direct student attention and foster achievement.

Decisions That Influence Interactive Behaviors and Achievement

Besides deciding what to pay attention to and whether to concentrate, students make many other decisions that have a powerful effect on their interactive behaviors during classes and ultimately determine what they learn. Examples of decisions that students make with regard to their interactive behavior are deciding whether to

a. engage in the achievement task,

b. exert effort,

c. work at a challenging level,

d. persist when they encounter difficulty, and

e. use strategies to improve performance.

Making the "right" choices has the potential to enhance student learning, and selecting alternatives to the "right" choices equates to student withdrawal from learning activities.

Students' attitudes, perceptions, and levels of attention and concentration can all play roles in the decisions that students make about their engagement. Studies that have examined quantity and quality of practice trials that students attempt in physical education classes demonstrate a high degree of variability among students (Silverman, 1993; Solmon & Lee, 1996), indicating that students do make choices about their level of engagement. Students who intend to avoid participation are usually able to do so, a phenomenon described almost two decades ago by Tousignant and Siedentop (1983) as being a "competent bystander." In large classes, individuals can easily avoid engaging in activity without drawing any attention to themselves. Skill level is one factor that influences whether students choose to engage in tasks, exert effort, and persist during activity (Silverman, 1993; Solmon & Lee, 1996). When students experience success, they report that they are more likely to exert effort (Hebert, Landin, & Solmon, 2000).

MOTIVATION AS A COGNITIVE CONSTRUCT UNDERLYING COGNITION

As pointed out earlier in this chapter, motivation is recognized as a cognitive process (Roberts, 1992), and, consistent with the line of thinking in the previous section, motivation is a decision-making process. I have heard physical education teachers say, "Oh, I can motivate my students to do whatever I want them to do," when they really meant that they could *make* students comply with orders. Motivation is a concept distinct from class control. Motivation is creating an environment that encourages students to make decisions to engage in learning activities actively and with effort, and that includes fostering positive attitudes about class and eliciting cognitions that will produce achievement. Motivation cannot be measured directly, so we make inferences concerning whether individuals are motivated by observing their actions. Actions that reflect motivated behavior are exerting effort, persisting in the face of difficulty, and making particular choices about activities (such as working at a challenging level). Ultimately, performance is viewed as an indicator of motivation (Roberts, 2001). I will draw on some of the powerful theories of achievement motivation to illustrate major points and draw conclusions about how physical education teachers can approach this task. Although prerequisites for motivation may apply to specific activities or achievement settings, I have identified two conditions that seem to hold true across settings. Differing theoretical perspectives may offer other prerequisites, but using expectancy-value theory (Wigfield & Eccles, 1993), a strong argument can be made across major theories that two prerequisites exist: valuing the task and believing in the possibility of achieving success.

Valuing the Task

Unless a task or activity has some inherent value, it is unlikely that anyone can be or will be motivated to engage in an activity. Wigfield and Eccles (1993) have identified four aspects of task values that can influence motivation:

    a. Attainment value or the importance of doing well on a task

    b. Utility value reflecting how the task related to future goals

    c. Perceived cost, or the negative aspects of the activity such as anxiety and the amount of effort required

    d. Intrinsic value or the enjoyment derived from the activity

A growing body of evidence supports the notion that value is an especially important issue for students in secondary physical education classes (Cothran & Ennis, 1997; Ennis, 1996; Solmon, in review; Tannehill et al., 1994). Substantial numbers of high school students in these studies have indicated that they see no value in the physical education curriculum, that they do not know why they have to take the class, and that they do not believe they should be required to take the class.

Perhaps the most influential dimension of value, and the one that we might aspire to advance, is intrinsic value. Although we might engage in activities that will help us attain something, or that we find useful, we are most likely to persist in activities that we value as an end in themselves. Intrinsic value is related to the activity as an end in itself, and it relates strongly to interest and enjoyment. Intrinsic motivation has been directly linked to effort and persistence in physical education classes (Ferrer-Caja & Weiss, 2000). Self-determination theory (Deci & Ryan, 1985; Vallerand, 2001) provides a rationale to understand why this dimension of value is important. In this hierarchical view of motivation, extrinsic, or externally controlled, motivation may be seen as a way to entice individuals to become involved in an activity on a short-term basis. According to self-determination theory, however, only when we are intrinsically motivated and feel a sense of autonomy and competence are we likely to engage in a behavior of our own volition over a long period. Chen's (2001) work related to interest in physical education settings has applicability here. As he reports, students are more likely to engage in activities that are novel, cognitively challenging, and generate instant enjoyment. He recommends that we strive to make tasks in physical education interesting, linking motivation to the learning setting, the curriculum, and the socioeconomic and cultural environment.

Believing in the Ability to Be Successful

Besides attaching some form of value to an activity, individuals, if they are to be motivated, must believe that some measure of success is a realistic possibility. Simply stated, we do things that we think we are good at, and we tend to withdraw from activities when we feel that we are unsuccessful, especially when we do not think success is a realistic possibility, even with practice and hard work. Harter's (1978) competence motivation theory illustrates this point. According to that theory, even if I value something, if I find myself in a situation where I do not believe I can feel successful or competent, I am unlikely to be motivated to engage. Two important issues are inherent in the consideration of the ability to be successful: beliefs about ability and how success is referenced or defined.

Beliefs About Ability

The nature of ability is a complex concept (Dweck, 2000). Perception of ability is defined as one's evaluation of current capacity. According to Harter (1978), individuals with a high perception of ability are more likely to persist in an activity, so it is important to foster high perceptions of ability. Conceptions of ability, or beliefs about the stability of ability, are also influential factors in the motivational process. Young children are unable to differentiate between ability and effort (Fry, 2001). They equate the two concepts and conclude that individuals who try hard are doing well. As children develop the ability to compare socially, they begin to be able to differentiate between effort and ability, but they also develop beliefs about whether ability is fixed (innate) or malleable (acquired). Several different terminologies have been used to describe conceptions of ability (Dweck, 2000; Nicholls, 1984, 1989; Roberts, 2001), but the terms *innate* and *acquired* are used here for clarity. Individuals who have an innate conception believe that ability is stable and cannot be changed, whereas those with an acquired conception believe that ability can be improved with effort. For individuals who have a high perception of their own ability, the conception of ability may not be a critical factor. In cases where the perception of ability is low, however, the conception of ability can become a critical variable. If an individual believes that she or he lacks ability and cannot change that level of ability, then the person has no reason to exert effort. Individuals who express a belief in the efficacy of effort are more likely to exert effort (Xiang & Lee, 1998).

Self-efficacy (Bandura, 1986), described as a specific kind of perceived competence reflected by an individual's confidence that he or she can effectively use his or her ability in a specific situation, is a useful concept in fostering perceptions of high ability and an acquired conception of ability. Hebert et al. (2000) investigated task progressions as a way to increase self-efficacy. Their results indicate that using an incremental approach when teaching a complex skill so that students experience success in the early stages of practice, is one way to enhance students' self-efficacy and motivation. Higher levels of self-efficacy are associated with attributing failure to lack of effort, whereas individuals with lower self-efficacy tend to attribute failure to lack of ability (Chase, 2001).

How Success Is Defined

In the complex web of evaluating the relationship between ability and effort, another critical variable is how success is defined. Achievement goal theory has dominated research in motivation in sport and exercise over the last decade (Roberts, 2001), and that framework illustrates how definitions of success can affect student motivation. Goal theory assumes that individuals enter achievement settings with the goal of demonstrating competence. Two dimensions of goals operating in achievement contexts have been identified (Nicholls, 1984; 1989). A task-oriented goal perspective focuses on learning, mastering a skill, individual improvement, and a self-referenced criterion for success. A focus on task orientation has been associated with patterns of adaptive behavior, such as exerting effort, choosing challenging tasks, persisting in the face of difficulty, and attributing success to effort. Because of the internally referenced criteria for success, a sense of achievement is always possible, based on improved performance, successful completion, or mastery of a task. In contrast, within an ego-oriented goal perspective, success is externally referenced, and outperforming others is the primary goal. Students operating in an ego-involved context are more at risk to display maladaptive behavior patterns, such as avoiding challenge, refusing to exert effort when encountering difficulty, and attributing success to ability. Because such students reference success based on social comparison with peers' performance, improved skill or mastery of a task is not sufficient to produce feelings of competence. One must outperform others to evoke a sense of achievement, and consequently success is not always a possibility. The individual who perceives himself or herself to lack the ability to succeed (outperform others) has little or no reason to exert effort.

A convincing body of evidence (for reviews see Biddle, 2001; Roberts, 2001) indicates that a task-involved climate in physical education classes is preferable for all students.

Note that competition and ego involvement are not interchangeable concepts. Individuals who are highly task involved can also be very competitive, in that they may want to win games or outperform others as a measure of their success. It is when beating others is the sole criterion for success and competition is overemphasized or misused that some individuals are likely to withdraw effort. In a recent study by Solmon et al. (2001), fifth-grade students were asked to evaluate teaching practices used in physical education classes. Students overwhelmingly indicated a preference for classes with a focus on effort and improvement rather than an emphasis on outperforming others. The rationales for their evaluations of the teaching practices clearly indicated that the children realized that the best students would be motivated under any of the circumstances described, but that students who were lower in ability would be motivated only in task-involved settings where the focus was on personal improvement rather than social comparison.

IMPLICATIONS FOR RESEARCH AND PRACTICE
Structuring the Environment in Physical Education Classes to Maximize Engagement

Motivation is a complex construct influenced by a number of variables. I have discussed several important considerations for teachers in this chapter, such as gender, skill level, and prior experiences, but I have not been able to include many others, such as race, cultural factors, and disabilities. Although the context of individual achievement settings varies, and teachers must evaluate each situation to determine what will work best, research on student issues supports several recommendations.

The issue of attitude, interest, and value of physical education must be addressed before students will be motivated to learn. Teachers, the curriculum, the context, and student characteristics are all factors in developing positive attitudes, high levels of interest, and value of the activity. If students are to be motivated, the teacher must design activities that are personally meaningful and relevant from the students' perspective.

Teachers should take into account what students bring with them to class in the way of prior knowledge and experiences. Being aware of what students already know and what they do not know should enable teachers to plan and implement meaningful instruction. If motivation is to be initiated and sustained, teachers must provide clear instruction and construct learning activities to direct students' attention and concentration to task-focused elements. Teachers should use frequent checks for understanding to ensure that students understand the instructions as they intended. Structuring tasks and activities so that students can experience success fosters motivation. Although it is important to challenge students, task progressions that enable students to experience success in the early stages of learning should foster student motivation and engagement.

Reinforcing a belief in effort, rather than innate ability, as a cause of success and as means of improving ability should have positive consequences. References to the influence of innate ability on performance can reduce effort and motivation for individuals who believe they lack ability. If ability is the cause of success and effort cannot improve ability, then students have no reason to exert effort. This issue sometimes leads to a discussion of the merits of grading on effort and improvement rather than on mastery of content or skills. Although I am in favor of encouraging effort, it is difficult if not impossible to quantify effort objectively for the purpose of evaluation. Math or English teachers do not give students grades because they try hard. They hold students accountable for demonstrating mastery of important content, and if we are to be considered a valuable curricular area, physical education teachers should do the same.

A focus on personal improvement and mastery of a task is preferable to stressing social comparison as the reference point for success. An overemphasis on class rankings or winning can lead to decreased motivation and effort for individuals in the lower percentiles, who are the ones most in need. In reference to the earlier statement about grading on effort, I also believe that it is probably not best teaching practice to grade solely on physical performance measures, especially if only a certain percentage of highly skilled performers can earn the best grades. Evaluating students on the mastery of skills and content in a criterion-referenced system would be preferable to using normative or social comparison standards for grades. For example, suppose that scores on the mile run are to be used as a factor in determining student grades. Rather than giving A's to the fastest 25% of the students in a class, an alternative that would likely be more motivating to all students would be to set a standard for an A that is challenging but attainable for all individuals who exert effort during extended fitness instruction, such as completing a mile in nine minutes.

These strategies reflect a focus on structuring a task-involved climate that will foster student motivation. Perhaps the most important issue with regard to student issues, though, is simple: Listen to your students. Over the course of my teaching career I have often been amazed at the sophisticated insight that students show concerning the educational process, both in public schools and at the university level. I have been able to improve my teaching and the quality of the courses that I teach by asking students for feedback at the end of a class. I do not always take their suggestions, but when I review student evaluations, I invariably learn something from their comments that helps me as I prepare for my next class. Just as you can provide valuable feedback concerning your job situation to your principal, supervisor, or department chair, your students can be a valuable resource as you strive to be an effective teacher. Teachers who are discouraged and leave the profession may say, "Kids are just not like they used to be," and they are not. Just as physicians must learn new techniques and adjust to the changing needs of their patients, so too must teachers adjust based on changing student populations, and teachers must understand their viewpoints if educational programs are to be successful. Listening to students' views is one important aspect in learning how to design and implement quality physical education programs that are meaningful and valuable to all students.

IMPLICATIONS FOR PRACTICE

1. Student attitude, interest, and value of physical education must be addressed before students will be motivated to learn. Teachers, the curriculum, the context, and student characteristics are all factors in developing positive attitudes, high levels of interest, and value of the activity. If students are to be motivated, the teacher must design activities that are personally meaningful and relevant from the students' perspective.

2. Students' prior knowledge and experiences should be considered in selecting content, planning lessons, and deciding how quickly to move to the next topic or task. Being aware of what students already know and what they do not know should enable teachers to plan and implement meaningful instruction.

3. If motivation is to be initiated and sustained, teachers should provide clear instruction and organize learning activities to direct students' attention and concentration to task-focused elements. Teachers should use frequent checks for understanding to ensure that students understand the instruction as they intended.

4. Structuring tasks and activities so that students can experience success fosters motivation.

Although it is important to challenge students, task progressions that enable students to experience success in the early stages of learning should foster student motivation and engagement.

5. Reinforcing a belief in the efficacy of effort in physical activity should facilitate student engagement. If students believe that success in physical activity is primarily dependent on natural ability, they are likely to withdraw effort in challenging situations when they think they lack natural ability. Conversely, if effort rather than natural ability is emphasized as a primary cause of success, then students will be more likely to exert effort during physical activity, even when perceptions of ability are low.

6. A focus on personal improvement and mastery of a task is preferable to an emphasis on social comparison as the reference point for success. An overemphasis on class rankings or winning can lead to decreased motivation and effort for individuals who are weaker, lower skilled performers or are in the lower percentiles. Those individuals need positive reinforcement and encouragement the most. Although competition can be motivating for some students, it should be used in a positive way.

7. Listening to students' views is an important aspect in learning how to design and implement quality physical education programs that are meaningful and valuable to all students. Of course, teachers must ultimately decide what is in the best interests of their students, but student input can be a valuable information source in that decision-making process.

REFERENCES

Ajzen, I. (1988). *Attitudes, personality, and behavior.* Chicago: Dorsey Press.

Ajzen, I. (1993). Attitude theory and the attitude behavior relation. In D. Krebs & P. Schmidt (Eds.), *New directions in attitude measurement* (pp. 41-57). New York: de Gruyter.

Bain, L.L. (1989). Implicit values in physical education. In T.J. Templin & P.G. Schempp (Eds.). *Socialization into physical education: Learning to teach* (pp. 289-314). Indianapolis: Benchmark.

Bandura, A. (1986). *Social foundations of thought and action: A social cognitive theory.* Englewood Cliffs, NJ: Prentice Hall.

Biddle, S.J.H. (2001). Enhancing motivation in physical education. In G.C. Roberts (Ed.), *Advances in motivation in sport and exercise* (pp.101-127). Champaign, IL: Human Kinetics.

Brodie, D.A., & Britwistle, G.E. (1990). Children's attitude to physical activity, exercise and health and fitness before and after a health-related fitness measurement program. *International Journal of Physical Education, 27*(2), 10-14.

Carlson, T.B. (1995). We hate gym: Student alienation from physical education. *Journal of Teaching in Physical Education, 14,* 467-477.

Chase, M.A. (2001) Children's self-efficacy, motivational intentions, and attributions in physical education and sport. *Research Quarterly for Exercise and Sport, 72,* 47-54.

Chen, A. (2001). A theoretical conceptualization for motivation research in physical education: An integrated perspective. *Quest, 53,* 59-76.

Cothran, D.J., & Ennis, C.D. (1997). Students and teachers' perceptions of conflict and power. *Teaching and Teacher Education, 13,* 541-553.

Deci, E.L., & Ryan, R.M. (1985). *Intrinsic motivation and self-determination in human behavior.* New York: Plenum Press.

Doyle, W. (1977). Paradigms of research for teacher effectiveness. *Review of Research in Education, 5,* 163-198.

Dweck, C.S. (2000). *Self-theories: Their role in motivation, personality, and development.* Philadelphia: Taylor & Francis.

Ennis, C.D. (1996). Students' experiences in sport-based physical education: [More than] apologies are necessary. *Quest, 48,* 453-456.

Ennis, C.D., Cothran, D.J., Davidson, K.S., Loftus, S.J., Owens, L., Swanson, L., & Hopsicker, P. (1997). Implementing curriculum within a context of fear and disengagement. *Journal of Teaching in Physical Education, 14,* 52-71.

Ferrer-Caja, E., & Weiss, M.R. (2000). Predictors of intrinsic motivation among adolescent students in physical education. *Research Quarterly for Exercise and Sport, 71,* 267-279.

Figley, G.E. (1985). Determinants of attitudes toward physical education. *Journal of Teaching in Physical Education, 4,* 229-240.

Fry, M.D. (2001). The development of motivation in children. In G.C. Roberts (Ed.), *Advances in motivation in sport and exercise* (pp.51-78). Champaign, IL: Human Kinetics.

Gage, N.L. (Ed.). (1963). *Handbook of research on teaching.* Chicago: Rand McNally.

Graham, G. (Ed.). (1995). Physical education through

students' eyes and in students' voices [Monograph]. *Journal of Teaching in Physical Education, 14*(4).

Griffin, L.L., Dodds, P., Placek, J.H., & Tremino, F. (2001). Middle school students' conceptions of soccer: Their solutions to tactical problems. *Journal of Teaching in Physical Education, 20*, 324-340.

Griffin, L.L., & Placek, J.H. (Eds.). (2001). The understanding and development of learners' domain-specific knowledge [Monograph]. *Journal of Teaching in Physical Education, 20*(4).

Hare, M.K., & Graber, K.C. (2000). Student misconceptions during two invasion game units in physical education: A qualitative investigation of student thought processing. *Journal of Teaching in Physical Education, 20*, 55-77.

Harter, S. (1978). Effectance motivation reconsidered: Toward a developmental model. *Human Development, 21*, 34-64.

Hebert, E.P., Landin, D., & Solmon, M.A. (2000). The impact of task progressions on students' practice quality and task-related thoughts. *Journal of Teaching in Physical Education, 19*, 338-354.

Langley, D.J. (1995). Student cognition in the instructional setting. *Journal of Teaching in Physical Education, 15*, 25-40.

Lee, A.M. (1997). Contributions of research on student thinking in physical education. *Journal of Teaching in Physical Education, 16*, 262-277.

Lee, A.M., Landin, D.K., & Carter, J.A. (1992). Student thoughts during tennis instruction. *Journal of Teaching in Physical Education, 11*, 256-267.

Lee, A.M., & Solmon, M.A. (1992). Cognitive conceptions of teaching and learning motor skills. *Quest, 44*, 57-71.

Luke, M.D., & Sinclair, G.D. (1991). Gender differences in adolescents' attitudes toward physical education. *Journal of Teaching in Physical Education, 11*, 31-46.

Martin, L.T. (2000, April). *Perceptions of high, average, and low performance second graders about physical education and physical education teachers.* Paper presented at the annual meeting of the American Educational Research Association, New Orleans.

Martinek, T.J. (1988). Confirmation of a teacher expectancy model: Student perceptions and casual attributions of teaching behaviors. *Research Quarterly for Exercise and Sport, 59*, 118-126.

McKenzie, T.L., Alcaraz, J.E., & Sallis, J.F. (1994). Assessing children's liking for activity units in an elementary school physical education curriculum. *Journal of Teaching in Physical Education, 13*, 206-215.

Merriam-Webster. (1969). *Webster's seventh new collegiate dictionary.* Springfield, MA: G. & C. Merriam.

Nevett, M., Rovegno, I., & Babiarz, M. (2001). Fourth-grade children's knowledge of cutting, passing and tactics in invasion games after a 12-lesson unit of instruction. *Journal of Teaching in Physical Education, 20*, 389-401.

Nicholls, J.G. (1984). Conceptions of ability and achievement motivation. In R. Ames & C. Ames (Eds.), *Research on motivation in education: Vol. 1. Student motivation* (pp. 39-68). New York: Academic Press.

Nicholls, J.G. (1989). *The competitive ethos and democratic education.* Cambridge, MA: Harvard University Press.

Peterson, P.L. (1988). Teachers' and students' cognitional knowledge for classroom teaching and learning. *Educational Researcher, 17*(5), 5-14.

Placek, J.H., Griffin, L.L. Dodds, P., Raymond, C., Tremino, F., & James, A. (2001). Middle school students conceptions of fitness: The long road to a healthy life style. *Journal of Teaching in Physical Education, 20*, 314-323.

Portman, P.A. (1995). Who is having fun in physical education classes? Experiences of six grade students in elementary and middle schools. *Journal of Teaching in Physical Education, 14*, 445-453.

Rice, P.L. (1988). Attitudes of high school students toward physical education activities, teachers, and personal health. *Physical Educator, 45*, 94-99.

Richardson, V. (Ed.). (2001). *Handbook of research on teaching* (4th ed.). Washington, DC: American Educational Research Association.

Roberts, G.C. (1992). Motivation in sport and exercise: Conceptual constraints and convergence. In G.C. Roberts (Ed.), *Motivation in sport and exercise* (pp. 3-29). Champaign, IL: Human Kinetics.

Roberts, G.C. (2001). Understanding the dynamics of motivation in physical activity: The influence of achievement goals on motivational processes. In G.C. Roberts (Ed.), *Advances in motivation in sport and exercise* (pp. 1-50). Champaign, IL: Human Kinetics.

Sanders, S., & Graham, G. (1995). Kindergarten children's initial experiences in physical education: The relentless persistence for play clashes with the zone of acceptable responses. *Journal of Teaching in Physical Education, 14*, 372-383.

Shulman, L.S. (1986). Paradigms and research programs in the study of teaching: A contemporary perspective. In M.C. Wittrock (Ed.), *Handbook of research on teaching* (3rd ed., pp. 3-36). New York: Macmillan.

Silverman, S. (1993). Student characteristics, practice, and achievement in physical education. *Journal of Educational Research, 87*, 54-61.

Silverman, S., & Subramaniam, P.R. (1999). Student attitude toward physical education and physical activity: A review of measurement issues and outcomes. *Journal of Teaching in Physical Education, 19*, 97-125.

Solmon, M.A. (in review). *Goal theory in physical education classes: Examining goal profiles to understand achievement motivation.*

Solmon, M.A., & Carter, J.A. (1995). Kindergarten and first-grade students' perceptions of physical education in one teacher's classes. *Elementary School Journal, 95*, 355-365.

Solmon, M.A., & Lee, A.M. (1996). Entry characteristics, practice variables, and cognition: Student mediation of instruction. *Journal of Teaching in Physical Education, 15*, 136-150.

Solmon, M.A., Lee, A.M., Rukavina, P., Landry, J., Harrison, L. Jr., & Li, W. (2001, April). *Children's critiques of teaching practices in physical fitness.* Paper presented at the annual meeting of the American Educational Research Association, Seattle.

Subramaniam, P.R., & Silverman, S. (2000). Validation of scores from an instrument assessing student attitude toward physical education. *Measurement in Physical Education and Exercise Science, 4*, 29-43.

Subramaniam, P.R., & Silverman, S. (2002). Using complimentary data: An investigation of student attitude in physical education. *Journal of Sport Pedagogy, 8*, 74-91.

Tannehill, D., Romar, J., O'Sullivan, M., England, K., & Rosenberg, D. (1994). Attitudes toward physical education: Their impact on how physical educators make sense of their work. *Journal of Teaching in Physical Education, 13*, 78-84.

Tjeerdsma, B.L. (1997). A comparison of teacher and student perspectives of tasks and feedback. *Journal of Teaching in Physical Education, 16*, 388-400.

Tjeerdsma, B.L., Rink, J.E., & Graham, K.C. (1996). Student perceptions, values and beliefs prior to, during, and after badminton instruction. *Journal of Teaching in Physical Education, 15*, 464-476.

Tousignant, M., & Siedentop, D. (1983). A qualitative analysis of task structures in required secondary physical education classes. *Journal of Teaching in Physical Education, 3*(1), 47-57.

Travers, R.M.W. (Ed.). (1973). *Second handbook of research on teaching.* Chicago: Rand McNally.

Vallerand, R J. (2001). A hierarchical model of intrinsic motivation and extrinsic motivation in sport and exercise. In G.C. Roberts (Ed.), *Advances in motivation in sport and exercise* (pp. 1-50). Champaign, IL: Human Kinetics.

von Glasersfeld, E. (1987). Learning as constructive activity. In E. von Glasersfeld (Ed.), *The construction of knowledge: Contributions to conceptual semantics* (pp. 307-333). Salinas, CA: Intersystems Publications.

Wigfield, A., & Eccles, J.S. (1993). The development of achievement task values: A theoretical analysis. *Developmental Review, 12*, 265-310.

Wittrock, M.C. (Ed.). (1986a). *Handbook of research on teaching* (3rd ed.). New York: Macmillan.

Wittrock, M.C. (1986b). Students' thought processes. In M.C. Wittrock (Ed.), *Handbook of research on teaching* (3rd ed., pp. 297-314). New York: Macmillan.

Wittrock, M.C. (1987). Teaching and student thinking. *Journal of Teacher Education, 38*(6), 30-33.

Xiang, P., & Lee, A.M. (1998). The development of self-perceptions of ability and achievement goals and their relations in physical education. *Research Quarterly for Exercise and Sport, 69*, 231-241

Zimbardo, P.G., & Leippe, M.R. (1991). *The psychology of attitude change and social influence.* Philadelphia: Temple University Press.

CHAPTER TEN

EFFECTIVE INSTRUCTION IN PHYSICAL EDUCATION

Judith E. Rink

Identifying good teaching has always been a problem for educators. We tend to say that good teaching is something we cannot describe or define, let alone prescribe. The problem is that if we cannot describe good teaching, then any teaching is as good as any other. We need to be able to describe good teaching so that we can help teachers to become better at what they do and so that we have a knowledge base from which to train and educate new teachers. The increasing research base on teacher effectiveness has helped us to describe good teaching more fully than ever before.

WHAT IS EFFECTIVE TEACHING?

Although the terms *effective teaching* and *good teaching* have been used interchangeably at times, more often the former has been used to describe teaching that results in intended learning (Berliner, 1987; Brophy, 1979; Rosenshine, 1987). Students learn a lot through experience. They learn a lot in schools that is not intended, some of it desirable and some of it not, but the primary function of schools is to produce intended learning. Effective teaching, then, is teaching that results in more intended learning than does less effective teaching (Gage, 1978). With the current emphasis on standards, assessment, and accountability in schools, the notion of intended learning takes on an even more important role. Teachers must not only teach to standards but also produce student learning in these standards. They must be both good teachers and effective teachers.

Most of what we know about effective teaching comes to us from well-conducted classroom research studies that identify what teachers do who produce the most learning (Brophy & Evertson, 1974; Brophy & Good, 1986; Good & Grouws, 1975; McDonald & Elias, 1976; Stallings & Kaskowitz, 1974). These efforts were large, correlational studies conducted primarily in a process-product research design. Process-product research designs examine the relationship between characteristics of the teaching process and the products of teaching (most often student learning). Primarily using highly structured subject matter and short-term teaching objectives, these studies consistently identified particular variables as important to effective classroom teaching. The physical education literature includes studies with similar findings. A set of teaching principles that describe what effective teachers do has evolved from this research base (Berliner, 1987; Brophy & Good, 1986; Gage, 1978).

As you read this material you will need to keep in mind that we are talking about studies based on highly structured content and short-term objectives. Highly structured subject matter lends itself to being broken down into small parts. The effective teaching literature has identified primarily generic variables related to teacher effectiveness, that is, those variables that seem to discriminate effective teaching across content and settings. More recent research in the classroom as well as in physical education has been concerned primarily with the identification of context-specific ideas that describe how effective teachers teach particular content to particular learners in particular settings (Griffin & Placek, 2001).

The effective teaching literature is also based on research procedures that identify how *most* students learn best. Recent literature focusing on individual learners makes clear the unique learning experience of all students (Lee, 2002). Nevertheless, a teacher works with groups, and the issue of how to meet the needs of most students within that group while accommodating individual differences is the challenge of teaching. The problem, of course, in defining effective teaching in terms of what most students learn is that goals for student learning are often complex, long-term, multidimensional, and not easily measured. What makes a multiobjective setting complex from a measurement perspective is that teachers can be effective in meeting one objective and ineffective in meeting another. The multiobjective problem is compounded by the idea that there may be real differences in what is effective in the short run and what is effective with time. The National Association for Sport and Physical Education (NASPE) Outcomes Project (1992) and the NASPE Standards and Assessment Project (1995; also see chapter 8 by Leslie Lambert) reinforce the multifaceted goals of a comprehensive physical education program. These materials describe skill development, fitness, participation in physical activity, and cognitive and affective concerns. The aim of the physical education program is clearly identified as developing students who lead a physically active lifestyle. The idea of a physically active lifestyle is a long-term goal. All the standards are considered essential to this long-term goal, but teachers may accomplish short-term objectives in a way that jeopardizes the long-term goal (e.g., making students fit but destroying their love for activity, acquiring motor skills as opposed to retaining motor skills).

Some teachers may not have student learning as the goal of teaching (Ennis, 1994). Under those conditions the concept of effective teaching is a moot point. Most educators accept the idea that it is their responsibility to facilitate student learning in some way. With teacher accountability for student learning moving in clearly articulated directions, teachers may have no choice but to learn to teach a more prescribed content effectively.

PROPOSITIONAL RULES AND PRINCIPLED PRACTICE

In spite of the complexity of trying to sort out issues related to what effective teachers actually do, we must try to understand the teaching-learning process in depth. A search for rigid prescriptions of the right way to teach has largely been replaced with the search for propositional rules and principles to guide practice. The effective teacher needs a wide variety of teaching strategies that he or she can use effectively (Freiberg & Driscoll, 2000). Propositional rules and principles of teaching largely transcend teaching strategies. Principles of teaching are general guidelines for practice that teachers can apply situationally (Berliner, 1987; Ornstein & Levine, 1981; Rosenshine & Stevens, 1986).

In this perspective what the teacher does is seen in terms of the function of a particular teaching act in a particular setting. Teaching functions have been identified at three domains in terms of the preactive, interactive, and postactive decisions teachers have to make (Rosenshine & Stevens, 1986). More specifically, several teaching functions for physical education have been described:

- Identifying intended outcomes for learning
- Planning learning experiences to accomplish those outcomes
- Presenting tasks to learners
- Organizing and managing the learning environment
- Monitoring the learning environment
- Developing the content
- Evaluating the effectiveness of the instructional-curricular process (Rink, 2002)

Principles of teaching can describe in broad terms the characteristics of these functions when they are performed well. Principles of teaching cannot prescribe particular behaviors because many behaviors can perform the same function. Furthermore, the same behavior can perform different functions in different settings. For example, learners can receive the information they need to perform a skill through teacher explanation, student or teacher demonstration, media, computers, or peers. Expertise involves knowing when and how to apply a principle of teaching to accomplish particular objectives in particular settings.

TEACHER EFFECTIVENESS IN PHYSICAL EDUCATION

Because physical education is concerned with the psychomotor domain, it has a unique position in the educational community. Principles of teaching physical education are drawn from the effective teaching literature in physical education and the classroom and, to some extent, from motor-learning theory and research. The rest of this chapter outlines the critical variables from the effective teaching research in physical education. Several chapters of this text include issues related to effective teaching that will not appear here, including issues of context (chapter 4), gender (chapter 5), students with disabilities (chapter 6), health-related physical activity goals (chapter 12), teaching sport (chapter 13), and teaching personal and social responsibility (chapter 14). The information on effective instruction has been organized as principles of practice and is discussed both in terms of the limitations of the knowledge base as well as the implications of that knowledge base for teaching physical education.

Students Who Spend More Time in Good Practice Learn More

The fact that students learn more when they practice more should not surprise anyone, particularly when it comes to learning motor skills. Initially, researchers investigated this variable in terms of the amount of time a teacher allocated for practice (Anderson, 1980; Metzler, DePaepe, & Reif, 1985). Gradually, the construct has evolved to the idea that if we want students to learn a motor skill they have to be engaged at a high level and be successful at an appropriate task for a sufficient amount of time (Cousineau & Luke, 1990; Goldberger & Gerney, 1990; Metzler, 1989; Silverman, 1985, 1990; Silverman, Devillier, & Ramírez, 1991).

Research

The first descriptive studies in physical education outlined a rather dismal picture. Students in physical education classes were active only about a third of the class time (Anderson, 1980; Costello, 1977). Newer descriptive studies using an instrument called Academic Learning Time Physical Education (ALT-PE) (Metzler, 1979) describe the amount of time students are engaged in activity at an appropriate level of difficulty. The results of these studies continue to show that students in physical education classes are not spending a great deal of time engaged in appropriate practice of physical skills and therefore do not have much opportunity to become skillful.

More specific measures of practice that look at the number of actual practice trials, as opposed to time only, and efforts that look at the quality of the practice have been more productive in identifying a strong, positive relationship between practice and learning (Ashy, Lee, & Landin, 1988; Buck, Harrison, & Bryce, 1991; Silverman, 1985, 1990; Werner & Rink, 1989). A relationship exists between the motor-appropriate variable in the ALT-PE instrument (as well as other measures of time) and the content and learning, although this relationship is not as close as we might have expected (Godbout, Burnelle, & Tousignant, 1983; Silverman et al., 1991). The idea that time in practice is not a sufficient predictor of effectiveness is most likely because other factors of engagement influence the quality of practice and determine whether or not a student learns.

Implications

The message from most process-product studies using complex motor skills, such as those most frequently taught in physical education, is that learning takes time. Physical education units planned for a period of three weeks may assign one class period to the development of each skill. If students are to learn a skill well enough to use it in game situations or to become a participant in a given activity, sufficient time must be allocated for learning, particularly if the goal is competence in sports that involve complex and difficult motor skills. This idea has serious implications for curriculum planning in physical education. Teachers must either increase the time spent teaching one activity and teach fewer of them or change the activities they teach so that students can master a skill or activity in the time allowed. Sport education (see chapter 13 by Peter Hastie) models of teaching sport and games to students do two things to make the program more effective. First, they recommend much longer units of instruction, and second, they reduce the complexity of the sport considerably by having students play small-sided games with modified rules. This curricular issue, identified primarily from instructional research, is perhaps the most significant issue facing physical educators with limited program time who continue to try to teach a comprehensive curriculum.

Practice Should be Appropriate to the Goal of Learning and the Individual Student

Tasks must be appropriate if students are to learn them. First, the tasks students do must relate to an objective or measurement. If, for instance, you are interested in teaching students how to use a forearm pass in volleyball and the practice never goes beyond a soft toss from the partner, you will not likely see much progress in the execution of a forearm pass in a game. Transfer of practice to game conditions depends on the extent to which the practice resembles the game (Magill, 2001). A key question teachers should ask themselves about student tasks is "Will this task develop the objective I want to develop?" If the answer to this question is no, the next question is "How can I make the task and the practice more appropriate?" or "How can I gradually move students from where they are to where I want them to be?"

A second factor related to appropriateness is the characteristics of the individual learner. If students do not have the prerequisites to learn a skill, they could practice forever and probably not make much progress. Students who do not have sufficient abdominal strength cannot do a hip circle on a bar no matter how hard they try.

Research

Research on teaching volleyball in high school and middle school found that about one-third of the student population from the studies made no progress over six days of practice in their ability to use a forearm pass or an overhand serve pattern in rather simple conditions. (French et al., 1991; French, Rink, & Werner, 1990; Rink, French, Werner, Lynn, & Mays, 1992). A simple to complex progression of tasks was used, but low-skilled students were not able to generate enough force in the testing conditions, which were more gamelike. What are the long-term implications of presenting to learners tasks that are not within their capabilities?

Implications

If students do not practice in gamelike conditions, they will not be able to play the game. If practice conditions are too gamelike, beginning learners may not improve because the practice conditions may be too difficult for them. These two statements present the major problem physical education teachers have in trying to teach the skills of complex games and sports to students in a typical physical education class. Practice must occur at a level that incorporates as much of the game as students can manage successfully. More effective articulation of expectations for students at different levels and grades in our curriculums should facilitate more appropriate content for students, but that approach will not be effective unless teachers teach to that level. Past practices of teaching to directional goals far above the level of a large number of students, rather than teaching so that all students in a class accomplish the goals, are difficult to change.

Students Who Practice at a Reasonably High Success Level Learn More

The issue of success rate is related to task appropriateness. The students in the volleyball example were not successful at even minimal levels. From the classroom literature we have learned that students should be engaged in the content with a success level approaching 80% (Berliner, 1987). Although the physical education research supports the importance of successful practice, indications are that applying an 80% success rate for motor skills may be inappropriate for many motor tasks.

Research

The type of motor skill being practiced is a factor in determining an appropriate success rate for practice. Consider basketball shooting. The expectation that beginners should have an 80% success rate would not be appropriate. An 80% success rate in many shots would be unheard of even for professional players. We are less able to be consistent when performing skills in a changing environment or when performing complex skills that require a great deal of eye-hand or eye-foot coordination, such as tennis serves, golf drives, volleyball spikes, and so on. As discussed in a later section on progressions, teachers can reduce the level of complexity of skills to increase the likelihood of success.

A more recent issue related to success rate has been raised in the motor-learning literature: Does more successful practice always mean more learning (Magill, 2001)? To understand the implications of this idea, we must make the distinction between acquisition and retention. Acquisition refers to the success of learners while they are learning a motor skill. Retention refers to their ability to perform after they have learned a motor skill. Some evidence supports the idea that a very high success rate during the acquisition phase of learning does not always lead to increased retention or learning. From a motor-skill perspective, "errorless practice and rote repetition are poor learning strategies" (Lee, Swinnen, & Serrien, 1994, p. 338). Although work in this area is at an early stage, theorists suspect that the reason for this may be related to cognitive processing, as discussed in the next section.

Physical educators often talk about trying to find the balance between tasks that are not challenging enough for students and those that are too difficult to sustain practice. Finding that balance for all students is difficult because the appropriate level of challenge is likely to be different for different students and performance in many motor skills is much more variable than performance in cognitive learning. In addition, some students are more willing to practice at lower success rates than other students are. This willingness is most likely related to the age of the learner, the particular skill they are practicing, and personality characteristics.

Implications

As Melinda Solmon indicates in chapter 9, most educators believe that students will not continue to do that at which they are not successful, either short-term practice of skills or long-term program goals. Teachers can determine appropriate task difficulty by weighing effort against degree of success. If the learner can be successful with effort, then the task is appropriate. If success requires no effort or if learners try hard but cannot be successful, then the task is probably not appropriate. Although teachers work with groups, success rate pertains to the appropriateness of the task for an individual. Effective teachers find ways to help individual students be successful by manipulating the demands of motor tasks. In many instances teachers can break down skills (e.g., start with the toss in the tennis serve), change the conditions of practice (e.g., move partners closer together), or modify the equipment (e.g., use lighter volleyballs or shorter rackets). Developing the ability to design learning experiences within a class so that different students can be working at different levels takes preparation and a real commitment to the importance of student success rate in learning.

Students Who Practice at a Higher Level of Processing Learn More

One of the characteristics of quality practice is related to the learner's level of cognitive effort. Learner attention to the task was identified early on as an important ingredient in learning. Fitts and Posner (1967) identified the first stage of motor learning as being cognitive, which means that the learner must translate information on how to perform into a motor program. The last stage of motor learning is automatic, which means that the movement response requires a lower level of cognitive functioning. Students cannot get to the later stages of learning without processing responses and attending to their actions.

Research

The importance of cognition becomes apparent at the point when the learner is trying to determine how to attempt the skill (the initial motor program), as well as during practice. Although we do not have consensus on the specific, underlying cognitive mechanisms governing motor performance, the importance of cognitive processes in anticipating, planning, regulating, and interpreting motor performances has received increased attention from researchers in both motor-learning theory and pedagogy (French et al., 1990; Housner & French, 1994; Lee et al., 1994; Sweeting & Rink, 1999).

The critical role of learner cognition has long been the justification for many of the variables we have identified as important to instructing learners on how to perform

(Magill, 2001; Rink, 2001). The intent has been to present information on performing a task to learners in a way that helps them design an accurate motor plan for a movement response. If a student has the prerequisites to perform a motor skill correctly and does not, the assumption is that the learner does not have a clear idea of how to perform that skill. The failure occurs not because the muscular-skeletal system is not functioning correctly but because the cognitive plan being executed is not correct. Obviously, the nature and manner in which information is communicated to learners can facilitate the development of accurate motor plans. This information appears later in this chapter (see the section on task presentation).

Teachers facilitate cognitive processing not only by the manner in which they present tasks but also by the way in which they arrange practice (Good & Magill, 1986; Lee et al., 1994). Mere repetition of responses without processing is unlikely to be as effective for learning as practice in which the student must continue to process or review their actions during each trial.

Implications

The idea that students should be engaged with the content at a high level for prolonged periods should surprise no one. When practice fails to produce student learning we can only suggest that what they practiced, or how they practiced it, was not appropriate, assuming that the measure of learning and the learning objective was appropriate. In one sense, the ability of the teacher to increase the quantity and quality of practice is the ultimate teaching skill. As Silverman and Tyson (1994) have said, most other teaching skills affect learning through their influence on practice. Student engagement is the goal, engagement not only in quantity of time but also in quality of time. One of the ideas that makes more indirect styles of teaching appealing to teachers is the belief that students will be engaged at a higher level when teachers transfer some teacher control and use more indirect styles of teaching. Although this idea is intuitively appealing, teachers must seek evidence that students are actually engaged in the processes that they have intended (Rink, 2001). Until we know more about how to engage students appropriately, we will not know enough to help teachers. Many of the variables that follow provide insight into how to engage students appropriately with the content.

Effective Teachers Create an Environment for Learning

Although management is often contrasted with the substantive content of instruction, the two are integrally related. Good managers are not necessarily effective teachers, but effective teachers must be good managers. Management was an early focus of research on teaching, both in the classroom as well as in the gymnasium, and it is a continuous concern for practicing teachers in public school settings. Most often you cannot see good management, but you will see the effects of poor management. Good managers have a learning environment in which students are highly engaged in the intended content. Good managers are able to use a variety of teaching strategies because they have developed the independent working skills of students and have been able to transfer some teacher control to the student.

Research

Management has come to be thought of as a process of obtaining and maintaining order (Doyle, 1986). Management usually involves two dimensions. The first relates to the ability of the teacher to develop and maintain a learning climate, and the second relates to the teacher's organizational skills (Emmer, Evertson, & Anderson, 1980; Evertson & Emmer, 1982; Soar & Soar, 1979). A positive learning climate is one in which students are focused and motivated to learn. The classroom climates of effective teachers are task oriented, businesslike, and slightly warm in their affective tone (Soar & Soar, 1979). Effective learning environments are not necessarily high affect. The teacher must motivate students to engage in academic content at a high level of engagement and avoid offering criticism (which is negative affect), but such an environment is not necessarily totally student centered.

Studies describing the classrooms of effective managers identified the critical role of teaching students rules and procedures and using these in a consistent fashion (Brophy, 1983; Doyle, 1986). Effective managers monitor student behavior, develop systems and methods of holding students accountable for their work, present information clearly, and organize instruction so that students spend more time on academic tasks rather than nonacademic tasks (Emmer et al., 1980; Evertson & Emmer, 1982).

Early work on teacher management probably spent too much time concerned with the teacher's responsibility for behavior and student compliance with rules. More recent efforts in studying teacher management have focused on trying to understand differences between settings and individual students as well as ways to transfer the responsibility for student behavior to the student (Freiberg & Driscoll, 2000; McCaslin & Good, 1992). Motivating students to learn requires that the teacher develop sympathy with the abilities and needs of particular students in particular settings without abandoning the comprehensive goals of the physical education program or the broader curricular goals of a school.

Implications

Management is important because time spent managing behavior or the learning environment is time taken away from providing substantive content. Management is important because teachers who have not developed control cannot release that control and use more effective teaching strategies. Teachers who are good managers organize for high levels of practice and develop a learning environment that maintains a high level of student engagement in that practice. Effective managers are in charge. Students are not simply let go; teachers hold them accountable for their work, and they are on task during class time. Teachers who teach and maintain rules and procedures in their class, use stop and start signals, and respond to inattentive and disruptive behavior quickly are more likely to be effective teachers.

Management continues to be a major problem and concern for physical education teachers who have not been able to develop a learning environment that enables them to focus students on learning. Many physical education environments include a great deal of student off-task behavior or a predominant teacher focus on student compliance. Many physical education environments have no learning expectations. Students are not off task—they are simply not engaged in learning. In some cases teachers have lost their belief that students can learn or want to learn physical education content, a circumstance that has produced subtle but substantial changes in curriculum (Ennis, 1994). Teachers have been unable to create an environment that enables them to teach motor or fitness content, which may be why they are looking elsewhere for program justification.

When teachers have not produced a learning environment conducive to learning, the teacher's choice of learning experiences is limited. Many of the exciting teaching strategies and curriculum approaches that are often recommended for physical education require a degree of student independence not developed in most physical education teaching environments. Students need a degree of independence to work in cooperative learning environments or to work independently at their own level with tasks. Teachers who do not develop a learning environment that minimally supports a level of student self-control (Hellison, 1995) will not be able to use alternative teaching strategies critical to the development of many important goals of physical education.

Effective Teachers Are Good Communicators

Much of the classroom research related to communication has taken the form of investigations of teacher clarity (Kennedy, Cruickshank, Bush, & Meyers, 1978; Land, 1981). The teacher's ability to communicate with the learner is critical to effective physical education. In terms of instructional events, the presentation of the instructional task is critical. The teacher must be able to select important information for the learner, organize that information, and communicate it to the learner. When students are not doing what the teacher intended, the problem can usually be traced back to poor communication and inadequate task presentations.

Research on Presentations

Rosenshine and Stevens (1986) have described several aspects of clear presentations from classroom research. Figure 10.1 summarizes these ideas. There is no reason to assume that these generic aspects of clarity are not appropriate for physical education. Teachers need to (a) have explicit goals for their classes that are clearly communicated,

---

Rosenshine and Stevens' Aspects of Clear Presentations

1. Clarity of goals and main points
   a. State the goals and objectives of the presentation.
   b. Focus on one thought, point, or direction at a time.
   c. Avoid digressions.
   d. Avoid ambiguous phrases and pronouns.

2. Step-by-step presentations
   a. Present the material in small steps.
   b. Organize and present the material so that one point is mastered before the next point is given.
   c. Give explicit step-by-step directions (when possible).
   d. Present an outline when the material is complex.

3. Specific and concrete procedures
   a. Model the skill or process (when appropriate).
   b. Give detailed and redundant information for difficult points.
   c. Provide students with concrete and varied examples.

4. Checking for students' understanding
   a. Be sure that students understand one point before proceeding to the next point.
   b. Ask the students questions to monitor their comprehension of what has been presented.
   c. Have students summarize the main points in their own words.
   d. Reteach the parts of the presentation that the students have difficulty comprehending, either by further teacher explanation or by students tutoring other students.

FIGURE 10.1   Summary of Rosenshine and Stevens' characteristics of clear presentations.

(b) organize and present material logically, in step-by-step progressions, (c) take material to concrete levels, and (d) check to make sure that students understand what they are saying (Rink, 1994). Almost all the work on task presentation in physical education has assumed a direct approach to teaching, the assumption being that the teacher must give explicit information to the learner on what to do and how to do it. What differentiates physical education from classroom subjects is its emphasis on presenting motor skills. Several instruments have been developed to describe task presentation characteristics in a physical education setting. The Qualitative Measures of Teaching Performance Scale (QMTPS) (Rink & Werner, 1989) was primarily designed to describe the manner in which the teacher presents tasks to learners. Figure 10.2 describes the categories of the scale. The initial work validating the relationship between this instrument and student learning has been encouraging. The total score on the QMTPS was highly correlated with student learning in a middle school volleyball setting, supporting results of earlier studies with elementary children (Gusthart, Kelly, & Rink, 1997). Silverman and his colleagues (Silverman, Kulinna, & Crull, 1995) have also identified and supported task explicitness, including communicating to the learner the situation, the criterion for performance, and the outcome of the desired performance, as a critical dimension of effective teaching.

Kwak (1993) conducted a study that provided a great deal of support for a direct approach to task presentation. Five different task presentations were compared in terms of their effects on process characteristics (form), the product characteristics of learning, and the learner's ability to verbalize how to perform an unfamiliar, complex, gross motor skill (lacrosse throw). The five different treatments were

1. verbal explanation with partial demonstration;
2. full demonstration only;
3. overload explanation with partial demonstration;
4. verbal explanation with full demonstrations and summary cues, visual-verbal rehearsal task presentation; and
5. control group with no task presentation.

The results of the study strongly support the use of full demonstration, summary cues, and student rehearsal. The students in the control group had higher product and process scores and were better able to verbalize how to perform the skill.

Graham and her colleagues (Graham, 1988; Graham, Hussey, Taylor, & Werner, 1993) have studied the task presentations of effective teachers in physical education and have identified eight dimensions of effective task presentations:

1. Making instruction explicit
2. Emphasizing the usefulness of the content being presented
3. Structuring new content
4. Signaling student's attention
5. Summarizing and repeating information
6. Checking for understanding
7. Creating a productive climate for learning
8. Presenting accountability measures

You will recognize the overlap of teaching functions in this list. These authors have identified not only the clarity of the information as being important to task presentation but also the need to structure content and organize to motivate learners.

QMTPS Task Presentation Categories

1. Clarity

Teacher's verbal explanation/directions communicated a clear idea of what to do and how to do it. This judgment is confirmed on the basis of student movement response to the presentation and is relative to the situation.

> **Yes:** Students proceed to work in a focused way on what the teacher asked them to do.
> **No:** Students exhibited confusion, questions, off-task behavior, or lack of intent to deal with the specifics of the task.

2. Demonstration

Visual information modeling desired performance executed by teacher, student(s), and/or visual aids.

> **Yes:** Full model of the desired movement.
> **Partial:** Incomplete model of task performance exhibiting only part of the desired movement.
> **No:** No attempt to model the movement task.

3. Appropriate Number of Cues

The degree to which the teacher presented sufficient information useful to the performance of the movement task without overloading the learner.

> **Appropriate:** Three or fewer new learning cues related to the performance of the movement task.
> **Inappropriate:** More than three new learning cues related to the performance of the movement, or none given when needed.
> **None given:** No attempt at providing learning cues was made.

4. Accuracy of Cues

The degree to which the information presented was technically correct and reflected accurate mechanical principles.

> **Accurate:** All information present was correct.
> **Inaccurate:** One or more instances of incorrect information.
> **None given:** No cues given.

5. Qualitative Cues Provided

Verbal information provided to the learner on the process or mechanics of movement.

> **Yes:** Teacher's explanation or direction included at least one aspect of the process of performance.
> **No:** Teacher's explanation or direction included no information on the process of performance.

6. Appropriate to the Focus

The degree to which student responses reflected an intent to perform the task as stated by the teacher.

> **All:** One—no more than two students viewed on the screen exhibited inappropriate responses.
> **Partial:** Two—three or more students viewed on the screen exhibited inappropriate behavior.
> **None:** Three—no students exhibited appropriate behavior.

7. Specific Congruent Feedback

The degree to which teacher feedback during activity was congruent with (matched) the focus of the task.

> **Yes :** More than two instances were evident of teacher feedback being congruent with the task.
> **Partial:** One or two instances of congruent feedback were evident.
> **No:** No congruent feedback was given.

FIGURE 10.2   QMTPS task presentation categories designed to describe how a teacher presents tasks to learners.

Research on Demonstrations

Demonstration (modeling) has received a great deal of research support in social learning, classroom research, motor-learning laboratory research, and research on teaching physical education. Demonstration has long been recognized as a critical aspect of presenting information to learners (Martens, Burwitz, & Zuckerman, 1976; McCullagh, Stiehl, & Weiss, 1990). In spite of the evidence supporting the use of demonstration in physical education settings, teachers present a large percentage of motor tasks to learners without the help of a visual demonstration of the movement (Gusthart & Sprigings, 1989; Gusthart et al., 1997; Werner & Rink, 1989).

Some effort has gone into trying to define the characteristics of good demonstrations in both laboratory and physical education settings. Most experts support the idea that the model should be accurate and suggest that a high-status model of the same gender as the learner is more likely to be an effective demonstrator (Gould & Roberts, 1982). If tasks need to be broken down, they should be demonstrated in sequence, and learners need to see complex movements more than once. In reviewing this research Lee et al. (1994) suggest that rather than search for expert models of a movement, teachers may want to use a learner to demonstrate, suggesting that although the expert model produces "learning by imitation," the learner model is more likely to promote greater cognitive processing of the skill by the learner. Unless the learner already has a clear idea of how to perform, however, it is not likely that he or she will be able to contrast his or her attempts with accurate performance of the motor response. The use of demonstration is part of a larger issue related to presenting information clearly to learners and is better understood as part of a process of communication. In this respect, the combination of verbal and visual information and the use of verbal rehearsal are most effective when the objective is to give the learner a clear idea of how to perform a motor task.

Research on Verbal Cues

The use of verbal learning cues is another aspect of presenting information to learners that has received a great deal of support in the motor-learning literature (Landin, 1994; Magill, 2001) and encouraging support in the pedagogy literature (Kwak, 1993; Masser, 1993). Learning cues are verbal words or phrases that describe the critical features of a skill, such as the term *squash* for the giving action in landing from height or the phrase *sit into it* for the ready position for a volleyball forearm pass. The theoretical support for learning cues comes primarily from research on attention and information processing (Housner & French, 1994; Landin, 1994). Learning cues help the learner to sort out and attend to what is relevant in a response and to compress many parts of a movement skill into a single response. *Squash*, for instance, might replace a description of how to land that involves remembering how to reach with the toes and give gradually with the ankles, knees, and hips. Use of the term *squash* helps produce the combined response.

The literature also offers ample evidence that student involvement in the learning process and therefore student learning increase if the learner verbalizes rehearsal strategies. Verbal rehearsal strategies (Madigan, Frey, & Matlock, 1992) and self-talk regimens (Landin, 1994) involve the learner in using spoken verbal cues to rehearse the sequence either before or during performance. A student learning a tennis serve might say, for instance, "Stretch down and back stretch," as he or she practices the serve.

Implications

Selecting good learning cues to explain or demonstrate what students should know or be able to do is part of the art of teaching. Expertise is knowing how to break down, organize, and present content for particular learners. For most physical education tasks, teachers will want to communicate not only the sequence of action but also the characteristics of good performance. Good learning cues accurately and richly reflect the movement characteristics that teachers want to convey. A learning cue may only describe or order parts of a skill, such as "1-2-3," a cue often used in teaching dance steps to indicate the timing as well as the sequence of actions. Numbers or words are useful if they help the learner perform a skill accurately. Most students find it more meaningful for teachers to use words or expressions that communicate a visual impression. The teacher who says "Make like a chicken" instead of "Keep your elbows out" is likely to receive a better response from more motivated learners.

The selection of learning cues depends on the age of the learner, the stage of the learner, and type of task she or he is performing. Learning cues break a skill down into phases, which is a useful approach for the beginning stages of most tasks. Continued reliance on sequenced practice, however, might interfere with skills that learners must perform without clear breaks, so the teacher may want to change the learning cues for some motor skills according to the stage of learning. For example, in teaching a jumping action, the teacher may replace initial cues for the preparation, execution, and recovery of the action with the simple cue "Explode" to produce a more holistic response.

Summary on Effective Communication

A major conclusion of the work on presenting information to learners—particularly the work on initially instructing learners on what they are to do—is that the teacher must select and organize learning cues and demonstrate the skill. Most teachers would not have difficulty with these ideas, yet teachers in physical education classes present a large percentage of movement tasks to learners without selected cues or a demonstration of what students are to do. The result is that although teachers intend that the learners replicate a movement response in a particular way, learners end up practicing movement responses without a clear idea of what they are trying to do. Effective teachers use the technique of checking to see if students understand what they were asked to do before they practice it (checking for understanding). Alternatively, teachers can determine the clarity of the information presented by noting as the students practice how many of them are using the information.

One of the important issues is deciding how much information learners need and when they need it. Several orientations to teaching movement skill and sport suggest there are times when the learner should not be given detailed information on how to perform (process characteristics of performance). These orientations include inner-game strategies, a games-for-understanding approach (see chapter 13 by Peter Hastie for further information), and environmental approaches to teaching motor skills and games (Bunker & Thorpe, 1982; Madden & McGowen, 1989; Sweeting & Rink, 1999). All these strategies approach learning a motor skill without focusing the learner on how to do a movement. They are indirect teaching strategies.

We do not have a great deal of information on how to present tasks when it is not the teacher's intent that learners replicate a movement response. The intent of a good task presentation, however, is to make explicit to the student the expectations for a learning experience. Many teachers who seek to have the students explore something have not considered how to communicate effectively what it is they want students to explore. If, for instance, a teacher wants students to explore different balances, the students need to know what the concept of balance is from a definitional perspective (e.g., still and extended shapes). They also need to have enough examples of the idea of balance so that the concept is not too narrow (e.g., only support on feet, only high levels, only inverted). When a teacher is working with concepts, student projects, or student discovery, the teacher does not identify one appropriate response but instead communicates what makes an appropriate response, often with many examples. The important criterion for good communication is whether the learners have a clear idea of what they are trying to do after the teacher has asked them to do it.

Teacher Feedback

Physical educators early on identified teacher feedback as a critical variable in learning motor skills. Learning was assumed to be enhanced if the learner was given information on performance. The justification for this variable came initially from work in motor-learning laboratory settings, and the classroom literature on the use of teacher feedback reinforced it. Virtually all motor-learning and teaching-methodology textbooks in physical education identified teacher feedback as critical to learning.

Research

The research support for teacher feedback in physical education settings has not been strong (Rink, 2002; Silverman & Tyson, 1994). We do not have any support for a direct link of this variable with student learning. Among the many reasons for this is the idea that most students in physical education classes receive little skill-related feedback (Toby, 1974; Yerg, 1978). For skill feedback to change student movement responses, the teacher would have to observe several movement trials of a single student to identify consistent errors and then stay with that student long enough to ensure that the student understood the feedback and was able to make the necessary changes. A teacher with a large number of students finds it impossible to give effective individual feedback.

Classroom research has explored the effects of different kinds of teacher feedback on learners with different characteristics. The idea of teacher feedback in this literature reflects a broad concept of reactions to student behavior beyond the correctness of the response, such as teacher praise and criticism. Brophy (1982) indicated that for the most part students assume they are correct unless told otherwise. Criticism and praise have an affective dimension attached to knowledge of performance. Research has consistently shown that teacher criticism has negative effects on student learning, and most educators would agree that criticism does not have a place in an educational setting. At one time, most educators thought that the more praise (positive evaluative comments to the learner) the teacher gave, the more effective that teacher would be.

Feedback is a form of teacher attention. Several studies have focused on the amount of feedback given to different types of learners and its effects on them. To a low-skilled or insecure learner, feedback can be assuring and motivating. To a high-skilled or self-assured learner, too much teacher feedback can be detrimental to learning. Some evidence indicates that although low-skilled students may profit from more teacher praise and feedback, more highly skilled students may be adversely affected by the feedback (Berliner, 1987; Brophy, 1981; Rickard, 1991; Silverman, Tyson, & Krampitz, 1993). Evidence also shows that teachers do not dispense attention to students equitably. Teachers in physical education tend to give more attention to the students they like, to high achievers, and to boys (Allard, 1979; Crowe, 1979; Martinek, Crowe, & Rejeski, 1982). Race does not seem to affect the amount of attention students receive (Williams, 1998).

Motor-learning theorists have been interested primarily in the use of teacher feedback to provide information to the learner on performance. Magill (1994) suggests that the influence of augmented teacher feedback on skill learning depends on the characteristics of the skill and the learner. According to Magill, augmented feedback is necessary for skills in which the learner is not able to access sensory information. For many complex skills in physical education settings, the learner does not have visual information on where different parts of the body are at different points in a movement and therefore cannot profit from feedback on limb position. Although kinesthetic information on limb position is always available to learners, the beginner usually cannot access it. Magill suggests that if the learner does not have prior information on the relationship of the movements required to reach a goal, then teacher feedback would be necessary (speed of performance). Teacher feedback may not be necessary if learners receive feedback directly from performance or have a clear enough idea of how to perform (through demonstration) so that they may compare their own performance with correct performance. Magill goes on to suggest that feedback can at times enhance learning although it is not necessary. In situations where learners receive feedback from the task itself, learning can be enhanced if the teacher also gives learners feedback that causes them to change some aspect of their response. In some situations feedback can hinder learning. For instance, if teachers give so much feedback that learners become dependent on it, they will not learn to use feedback intrinsic to the task.

In terms of Magill's classification, most learners in most physical education settings would profit from teacher-augmented feedback. The fact that pedagogy research has not been able to establish direct links between teacher feedback and learning probably has more to do with teaching situations than it does with learner needs. Giving accurate and well-timed feedback to individual learners in large groups on their skill performance is not possible in many teaching settings.

Implications

Most experts in pedagogy continue to recommend the use of specific feedback to learners, probably because specific feedback in a teaching setting is thought to provide learners with more than mere information on performance (van der Mars, 1989). Teachers also use feedback to motivate and keep practice focused in large-group instruction, which is a valid and important function of the teacher. Settings with large numbers of learners and one teacher require teachers to look for alternative ways to provide learners with information on performance when it can enhance learning. The refining task (corrective feedback to the total class) is just one alternative to the teacher's moving quickly from one student to another. A second alternative is to look toward other teaching strategies for ways to provide individual learner feedback.

If for most tasks in physical education learning is enhanced if students can make use of feedback intrinsic to the task, then pedagogy needs to focus on ways in which students can learn to use the feedback intrinsic to the task—either external or internal. If external feedback is critical to the task, then teachers need to focus on ways in which this kind of feedback can be provided in group settings, for example, by using peer feedback strategies, videotapes of performance, or computer-generated images to be viewed by the learner immediately after the performance.

Good Content Development Can Increase Learning

One of the characteristics of expertise in teaching is the ability to organize content for learners and develop that content through a process of interactive decision making. The process of development as it plays out in a class has been referred to as content development (Rink, 2002). As part of this process, teachers can establish a sequence of tasks or learning experiences that increase or decrease in complexity. Teachers can also refine what students do by emphasizing the quality of the response. Or they can apply and assess learning to a game or performance. Developing content includes giving information on how to perform a task, changing the complexity or difficulty of that task, refining performance, and applying what has been learned. When teachers add a player, increase distance between players, or change the rules, they are manipulating the difficulty of movement tasks (extending tasks). When teachers focus the learner on an aspect of performance, such as keeping the shoulders square or staying with the player who has the ball, they are refining performance (refining task). Studies in this area are few, but those we have seem to support the use of progressions that move from simple to complex and the use of tasks with a refining focus.

Research

One of the more difficult decisions teachers have to make about the content they want to teach is when and how to break it down into smaller, progressive units for students. Many teachers continue to believe that students will learn the complex motor skills of many games by playing the game, despite the evidence that this is not so (Buck & Harrison, 1990; Earls, 1983; French & Thomas, 1987; Parker & O'Sullivan, 1983). Ordering appropriate progressions for learners is a critical function of effective teaching. Research on progressions in physical education is not voluminous, but in the skills studied ample evidence suggests that students profit from progressions of content going from simple to complex (French et al., 1990, 1991; Masser, 1985; Rink et al., 1992). Students do not profit from progressions that are inappropriate for them, and poor progressions may cause a regression in performance (Earls, 1983).

Even fewer studies have investigated the use of the refining task in content development. Teachers who use the refining task select a prescriptive focus for practice based on observation of what the class as a whole needs to correct their practice. For example, a teacher may say, "When you go back to practice, make sure your weight is on the forward foot by stepping into your swing." Masser (1985) studied the use of the refining task in an elementary school skill and found that students who received refining tasks did better than students who did not. Rink et al. (1992) found that the use of the progression with the refining task was most effective in producing student skill acquisition. At times a good progression may be sufficient to maintain student success at increasing levels of difficulty. At other times the learner does not seem to adjust adequately to more complex conditions without the help of the teacher's refining task. In other words, appropriate progressions are important, but students may often need more specific help in adjusting their movement to increased task demands.

In dealing with the problem of trying to maintain accountability and focus on skill performance, Rink (2002) has suggested that the refining task in which the teacher provides corrective feedback to the class is a useful strategy for large-group instruction. Students focus when the teacher asks a class to adjust some aspect of their response, and the class can be observed actually working on the substantive content of the refining task. Although refining tasks help a teacher maintain accountability for performance, they can improve skill performance only to the degree that their focus is appropriate—when most of the students can profit from the same information. When this assumption cannot be made, feedback of this nature can be inappropriate.

Implications

The issue of content development is related to the issue of appropriate practice. The progression a teacher uses and the refining focus determine the success rate of the learner and the relationship of the practice to the teaching objective. Most of the complex skills in a physical education program should be taught in a progressive manner. The teacher can break down skills either into parts of the skill itself (such as the toss, swing, and execution of the tennis serve) or into conditions of practice (from a toss, from a hit, to particular areas of the court). Although some skills should not be broken down for extensive practice because division into parts destroys the timing of the movement, beginners can benefit from the breaking down of most complex motor skills.

Progressions for open skills—particularly complex open sport skills—need to occur in gradually more gamelike conditions. If, for instance, a teacher wants a learner to be able to use the forearm volleyball pass to receive a serve, practice will eventually have to include a ball coming across the net at a speed and force equivalent to a serve and the player will have to be able to place a pass to different parts of the court. Practice from a soft toss to a partner is many steps away from game conditions.

One question teachers always ask regarding the issue of progression is "How do I know when to move on to the next step, particularly when I have a variety of skill levels within one class?" If we had a definitive answer to the success rate question, we would be able to tell the teacher when to move on. A study by French et al. (1991) compared groups of students who were required to reach an 80% success rate before moving on to the next step in a progression with those students who moved on when they had performed a particular number of practice trials. The groups did not differ on a final test in this situation, which kept the amount of practice trials consistent for both groups. We simply do not know enough about how much success learners need at lower levels of movement tasks before they can profit from more advanced levels of movement tasks.

Issues regarding teaching progressions have a great deal of significance for both instruction and curriculum. How refined do progressions for skill learning have to be? When can the learner expect to take "leaps" from one level to another? What would be the long-term curricular effects of physical education programs if teachers taught less content more effectively at each grade? Even though we lack answers to many of these questions, we suspect that students would be far more skillful if teachers used progressions that helped learners be successful and taught all students for success. Teachers often respond that if they stay on skills too long the students become bored. In the volleyball studies on content development, however, the highly skilled students were the ones who quickly decreased their effort when confronted with a situation in which they were not immediately successful (French et al., 1990, 1991). The low-skilled student achieved even less success, yet they persevered. Teachers should know what drives the decision to move on. The teacher must be able not only to plan progressions that go from simple to complex but also to design many ways to practice skills at the same level.

Teachers Need to Try to Understand Student Perceptions of What They Ask Students to Do

We end this discussion of important teaching variables by looking at the role of the student in the teaching-learning process. No direct link exists between what the teacher does and student learning. The student is the mediator of instruction. The cognitive mediational perspective on student learning, as Melinda Solmon discusses in chapter 9, is primarily attributed to the work of Doyle (1977). This perspective emphasizes the critical role that the individual student plays in his or her learning. Students decide to attend to what teachers are saying. They decide to put effort into learning experiences. They largely decide whether they can or want to be engaged before a task even begins.

Research

Although many contextual variables play a major role in the response of individual students to any particular learning experience on any particular day, research in both education and physical education has identified several critical student characteristics that influence student involvement in learning (Chen, 1996; Duda, 1996; Lee, 1997; Lee & Solmon, 1992; Mitchell & Chandler, 1993; Wilkerson & Allen, 1995). The past experiences learners have had with the content and physical education and the way in which they have come to think of their roles in the physical education setting have a lot to do with how students respond to what teachers do (Lee & Solmon, 1992). Unfortunately, for the most part, students in physical education do not fully understand why they are participating in physical education (Greenockle, Lee, & Lomax, 1990). This lack of awareness means that teachers have not done a good job of helping students understand the importance of their subject matter or the contribution of different learning experiences to achieving the goals of physical education. We do know that students decide whether they like or dislike physical education largely based on the specific content they are studying (e.g., I like basketball; I do not like fitness).

One of the most important characteristics of students that affects their participation patterns is the extent to which student feels they can be successful at what the teacher asks them to do. The perceived competence of the student relates strongly to his or her engagement. Students develop a sense of competence or lack of it largely through previous experiences of success and failure. We typically attribute our success or failure in achievement situations to our ability, luck, effort, or the difficulty of the task. Students who attribute their success or failure to internal things (ability and effort) are more likely to engage in learning experiences with a high degree of motivation and show greater confidence than students who attribute their successes or failure to things that are out of their control (luck or the task). Attribution theorists refer to these ideas as locus of control. Students who are not success oriented tend to blame their lack of ability for their failures but do not take credit for their successes. They also tend to avoid trying because trying and failing puts them more at risk than not trying does.

Implications

For the teacher, understanding the critical role of success and the perceived confidence of individual students in the subject area is a first step. Working with students to help them want to achieve the task for internal rather than imposed reasons (e.g., grades or to avoid disciplinary action) is a next step. Students have a better chance of being motivated to achieve the tasks that teachers present if the tasks are of moderate difficulty and the students can accomplish them with reasonable effort. We also know if we can remove the threat of how others will perceive student performance, we have a better chance of getting high levels of engagement. Alleviating concern about the perceptions of others is particularly critical for the physical education setting because so much of what we do is public. Teachers have many reasons for having all students working at one time on a task or tasks. Perhaps as important as increasing the practice time for students is the idea that each student's practice is likely to be much less of a public performance for others. None of us likes to be seen failing in front of others. Unfortunately, one cannot learn without making errors.

Direct Instruction

We began this chapter with an introduction that described the research base for effective teaching as having its foundation in a group of research studies on highly structured content and rather short-term objectives. The collection of teaching behaviors identified by this research have come to be associated with the construct of direct instruction or explicit teaching. Direct instruction usually means that the teacher teaches in small steps, gives explicit directions or instructions on what the student is to do, maintains a task-oriented and teacher-monitored environment with high student engagement with the content, and provides immediate feedback to students.

Most of the principles identified in this chapter are associated with direct instruction. Direct instruction is appropriate when subject matter is highly structured and when teachers can describe specifically what they want students to learn (Peterson, 1979a, 1979b) Most of the process-product research in physical education has identified direct instruction as an effective way to teach motor skills, which should not surprise anyone. The intent of most physical education instructional lessons is for students to perform in a particular way identified by the teacher. Under these conditions, teachers would be most effective if they used the principles of teaching described in this chapter. More students would successfully learn skills if teachers developed and used these skills. Although we are less clear in prescribing effective teaching in physical education when we may not want every student doing the same thing in the same way, many of the characteristics of effective teaching described in this chapter are likely to be generic to both direct and indirect teaching.

SUMMARY

This chapter has provided a set of basic and generic principles for teaching. Research on the teaching process has continued to identify contextual variables that affect relationships between what we do as teachers and how different learners respond in different contexts with different content. The material in this chapter has been presented with the intent to help the reader develop an understanding of the more generic principles of teaching. The research presented is stronger in some areas than in others, but it is the best information we currently have. We have more to learn, but the principles we have established can provide guidance for teaching in a motor context. Thoughtful practitioners will carefully select what they will teach and will select just as carefully the manner in which they will teach it.

IMPLICATIONS FOR PRACTICE

1. Design practice so that students are engaged at a high level and are successful with effort for sufficient time to produce learning.
2. Design practice conditions to be as gamelike as students can cope with successfully.
3. Design curriculum so that students develop skills through careful articulation of progressions over the grade levels.
4. Design tasks so that the learner can achieve them with effort.
5. Plan progressions that go from simple to complex and have available many ways to practice skills at the same level.
6. Manipulate the demands of motor tasks by manipulating the context (conditions of practice) of the task for individual learners.
7. Develop good management skills so that you can teach using a variety of effective teaching methods.
8. When the objective is to give the learner a clear idea of how to perform a motor task, use a combination of verbal and visual information and verbal rehearsal.
9. Design learning cues for skills that accurately and richly reflect the required movement characteristics.
10. Use specific feedback to provide information to learners and to motivate and keep practice focused in large-group instruction.
11. Understand the critical role of success and the perceived confidence of individual students and work with students to help them want to achieve the task for internal rather than imposed reasons.

REFERENCES

Allard, R. (1979). A need to look at dyadic interactions. In *American Alliance for Health, Physical Education, Recreation and Dance, Research Consortium Symposium Papers:* *Teaching behavior and women in sports* (Vol. 2, Book 1). Washington, DC: American Alliance for Health, Physical Education, Recreation and Dance.

Anderson, W. (1980). *Analysis of teaching physical education.* St. Louis: Mosby.

Ashy, M., Lee, A., & Landin, D. (1988). Relationship of practice using correct technique to achievement in a motor skill. *Journal of Teaching in Physical Education, 7,* 115-120.

Berliner, D. (1987). Simple views of classroom teaching and a simple theory of classroom instruction. In D. Berliner & B. Rosenshine (Eds.), *Talks to teachers* (pp. 93-110). New York: Random House.

Brophy, J. (1979). Teacher behavior and its effects. *Journal of Educational Psychology, 71,* 733-750.

Brophy, J. (1981). Teacher praise: A functional analysis. *Review of Educational Research, 51,* 5-32.

Brophy, J. (1982, January). On praising effectively. *Education Digest, 47*(5), 16-19.

Brophy, J. (1983). Classroom organization and management. *Elementary School Journal, 83,* 265-286.

Brophy, J., & Evertson, C. (1974). *Process product correlations in the Texas teacher effectiveness study (final report).* Austin, TX: The University of Texas at Austin, Research and Development Center for Teacher Education.

Brophy, J., & Good, T. (1986). Teacher behavior and student achievement. In M. Wittrock, (Ed.), *Handbook of research on teaching* (3rd ed., pp. 328-375). New York: Macmillan.

Buck, M., & Harrison, J. (1990). An analysis of game play in volleyball. *Journal of Teaching in Physical Education, 10,* 38-48.

Buck, M., Harrison, J., & Bryce, G. (1991). An analysis of learning trials and their relationship to achievement. *Journal of Teaching in Physical Education, 10,* 134-152.

Bunker, D., & Thorpe, R. (1982). A model for the teaching of games in secondary schools. *Bulletin of Physical Education, 18,* 5-8.

Chen, A. (1996). Student interest in activities in secondary physical education curriculum: An analysis of student subjectivity. *Research Quarterly for Exercise Science and Sport, 67,* 424-432.

Costello, J. (1977). A *descriptive analysis of student behavior in elementary school physical education classes.* Unpublished doctoral dissertation, Columbia University Teachers College, New York.

Cousineau, W., & Luke, M. (1990). Relationships between teacher expectations and academic learning time in sixth grade physical education basketball classes. *Journal of Teaching in Physical Education, 9,* 262-271.

Crowe, P. (1979). An observational study of teachers' expectancy effects and their mediating mechanisms. In *American Alliance for Health, Physical Education, and Recreation, Research Consortium Symposium Papers: Teaching behavior and women in sports* (Vol. 2, Book 1, pp. 17-21). Washington, DC: American Alliance for Health, Physical Education, Recreation and Dance.

Doyle, W. (1977). Paradigms of research on teacher effectiveness. *Review of Research in Education, 5,* 163-198.

Doyle, W. (1986). Classroom organization and management. In M. Wittrock (Ed.), *Handbook of research on teaching* (3rd ed., pp. 392-441). New York: Macmillan.

Duda, J. (1996). Maximizing motivation in sport and physical education among children and adolescents: The case for greater task involvement. *Quest, 48,* 290-302.

Earls, N. (1983). Research on the immediate effects of instructional variables. In T. Templin & J. Olson (Eds.), *Teaching in physical education* (pp. 254-264). Champaign, IL: Human Kinetics.

Emmer, E., Evertson, C., & Anderson, L. (1980). Effective classroom management at the beginning of the school year. *Elementary School Journal, 80,* 219-231.

Ennis, C. (1994, April). *They just don't want to learn anymore. What can you do?: Teachers' resistance to curricular change.* Paper presented at the annual meeting of the American Educational Research Association, New Orleans.

Evertson, C., & Emmer, E.T. (1982). Effective management at the beginning of the year in junior high school classes. *Journal of Educational Psychology, 74,* 485-498.

Fitts, P.M., & Posner, M.I. (1967). *Human performance.* Belmont, CA: Brooks/Cole.

Freiberg, H.J., & Driscoll, A. (2000). *Universal teaching strategies* (3rd ed.). Boston: Allyn and Bacon.

French, K., Rink, J., Rickard, L., Mays, A., Lynn, S., & Werner, P. (1991). The effects of practice progressions on learning two volleyball skills. *Journal of Teaching in Physical Education, 10,* 261-275.

French, K.E., Rink, J.E., & Werner, P.H. (1990). Effects of contextual interference on retention of three volleyball skills. *Perceptual and Motor Skills, 71,* 179-186.

French, K., & Thomas, G. (1987). The relation of knowledge development to children's basketball performance. *Journal of Sport Psychology, 9,* 15-32.

Gage, N.L. (1978, November). The yield of research on teaching. *Phi Delta Kappan,* 230-235.

Godbout, P., Burnelle, J., & Tousignant, M. (1983). Academic learning time in elementary and secondary physical education. *Research Quarterly for Exercise and Sport, 54,* 11-19.

Goldberger, M., & Gerney, P. (1990). Effects of learner use of practice time on skill acquisition. *Journal of Teaching in Physical Education, 10,* 84-95.

Good, S., & Magill, R.A. (1986). Contextual interference effects in learning three badminton serves. *Research Quarterly for Exercise and Sport, 57,* 308-315.

Good, T., & Grouws, D. (1975). *Process-product relationships in fourth grade mathematics classrooms: Final report of National Institute of Education grant* (NE-G-00-0123). Columbia, MO: University of Missouri.

Gould, D., & Roberts, G. (1982). Modeling and motor skill acquisition. *Quest, 33,* 214-230.

Graham, K.C. (1988). A qualitative analysis of an effective teacher's movement task presentations during a unit of instruction. *Physical Educator, 11,* 187-195.

Graham, K.C., Hussey, K., Taylor, K., & Werner, P. (1993). A study of verbal presentations of three effective teachers. *Research Quarterly for Exercise and Sport, 64,* 87A (Abstract).

Greenockle, K., Lee, A., & Lomax, R. (1990). The relationship between selected student characteristics and activity patterns in a required high school physical education class. *Research Quarterly for Exercise and Sport, 61,* 59-69.

Griffin, P., & Placek, J. 2001. (Eds.). The understanding and development of learner's domain-specific knowledge [Mongraph]. *Journal of Teaching in Physical Education, 20*(4).

Gusthart, J.L., & Sprigings, E. (1989). Student learning as a measure of teacher effectiveness. *Journal of Teaching in Physical Education, 8,* 298-311.

Gusthart, L., Kelly, I., & Rink, J. (1997). The validity of the Qualitative Measures of Teacher Performance Scale (QMTPS) as a process measure of achievement. *Journal of Teaching in Physical Education, 16,* 196-210.

Hellison, D. (1995). *Teaching responsibility through physical activity.* Champaign, IL: Human Kinetics.

Housner, L.D., & French, K.E. (Eds.) (1994). Expertise in learning, performance, and instruction in sport and physical activity [Monograph]. *Quest, 46*(2).

Kennedy, J., Cruickshank, D., Bush, A., & Meyers, B. (1978). Additional investigations into the nature of teacher clarity. *Journal of Educational Research, 72,* 3-10.

Kwak, C. (1993). *The initial effects of various task presentation conditions on students' performance of the lacrosse throw.* Unpublished doctoral dissertation, University of South Carolina, Columbia.

Land, M. (1981). Combined effect of two teacher clarity variables on student achievement. *Journal of Experimental Education, 50,* 14-17.

Landin, D. (1994). The role of verbal cues in skill learning. *Quest, 46,* 299-313.

Lee, A.M. (1997). Contributions of research on student thinking in physical education. *Journal of Teaching in Physical Education, 16,* 262-277.

Lee, A.M. (2002). 2001 C.H. McCloy Research Lecture: Promoting quality school physical education: Exploring the root of the problem. *Research Quarterly for Exercise and Sport, 73,* 118-124.

Lee, A., & Solmon, M. (1992). Cognitive conceptions of teaching and learning motor skills. *Quest, 44,* 57-91.

Lee, T., Swinnen, S., & Serrien, D. (1994). Cognitive effort and motor learning. *Quest, 46,* 328-344.

Madden, G., & McGowan, C. (1989). The effect of the inner game method versus the progressive method on learning motor skills. *Journal of Teaching in Physical Education, 9,* 39-48.

Madigan, R., Frey, R., & Matlock, T. (1992). Cognitive strategies of university athletes. *Canadian Journal of Sport Science, 17,* 135-140.

Magill, R.A. (1994). The influence of augmented feedback during skill learning depends on characteristics of the skill and the learner. *Quest, 46,* 314-327.

Magill, R.A. (2001). *Motor learning: Concepts and applications* (6th ed.). New York: McGraw-Hill.

Martens, R., Burwitz, L., & Zuckerman, J. (1976). Modeling effects on motor performance. *Research Quarterly, 47,* 277-291.

Martinek, T., Crowe, P., & Rejeski, W. (1982). *Pygmalion in the gym: Causes and effects of expectations in teaching and coaching.* West Point, NY: Leisure Press.

Masser, L. (1985). The effect of refinement on student achievement in a fundamental motor skill in grades K–6. *Journal of Teaching in Physical Education, 6,* 174-182.

Masser, L. (1993). Critical cues help first grade students' achievement in hand-stands and forward rolls. *Journal of Teaching in Physical Education, 12,* 301-312.

McCaslin, M., & Good, T. (1992). Compliant cognition: The misalliance of management and instructional goals in current school reform. *Educational Researcher, 21*(3), 4-16.

McCullagh, P., Stiehl, J., & Weiss, M. (1990). Developmental modeling effects on the quantitative and qualitative aspects of motor performance. *Research Quarterly for Exercise and Sport, 61,* 344-350.

McDonald, F., & Elias, P. (1976). *The effects of teacher performance on student learning. Beginning teacher evaluation study—phase II final report* (Vol. 1). Princeton, NJ: Educational Testing Service.

Metzler, M. (1979). The measurement of academic learning time in physical education. *Dissertation Abstracts International, 40,* 5365A. (University Microfilms No. 8009314)

Metzler, M. (1989). A review of research on time in sport pedagogy. *Journal of Teaching in Physical Education, 8,* 87-103.

Metzler, M., DePaepe, J., & Reif, G. (1985). Alternative technologies for measuring academic learning time in physical education. *Journal of Teaching in Physical Education, 6,* 271-285.

Mitchell, S., & Chandler, T. (1993). Motivating students for learning in the gymnasium: The role of perception and meaning. *Journal for Teaching Physical Education, 15,* 369-383.

National Association for Sport and Physical Education. (1992). *Outcomes of quality physical education.* Reston, VA: American Alliance for Health, Physical Education, Recreation and Dance.

National Association for Sport and Physical Education. (1995). *Moving into the future: National physical education standards: A guide to content and assessment.* Reston, VA: American Alliance for Health, Physical Education, Recreation and Dance.

Ornstein, A., & Levine, D. (1981, April). Teacher behavior research: Overview and outlook. *Phi Delta Kappan,* 592-596.

Parker, M., & O'Sullivan, M. (1983). Modifying ALT-PE for game play contexts and other reflections. *Journal of Teaching Physical Education, 3*(monograph 1), 8-10.

Peterson, P. (1979a). Direct instruction: Effective for what and for whom? *Educational Leadership, 37*(1), 46-48.

Peterson, P. (1979b). Direct instruction reconsidered. In P. Peterson & H. Walberg (Eds.), *Research on teaching: Concepts, findings, and implications* (pp. 57-69). Berkeley, CA: McCutchan.

Rickard, L. (1991). The short term relationship of teacher feedback and student practice. *Journal of Teaching in Physical Education, 10,* 275-285.

Rink, J. (1994). Task presentation in pedagogy. *Quest, 46,* 270-280.

Rink, J. (2001). Investigating the assumptions of pedagogy. *Journal of Teaching in Physical Education, 20,* 112-128.

Rink, J. (2002). *Teaching physical education for learning.* St. Louis: Mosby Year Book.

Rink, J., French, K., Werner, P., Lynn, S., & Mays, A. (1992). The influence of content development on the effectiveness of instruction. *Journal of Teaching in Physical Education, 11,* 139-149.

Rink, J., & Werner, P. (1989). Qualitative measures of teaching performance scale (QMTPS). In P. Darst, D. Zakrajsek, & V. Mancini (Eds.), *Analyzing physical education and sport instruction* (2nd ed., pp. 269-276). Champaign, IL: Human Kinetics.

Rosenshine, B. (1987). Explicit teaching. In D. Berliner & B. Rosenshine (Eds.), *Talks to teachers* (pp. 75-92). New York: Random House.

Rosenshine, B., & Stevens, R. (1986). Teaching functions. In M. Wittrock (Ed.), *Handbook of research on teaching* (3rd ed., pp. 376-391). New York: Macmillan.

Silverman, S. (1985). Relationship of engagement and practice trials to student achievement. *Journal of Teaching in Physical Education, 5,* 13-21.

Silverman, S. (1990). Linear and curvilinear relationships between student practice and achievement in physical education. *Teaching and Teacher Education, 6,* 305-314.

Silverman, S., Devillier, R., & Ramírez, T. (1991). The validity of academic learning time–physical education (ALT-PE) as a process measure of student achievement. *Research Quarterly for Exercise and Sport, 62,* 319-325.

Silverman, S., Kulinna, P., & Crull, G. (1995). Skill-related task structures, explicitness, and accountability: Relationships with student achievement. *Research Quarterly for Exercise and Sport, 66,* 32-40.

Silverman, S., & Tyson, L. (1994, April). *Modeling the teaching learning process in physical education.* Paper presented at the annual meeting of the American Educational Research Association, New Orleans.

Silverman, S., Tyson, L., & Krampitz, J. (1993). Teacher feedback and achievement: Mediating effects of initial skill and sex. *Journal of Human Movement Studies, 24,* 97-118.

Soar, R., & Soar, R.M. (1979). Emotional climate and management. In P. Peterson & H. Walberg (Eds.), *Research on teaching: Concepts, findings and implications* (pp. 97-119). Berkeley, CA: McCutchan.

Stallings, J., & Kaskowitz, D. (1974). *Follow through classroom observation evaluation, 1972-1973* (Office of Education contract OEC 08522480-4633-1001). Menlo Park, CA: Stanford Research Institute.

Sweeting, T., & Rink, J. (1999). Effects of direct instruction and environmentally designed instruction on the process and product characteristics of a fundamental skill. *Journal of Teaching in Physical Education, 18,* 216-233.

Toby, C. (1974). A *descriptive analysis of the occurrence of augmented feedback in physical education classes.* Unpublished doctoral dissertation, Columbia University Teachers College, New York.

van der Mars, H. (1989). Effects of specific verbal praise on off-task behavior of second grade students in physical education. *Journal of Teaching in Physical Education, 8,* 162-169.

Werner, P., & Rink, J. (1989). Case studies of teacher effectiveness in physical education. *Journal of Teaching in Physical Education, 4,* 280-297.

Wilkerson, S., & Allen, J. (1995). Learning to like physical education: Changes in perceptions and attitudes toward activity. *Research Quarterly for Exercise and Sport, 66,* A-72.

Williams, C. (1998). *The relationship between teacher's race and student race and teacher-student interactions.* Unpublished doctoral dissertation, University of South Carolina, Columbia.

Yerg, B. (1978). Identifying teacher behavior correlates of student achievement. In C.B. Corbin (Ed.), *AAHPERD Research Consortium Symposium Papers: Teaching behavior and sport history* (Vol. 1, Book 1, pp. 39-43). Washington, DC: American Alliance for Health, Physical Education and Recreation.

CHAPTER ELEVEN

ASSESSMENT IN PHYSICAL EDUCATION: THE FUTURE IS NOW!

Terry M. Wood

In the six years since publication of the first edition of this text, much has changed in the realm of educational assessment. The seeds of the educational reform movement sown in the early 1980s have germinated and are beginning to bear fruit in the first decade of the new millennium. New terminology such as content standards, benchmarks, performance assessments, and rubrics is becoming commonplace among teachers, administrators, students, and parents. Teachers are struggling to keep abreast of the rapidly changing landscape of the reform movement and its emphasis on integrating assessment into the teaching-learning process. Students and parents are adjusting to integrated teaching and assessment aimed at common learning targets. Administrators, faced with an unstable resource base, are striving to implement the new reforms.

Assessment plays a pivotal role in this latest round of educational reform. At the classroom level, teachers are expected to link instruction and assessment to student mastery of common learning targets. At the district and state levels, assessment of student mastery in core subject areas is being used to evaluate school, district, and state performance in so-called high-stakes assessment. The focus on assessment has become so concentrated that a new strategy termed *assessment-based education* has evolved. This strategy suggests that instruction aim at assisting students to master predefined assessments. That is, after common learning targets have been established, assessment devices are constructed to indicate level of student mastery relative to the learning targets. Instructional strategies are then developed to help students meet the learning targets (i.e., pass the assessments). This process is a radical shift from the more traditional practice of formulating curriculum and instruction and then constructing assessments to determine if learning objectives have been met.

In physical education, response to educational reform and the increased role of assessment has been mixed. At the national level the National Association for Sport and Physical Education (NASPE) led the charge toward educational reform with the development of national content standards for physical education (NASPE, 1995) and a series of publications on assessment for K–12 physical education aimed at helping professionals implement new assessment practice (e.g., Lambert, 1999; Lund, 2000; Mitchell & Oslin, 1999). At the state level, physical education standards were recognized along with other core subject areas in states such as Kentucky and Wyoming (Deal, Byra, Jenkins, & Gates, 2002), and grassroots advocacy movements in several states such as New York (Fay & Doolittle, 2002), South Carolina (Rink et al., 2002), and Oregon required several years of intense effort to establish state-level content standards for physical education. Among teaching professionals, response has ranged from wholehearted acceptance to the hope that if the reform efforts are ignored they will eventually go away. The latter position prompted a passionate and reasoned response from Lambert (1998) who argued that "assessment reform has been the major catalyst of change in the nearly decade-long school restructuring movement. In many ways it has created new-found energy in education and has caused us to think about and devise new ways of seeking evidence of learning" (p. 14).

In a real sense, the future is now. Currently, we have a clear picture of what appropriate assessment practice should entail under the current educational reform movement. Less clear is how teachers, districts, and states can effectively implement such practices. The purposes of this chapter are to (a) examine the new assessment building blocks and assessment practice, (b) describe recent advances in grading practice, and (c) outline the challenges that can arise when implementing standards-based physical education.

NEW ASSESSMENT BUILDING BLOCKS

The core of the current round of educational reform is the creation of common learning targets (i.e., content standards and benchmarks) for all students across all subject areas, coupled with assessments that indicate the degree to which students are mastering the targets. Moreover, assessments of student mastery focus on what students know and are able to do in real world settings (i.e., authentic assessments). As Rothman (1995) eloquently put it:

> More fundamentally, the shift in view about student assessment is turning the traditional notion of education itself on its head. For most of this century we have defined education by what goes into the system—the number of teachers, library books, and courses we provided—and tests have indicated which students got more out of the system and which got less. The revamped system, by contrast, begins with outcomes—what students should leave school knowing and be able to do. The inputs are important only to the extent that they lead students to the desired outcomes. Such a transformation, if widely adopted, would be truly radical. It would change the definition of an educated student from one who went through school to one who could demonstrate valued knowledge and skills. (p. xii)

We should not be surprised that new concepts and technology accompany such a radical shift in the way we view education. The aim of this section is to look briefly at the concepts directly related to assessment to prepare readers for subsequent discussion.

Content Standards

Content standards are general statements describing what students should know and be able to do in a given subject area. For example, NASPE (1995) published seven content standards for physical education (see chapter 8 by Leslie Lambert). These standards describe what physically educated people should know and be able to do as they exit the public school system. Specifically, "they include the knowledge and skills—the ways of thinking, communicating, reasoning, and investigating, and the most enduring ideas, concepts, issues, dilemmas, and information that characterize each discipline" (NASPE, p. vi). The NASPE national standards document also recognizes the developmental nature of the behavior described in the standards and thus provides descriptions of behavior expected relative to each standard for grades K, 2, 4, 6, 8, 10, and 12. Many states have used the NASPE national standards as a foundation for state standards.

Benchmarks

Some confusion concerning the meaning of *benchmark* exists in the literature. For example, the NASPE (1995) national standards document speaks to "performance benchmarks" defined as "behavior that indicates progress toward a performance standard" (p. vi) and "which describe developmentally appropriate behaviors representative of progress toward achieving the standard . . ." (p. viii). Similarly, Marzano and Kendall (1996) describe benchmarks "as statements of developmental levels of information and skill that define the general categories of knowledge articulated by the standards" (p. 47). In contrast, Hibbard et al. (1996) use *benchmark* to denote "models of excellence" or "products that represent excellent work for the grade level" (p. 165).

Unless otherwise indicated, this chapter uses the NASPE definition of benchmark. That is, benchmarks are signposts that indicate more directly if students are mastering a content standard at a given grade level. For example, in 2001 the state of Oregon adopted six content standards for physical education (Oregon Department of Education, 2001) based on the NASPE national standards. In addition, the state mandated district-level assessment of the content standards at grades 3, 5, 8, and 10. The Oregon Department of Education created benchmarks for content standards at each of these grade levels as signposts to indicate if students were achieving mastery of the content standards. Table 11.1 presents benchmarks identified for the state's sixth content standard, "Demonstrates responsible behavior and respect for differences among people during physical activities."

TABLE 11.1

SAMPLE BENCHMARKS FROM THE OREGON DEPARTMENT OF EDUCATION PHYSICAL EDUCATION CONTENT STANDARDS

Third Grade	Fifth Grade	Eighth Grade	Tenth Grade
Identify rules, procedures, and etiquette in a specified physical activity.	Explain and demonstrate safety, rules, procedures, and etiquette to be followed during participation in physical activities.	Apply rules, procedures, and etiquette that are safe and effective for specific activities and situations.	Analyze and apply rules, procedures, and etiquette that are safe and effective for specific activities and situations.
Identify positive ways to resolve conflict.		Identify the elements of socially acceptable conflict resolution and sportsmanship.	Apply conflict resolution strategies in appropriate ways and analyze potential consequences when confronted with unsportsman-like behavior.

Alternative Assessment, Performance Assessment, and Authentic Assessment

Content standards and benchmarks are the explicit learning targets that all students aim for. Assessment is the process used to determine where on the target the student has landed and how close she or he is to obtaining mastery.

Alternative assessment takes its name from assessment that is alternative to more traditional modes. In 1996 I contrasted traditional assessment and alternative assessment as follows:

> Traditional assessment devices tend to measure narrowly defined cognitive, affective, and psychomotor characteristics; treat the three behavioral domains separately; and often fail to measure higher order performance processes under realistic or authentic conditions. An increased emphasis on assessing what students know and can actually do as they exit various grade levels and integrating higher order cognitive, affective, and psychomotor processes has led to dissatisfaction with traditional tests, resulting in the development of various alternative assessment strategies. (p. 213)

Traditional assessment includes multiple-choice tests and motor-skill tests, and alternative assessment examples include portfolios (Collins & Dana, 1993; Danielson & Abrutyn, 1997; Kirk, 1997; Melograno, 1994) journals (Cutforth & Parker, 1996), student logs, role playing, and oral presentations (see Bartz, Anderson-Robinson, & Hillman, 1994; Feuer & Fulton, 1993; NASPE, 1995; and Ornstein, 1994). Wood (1996) provided further discussion of the promises and challenges of alternative assessments.

Performance assessments are alternative assessments in which "the student completes or demonstrates the same behavior that the assessor desires" (Meyer, 1992, p. 40). Authentic assessments are performance assessments administered in real-life contexts (Meyer, 1992). Lund (1997) offered seven characteristics of authentic assessment, which are presented in figure 11.1.

Characteristics of Authentic Assessment

1. Involves the presentation of worthwhile or meaningful tasks designed to be representative of performance in the field.
2. Emphasizes higher-level thinking and learning that is more complex.
3. The criteria are articulated in advance so that students know how they will be evaluated.
4. Assessments are practically indistinguishable from instruction.
5. Changes the role of teacher from adversary to ally.
6. Students are expected to present their work publicly.
7. Assessment involves the examination of process as well as products of learning.

FIGURE 11.1 Characteristics of authentic assessment (Lund, 1997).

The following example will help distinguish these types of assessment. In a high school physical fitness unit, the physical education teacher desired to assess student mastery of the FITT (frequency, intensity, time, and type) principle of exercise. Using traditional assessment, the teacher could administer a multiple-choice test. Results of this assessment indicate students' knowledge of the concepts but give little information concerning their ability to apply the concepts in a meaningful way. An alternative approach requires students to demonstrate the FITT principle on a stationary bicycle. This method is an example of a performance assessment because it directly assesses desired behavior and focuses on both content and application. The performance assessment could be made more authentic by requiring students to use the FITT principle to develop a tailored training program for another individual in the class or for their parents.

Scoring Alternative Assessments: Scoring Guides, Performance Standards, Performance Cutoffs

Perhaps no other facet of alternative assessment has received the high degree of scrutiny as the topic of scoring. The term *rubric* is often used to describe scoring rules for alternative assessments, but many practitioners, including me, are replacing it with the more descriptive term *scoring guide*. The latter term is more useful when communicating with students and parents.

Soundly constructed scoring guides are critical for the success of alternative assessments. Valid and reliable scoring guides reflect the behaviors that teachers deem important, students use the scoring guides to set goals and as markers of progress toward those goals, and the scoring guides provide a basis for determining standards of minimal competency (Taggart, Phifer, Nixon, & Wood, 1998).

Scoring guides come in many different flavors—checklists, rating scales, holistic guides, analytical guides, general guides, and task-specific guides. Checklists and rating scales are popular among physical educators when assessing basic movement patterns and complex sport skills (see Safrit & Wood [1995] for a discussion of constructing these types of scoring guides and Schincariol & Radford [1998] for samples of scoring guides in a university volleyball activity course). Many authors, most notably Lund (2000), Arter and McTighe (2001), and Taggart et al. (1998), have described in detail the construction of holistic guides and analytical guides. Both guides contain performance criteria that "describe what to look for in student performances or products to judge quality" (Arter & McTighe, 2001, p. 4) and a performance scale that maps a score onto the performance criteria.

What distinguishes holistic scoring guides from analytical scoring guides is the way the information is packaged. Holistic guides package all the performance criteria at each score on the performance scale, whereas analytic guides provide separate performance scales for each criterion. For example, in a high school advanced tennis class, students are asked to develop a videotape of the forehand and backhand ground strokes, the topspin serve, and the volley along with an explanation and demonstration of the critical elements for each stroke. Figure 11.2 presents a holistic scoring guide. Notice that

---

Holistic Scoring Guide

Level 4: Distinguished

The student makes the videotape of the four strokes, and all four are correctly explained and demonstrated.

Level 3: Proficient

The student makes the videotape of the four strokes, but the explanation and demonstration of critical elements show minor errors.

Level 2: Basic

The student makes the videotape and includes only one or two strokes, and the explanation and demonstration of critical elements show major errors.

Level 1: Novice

The student says he or she chose not to make a videotape or made a videotape of the wrong strokes.

FIGURE 11.2 Holistic scoring guide.

for each level of the performance scale, descriptions accompany each performance criteria (i.e., presence of videotape, correct number and identification of strokes, quality of explanations and demonstrations). Performance standards encompass a point on the performance scale and its accompanying description of performance criteria. For example, in figure 11.2 the descriptions accompanying Level 1: Novice, Level 2: Basic, Level 3: Proficient, and Level 4: Distinguished are performance standards. In contrast, an analytic scoring guide would identify each important performance criterion and provide a separate score for each criterion.

General scoring guides can be used across similar assessments, whereas task-specific scoring guides are used for single assessments. For example, the holistic scoring guide presented in figure 11.3 is a general guide used for assessing performance in a physical fitness unit.

Fitness Scoring Guide

Level 4: Exemplary

Exceeds criterion-referenced standard. Always uses proper form and technique. Knows how to administer the assessment.

Level 3: Proficient:

Meets criterion-referenced standard. Uses proper form and technique most of the time. Knows how to administer the assessment.

Level 2: Emerging

Does not meet criterion-referenced standard. Uses proper form and technique some of the time. Makes errors in administering the assessment

Level 1: Beginning

Does not meet criterion-referenced standard. Does not use proper form and technique. Does not know how to administer the assessment.

FIGURE 11.3   General scoring guide for physical fitness assessment.

Choosing a scoring guide depends on several factors including the nature of the assessment, the skills of the guide developers, and the number of students to be assessed. General and holistic scoring guides are popular when a large number of students must be assessed and speed of assessment is critical, when the assessments are relatively simple, and when a general assessment of achievement is required. Analytic guides are useful when students require detailed feedback, when the number of students is few, when speed of assessment is not critical, and when the focus is teaching students the components of quality performance (Arter & McTighe, 2001). Whichever scoring guide is used, however, users of the guide must be carefully trained in its use to maximize reliability of scoring (Joyner & McManis, 1997).

Growing pains often accompany rapid growth and change. Evidence of this is the confusion in terminology found in the performance assessment literature. A case in point is the current confusion over the terms *performance standards* and *performance cutoffs* (Kane, 2001). As noted earlier, a performance standard "describes a level of performance in terms of what examinees at that level know and can do" (Kane, p. 55) (e.g., descriptions of novice, basic, proficient, and advanced on a scoring guide). Performance cutoffs, or cutscores, are "points on the score scale, with one cutscore associated with one performance standard" (Kane, p. 55). For example, the fitness scoring guide in figure 11.3 has four cutscores (4 = exemplary, 3 = proficient, 2 = emerging, and 1 = beginning). Each cutscore has associated with it a qualitative description of the behavior expected from students. This description is the performance standard. The distinction is important because decisions about student mastery of content standards are made based on the cutscores, not on the performance standards.

Arguably, the greatest challenge facing teachers is the task of determining the cutscore on an assessment that reflects mastery of the measured characteristic. Put simply, when students are aiming at the common learning targets (i.e., content standards and benchmarks), how close to the bull's eye must they get? How good is good enough? The literature concerning this topic has increased exponentially since the focus on criterion-referenced tests and minimal competency testing began in the 1970s. The more recent emphasis on greater accountability in the classroom and high-stakes assessment has fueled the fire. (Readers can read Cizek [2001] for a contemporary view of this burgeoning literature.) Teachers are being asked to determine the cutscore that reflects minimal competency or mastery of the benchmark. Students failing to reach this mastery cutscore may not graduate from high school. For example, beginning in 2004 high school students in Oregon will be required to show mastery of the Oregon Content Standards for Physical Education to attain a Certificate of Initial Mastery. Physical educators in Oregon are currently grappling with the challenge of developing appropriate assessments, scoring guides, and mastery cutscores. Not surprisingly, controversy surrounds the issues related to setting valid mastery cutscores.

NEW ASSESSMENT PRACTICE

Assessment practice in the educational reform movement is authentic and fully integrated into the instructional process (Melograno, 1997). Educational reform involves the intertwining of standards-based curricula, performance assessment, assessment-driven instruction, and authentic learning into what has been coined "the achievement cycle" (Glatthorn, Bragaw, Dawkins, & Parker, 1998). The achievement cycle has as its goal authentic learning or "high-order learning used in solving contextualized problems" (Glatthorn et al., 1998, p. 11). Standards-based curricula, performance assessment, and assessment driven instruction interact to achieve authentic learning.

> The stubborn problems in assessment reform have to do with a pervasive thoughtlessness about testing and a failure to understand the relationship between assessment and learning. We have the tests we deserve because we are wont to reduce "assessment" to "testing" and to see testing as separate from learning—something we do expediently, after the teaching is over, to see how students did (usually for *other* people's benefit, not the performer's). (Wiggins, 1993, p. 3)

Standards-based curricula are based on content standards and benchmarks. From a teacher's perspective, a standards-based curriculum provides the focus for developing lesson plans and instructional strategies. The degree to which students have mastered the standards-based curriculum is determined through a combination of traditional and performance-based assessments.

Assessment-driven instruction involves "teaching and planning for teaching that are based on, derived from, and focused on performance assessment" (Glatthorn et al., 1998, p. 7). In assessment-driven instruction, performance assessments are developed to assess students' mastery of content standards and benchmarks. The teacher's focus is to develop creative and effective instructional strategies to prepare students to be successful in mastering the performance assessment.

Assessment-driven instruction has been criticized as teaching to the test. But this criticism is unwarranted because the nature of performance assessment is to assess what students know and are able to do in real-life settings. If the performance assessments are challenging and properly constructed, they become a proper focus for instruction (Glatthorn et al., 1998). As Melograno (1997) pointed out, the construction of assessment devices themselves can be an important learning task for students.

COMMUNICATING STUDENT LEARNING: MORE THAN A GRADE

Issues surrounding the grading process have captured the attention of physical educators for decades. Over the past 30 years we have seen major shifts from norm-referenced to criterion-referenced grading and from reliance on high-inference grading criteria such as participation and effort to reliance on low-inference grading criteria such as motor-skill performance and scores on cognitive tests.

The educational reform movement is adding its own contributions to evaluation methodology. Driven in part by the renewed emphasis on accountability and in part by the radical shift to and complexity of standards-based and assessment-driven instruction, the evolution of grading practice is changing the way we view student learning. For example, the term *grading* is being supplanted by the encompassing notion *communicating student learning* (Guskey, 1996a), implying that simply reporting a letter grade is no longer sufficient. Moreover, the perspectives that effective assessment systems (a) involve student input and (b) are used to assist and inform instruction are becoming more widespread. (Readers can review *Natural Classroom Assessment: Designing Seamless Instruction and Assessment* by Smith, Smith, & De Lisi [2001] for a comprehensive look at these perspectives.)

Two issues that have captured the attention of educators are the types of assessment information that should be reported and how this information should be reported. The issue of what to report depends in part on the intended audience and purpose. For example, minimal reporting (e.g., letter grades and grade point average) is sufficient for admission to institutions of higher learning, but for classroom purposes "grades are so imprecise that they are almost meaningless" (Marzano, 2000, p. 1). Students and parents require more extensive information about student learning. Guskey (1996b) outlines three learning criteria used for grading and reporting:

- Product criteria reflect performance relative to content standards and benchmarks. These criteria are assessed by traditional and performance assessments of benchmarks.
- Process criteria reflect performance relative to how students reached mastery of product criteria. Criteria such as participation, effort, work habits, homework, and attendance fall into this category.
- Progress criteria reflect how much student learning has changed over time.

Arguments abound supporting each of these criteria. Measurement specialists in physical education have traditionally defended the use of product criteria as the most objective evidence, whereas teachers challenged by classroom management issues gravitate towards process criteria. As in many aspects in life, the answer lies in a balance of the three, each receiving its own evaluation (Stiggins, 1994).

Reporting formats for communicating student learning, therefore, should include product, process, and progress. Figure 11.4 presents an example of such a reporting format. The benchmark performance assessments and their scores relative to the mastery

Benchmark Mastery Profile

Name:	John Doe					
Class:	Period 3	**Attendance:**	5	Days absent		
Date:	11/29/03	**Behavior:**	4	SR level		
Performance tests		**Score**	**Mastery cutoff**	**Standard**		
	Benchmark 1	5	3		P	
	Benchmark 2	3	4	D		
	Benchmark 3	5	3		P	Proficient
	Benchmark 4	25	20		C	Competent
	Benchmark 5	5	3		P	Developing
	Benchmark 6	5	3		P	Emerging
	Benchmark 7	21	15		P	Beginning
	Benchmark 8	1	3	E		

Comments:
John is performing above the standard for all benchmarks with the exception of knowledge and interpretation of physical fitness components.
We have discussed his performance and have scheduled time to discuss the topics he is having difficulty with.

Mastery Profile

FIGURE 11.4 Sample reporting format for communicating student learning.

cutoff scores give product criteria. Process criteria include days absent and the student's current level of personal and social responsibility (see chapter 14 by Don Hellison), while anecdotal comments at the bottom of the report describe progress. Guskey (1996a) and Guskey and Bailey (2001) provide examples of model reporting formats for various grade levels and academic subjects.

More complete reporting formats enhance student learning, but the benefits of such reporting do not come without cost. Of primary concern to physical educators are time constraints related to large class size and frequency of class meetings. In addition, use of extended reporting formats will necessitate staff development and increased use of technology, particularly computers. Last, because physical educators may face challenges from students, parents, and administrators who do not fully understand the need for extended formats, advocacy and promotion of the methods used to communicate student learning are a necessary part of the implementation process.

IMPLEMENTING NEW ASSESSMENT PRACTICE: CHALLENGES FOR PRACTITIONERS

Physical educators faced with implementing new assessment practice in a standards-based education framework will encounter a number of significant challenges. Meeting these challenges takes patience, persistence, and in some cases assistance from other professionals.

Aligning the Physical Education Curriculum

Content standards and benchmarks are developmentally appropriate learning goals for students at each grade level (NASPE, 1995). Proper implementation of standards-based physical education therefore implies that (a) the K–12 physical education curriculum is developmentally appropriate and (b) the curriculum is delivered so that as students progress through the school system they will have the maximum potential for meeting content standards and benchmarks.

Articulation of the curriculum across grade levels thus becomes a primary concern when implementing standards-based education. For example, one of the first steps in implementing the state-mandated content standards for physical education in Oregon is curriculum alignment across grade levels. Using a process known as curriculum mapping (see Jacobs, 1997), teachers, schools, and school districts examine their physical education curriculum for the content and assessments that they deliver each month over the school year. They then align benchmarks to the curriculum map to identify any redundancies across grade levels or any instructional gaps that would reduce students' chances of meeting required benchmarks.

Overcoming Classroom Logistics

The logistical barriers to effective instruction and assessment in physical education are well documented (e.g., Griffin, 1985; Hastie, Sanders, & Rowland, 1999). Elementary school physical educators commonly serve several hundred students in a single week. At first glance, large class size and sheer numbers of classes coupled with reduced instructional time seem to be an insurmountable barrier to new assessment practice. Careful planning and seamless integration of assessment into the instructional process can assist in overcoming this obstacle (Melograno, 1997). In addition, keeping the assessments simple will help teachers cope with logistical constraints. For example, Schiemer (1996) describes a number of one-minute assessment tools for grades 1 through 5 and offers the following useful suggestions for implementing new assessment practice: Start slowly, start small, expect failure, share with colleagues, and begin with assessment formats that are familiar to students. In addition, many resources that focus on implementing standards-based education and performance assessments are available (e.g., Baron & Boschee, 1995; Glatthorn et al., 1998; Marzano & Kendall, 1996; Smith et al., 2001).

Validity and Reliability of Assessments

Although the literature abounds with examples of alternative assessments, researchers have not provided much evidence of the validity and reliability of these methods. Joyner and McManis (1997) provide one of the few discussions of these topics in the physical education literature. Alternative and traditional assessments face many of the same measurement concerns, but of particular importance for alternative assessments are ensuring that (a) the behaviors included in the assessment align with what was taught in the class and with important curricular objectives and (b) evidence is provided for interrater and stability reliability of the scoring method. See Dunbar, Koretz, and Hoover (1991) and Burger and Burger (1994) for comprehensive discussions of these issues.

Setting Valid Performance Standards

The thorniest issue facing those implementing standards-based physical education and assessment-driven instruction involves setting valid performance mastery cutoff scores for each assessment. Considering that the decisions about students resulting from using mastery cutoffs can have serious ramifications (e.g., high school graduation), it is little wonder that students, teachers, parents, and administrators are looking carefully at how these indicators of student mastery are determined. Fortunately, a wealth of information describes (a) various methodologies for determining mastery cutoffs and (b) procedures for ensuring that the cutoff-setting process is defensible (e.g., Cizek, 2001).

Most cutoff-setting methods were developed for the more cognitive-oriented subject areas and can be generalized as test-centered or examinee-centered methods (Jaeger, 1989). One of the oldest test-centered methods, and one that remains popular in various forms, is the Angoff method (Angoff, 1971). For example, to determine the mastery cutoff of a 10-question multiple-choice test of basketball rules, qualified experts determine for each test question the probability that a student with mastery of the content would supply the correct answer. The mastery cutoff is the sum of the probabilities. Alternatively, the experts could award a "1" to questions that a student with mastery would answer correctly, give a "0" to those questions that this student would not answer correctly, and simply total the number of correct responses.

A drawback of test-centered methods is their failure to use actual student performance in determining mastery cutoff scores. Examinee-centered methods circumvent this issue by using test data from students to determine the mastery cutoff score. For example, test responses from a representative sample of students are scored and the scores are filed away. The test responses are then given to a panel of experts who review each test and choose those test responses that are most representative of students who have content mastery. The actual test scores are then reviewed, and the frequency of scores on the selected mastery performances in each assessment are used to determine a cutoff score (see Kingston, Kahl, Sweeney, & Bay [2001] and Plake & Hambleton [2001] for more complete descriptions of examinee-centered methods).

A more statistically oriented examinee-centered approach described in the physical education literature (see Safrit, 1989 and Safrit & Wood, 1995) is the contrasting groups method. This method first identifies a group of masters (skilled performers) and nonmasters (unskilled performers) by the ratings of experts. The test is then administered to these students to determine which test score most accurately predicts students into their identified mastery state. Consider, for example, scores with a possible range of 0 to 10 points for a test of volleyball spiking ability of high school students in an intermediate-level volleyball class. Assume that we have used the school volleyball coach to determine which students in the volleyball class are masters (skilled) or nonmasters (unskilled) at volleyball spiking. We then administer the volleyball-spiking test to each student and compare his or her test score to a cutoff score (e.g., 8). Students achieving a score of 8 or higher on the test are deemed masters (skilled), and those with test scores below 8 are categorized as nonmasters (unskilled). The most accurate cutoff score is one that most frequently predicts the mastery state estimated by the volleyball coach.

The procedures used to set performance mastery cutoff scores are critically important because (a) important decisions about students are made based on cutoff scores and (b) adequacy of these procedures provide the yardstick by which we judge the overall validity and fairness of the cutoffs. Research concerning the adequacy of cutoff-setting procedures is therefore burgeoning (see, for example, Hambleton, 2001; Raymond & Reid, 2001; and Reckase, 2001).

Six steps are typically suggested when setting cutoff scores:

1. Choose a review panel.
2. Choose a method or methods for setting cutoff scores (e.g., contrasting groups, Angoff).
3. Train panelists.
4. Set cutoff scores.

5. Compile evidence for validity and generalizability of cutoff scores.

6. Carefully document the process.

Although all steps are important, the first and the last deserve special mention. The review panel is the group of individuals who will set the performance cutoff scores. From a logistical perspective, this panel will most likely be the same group that oversees aligning the curriculum and developing performance assessments. Therefore, the review panel must be chosen carefully. For example, review panels for physical education should include representation from both genders; content specialists from primary, middle, and high school levels; at least one elementary or middle school classroom teacher; students; administrators; parents; and other stakeholders from the community. Although the literature concerning the number of panelists to include is equivocal, a panel of size 10 to 20 appears to optimize dependability and minimize errors of measurement (Raymond & Reid, 2001).

Setting mastery cutoff scores is a difficult and complex process complicated by the presence of subjectivity in all methods for setting cutoff scores. Subjectivity in the method leaves the process vulnerable to challenges from stakeholders. Review panels must therefore provide complete and detailed documentation of the process used to set mastery cutoffs. This documentation provides a record of fairness and use of accepted cutoff-setting practice. From a legal perspective, Phillips (2001) concluded that "courts will uphold a state's passing standards if all the facts and circumstances indicate that the resulting standard is not arbitrary or capricious and has been adopted by the requisite authorities based on legitimate goals and relevant information" (p. 420).

Overcoming Opportunity Bias or Can One Shoe Fit All?

Assume that a state or school district mandates content standards for physical education along with performance assessment of students to monitor progress towards benchmarks. An issue of some importance concerns the adequacy of facilities, personnel, class time, and instruction for meeting those goals. In other words, do all students have comparable opportunity to master the standards and successfully complete the assessments? If a benchmark mandates that students demonstrate proficiency in swimming, is it reasonable to expect students with no access to swimming facilities to meet this benchmark? Or, if a district reacts to a budget shortfall by dismissing physical education specialists or by reducing the time devoted to physical education instruction, will students have grounds for claiming that they did not have sufficient opportunity to master physical education benchmarks? Add to this scenario the likelihood that mastery of physical education benchmarks at the high school level are required for graduation, and it is clear that opportunity bias is an issue that must be considered when mandating standards-based education and assessment-driven instruction.

Opportunity bias is not a new issue. Physical educators have been addressing the issue in multicultural gymnasiums and when delivering instruction to individuals with disabilities. The scope of the challenge, however, is widening as we begin to expect all students to master common learning targets. Those responsible for developing and implementing content standards, benchmarks, and performance assessments must keep in mind the potential for opportunity bias and develop flexible policies for dealing with diverse student needs.

Professional Development Activities

Given the increased emphasis on standards-based education and assessment-driven instruction, a myriad of new terminology and methodologies, and a challenge to change the very way we deliver physical education, one of the most pressing challenges in implementing standards-based physical education and assessment-driven instruction is continuing education and professional development. The significance of professional development in the New York State implementation process led Fay and Doolittle (2002) to conclude that "the state's goal of changing to a standards-based paradigm for curriculum, instruction, and assessment was doomed unless a strategy could be found to bring the standards to each school district in the state" (p. 32).

Strategies for accomplishing professional development vary by state. The Wyoming Health and Physical Education School Network (Deal et al., 2002) directed the development of state standards. Professional development activities in this rural state with relatively sparse population were enhanced by creation of a Web site and e-mail list server to facilitate dissemination of information and communication among teachers. Presentations at state conferences and district in-service workshops introduced the standards and helped districts align the standards with current curriculum. Subsequent regional workshops assisted districts in developing assessments. In New York, the New York State Association for Health, Physical Education, Recreation, and Dance developed a workshop format and trained four to six physical educators in each state geographic zone to act as workshop leaders. The New York strategy served to give physical education teachers ownership of the process while maintaining professional control over the nature and consistency of the content (Fay & Doolittle, 2002).

Educating Stakeholders

One of the most neglected facets of implementing standards-based education and assessment-driven instruction is educating students, parents, and the community. In her book *Developing Parent and Community Understanding of Performance-Based Assessment*, Alvestad (2000) provides one of the few comprehensive treatments of this topic. She begins by noting that significant changes in educational practice can result in expectations that student performance will decline, confusion among students, and criticism from parents and the community. Her "proactive approach" to planning long-term and comprehensive parental and community involvement in the process of change uses the following four-step process:

1. Informally introducing performance-based assessment succinctly and calmly to as many people as possible
2. Sharing knowledge about performance based assessment through handouts such as parent handbooks
3. Teaching performance-based assessment to parents through more formal venues such as workshops
4. Helping parents practice performance-based skills

In addition, Alvestad advocates maintaining continuous communication with parents through newsletters and with other stakeholders through newspaper articles and speaking engagements at local organizations. The significance of maintaining the support of stakeholders should not be underestimated because it has been shown repeatedly that a persistent and vocal opposition, no matter how small in number, can derail a well-intentioned program.

RESEARCH TO PRACTICE OR PRACTICE TO RESEARCH?

At its core, the assessment practice and products of the latest round of educational reform arise from grassroots efforts of teachers. With the exception of interest in methodologies for constructing performance tests for large-scale high-stakes assessments and the evolving research in setting performance mastery cutoff scores, literature concerning assessment methods and practice has been descriptive and focused on a how-to approach aimed at in-service teachers.

Since 1996, research regarding performance assessment methods and practice in physical education has been conspicuous by its absence. Although several features focusing on the practical application of content standards and performance assessment along with articles offering practical advice for implementing alternative assessments have appeared in the *Journal of Physical Education, Recreation and Dance* (see, for example, the September 1997, October, 2001, November/December 2001, and March 2002 issues) and two articles have appeared in *The Physical Educator* (Pennington, Manross, & Poole, 2001; Woods & Anderson, 2002), the topic has been virtually ignored in research-oriented journals such as the *Journal of Teaching in Physical Education* and *Measurement in Physical Education and Exercise Science* (see the tutorial on developing portfolio systems by Melograno [2000] and a description of issues involved in developing quality performance assessments by Stiggins [1997] for two exceptions). This lack of attention may become problematic given the potential for new assessment practice to change the way physical educators deliver instruction. As more states and school districts mandate standards-based physical education and assessment-driven instruction, teachers will require guidance on the most effective and efficient ways to integrate curriculum, instruction, and assessment practice.

The latest wave of educational reform and its emphasis on standards-based education and assessment of learning in real-life contexts has accomplished much in the realm of teacher and student accountability for learning. Physical educators are beginning to see the potential of reform for establishing the rightful place of physical education in the school curriculum. Yet successful implementation of such reforms will require a systematic investigation into issues such as (a) how to organize effective and efficient professional development, (b) how to overcome logistical barriers to implementation and integration of assessment-driven instruction in the gymnasium (Ward & Doutis, 1999), and (c) how to develop valid and reliable performance assessments, associated scoring guides, and mastery cutoff scores. The wave of educational reform is much like a surfing competition. Those who catch the big wave and ride it successfully reap the rewards. Those who miss the wave fall behind.

IMPLICATIONS FOR PRACTICE

1. Educational reform is changing what we teach, how we teach, and what the role of student assessment is in the teaching-learning process.
2. The core of the current round of educational reform is the development of common learning targets (i.e., content standards and benchmarks) for students at each grade level, coupled with assessments that indicate the degree to which students are mastering the targets.
3. Assessment of student mastery focuses on what students know and should be able to do in real-life contexts (i.e., authentic assessment).
4. Assessment practice is fully integrated into the instructional process (i.e., assessment-driven instruction).
5. Valid and reliable scoring guides with clearly defined performance standards are a critical component of effective authentic assessment.
6. Determining the performance level (i.e., performance cutscore) that reflects mastery of a benchmark may prove to be the most challenging hurdle for physical educators. Subjectivity inherent in the process of setting mastery cutscores requires that physical educators use

recognized methods accompanied by careful documentation of the process used for setting cutscores.

7. Effectively communicating student learning to parents, students, and administrators will involve changes in the way we evaluate students. Expanded reporting formats will include product criteria, process criteria, and progress criteria.

8. Implementing new assessment practice will require careful attention to aligning the physical education curriculum, overcoming classroom logistics (e.g., large class size, reduced instructional time), developing valid and reliable assessments, setting valid performance standards and cutoffs, educating stakeholders, providing sufficient professional development activities, and overcoming opportunity bias.

REFERENCES

Alvestad, K.A. (2000). *Developing parent and community understanding of performance-based assessment.* Larchmont, NY: Eye on Education.

Angoff, W.H. (1971). Scales, norms, and equivalent scores. In R.L. Thorndike (Ed.), *Educational measurement* (2nd ed., pp. 508-600). Washington, DC: American Council on Education.

Arter, J., & McTighe, J. (2001). *Scoring rubrics in the classroom: Using performance criteria for assessing and improving student learning.* Thousand Oaks, CA: Corwin Press.

Baron, M.A., & Boschee, F. (1995). *Authentic assessment: The key to unlocking student success.* Lancaster, PA: Technomic.

Bartz, D., Anderson-Robinson, S., & Hillman, L. (1994). Performance assessment: Make them show what they know. *Principal, 73*(3), 11-14.

Burger, S.E., & Burger, D.L. (1994). Determining the validity of performance-based assessment. *Educational Measurement: Issues and Practice, 13*, 9-15.

Cizek, G.J. (Ed.). (2001). *Setting performance standards: Concepts, methods, and perspectives.* Mahwah, NJ: Erlbaum.

Collins, A., & Dana, T.M. (1993). Using portfolios with middle grades students. *Middle School Journal, 25*(2), 14-19.

Cutforth, N., & Parker, M. (1996). Promoting affective development in physical education. *Journal of Physical Education, Recreation and Dance, 67*(7), 19-23.

Danielson, C., & Abrutyn, L. (1997). *An introduction to using portfolios in the classroom.* Alexandria, VA: Association for Supervision and Curriculum Development.

Deal, T.B., Byra, M., Jenkins, J., & Gates, W.E. (2002). The physical education standards movement in Wyoming: An effort in partnership. *Journal of Physical Education, Recreation and Dance, 73*(3), 25-28.

Dunbar, S.B., Koretz, D.M., & Hoover, H.D. (1991). Quality control in the development and use of performance assessments. *Applied Measurement in Education, 4*, 289-303.

Fay, T., & Doolittle, S. (2002). Agents for change: From standards to assessment to accountability in physical education. *Journal of Physical Education, Recreation and Dance, 73*(3), 29-33.

Feuer, M.J., & Fulton, K. (1993). The many faces of performance assessment. *Phi Delta Kappan, 74*, 478.

Glatthorn, A.A., Bragaw, D., Dawkins, K., & Parker, J. (1998). *Performance assessment and standards-based curricula: The achievement cycle.* Larchmont, NY: Eye on Education.

Griffin, P. (1985). Teaching in an urban multicultural junior high school physical education program: The power of context. *Quest, 37*, 154-165.

Guskey, T.R. (Ed.). (1996a). *Communicating student learning.* Alexandria, VA: Association for Supervision and Curriculum Development.

Guskey, T.R. (1996b). Reporting on student learning: Lessons from the past—prescriptions for the future. In T.R. Guskey (Ed.), *Communicating student learning* (pp. 13-24). Alexandria, VA: Association for Supervision and Curriculum Development.

Guskey, T.R., & Bailey, J.M. (2001). *Developing grading and reporting systems for student learning.* Thousand Oaks, CA: Corwin Press.

Hambleton, R.K. (2001). Setting performance standards on educational assessments and criteria for evaluating the process. In G.J. Cizek (Ed.), *Setting performance standards: Concepts, methods, and perspectives* (pp. 89-116). Mahwah, NJ: Erlbaum.

Hastie, P.A., Sanders, S.W., & Rowland R.S. (1999). Where good intentions meet harsh realities: Teaching large classes in physical education. *Journal of Teaching in Physical Education, 18*, 277-289.

Hibbard, K.M., Van Wagenen, L., Lewbel, S., Waterbury-Wyatt, S., Shaw, S., Pelletier, K., Larkins, B., O'Donnell-Dooling, J., Elia, E., Palma, S., Maler, J., Johnson, D., Honan, M., McKeon-Nelson, D., & Wislocki, J.A. (1996). *A teacher's guide to performance-based learning and assessment.* Alexandria, VA: Association for Supervision and Curriculum Development.

Jacobs, H. (1997). *Mapping the big picture: Integrating curriculum and assessment K–12.* Alexandria, VA: Association for Supervision and Curriculum Development.

Jaeger, R.M. (1989). Certification of student competence. In R.L. Linn (Ed.), *Educational measurement* (3rd ed., pp. 485-514). New York: American Council on Education and Macmillan.

Joyner, A.B., & McManis, B.G. (1997). Quality control in alternative assessment. *Journal of Physical Education, Recreation and Dance, 68*(7), 38-40.

Kane, M.T. (2001). So much remains the same: Conception and status of validation in setting standards. In G.J. Cizek (Ed.), *Setting performance standards: Concepts, methods, and perspectives* (pp. 53-88). Mahwah, NJ: Erlbaum.

Kingston, N.M., Kahl, S.R., Sweeney, K.P., & Bay, L. (2001). Setting performance standards using the body of work method. In G.J. Cizek (Ed.), *Setting performance standards: Concepts, methods, and perspectives* (pp. 219-248). Mahwah, NJ: Erlbaum.

Kirk, M. (1997). Using portfolios to enhance student learning and assessment. *Journal of Physical Education, Recreation and Dance, 68*(7), 29-33.

Lambert, L.T. (1998). This too shall pass—or will it? [Editorial]. *Journal of Physical Education, Recreation and Dance, 69*(1), 13-14.

Lambert, L.T. (1999). *Standards-based assessment of student learning: A comprehensive approach.* Reston, VA: National Association for Sport and Physical Education.

Lund, J. (1997). Authentic assessment: Its development and applications. *Journal of Physical Education, Recreation and Dance, 68*(7), 25-28, 40.

Lund, J.L. (2000). *Creating rubrics for physical education.* Reston, VA: National Association for Sport and Physical Education.

Marzano, R.J. (2000). *Transforming classroom grading.* Alexandria, VA: Association for Supervision and Curriculum Development.

Marzano, R.J., & Kendall, J.S. (1996). *Designing standards-based districts, schools, and classrooms.* Alexandria, VA: Association for Supervision and Curriculum Development.

Melograno, V.J. (1994). Portfolio assessment: Documenting authentic student learning. *Journal of Physical Education, Recreation and Dance, 65*(8), 50-55, 58-61.

Melograno, V.J. (1997). Integrating assessment into physical education. *Journal of Physical Education, Recreation and Dance, 68*(7), 34-37.

Melograno, V.J. (2000). Designing a portfolio system for K–12 physical education: A step-by-step process. *Measurement in Physical Education and Exercise Science, 4,* 97-115.

Meyer, C.A. (1992). What's the difference between authentic and performance assessment? *Educational Leadership, 49*(8), 39.

Mitchell, S.A., & Olsin, J.L. (1999). *Assessment in games teaching.* Reston, VA: National Association for Sport and Physical Education.

National Association for Sport and Physical Education. (1995). *Moving into the future: National physical education standards: A guide to content and assessment.* St. Louis: Mosby.

Oregon Department of Education. (2001). *Physical education common curriculum goals and content standards.* Salem, OR: Author.

Ornstein, A.C. (1994). Assessing without testing. *Principal, 73*(3), 24-26.

Pennington, T.R., Manross, D., & Poole, J. (2001). Exploring alternative assessment in college physical activity classes. *The Physical Educator, 58,* 206-210.

Phillips, S.E. (2001). Legal issues in standard setting for K–12 programs. In G.J. Cizek (Ed.), *Setting performance standards: Concepts, methods, and perspectives* (pp. 411-426). Mahwah, NJ: Erlbaum.

Plake, B.S., & Hambleton, R.K. (2001). The analytic judgment method for setting standards on complex performance assessments. In G.J. Cizek (Ed.), *Setting performance standards: Concepts, methods, and perspectives* (pp. 283-312). Mahwah, NJ: Erlbaum.

Raymond, M.R., & Reid, J.B. (2001). Who made thee a judge? Selecting and training participants for standard setting. In G.J. Cizek (Ed.), *Setting performance standards: Concepts, methods, and perspectives* (pp. 119-157). Mahwah, NJ: Erlbaum.

Reckase, M.D. (2001). Innovative methods for helping standard-setting participants to perform their task: The role of feedback regarding consistency, accuracy, and impact. In G.J. Cizek (Ed.), *Setting performance standards: Concepts, methods, and perspectives* (pp. 159-173). Mahwah, NJ: Erlbaum.

Rink, J., Mitchell, M., Templeton, J., Barton, G., Hewitt, P., Taylor, M., Dawkins, M., & Hohn, R. (2002). High stakes assessment in South Carolina. *Journal of Physical Education, Recreation and Dance, 73*(3), 21-24, 33.

Rothman, R. (1995). *Measuring up: Standards, assessment, and school reform.* San Francisco: Jossey-Bass.

Safrit, M.J. (1989). Criterion-referenced measurement: Validity. In M.J. Safrit & T.M. Wood (Eds.), *Measurement concepts in physical education and exercise science* (pp. 119-135). Champaign, IL: Human Kinetics.

Safrit, M.J., & Wood, T.M. (1995). *Introduction to measurement in physical education and exercise science.* St. Louis: Mosby.

Schiemer, S. (1996). Efficient and effective assessment techniques. *Journal of Physical Education, Recreation and Dance, 67*(9), 26-28.

Schincariol, L.M., & Radford, K.W. (1998). Checklists and rubrics: An alternative form of assessment in a university volleyball activity course. *Journal of Physical Education, Recreation and Dance, 69*(1), 25-32.

Smith, J.K., Smith, L.F., & De Lisi, R. (2001). *Natural classroom assessment: Designing seamless instruction & assessment.* Thousand Oaks, CA: Corwin Press.

Stiggins, R.J. (1994). Communicating with report card grades. In R.J. Stiggins, *Student-centered classroom assessment* (pp. 363-396). New York: Macmillan.

Stiggins, R.J. (1997). Dealing with the practical matter of

quality performance assessment. *Measurement in Physical Education and Exercise Science, 1,* 5-17.

Taggart, G.L., Phifer, S.J., Nixon, J.A., & Wood, M. (1998). *Rubrics: A handbook for construction and use.* Lancaster, PA: Technomic.

Ward, P., & Doutis, P. (1999). Chapter 2. Toward a consolidation of the knowledge base for reform in physical education. *Journal of Teaching in Physical Education, 18,* 382-402.

Wiggins, G.P. (1993). *Assessing student performance: Exploring the purpose and limits of testing.* San Francisco: Jossey-Bass.

Wood, T.M. (1996). Evaluation and testing: The road less traveled. In S.J. Silverman & C.D. Ennis (Eds.), *Student learning in physical education: Applying research to enhance instruction* (pp. 199-219). Champaign, IL: Human Kinetics.

Woods, M.L., & Anderson, D. (2002). Students designing and applying evaluation rubrics in an aerobics unit. *The Physical Educator, 59,* 38-56.

PART IV

PROMOTING VALUED OUTCOMES AND ATTITUDES

CHAPTER TWELVE

HEALTH-RELATED PHYSICAL EDUCATION: PHYSICAL ACTIVITY, FITNESS, AND WELLNESS

Thomas L. McKenzie

Health, wellness, physical fitness, and physical activity are inextricably connected. Of these, physical fitness has long been an important goal of physical education and is the goal that physical educators most frequently assess in schools. Physical fitness is related to improved health and well-being and is extremely important in sport skill performance. Physical activity, a process, is also related to health and wellness. Additionally, only through active participation do people achieve and maintain physical fitness and motor skills. With the increased evidence of the positive contribution of physical activity to health and well-being (U.S. Department of Health and Human Services [USDHHS], 1996), the primary focus of this chapter is on the promotion of physical activity through school physical education.

WARMING UP: AN INTRODUCTION

The costs and consequences of sedentary living are tremendous (Booth & Chakravarth, 2002). For example, physical inactivity is a risk factor for cardiovascular disease (CVD), which accounts for more than half of the adult deaths in the United States each year. Meanwhile, approximately 29% of the adult population report participating in no leisure time physical activity, and another 41% report activity levels insufficient for health purposes ("Physical Activity Trends," 2001). Thus, the costs of health care and premature deaths could decline if individuals made changes in their physical activity habits. By engaging children and adolescents in enjoyable physical activity and teaching them the skills related to developing and maintaining appropriate physical activity, physical education could help future generations of adults avoid becoming so sedentary.

Physical education is increasingly being considered as an important component of a coordinated school health program (Allensworth, Lawson, Nicholson, & Wyche, 1997). Because most students have about nine years of required physical education, schools are the institutions with primary responsibility for physical activity promotion (Sallis & McKenzie, 1991). Reorienting school programs to promote physical activity could have a major effect on public health. Therefore, the notion of health-related physical education (HRPE) has been advanced (Pate & Hohn, 1994; Sallis & McKenzie, 1991). The main goal of HRPE is to prepare children and adolescents for a lifetime of physical activity. Although this is not a new goal for physical education, reaching it will require the implementation of both curricular and instructional strategies that are substantially different from those in traditional fitness and sport-oriented programs (McKenzie, 2001).

The second section of this chapter, "Serious Preparation: A Review of Related Literature," provides a brief overview of research related to physical activity and fitness and describes the status of HRPE in schools. The third section, "Exercising Opinions: A Health-Related View," discusses the conduct of physical education and the preparation of teachers from a health-related viewpoint. The fourth, "SPARKing up Physical Education," describes Sports, Play, and Active Recreation for Kids (SPARK), an experimental elementary school physical education program designed with a health-related focus. The fifth section, "Cooling Down: Further Implications for Research and Practice," summarizes the chapter and encourages teachers to redirect physical education and physical fitness instruction toward reaching public health objectives.

SERIOUS PREPARATION: A REVIEW OF RELATED LITERATURE

This section describes the status of HRPE in schools and provides a brief overview of research related to physical activity and fitness in youth. Connections between physical activity, physical fitness, and health and wellness are identified, and several questions related to the appropriateness of current levels of physical activity in youth are answered.

Status of the Field

Although sports typically dominate school programs after the third grade, physical fitness is usually advanced as a major goal of physical education, particularly during threats of program elimination. In 1992, 25% of states reported mandatory testing in physical education, and these consisted primarily of physical fitness assessments conducted only at designated grade levels (Bennett & Peel, 1994). State, district, and school regulations for the content and delivery of physical education vary tremendously, with individual teachers being the major decision makers for what happens during classes. Most physical educators at least provide lip service to physical fitness and use various approaches to include it in their curricula. Some incorporate several minutes of general fitness activities into each class, some match fitness activities to the sport unit they are teaching, some offer specialized fitness units, and some conduct obligatory annual fitness tests. Currently seven states (e.g., Florida, South Carolina, Texas) and the Department of Defense Dependent Schools (schools for military and U.S. government employees worldwide) require a personal fitness class during high school. These jurisdictions all have standards requiring such a course, but not all provide money to supply students with textbooks.

Most popular general texts on elementary and secondary school physical education include sections or chapters on physical fitness, and several books specifically teach physical fitness. Two examples are *Fitness for Life* (Corbin & Lindsey, 2002), a textbook for junior and senior high schools, and *Teaching Strategies for Improving Youth Fitness* (Pangrazi & Corbin, 1994), which is geared for all grades. The latter text includes information on the FITNESSGRAM, an assessment and recognition system to motivate physical activity, and on family involvement in students' fitness activities. Additionally, Pate and Hohn (1994) include several chapters on physical fitness curriculum and methods, as well as descriptions of special school programs. Although many theoretically sound curricula and instructional strategies have been promoted, few have been examined empirically, and rarely have their long-term effects been investigated. As a result, the effects of different physical fitness programs on either students' out-of-school physical activity or their future physical fitness are relatively untested.

Historically, being physically fit has been associated with being good at sports. A distinction is now made among the various components of physical fitness, and they are classified according to whether they develop skill fitness or health-related fitness. Skill fitness is considered activity-specific or sport-specific and includes components such as accuracy, agility, balance, coordination, power, reaction time, and speed. Health-related physical fitness is more general and encompasses components directly related to reduced risk of hypokinetic disease, including cardiovascular fitness, muscular strength and endurance, flexibility, and body composition. The most widely used fitness testing programs (e.g., the FITNESSGRAM) at schools measure health-related components (Pate & Shephard, 1989). Although the various components of skill- and health-related fitness are distinct and can be measured separately, they do affect one another. For example, health-related fitness aids most sports performance, and sports participation reciprocally contributes to health-related physical fitness.

Physical Fitness, Physical Activity, Health, and Wellness Connections

Physical fitness, physical activity, health, and wellness are interconnected, but the full relationship remains unclear. Physical fitness is typically viewed as one of the variables that have an influence on how physical activity affects both health (Bouchard, Shephard, & Stephens, 1994) and wellness, which refers to a broader concept of health that includes participation in a positive, active, healthy lifestyle. Children's habitual physical activity relates significantly to multiple health-related fitness components, including cardiovascular endurance and muscular strength and endurance (Malina, 1994; Sallis, McKenzie, & Alcaraz, 1993). Increases in both physical activity and physical fitness are also associated with improved health measurements (Malina, 1994; Riddoch, 1998). The effects of physical activity on health and wellness, however, appear to have multiple mechanisms, some of which do not depend on fitness (Bouchard et al., 1994). Additionally, other factors, including heredity, environment, and general lifestyle behaviors, influence all four.

Training programs specifically designed to influence one or more components of health-related physical fitness can be successful (Malina, 1994; Riddoch, 1998). Resistance-training programs have been shown to bring about substantial gains in static and functional strength measures in both prepubescent and adolescent boys and girls, although the data on girls are limited. Endurance training programs affect both boys and girls, but the data suggest that even intensive programs do little to change the maximal aerobic power of children younger than 10 years of age. Although these studies have design problems, it is generally agreed that structured, vigorous training programs can improve most fitness components in children. Because children have relatively high levels of fitness compared with adults (Simons-Morton, O'Hara, Simons-Morton, & Parcel, 1987), some health professionals consider it more important that children maintain a good level of fitness rather than reach extremely high levels, particularly if the process of becoming maximally fit turns them off to engagement in physical activity.

Health Benefits of Physical Activity in Youth

Physical activity seems to have beneficial effects on many bodily systems (Bouchard et al., 1994; USDHHS, 1996), but we are just beginning to understand its effects on youth (Riddoch, 1998). Reviews of the scientific literature have shown that physical activity in adolescence (defined as ages 11 to 21) reduces the risk of obesity and aids in its treatment (Bar-Or & Baranowski, 1994). In addition, activities that work against gravity help increase the density of bones, which may prevent osteoporosis later in life (Bailey & Martin, 1994), and vigorous exercise helps improve psychological health and mood (Calfas & Taylor, 1994). Among high-risk youth, physical activity can reduce blood pressure (Alpert & Wilmore, 1994) and increase HDL-cholesterol (Armstrong & Simons-Morton, 1994).

Improvement in children's flexibility, muscular strength, and bone health is thought to be related to reduced occurrences of back pain and fractures in adulthood. The strongest rationale for health-related physical education, however, appears to be the prevention of CVD (Riddoch, 1998). Cardiovascular risk in childhood predicts risk in young adulthood (Cresanta, Burke, Downey, Freedman, & Berenson, 1986), so decreasing risk factors in children is important. CVD risk associations are similar for children and adults (Sallis, Patterson, Buono, & Nader, 1988), so it may be possible that children can reduce their risk of future heart disease through regular physical activity.

Health Goals for the Nation

Public health objectives designed to reduce preventable death, disease, and disability in the United States have been established, and these are likely to influence the conduct of school physical education in the future. *Healthy People 2000: National Health Promotion and Disease Prevention Objectives* (USDHHS, 1991) and *Healthy People 2010* (USDHHS, 2000) describe the objectives and their rationale. Figure 12.1 presents in abbreviated form objectives pertinent to the conduct of physical education in schools. The number preceding the objective in the table provides a reference (chapter and number) for the complete objective in the *Healthy People 2010* document.

Are Students Physically Fit and Active Enough?

Substantial public concern has been expressed about how physically inactive and unfit American children are becoming. Despite the negative press, little scientific information is available to indicate that today's children are either less fit than those of previous generations or that they compare badly to age-matched youth in other industrialized nations (Falls & Pate, 1993). Levels of obesity in both children (Rocchini, 2002) and adults (James, Leach, Kalamara, & Shayeghi, 2001) are increasing at a rate high enough to be termed an epidemic. This health problem, however, could be partially solved if individuals were more active. Simons-Morton et al. (1987) found children to be substantially more fit than adults, and they concluded that increasing cardiopulmonary fitness was not a health priority for children. They recommended that programs for children focus on promoting physical activity habits that would carry over from childhood to adulthood rather than emphasizing physical fitness.

To be able to judge whether children are active enough, a standard must be available to which they are compared. In 1994 an international consensus statement was developed for physical activity guidelines for adolescents (Sallis & Patrick, 1994). The first recommendation was that adolescents do some activity, regardless of intensity, daily or nearly every day. A reasonable guideline is 30 minutes per day. National surveys

Selected *Healthy People 2010* Objectives
Related to School Physical Activity
and Physical Education (USDHHS, 2000)

22-6

Increase the proportion of adolescents who engage in moderate physical activity for at least 30 minutes on five or more of the previous seven days.
(Target = 30%; 1997 Youth Risk Behavior Surveillance System (YRBSS) baseline = 20%)

22-7

Increase the proportion of adolescents who engage in vigorous physical activity that promotes cardiorespiratory fitness three or more days per week for 20 or more minutes per occasion.
(Target = 85%; 1997 YRBSS baseline = 64% of students in grades 9–12)

22-8

Increase the proportion of the nation's public and private schools that require daily physical education for all students.
(Middle school target = 25%; 1994 School Health Policies and Program Study (SHPPS) baseline = 17%; Senior high target = 5%; 1994 SHPPS baseline = 2%)

22-9

Increase the proportion of adolescents who participate in daily school physical education.
(Target = 50%; YRBSS baseline = 27% of students in grades 9–12 in 1997)

22-10

(also Healthy People 2000 objective 1.9) Increase the proportion of adolescents who spend at least 50% of school physical education class time being physically active.
(Target = 50%; 1997 YRBSS baseline = 33% of students in grades 9–12 were physically active in physical education class more than 20 minutes, three to five times per week)

22-11

Increase the proportion of children and adolescents who view television two or fewer hours per day.
(Target = 75%; Baseline 1988–94 = 60% of persons aged 8–16 years viewed TV two or fewer hours per day)

22-13

Increase the proportion of worksites offering employer-sponsored physical activity and fitness programs.
(Target = 75%; Baseline = 48% of worksites with 50 or more employees in 1998)

22-14

Increase the proportion of trips made by walking.
(Target = 50%; Baseline = 28% of trips to school less than one mile by those aged 5–15.)

22-15

Increase the proportion of trips made by bicycling.
(Target = 5%; Baseline = 2.2% of trips to school less than one mile by those aged 5–15.)

FIGURE 12.1 Abbreviated objectives from *Healthy People 2010.*

of adolescents indicate that the vast majority are meeting this guideline (Pate, Long, & Heath, 1994). The second recommendation is that adolescents engage in vigorous exercise, three or more times a week, for 20 minutes or more at a time. Only about one-half of adolescent boys and one-quarter of adolescent girls meet this standard (Pate et al., 1994). More recently published guidelines recommend that youth engage in 60 or more minutes of physical activity daily (Corbin & Pangrazi, 1998; Health Education Authority, 1998).

Sallis (1993) found variations in both physical activity and aerobic power related to age and gender. Aerobic power remained stable from ages 6 to 16 for boys but declined about 2% per year in girls. Overall, boys were about 25% more fit than girls. Reviews of studies using both self-reports and objective measures revealed that boys were from 15 to 25% more physically active than girls were. A constant decline in physical activity engagement over time occurred, with boys decreasing engagement about 2.7% per year and girls decreasing engagement 7.4% per year. These results suggest that older students and females are at increased risk because of a more sedentary lifestyle. Minority and economically disadvantaged adults are relatively inactive compared with majority and more affluent adults. This pattern may start in childhood. For example, four-year-old Mexican American boys and girls were found to be less physically active than their Anglo-American counterparts, both at home and during school recess (McKenzie, Sallis, Nader, Broyles, & Nelson, 1992).

Observations of Physical Activity in Elementary and Middle Schools

Direct observation of physical education classes may reveal relatively little physical activity. Several studies have shown that children, particularly boys, may be more active during recess than they are during physical education classes (e.g., Sarkin, McKenzie, & Sallis, 1997), and one study found the average child in 30-minute classes to be vigorously active for only 2 minutes (Parcel et al., 1987). Faucette, McKenzie, and Patterson (1990) found that physical education classes of classroom teachers consisted mainly of game play in which a few children were active while the remainder waited for a turn. Only 5% of these classes had fitness activities as the major focus. A baseline Child and Adolescent Trial for Cardiovascular Health (CATCH) study (McKenzie et al., 1995) of third-grade physical education in 95 schools in four states found children engaged in moderate to vigorous physical activity (MVPA) 36% of class time, far short of the 50% recommended by the *Healthy People 2010* objectives. Outdoor classes provided significantly more physical activity than those held indoors. For children in this study, physical education classes provided only 25% of the vigorous activity and 12% of the amount recommended per week for health purposes by national objectives. As the children moved from third to fifth grade, the proportion of time they were active in class increased (Levin, McKenzie, Hussey, Kelder, & Lytle, 2001). A similar study of 878 third-grade children in 10 study centers in nine states found children engaged in MVPA 37% of lesson time. These children participated in an average of only 2.1 physical education lessons per week, and the lessons had a mean length of 32 minutes (National Institute of Child Health and Human Development [NICHD], 2003).

A study (Middle School Physical Activity and Nutrition, M-SPAN) using the same instrument in 24 middle schools in southern California showed that students spent 48% of lesson time in MVPA (McKenzie, Marshall, Sallis, & Conway, 2000a). The apparent increase in the proportion of class time that children engage in MVPA in higher grades could be because of several factors, such as more active curricula, active participation by older students without direct control over them by teachers, and children's personal motivation. Both the CATCH and M-SPAN studies showed substantial differences in physical activity engagement during different lesson contexts. For example, time allocated for fitness activities provided substantially more MVPA than game play, skill drill, and knowledge contexts.

Do Current Physical Education and Athletic Programs Motivate Youth to Engage in Physical Activity Into Adulthood?

Only a few studies have attempted to determine whether physical education and athletic programs motivate youth to engage in physical activity into adulthood, and they have produced conflicting findings (Powell & Dysinger, 1987). One study found participation in physical activities during childhood and adolescence to be one of the lowest of 25 correlates of adult vigorous activity (Sallis et al., 1989). Because most adult physical activities are solitary and noncompetitive, one might not expect too much carryover from physical education programs that emphasize team sports. *Healthy People 2000* Objective 1.9 recognizes this possibility and recommends (in part) that students in physical education classes spend more time being active, preferably "engaged in lifetime activities" (US-DHHS, 1991). Along the same lines, both the American Academy of Pediatrics (1987) and the American College of Sports Medicine (1988) suggest that physical education adopt more health-related goals. Meanwhile, except for the research conducted in Trois Rivieres, Quebec, long-term studies in North America of most of the objectives of physical education have not been reported (Shephard & Trudeau, 2000; Trudeau, Laurencelle, Tremblay, Rajic, & Shephard, 1999).

Health-Related Physical Activity Interventions: School-Based Programs

A recent review paper summarized large-scale studies that specifically targeted physical activity as a dependent variable in youth (Stone, McKenzie, Welk, & Booth, 1998), and another examined maintenance effects of activity interventions in several settings (Marcus et al., 2000). School programs specifically targeting knowledge, attitudes, and physical fitness as part of the interventions were generally successful in these areas. Studies conducted during school physical education classes found the most positive effects for physical activity. The most successful interventions in this setting included components that provided an active physical education curriculum, staff development, and on-site follow-up. Several of these interventions significantly increased both the number of minutes and percentage of lesson time that children were vigorously active during classes (McKenzie et al., 2001; Sallis et al., 1997; Sallis et al., 2002; Simons-Morton, Parcel, & O'Hara, 1988). In the CATCH study, MVPA during lessons in intervention schools increased from 37 to 52%, and MVPA in M-SPAN increased by 18%, both without modifying either the frequency or duration of lessons. Compared with students in control schools, those in CATCH intervention schools continued to report increased daily activity up to three years later (Nader et al., 1999).

Other studies have shown that physical education programs emphasizing physical activity and cardiovascular fitness can work successfully in schools (Riddoch, 1998; Stone et al., 1998). At least five studies found that children who participated in health-related physical education improved their cardiovascular fitness, and several showed that children reduced their skinfold thickness. Programs that are specifically targeted and implemented as planned appear to produce improvements in health-related outcomes.

Meanwhile, health promotion programs targeting children's physical activity without directly influencing physical education classes are less successful. Coates, Jeffery, and Slinkard (1981) reported the results of a classroom-based diet and physical activity change program designed to reduce CVD risk factors in fourth- and fifth-grade students.

Behavioral self-management procedures were used to help children change health-related behaviors, and the program produced significant effects on dietary behavior. The six-session component targeting increased physical activity during daily recess, however, produced no observed effects. Similarly, the five-year, classroom-based "Know Your Body" program produced significant changes in total cholesterol, dietary intake, and health knowledge, but not in physical fitness (Walter, Hofman, Vaughan, & Wynder, 1988). These data suggest that school efforts to modify children's physical activity and fitness must target physical education and physical activity directly.

A major barrier to improving physical education is the concern by administrators that spending more time in physical education takes time away from scholastic work. Two studies, one in Canada and one in the United States, show that this concern is not justified. Even when more time is allocated for physical education in the school day, a decline in academic performance does not occur (Shephard, Lavallee, Volle, LaBarre, & Beaucage, 1994; Sallis et al., 1999).

The National Institutes of Health has funded several multidisciplinary and multifaceted programs that included physical activity as a target. Three of them are currently being disseminated to nonstudy schools. All three had similar intervention components: (a) curricula and materials, (b) staff development (i.e., teacher training), and (c) on-site assistance provided to school personnel. Each of these complex projects used numerous formative, process, and outcome assessments. A brief description follows.

Child and Adolescent Trial for Cardiovascular Health (CATCH)

CATCH was initially studied in third through fifth grades in 96 schools in California, Louisiana, Minnesota, and Texas (Nader et al., 1999). The program targeted physical activity, eating, and smoking behavior and included classroom curricula, school environment changes involving physical education and food service, and family involvement components. Follow-up measures of the children were obtained in 8th and 12th grades, and physical education in the schools was investigated after the intervention ended. Positive effects of the intervention were seen in physical education five to seven years postintervention, even though less than half the current teachers had received CATCH PE training. Student energy expenditure levels and proportion of physical education time spent in MVPA in intervention schools were maintained, but vigorous activity levels declined (McKenzie et al., in press). Use of CATCH PE curricula was associated with increased levels of teacher training and school support for physical education in both former intervention and control schools.

Sports, Play, and Active Recreation for Kids (SPARK)

SPARK curricula included a physical education program that emphasized physical activity, physical fitness, and motor-skill development and an innovative self-management program for children. The program was tested with physical education specialists and classroom teachers in seven elementary schools over a five-year period. Besides participating in physical education, children took part in self-management workshops in which they learned to plan and be responsible for out-of-school physical activity (Marcoux et al., 1999). Outcomes included student activity levels, lesson context, and teacher behavior during physical education lessons plus assessments of physical fitness and out-of-school physical activity (Sallis et al., 1997), manipulative skills (McKenzie et al., 1998), and academic achievement (Sallis et al., 1999). Generally, intervention conditions were superior to controls on most variables, with trained physical educators most often producing greater gains than trained classroom teachers did. The amount of class time for physical education was doubled in intervention schools without any reductions on standardized academic achievement tests, and sometimes gains occurred (Sallis et al., 1999). Observations of physical education lessons indicated substantial retention of program elements by trained classroom teachers at least one and a half years after the intervention ended (McKenzie et al., 1997).

Middle School Physical Activity and Nutrition (M-SPAN)

M-SPAN is a four-year study of a physical activity and nutrition intervention in 24 middle schools (26,000 students, grades 6 through 8) in San Diego County, California. The overall goal is to investigate whether environmental changes can lead to improved physical activity and dietary habits of students throughout the school day. Intervention schools receive staff development, materials, and services to increase student activity levels and promote the consumption of less dietary fat. Control schools continue with their usual physical activity and nutrition programs. Besides targeting physical education classes, M-SPAN promotes physical activity throughout the school day. Baseline data showed that boys were significantly more active in physical education than girls were, particularly during skill drills, games, and free play, and that activity levels during lessons were related to class size (McKenzie et al., 2000a). The two-year intervention increased MVPA in physical education by 18% without requiring an increase in either the frequency or the duration of classes. MVPA was higher during the second year of the intervention than it was during the first, showing that the program had cumulative effects (Sallis et al., in press). Examination of physical activity on school campuses outside of physical education showed that few students, particularly girls, participated in MVPA, even though ample space was available (McKenzie, Marshall, Sallis, & Conway, 2000b)

EXERCISING OPINIONS: A HEALTH-RELATED VIEW OF PHYSICAL EDUCATION

New research on the benefits of physical activity has produced a conceptual shift regarding the relative importance of physical fitness and physical activity. Physical activity has been recognized as a CVD risk factor, although physical fitness has not. Physical fitness is transitory, and only regular physical activity can maintain it. As a result, several reviewers argue from a public health perspective that increasing the physical activity of children is more important than improving their physical fitness (Sallis & McKenzie, 1991; Simons-Morton et al., 1987). This notion has many implications for the conduct of physical education, with a major distinction being whether the primary outcome of programs should be a behavior (physical activity engagement) or a biological characteristic (e.g., physical fitness). This section discusses various aspects of the conduct of physical education and the preparation of teachers from a health-related viewpoint.

Moderate Versus Vigorous Intensity Activities

Improvements in physical fitness and sport performances (especially those involving cardiovascular endurance) require high-intensity or vigorous physical activity. On the other hand, the clear message from recent research, put forth in the *Healthy People 2010* objectives, is that people need not exercise vigorously to receive health benefits. Cardiovascular, musculoskeletal, and mental health improvement also result from engaging in lower- or moderate-intensity physical activity.

When developing programs and conducting classes, physical educators should consider the implications of the results from a large number of studies that have demonstrated the lack of adherence by adults to high-intensity exercise programs (Dishman & Sallis, 1994). Adults are less likely to comply with high-intensity exercise programs than they are with low-intensity programs, and a public health benefit is more likely to result from inducing sedentary individuals to move rather than by increasing the activity levels of those already physically active (Blair, Kohl, Gordon, & Paffenbarger, 1992). Studies of obese children suggest that moderate-intensity activities incorporated into a daily lifestyle are more effective at maintaining weight loss than vigorous exercise (Epstein, Wing, Koeske, & Valoski, 1985). At least one study has reported that upper-elementary school children preferred moderate-intensity physical activity units of instruction to more strenuous ones (McKenzie, Alcaraz, & Sallis, 1994). These studies suggest that for long-term public health, regular, moderate-intensity activity may be a more appropriate goal for some students in schools than vigorous exercise is. Some students may be turned off to physical education (and physical activity) because classes demand high-intensity exercise.

The recommendation that teachers include lower-intensity activities does not mean that physical education should be devoid of strenuous activity or that programs should not strive for students to become fit and highly skilled. Becoming physically fit and highly skilled are important outcomes that provide substantial personal benefits (Pate, Trost, Levin, & Dowda, 2000), but these may not be important goals for all students. Alternative programs and activities are needed if public health objectives are to be met.

Time for Physical Activity and Fitness

Low-intensity activity does not produce health benefits as quickly as high-intensity activity does. For example, more time is required to achieve weight loss from walking than from running. Subsequent modifications in the frequency and duration of physical education classes might be necessary if health objectives are to be met, particularly for programs that strive to reach all the standard objectives of physical education.

Students do not have enough time in physical education to meet fitness and physical activity objectives, let alone reach the other objectives assigned to physical education programs. Most fifth- and sixth-grade students have some physical education, of approximately 100 minutes each week (Ross & Gilbert, 1985; Ross & Pate, 1987), but children in some schools may have no physical education at all (NICHD, 2003). Enrollment declines with each successive grade. In 1997 only 23% of boys and 14% of girls in 12th grade had physical education daily (USDHHS, 2000).

Although it is clear that elementary school physical education classes may not be particularly active, fewer data are available for secondary schools. Classes at this level, however, typically allocate large amounts of time for dressing and showering. One middle school study showed that students with daily physical education accrued an average of 25 vigorous activity minutes and 83 MVPA minutes per week (McKenzie et al., 2000a). Direct observation showed that lesson length (mean = 34.3 minutes) was 69% of scheduled class length (mean = 49.8 minutes). After lessons start, students spend considerable time in sedentary activities, including being managed, waiting a turn, and receiving knowledge. At the beginning of classes, students often warm up in preparation for skill learning only to cool down while they sit and listen to lengthy instructions. This sequence may be medically unsound and could turn students off to physical education—evidenced by measures of enrollment, absenteeism, and tardiness.

A Place for Fitness Knowledge

Fitness and health knowledge are important aspects of physical education. Most knowledge could be taught in an environment more conducive to learning than a gymnasium or a playing field is. Classrooms are more suitable for engaging in cognitive learning.

They are more comfortable, provide fewer distractions, and have more instructional aids. Expectations for student knowledge gains are already present. Classes conducted in gymnasia and on playing fields should be primarily reserved for students to engage in physical activity and develop motor skills.

With the newly available evidence of the benefits of physical activity, it would also be appropriate to teach students how much time they should spend being active for health purposes. Advanced high school students should be taught that energy expenditure is expressed in calories, and that they, as adults, can substantially improve their health and reduce risk of death from cardiovascular disease by being active.

Physical education and athletic programs are also important vehicles for delivering relevant messages about steroids, eating disorders, and other sport and exercise practices related to health. Secondary school students should be taught to be informed consumers so that they can make appropriate decisions about sports drinks, exercise equipment, and exercise clubs.

Of course, knowledge itself is insufficient to change behavior. Prompts and reinforcement for engaging in appropriate health-related behavior should accompany knowledge dissemination, but this is rarely done. Behavior-change skills, such as planning, setting goals to be physically active outside school, and resisting peer pressure to engage in unhealthy habits, can be taught in school settings to children as young as fourth-graders. Young children, however, may not have the opportunity to use these skills at home, so it is more advisable to teach these skills in secondary schools (Marcoux et al., 1999).

Involving the Family in Physical Education

Family members influence each other's physical activity in many ways (Sallis & Nader, 1988). School programs that promote physical activity and fitness might do well to involve the entire family. One successful family-based program identified fourth- through sixth-grade students with low fitness levels and involved their parents in a 12-week home reinforcement program (Taggart, Taggart, & Siedentop, 1986). Parents worked with behavioral consultants who trained and assisted them to develop individualized programs to promote their children's physical activity. Almost all children increased both their physical activity and their fitness, and it was noted that the availability of appropriate facilities for activity and weekly contact with consultants were felt to enhance the effectiveness of the program. Some of the methods of this intensive, individualized treatment could be implemented more broadly in schools.

School could involve families in physical education in several ways, such as offering special events and evening programs, sending home newsletters, and prompting parents to encourage and reward their children's physical activity. Although several publications have described these strategies, data on their effectiveness are limited. Meanwhile, many impediments to family-oriented programs need to be considered and overcome (Nader et al., 1996). Money, time, and staff training are the most conspicuous barriers, but parents must also perceive programs as relevant or they will not participate. Families are more likely to participate in programs for younger children. Many adolescents are unlikely to appreciate being involved with their parents in programs conducted on the school site.

Assessing Physical Fitness

About 25% of U.S. states mandate some physical fitness testing in schools (Bennett & Peel, 1994). Regular fitness testing is useful in determining the effectiveness of programs and can aid in assessing how students compare both to health-related standards and to the performance of others. Fitness testing in schools is controversial, however, with some leading professionals proposing more of it and others suggesting that it be abolished completely. Using physical fitness test results in determining physical education grades is a problem. Heredity plays a major role in the level of performance on fitness tests, and some students may not be able to reach either their own expectations or health-related standards, no matter how hard they try or how long they practice.

Unless administered judiciously, fitness testing could discourage students from participating in physical activity. To produce a valid measure of fitness, tests require that students do their best in school, which means performing publicly in front of peers. Rarely do people look, smell, or sound good when going all out on a physical test, and doing so may be embarrassing, particularly for adolescents in coeducational classes. Little effort is made to be discrete about how well students perform on tests. Results are frequently posted publicly, and rewards are sometimes distributed at assemblies.

Fitness tests should be administered periodically and humanely. For example, measures of adiposity should be taken privately, and students should be told that their scores are personal and highly affected by heredity, practice, and effort. They should be encouraged to meet standards for good health and make individual improvements rather than be compared with others. Students should also learn how to assess themselves and have opportunities to practice the school-administered tests. Before testing, they should be informed of tactics that will help them do well. After testing, students should receive feedback on how their scores compare with health-related standards and how to overcome performance deficits. Computerized feedback is now available to assist teachers who use some of the widely available, standard test batteries.

Assessing Physical Activity

Although physical educators are typically knowledgeable about field-based measures of physical fitness, they are generally less informed about how they can assess students' physical activity levels or how much activity their school programs provide. A variety of methods and techniques for measuring physical activity are available, including self-report, electronic motion sensors and heart rate monitors, and direct observation. A special issue of the *Journal of School Health* (1991) and a new text, *Physical Activity Assessments for Health-Related Research* (Welk, 2002), describe the purpose, validity, and reliability of various instruments, as well as guidelines for their use.

Although some techniques are designed for use in large-scale epidemiology studies, most can be adapted for assessing the amount or intensity of students' physical activity. Self-reports are reasonably reliable with children over age 10 and can be used to assess the out-of-school physical activity, including that done on weekends and vacations. Use of this technique could provide a measure of the generalizability of programs to promote physical activity beyond the physical education class.

Heart rate monitors, pedometers, and accelerometers can provide measures of activity that are more objective. Of these, pedometers are the least expensive and least burdensome. Nonetheless, instructors could place heart rate monitors and accelerometers on randomly selected students during class time to provide feedback to teachers on how active their classes are.

A number of direct observation instruments (McKenzie, 2002) have been used to assess physical education interventions. These tools are particularly useful because they can provide simultaneous measures of student activity, lesson context, and teacher behavior. Trained observers typically use these instruments in research studies, but with the increased availability of videotaping, conscientious physical educators could assess their own classes. An easier but less sophisticated method to assess activity levels is for teachers to use placheck (momentary time sampling) recording and periodically record the number of students being sedentary versus being physically active during classes and leisure time. Teachers could also use checklists to assess periodically whether their own behavior matches proposed goals.

Assessing the Pulse of the Class

The heart rate is the most frequent method for determining the intensity of student engagement in cardiovascular exercise. Various target zones have been set. Physical education curricula frequently call for students to learn about the frequency, intensity, time, type (FITT) principle and to exercise a minimum of three times per week, at 60 to 80% of their maximum heart rate for at least 20 minutes at a time. Students commonly learn how to take pulse rates and calculate how well they are doing during fitness classes. This exercise is best reserved for older students. Elementary school students can learn these skills, but younger students are not particularly accurate. The time it takes to teach and use the procedures could probably be better spent engaging children directly in activity. More global and less time-consuming indicators of intensity, such as sweating and breathing hard, are probably more useful in elementary schools.

Strength Training

Many high schools and some junior high schools offer specialized units targeted at producing increases in strength and power. These courses are particularly popular with male adolescents interested in athletic performance and bodybuilding, although information and practice in strength development activities are important for all students. A study indicated that weightlifting was the most prevalent physical activity engaged in by male adolescents (Sallis, Zakarian, Hovell, & Hofstetter, 1996). Strength training not only improves the function of muscles but also strengthens bones, ligaments, and tendons, which might help decrease risk of injuries, poor posture, and lower back pain.

The efficient development of strength through progressive resistance training requires substantial amounts of equipment. Only a few schools have the newly developed, sophisticated, and expensive variable resistance machines; free weights and constant resistance machines are more common. Strength development equipment requires a special location (i.e., weight room) that can be properly monitored and secured when supervision is not available. Interscholastic teams often receive priority for using these facilities. Because the amount of weight-training equipment is usually limited, a substantial percentage of students may be inactive during class time. Circuit training can accommodate more users, and some schools are able to use private fitness facilities during off-peak hours. Using off-campus exercise facilities should promote the generalization of physical activity beyond graduation.

Substantial evidence indicates that some athletes and bodybuilders use illegally obtained anabolic steroids to produce rapid gains in strength and muscle size. Junior and senior high school students may be generally aware of some of these benefits of steroids, but they do not necessarily know about accompanying undesirable side effects. Reducing the proportion of male high school seniors who use anabolic steroids is one of the objectives of *Healthy People 2000*.

PE: A Place To Be

To promote physical activity successfully in both the short and long term, physical education classes need to be enjoyable. Low enrollments and high rates of tardiness and absenteeism in classes at secondary schools may be indicative of students' negative feelings toward physical education. School administrators and physical educators, particularly at the secondary level, need to begin to think about students as consumers. Consumers do not *all* want or *all* need the same product; they need options. Events and activities that motivate the highly skilled and highly fit in physical education are not necessarily effective with those who are inactive or unfit. Some students do not enjoy competing against others, so the role of competition in classes needs to be examined. Support from friends and peers is known to reinforce exercise maintenance, so it would seem to be appropriate for teachers to allow friends to participate together. But what effect does allowing students to work in self-determined groups have on other class goals? Success enhances activity maintenance, but does exposure to large numbers of activities and sports in a curriculum enhance the generalization of physical activity out of school? Is generalization hindered because students are not skilled enough to be successful and feel comfortable in any one activity area? Empirical study and debate about these curricular questions are needed. In the meantime, it is reasonable to expect that consumers of physical education would like to participate in a clean, friendly environment and would enjoy participating in classes that are small enough to allow teachers to both recognize them and plan an activity program that meets their individual needs.

SPARKING UP PHYSICAL EDUCATION: A SAMPLE PROGRAM

Sports, Play, and Active Recreation for Kids (SPARK) is a health-oriented physical education program that teaches carry-over activities and behavioral skills to upper-elementary school children. The Heart, Lung, and Blood Institute of the National Institutes of Health funded SPARK for seven years, and the Program Effectiveness Panel of the National Diffusion Network, United States Department of Education has validated SPARK as a "program that works." Two SPARK curricula were tested, the SPARK Physical Education Program and the SPARK Self-Management Program. These curricula blend science and theory into practical programs. Because many states do not require that specialists teach physical education (National Association for Sport and Physical Education, 2001), the curricula were written for and tested with both classroom teachers and physical education specialists.

SPARK Physical Education Program

The SPARK physical education curriculum is a comprehensive program with the student goal of learning to enjoy and seek out physical activity. SPARK PE classes are designed to promote high levels of physical activity that will improve health-related fitness, promote movement skills that add to success and enjoyment in physical activity, and engender positive socialization.

Both the selection of activities and the way they are taught promotes maximum student participation during class time. The program excludes inactive sports and drills, elimination games, and activities that require specialized and expensive equipment (e.g., formal gymnastics) or demand inordinate amounts of time to set up.

The curriculum promotes individual improvement and encourages students to monitor their progress over time. Eight times per year students participate in "Personal Best Day" to self-assess and track their cardiovascular fitness and upper-body and abdominal strength and endurance.

A standard elementary school SPARK lesson is 30 minutes long and has two parts: (a) a health-fitness activity, which includes an introduction (warm-up) with a transition to a health-fitness activity (15 minutes) and (b) a skill-fitness activity with a transition to closure (cool-down) (15 minutes).

Health-Fitness Activities

The health-fitness portion of the lesson focuses on developing health-related fitness and locomotor skills. The SPARK PE curriculum includes numerous units, including aerobic dance, aerobic games, and jump rope. Modifying the intensity, duration, and complexity of the activities develops progression. Although the focus is on developing cardiovascular endurance, activities to develop abdominal and upper-body strength are also included.

Sport-Fitness Activities

The second part of a SPARK lesson focuses on developing skill-related fitness, particularly as it relates to the development of body-limb-object coordination and specialized sport skills (e.g., basketball, soccer). The SPARK PE curriculum includes sports units that have the most potential for development of cardiovascular fitness and movement skills that will carry over into the child's community.

SPARK Self-Management Program

The goal of the self-management component is to provide children with cognitive and behavioral skills that will help them stay physically active on their own and to promote parental support for the children's activity. Children learn specific methods to help themselves achieve personal goals. Because many studies show that knowledge gains are usually insufficient to produce changes in behavior, this component emphasizes teaching behavior-change skills related to physical activity rather than teaching knowledge. Hundreds of studies (e.g., Kanfer & Goldstein, 1980) support the effectiveness of self-management skills, and these skills can be used to enhance the generalization and maintenance of physical activity.

Self-management skills and related topics are taught during classroom sessions. Beginning and advanced curricula, each with 22 scripted lessons, has been developed and implemented with fourth and fifth grades.

A standard, 30-minute self-management session begins with a brief review of the skills or information presented during the previous session and a discussion of the students' progress on activity goals during the previous week. Goal attainment is praised, and lack of progress is approached as a problem-solving opportunity. After the review, approximately 15 to 20 minutes are spent on the presentation of a new topic. Students usually spend much of this time working in small groups or playing games designed to convey the information and provide practice using the targeted skills. The next 4 to 5 minutes are spent setting physical activity goals for the coming week. On occasion, teachers assign homework designed to reinforce the skill or information provided during the session. At the end of the session, students who have achieved their goals receive rewards.

Students receive reinforcement for meeting activity goals. They are provided with a chart that indicates the points they can receive for specific amounts of time spent in various physical activities. The number of points that a student can earn each day and each week is limited, encouraging moderate levels of regular physical activity instead of excessive amounts. The reward system for progress is recommended initially, but because the aim is to prepare students to be active on their own, it should be phased out.

The self-management program strongly encourages family involvement. Students are instructed to share and discuss handouts and homework assignments with their parents. To receive points for activities, a parent's signature is required on each goal sheet, and many homework assignments require family participation. Students can receive extra points for having family members be active with them. Monthly newsletters to families encourage this behavior and instruct family members how to promote children's physical activity.

COOLING DOWN: FURTHER IMPLICATIONS FOR RESEARCH AND PRACTICE

This chapter has introduced the notion of health-related physical education, provided an overview of research related to physical activity and fitness, described the current status of health-related physical education in schools, discussed various aspects of the conduct of physical education and the preparation of teachers from a health-related viewpoint, and described one experimental elementary school physical education program designed with a health-related focus. This final section reorients the reader to the purpose of health-related physical education and the place it might play in reaching public health objectives.

The goal of HRPE is to prepare children and adolescents to develop and maintain physically active lifestyles. It goes far beyond the traditional notion of getting students fit and teaching them physical fitness concepts. HRPE also includes arranging the entire school environment to ensure that all students have many opportunities to participate in physical activity and learn the behavioral and cognitive skills necessary for maintaining physical activity outside the school setting. A reorientation of physical education to make it a vehicle for physical activity promotion would go a long way toward reaching the public health goals of the nation.

The goals of physical education in promoting physical activity align closely with public health priorities. These common purposes can lead to increased appreciation for, and support of, school physical education. How the *Healthy People 2010* objectives will influence physical education is unknown, but many policy makers are now aware of the benefits of regular physical activity. Meanwhile, the data clearly show that if schools are to carry the major responsibility for activity promotion for youth, changes need to be made. The time allocated to physical education is simply insufficient for it to be able to reach physical activity promotion goals, let alone all the other outcomes expected of it. Increasing the frequency and length of physical education classes and increasing the proportion of time that students are physically active during them could create more opportunities for students to be active. These changes would still not provide enough physical activity for students to reach recommended standards for health purposes, so additional early morning, noontime, and after-school programs will be needed.

A primary question at this time is how, not whether, schools should become involved in health-related physical education. The content of health-related physical education and the best way to teach it is still to be determined. We have no clear-cut answers about what an effective health-oriented physical education program at either the elementary or secondary level looks like. How much will current practices have to change? How will traditional goals of physical education be accommodated? Will students like health-related physical education? How will athletic coaches receive it? Will the movement and behavioral skills taught in these classes generalize to out-of-school settings during the holidays and summers? Will students maintain these skills into adulthood? Practitioners and researchers alike must discuss these questions, and they must develop and empirically test more sample programs. In the interim, all physical educators have the responsibility to assess each class they teach to determine whether what they did today is likely to increase the probability that their students will be physically active tomorrow and in the future.

IMPLICATIONS FOR PRACTICE

1. Schools, primarily through physical education classes, bear major responsibility for the promotion of youth physical activity that will continue throughout adulthood.
2. *Healthy People 2010, Health Objectives for the Nation* has established goals for physical education frequency (i.e., daily) and quality (e.g., include 50% activity time).

3. School physical education has multiple objectives, not all of which can be reached in the short time currently allocated to the subject matter.

4. Substantial research indicates that student engagement in moderate to vigorous physical activity during lesson time is low.

5. A reorientation of physical education toward physical activity promotion would help the nation reach health goals and likely find increased support for programs.

6. The main goal of health-related physical education (HRPE) is to prepare students for a lifetime of physical activity engagement.

7. HRPE goes beyond teaching about fitness to include many opportunities for engaging in enjoyable physical activity.

8. Self-management skills are an important component of HRPE, but their inclusion in school programs has rarely been tested.

9. Physical education occurs too infrequently, so the entire school environment needs to be arranged to support physical activity opportunities.

10. To help students meet national recommendations for physical activity, physical educators need to involve parents and the community.

Notes

I would like to acknowledge the contributions of James F. Sallis, PhD to this and other work. Dr. Sallis, a health psychologist at San Diego State University, coauthored an earlier version of this chapter. He is a strong proponent of quality physical education and the study of it. A list of his publications is available at www-rohan.sdsu.edu/faculty/sallis/index.html.

Additional information on the SPARK physical education, self-management, and staff development programs may be obtained at www.foundation.sdsu.edu/projects/spark/index.html or from SPARK, 438 Camino Del Rio South, Suite 110, San Diego, CA 92108 (1-800-SPARKPE, ext. 208).

REFERENCES

Allensworth, D., Lawson, E., Nicholson, L., & Wyche, J. (Eds.). (1997). *Schools and health: Our nation's investment.* Washington, DC: Institute of Medicine, National Academy Press.

Alpert, B.S., & Wilmore, J.H. (1994). Physical activity and blood pressure in adolescents. *Pediatric Exercise Science, 6,* 361-380.

American Academy of Pediatrics. (1987). Physical fitness and the schools. *Pediatrics, 80,* 449-450.

American College of Sports Medicine. (1988). Physical fitness in children and youth. *Medicine and Science in Sports and Exercise, 20,* 422-423.

Armstrong, N., & Simons-Morton, B. (1994). Physical activity and blood lipids in adolescents. *Pediatric Exercise Science, 6,* 381-405.

Bailey, D.A., & Martin, A.D. (1994). Physical activity and skeletal health in adolescents. *Pediatric Exercise Science, 6,* 330-347.

Bar-Or, O., & Baranowski, T. (1994). Physical activity, adiposity, and obesity in adolescents. *Pediatric Exercise Science, 6,* 348-360.

Bennett, J.P., & Peel, J.C. (1994). Health and physical education teacher certification practices in the United States 1988–1992. *Journal of Health Education, 25,* 239-243.

Blair, S.N., Kohl, H.W., Gordon, N.F., & Paffenbarger, R.S. (1992). How much physical activity is good for health? *Annual Review of Public Health, 13,* 99-126.

Booth, F.W., & Chakravarth, M.V. (2002). Costs and consequences of sedentary living: New battleground for an old enemy. *Research Digest,* Series 3(16), 1-8. Washington, DC: President's Council and Physical Fitness and Sports.

Bouchard, C., Shephard, R., & Stephens, T. (1994). *Physical activity, fitness, and health: International proceedings and consensus statement.* Champaign, IL: Human Kinetics.

Calfas, K.J., & Taylor, W.C. (1994). Physical activity and psychological health in adolescents. *Pediatric Exercise Science, 6,* 406-423.

Coates, T.J., Jeffery, R.W., & Slinkard, L.A. (1981). Heart healthy eating and exercise: Introducing and maintaining changes in health behaviors. *American Journal of Public Health, 71,* 15-23.

Corbin, C.B., & Lindsey, R. (2002). *Fitness for life* (Updated 4th edition). Champaign, IL: Human Kinetics.

Corbin, C.B., & Pangrazi, R.P. (1998). *Physical activity for children: A statement of guidelines.* Reston, VA: NASPE.

Cresanta, J.L., Burke, G.L., Downey, A.M., Freedman, D.S., & Berenson, G.S. (1986). Prevention of atherosclerosis in childhood: Prevention in primary care. *Pediatric Clinics of North America, 33,* 835-858.

Dietary and Physical Acitivity Assessment in School-Aged Children [Special issue]. (1991). *Journal of School Health, 61.*

Dishman, R.K., & Sallis, J.F. (1994). Determinants and interventions for physical activity and exercise. In C. Bouchard, R. Shephard, & T. Stephens (Eds.), *Physical activity, fitness, and health* (pp. 214-238). Champaign, IL: Human Kinetics.

Epstein, L.H., Wing, R.R., Koeski, R., & Valoski, A. (1985). A comparison of lifestyle exercise, aerobic exercise, and calisthenics on weight loss in obese children. *Behavior Therapy, 16,* 345-356.

Falls, H.B., & Pate, R.R. (1993). Status of physical fitness in U.S. children. In M. Leppo (Ed.), *Healthy from the start: New perspectives on childhood fitness* (pp. 3-23). Washington, DC: ERIC Clearinghouse on Teacher Education.

Faucette, N., McKenzie, T.L., & Patterson, P. (1990). Descriptive analysis of nonspecialist elementary physical education teachers' curricular choices and class organization. *Journal of Teaching in Physical Education, 9,* 284-293.

Health Education Authority (1998). *Young and active? Policy framework for young people and health-enhancing physical activity.* London: Health Education Authority.

James, P.T., Leach, R., Kalamara, E., & Shayeghi, M. (2001). The worldwide obesity epidemic. *Obesity Research, 9*(Supplement 4), S228-233.

Kanfer, F.H., & Goldstein, A.P. (1980). *Helping people change.* New York: Pergamon.

Levin, S., McKenzie, T.L., Hussey, J.R., Kelder, S., & Lytle, L. (2001). Variability of physical activity in physical education lessons across elementary school grades. *Measurement in Physical Education and Exercise Science, 5,* 207-218.

Malina, R.M. (1994). Physical activity: Relationship to growth, maturation, and physical fitness. In C. Bouchard, R. Shephard, & T. Stephens (Eds.), *Physical activity, fitness, and health* (pp. 918-930). Champaign, IL: Human Kinetics.

Marcoux, M.F., Sallis, J.F., McKenzie, T.L., Marshall, S., Armstrong, C.A., & Goggin, K. (1999). Process evaluation of a physical activity self-management program for children: SPARK. *Psychology and Health, 14,* 659-677.

Marcus, B.H., Dubbert, P.M., Forsyth, L.H., McKenzie, T.L., Stone, E.J., Dunn, A.L., & Blair, S.N. (2000). Physical activity behavior change: Issues in adoption and maintenance. *Health Psychology, 19*(Supplement 1), 32-41.

McKenzie, T.L. (2001). Back to the future: Health-related physical education. In P. Ward & P. Doutis (Eds.), *Physical education for the 21st century* (pp. 113-131). Lincoln, NE: University of Nebraska.

McKenzie, T.L. (2002). The use of direct observation to assess physical activity. In G. Welk (Ed.), *Physical activity assessments for health-related research* (pp. 179-195). Champaign, IL: Human Kinetics.

McKenzie, T.L., Alcaraz, J., & Sallis, J.F. (1994). Assessing children's liking for activity units in an elementary physical education curriculum. *Journal of Teaching in Physical Education, 13,* 206-215.

McKenzie, T.L., Alcaraz, J.E., Sallis, J.F., & Faucette, F.N. (1998). Effects of a physical education program on children's manipulative skills. *Journal of Teaching in Physical Education, 17,* 327-341.

McKenzie, T.L., Feldman, H., Woods, S., Romero, K., Dahlstrom, V., Stone, E., Strikmiller, P., Williston, J., & Harsha, D. (1995). Student activity levels and lesson context during third grade physical education. *Research Quarterly for Exercise and Sport, 66,* 184-193.

McKenzie, T.L., Li, D., Derby, C., Webber, L., Luepker, R., & Cribb, P. (in press). *Maintenance of effects of the CATCH physical education program.* Health Education and Behavior.

McKenzie, T.L., Marshall, S., Sallis, J.F., & Conway, T.L. (2000a). Student activity levels, lesson context, and teacher behavior during middle school physical education. *Research Quarterly for Exercise and Sport, 71,* 249-259.

McKenzie, T.L., Marshall, S.J., Sallis, J.F., & Conway, T. (2000b). Measuring leisure-time physical activity in school environments: SOPLAY. *Preventive Medicine, 30,* 70-77.

McKenzie, T.L., Sallis, J.F., Kolody, B., & Faucette, N. (1997). Long term effects of a physical education curriculum and staff development program: SPARK. *Research Quarterly for Exercise and Sport, 68,* 280-291.

McKenzie, T.L., Sallis, J.F., Nader, P.R., Broyles, S.L., & Nelson, J.E. (1992). Anglo- and Mexican-American preschoolers at home and at recess: Activity patterns and environmental influences. *Developmental and Behavioral Pediatrics, 13,* 173-180.

McKenzie, T.L., Stone, E.J., Feldman, H.A., Epping, J.N., Yang, M., Strikmiller, P.K., Lytle, L.A., & Parcel, G.S. (2001). Effects of the CATCH physical education intervention: Teacher type and lesson location. *American Journal of Preventive Medicine, 21,* 101-109.

Nader, P.R., Sellers, D.E., Johnson, C.C., Perry, C.L., Stone, E.J., Cook, K.C., Bebchuk, J., & Luepker, R.V. (1996). The effect of adult participation in a school-based family intervention to improve children's diet and physical activity: The child and adolescent trial for cardiovascular health. *Preventive Medicine, 25,* 455-464.

Nader, P.R., Stone, E.J., Lytle, L.A., Perry, C.L., Osganian, S.K., Kelder, S., Webber, L., Elder, J., Montgomery, D., Feldman, H., Wu, M., Johnson, C., Parcel, G., & Luepker, R.V. (1999). Three-year maintenance of improved diet and physical activity: The CATCH cohort. *Archives of Pediatrics and Adolescent Medicine, 153,* 695-704.

National Association for Sport and Physical Education. (2001). *Shape of the nation report. A survey of state physical education requirements.* Reston, VA: AAPHERD.

National Institute of Child Health and Human Development (NICHD) (2003). Study of Early Child Care and Youth Development Network. Frequency and intensity of activity of third grade children in physical eucation. *Archives of Pediatrics and Adolescent Medicine, 157,* 185-190.

Pangrazi, R.P., & Corbin, C.B. (1994). *Teaching strategies for improving youth fitness* (2nd ed.). Reston, VA: AAH-PERD.

Parcel, G.S., Simons-Morton, B.G., O'Hara, N.M., Baranowski, T., Kolbe, L.J., & Bee, D.E. (1987). School promotion of healthful diet and exercise behavior: An integration of organizational change and social learning theory interventions. *Journal of School Health, 57,* 150-156.

Pate, R.R., & Hohn, R.C. (Eds.). (1994). *Health and fitness through physical education.* Champaign, IL: Human Kinetics.

Pate, R.R., Long, B.J., & Heath, G. (1994). Descriptive epidemiology of physical activity in adolescents. *Pediatric Exercise Sciences, 6,* 434-447.

Pate, R.R., & Shephard, R.J. (1989). Characteristics of physical fitness in youth. In C.V. Gisolfi & D.R. Lamb (Eds.), *Perspectives in exercise science and sports medicine: Vol. 2. Youth, exercise, and sport* (pp. 1-46). Indianapolis: Benchmark.

Pate, R.R., Trost, S.G., Levin, S., & Dowda, M. (2000). Sports participation and health-related behaviors among U.S. youth. *Archives of Pediatric and Adolescent Medicine, 154,* 904-911.

Physical activity trends—United States, 1990–1998. (2001). *Morbidity and Mortality Weekly, 50,* 166-169.

Powell, K.E., & Dysinger, W. (1987). Childhood participation in organized school sports and physical education as precursors of adult physical activity. *American Journal of Preventive Medicine, 3,* 276-281.

Riddoch, C. (1998). Relationships between physical activity and health in young people. In S. Biddle, J. Sallis, & N. Cavill (Eds.), (pp. 17-48) *Young and active? Young people and health-enhancing physical activity—evidence and implications.* London: Health Education Authority.

Rocchini, A.P. (2002). Childhood obesity and a diabetes epidemic. *New England Journal of Medicine, 346,* 854-855.

Ross, J.G., & Gilbert, G.G. (1985). The National Children and Youth Fitness Study: A summary of findings. *Journal of Physical Education, Recreation and Dance, 56*(1), 45-50.

Ross, J.G., & Pate, R.R. (1987). The National Children and Youth Fitness Study II: A summary of findings. *Journal of Physical Education, Recreation and Dance, 58*(9), 51-56.

Sallis, J.F. (1993). Epidemiology of physical activity and fitness in children and adolescents. *Critical Reviews in Food Science and Nutrition, 33,* 403-408.

Sallis, J.F., Hovell, M.F., Hofstetter, C.R., Faucher, P., Elder, J.P., Blanchard, J., Casparsen, C.J., Powell, K.E., & Christenson, C.M. (1989). A multivariate study of exercise determinants in a community sample. *Preventive Medicine, 18,* 20-34.

Sallis, J.F., & McKenzie, T.L. (1991). Physical education's role in public health. *Research Quarterly for Exercise and Sport, 62,* 124-137.

Sallis, J.F., McKenzie, T.L., & Alcaraz, J.E. (1993). Habitual physical activity and health related physical fitness in fourth-grade children. *American Journal of Diseases of Children, 147,* 890-896.

Sallis, J.F., McKenzie, T.L., Alcaraz, J.E., Kolody, B., Faucette, N., & Hovell, M.F. (1997). The effects of a 2-year physical education program (SPARK) on physical activity and fitness in elementary school students. *American Journal of Public Health, 87,* 1328-1334.

Sallis, J.F., McKenzie, T.L., Conway, T.L., Elder, J.P., Prochaska, J.J., Brown, M., Zive, M.M., Marshall, S.J., & Alcaraz, J.E. (in press). Environmental and policy interventions to improve eating and physical activity on middle school campuses: Outcomes of Project M-SPAN. *American Journal of Preventative Medicine.*

Sallis, J.F., McKenzie, T.L., Kolody, B., Lewis, M., Marshall, S., & Rosengard, P. (1999). Effects of health-related physical education on academic achievement: Project SPARK. *Research Quarterly for Exercise and Sport, 70,* 127-134.

Sallis, J.F., & Nader, P.R. (1988). Family determinants of health behavior. In D.S. Cochman (Ed.), *Health behavior: Emerging research perspectives* (pp. 107-124). New York: Plenum.

Sallis, J.F., & Patrick, K. (1994). Physical activity guidelines for adolescents: Consensus statement. *Pediatric Exercise Sciences, 6,* 302-314.

Sallis, J.F., Patterson, T.L., Buono, M.J., & Nader, P.R. (1988). Relation of cardiovascular fitness and physical activity to cardiovascular disease risk factors in children and adults. *American Journal of Epidemiology, 127,* 933-941.

Sallis, J.F., Zakarian, J.M., Hovell, M.F., & Hofstetter, C.R. (1996). Ethnic, socioeconomic, and sex differences in physical activity among adolescents. *Journal of Clinical Epidemiology, 49,* 125-134..

Sarkin, J.A., McKenzie, T.L., & Sallis, J.F. (1997). Gender differences in physical activity during fifth-grade physical education and recess periods. *Journal of Teaching in Physical Education, 17,* 99-106.

Shephard, R.J., Lavallee, H., Volle, M., LaBarre, R., & Beaucage, C. (1994). Academic skills and required physical education: The Trois Rivieres experience. *CAHPERIAC-SEPL Research Supplement, 1*(1), 1-12.

Shephard, R.J., & Trudeau, F. (2000). The legacy of physical education: Influences on adult lifestyle. *Pediatric Exercise Science, 12,* 34-50.

Simons-Morton, B., O'Hara, N.M., Simons-Morton, D., & Parcel, G.S. (1987). Children and fitness: A public health perspective. *Research Quarterly for Exercise and Sport, 58,* 295-302.

Simons-Morton, B.G., Parcel, G.S., & O'Hara, N.M. (1988). Implementing organizational changes to promote healthful diet and physical activity at school. *Health Education Quarterly, 15,* 115-130.

Stone, E.J., McKenzie, T.L., Welk, G.J., & Booth, M.L. (1998). Effects of physical activity interventions in youth: Review and synthesis. *American Journal of Preventive Medicine, 15,* 298-315.

Taggart, A.C., Taggart, J., & Siedentop, D. (1986). Effects of a home-based activity program: A study with low fitness elementary school children. *Behavior Modification, 10,* 487-507.

Trudeau, F., Laurencelle, L., Tremblay, J., Rajic, M., & Shephard, R.J. (1999). Daily primary school physical education: Effects on physical activity during adult life. *Medicine and Science in Sports and Exercise, 31,* 111-117.

U.S. Department of Health and Human Services (US-DHHS). (1991). *Healthy people 2000: National health promotion and disease prevention objectives* (DHHS Publication No. 91-50212). Washington, DC: Author.

U.S. Department of Health and Human Services (USD-HHS). (1996). *Physical activity and health: A report of the Surgeon General.* Atlanta: Centers for Disease Control and Prevention.

U.S. Department of Health and Human Services (USD-HHS). (2000). *Healthy people 2010* (conference edition, in two volumes). Washington, DC: U.S. Government Printing Office. Available: http://web.health.gov/healthypeople/Document/tableofcontents.htm.

Walter, H.J., Hofman, A., Vaughan, R.D., & Wynder, E.L. (1988). Modification of risk factors for coronary heart disease: Five-year results of a school-based intervention trial. *New England Journal of Medicine, 18,* 1093-1100.

Welk, G. (Ed.). (2002). *Physical activity assessments for health-related research.* Champaign, IL: Human Kinetics.

CHAPTER THIRTEEN

TEACHING SPORT WITHIN PHYSICAL EDUCATION

Peter A. Hastie

One of the significant events of the new millennium was an Olympic Games that seemed able to divorce itself from the extensive politics that were so pernicious during the 1970s and early 1980s. The events of Salt Lake City, however, again reminded us to take stock of the place of sport in our lives and ask ourselves a number of questions.

The first of these questions is "Has sport ever been more institutionalized?" We see players earning millions of dollars in all aspects of competition and endorsements—in golf, in professional football, in baseball, and even in figure skating. We see rules and sanctions codifying sport institutions like never before. Sport, too, is now legitimately part of the global economy. A teenager in Malaysia can easily obtain a Manchester United or Los Angeles Lakers T-shirt. We also see sport being institutionalized with increasingly younger competitors. In the United States, for example, some schools receive sanctions for violations of particular athletic association rules for children in the sixth grade.

The second question we may ask is "Has sport ever been more public?" The Super Bowl is the most watched television event on the planet. With the incredible growth of the Internet we can access sports results from around the globe at the click of a button. Sports fans in the United States can now listen live through the Internet to cricket broadcasts from India or rugby football matches in Australia.

Not only is sport more public through the various reporting mechanisms of the print and electronic media, but athletes' lives are also under more scrutiny. What was once a private domain of the athletes' world off the court or field has now become part of the entire sport process. We seem to have a need to know everything about every athlete and every component of his or her life. Indeed, we even become indignant when certain associations will not release drug-testing data. The fan's "right to know" has now usurped a fundamental human right of privacy within common law.

We can also ask ourselves "Has sport ever been more scrutinized?" In the past, the task of the media was to report scores, discuss the reasons for victories and losses, and make predictions about future outcomes. Nowadays, we have a vast increase in the critical reflective nature of the sports magazine business, radio talk shows, and other forums that examine the role and place of sport in society.

We also may ask ourselves a potentially disturbing question, "Has sport ever been more alienating or exclusionary?" Within the United States in particular, fewer youth have the opportunity to play sports. First, schools typically have only one or at most two football teams, whereas Australian grammar schools (grades 8 through 12) may have as many as 40. In the United States the mentality seems to be that only the best shall play. Add this to the prospect that sport participation will become more expensive and that some schools have "pay-to-play" schemes, and the result is that economically disadvantaged students have less opportunity to participate. White students already use the system more than minority students do.

PURPOSE OF THIS CHAPTER

The purpose of this chapter is to examine the conduct of sport within physical education, particularly as it applies to those questions about sport in general. Specific differences are found between the histories of team sports and individual sports. Although sport itself has been part of many cultures for thousands of years, team sport is a relatively recent phenomenon, and only in the last century have many sports become common. Basketball, for example, was invented in 1891, and volleyball first appeared in 1895. In contrast, boxing, wrestling, and the running events of the ancient Crown festivals have been documented for over 1,500 years. The Egyptians had many individual sporting contests well before that time.

EARLY SCHOOL PHYSICAL EDUCATION

The earliest physical education lessons in 19th century American schools were derived from the formal gymnastics movements based on the philosophies of Jahn and Ling. A medical framework formed the basis of these physical education programs, and the development of fitness and movement grace were the prized objectives. Indeed, many of the early leaders in the field were trained in medicine. In fact, in the earliest physical education programs, attempts were made to keep sport *out* of the curriculum. During the famous Boston Conference of 1889, where the leaders of the various systems of training first gathered to argue their objectives, sport did not even warrant a mention (Lee & Bennett, 1985).

It was not until the early 20th century, with the advent of the developmental model of the progressive education theorists, that the concept of "education through the physical" provided a vehicle for the teaching of games and sports. In this model, the objectives for physical education expanded from simply organic to include psychomotor, cognitive, and character objectives as well (see Hetherington, 1910). The development of La Porte's (1937) Physical Education Curriculum would change the face of the practice of physical education (and with it a strong focus on sport) for the next 50 years. As Siedentop (1998, p. 52) notes, "the curriculum model advocated in the La Porte monograph was a *block* or *unit* approach in which activities were offered for periods lasting from 3 to 6 weeks, allowing for initial instruction and skill development, and culminating in game play." This standard approach of skill development and game play became the beginning of what we know as the multiactivity curriculum.

STUDENT PARTICIPATION WITHIN THE MULTIACTIVITY MODEL

As noted in the introduction to this chapter, the conduct and practice of sport in the 21st century is coming under substantial scrutiny. Ironically, the multiactivity model of physical education went unchallenged for decades. It was not until the early 1980s that researchers in physical education pedagogy began to describe, and then question, many of the practices involved with the conduct of sport in physical education. These criticisms could be grouped under the following headings: (a) lack of content mastery, (b) discriminatory and abusive practices, and (c) irrelevant content.

Lack of Content Mastery

The first criticism of the multiactivity model is that the units of instruction are too short for the development of substantive learning outcomes. As Taylor and Chiogioji (1987) note,

> the proliferation of and emphasis on teaching too many activities in too short a time—has made these goals (fitness, self-esteem, and cognitive/social development) more difficult to attain. The smorgasbord approach of requiring team sports, individual sports, dance, physical fitness activities, all within the space of one year lessens those student's opportunities to master any one activity through which they can meet the stated goals (p. 22).

Silverman's (1985; Silverman, Tyson, & Morford, 1988) research on the relationship of students' practice time and skill achievement provides empirical support for those who suggest the short length of units within the multiactivity curriculum are insufficient to develop substantive skills.

Discriminatory and Abusive Practices

Although the multiactivity curriculum itself does not propagate exclusionary practices, many authors have described a number of such practices that seem to be consistent within sports units conducted under this model. Team sports taught within a traditional multiactivity format often permit dominant aggressive male players to control the game, marginalizing and alienating low-skilled girls and boys (Ennis, 1999). Indeed, Napper-Owen, Kovar, Ermler, and Mehrhoff (1999) note that as many as 25% of schools in their regional sample had programs with a primary emphasis on competitive, contact, male-oriented team activities.

Several authors note that associated with teaching practices that allow the dominance of the elite few are participation patterns of avoidance of lower-skilled students (e.g., Ennis, 1996). Tousignant and Siedentop (1983) wrote eloquently of "competent bystanders," those students who would migrate to areas of lesser involvement. Griffin (1984) noted that during team sports units, many girls would also take roles that served to reduce their playing involvement. These included categories such as "cheerleader" (or vicarious involvement), "lost soul" (or invisible noninvolvement), and "femme fatale" (or blatant noninvolvement). Griffin (1984) further remarked that not only would many girls decline to participate but those who did were generally nonassertive. To this end, she described four kinds of nonassertive behavior typically exhibited by lower-skilled girls, including "giving up," "giving away," "hanging back," and "acquiescing."

Boring and Irrelevant Content

Criticisms of sport units come not only from academic sources but also from students, with claims of boring, repetitive content (Carlson, 1995b). Students also claim that content is irrelevant when activities are alien to their homes and communities. Students identify much of what teachers present to them as irrelevant and boring, yet teachers view it as subject matter worth learning. Tinning, Macdonald, Wright, and Hickey (2001) list a number of scenarios of the apparent disjunction between school physical education and the lives of young people that mirror these different agendas. Particularly relevant from these scenarios is that many teens are serious about their engagement with sport outside school but find their in-school experiences unattractive.

Contemporary Curriculum Models

As Ennis (2000) comments, "like canaries kept in the coal mines, disengaged students warn us of the danger of continuing with current policies that fail to meet current students' needs (p. 119)." To this end, a number of curriculum models have been developed that all aim to address one or more of the limitations seen in the multiactivity curriculum. These include "Teaching games for understanding" and its variations, and "Sport education" and its variations.

SEARCH FOR A MORE "INTELLIGENT" SPORTS PLAYER—GAMES FOR UNDERSTANDING

The traditional model for teaching games within a multiactivity curriculum typically follows the process of (1) teacher explanation, (2) teacher demonstration, (3) teacher-led drill on basic skills, and (4) full game play. In the 1980s a number of British authors began to criticize this particular sequence of instruction. These criticisms ranged from the notion of the failure of the traditional model to observe developmentally appropriate considerations (Thorpe, 1983), to a lack of skill transfer (Bailey, 1982), to a lack of vision and a basic conservatism of many teachers (Jackson, Jones, & Williamson, 1983). For example, Thorpe (1983) commented that although this sequence might be suitable for small numbers of talented and motivated players in the coaching situation, it is unlikely to be appropriate in the physical education class of 30. Bailey (1982) was critical of a teaching approach that was "blinkered to producing skills practices that are scarcely evidence in play" (p. 135).

Metheny's (1968) concept of sport and games, however, provided the greatest emphasis for the change in the manner in which games were taught. In Metheny's notion, the skills that make up a game are not the essential feature of a game but simply the forms that are most appropriate as defined by the rules. To understand a game, and to make meaning out of playing an activity, participants must understand what makes that activity unique. We can do this only by investigating the rules of the game and exploring how the rules affect and delimit performance, and through playing the game and analyzing the decisions that confront us to appreciate "intelligent performance" when we see it.

With this notion in mind, Thorpe and Bunker (1983) developed a model to provide a workable teaching progression for teaching games. In this model the idea that the student should have an understanding of the game replaced the idea of having skill techniques as the center of a games curriculum. This emphasis included appreciation of the rules, comprehension of the tactics implicit in the game, and development of some ability to make decisions about how to win and how not to lose, in order to become an intelligent performer.

Teaching for Understanding—a Brief History

Bunker and Thorpe (1983) suggested the main emphasis on teaching games should be an understanding of the game *as it exists*. This idea developed from their beliefs that few players, spectators, or administrators know much about playing anything except the technique of a game. Thorpe and Bunker (1983) criticized the traditional approach in that the common lesson structure in this approach saw the game itself as a mere appendage to technique. They also wrote that the traditional lesson structure focuses on games that are inappropriate for many students and on technique sessions seen as essential by the teacher but not the students.

Bunker and Thorpe's (1983) model starts with a game form and then seeks to develop an appreciation of that game. Developed from the questions concerning the game's rules, delimitations, and aims, are problems of tactical awareness and decision making. Note also that students develop and perform skills after they understand the concepts of the game. Indeed, the central aim proposed by the model is to place the spotlight on the player's *knowing* rather than "simply doing." Figure 13.1 presents a conceptualization of that model.

According to Bunker and Thorpe (1983), games fall into in three categories: net games, striking or fielding games, and invasion games. Games in each of these categories have both structural and strategic similarities. Spackman (1983a) presented the concepts or principles as the basis of tactical solutions to strategic problems. She stated that playing games is about solving problems and comments that the teaching-for-understanding approach encourages (a) the identification of these problems and (b) the subsequent consideration of tactical solutions.

FIGURE 13.1   A conceptualization of teaching sport for understanding.

Booth (1983) outlined the key principles of invasion games as possession, invasion-progression, and scoring. She examined netball in the light of these principles as having attacking and defensive play. Indeed, we could analyze most invasion games in that way. In general, these principles of games place attention on the two important aspects of competitive games: knowing how to win, and later, knowing how not to lose.

Doolittle (1983) and Jackson (1983) conducted the earliest research projects on the efficacy of the teaching games for understanding approach. Both authors monitored teachers who were experimenting with a teaching for understanding approach. The advantages reported by those teachers included increased student enthusiasm, increased involvement and success of low ability pupils, greater knowledge about games because of the different perspective taken, and a greater sense of achievement by students. Thorpe, Bunker, and Almond (1984) also examined the specific problems encountered by teachers when beginning to teach games for understanding. He stated that the two main difficulties were (a) breaking from traditional teaching styles and (b) the difficulty in finding resources relating to alternative games teaching. In response to these difficulties, Spackman (1983b) together with Bailey and Almond (1983) suggested that teaching children to design their own games provided the teacher with a useful tool to help develop students' understanding of the function of rules and analysis of strategies and tactics.

In an attempt to provide an overall theory to describe the "understanding" approach, Kirk (1983) developed the concept of "intelligent performance." He suggested that there is more to understanding than simply knowing facts or being able to reproduce skills. As a result, he distinguished between competent performance and intelligent performance. An intelligent performance can accommodate both the familiar and the unfamiliar. He or she can select which skill to use at the appropriate time and can "read" a game. Kirk concluded that teaching for understanding is not a prescriptive model that might be the case in teaching technique but is rather a process of bringing to students the principles of play.

Renaissance of the Model and Its Updated Research Findings

Although many authors espoused the model in teaching-focused journals (e.g., Smith, 1991; Werner, 1989), the first empirical research of teaching games for understanding was not completed until the 1990s. Research was conducted comparing the effectiveness of games for understanding with the more traditional approach of skill development followed by game play.

Turner and Martinek (1995, 1999) and Allison and Thorpe (1997) provided evidence of some advantages of the understanding approach. Specifically, the games for understanding model provides a more feasible way of teaching strategic decision making for game players. Rink (1996) and Rink, French, and Graham (1996) conducted the most indepth and sophisticated analysis of various instructional methods in a 1996 monograph in the *Journal of Teaching in Physical Education*. Comparing the effects of a three-week and six-week unit of tactical, skill, or combined tactical and skill instruction on badminton performance of ninth-grade students, Rink's group found no treatment differences for game performance measures between the tactic or skill instruction approaches. They did find, however, significant improvement in students who learned the game over six weeks compared with those who received instruction for only three weeks.

Since the studies that examined the efficacy of the games for understanding approach, researchers have begun to examine the concepts of skillfulness. Turner, Allison, and Pissanos (2001) reported that the instructional context of games for understanding contributed to students' constructions of skillfulness, which included tactical knowledge inherent in invasion game play.

Derivations of the Teaching Games for Understanding Principle

Griffin, Mitchell, and Oslin (1997) have developed a modification of the teaching games for understanding approach. Calling the innovation a "tactical approach to games education," this approach to games teaching focuses on using small-sided games to highlight a predetermined tactical problem. Specifically, this problem is one that would occur within the real game. The game-practice-game format is then used to let students experience game play before they begin practicing specific skills. Like games for understanding, the tactical approach takes a problem-solving approach to mastering skills with the ultimate aim of having students understand why each skill is important.

SEARCH FOR AN "AUTHENTIC" SPORT EXPERIENCE IN PHYSICAL EDUCATION— SPORT EDUCATION

One of the most striking criticisms of team sports in physical education has been that sports are often presented in inauthentic and decontextualized ways. That is, skills are taught in isolated situations. For example, rarely in games do we see players following preset patterns by dribbling in and out of markers. We see large-sided games create demands that do not match the skill development of the players. Common in many programs are 8-a-side volleyball and 15-a-side volleyball. In these large-sided games and in shorter units of sports, strategy is notably absent.

In response to this criticism of team sports within physical education, an alternate sport-based curriculum model has been developed. This model, known as sport education, attempts to provide a culturally responsive and engaging curriculum for students within units of sport.

As a Curriculum Model

Sport education has as its premise that modern physical education fails to present an authentic sport experience (Siedentop, 1994). When we examine an authentic sport experience that we might witness, for example, in the Sheffield Shield cricket competition in Australia or in major league baseball in the United States, we see that sport is performed by seasons. After a definite starting point when teams come together to practice and prepare, they finally play games. An authentic sport experience includes team affiliation, with players remaining on the same team throughout a season. We see formal competition with formalized rules, referees who are responsible for the conduct of the event, and results that count toward some specific reward system at the end of the season. In authentic sport, we see a culminating event in which two teams engage in championship games like the Football Association Cup final, the World Series, or the Super Bowl.

Authentic sport is characterized by extensive record keeping that upholds the traditions of the sport by noting outstanding performances throughout history. Those records allow us to make comparisons between the players of today and those of yesterday. Authentic sport is also conducted with a festive nature, including extensive celebration. Spectators and fans wear their team's colors to games, they paint their faces, and they celebrate victories. The sporting experience is conducted in an atmosphere of enthusiasm and passion. Rarely do we see such enthusiasm and passion in the typical sport unit of physical education.

Sport education as a curriculum model aims to provide such an authentic experience by incorporating many of the features of authentic sport within physical education settings. First, sport education follows a season rather than unit format—and this implies and requires a commitment to an extended number of allocated lessons. No longer are three-week units of 9 total lessons adequate. During this season of 20 or more lessons, we try to replicate the phases of a season that we see in formal sport. In the early stages, players get together to practice skills, develop new strategies, identify team strengths and weaknesses, and develop team tactics. The next stage is a series of lessons in which teams engage in practice matches. Scores do not count, players experiment in different playing roles, and teams use the results of these games to reevaluate their skills. Formal competition follows, with the games counting toward some final season ranking, after which playoffs occur to determine champions. Thus, like players in formal sport, students learn skills and tactics in no-consequence scrimmages and play in the more important games later in the season.

In designing the model, Siedentop (1994) stated that sport education has as its main goal "to educate students to be players in the fullest sense, and to help them develop as competent, literate and enthusiastic sportspeople" (p. 4). In this context, the following definitions apply:

- A competent sportsperson: one who has developed the skills and strategies to such a level that he or she can participate successfully in a game
- A literate sportsperson: one who understands and values the rules, traditions, and values of a sport and can distinguish between good and bad sport practices
- An enthusiastic sportsperson: one who plays and behaves in ways that preserve, protect, and enhance the sport culture

Sport education, however, has three fundamental differences from formal sport. The first is that participation required. In sport education, full participation by all players at all times is a fundamental ethic of the model. As a result, large-sided teams are inappropriate because these typically provide those with lesser skill fewer opportunities to play. Soccer games in sport education are more likely to be between teams of 4 rather than 11, and 5-a-side softball is the norm rather than 9-a-side. The culminating event in sport education also involves all students, and seasons are designed so that all teams participate in the final games. In addition, students have significant input and involvement in this celebratory end to a season.

The second fundamental difference is the notion of developmentally appropriate competition. Equipment and rules are modified to make the game more accessible and attractive for students. Games are played over a shorter period, requiring a high level of intensive play.

The third and perhaps most fundamental component of sport education is the engagement of students in diverse roles. In nearly all previous sport experiences, students would have participated only as players. In sport education, a student will become not only a player but also a referee, a statistician, a member of a sport board or rules committee, a coach, a team manager, a journalist, or any of the other professional nonplaying roles that are part of the sporting experience. Participation in these roles allows students to become more literate about the structure and function of the sport they are playing.

Student Responses to Sport Education

Student responses to sport education have been particularly informing. Moreover, researchers have found similar outcomes across diverse settings (see Hastie & Carlson, 1998). First, students perceive that they improve in their skill over the phases of a season, and lower-skilled children hold this as their strongest perception. Empirical studies have also shown that students do indeed improve in skills (Hastie, 1998a). Students also have a strong preference for the persisting team concept. They enjoy playing with the same players over a long period (Hastie, 1998a). For the lower skilled, this is an attractive component of sport education (Carlson, 1995a). For those who are frequently picked last and are alienated in large teams, being on a small team of four or five in which they have some responsibility and their teammates are helping them improve is empowering (see Hastie, 1998b). Students prefer the instruction of peer coaches to that of teachers and other adults. They also perceive that they have increased responsibility for leadership, teamwork, and administrative roles (Hastie, 1997).

Explanation of Student Attraction

So what are the features that make this particular presentation of sport so attractive to students? One explanation seems to lie within the student social system that operates during a season (Carlson & Hastie, 1997). In the traditional games unit, the social tasks of lessons often interfere with the teacher's agenda, the instructional component. Within sport education, students socialize in a different way during class, with particular emphasis on the development of teamwork and cooperation. Students have leadership positions, and the instructional and managerial systems that normally are the total domain of the teacher become part of the students' world. Working hard together as a team to be successful is a way of having fun. These kinds of experiences have also occurred for students in collegiate settings as well as in the more often studied secondary and middle school settings (Bennett & Hastie, 1997).

The student social system is, nonetheless, one part of a multidimensional program of action operating in sport education. I previously suggested (Hastie, 2000) that the high level of enthusiastic student engagement was because of the presence of three vectors, all of which make positive contributions to sustaining the program of action. These vectors include the student social system, the teacher's managerial task system, and the content-embedded accountability inherent in the curriculum model.

Perceptions of Teachers

One of the major attractions for teachers of sport education is that it frees the teacher from much of the formal instructional demands of lessons (Alexander & Luckman, 2001). The teacher can attend to pressing needs that otherwise do not receive attention. These include conducting student assessment, working with individual students in skill development, or attending to the affective domain. All these features have revitalized teachers' enthusiasm toward teaching physical education, which Alexander, Taggart, and Thorpe (1996) described as giving teachers "a spring in their steps."

In delivering seasons of sport education, teachers face some challenges. First, they need to develop a strong management system and establish numerous protocols. A number of new tasks need to be taught formally and practiced early. The fate of an entire season will depend on how well students can perform their nonplaying roles (Hastie, 2000).

With the transfer of much of the instruction to students, we see some differences in the style of student leaders. Peer coaches typically spend more time playing games with their teams than they do teaching skills. Although teachers spend more time refining and extending tasks, peer coaches spend more time in organization, demonstration, and application tasks (Hastie, 2000). Therefore, teachers may need to monitor the tasks that peer coaches implement to help students develop skill.

Sport education is a flexible model that allows for reinforcement of whatever instructional focus the teacher wishes. The scoring systems of leagues in sport education can include rewards for fair play, for personal and team responsibility, and for cognitive learning. Sport education also gives students considerable power to determine learning priorities. In some cases teachers will engage a sport advisory board that will have a significant influence on the conduct of seasons. The students on this board determine many key features of the season. The only caveat to the flexible nature of the model is that the season must include an extended number of lessons, teams must persist, and students must take roles other than player during a season.

Situation Specific Applications of the Sport Education Model

The attractiveness of sport education as a model that can legitimately address multiple objectives has gained the interest of a number of researchers. Indeed, a number of studies have used the template of sport education to focus on specific issues seen as problematic in the presentation of sport to students. These studies used the sport education principles of persisting teams, developmentally appropriate competition, and the empowerment of students by using roles but added an additional focus to address situation specific concerns.

The study by Hastie and Sharpe (1999) used sport education to address an explicit outcome. In this case, a sport education curriculum included two specific fair-play interventions that focused on student compliance as well as interpersonal and leadership behaviors. The results indicated increased positive peer interactions as well as accurate self-monitoring by the students of their social interactions.

More recent studies founded on sport education resulted in the creation of new models. Like the study of Hastie and Sharpe (1999), these derivations of sport education tackled situations seen as problematic, namely, the conduct of sport within urban settings (see Ennis et al., 1999), and the development of personal and social responsibility within competitive game play (see Hastie & Buchanan, 2000).

Ennis and her colleagues (1999) were interested in addressing two particular concerns of the conduct of sport within urban schools. First, they wished to enhance girls' satisfaction in physical education. Second, they hoped to address the difficulty that many urban students experience with regard to engaging in learning and affiliating with others. To this end, Ennis et al. (1999) developed a model that they named Sport for Peace.

Sport for Peace

Sport for Peace incorporates all the essential curricular structures associated with sport education, that is, player roles and responsibilities, skill development, and developmentally appropriate, authentic competition. Additional curricular structures include strategies for conflict negotiation, the requirement that all students play during every class, and rules that require students to rotate through every position and responsibility (except that of coach). The model specifically aims to create moderate levels of authentic conflict and then provide strategies to facilitate and teach students to negotiate and compromise.

In the research of Ennis et al. (1999) seven urban schoolteachers were trained to use Sport for Peace, and each implemented the model with two classes within his or her school. On a global level the curricular structures of Sport for Peace were found to foster shared responsibility for learning, trust, respect, and a sense of family (Ennis et al., 1999). The authors reported that both high- and low-skilled girls and boys felt successful and responded positively, creating a class community more conducive to engagement and participation. In addition, Sport for Peace enhanced the students' perceptions of success, promoted ownership of the sport content and the class processes, and created authentic cooperative environments for boys and girls, particularly through the use of second chances to promote understanding and learning (see Ennis, 1999).

Focus on Personal and Social Responsibility: Empowering Sport

The study of Hastie and Buchanan (2000) followed an agenda similar to that of Ennis. Their aim was to improve the performance of middle school students (particularly boys) with regard to the fair play requirements of sport education. Using a strong infusion of Hellison's "teaching for personal and social responsibility" model (see Hellison, 1995, and chapter 14 in this text), they created a hybrid model named Empowering Sport.

A template of Empowering Sport would be the following:

> Units begin with a series of work related problems—the major ones being the creation of even teams as well as a game. This game is born from either a skeleton of primary rules (as was the case in this experience) or may even be totally student-centered. The teacher may then provide some leadership in the form of direct skill instruction or may further facilitate team captains (or practice leaders), with the primary agenda being to assist lower skilled students to become more competent and with an increased sense of self-efficacy. The competition format is one in which teams negotiate to play or scrimmage, again within certain parameters put in place by the teacher. . . . Decisions concerning more formal competition within this hybrid model would be a function of the teacher's primary Sport Education agenda in combination with the students' goals for their sport experience. However, the global objective of this model is personal empowerment, particularly through making appropriate personal and social responses. (Hastie & Buchanan, 2000, p. 34)

Empowering Sport, then, is a model that allows for achievement within a powerful triangle of goals—sport, skill competence, and social responsibility.

IMPLICATIONS OF THE RESEARCH FOR PRACTICE

The preceding sections of this chapter attest to the idea that a significant change has occurred in the way we think about the presentation of sport within physical education. The once-unquestioned traditional multiactivity model of brief periods of skill practice followed by game play has been transformed to one in which students make decisions about the games they play or even design those games. Students now take significant responsibility for the organization of play and the conduct of sport as a whole. We have also seen a substantial change in the role of the teacher during units of sport instruction. With this in mind, research into game play has a number of implications for the practice of sport within physical education. These can be classified as issues of curriculum or issues of instruction.

Curriculum Design Issues

Rink et al. (1996) suggested that several key principles should guide the selection of sport content in physical education. The first is to select only sports that will lead to student success. By this they mean that we should modify the rules of games and reduce team size so that students have maximum opportunity to participate. Both changes serve to maximize opportunities for students to develop an understanding of the key tactics and techniques that guide successful game play.

The second principle is to give students time to play. That is, we need to allocate time during *each* lesson for some game-playing contests. These contests may be simply a series of application tasks using the skills learned during the lesson, or they may be in the form of two-versus-two challenges. The point is that we should not leave the issue of skills transfer until later in the unit. Students should be transferring skills into some applied context at all phases during the unit. With that in mind, we should teach skills that transfer to game settings. Consequently, in designing skill development tasks, we should avoid including tasks that present a skill in a way that students would never experience in the real game. In designing these tasks, we should be asking whether the particular action actually occurs in a game.

In designing these skills tasks we may want to use a unique game segment, such as setting up the ball for a smash in volleyball or cutting to an open space and receiving a lead pass in any of the invasion games (e.g., hockey, soccer, or basketball). A wonderful resource for the teaching of this potential for transfer is found in the monograph by Rovegno, Nevett, and Babiarz (2001).

Instructional Issues

Besides making these game modifications, we must avoid using short units of instruction. With the large amount of learning involved in the contemporary sport models discussed in this chapter, an essential edict would have to be "It takes time." It takes time for students to learn the nonplaying roles that are involved in the sport models that empower students. It takes time for students to develop the necessary interpersonal and social skills required for a team to develop significant affiliation and the benefits involved in a persisting team. It takes time for students to learn to receive instruction from their peers in ways that they believe are helpful. It takes time for students to become sufficiently empowered that they can successfully make decisions that will benefit all students, not just the elite.

From an instructional perspective, the role of the teacher in the curriculum models presented shifts from one of director to one of facilitator. Rather than being concerned solely with the development of students' skill and knowledge of game rules, teachers must help students learn the new roles they are taking and new ways of examining sport problems.

Teachers need to be able to step back and allow students to make decisions, allow students to make mistakes, and give opportunities for students to have a voice. In doing so, however, they should remember the counsel of Holdsworth (1999), who comments that for students, having a real voice is much more than being consulted; it is having a valued and recognized role within that community (in this case, the physical education class.) Notably, most of the recent research into sport instruction is strongly grounded in student voice. So, too, should your teaching.

But the role of the teacher is not diminished. Teachers have significantly more opportunities to be involved in formative assessments and work at an individual level rather than at a whole class level. Nonetheless, teachers also need to be expert planners and class managers. The curriculum models discussed offer significant potential for student engagement with the content, provided that the teacher has all the instructional materials ready and has developed specific protocols so that students can successfully complete their managerial roles. The successful teachers in these sport forms have developed class protocols that allow students to maximize their time with the solving of sport problems.

A NOTE TO THE FUTURE

Our study and concern with sport within physical education has given birth to a number of curriculum models that have made strong attempts to counter the criticisms of inequitable practices and the dominance of highly skilled students. These models have made an effort to produce sports players who are both more literate and more competent. Regardless of the model, students are now being asked to do more than "just play." They are being asked to think strategically, to play with consideration for those with lesser skill, and, in many cases, to assume more responsibility for the conduct of sport.

These advances in the teaching and presentation of sport within physical education can only result in positive student attitudes toward sport participation. Indeed, research to date confirms significant student appreciation of curriculum models discussed in this chapter. To this end, we have achieved positive immediate outcomes. Of more consequence, however, is Siedentop's (1994) objective of producing students who will eventually change the sport culture to one characterized by greater tolerance and inclusion. We can look forward to seeing the graduates of positive sporting programs take significant leadership roles in community and sport settings and facilitate opportunities for *all* individuals to find success and fulfillment through sport.

IMPLICATIONS FOR PRACTICE

1. Sport in physical education in and of itself does not promote positive student interactions. Teachers must specifically and deliberately promote these behaviors.
2. Whatever curriculum model is used to present sport in physical education, there seems to be no justification for playing full-sided, nonmodified games such as a nine-a-side softball or six-a-side volleyball.
3. Teachers' first efforts to introduce teaching games for understanding or sport education should probably be with a sport that they know well and feel comfortable teaching.
4. Although efficient sport education seasons appear to run smoothly without specific teacher direction, teachers are instrumental in planning and organizing the unit and facilitating relevant student experiences. The program is not an advanced version of "roll out the ball."

5. Of all the components of the sport education model, the one variable that cannot be compromised is the extended length of the season.

6. The success of a season of sport education requires the teacher to develop robust managerial tasks systems in the early lessons.

7. Providing that they maintain the concepts of persisting teams, authentic competence, and student responsibility, teachers can develop situation-specific derivations of sport education to meet local needs.

8. If we wish students to take their sport roles seriously (e.g., leadership roles, problem-solving roles, or managerial and other nonplaying roles), they need some form of formal accountability for their performance in these roles.

REFERENCES

Alexander, K., & Luckman, J. (2001). Australian teachers' perceptions and uses of the sport education curriculum model. *European Physical Education Review, 7*, 243-267.

Alexander, K., Taggart, A., Thorpe, S. (1996). A spring in their steps? Possibilities for professional renewal through sport education in Australian schools. *Sport, Education and Society, 1*(1), 23-46.

Allison, S., & Thorpe, R.A. (1997). Comparison of the effectiveness of two approaches to teaching games within physical education. A skills approach versus a games for understanding approach. *British Journal of Physical Education, 28*(3), 9-13.

Bailey, L. (1982). Netball: Are we playing the game? *Action: British Journal of Physical Education, 13*(5), 135, 150.

Bailey, L., & Almond, L. (1983). Creating change: By creating games? *Physical Education Review, 6*(1), 16-18.

Bennett, R.G., & Hastie, P.A. (1997). A sport education curriculum model for a collegiate physical activity course. *Journal of Physical Education, Recreation and Dance, 68*(1), 39-44.

Booth, K. (1983). An introduction to netball: An alternative approach. *Bulletin of Physical Education, 19*(1), 27-31.

Bunker, D., & Thorpe, R. (1983). A model for the teaching of games in secondary schools. *Bulletin of Physical Education, 19*(1), 32-35.

Carlson, T. (1995a). "Now I think I can." The reaction of eight low-skilled students to sport education. *ACHPER Healthy Lifestyles Journal, 42*(4), 6-8.

Carlson, T.B. (1995b). We hate gym: Student alienation from physical education. *Journal of Teaching in Physical Education, 14*, 467-477.

Carlson, T., & Hastie, P.A. (1997). The student social system within sport education. *Journal of Teaching in Physical Education, 16*, 176-195

Doolittle, S. (1983). Reflecting on an innovation. *Bulletin of Physical Education, 19*(1), 36-38.

Ennis, C.D. (1996). Students' experiences in sport-based physical education: (More than) apologies are necessary. *Quest, 48*, 453-456.

Ennis, C.D. (1999). Creating a culturally relevant curriculum for disengaged girls. *Sport, Education and Society, 4*, 31-49.

Ennis, C.D. (2000). Canaries in the coal mine: Responding to disengaged students using theme-based curricula. *Quest, 52*, 119-130.

Ennis, C.D., Solmon, M.A., Satina, B., Loftus, S., Mensch, J., & McCauley, M.T. (1999). Creating a sense of family in urban schools using the Sport for Peace curriculum. *Research Quarterly for Exercise and Sport, 70*, 273-285.

Griffin, L., Mitchell, S., & Oslin, J. (1997). *Teaching sport concepts and skills: A tactical games approach.* Champaign, IL: Human Kinetics.

Griffin, P.S. (1984). Girls' participation patterns in a middle school team sports unit. *Journal of Teaching in Physical Education, 4*, 30-38.

Hastie, P.A. (1997). Student role involvement during a unit of sport education. *Journal of Teaching in Physical Education, 6*, 88-103.

Hastie, P.A. (1998a). Skill and tactical development during a sport education season. *Research Quarterly for Exercise and Sport, 69*, 368-379.

Hastie, P.A. (1998b). The participation and perceptions of girls within a unit of sport education. *Journal of Teaching in Physical Education, 17*, 157-171.

Hastie, P.A. (2000). An ecological analysis of a sport education season. *Journal of Teaching in Physical Education, 19*, 355-373.

Hastie, P.A., & Buchanan, A.M. (2000). Teaching responsibility through sport education: Prospects of a coalition. *Research Quarterly for Exercise and Sport, 71*, 25-35.

Hastie, P.A., & Carlson, T.B. (1998). Sport education: A cross cultural comparison. *Journal of Comparative Physical Education and Sport, 20* (2), 36-43.

Hastie, P.A., & Sharpe, T. (1999). Effects of a sport education curriculum on the positive social behavior of at-risk rural adolescent boys. *Journal of Education for Students Placed at Risk, 4*, 417-430.

Hellison, D. (1995). *Teaching responsibility through physical activity.* Champaign, IL: Human Kinetics.

Hetherington, C. (1910). Fundamental education. *American Physical Education Review, 15*, 629-635.

Holdsworth, R. (1999). Enhancing effective student participation: 33 curriculum approaches. *Connect, 116,* 6-9.

Jackson, S. (1983). Teaching for understanding in invasion games. In L. Spackman (Ed.), *Games teaching for understanding* (pp. 27-28). Cheltenham: Cheltenham College CDC.

Jackson, S., Jones, D., & Williamson, T. (1983). It's a different ball game! A critical look at the games curriculum. *Bulletin of Physical Education, 18*(1), 23-26.

Kirk, D. (1983). Theoretical guidelines for "teaching for understanding." *Bulletin of Physical Education, 19*(1), 41-45.

La Porte, W.R. (1937). *The physical education curriculum (a national program).* Los Angeles: University of Southern California Press.

Lee, M., & Bennett, B. (1985). 1885–1900: A time of gymnastics and measurement. *Journal of Physical Education, Recreation & Dance, 56*(4), 19-26.

Metheny, E. (1968). *Movement and meaning.* New York: McGraw-Hill.

Napper-Owen, G.E., Kovar, S.K., Ermler, K.L., & Mehrhof, J.H. (1999). Curricula equity in required ninth-grade physical education. *Journal of Teaching in Physical Education, 19,* 2-21.

Rink, J.E. (1996). Tactical and skill approaches to teaching sport and games: Introduction. *Journal of Teaching in Physical Education, 15,* 397-398.

Rink, J.E., French, K.E., & Graham, K.C. (1996). Implications for practice and research. *Journal of Teaching in Physical Education, 15,* 490-516.

Rovegno, I., Nevett, M., & Babiarz, M. (2001). Learning and teaching invasion-game tactics in 4th grade: Introduction and theoretical perspective. *Journal of Teaching in Physical Education, 20,* 341-351.

Siedentop, D. (1994). *Sport education: Quality PE through positive sport experiences.* Champaign, IL: Human Kinetics.

Siedentop, D. (1998). *Introduction to physical education, fitness and sport* (3rd ed.). Mountain View, CA: Mayfield.

Silverman, S. (1985). Relationship of engagement and practice trials to student achievement. *Journal of Teaching in Physical Education, 5,* 13-21.

Silverman, S., Tyson, L., & Morford, L.M. (1988). Relationships of organization, time, and student achievement in physical education. *Teaching and Teacher Education, 4,* 247-257.

Smith, M.D. (1991). Utilizing the games for understanding model at the elementary school level. *Physical Educator, 48,* 184-187.

Spackman, L. (1983a). Invasion games: An instructional strategy. In L. Spackman (Ed.), *Games teaching for understanding* (pp. 37-41). Cheltenham: Cheltenham College CDC.

Spackman, L. (1983b). Games making at the Colleges of St. Paul and St. Mary, Cheltenham. In L. Spackman (Ed.), *Games teaching for understanding* (pp. 64-69). Cheltenham: Cheltenham College CDC.

Taylor, J., & Chiogioji, E. (1987). Implications of physical education report on high school programs. *Journal of Physical Education, Recreation and Dance, 54*(8), 22-23.

Thorpe, R. (1983). An "understanding approach" to the teaching of games. *Bulletin of Physical Education, 19*(1), 12-19.

Thorpe, R., & Bunker, D. (1983). From theory to practice: Two examples of an understanding approach to the teaching of games. In L. Spackman (Ed.), *Games teaching for understanding* (pp. 5-10). Cheltenham: Cheltenham College CDC.

Thorpe, R., Bunker, D., Almond, L. (1984). Four fundamentals for planning a games curriculum. *Bulletin of Physical Education, 20*(1), 24-28.

Tinning, R., Macdonald, D., Wright, J., & Hickey, C. (2001). *Becoming a physical education teacher: Contemporary and enduring issues.* Sydney: Pearson Education Australia.

Tousignant, M., & Siedentop, D. (1983). A qualitative analysis of task structure in required secondary physical education classes. *Journal of Teaching in Physical Education, 3,* 47-57.

Turner, A.P., Allison, P.C., & Pissanos, B.W. (2001). Constructing a concept of skillfulness in invasion games within a games for understanding context. *European Journal of Physical Education, 6*(1), 38-54.

Turner, A., & Martinek, T.J. (1995). Teaching for understanding: A model for improving decision making during game play. *Quest, 47,* 44-63.

Turner, A.P., & Martinek, T.J. (1999). An investigation into teaching games for understanding: Effects on skill, knowledge, and game play. *Research Quarterly for Exercise and Sport, 70,* 286-296.

Werner, P. (1989). Teaching games: A tactical perspective. *Journal of Physical Education, Recreation and Dance, 60*(3), 97-101.

CHAPTER FOURTEEN

TEACHING PERSONAL AND SOCIAL RESPONSIBILITY IN PHYSICAL EDUCATION

Don Hellison

"Kids aren't the same anymore," a veteran physical education teacher recently lamented. He is right, of course. Changes in the diversity of student backgrounds, more varied family structure, and greater incidence of at-risk behaviors such as drug use, violence, and dropping out (or staying in school and "cruisin' in neutral") have created problems for teachers and students alike. Students have more unsupervised discretionary time, more access to guns and drugs, and more exposure to the electronic media (including the music industry), which bombards them with messages about dress, money, fame, and violence when they are perhaps most vulnerable, most interested in being "cool" and "looking good." These problems are exacerbated for kids who live in inner-city "war zones" (Garbarino, Dubrow, Kostelny, & Pardo, 1991; Walberg, Reyes, & Weissberg, 1997), face poverty and racism every day, and are not well served by bureaucratic, unresponsive schools (Weiner, 1993). Although the inner city has special needs, the problems this nation's children and youth face are now surfacing in all communities (Benson, 1997).

Children and youth today need more guidance, and criticism for failing to meet students' needs has spread beyond urban schools to schools in general (Des Dixon, 1994) as well as community agencies (Carnegie Council on Adolescent Development, 1992; McLaughlin & Heath, 1993).

WHAT IS OUR RESPONSIBILITY?

The central question for us is this: To what extent and in what ways can physical education help meet the needs of today's kids? What is our responsibility, and how can we meet this challenge?

Toward a More Holistic Approach

In-school physical education has the potential to reach far more children and youth than any other kind of physical activity structure. This advantage, however, has to be weighed against such disadvantages as large classes, large numbers of students assigned to teachers every day, and bureaucratic policies not always in the best interests of kids. To broaden and deepen our potential influence, physical education is better conceived as a community-wide undertaking with community youth organizations taking their place alongside schools in providing physical activity programs for children and youth (Ianni, 1989; Lawson, 1994; McLaughlin, 2000).

We need more than classroom management to address the problems that children and youth bring to school and community programs. To help today's kids, we need to deliver on our holistic rhetoric about such things as character development and the affective domain. Of course, physical activity is central to physical education, but the world today requires that teachers put kids ahead of physical activity, that they teach for personal and social development much more than teachers have in the past. Although many current social problems are rooted in social, economic, and political policy and are beyond the reach of most teachers and youth workers, each of us can investigate the possibility of introducing alternative physical activity models and structures into our programs. Margaret Mead (National Clearinghouse on Families and Youth, 1996, p. 22) offered us hope with this remark: "Never doubt that the efforts of one person can change the world. . . . Indeed, it's the only thing that ever has."

Alternative Program Model

In this chapter I describe one such alternative program model along with applications to both in-school physical education and community extended-day programs and structures. Nearly 30 years of interplay among my beliefs and values, my fieldwork with underserved and so-called at-risk kids, and self-reflection support this approach. I have been joined by many teachers and youth workers who have applied these ideas in a variety of K–12 and community settings with students of all socioeconomic classes throughout the United States and in other countries.

TEACHING PERSONAL AND SOCIAL RESPONSIBILITY IN PHYSICAL EDUCATION: PROGRAM PRINCIPLES

What I learned in my early years of teaching was that although I could not change the experience of poverty, racism, and violence that my students brought to the gym, I could, through activity experiences and discussions, help them be more reflective about the personal and social-moral decisions they were making. I gradually came to understand that teaching personal and social responsibility in physical education meant helping children and youth become more personally responsible for their own well-being and more socially and morally responsible for contributing to the well-being of others.

Until recently (Hellison et al., 2000) the fundamental principles for teaching personal and social responsibility have been largely implicit. Unfortunately, this circumstance has led to some weak and even erroneous interpretations and applications by teachers.

Some general guidelines for teaching physical education help set the stage for a personal and social responsibility program. You can compare your beliefs and practices with these guidelines to determine to what extent teaching personal and social responsibility makes sense to you, as well as the changes you would need to make to use this approach (see also the questionnaire in Hellison et al., 2000, pp. 45-46):

- Because physical activity is central to physical education, the teacher must be competent in teaching physical activities.

- Physical education should not only be active but educational as well; it should put kids first and promote holistic development. Holistic development, however, needs to be focused. Following Sizer's (1992) less-is-more guideline, a few focused program goals will have greater effect on kids than many diffuse goals.

- Physical activity programs—because they involve action, interaction, and a range of emotional states—offer unique personal and social development opportunities, and people often make claims about these kinds of contributions. Personal and social development, however, is not an automatic outcome of participation in sport and exercise; such development requires specific goals, strategies, and teacher qualities.

These assumptions lead us to the essence of teaching personal and social responsibility:

First, a certain kind of teacher-student relationship is essential. Although terms such as *caring* and *empathy* dot the literature and are certainly important, the key to teaching responsibility is to be able to recognize and respect the following qualities in one's students:

- That they all have strengths, not just weaknesses

- That each is an individual and wants to be recognized as such, despite the uniformity of attire, slang, gestures, and so on

- That each knows things the teacher does not; each has a voice, a "side," that needs to be heard

- That each has the capacity, if not the experience, to make good decisions; often, they just need practice (as they do in learning a motor skill)

These last two, voice and decision-making capacity, are especially crucial if responsibility is to be put into practice.

Second, the teacher must integrate personal and social responsibility goals and strategies into the physical activity lesson rather than teach them separately. This requires the teacher to be competent not only in teaching physical activities but also in teaching students to become more personally and socially responsible. Further, the teacher must be able to integrate the two sets of content.

Third, teaching responsibility means empowering students—that is, gradually shifting power from the teacher to students (accompanied by self-reflection). Teaching responsibility means helping them learn to make wise personal and social-moral decisions and giving them opportunities to do so.

Fourth, transfer from the activity setting to other arenas of life—school, playground, street, home—is crucial if responsibility is to become an integral part of kids' lives.

GOALS AND GOAL MODIFICATIONS FOR TEACHING RESPONSIBILITY

The program goals shown in figure 14.1 give students a clearer, more specific sense of what they are to take responsibility for. These goals are often referred to as levels, because they represent a loose progression from one to five. The first two goals (or levels), respect and effort, are the beginning stage of responsibility development; both are essential to establishing a positive learning environment. The next two, self-direction and helping, are an advanced stage that, while enhancing the learning environment, provides students choices to explore and expand if carried out successfully. Transfer outside the gym is the most advanced stage; it involves exploring the preceding four responsibilities in school, at home, with friends, and so on to evaluate whether they work better than what the student has been thinking, feeling, and doing. Unfortunately, teachers often exclude this goal.

Goals for Teaching Personal and Social Responsibility

1. Respect for the rights and feelings of others
   a. Self-control of temper and mouth
   b. Respect everyone's right to be included
   c. Involvement in peaceful and democratic conflict resolution
2. Effort
   a. Self-motivation
   b. Explore self-effort and try new tasks
   c. On-task persistence
3. Self-direction
   a. Work independently
   b. Goal-setting progression
   c. Courage to resist peer pressure
4. Helping others and leadership
   a. Caring and compassion
   b. Sensitivity and responsiveness
   c. Inner strength
5. Outside the gym
   a. Trying these ideas outside the physical activity program
   b. Being a role model

FIGURE 14.1   Goals for teaching personal and social responsibility.

Teaching personal and social responsibility encompasses more than observable behaviors; it also includes attitudes, beliefs, values, and intentions. For example, when a student helps another student, is she motivated by an external reward or by caring and compassion? This focus on the inside self as well as outside self makes teaching infinitely more complicated, but then teaching is exactly that (McDonald, 1992; Tom, 1984).

Because empowerment is a fundamental value of this approach, teachers like yourself—not just students—must be empowered to modify the goals and strategies to meet the needs of their students, settings, and personal styles, as long as such modifications take place within the scope of the basic principles for teaching personal and social responsibility. Of course, you are free to interpret responsibility in a different way as long as you understand that you are doing something other than the approach I am describing here.

Cumulative levels, shown in figure 14.2, are particularly popular with in-school teachers, because they provide a shortcut in dealing with large classes and large numbers of kids every day. The disadvantage is that students don't conform well to the concept of cumulative levels. A student may show some helping and leadership and later laugh at someone who made a mistake or decide not to participate for a while. As a result, they probably work better as goals toward which kids can work—"I made it through the class at level two yesterday, maybe I can do level three today"—than as an evaluation tool. But this choice is up to the individual teacher, some of whom—like Pete Hockett, a PE teacher in Wisconsin who painted the cumulative levels on the gym wall so that students can tap their goal for the day when coming into the gym and, on the way out, tap the level they actually were at—have come up with creative ways of using the cumulative levels for both goal setting and self-evaluation.

The Cumulative Levels

Level 0: Irresponsibility

Students who operate at Level 0 make excuses and blame others for their behavior and deny personal responsibility for what they do or fail to do.

Level I: Respect

Students at Level I may not participate in the day's activities or show much mastery or improvement, but they are able to control their own behavior enough so that they don't interfere with other students' right to learn or the teacher's right to teach. And they do this without being prompted by the teacher very much and without constant supervision.

Level II: Participation

Students at Level II not only show minimal respect to others but also participate in the subject matter. They willingly, even enthusiastically, play, accept challenges, practice motor skills, and train for fitness under the teacher's supervision.

Level III: Self-Direction

Students at Level III not only show respect and participation, but they are also able to work without direct supervision. They can identify their own needs and can begin to plan and execute their own physical education programs.

Level IV: Caring

Students at Level IV, in addition to respecting others, participating, and being self-directed, are motivated to extend their sense of responsibility beyond themselves by cooperating, giving supports, showing concerns, and helping.

FIGURE 14.2   The cumulative levels.

Adapted, by permission, from D. Hellison, 1985, *Goals and Strategies for Teaching Physical Education* (Champaign, IL: Human Kinetics), pp. 6-8.

I have found that simply referring to the five goals or levels as the students' responsibilities best captures the intent of this approach. This approach shifts the goals to them, and the teacher becomes a facilitator. Like all these ideas, however, this is only a suggestion.

These responsibilities are not etched in stone. Teachers can change the terminology, and sometimes a responsibility itself, depending on the kids, setting, and physical activity content. For example, in our extended-day team sport programs, most of the students are highly motivated but lack interest and experience in teamwork and cooperation, so we substitute teamwork for effort (Hellison et al., 2000). Following the less-is-more guideline, however, we never add more goals.

Sharing power with students means allowing them to make and reflect on decisions, and negotiating issues with them. Sharing power with students, taken to its logical conclusion, means that for each student the five responsibilities (levels) eventually become provisional goals, to be learned, experienced, reflected upon, and eventually validated, changed, or even rejected.

STRATEGIES FOR TAKING RESPONSIBILITY

The principles for teaching responsibility provide a holistic, relational, student-centered perspective for teaching responsibility, and the five goals (or levels) spell out what students are to take responsibility for—in other words, their responsibilities. Together they describe *what* teaching responsibility is about and provide some broad guidelines for *how* to put the model into practice. Although you can use your imagination in applying these ideas, I offer specific instructional strategies both to spark the imagination and to provide ideas for specific settings and kids.

Format

A specific format for every class provides a strategic framework to ensure routine implementation of personal and social responsibility. The format involves six sequential parts:

- Counseling time (before the formal program begins, to the extent that time and other duties permit): Because teaching this way is at its heart relational, teachers must attempt to touch base with as many individual students as possible, sometimes briefly discussing a positive or negative incident that occurred in the last lesson, sometimes just checking in or commenting on new hair style or a particularly happy or unhappy face.

- Awareness talk: Next, the teacher brings students together briefly, standing or sitting, to teach the five responsibilities. In most settings the teacher should do this gradually, beginning with respect and effort, eventually adding self-direction and helping, and even later including transfer outside the gym. Following the initial teaching, the awareness talk is an opportunity to remind students about their responsibilities that day. After students learn the levels and have had some experience with them, they can conduct the awareness talk, describing what the program is about in their own words (rather than mimicking the teacher).

- The lesson: The majority of time is spent on the physical activity lesson. During the lesson the teacher uses instructional strategies (see the next section) to integrate teaching responsibility with teaching the physical activities, which may mean changing longstanding patterns of teaching physical activities.

- Group meeting: Near the end of the period students gather around the teacher, standing or sitting depending on the time available. The purpose of the group meeting is to give students the opportunity to express their views about the day's lesson, how their peers as a whole did, and perhaps even how effective the teacher's instruction and leadership were. They can also raise issues and suggest possible solutions, or the teacher can suggest a solution and ask for advice. Students can discuss problems they have with one or more of their peers during counseling time or, if handled carefully, during group meetings. If the time is limited, teachers can ask a question and ask one or two volunteers to say what they liked or disliked about the class that day, perhaps followed by a show of hands of those who agree. The important point is that students have a chance to share their points of view.

- Reflection time: The last activity students engage in before they leave gives them an opportunity to evaluate their own attitudes, intentions, and behaviors in relation to their five responsibilities. Whereas the group meeting empowers students to become part of the program evaluation process, reflection time is designed so that students can reflect on and evaluate themselves—that is, how well they respected others' rights and feelings, the extent of their success at self-motivation and self-direction, their contribution to others and to making the lesson a positive experience for everyone, and whether they put some of these things into practice outside the program. Many self-evaluation methods have been used, including brief journal entries, raised hands, thumbs (up, down, or sideways), checklists, and comments on the way out of the gym. The teacher can also ask students to share examples of taking responsibility into areas of their lives outside the gym.

- Counseling time (after the formal program ends to the extent that time permits): After class the teacher sometimes has an opportunity for brief one-to-one meetings in the same ways and for the same reasons as counseling time before class, as well as a time for immediate follow-up of individual student successes and problems that day.

Instructional Strategies

Instructional strategies for teaching personal and social responsibility can be grouped according to four strategy clusters. In the beginning, awareness and direct instruction strategies dominate the lesson. Gradually, the time allotted for individual and group decision making expands to facilitate the shift of power from teacher to students, until eventually most of the lesson is empowerment based. Teachers report that adopting this approach is harder at first, because it is new to them and to students, but when students begin to be self-directed and take on leadership roles, it becomes easier than traditional teaching. This process, however, progresses unevenly and requires what I call the accordion principle, which means gradually progressing toward more empowerment but tightening and loosening the reins as necessary, both with the entire group and with individuals who require more or less structure.

- **Awareness strategies:** These strategies include awareness talks, wall charts, and other "teachable moments" that teachers can take advantage of to teach or reinforce the five responsibilities. Students need to know the goals of the program if they are to take more responsibility for their own development as well as the development of peers and of the program itself.

- **Direct instruction:** Direct instruction is important in helping students experience taking responsibilities that they may not choose to do on their own. For example:
  - For respecting others' rights to participate, using modified game rules—such as requiring two hits before returning the ball to the other team in volleyball or requiring all players on a basketball team to receive a pass before anyone shoots—helps students experience respecting others' right to be included.
  - For effort, structuring a lesson around self-paced challenges—for example, having students perform a progression of basketball-dribbling tasks that they work through at their own pace, or having students do as many push-ups as they can instead of a specified number for the whole class—adjusts the task to the student's ability and encourages improvement and self-motivation rather than outdoing others. This sort of lesson also introduces students to individual decision making.

- For helping others, reciprocal coaching (adapted from Mosston and Ashworth, 2002), in which students learn to give feedback to each other during a skill drill, helps all students experience helping each other. The notion of helping others is further enhanced if students later evaluate each other as coaches (Did they say anything? Were they helpful? Were they positive?).

- **Individual decision making:** Infusing individual decision-making skills is more difficult for teachers who have not experienced much empowerment as students, athletes, or preservice teachers and who have therefore not taught that way either. The list of possibilities is lengthy, a number of which are described elsewhere (Hellison, 1995). Here is an example for each goal:

  - For students who have difficulty respecting the rights and feelings of others, negotiating a plan to deal with a recurring respect issue or giving students who lose self-control the option of sitting out to regain control (and coming back in on their own) as part of a sit-out progression helps empower them to handle their own problems.

  - For effort, having students choose their own intensity level in a game situation— for example, by offering competitive, recreational, and practice options in class—shifts the effort decision to them. Coupled with a brief reflection time, this strategy and others like it encourage students to decide what best motivates them to participate (or what they value most), how much effort they want to put into an activity, and whether their decision worked for them.

  - Self-direction can be developed gradually by offering a self-direction progression, perhaps by having students first work independently on an assigned task and later work on a self-selected skill and drill that they think will help them improve. Reflection time should follow for students to assess how dedicated they were to the task and whether it helped them. Those who are successful can proceed to take charge of their own physical education programs. Those who aren't can return to the teacher's direct instruction until they are prepared to try again.

  - Many opportunities for helping and providing leadership for peers potentially exist in any physical activity program, for example, by first teaching students how to coach and then giving them a progression of coaching responsibilities.

  - The goal outside the gym is designed so that students can explore possible applications of these goals in other aspects of their lives. Individual decision making resides in deciding whether something, for example, practicing self-control in the classroom, works better for them than what they have been doing.

- **Large and small group decision making:** The group meeting facilitates students' voices so that they can become an active part of the program evaluation process, including raising issues and suggesting solutions. If the teacher adopts some, or even a few, of their solutions, students gain confidence in the process. In addition to the group meeting, small groups such as a coaches' meeting or team meeting can make decisions that solve a conflict, change how teams conduct practice or games, determine what tasks they will do, settle on whether to be more or less competitive, and so on.

Assessment

The recent emphasis (or overemphasis) on school test scores has elevated the priority of assessment and outcomes in schools and even in community youth organizations (McLaughlin, 2000). In many states, as Terry Wood indicates in chapter 11, rubrics are the in-school assessment tool of choice. If so, teachers can create a responsibility rubric—

for example, categories such as "consistently," "sometimes," "seldom," and "never" for the five responsibilities. Teachers can use this rubric to assess students' responsibility, but based on the empowerment principle, they should gradually shift the assessment responsibility to students. This shift of responsibility might first go to student leaders, but eventually all students should have the opportunity to share with the teacher their perception of the extent to which they carry out their responsibilities. Hellison (1995) offers several creative self-assessment tools as alternatives to rubrics.

Teacher Qualities

Because teaching personal and social responsibility is, at its heart, relational (as reflected in the program principles), the qualities that the teacher possesses and puts into practice is of overriding importance. Bill Ayers (1989) points out that teaching is not simply what one does; it is who one is. If you want to teach for personal and social responsibility, you have to put kids first, care about them as individuals, see their strengths, and be able to listen as well as talk. You have to size up students' readiness for additional responsibility and know when to tighten as well as loosen the reins (the accordion principle). You also need to know when to back off, when you are pushing too hard, without caving in to students' demands to "just play the game." Teaching personal and social responsibility is a matter of outlasting them while at the same time continually fine-tuning the extent of responsibility-based instruction possible at a given time. As noted earlier, a brief questionnaire (Hellison et al., 2000, pp. 45-46) can help you assess these qualities in yourself. See also Hellison (1995) for an extended discussion of teacher qualities relevant to teaching responsibility.

APPLICATIONS

In this section I will outline how you can start applying personal and social responsibility in your physical education classrooms or extended-day programs.

School Physical Education Applications

Because in-school physical education teachers face many students in large classes each day, full implementation of personal and social responsibility is difficult. For that reason the cumulative levels described earlier come in handy. And that's why, despite my dim view in this chapter about controlling kids, many teachers face the daily reality of managing large numbers of students and the fear that they will lose control.

Despite this bleak outlook, numerous teachers have adopted many of these ideas. Some have even created new strategies that I in turn have adopted! If this approach makes sense to you, my advice is to start small, perhaps with one class or with something you think you can pull off, such as reflection time, and build from there (Hellison et al., 2000). As long as you remain true to the core convictions of the model, anything you do will advance kids' ability to become more personally and socially responsible.

In general, the daily format will help in organizing the lesson, and the instructional strategy suggestions will facilitate the exploration of responsibility-based tasks, such as how to empower students to develop their own fitness programs, how to make motor-skill drills more user friendly and progressively independent, how to introduce games so that students not only play fairly and cooperatively but also play in line with their skill and interest levels, and how to help students learn and transfer life lessons that occur in the gym. Teachers can certainly introduce young kids to the ideas of being responsible and taking responsibility, and some teachers have seen the potential in young children for taking considerable responsibility as early as first grade.

Extended-Day Programs

Compared with in-school physical education, community youth programs generally have more flexibility in determining curriculum, class size, meeting times, and so on. Traditional in-school physical education expectations (e.g., uniforms) generally are not as deeply rooted, and voluntary participation reduces motivation problems. On the other hand, these programs face other issues, such as funding, student recruitment, staff turnover, and variable staff training and education (DeWitt Wallace–Reader's Digest Fund, 1996).

As incidence of violence, sex, drugs, and peer pressure escalate in after-school hours, extended-day programs have received more attention. One apparent result is the emergence of the field of youth development (DeWitt Wallace–Reader's Digest Fund, 1996; Hudson, 1997; Hughes & Curnan, 2000), which has sought to replace traditional community youth programs mostly limited to having fun in a safe environment. Youth development is perhaps best described by recent studies that identify common convictions and characteristics of successful extended-day youth development programs—recognition of student strengths and individuality, holistic (e.g., physical, cognitive-creative, psycho-social) student development and empowerment within an explicit set of values, and small class sizes that encourage a sense of belonging and participation over a long period (Hellison & Cutforth, 1997; McLaughlin, 2000).

Unfortunately, this youth development approach often fails because its holistic agenda is broader than the existing youth services framework into which it must fit (National Clearinghouse on Families and Youth, 1996). In particular, these youth development criteria are absent in most sport programs (Kahne et al., 1998; Lawson, 1994), although the one sport program in the Kahne et al. study that teaches personal and social responsibility did reflect a youth development orientation (see also Walsh, 1999).

Perhaps the most important advantage of extended-day programs is the flexibility to change program structure. The following program structures, which are described at length elsewhere (Hellison et al., 2000), have been created or adapted specifically for teaching personal and social responsibility.

- Coaching clubs are before- or after-school team sport clubs in which members play games only with other club members. Club membership is restricted to no more than 15 students, but students of all skill levels, both boys and girls, are welcome. Club members learn not only how to play the sport, especially team offense and defense, but also how to control their temper and mouths, how to coach themselves and each other, how to solve conflicts, and how to make a variety of proactive sport-related and nonsport decisions that help all members have a positive experience.

- Other clubs may form around nonteam sport activities such as fitness, martial arts, outdoor and adventure activities, tennis, and a variety of physical activities (e.g., a sport or exercise club).

- Cross-age teaching and coaching programs place advanced students in leadership roles with younger students, in which they help conduct awareness talks, group meetings, and reflection times as well as provide leadership in lessons.

- The neighborhood scholar program funds postsecondary education and youth work internships for former cross-age leaders and club or program members. The career club and career night help younger club and program members explore possible futures, another characteristic of youth development.

IMPLICATIONS OF THE RESEARCH FOR PRACTICE

Evidence of one kind or another supports everything reported in this chapter. But what evidence really counts? Program evaluation research, despite its popularity, is rife with uncertainties and debates (e.g., Cook, 2000; Schön, 1990). Personal and social development outcomes are especially difficult to evaluate (McLaughlin & Heath, 1993), to the point that McLaughlin (2000) argues for more emphasis on evaluation of process—for example, attendance, climate, and program focus. Dealing with such "softer" outcomes involves complex issues such as changes that occur inside kids rather than observable behavior (Shabazz in Ascher, 1992), as well as the "sleeper effect," that is, changes that don't occur until years later (Lickona, 1991).

Tom (1984), McDonald (1992), and Kliebard (1993) offer compelling arguments for approaching curriculum work as a craft, and Kirk (1993) and Georgiadis (1992) apply this notion to the responsibility model, praising the reflective, craft-oriented process of its development. Much of the evidence in support of the responsibility model is based on my reflective fieldwork over the past 30 years as well as that of many other teachers, youth workers, and scholar activists (e.g., Hellison et al., 2000). Martinek and I (1997) developed a hybrid research approach, service-bonded inquiry, to describe the craft process.

Several studies have investigated the outcomes of responsibility-based physical activity programs (e.g., Compagnone, 1995; Cutforth & Puckett, 1999; DeBusk & Hellison, 1989; Eddy, 1998; Galvan, 2000; Hellison, 1978; Kallusky, 1997; Lifka, 1989). As a result, considerable qualitative evidence shows that students in responsibility model programs learn, experience, and practice the goals and the empowerment process while participating in these programs, although weaker evidence suggests that the model has influenced students' lives outside physical activity.

Recently, mixed methodology (Tashakkori & Teddlie, 1998), which combines quantitative and qualitative methods, has been used to explore the effect of the responsibility model. Cummings (1998), for example, found that responsibility-based coaching club participants dropped out of high school far less often than did students in their classes at school who did not participate in the coaching club. Her study—as well as the work of Martinek and his associates (Martinek, Schilling, & Johnson, 2001), the extended-day program studies of Walsh (1999) and Wright (1998), and Keramidas's (1991) study of an organized sport program in Greece—demonstrated that quantitative data can be useful in assessing outcomes of responsibility-based programs, especially in concert with qualitative data.

Adoptions of the responsibility model have spread beyond the United States to several other countries, for example, the successful Northern Fly-In Sports Camps serving native Canadians in northern Manitoba (Searle, Winther, & Reed, 1994). From England, David Kirk (1992, p. 4) makes this point about the contribution of the responsibility model to social problems: "Hellison . . . [offers] genuinely alternative forms of social organization in physical education classes in an attempt to constructively redress the social conditions placing some young people's well-being at risk."

WHAT'S WORTH DOING?

Classroom management and rhetoric about building character through sport and exercise are ineffective in addressing the social problems and needs of kids today. Teaching personal and social responsibility is one of several approaches that hold promise for doing more to help youngsters grow personally and socially. Based on three decades of field experience and numerous studies and reflections by teachers, youth workers, and scholars, the responsibility model offers ideas for teaching kids to take more responsibility for their well-being and their relationships with others. Putting this approach into practice, however, demands more than how-to knowledge. It requires reflecting on the question "What's worth doing?"

Certainly, fundamental social, economic, and political changes are necessary to create a more hospitable environment for teaching responsibility. But some of us, whether such changes are forthcoming or not, will continue to press our case with kids as Margaret Mead has urged us to do. For us, it's what's worth doing.

IMPLICATIONS FOR PRACTICE

Teaching personal and social responsibility through physical activity includes several essential points:

1. The curricular purpose should include taking personal responsibility for one's own well-being and social responsibility for contributing to the well-being of others.

2. The teacher should be able to recognize and respect students' strengths, individuality, voices, and capacity for decision making.

3. The teacher must master two sets of content, physical activity and personal-social responsibility, and integrate them into each lesson.

4. The lesson plan format as well as existing strategies (or newly created ones) should gradually empower students to take more responsibility individually and collectively.

5. The teacher should progressively introduce specific responsibilities—respect for the rights and feelings of others, effort and motivation, self-direction, and helping and leadership.

6. The teacher should gradually introduce the concept of transferring these responsibilities outside the gym to other areas of students' lives so that they at least try out these responsibilities to see if they work better than what they had been doing.

7. These guidelines can be (and have been) implemented in both in-school physical education and extended-day youth programs.

8. For in-school physical education, assessments should gradually involve students in self-assessment.

REFERENCES

Ascher, C. (1992). School programs for African-American males . . . and females. *Phi Delta Kappan, 73,* 777-782.

Ayers, W. (1989). *The good preschool teacher: Six teachers reflect on their lives.* New York: Teachers College Press.

Benson, P.L. (1997). *All kids are our kids: What communities must do to raise caring and responsible children and adolescents.* San Francisco: Jossey-Bass.

Carnegie Council on Adolescent Development (1992). A matter of time: Risk and opportunity in the nonschool hours. *Report of the task force on youth development and community programs.* New York: Carnegie Corporation of New York.

Compagnone, N. (1995, May/June). Teaching responsibility to rural elementary youth: Going beyond the at-risk boundaries. *Journal of Physical Education, Recreation and Dance, 66,* 58-63.

Cook, T.D. (2000). The false choice between theory-based evaluation and experimentation. In P.J. Rogers, T.A. Hasci, A. Petrosino, & T.A. Huebner (Eds.), *Program theory in evaluation: Challenges and opportunities* (pp. 27-34). San Francisco: Jossey-Bass.

Cummings, T.K. (1998). *Testing the effectiveness of Hellison's personal and social responsibility model: A dropout, repeated grade, and absentee rate comparison.* Unpublished master's thesis, California State University, Chico.

Cutforth, N., & Puckett, K. (1999). An investigation into the organization, challenges, and impact of an urban apprentice teacher program. *Urban Review, 31,* 153-172.

DeBusk, M., & Hellison, D. (1989). Implementing a physical education self-responsibility model for delinquency-prone youth. *Journal of Teaching in Physical Education, 8,* 104-112.

Des Dixon, R.G. (1994). Future schools and how to get there from here. *Phi Delta Kappan, 75,* 360-365.

DeWitt Wallace–Reader's Digest Fund (1996). *Strengthening the youth work profession.* New York: DeWitt Wallace–Reader's Digest Fund.

Eddy, M. (1998). The role of physical activity in educational violence prevention programs (Doctoral dissertation, Columbia University Teachers College, 1998). *Dissertation Abstracts International, 59-10,* A3771.

Galvan, C. (2000). *The impact of the responsibility model on underserved elementary students in physical education classes: A university-community collaboration.* Unpublished master's thesis, California State University, Los Angeles.

Garbarino, J., Dubrow, N., Kostelny, K., & Pardo, C. (1991). *Children in danger: Coping with the consequences of community violence.* San Francisco: Jossey-Bass.

Georgiadis, N. (1992). *Practical inquiry in physical education: The case of Hellison's personal and social responsibility model.* Unpublished PhD dissertation, University of Illinois at Chicago.

Hellison, D. (1978). *Beyond balls and bats: Alienated (and other) youth in the gym.* Washington, DC: American Association of Health, Physical Education, & Recreation.

Hellison, D. (1995). *Teaching responsibility through physical activity.* Champaign, IL: Human Kinetics.

Hellison, D., & Cutforth, N. (1997). Extended day programs for urban children and youth: From theory to practice. In H.J. Walberg, O. Reyes, & R.P. Weissberg (Eds.), *Children and youth: Interdisciplinary perspectives* (pp. 223-249). Thousand Oaks, CA: Sage.

Hellison, D., Cutforth, N., Kallusky, J., Martinek, T., Parker, M., & Stiehl, J. (2000). *Youth development and physical activity: Linking universities and communities.* Champaign, IL: Human Kinetics.

Hudson, S.D. (1997, November/ December). Helping youth grow. *Journal of Physical Education, Recreation and Dance, 68,* 16-17.

Hughes, D.M., & Curnan, S.P. (2000). Community youth development: A framework for action. *Community Youth Development Journal, 1,* 7-13.

Ianni, F.A.J. (1989). *The search for structure: A report on American youth today.* New York: Macmillan.

Kahne, J., Nagaoka, J., Brown, A., O'Brien, J., Quinn, T., & Thiede, K. (1998). *A comparison of school-day and after-school programs in terms of supports for youth development.* Unpublished report from the Center of Urban Educational Research and Development, University of Illinois at Chicago.

Kallusky, J. (1997). *Constructing an urban sanctuary for at-risk youth in physical education: An artistically crafted research project in an inner city high school.* Unpublished doctoral dissertation, University of Northern Colorado.

Keramidas, K. (1991). *Strategies to increase the individual motivation and cohesiveness of a junior male basketball team.* Unpublished master's thesis, University of Illinois at Chicago.

Kirk, D. (1992). *Articulations and silences in socially critical research on physical education: Towards a new agenda.* Paper presented at the Australian Association for Research in Education Annual Conference, Geelong, Australia.

Kirk, D. (1993). Curriculum work in physical education: Beyond the objectives approach? *Journal of Teaching in Physical Education, 12,* 244-265.

Kliebard, H.M. (1993). What is a knowledge base, and who would use it if we had one? *Review of Educational Research, 63,* 295-303.

Lawson, H.A. (1994). *International changes and challenges: Their import for new models for practice.* Paper presented at AIESEP World Congress, Berlin, Germany.

Lickona, T. (1991). *Educating for character: How our schools can teach respect and responsibility.* New York: Bantam.

Lifka, R. (1989). *Implementing an after-school alternative wellness/activities program for at-risk Hispanic youth.* Unpublished master's thesis, University of Illinois at Chicago.

Martinek, T., & Hellison, D. (1997). Service-bonded inquiry: The road less traveled. *Journal of Teaching in Physical Education, 17,* 107-121.

Martinek, T., Schilling, T., & Johnson, D. (2001). Transferring personal and social responsibility of underserved youth to the classroom. *Urban Review, 33,* 29-45.

McDonald, J.P. (1992). *Teaching: Making sense of an uncertain craft.* New York: Teachers College Press.

McLaughlin, M.W. (2000). *Community counts.* Washington, DC: Public Education Network.

McLaughlin, M.W., & Heath, S.B. (1993). Casting the self. Frames for identity and dilemmas for policy. In S.B. Heath & M.W. McLaughlin (Eds.), *Identity and inner city youth: Beyond ethnicity and gender* (pp. 210-239). New York: Teachers College Press.

Mosston, M., & Ashworth, S. (2002). *Physical education: From intent to action.* Columbus, OH: Merrill.

National Clearinghouse on Families and Youth (1996). *Reconnecting youth and communities: A youth development approach.* Washington, DC: U.S. Department of Health and Human Services.

Schön, D.A. (1990). *Educating the reflective practitioner: Toward a new design for teaching and learning in the professions.* San Francisco: Jossey-Bass.

Searle, M.S., Winther, N.R., & Reed, M. (1994). *An assessment of the daily life experiences of Native youth: Implications for Northern Fly-In Sports Camps, Inc.* Winnipeg, MB: Health, Leisure, and Human Performance Research Institute, University of Manitoba.

Sizer, T.R. (1992). *Horace's school: Redesigning the American high school.* Boston: Houghton Mifflin.

Tashakkori, A., & Teddlie, C. (1998). *Mixed methodology: Combining qualitative and quantitative approaches.* Thousand Oaks, CA: Sage.

Tom, A.R. (1984). *Teaching as a moral craft*. New York: Longman.

Walberg, H.J., Reyes, O., & Weissberg, R.P. (Eds.) (1997). *Children and youth: Interdisciplinary perspectives*. Thousand Oaks, CA: Sage.

Walsh, D. (1999). *A comparative analysis of extended day programs for inner city youth*. Unpublished master's thesis, University of Illinois at Chicago.

Weiner, L. (1993). *Preparing teachers for urban schools: Lessons from thirty years of school reform*. New York: Teachers College Press.

Wright, P.M. (1998). *The impact of a responsibility-based martial arts program on violence prevention*. Unpublished master's thesis, University of Illinois at Chicago.

CHAPTER FIFTEEN

INTERDISCIPLINARY CURRICULUM IN PHYSICAL EDUCATION: POSSIBILITIES AND PROBLEMS

Judith H. Placek

When the words *interdisciplinary curriculum in physical education* are used, what type of curriculum is envisioned? Consider the following examples:

- Teaching a Korean folk dance in a fifth-grade social studies unit on other cultures
- Offering a course titled "Personal Fitness" as part of a high school PE curriculum
- Teaching Newton's laws in a PE soccer unit
- Using prominent sports figures as examples in a middle school interdisciplinary unit on heroes and heroines
- Teaching reading as a part of a fundamental movement unit
- Studying the opportunities for sport and recreation in students' own city as a part of a unit examining problems of modern cities

Are these all examples of interdisciplinary curriculum? In this chapter I will address that question by reviewing the idea of interdisciplinary curriculum and discussing the main issues among theorists who write about curriculum integration. I will then discuss the state of interdisciplinary PE through a review of selected literature, including curriculum models and research. Finally, I will consider the possibilities and potential problems arising from the adoption of an interdisciplinary curriculum and how teachers and teacher educators might begin to implement an interdisciplinary curriculum.

BRIEF HISTORY

Although the concept of interdisciplinarity can be traced to Plato (Klein, 1990), the term itself did not emerge until the 20th century, and the brief review that follows will be limited to this latter period. Tanner, using the term *integrative*, describes the ebb and flow of the integrative tide over the years—calls for integration alternating with the proposals for a return to basics (Tanner, 1989, 1992). In the early 20th century influential progressives such as John Dewey and Alfred North Whitehead recognized the need for integrative education. Shortly thereafter, the results of the Eight Year Study (from 1933 to 1941) were published. This work is often cited as one of the first studies showing positive results for integration. Students with an integrative education, based, for example, on a problem-focused core curriculum, were found to score better on a number of factors (e.g., attitude toward learning, success in college) than were students pursuing a traditional college preparation program (Aikin, 1942). Aikin notes, however, that although the results looked good on paper, a number of problems occurred in practice (e.g., attempts to integrate mathematics and science were unsuccessful, and English became subservient to history).

Post-World War II America, however, saw a back-to-basics movement. Then, because of Soviet achievements, education in the 1950s and 1960s emphasized math, science, and foreign languages. Educators eventually realized that these efforts at "new math" and "new physics" had not produced the promised results and again began thinking of integrative formats. In the 1960s campus unrest related to the civil rights movement and the Vietnam War sparked a call for curriculum "relevance." Although elective courses in both colleges and high schools were added in response to these demands, the additions did not change the basic offerings. The disciplines remained the primary basis for curriculum structure in secondary schools. The mid-1970s saw dwindling concern for relevance, and the perceived "Japanese challenge" lent new energy to the isolation of disciplines in the back-to-basics movement through the 1980s and into the 1990s.

Although many curriculum writers are currently encouraging interdisciplinary and integrative curriculum, many states are taking quite the opposite approach by implementing high-stakes testing (e.g., Massachusetts Comprehensive Assessment System). Most states test students by individual subjects such as history and math. So, deliberations about an interdisciplinary or integrated curriculum continue. Teachers (especially middle school teams) and university faculty promote interdisciplinary curriculum, but the political reality of subject matter tests often drives curriculum (George, 2000–2001; Renyi, 2000).

DEFINING INTEGRATION

Although many terms (e.g., *multidisciplinary, cross-disciplinary, interdisciplinary, integrative*) are used to describe the broad idea of cutting across disciplinary boundaries, two terms, *integrative* and *interdisciplinary*, are used most often in the education literature. Although, in general, *interdisciplinary* denotes the use of more than one discipline in pursuing a particular topic, that is, the linking of existing categories or disciplines, *integration* is understood to describe a higher, more powerful conceptual synthesis or unity between forms of knowledge and their respective disciplines. Agreement is lacking, however, on actual definitions of these terms. Grossman, Wineburg, and Beers (2000) note that "the problem is not a shortage of schemes . . . but rather the inability of any one of these schemes to impose conceptual order among multiple audiences" (p. 10).

Most schemes or models for integration present integration as a continuum beginning with subjects taught as separate disciplines (nonintegration), continuing to complete integration of all subjects (Fogarty, 1991; Jacobs, 1989; Vars, 1987). The models differ considerably in their complexity, suggesting a varying number of intermediate stages between the two poles. For example, Vars's model (1987) suggests 3 stages (correlation, fusion, and core); Jacobs (1989) has 6 stages (disciplines, parallel, complementary, interdisciplinary, integrated day, and complete day); Fogarty (1991) tops the list with 10 stages (fragmented, connected, nested, sequenced, shared, webbed, threaded, integrated, immersed, and networked).

James Beane (1995, 1997), an influential voice on the topic of integration, provides a strong critique of the various models of integration that merely correlate several subjects, sometimes around a specific theme. He considers this type of integration a limited and flawed approach to integration because he defines integration as a "curriculum design that is concerned with enhancing the possibilities for personal and social integration through the organization of curriculum around significant problems and issues, collaboratively identified by educators and young people, without regard for subject-area boundaries" (p. x). This definition offers a far more complex and encompassing view of integration because it emphasizes organizing themes that have personal and social significance to students and collaborative planning between teachers and students.

Erickson (1998) and Glasgow (1997) also endorse the importance of a coherent integrated curriculum driven by conceptual themes. Concepts, or what Beane calls "big ideas" such as pollution, technology, leadership, conflict-cooperation, and beliefs-values, are suggested as themes that are relevant to students and useful in developing the knowledge and skills they need for the present and in the future (Beane, 1997; Erickson, 1998; Glasgow, 1997). Thus, a truly integrated curriculum must go beyond themes such as dinosaurs or colonial America. As Beane (1997) notes,

> organizing centers that are not related to significant self and social issues may be interesting, fun, exciting, and even likely context for correlating separate-subject content, but they will not do if we really mean to engage in curriculum integration. (p. 15)

This type of concept-driven curriculum is clearly at one end of the continuum of writers' definitions of an integrated curriculum. Most attempts to integrate curriculum, especially in physical education, are examples of interdisciplinary curriculum at various levels (e.g., connected, sequenced). Thus, the term *interdisciplinary* will be used because most examples in this chapter do not meet Beane's definition of an integrated curriculum. Note, however, that separating perfectly integrative efforts from those that are interdisciplinary is difficult.

INTERNAL INTERDISCIPLINARY CURRICULUM IN PHYSICAL EDUCATION

Fogarty (1991) states that "both integration within a discipline and integration across disciplines are necessary to fully integrate the curricula" (p. xiv). Authors who try to define interdisciplinary or integrated curriculum in physical education view integration from both perspectives—primarily as internal or intradisciplinary (Kirk, Burgess-Limerick, Kiss, Lahey, & Penney, 1999; Mohnsen, 1998), as external or across disciplines (Cone, Werner, Cone, & Woods,1998), or as an idea that includes both designs (Housner, 2000; Placek, 1996). Although integrating physical education with other subjects such as science and history (external) is relatively easy to understand, integrating within our own subject matter (internal) requires some consideration of our subject matter and possible topics for integration (see table 15.1).

During the past 30 years, enormous changes have taken place in physical education departments in colleges and universities. Physical education evolved from a major that focused on sport skill instruction and training physical education teachers to a multifaceted configuration that includes specialized study in subdisciplines (e.g., sport psychology, biomechanics) and a variety of career options, such as athletic training and sport management. The change in names from Department of Physical Education to

TABLE 15.1 ██

TYPES OF INTERDISCIPLINARY PHYSICAL EDUCATION

Internal
(expands goals of physical education beyond physical activity and a physically active lifestyle)

- Movement concepts & principles
- Responsible personal & social behavior
- Enjoyment, challenge, & self expression

External
(linking physical education with other subjects)

- Physical education content into other subjects
- Others subjects into physical education
- Integrated curriculum

Department of Kinesiology or Department of Exercise and Sport Studies indicates the evolving nature of physical education in higher education.

Physical education in the schools remained virtually untouched by this evolution as it retained a multiactivity model (Napper-Owen, Kovar, Ermler, & Mehrhof, 1999; Siedentop, Mand, & Taggart, 1986), particularly in the secondary schools. The multiactivity model is a curriculum organized around a series of short units in which the skills and strategies of sports and games are taught. Although different models for thinking about how to teach these sports have been proposed (e.g., Rink, 2002; Siedentop, 1994: Vickers, 1990), sport skill classes in secondary schools today look much the same as they did 25 years ago. Elementary physical education typically focuses on basic skills, sports, and games but also has explored a number of different models (e.g., movement education, skill themes, teaching for understanding). Although some programs incorporate fitness, K–12 physical education continues to focus on sport skills and games.

This disjuncture in scope between physical education at the college level and the continuing K–12 focus on sports and games has limited students' opportunities to learn about the wide-ranging current body of knowledge in physical education. Although physical education goals traditionally have included psychomotor, cognitive, and affective objectives, in reality psychomotor skills relating to sports and games have dominated our curriculum. Thinking about expanding students' experiences in physical education to include the current broad knowledge base in physical education helps to define internal interdisciplinary physical education. For the purposes of this chapter, an internal interdisciplinary curriculum in physical education will be defined as curricula that expand the goals of physical education beyond teaching students motor skills, games, and sports and encouraging a physically active lifestyle. Interdisciplinary curriculum can include concepts from the disciplinary base of physical education such as exercise science, biomechanics, sport psychology, or sport sociology or incorporate other goals such as personal development or social interaction.

Since the first edition of this chapter was published (Placek, 1996), written material focused on interdisciplinary curriculum in physical education has increased exponentially. Although material promoting and suggesting ways of integrating the disciplinary base of physical education into K–12 curricula had been available for more than 20 years (Dodds, 1987; Hoffman, Young, & Klesius, 1981; Kneer, 1981; Lawson & Placek 1981), much of the impetus for this recent interest can be traced to the National Association of Sport and Physical Education (NASPE) standards for physical education (1995; see chapter 8 by Leslie Lambert for a listing of the standards). Although the degree of implementation of interdisciplinary curriculum in schools is not known, the amount of material available for teachers who want to design and teach interdisciplinary curriculum has increased dramatically. Curriculum developers have used the NASPE standards (1995) extensively to redefine the broad goals of physical education. Indeed, a number of state curriculum guidelines use the NASPE standards to structure their curriculum (e.g., Florida [www.firn.edu]; South Carolina [www.sde.state.sc.us]). Even states that do not use the NASPE standards have a variety of interdisciplinary goals (e.g., Missouri, California, Washington, Montana). The main purpose of physical education is no longer considered to be teaching sports and games with a few fitness activities thrown in for good measure. A broad consensus at the national level is that learning and applying concepts, demonstrating responsible personal and social behavior, and demonstrating understanding and respect for a variety of people should be an integral part of physical education (NASPE, 1995).

Recently published student textbooks with accompanying teacher's editions include a great deal of interdisciplinary material (e.g., Spindt, Monti, & Hennessy, 1997; Weinberg, Monti, Spindt, Hennessy, & Holyoak, 2002a, 2002b, 2002c). Mohnsen's book (1998), an updated version of the Basic Stuff series (Kneer, 1981) that suggested disciplinary content for integration, includes chapters on almost all the subdisciplines of our field—motor learning, motor development, biomechanics, exercise physiology, history, social psychology, and aesthetics. Articles with ideas for teaching interdisciplinary PE appear in the *Journal of Physical Education, Recreation and Dance (JOPERD)*, *Strategies*, and *Teaching Elementary Physical Education*.

Two physical education Web sites also offer additional options for accessing interdisciplinary curriculum. PELINKS4U (www.pelinks4u.org) includes a section on integrative physical education, and PE Central (www.pecentral.org) offers ideas for integrated lessons. Those interested in interdisciplinary curriculum don't have to look far or hard.

Internal Interdisciplinary Physical Education and the NASPE Standards

The next section will detail the most recent topics and concepts commonly suggested by physical educators for creating interdisciplinary physical education and report on research conducted in those areas. The NASPE standards provide a means of organizing the literature. First, literature relating to standard 2 (applies movement concepts and principles to the learning and development of motor skills) will be described. Second, standard 5 (demonstrates responsible personal and social behavior in physical activity settings) will be examined through the work of Hellison and others. Third, standard 7 (understands that physical activity provides opportunities for enjoyment, challenge, self-expression, and social interaction) will be examined through the adventure education model and others (e.g., Glover & Midura, 1992; Grineski, 1996).

Standard 2: Movement Concepts and Principles

The topic most often suggested for integrating movement concepts and principles appears to be physiology and fitness. All the textbooks mentioned previously include the topic, and many specific texts for students and teacher focus solely on fitness (e.g., Baker, 2001; Harris & Elbourn, 1997; *Physical Best*, 1999a, 1999b; Richmond, 2000). In addition, numerous articles are available on a variety of fitness topics. These include suggestions for secondary fitness units (Bycura & Darst, 2001; Ward, Everhart, Dunaway, Fisher, & Coates,1998), guidelines for strength training for children (Faigenbaum, 2001), and ways of assessing physical activity in PE (Beighle, Pangrazi, & Vincent, 2001; Deal & Deal, 1995; Welk & Wood, 2000). The number of resources available may overwhelm teachers looking for ideas for including fitness concepts in their curricula.

Other topics from subdisciplines such as biomechanics and sport psychology have received attention in books designed for teachers and students (e.g., Spindt et al., 1997; Mohnsen, 1998). But in contrast to information available on fitness in journals designed for teachers, such as *JOPERD*, almost no information is available suggesting how to teach these other concepts. Biomechanics is strangely absent from journal articles describing curriculum. Van Oteghen (1996) suggests using oral history interviews to enliven a college course in history and philosophy of education. The activity could easily be adapted for use in K–12 physical education.

Several current examples of a more integrated curricular approach engaging students in issues around sport and society are available. In a sports studies unit, high school students "reflected on their own physical activity biographies, reviewed and critiqued the sport culture of their high school, and addressed the role of sport in the larger society" (Placek & O'Sullivan, 1997, p. 22). This unit was refined and expanded to a cultural studies unit that students reported to be both relevant and significant (Kinchin & O'Sullivan, 1999). Another school developed a curriculum that included an exploration of various careers in health, sport, recreation, and allied medical fields (Placek & O'Sullivan, 1997).

Research on fitness and physical activity has received the most attention of any internal interdisciplinary topic in PE. See chapter 12 by Thom McKenzie for information about research conducted by physical educators and other health professionals.

With the exception of health-related fitness, almost no research has been done on this type of internal interdisciplinary curriculum in physical education. Thus, many of the questions asked in the first edition of this chapter remain unanswered. First and perhaps most fundamentally, we don't even know to what extent material from these subdisciplines is being taught in the schools. Although an early study on Basic Stuff indicated that the inclusion of concepts was limited (Placek, 1989), no recent regional or national studies have examined the implementation of this type of curriculum. Other possible questions include the following:

- What knowledge do students learn in an internal interdisciplinary curriculum?
- Are students able to apply the concepts to improve movement?
- Can concepts be taught without detriment to the development of psychomotor skills?
- Will students use the conceptual material later in life?
- What is the best way to teach concepts in different settings?
- Are teachers willing to change their teaching to include concepts?
- How will students respond to the integration of concepts into physical education?

These questions need answers because the NASPE standards, including learning and applying movement concepts, are now frequently cited as the appropriate yardstick for physical education in the United States.

Standard 5: Responsible Personal and Social Behavior

The topics included in standard 5 include cooperation and teamwork, ethical behavior, and positive social interactions. Curriculum writers and teachers have long promoted the capacity of physical education to promote these goals. In many cases, however, these goals were assumed to accrue through osmosis or incidental learning, that is, from students' participation and instruction in sports and games rather than through direct instruction (Espiritu, 1987; Hellison, 1995). This perspective seems to have changed recently. The literature now includes many more calls for teaching this material directly. Don Hellison's model for teaching personal and social responsibility is the best known work in this area. Hellison's chapter in this book, "Teaching Personal and Social Responsibility in Physical Education," provides a complete review of his ideas.

Review of the Literature.   Organizing the literature dealing with integrating topics such as cooperation and positive social interactions is analogous to herding cats—an unenviable task. Suggestions for teaching these topics appear in *JOPERD* articles dealing with moral development, character development, teaching fair play, responsibility, social skills, and cooperative learning (Butler, 2000; Fisher, 1998; Gough, 1998; McHugh, 1995; Parker, Kallusky, & Hellison, 1999; Solomon, 1997a, 1997b). Two terms occur most frequently—*cooperative learning* and *character development*.

The notion that physical education teaches cooperation has been part of our vocabulary for many years. Ideas for specifically teaching cooperation as a part of physical education are now widely available. Grineski's book, *Cooperative Learning in Physical Education* (1996), outlines the ingredients necessary for cooperative learning and provides examples of cooperative activities in games, dance, gymnastics, and fitness. The PE Central Web site offers a book summarizing many ideas for cooperative activities that were published on the Web site. Dyson and Grineski (2001) offer a brief review of the cooperative learning literature in general and specific ideas based on a number of different cooperative learning models.

Character development is considered important enough to warrant a three-part series in *JOPERD* (November/December 1997, January 1998, February 1998). Character development as a component of moral development is defined by Solomon (1997a) as the process individuals experience as they develop the capacity to reason about moral issues. Gough (1998) suggests that "well-organized sport and physical education activities can provide powerful contexts for teaching students about the development of good moral habits" (p. 18). The nature of character development becomes less clear, however, when Fisher (1998) describes a character education program encompassing topics such as respect, responsibility, cooperation, tolerance, trustworthiness, self-discipline , and caring. Character education in physical education is as muddy as the Yellowstone River during spring flood.

Research.   The term *cooperative learning* has a standard definition in the educational literature, from which rise many of the ideas in physical education. Although Dyson & Grineski (2001) note that research on cooperative learning in physical education is limited, there is no reason to believe that, if implemented properly, the benefits cited in the general education literature by Dyson and Grineski (e.g., higher achievement scores, improved group relations, increased ability to work with others) would not be found in physical education. In fact, Dyson (2001) noted benefits such as improved psychomotor and social skills cited by teachers and students after implementation of a curriculum including cooperative learning.

Two studies examining moral reasoning found that an intervention did produce an increase in indexes in moral development of elementary school students (Gibbons, Ebbeck, & Weiss, 1995; Romance, Weiss, & Bockoven, 1986). Although Solomon (1997a) cites several studies of character education that show an increase in students' moral reasoning after an intervention program, the studies were not published in peer-refereed research journals so their findings cannot be viewed with confidence. If our goals in physical education are to include topics such as those cited above, we need to clarify what we mean by character education and set a research agenda to examine what physical education can contribute to this area.

Standard 7: Enjoyment, Challenge, Self-Expression, and Social Interaction

The NASPE standards (1995) suggest that "physical activity can provide opportunity for self-expression and social interaction and can be enjoyable, challenging, and fun" (p. 4).

This potpourri of goals makes organizing literature on these topics difficult. One model that encompasses a number of these goals, however, has a long-standing body of literature—that of adventure education programs.

Adventure Education Program.   Adventure education (Rohnke, 1984, 1989; Rohnke & Butler, 1995) is a well-known model that includes goals such as increasing participants' sense of personal confidence, increasing mutual support within a group, and developing an increased joy in one's physical self and in being with others. Participants pursue these goals through various individual and group physical activities (games, stunts, initiative problems, trust activities, rope courses). The model, although developed as an alternative physical education curriculum, has been adapted and used in a number of different settings, including traditional academic settings, marriage and family therapy, adolescent counseling, and corporate training (Bronson, Gibson, Kichar, & Priest, 1992; Gillis, 1985; Gillis & Gass, 1993; Nassar-McMillan & Cashwell, 1997; Paling, 1984–85).

Several descriptions of adventure activities and programs in physical education are available in the literature. Halliday (1999) provides a comprehensive overview of components of challenge education. *Team Building Through Physical Challenges* (Glover & Midura, 1992) suggests that teamwork can help build a positive self-concept, help students learn different roles, and help develop team communication. Challenges at different levels such as "teamwork walk" and "the black hole" offer ideas for teachers. In other descriptions of school programs incorporating adventure education (O'Donnell, 1997; Panicucci, 2000), students, teachers, and administrators offer glowing reviews of the effects of these programs.

Research on Adventure Education.   Research on adventure education was reported in the late 1970s after two years of implementation at a single high school (Fersch & Smith, 1978). Although cautioning that the findings might be the result of many factors, the evaluation at the end of both years showed a number of positive changes in students' attitudes toward school, self-concept, and willingness to try new things.

Research on adventure education in physical education has increased over the past several years. Dyson (1995, 1996) reports on generally positive student and teacher perceptions of a Project Adventure curriculum in which the entire school curriculum of two magnet elementary schools was integrated around the five concepts of adventure education (risk, trust, cooperation, challenge, problem solving). Ebbeck and Gibbons (1998) provide data to show that sixth- and seventh-grade students who participated in the Team Building Through Physical Challenges program scored significantly higher on self-perceptions of global self-worth, athletic competence, physical appearance, and social acceptance than a control group did.

Summary of Internal Interdisciplinary Curriculum in Physical Education

Although material about interdisciplinary physical education has been available for many years, I believe that the emphasis of the NASPE standards on a variety of objectives besides traditional sports and games has been influential in promoting interdisciplinary physical education. A great deal of material is now readily available for curriculum writers and teachers who want to develop and implement an interdisciplinary physical education curriculum. Research in this area also is increasing, although at a less accelerated pace. Researchers and teachers need to work together to design studies in school settings to show the effects of this type of curriculum.

EXTERNAL INTERDISCIPLINARY PHYSICAL EDUCATION: PHYSICAL EDUCATION AND OTHER SCHOOL SUBJECTS

The linking of physical education with other subjects may be thought about in three ways—first, the incorporation of physical education content (however defined) into other subjects, second, the addition of material from other subjects into physical education, and third, a truly integrated curriculum that uses themes to address a number of subjects. The distinction between the categories, although somewhat artificial, is important to consider. Is an interdisciplinary curriculum defined as teaching material related to physical education in other subject areas or using the physical education environment as a means of teaching concepts from math, science, or language arts? Or are the subjects truly integrated rather than interdisciplinary with themes or big ideas driving the curriculum? The following review, although not exhaustive, provides a representative sampling of the recent available literature.

Review of the Literature

Certainly, there is no lack of literature written by physical educators showcasing ideas about how physical education can help teach content from other subjects. Authors suggest ways of incorporating other subjects into a movement environment, and their ideas range from helping students learn the alphabet by making letters with their bodies to understanding fractions by using a parachute.

Two recent books provide an array of ideas for including material from other subjects into physical education (Cone et al., 1998; Housner, 2000). *Integrated Physical Education: A Guide for the Elementary Classroom Teacher* (Housner, 2000), designed for elementary classroom teachers who may be required to teach physical education, includes ideas for teaching fitness, fundamental movement, education rhythms and dance, educational gymnastics, and educational games and sport. The chapters include short sections that suggest ways to integrate academic content into physical education lessons. For example, concepts related to base of support and center of gravity can be taught in educational gymnastics, and students can read and write about sport as part of a sport education unit.

Interdisciplinary Teaching Through Physical Education (Cone et al., 1998) is a comprehensive text designed for physical education teachers, although teachers of any subject could get ideas for active learning. The book offers hundreds of activities to help teachers include language arts, mathematics, science, social studies, music, theater arts, and visual arts in a physical education curriculum. Most chapters also include a section reviewing research on integrating physical education and that subject.

Some authors have refined their view of the role of physical education in working with other subjects. Although the time-worn idea of incorporating physical education into social studies by teaching games and dances from holidays or other eras or cultures is still popular (Buell & Reekie, 1993; Troisi, 1995), writers dealing with literacy and mathematics make different theoretical cases for including their topics as part of physical education. For example, literacy skills are suggested to be an integral part of content literacy—the ability to use reading and writing for the acquisition of new content in physical education (Buell & Whittaker, 2001). Block (2001) suggests that motor-learning theory can be used to support reading in physical education. And working on spatial ability and awareness in physical education has been suggested as a way of improving the teaching of mathematics (Lambdin & Lambdin, 1995; Nilges & Usnick, 2000).

Thus, curriculum writers have become more sophisticated in their understanding of how physical activity and other subjects can work in concert to promote student learning.

Research

Although a wide range of material is available for physical educators who wish to include other subjects in physical education or attempt to work with other teachers to implement physical education activities into their classrooms, research on external integration has not kept pace with ideas for interdisciplinary curriculum. The limited research cited in the first edition of this chapter (Placek, 1996) showed mixed results with generalization because many different academic and physical education related variables were measured. Only a few studies can be added here. Two studies examined the integration of language and physical education. Owens and Yoder (1999) studied the integration of literacy with music, visual arts, and physical education to see if the reading and writing skills of low-achieving first graders would improve. Although they reported generally favorable results, problems with study design (e.g., no control group) make interpretation difficult. On the other hand, a well-designed study by Connor-Kuntz & Dummer (1996) found that the addition of language instruction to physical activity settings for four- to six-year-olds did not require additional instructional time and did not affect improvement in motor-skill performance.

One article described a truly integrated program in Ontario in which 12th grade students enrolled in four courses that made up their curriculum for the semester: environmental science, physical education, English, and human relations–peer helping. The program was conducted on an integrated basis. In the physical education part of the program, students prepared for and participated in outdoor activities such as a wilderness canoe trip, snowshoeing, backpacking, cycling, and rock climbing (Patterson, 1995). Research reported on this program showed that students felt that integration was not merely because of the combining of subjects but that complete process, authenticity, community, and responsibility were the critical factors that cut across the subjects (Horwood, 1994).

The need for more studies seems clear. For example, in what ways does the subject matter affect its integration with physical education? Will results differ depending on where the integration takes place (physical education or the classroom)? What are the benefits for physical education if it is included in a true integrated (rather than interdisciplinary) program? The major problem in this type of research may prove to be methodological. It may be impossible to confirm differences based on standard forms of experimental research for multifaceted processes like integration.

PROBLEMS AND POSSIBILITIES IN INTERDISCIPLINARY PHYSICAL EDUCATION CURRICULUM

Interdisciplinary physical education offers many possibilities for students, teachers, administrators, and parents. But along with the possibilities are problems. In this section, I will outline the possibilities and problems.

Possibilities

Given the long tradition of discrete disciplines and the enormous effort required to design, implement, and evaluate any type of interdisciplinary curriculum, what arguments are used to promote the use of interdisciplinary curriculum? First, the rate of knowledge growth and the finite time available for students to learn that knowledge requires us to rethink the way we select appropriate content for the curriculum. If we add new knowledge to the curriculum, we must decide what to eliminate (Jacobs, 1989). An integrated curriculum should "condense" the subject matter and thus provide a significant improvement in economy.

Second, the isolation and fragmentation of knowledge represented by a traditional curriculum does not match real life. The world outside school doesn't exist in discrete, disciplinary chunks, and real problems don't come in neat, discipline-bound packages that require a change of location and mind-set every 40 minutes (Cone et al., 1998; Grossman et al., 2000; Jacobs, 1989; Tanner, 1989).

Third, an integrated curriculum may help overcome the common complaint of students that school is irrelevant to their lives. Integrating school subjects and emphasizing their connection to the larger world will help students see the value of school and learning (Cone et al., 1998; Jacobs, 1989; Werner, 1996).

Additional reasons include the idea that administrators, teachers, and parents may value interdisciplinary curriculum because it is seen as progressive and being the forefront of education (Wineburg & Grossman, 2000). In addition, Werner (1996) suggests that interdisciplinary curriculum can enhance and enrich student learning, and Wineburg and Grossman (2000) suggest that teachers may benefit because working with others combats the traditional culture of privatism that had been the norm in schools. We should recognize that although the sincerity of these arguments cannot be doubted, their veracity has been little tested in schools.

What possibilities does an interdisciplinary curriculum offer to physical education? What reasons, other than those offered earlier, support the inclusion of physical education in interdisciplinary curriculum efforts? One reason is the marginal status of physical education in our schools. In a previous paper (Placek, 1992) I suggested that one way of alleviating our marginality in middle schools is by working toward an integrated curriculum. Dyson's (1994) study of two elementary schools that were organized around the principles of adventure education support this view.

Why might this be beneficial? Integration, both internal and external, may force us to examine our subject matter and define both our unique contribution to the schools and areas in which we reinforce common schools goals. The publication of the NASPE standards (1995) and subsequent curriculum revisions by many states to include the interdisciplinary ideas in the standards have already begun the process of internal integration, at least on paper. If the written curriculum is enacted, students will have richer learning experiences and increase their knowledge about physical education.

External integration, which forces us to work with teachers of other subjects, may force more introspection. Although physical educators may fool themselves into thinking that they have created an interdisciplinary curriculum by adding a new activity to "meet student needs" or by requiring students to cooperate on a team, developing curriculum with other teachers will require the examination and explanation of the basic assumptions behind physical education. Perhaps other teachers will come to view us not just as "gym teachers" but as contributors to all-school goals. In addition, students may come to see physical education as an important and legitimate part of the school curriculum and life rather than as a subject they don't consider "real" (Carlson, 1994).

Potential Problems

This section considers potential problems for teachers, teacher education programs and teacher educators, preservice teachers, and students if interdisciplinary curricula is developed and implemented.

Teachers

Physical education teachers have a number of obstacles to overcome in developing an interdisciplinary curriculum. They must believe that it is in the interest of both themselves and their students, and they must have time to plan and implement a curriculum that may be vastly different from their current one. Many physical education teachers coach and, indeed, became teachers because teaching is the only route to coaching. Therefore, coaching receives most of their time and attention, and they relegate physical education to secondary status. Physical education teachers also have little experience in designing and teaching either an internal or an external interdisciplinary curriculum. Expecting a level of sophistication beyond rudimentary linking of topics (e.g., dances of other countries) therefore seems optimistic. Given the knowledge obsolescence that occurs (Kelly & Lindsay, 1980; Kneer, 1986) and the constant flood of new knowledge, teachers must be willing to devote time to professional development to keep current.

The fact that teachers have not been trained to think about, develop, or teach an interdisciplinary or integrated curriculum (internal or external) presents a formidable set of constraints. For example, working with other teachers requires more than good social skills to solve problems that arise. Significant differences may arise due to teachers' different understanding of the subjects they are attempting to integrate. Wineburg and Grossman (2000) discovered that integrating even such seemingly closely related subjects as English and history was extraordinarily difficult because the teachers tended to cast their disagreements as personality conflicts rather than understanding the deep epistemological differences in how they interpreted their subject.

In conjunction with these strongly held views of their discipline, teachers' identities, particularly in secondary schools, are strongly associated with departments. This often unacknowledged role that departments play in teachers' identity can impede attempts to develop interdisciplinary curriculum (Siskin, 1995; Wineburg & Grossman, 1998). The combination of disciplinary understanding and departmental loyalty offer a possible explanation about why external interdisciplinary curriculum development and teaching can be so difficult for physical education. Because physical education is really a multidisciplinary field, physical education teachers may not hold a strongly disciplinary view, but if other teachers regard physical education as only "gym," the potential for misunderstanding is enormous.

Two interrelated concerns may also contribute to problems teachers see in implementing an interdisciplinary curriculum. First, teachers may fear that their content will not be covered. Second, they may worry that their subject will become the handmaiden of another (Allen, 1996; Brophy & Alleman, 1991; Werner, 1996). For example, in a fifth-grade interdisciplinary language arts and social studies curriculum, social studies dominated the curriculum; in a science and math integration, science drove the curriculum (Applebee, Burroughs, & Cruz, 2000).

Teacher Education Programs

Teacher education programs might require significant modifications to teach students about interdisciplinary curricula. Programs could take a significant first step by basing part of their curriculum on the national standards and teaching preservice students how to teach to those goals. Besides making changes in teacher education programs, teacher educators need more professional development. How many teacher educators are knowledgeable about interdisciplinary and integrative curriculum, much less knowledgeable about the best way to teach preservice teachers to develop, teach, and evaluate this type of curriculum (Lawson, 1993)?

Preservice teachers perceive a number of the disciplinary-based classes (in particular, sociocultural courses) as not relevant to their future roles as teachers because knowledge from these courses is not easily applied to performance (Dewar, 1987; Macdonald &

Tinning, 1995). In addition, these classes usually are not taught in a manner that allows easy transfer of their content knowledge to pedagogical content knowledge. In other words, how are preservice students expected to figure out how to teach biomechanics to K–12 students, much less envision how to integrate it with other subject matter in the schools? Given what we know about why students choose to teach physical education (e.g., stay associated with sport, coach, continue participation in sport) (Dodds et al., 1992), what is the likelihood they would accept or be interested in teaching this different, interdisciplinary version of physical education? One discouraging clue comes from a study by O'Brien & Stewart (1990), which indicates that physical education majors may resist teaching subject matter other than physical education.

Student Issues

Even if the issues surrounding teachers and teacher education programs can be resolved, students' expectations of physical education as a nonacademic subject may be the most difficult barrier to overcome. Students who view physical education as requiring only dressing out and participating may resist an academic component to the program, whether through internal or external integration (Cothran & Ennis, 2001; Lawson & Placek, 1981; Macdonald & Leitch, 1994). We know that teachers view students as a major influence on their teaching. Thus, if students are unhappy with an interdisciplinary or integrated curriculum, teachers may quickly abandon it as unworkable. Ironically, in my opinion, students may be less resistant if academic topics from physical education are integrated into other subjects rather than internally integrated into physical education.

Perhaps recitation of these problems paints an overpessimistic picture. Given the increase in available ideas and lesson plans and the NASPE standards, a number of leaders, teachers, and curriculum developers have been enthusiastic about developing interdisciplinary curricula. The picture is much less clear if we ask for proof that such curricula have been implemented and accepted by students and teachers, and even more opaque if we want evidence that they have been effective in producing student learning.

SUMMARY

Obviously, the answer to the question asked at the beginning of the chapter is, yes, all are examples of possible interdisciplinary curricula. What recommendations might be offered to teachers or teacher educators who are novices in developing and teaching interdisciplinary curricula? First, many types of interdisciplinary curricula are possible. An appropriate initial step is to become knowledgeable by reading and talking to experienced integrators. Begin slowly, perhaps teaching only one unit, and use a topic you know well. For example, developing an internal interdisciplinary unit using content from exercise physiology or sport psychology may provide a comfortable entree. Search the literature for ready-made ideas; you don't need to re-invent the wheel. Be flexible and change unsuccessful ideas or teaching strategies. Be persistent and willing to explain to students, parents, and other teachers why this type of curriculum is important.

When thinking about external interdisciplinary curricula, make natural connections between subject areas. Not every subject integrates well in every case—don't force a relationship that isn't there. For example, developing the natural connections between health and physical education will be easier than figuring out how physical education connects with American government. The middle school, with its emphasis on team teaching and core curriculum, may provide an easy access point. Finally, physical education teachers must leave the isolation of their locker-room offices and gyms and build alliances among themselves and with other teachers in their schools. Beginning the process of interdisciplinary work is difficult if you are talking only to yourself.

IMPLICATIONS FOR PRACTICE

1. Many terms, such as *multidisciplinary, interdisciplinary,* and *integrative,* are used to describe content or tasks that cut across disciplinary boundaries.

2. An interdisciplinary curriculum usually links existing categories or disciplines (e.g., math and physical education).

3. An integrated curriculum is a higher, more powerful form of synthesis often represented through significant themes such as leadership, technology, or conflict-cooperation. The literature includes few examples of true integrated curriculum in physical education.

4. Two types of interdisciplinary curriculum in physical education, internal and external, seek relevant content or disciplinary connections through concepts.

5. Internal interdisciplinary curricula in physical education are curricula that expand the goals of physical education beyond teaching students motor skills, games, and sport to include concepts from classes such as exercise science, biomechanics, and sport psychology.

6. External interdisciplinary curricula link physical education with other content and concepts in subjects such as math, science, and language arts. These curricula may be thought about in three ways:

   - physical education content may be incorporated into other subjects,
   - material from other subjects may be used in physical education, or
   - themes may be used to achieve true integration of subjects.

7. A great deal of literature is available to give teachers ideas and examples for constructing interdisciplinary curricula, but research on the effectiveness of both internal and external interdisciplinary curricula is limited and shows mixed results.

8. Several arguments are used to support the use of interdisciplinary curricula:

   - Time can be saved because subject matter is "condensed."
   - Interdisciplinary curricula match the complexity of the real world more closely than traditional subject matter divisions do.
   - These curricula may help students see the value of school and learning.

9. Curriculum developers should realize that potential problems exist for teachers, teacher education programs, and students when developing and implementing these types of curricula.

REFERENCES

Aikin, W.M. (1942). *The story of the eight-year study.* New York: Harper and Row.

Allen, V.L. (1996). A critical look at integration. *Teaching Elementary Physical Education, 7,* 12-14.

Applebee, A.N., Burroughs, R., & Cruz, G. (2000). Curricular conversations in elementary school classrooms. In S. Wineburg & P. Grossman (Eds.), *Interdisciplinary curriculum: Challenges to implementation* (pp. 93-111). New York: Teachers College Press.

Baker, D. (2001). *Elementary heart health: Lessons and assessment.* Champaign, IL: Human Kinetics.

Beane, J. (1995). Curriculum integration and the disciplines of knowledge. *Phi Delta Kappan, 76,* 616-622.

Beane, J. (1997). *Curriculum integration.* New York: Teachers College Press.

Beighle, A., Pangrazi, R.P., & Vincent, S.D. (2001). Pedometers, physical activity and accountability. *Journal of Physical Education, Recreation and Dance, 72*(9), 16-19, 36.

Block, B.A. (2001). Literacy through movement: An organization approach. *Journal of Physical Education, Recreation and Dance, 72*(1), 39-48.

Bronson, J., Gibson, S., Kichar, R., & Priest, S. (1992). Evaluation of team development in a corporate adventure training program. *Journal of Experiential Education, 15*(2), 50-53.

Brophy, J., & Alleman, J. (1991). A caveat: Curriculum integration isn't always a good idea. *Educational Leadership, 49*(2), 66.

Buell, C.M., & Reekie, S.H. (1993). Physical education and social studies—the natural alliance. *Social Studies Review, 32*(2), 29-34.

Buell, C., & Whittaker, A. (2001). Enhancing content literacy in physical education. *Journal of Physical Education, Recreation and Dance, 72*(6), 32-37.

Butler, L.F. (2000). Fair play: Respect for all. *Journal of Physical Education, Recreation and Dance, 71*(2), 32-35.

Bycura, D., & Darst, P.W. (2001). Motivating middle school students: A health-club approach. *Journal of Physical Education, Recreation and Dance, 72*(7), 24-26, 29.

Carlson, T.B. (1994). *Why students hate, tolerate, or love gym: A study of attitude formation and associated behaviors in physical education.* Unpublished doctoral dissertation, University of Massachusetts, Amherst, MA.

Cone, T.P., Werner, P., Cone, S.L., & Woods, A.M. (1998). *Interdisciplinary teaching through physical education.* Champaign, IL: Human Kinetics.

Conner-Kuntz, F.J., & Dummer, G.M. (1996). Teaching across the curriculum: Language-enriched physical education for preschool children. *Adapted Physical Activity Quarterly, 13*, 301-315.

Cothran, D.J., & Ennis, C.D. (2001). "Nobody said nothing about learning stuff": Students, teachers and curricular change. *Journal of Classroom Interaction, 36*(1), 1-5.

Deal, T.B., & Deal, L.O. (1995). Heart to heart: Using heart rate telemetry to meet physical education outcomes. *Journal of Physical Education, Recreation and Dance, 66*(3), 30-35.

Dewar, A. (1987). Knowledge and gender in physical education. In J. Gaskell & A. McLaren (Eds.), *Women and education: A Canadian perspective* (pp. 265-288). Calgary: Detselig Enterprises.

Dodds, P. (Ed.). (1987). *Basic Stuff Series I* (2nd ed.). Reston, VA: American Alliance for Health, Physical Education, Recreation and Dance.

Dodds, P., Placek, J.H., Pinkham, K.M., Doolittle, S.A., Ratliffe, T.A., Portman, P.A. (1992). Teacher/coach recruits: Background profiles, occupational decision factors, and comparisons with recruits into other physical education occupations. *Journal of Teaching in Physical Education, 11*, 161-176.

Dyson, B. (1994). *A case study of two alternative elementary physical education programs.* Unpublished doctoral dissertation, Ohio State University, Columbus.

Dyson, B. (1995). Students' voices in two alternative elementary physical education programs. *Journal of Teaching in Physical Education, 14*, 394-407.

Dyson, B. (1996). Two physical education teachers' experience of Project Adventure. *Journal of Experiential Education, 19*(2), 90-97.

Dyson, B. (2001). Cooperative learning in an elementary physical education program. *Journal of Teaching in Physical Education, 20*, 264-281.

Dyson, B., & Grineski, S. (2001). Using cooperative learning structures in physical education. *Journal of Physical Education, Recreation and Dance, 72*(2), 28-31.

Ebbeck, V., & Gibbons, S.L. (1998). The effect of a team building program on the self-conceptions of grade 6 and 7 physical education students. *Journal of Sport and Exercise Psychology, 20*, 300-310.

Erickson, H.L. (1998). *Concept-based curriculum and instruction.* Thousand Oaks, CA: Corwin.

Espiritu, J.E. (1987). Quality physical education programs—cognitive emphases. *Journal of Physical Education, Recreation and Dance, 58*(6), 38-40.

Faigenbaum, A.D. (2001). Strength training and children's health. *Journal of Physical Education, Recreation and Dance, 72*(3), 24-30.

Fersch, E., & Smith, M. (1978). *Project Adventure, year 11, final quantitative evaluation for 1972–73.* Washington, DC: Bureau of Elementary and Secondary Education. (ERIC Document Reproduction Service No. ED 173 060)

Fisher, S. (1998). Developing and implementing a K–12 character education program. *Journal of Physical Education, Recreation and Dance, 69*(2), 21-23.

Fogarty, R. (1991). *The mindful school: How to integrate the curricula.* Palatine, IL: Skylight.

George, P.S. (2000–2001). The evolution of middle schools. *Educational Leadership, 58*(4), 40-44.

Gibbons, S.L., Ebbeck, V., & Weiss, M.R. (1995). Fair Play for Kids: Effects on the moral development of children in physical education. *Research Quarterly for Exercise and Sport, 66*, 247-255.

Gillis, H.L. (1985, July). *An active adventure for groups.* Paper presented at the Georgia School Counselors Institute, St. Simons Island, GA. (ERIC Document Reproduction Services No. ED 260 879)

Gillis, H.L., & Gass, M.A. (1993). Bringing adventure into marriage and family therapy: An innovative experiential approach. *Journal of Marital and Family Therapy, 19*(3), 273-286.

Glasgow, N.A. (1997). *New curriculum for new times.* Thousand Oaks, CA: Corwin.

Glover, D.R., & Midura, D.W. (1992). *Team building through physical challenges.* Champaign, IL: Human Kinetics.

Gough, R.W. (1998). A practical strategy for emphasizing character development in sport and physical education. *Journal of Physical Education, Recreation and Dance, 69*(2), 18-20, 23.

Grineski, S. (1996). *Cooperative learning in physical education.* Champaign, IL: Human Kinetics.

Grossman, P., Wineburg, S., & Beers, S. (2000). Introduction: When theory meets practice in the world of school. In S. Wineburg & P. Grossman (Eds.), *Interdisciplinary curriculum: Challenges to implementation* (pp. 1-16). New York: Teachers College Press.

Halliday, N. (1999). Developing self-esteem through challenge education experiences. *Journal of Physical Education, Recreation and Dance, 70*(6), 51-58, 66.

Harris, J., & Elbourn, J. (1997). *Teaching health-related exercise.* Champaign, IL: Human Kinetics.

Hellison, D. (1995). *Teaching responsibility through physical activity.* Champaign, IL: Human Kinetics.

Hoffman, H.A., Young, J., & Klesius, S.T. (1981). *Meaningful movement for children.* Boston: Allyn & Bacon.

Horwood, B. (1994). Integration and experience in the secondary curriculum. *McGill Journal of Education, 29*(1), 89-102.

Housner, L.D. (Ed.) (2000). *Integrated physical education: A guide for the elementary classroom teacher.* Morgantown, WV: Fitness Information Technology, Inc.

Jacobs, H. (1989). Design options for an integrated curriculum. In H.H. Jacobs (Ed.), *Interdisciplinary curriculum: Design and implementation* (pp. 13-24). Alexandria, VA: Association for Supervision and Curriculum Development.

Kelly, E., & Lindsay, C. (1980). A comparison of knowledge obsolescence of graduating seniors and practitioners in the field of physical education. *Research Quarterly for Exercise and Sport, 54,* 636-644.

Kinchin, G.D., & O'Sullivan, M. (1999). Making physical education meaningful for high school students. *Journal of Physical Education, Recreation and Dance, 70*(5), 40-44, 54.

Kirk, D., Burgess-Limerick, R., Kiss, M., Lahey, J., & Penney, D. (1999). *Senior physical education: An integrated approach.* Champaign, IL: Human Kinetics.

Klein, J.T. (1990). *Interdisciplinarity: History, theory, and practice.* Detroit: Wayne State University Press.

Kneer, M. (Ed.). (1981). *Basic Stuff Series I.* Reston, VA: American Alliance for Health, Physical Education, Recreation and Dance.

Kneer, M. (1986). Description of physical education instructional theory/practice gap in selected secondary schools. *Journal of Teaching in Physical Education, 5,* 91-106.

Lambdin, D.V., & Lambdin, D. (1995). Connecting mathematics and physical education through spatial awareness. In P.A. House & A.F. Coxford (Eds.), *1995 yearbook connecting mathematics across the curriculum* (pp. 147-151). Reston, VA: National Council of Teachers of Mathematics.

Lawson, H.A. (1993). School reform, families, and health in the emergent national agenda for economic and social improvement: Implications. *Quest, 45,* 289-307.

Lawson, H.A., & Placek, J.H. (1981). *Physical education in the secondary schools: Curricular alternatives.* Boston: Allyn & Bacon.

Macdonald, D., & Leitch, S. (1994). Praxis in PE: The Queensland senior physical education syllabus on trial. *Journal of Physical Education New Zealand, 27*(2), 17-21.

Macdonald, D., & Tinning, R. (1995). Physical education teacher education and the trend to proletarianization: A case study. *Journal of Teaching in Physical Education, 15,* 98-118.

McHugh, E. (1995). Going "beyond the physical": Social skills and physical education. *Journal of Physical Education, Recreation and Dance, 66*(4), 18-21.

Mohnsen, B. (Ed.). (1998). *Concepts of physical education: What every student needs to know.* Reston, VA: National Association for Sport and Physical Education.

Napper-Owen, G.E., Kovar, S.E., Ermler, K.L., & Mehrhof, J.H. (1999). Curricula equity in required ninth-grade physical education. *Journal of Teaching in Physical Education, 19,* 2-21.

Nassar-McMillan, S.C., & Cashwell, C.S. (1997). Building self-esteem of children and adolescents through adventure-based counseling. *Journal of Humanistic Education and Development, 36*(2), 59-67.

National Association for Sport and Physical Education. (1995). *Moving into the future: National standards for physical education.* Reston, VA: AAHPERD.

Nilges, L., & Usnick, V. (2000). The role of spatial ability in physical education and mathematics. *Journal of Physical Education, Recreation and Dance, 71*(6), 29-33, 52-53.

O'Brien, D.G., & Stewart, R.A. (1990). Preservice teachers' perspective on why every teacher is not a teacher of reading: A qualitative analysis. *Journal of Reading Behavior, 22*(2), 101-129.

O'Donnell, M.D. (1997). Boston's Lewenberg Middle School delivers success. *Phi Delta Kappan, 78,* 508-512.

Owens, N., & Yoder, J. (1999). *Integrating literacy with music, art, and physical education. Target action research 1998–99.* (ERIC Document Reproduction Service No. ED 429 280)

Paling, D. (1984–1985). Project Adventure. *College Board Review, 134,* 21-24, 31.

Panicucci, J. (2000). This is the first time I ever liked gym! *Zip Lines: The Voice for Adventure Education, 41,* 13-18, 52-53.

Parker, M., Kallusky, J., & Hellison, D. (1999). High impact, low risk: Ten strategies to teach responsibility. *Journal of Physical Education, Recreation and Dance, 70*(2), 26-28

Patterson, B. (1995). The TAMARACK Program. *Green Teacher, 42,* 25-27.

Physical best activity guide elementary level. (1999a). Champaign, IL: Human Kinetics.

Physical best activity guide secondary level. (1999b). Champaign, IL: Human Kinetics.

Placek, J.H. (1989). An evaluation of the implementation of Basic Stuff. *Journal of Teaching in Physical Education, 8,* 152-161.

Placek, J.H. (1992). Rethinking middle school physical education curriculum: An integrated, thematic approach. *Quest, 44,* 330-341.

Placek, J.H. (1996). Integration as a curriculum model in physical education: Possibilities and problems. In S.J. Silverman & C.D. Ennis (Eds.), *Student learning in physical education: Applying research to enhance instruction* (pp. 287-311). Champaign, IL: Human Kinetics.

Placek, J.H., & O'Sullivan, M. (1997). The many faces of integrated physical education. *Journal of Physical Education, Recreation and Dance, 68*(1), 20-24.

Renyi, J. (2000). Hunting the quark. In S. Wineburg & P. Grossman (Eds.), *Interdisciplinary curriculum: Challenges to implementation* (pp. 39-56). New York: Teachers College Press.

Richmond, M. (2000). *The physiology storybook.* Northbrook, IL: Joie.

Rink, J. (2002). *Teaching physical education for learning.* Boston: WCB/McGraw Hill.

Rohnke, K. (1984). *Silver bullets: A guide to initiative problems, adventure games, and trust activities.* Hamilton, MA: Project Adventure.

Rohnke, K. (1989). *Cowstails and cobras II: A guide to games, initiatives, ropes courses, and adventure curriculum.* Dubuque, IA: Kendall/Hunt.

Rohnke, K., & Butler, S. (1995). *Quicksilver: Adventure games, initiative problems, trust activities and a guide to effective leadership.* Dubuque, IA: Kendall/Hunt.

Romance, T.J., Weiss, M.R., & Bockoven, J. (1986). A program to promote moral development through elementary school physical education. *Journal of Teaching in Physical Education, 5,* 126-136.

Siedentop, D. (1994) *Sport education: Quality PE through positive sport experiences.* Champaign, IL: Human Kinetics.

Siedentop, D., Mand, C., & Taggart, A. (1986). *Physical education teaching and curriculum strategies for grades 5–12.* Palo Alto, CA: Mayfield.

Siskin, L.S. (1995). Subject divisions. In L.S. Siskin & J.W. Little (Eds.). *The subjects in question: Departmental organization and the high school* (pp. 23-47). New York: Teachers College Press.

Solomon, G. (1997a). Does physical education affect character development in students? *Journal of Physical Education, Recreation and Dance, 68*(9), 38-41.

Solomon, G. (1997b). Fair play in the gymnasium: Improving social skills among elementary school students. *Journal of Physical Education, Recreation and Dance, 68*(5), 22-25.

Spindt, G.B., Monti, W.H., & Hennessy, B. (1997). *Moving for life.* Dubuque, IA: Kendall/Hunt.

Tanner, D. (1989). A brief historical perspective of the struggle for an integrative curriculum. *Educational Horizons, 68*(1), 7-11.

Tanner, D. (1992). Synthesis versus fragmentation: The way out of curriculum confusion. In J.M. Jenkins & D. Tanner (Eds.), *Restructuring for an interdisciplinary curriculum* (pp. 1-14). Reston, VA: National Association of Secondary School Principals.

Troisi, A., (1995). Native American culture: An interdisciplinary approach. *School Library Media Activities Monthly, 12*(3), 34-36.

Van Oteghen, S.L. (1996). Using oral history as a motivating tool in teaching. *Journal of Physical Education, Recreation and Dance, 67*(6), 45-48.

Vars, G.F. (1987). *Interdisciplinary teaching in the middle grades: Why and how.* Columbus, OH: National Middle School Association.

Vickers, J.N. (1990). *Instructional design for teaching physical activities.* Champaign, IL: Human Kinetics.

Ward, B., Everhart, B., Dunaway, D., Fisher, S., & Coates, T. (1998). Emphasizing fitness objectives in secondary physical education. *Journal of Physical Education, Recreation and Dance, 69*(1), 33-35.

Weinberg, H., Monti, W.H., Spindt, G.B., Hennessy, B., & Holyoak, C. (2002a). *Middle school physical education: Moving as a team.* Dubuque, IA: Kendall/Hunt.

Weinberg, H., Monti, W.H., Spindt, G.B., Hennessy, B., & Holyoak, C. (2002b). *Middle school physical education: Moving with confidence.* Dubuque, IA: Kendall/Hunt.

Weinberg, H., Monti, W.H., Spindt, G.B., Hennessy, B., & Holyoak, C. (2002c). *Middle school physical education: Moving with skill.* Dubuque, IA: Kendall/Hunt.

Welk, G.J., & Wood, K. (2000). Physical activity assessments in physical education. *Journal of Physical Education, Recreation and Dance, 71*(1), 30-40.

Werner, P. (1996). Interdisciplinary programming: An idea whose time has come again. *Teaching Elementary Physical Education, 7*(4), 28-30.

Wineburg, S., & Grossman, P. (1998). Creating a community of learning among high school teachers. *Phi Delta Kappan, 79,* 350-353.

Wineburg, S., & Grossman, P. (2000). Scenes from a courtship. In S. Wineburg & P. Grossman (Eds.), *Interdisciplinary curriculum: Challenges to implementation* (pp. 57-73). New York: Teachers College Press.

PART V

LEARNING TO TEACH: AN ONGOING PROCESS

CHAPTER SIXTEEN

LEARNING TO TEACH PHYSICAL EDUCATION

Mary O'Sullivan

This chapter begins with a discussion of the theoretical perspectives brought to bear on research on learning to teach and the conceptual orientations of teacher education programs, particularly physical education teacher education (PETE) programs. The chapter describes characteristics of quality teacher education programs and how the research findings relate to PETE. The discussion highlights key findings on teacher's knowledge, skills, and dispositions for teaching, the content and pedagogy debates in PETE, and what we know about the scope and sequence of quality field experiences. The chapter ends with recommendations for research in PETE and implications for the practice of teacher education.

Almost as soon as the first edition of this chapter was published in 1996, it was in some respects out of date. Several new initiatives that focused on teacher quality had begun. The National Commission on Teaching for America's Future (NCTAF, 1996, 1997) published two seminal reports bringing attention to the central importance of teachers in ensuring sustained and meaningful change in the nation's schools. Two of the commission's three premises have particular relevance for the work of teacher education and teacher educators.

1. What teachers know and can do is the most important influence on what students learn.

2. Recruiting, preparing, and retaining good teachers is the central strategy for improving our schools (NCTAF, 1996, p. vi).

These reports spawned other writings and teacher education intervention efforts. Scholars and policy makers alike seemed to reach a consensus that a critical component of school improvement, specifically improved student learning, was a caring and competent teacher in every classroom. The value-added assessment work of Ted Sanders (1998) in Kentucky schools demonstrated the critical role of quality teachers in student learning and the devastating effect that poor teachers can have on students' academic achievement. The commission, however, highlighted the critical shortage of qualified teachers in the nation's schools. Policy makers began to focus on quality teaching and quality teachers, their preparation for teaching, and relationships between quality teaching and student learning.

Although educational reformers agreed on the need for a major overhaul of how to prepare the next generation of teachers, there has been considerably less agreement on the scope of the problems or strategies for solving them. The United States Department of Education commissioned a report to summarize what rigorous, peer-reviewed research had to say about key issues in teacher preparation. The report summarized findings from research about subject matter and pedagogical preparation, clinical training, policy influences, and alternative certification to provide directions to improve teacher preparation nationally (Wilson, Floden, & Ferrini-Mundy, 2001). Although many, including the authors, noted the restrictive review of literature undertaken for that report, the authors noted

> a sharper sense of the gaps between claims we, as teacher educators, would like to make and evidence that those outside our field would find persuasive. We came away with the conviction that we, as a field must make changes that will, in the coming years, give us a better grounding for the practices we believe in or perhaps give us reasons to rethink some practices. (Wilson, Floden, & Ferrini-Mundy, 2002, p. 201)

TEACHER EDUCATION AND CONCEPTIONS OF TEACHER LEARNING

Answering the question about the most appropriate content and pedagogy for PETE poses another question: What do you see as the central issue of teacher education? The answer depends on what you consider the goals of teacher preparation and how you view the images of teacher development. In a review of teacher learning, Cochran-Smith and Lytle (1999) suggested three conceptions of teacher preparation that reflect different teacher education programs and policies nationwide. Each conception of teacher learning holds assumptions about quality teaching that results in different ideas about how to improve teacher education, teacher learning, and professional development. The following summary of these perspectives is an attempt to place current research on physical education teacher education in the respective categories. A caveat must accompany the presentation of distinct perspectives on teaching and teacher education. Although categories can be a useful heuristic, the real world rarely sees such distinctions. What might be helpful is to consider which of these perspectives was most grounded in your teacher education program or in the studies of teacher education you have reviewed. Alternatively, consider what you think ought to be the central goal of a teacher preparation program.

First Conception of Teacher Learning

The first conception of teacher learning that Cochran-Smith and Lytle (1999) describe is what they refer to as "knowledge for practice." This view of teacher learning suggests that knowing more about subject matter, pedagogy, and educational theory among other formal knowledge bases leads more or less directly to improved practice. The belief is that skilled teachers have a deep and thorough grounding in their subject matter and well-developed strategies of delivering this content to the students they teach. They learned these knowledge bases through various experiences in their teacher preparation program. Preservice physical education teachers implement, translate, use, adapt, and put into practice what they had learned of the knowledge bases. Cochran-Smith and Lytle (1999) suggest that Shulman's research program on teacher reasoning, first at Michigan State and later at Stanford, represents this view of teacher learning. This perspective is similar to the academic orientation to teacher education as suggested earlier by Feiman-Nemser (1990).

Cochran-Smith and Lytle argue that three decades of research by Shulman (1986, 1987, 2002), his colleagues, and students has "influenced the way most current teacher education programs are conceptualized and presented" (Cochran-Smith & Lytle, 1999, p. 256). They also suggested that most of the major initiatives for teacher learning such as the handbooks on teacher education (Houston, 1990; Richardson, 2001) are grounded in the assumptions of this view of teacher learning. As evidenced by aspects of their research programs, several researchers are advocates for such a view in physical education teacher education programs. Siedentop and his doctoral students studied *what teachers know* about physical education content areas (weak and strong content areas) and how they transform that knowledge in ways that are meaningful for their students (Romar, 1995; Siedentop, 2002). Rovegno has asked questions about *how preservice teachers learn* their content and pedagogy and the conditions that influence their choice and delivery of that content to children (see chapter 17 by Rovegno in this volume). The recent focus on didactics (the features of teaching that are specific to the knowledge taught) (Amade-Escot, 2000) and teaching games for understanding (Griffin & Placek, 2001; also see chapter 13 by Peter Hastie) reflects this conception of teacher learning.

Second Conception of Teacher Learning

The second conception of teacher learning relates to building "knowledge in practice." Teacher's practical knowledge is central to this perception (Clandinin & Connelly, 1995). The basic assumption is that "teaching is, to a great extent, an uncertain and spontaneous craft situated and constructed in response to particularities of everyday life in schools and classrooms" (Cochran-Smith & Lytle, 1999, p. 262). Thus, what physical education teachers need to teach well is embedded in the exemplary practice of experienced physical educators. This view of teacher learning is exemplified in Don Schön's (1987) notions of the reflective practitioner. Physical education teachers are viewed as problem solvers (and to a lesser extent problem setters). They pose and construct problems out of the uncertainty and complexity of life in schools and in particular in the gymnasium. Indeed, exemplary physical educators are generators of valuable tacit knowing in action. They make sense out of the complexity of the teaching-learning environment and choose actions that can best ensure student learning in their classrooms. Lawson (1999) and Tinning (1997) have been some of the more vocal advocates of such a view of teacher learning. Teaching is

> understood primarily as a process of acting and thinking wisely in the immediacy of classroom life, making split second decisions, choosing among alternative ways to convey the subject matter, interacting appropriately with an array of students, and selecting and focusing on particular dimensions of classroom problems. (Cochran-Smith & Lytle, 1999, p. 266)

Case-based teaching, journal writing, and other self-reflective activities are now common strategies in teacher education programs focused on the development of physical educators as reflective practitioners (Collier & O'Sullivan, 1997; Curtner-Smith, 1998; Tsangaridou & O'Sullivan, 1997). The goal of these teacher-learning pedagogies is to provide social and intellectual contexts to probe the teachers' knowledge and the wisdom of their own and others' ideas of teaching and teaching practices. The proceedings from the 1993 AIESEP conference provide further reading on this topic in physical education teacher education (Pare, 1995).

Third Conception of Teacher Learning

"Knowledge of practice" is the third conception of teacher learning. The basic assumption is that "the knowledge teachers need to teach well emanates from systematic inquiries about teaching, learning, learners and learning, subject matter and curriculum, and schools and schooling" (Cochran-Smith & Lytle, 1999, p. 174). Some physical educators who have grounded action research in their teacher education program could be seen as advocates for this conception of preservice teacher learning. Such teacher educators view the teacher's roles as "co-constructors of knowledge and creators of curriculum," and teachers in turn see themselves as active change agents and school leaders. Pedagogies that allow preservice teachers to challenge their assumptions about teaching, children, and schooling have the potential to transform gymnasia into teaching spaces that challenge existing inequities in physical education. In this way, teacher learning is linked to larger efforts of school change, school reorganization, and social justice. A number of physical education scholars have voiced support for this view of teacher learning in recent years (Fernandez-Balboa, 1997b; Hickey, 2001) and have attempted to incorporate these perspectives into PETE programs. See the Fernandez-Balboa text (1997b) for further reading on these ideas. This view of teacher learning may make more sense as a theoretical framework to ground professional development initiatives with experienced teachers than as a theoretical perspective for a preservice teacher education program.

Summary of Teacher Education and Conceptions of Teacher Learning

In comparing the three conceptions of teacher learning, note that although the methods used in teacher education programs may be similar (reflection, journal writing, internships, etc.), the experiences can serve very different functions in learning to teach depending on the purposes of these experiences or assignments. The first conception of teacher learning as knowledge for practice sees teachers using the existing knowledge bases to solve problems, represent content, and make decisions about physical education experiences for children in the gymnasium. Most PETE programs are probably represented here. The second conception emphasizes how teachers invent knowledge (as distinct from applying existing knowledge) in the midst of teaching to make wise choices in creating supportive learning environments for their students. Many of the reflective teaching studies seem to fit well here (Bolt, 1998; Collier & O'Sullivan, 1997; Tsangaridou & O'Sullivan, 1997). The third conception of teacher learning sees teachers as creators of curriculum who are informed by their stance as theorizers, activists, and school leaders. An "inquiry stance" for the preparation of teachers allows teachers to problematize their roles in the design and delivery of curriculum to their students. Teachers "challenge the purposes and underlying assumptions of educational change efforts rather than simply helping to carry out the most effective methods of predetermined ends" (Cochran-Smith & Lytle, 1999, p.295). Although many physical education teachers have the freedom (some might say they suffer from benign neglect) to teach almost any content they wish, little evidence shows that PETE programs support the notion of teacher as activists in the sense lauded by Cochran-Smith. Perhaps the ideas shared by Fernandez-Balboa (1997a) and Lawson (1999) might be the closest to such views among PETE scholars in the United States. One reads more about such efforts from our Australian colleagues (Hickey, 2001; Tinning, 1997). To address contemporary social issues in schools proactively and successfully, teachers need to be prepared not only in subject matter knowledge and pedagogy but also in child studies, community studies, and critical analyses of teaching and learning in physical education (O'Sullivan, Siedentop, & Locke, 1992). They should also spend sustained time teaching in schools and working with children and youth in the community.

CONCEPTIONS OF LEARNING IN PETE

Rink (1993) adapted and applied earlier conceptual orientations of teacher education (Feiman-Nemser, 1990) to PETE. These orientations included

- an academic orientation (a focus on the subject matter of games, sport, dance, fitness, etc.),
- a practical orientation (heavy reliance on field experience and practice),
- a technological orientation (emphasis on teacher effectiveness),
- a personal orientation (emphasis on personal meaning and growth as a teacher), and
- a critical-social orientation (emphasis on the moral basis of teaching and on equity and the social dimensions of teaching).

Rink (1993) suggested the orientations "can and do coexist in different aspects of the same program and perhaps should all be a consideration in program design" (p. 316) and they do not necessarily have to compete. Rink argued that we have spent too much energy in recent years debating the relative merits of what theorists have presented as competing conceptual orientations to teacher education in physical education and not enough energy presenting our visions of teacher education and how well we have realized those visions. Others, however, take a more purist stance and suggest that many of these visions of teacher education in physical education are mutually exclusive (Sparkes, 1989). Indeed, Sparkes (1992) looks on this positively, noting that such new visions and voices encourage us to consider different perspectives

> in a spirit of intellectual curiosity and respect [and this] is essential if theoretical vitality is to be nurtured within the PE community. In broadening our perspectives and becoming more aware of research paradigms that offer alternatives to our own, even if we disagree with them, we become far less parochial. (p. 49)

Earlier, I presented Cochran-Smith & Lytle's (1999) heuristic as a more useful conceptual framework to clarify respective visions for teacher education programs and operationalize what we expect our teacher candidates to know and be able to do as a consequence of successfully completing our preparation programs. Depending on your beliefs about teaching and learning to teach, you may emphasize one or more conceptions of teaching at the expense of others, thus making a judgment about the scope and content of the curriculum for teacher education.

CHARACTERISTICS OF TEACHER EDUCATION PROGRAMS

Using an in-depth, cross-institutional analysis of six highly regarded elementary teacher education programs, Howey and Zimpher (1989) identified a set of conditions and characteristics that appeared to contribute in substantial ways to the education of teachers. The teacher education programs demonstrated the following attributes:

1. Clear conceptions of schooling and teaching. Faculty shared beliefs about teaching and expectations of a prospective teacher.
2. Planned variations. Faculty coalesced around a set of planned variations, sharing a specific agenda for instruction and joint ownership and responsibility for the program.

3. Articulated program goals. Both the faculty and students clearly articulated program goals.

4. Rigorous and academically challenging program. The program communicated to students that quality work and a commitment to the program were expected.

5. Key concepts infused throughout the programs. The concepts provided students a framework to assist in developing their perspective on learning to teach.

6. Respect for and a balance of time for learning subject matter knowledge, pedagogy, pedagogical knowledge, and school experiences in learning to teach.

7. Student cohorts. Faculty noted this strength provided a greater sense of accountability when interacting with students over long periods.

8. Students socialized into teaching. Each program had a curricular event, which served to socialize students to their teaching career and reinforce their commitment to teaching.

9. Well-conceived set of laboratory and clinical experiences.

10. Program evaluation. Each program had a systematic plan for program evaluation and direct linkage to research and development in teacher education.

In a review of the PETE literature, Graham (1991) identified "four dimensions of teacher preparation that appeared to positively influence the development of preservice students' perspectives toward teaching" (p. 6). These included the following:

1. A shared vision of teacher education held jointly by university and school personnel (cooperating teachers, clinical faculty, and university supervisors) who worked hard to establish and maintain a relationship with practicing teachers.

2. The presence of an inquiry approach to teaching in which students, in a non-threatening, safe environment, were provided various types of "assignments" at different times during their programs to reflect on teaching (their own and others) and critically examine the nature of their values and beliefs about teaching and learning.

3. The structure and content of such experiences "were wed inextricably to the theoretical perspective under-girding the program" (p. 8).

4. The promotion of a critical approach to curriculum and instruction in which school was viewed as a place for questioning and transforming existing societal injustices and inequalities.

One implication of Graham's (1991) work for the practice of PETE is that the development of critical, inquiring teachers becomes a primary goal of all PETE programs, with works by Schön (1987) and Zeichner and Liston (1987) as guides in the development of these efforts. Work in physical education by Sebren (1995) and Tsangaridou and O'Sullivan (1994, 1997) are also useful here. Graham (1991) challenged teacher educators to determine at what stage in PETE programs each of the dimensions of reflection (technical as distinct from critical) might be emphasized. Note that in neither Howey and Zimpher's (1989) work nor Graham's (1991) work, nor indeed in most of the contemporary literature, does one find any substantive efforts to link the processes of teacher education to any dimensions of student learning as a consequence of the teaching by these teacher candidates. Establishing this link is perhaps one of the most significant challenges facing teacher education researchers and practitioners today.

BELIEFS OF TEACHER CANDIDATES

Our deliberations about quality teacher education cannot ignore the voices of prospective teachers. Scholars now remind us to listen to teacher voices (and prospective teacher voices) and address students' beliefs and values in teacher education programs (Devis-Devis & Sparkes, 1999). Doing so allows for the design of teacher preparation programs that can influence prospective teachers' views of teaching and learning in physical education (Hardy, 1999; Hutchinson, 1993; Laker & Jones, 1998).

Lortie (1975) suggested that biography and precareer experiences could be more important than the teacher education program itself. Preservice teachers enter professional training programs already having formed images of themselves as teachers. They then filter what their professional education exposes them to and adopt ideas that fit already existing beliefs derived from past experiences (Doolittle, Dodds, & Placek, 1993; Feiman-Nemser, 1990). Doolittle et al. (1993) found that incomplete physical education teaching perspectives often "constitute a weak base for the professional identities that formal training tries to shape" (p. 355). Hutchinson (1993) noted that they exude confidence in their own abilities to teach, and are often unrealistically optimistic that they will be better able to solve daily problems of teaching than their fellow recruits. Lawson (1983) suggested that "successful induction is one in which a recruit's inaccurate subjective warrant is replaced by a new self-image forged out of new ideological commitments and newly acquired knowledge and skill" (p. 13)

More recently, researchers have studied several different aspects of prospective teachers' beliefs and attitudes. These include studies about teaching diverse students (Hodge, 1998), attitudes toward cultural pluralism (Stanley, 1997), subject matter knowledge competence (Capel & Katene, 2000), pedagogical competence (Chedzoy, 2000), and understandings of the teaching learning process (O'Connor & Macdonald, 2002). A recent study of practicing teachers' perspectives on the characteristics of teaching recruits suggested that we need persons who are physically fit teachers with a love of physical activity and a liking for children (McCullick, 2001). Chedzoy's (2000) study is particularly instructive because it attempts (as few others do) to determine if the pedagogical and content goals of the program have been met by observing and interviewing teacher candidates about their planning and competence to teach. These studies offer some evidence that students are not confident about their pedagogical or content knowledge and abilities.

CONTENT OF PHYSICAL EDUCATION TEACHER EDUCATION PROGRAMS

What makes a coherent or effective professional preparation program for prospective physical education teachers? Let us start with the question "What do we know about how to prepare teachers who will conduct quality instructional programs in schools?" Any discussion of quality must first address the question "What or who determines quality?" Any teacher education program should be judged against the specific goals articulated for that program. In other words, a program that emphasizes an academic orientation ought to be judged on criteria pertinent to that program. The ultimate gauge of a teacher education program is the learning achieved by its graduates and their students. For technical (lack of equipment and facilities, limited time) and economic reasons (shortage of funds for expensive longitudinal research) such stringent criteria are difficult to apply in researching the effectiveness of teacher education programs. Regardless, with recent legislation in some states mandating universities to report Praxis II scores and in many states the scores of their graduates on Praxis III tests (teaching performance during their first years of teaching), such linkages, however tentative, will be evaluated. Praxis II measures knowledge of subject matter and principles of teaching and learning. Praxis III is an evaluation of beginning teachers' classroom performance by trained local observers. The United States Elementary and Secondary Education Act (ESEA) and the National Council for the Accreditation of Teacher Education (NCATE) requirements for performance-based standards will ensure greater attention to the links between teacher learning and student learning, and which teacher education practices are needed to better support teacher learning.

Subject Matter Knowledge Base

What are the essential elements of content knowledge in physical education? What kinds of subject matter preparation, and how much of it, do prospective teachers need? To address this issue, I have drawn on Shulman's (1987) framework of a knowledge base for teacher education and the findings from a review of the research on this question by Wilson et al. (2001). Shulman describes the knowledge base of teaching and different ways of knowing that are important for teachers and necessary for successful practice. Three of Shulman's categories of teacher knowledge are content knowledge, pedagogical knowledge, and pedagogical content knowledge.

What is the appropriate content knowledge for physical education trainees? Two decades ago, the *Academy Papers* (Corbin & Eckert, 1990) highlighted the struggle over the nature of essential subject matter in our profession. Some believed that the essential content for preservice teachers should be closely aligned to physical education in current K–12 schools such as sport, games, and fitness activities (Siedentop, 1990). Others argued that undergraduate curriculum content should focus on the subdisciplines of physical education (sport psychology, exercise physiology, biomechanics, etc.) and that teacher educators should help prospective teachers apply this "foundational knowledge base" to helping children learn sport, games, and physical education. Still others suggest alternative knowledge bases for physical education preparation (Daniel & Bergman-Drewe, 1998; Fernandez-Balboa, 1997b; Tinning, 2000).

Even those who advocate a teacher education content curriculum aligned with content in K–12 schools disagree about the nature of that content. Some support a sport and games content. Siedentop (1994) has been an advocate of this approach with his sport education curriculum model. Others advocate the need for a more balanced presentation of physical activities, recognizing the needs, interests, and abilities of all contemporary students, not just those girls and boys who benefit from a competitive, "male model of sport" (Tinning, 2000; Wright, 1995). Siedentop (1989) noted that "we have arrived at a point in our history where we can now prepare teachers who are pedagogically more skillful than ever, but who in many cases are so unprepared in the content area they would be described as 'ignorant' if the content were a purely cognitive knowledge field" (p. 3). The consequence, according to Siedentop, has been teachers who are "ill-equipped to teach anything beyond a beginning unit of activity" (p. 9).

In describing the decline of activity coursework in undergraduate physical education, Siedentop (1989) suggested that the root problem is that the study of

> sport skill and strategy through experiential learning is not considered of sufficient academic quality to form the core of an undergraduate degree program. Learning basketball, volleyball, and gymnastics—and all the associated issues of training, technique, performance, and strategy—are not worthy of formal academic credit as the central foci of a pre-professional program. If we cannot confront that core problem, and somehow resolve it, physical education in schools is doomed. (p. 8)

Tinning (1992) suggested that although prospective teachers must have practical experiences in sport forms that make up school curricula, performance competence was not absolutely necessary. Although teachers may have better insights and understandings of an activity if they can perform it themselves, Tinning believed time devoted to developing such competence is a luxury rather than a necessity. Thomas (1990) sees physical activity as a core of any physical education undergraduate program. Without such a focus, he asks, "What will happen to a field of study in which the scholars have not mastered and do not understand through experience the essential nature of the field-movement? . . . Simply stated, one who has no expertise in a sport cannot study the skilled nature of the behavior satisfactorily" (pp. 10-11).

Various positions have been presented as to the foundational knowledge bases for preservice teachers (McCullick, 2001; Rovegno, Nevett, & Babiarz, 2001; Schempp, Manross, Tan, & Fincher, 1998). One argument has been the importance of subject matter expertise (Housner & French, 1994; O'Sullivan & Doutis, 1994). Increasing evidence suggests, however, that less curricular time is devoted to the study and performance of physical activity, be it traditional sports or contemporary physical activities (e.g., adventure activities, and yoga) (Livingston, 1996; O'Sullivan, 1990). What might be the consequences when teachers are required to show evidence of student learning in this content? Will a focus on content (however defined) be demanded if not from within the profession then from without? What will be presented as the knowledge of most worth and by whom?

Several writers in recent years have criticized teacher education programs and NASPE's content standards for prospective physical educators because they are overconcerned with preparing teachers to be followers of social change rather than leaders of education reform in physical education programming (Fernandez-Balboa, 1997a; Kirk, 1997). Fernandez-Balboa (1997a) believes that teacher candidates should view themselves as transformative intellectuals engaged in professional reform and seems to be proposing a physical education version of the "knowledge-of-practice" view of teacher learning. Prospective teachers would develop leadership skills, political skills, and moral values (besides content knowledge and pedagogy skills) that would better prepare them for teaching in contemporary schools.

We need research about the types of activities that better support teachers to teach such ideals and how preservice physical educators can learn such practices. Regardless of which content is considered of most worth, little definitive research has been done on the kind or the amount of subject matter preparation needed. These answers are simply not available now in either the general teacher education literature or the physical education literature.

Pedagogical Knowledge and Pedagogical Content Knowledge Preparation

The ambivalence about the relative importance of content knowledge as compared with pedagogical knowledge in physical education teacher education programs may be representative of the confusion among pedagogy researchers about the relative importance of content, context, and pedagogy in improving PETE programs. The integration of methods courses with content course work with field experiences in schools has focused prospective teachers to align their knowledge of learning theory, instructional theory, and content for optimum student learning.

In making a case for the importance of both subject matter knowledge and pedagogical content knowledge in teaching physical education, Tinning (1992) drew on Arnold's (1988) distinction between weak and strong practical knowledge in physical education.

Practical knowledge in the weak sense is demonstrated by an individual who can perform an activity (is physically able to do something) but cannot articulate how to do it. Practical knowledge in the strong sense is demonstrated by an individual who can both physically perform an activity or skill and articulate how to do it (Tinning, 1992). Tinning noted that practical knowledge in the weak sense is of little use to teachers, but practical knowledge in the strong sense is to their advantage. Possessing knowledge about a movement or sport without being able to perform it is typical in the coaching world (for example, gymnastic coaches who teach stunts they cannot perform). As a result, Tinning (1992) argued that the

> essential knowledge for a physical education teacher is knowledge about (i.e., prepositional knowledge) how to perform a practical activity and the corresponding ways of organizing the graded progressive practice necessary to acquire the skill. Being able to also perform the skill might be a bonus but it is not a necessity. (p. II)

A growing body of literature on teachers' practical knowledge has highlighted the significance of helping undergraduates tie their knowledge of pedagogy to their knowledge of the subject matter and their knowledge of the learner—what Shulman (1986) has termed "pedagogical content knowledge" (PCK). Shulman defined pedagogical content knowledge as

> the most useful forms of representation of those ideas, the most powerful analogies, illustrations, examples, explanations, and demonstrations—in a word, the ways of transforming the subject that make it comprehensible to others. Pedagogical content knowledge also includes an understanding of what makes the learning of specific topics easy or difficult: the conceptions and preconceptions that students of different ages and backgrounds bring with them to the learning of those most frequently taught topics and lessons. (pp. 9-10)

I will now highlights key findings on PCK from the general and physical education literature. In a review of the literature on pedagogical content knowledge, Grossman (1991) laid out several implications for teacher education. First, teacher educators need to take "teachers' prior knowledge of a subject more seriously" (p. 212). Second, the mismatch between college coursework in a subject and the K–12 curriculum requires that courses on "subject specific methods can help bridge these gaps by incorporating substantive discussions about central topics in the field" (p. 212). According to Grossman, "teachers need pedagogical maps of content, the understanding of a subject from an explicitly pedagogical perspective that enables teachers to track students' misunderstandings and guide them toward new conceptions" (p. 213). Given the importance of content knowledge and pedagogical content knowledge, Grossman (1991) advocated a rethinking of the generalist view of an elementary and middle school teacher and exploring the potential for building subject matter expertise within collaborative teaching teams.

Dodds (1994) concluded that expert physical educators have richer, more substantive cognitive representations of their subject matter, instructional strategies, and their students than do novice teachers. Griffey and Housner (1991) demonstrated how novices reacted to surface issues in the classroom and were more prone to shift activities during lessons for no obvious curricular reasons. Novices seem to be caught up in the present moment. Although the routines of experienced teachers are few, novices do not yet possess them.

Given the space limitations of the chapter I refer readers to a fuller review of the contributions of pedagogical content knowledge (PCK) and the "didactics of physical education" for physical education content by Amade-Escot (2000). Like Grossman (1991) in the general literature, Amade-Escot suggested that PCK is highly domain specific to the physical activity content being taught. This issue requires careful research on the best representation of teaching various aspects of physical education content to learners in different contexts. Little research in the field informs us how best to develop such knowledge specificity, although some American (Griffin, Placek, and Rovegno among others) and international colleagues (Godbout, Grehaigne, and Mahut among others) have begun addressing these issues. Research on teaching games for understanding and how to teach for such understanding (Griffin & Placek, 2001) and tactical awareness (Griffin, Mitchell, & Oslin, 1997) also suggests a renewed focus on content and pedagogy issues in physical education (Holt, Strean, & Bengoechea, 2002).

Most teacher educators recognize the significant contribution of research on pedagogical knowledge (Doyle, 1990; Silverman, 1994) and pedagogical content knowledge (Griffey & Housner, 1991; Griffin & Placek, 2001; Rovegno, 1991) to our understanding of learning to teach. Several pedagogical strategies have been used to develop preservice teachers' understandings of pedagogy and content for specific curricular goals. To develop pedagogical skills, Berliner (1986) suggested the development and use of scripted lessons in early fieldwork so that student teachers could concentrate on presenting the content to students in meaningful and challenging ways. Livingston and Borko (1989) suggested students' pedagogical expertise might be developed with less fieldwork and more discussion and analysis of the teaching completed. They argued that it would be best to have teacher candidates assigned to teach in areas for which they have strong content preparation and know the content well in advance.

In physical education teacher education Collier and O'Sullivan (1997) and Bolt (1998) used case-based teaching to enhance teacher learning of when and why to use specific content to achieve desired learning outcomes with students. Hickey (2001) reported on the use of critical studies discourses to guide teaching candidates' practices. My colleagues and I have used community mapping (doing an on-site analysis of the physical recreation assets of the local community) to integrate the experiences and assets children bring from their family and community experiences to the learning environment in the gymnasium (O'Sullivan & Tsangaridou, 2001). We have also used the teacher work sample methodology to connect teacher learning with student learning (Stroot, Ward, O'Sullivan, Hodge, & Goodway, 2002). This methodology is a powerful tool that allows teacher candidates to consider the connections between the design and delivery of their instruction with student learning. The teacher work sample uses pupil learning to assess the performance of teacher candidates and their reflection on their pupils' learning. For further reading in this area in the general education literature, see Schalock (1998). Many critical issues have been presented along with a thumbnail sketch of how current research addresses them.

FIELD EXPERIENCE, STUDENT TEACHING, AND SUPERVISION

Much has been written about the role of fieldwork in learning to teach. Study after study confirms the critical role of this experience and the significant contribution of cooperating teachers to the preparation of neophyte teachers (Dodds, 1989; Hardy, 1999; O'Sullivan, 1990). Other studies recognize that, at times, the influence of poorly organized and unstructured fieldwork on prospective teachers can be weak, contradictory, and ambiguous (O'Sullivan & Tsangaridou, 1992). What types of field experiences should be structured for prospective teachers? When and how often should they be included in the program? Although the current literature provides few solid clues about these questions, it does offer the following key findings.

Jones (1992) found that positive student reactions and positive feedback from their cooperating teachers were two key factors that confirmed physical education teaching as their career choice. Three factors—off-task student behavior, off-task class behavior, and unmotivated students during lessons—caused preservice teachers to question their career choices. Jones's study reaffirmed the importance of careful attention to site selection for field experiences, appropriate training of cooperating teachers for their roles as teacher educators, and carefully designed opportunities for student teachers to be debriefed on their teaching experiences.

Earlier studies on field experiences have demonstrated that student teachers become more custodial during student teaching (Templin, 1979) and that sometimes field experiences, if not properly structured and supervised, can be misinterpreted, teaching trainees false ideas such as that pupil learning is not a high priority. Preservice teachers attend more to classroom management than to other topics and focus their attention on ensuring that children are busy, happy, and good (Placek, 1983). Recognizing this is one thing, but knowing how to intervene effectively is another matter. The university supervisor's limited observations and lack of time in the schools reduces the credibility of his or her feedback in the eyes of the cooperating teacher and student teacher. The direct tutelage of the cooperating teacher is the primary influence on teaching styles and attitudes of preservice teachers (Randall, 1992). We know that the willingness of cooperating teachers to buy into a collaborative educational mission with university personnel is critical. Assuring the provision of these collaborative opportunities, however, is not easy.

Obstacles to Effective Field Experience Supervision

Randall (1992) highlighted several key obstacles to the effective supervision of field experiences:

1. Students are not prepared for their teaching assignments in schools and do not exhibit the curiosity about the process of becoming a teacher.
2. University and school supervisors do not communicate well with one another.
3. There is a lack of a shared understanding of the respective role of each triad member (student, cooperating teacher, university supervisor) in the supervision process.
4. Student teachers lack the managerial and organizational skills considered necessary by cooperating teachers.
5. Goals for student teaching in the managerial and organizational areas are inconsistent.

In a review of the student-teaching literature Dodds (1989, p. 83) noted that research on field experience is scarce when it comes to providing professors clues about "how they might be more deliberate and effective in using field experiences to intensify their programmatic message to trainees." One study by O'Sullivan and Tsangaridou (1992) found that PETE programs that produce teachers who show concern for student learning advocate a shared vision and promote reflective inquiry. They also concluded that well-constructed, early field experiences provide opportunities for preservice teachers to explore their understandings of teaching, schooling, and the role of the teacher in educating youth. In a follow-up study Tsangaridou and O'Sullivan (1994) showed that carefully designed, reflective assignments can help prospective teachers focus on the social and ethical aspects of the teaching and learning setting as well as on the technical aspects of teaching. Such efforts are small but promising steps in equipping students with the "conceptual apparatus, understandings, and strategies to recognize and engage the hidden learnings present in all teaching" (Tinning, 1992, p. 17).

Whatever view of good teaching we hold, we must spend more time and energy studying how best to realize our specific visions of PETE programs and produce teachers who embody that view. We must pursue our visions of what it means to be a good teacher and what it means to have a program that produces such educators. In doing so, we can show that we are preparing professionals who can help students enjoy our subject matter in ways that are exciting, accessible, and attentive to their diverse needs and interests. Currently, the gap is too large between what we suggest ought to be the focus in preparing teachers, what we say we can do in such programs, and the evidence to show that our teacher candidates have such knowledge, skills, and dispositions.

Contemporary Challenges for PETE

In recent years two other issues have begun to receive some serious consideration in the teacher education literature. One addresses the best way to prepare teacher candidates to teach in diverse contexts and more specifically in urban schools. Although much has been written in the general literature (Ladson-Billings, 1994; Oakes & Lipton, 1999; Weiner, 2000), PETE scholars have not focused attention on what an urban PETE program might include and how it might be conceptualized. Finally, although many authors have recently written about the integration of technology into physical education teaching, little guidance is available for teacher educators on how best to prepare prospective teacher candidates to integrate technology into their physical education programs (Beighle, Pangrazi, & Vincent, 2001; Juniu, 2002; Silverman, 1997). Many list servers and Web sites are available for sport and physical education teachers and coaches (e.g., www.pecentral.org). A growing number of practitioner journals include articles about using various technologies in the gymnasium. Much less information focuses on questions about what technology is best for what purposes and how technology might—or even should—change the way we learn some aspects of physical education. These are central questions if we are to integrate technology in meaningful ways into teacher education programs.

DIRECTIONS FOR FUTURE TEACHER EDUCATION RESEARCH

Shulman's critique of three decades of his research on learning to teach follows:

> Understanding and improving teacher education is unlikely without the development and field testing of instruments for documenting and measuring the various important dimensions of both teacher learning and development and of the opportunities for teacher learning that are critical for future teachers. (Shulman, 2002, p. 252)

Although his work defines much of teacher education and PETE today, he has noted that along the way he and his colleagues (and most teacher education scholars) lost sight of

> a key principle in the product-process research . . . the importance of linking distinctive features of teaching to the quality of student learning. . . . The teacher education knowledge project did not seek to document connections between teacher knowledge and student achievement. (Shulman, 2002, p. 250)

In addition, teacher educators have not been particularly introspective about their own programs. But NCATE's shift to performance-based standards for teacher education programs will require teacher education programs to share evidence about the knowledge, skills, and dispositions that teacher candidates have acquired during their teacher preparation. The NASPE Task Force on Beginning Teacher Standards has revised the beginning teacher standards for physical educators to align them with the performance-based NCATE standards (NASPE, 2002a). The NASPE Task Force for Advanced Standards completely revised the existing expectations for graduate programs in physical education (masters programs for practicing teachers are the focus of these standards). The performance standards reflect the standards for the National Board for Professional Teaching Standards certification (www.nbpts.org) and NCATE's performance standards (NASPE, 2002b). Both sets of standards were unveiled in 2002 at the Annual Convention of the American Alliance for Health, Physical Education, Recreation and Dance (AAHPERD). The standards will affect how teacher education faculty think about their program goals and objectives and how their candidates demonstrate such knowledge, skills, and dispositions.

In recent years PETE scholars have been studying how best to measure the knowledge and skills their teacher candidates achieve upon completion of their teacher programs. They also want to use this information to improve their programs (Metzler & Tjeerdsma, 1998). Other PETE scholars have looked at how teacher education programs can help teacher candidates learn a specific curricular or instructional perspective on the teaching of physical education to young children (Graber, 1995; O'Bryant, O'Sullivan, & Raudensky, 2000; Rovegno, 1995). Physical education teacher education scholars need to pay closer attention to what it is teacher candidates actually know, can do, and value about teaching, children, and physical education as a result of their teacher preparation (National Academy of Education, 1999; Shulman, 2002). We need to better understand what kinds of experiences can prepare the caring and competent teachers we value most. For example, does your teacher education program emphasize knowledge for practice, knowledge in practice, or knowledge of practice (Cochran-Smith & Lytle, 1999)? We need more studies of teacher learning that are embedded within ongoing programs of teacher education with ties to student learning when and where possible. I suggest the need for long-term programs of scholarship in PETE to address the following research questions:

- What do we know about the connections between what preservice physical educators do and what students learn?

- What are the types of activities that better support teachers to teach physical education content to a diverse cohort of students? Which pedagogical strategies work better for specific program objectives, for specific children, or for specific contexts?

- How can preservice physical educators learn such practices?

- What instruments might physical education teacher education programs use to identify the connections between opportunities to learn and enduring changes in teacher capacities?

- What are the characteristics of PETE programs that connect opportunities to learn with enduring teacher capacities and student learning in physical education?

Shulman (2002) noted that although we don't need studies that compare the presence of teacher education with its absence, we do need studies of teacher education programs that employ "good instrumentation, careful measurement, scrupulously faithful ethnographic accounts and carefully reasoned inferences and arguments" (p. 252).

The passage of the ESEA in 2002 suggests more involvement of the federal government in K–16 education. College- and university-based education are no longer considered "the sole or required mode of preparation for teaching" (Cochran-Smith, 2002). A widespread view in government circles is that research on teacher preparation has been of low quality and incapable of producing knowledge that improves educational policy and practice. Thus, every teacher educator should take notice of what it means from the government perspective to do "scientifically based research." Conservative readings of the act seem to suggest that ESEA prefers "educational research that utilizes randomized experiments and related designs." That perspective is a much more conservative view of research than that put forth by the National Research Council's (2001) report titled *Scientific Inquiry in Education*. Space does not allow attention to these two important documents. As this chapter goes to press, however, a new era of teacher preparation research and initiatives is about to unfold. The implications of these documents for teacher education, and by implication for physical education, will be considerable.

SUMMARY

This overview of the teacher education research in the last decade makes it clear that teacher quality is of central importance to ensure sustained and meaningful change in schools. What teachers know is a key factor in what students learn. If we are to ensure quality physical education experiences for children and youth, then the recruitment and professional preparation of caring and competent teachers is of central importance. Although we have much work that provides some direction for the design of quality teacher education programs, we need to conduct substantial additional research to understand how best to prepare caring and competent physical educators who will positively influence student learning.

IMPLICATIONS FOR PRACTICE

The following implications for the design, delivery, and assessment of teacher education include a caveat. Although we have evidence to support these implications, the evidence is stronger in some areas than in others. In most cases, however, the research is not linked to any indices of pupil learning, a limitation of most of the current teacher education research (Shulman, 2002).

1. Little evidence is available to guide how much time should be devoted to content knowledge or to show what content is most critical. We should spend more time than we currently do, however, helping teacher candidates learn how to understand and transform physical activity content for the specific needs and abilities of students they teach.

2. Teacher candidates' beliefs about teaching act as a filter for the content and experiences they receive in a teacher education. These beliefs are resistant to change. Thus, teacher educators should provide several opportunities during their programs to clarify their values and beliefs and the alignment between their theories of action and theories in use. Journal writing and reflective assignments seem to be effective strategies to help teacher candidates question what they are teaching, what students are learning, and who is served best by what and how they delivered and assessed lesson content.

3. The establishment of cohorts of teacher candidates should be considered. Time should then be allocated for small groups within the cohort to function as learning communities by discussing their teaching and learning experiences and sharing data on their teaching and student learning. In these ways, teacher candidates can become socialized as a community of learners who see questioning as part of the task of teaching across the life span (Zeichner & Miller, 1997).

4. Teacher candidates should spend time getting to know and understand children's needs and interests. Time working with children in nonschool settings as well as in classroom settings

allows teacher candidates to develop both cultural competence (Ladson-Billings, 1994; Valenzuela, 2002; Weiner, 2002) and a better sense of how to align their subject matter with the experiences and dispositions students bring to school from their communities.

5. Frequent opportunities to teach in real schools in focused and supervised teaching experiences ought to be a central feature of any teacher education physical education program. Such clinical experiences work well in professional development schools devoted to teacher growth (preservice and in-service professional development) and pupil learning.

6. Dominant views of new recruits are that they perceive physical education as primarily motor-skill oriented, prefer coaching to teaching, and are more conservative than other teachers. Grounding teacher education programs in the experiences of new recruits and allowing them to develop awareness and appreciation for the legitimacy of their professional history is imperative (Graber, 1991; Hutchinson & Buschner, 1996).

7. Preservice programs should ensure that teachers are prepared to design programs that serve all students, not only the interests of the skilled and competitive students. Teacher educators must examine carefully what skills and beliefs prospective teachers take away from their programs, as distinct from the beliefs and skills that the programs intended to convey (Dewar, 1989).

8. Teacher education faculty must convince recruits that learning to teach is a career-long process that involves much more than a love for children, as important as that may be (Graber, 1989).

9. Teacher educators must provide opportunities for recruits to examine and challenge the structure and function of physical education and sport in a male-dominated society (Bain, 1990; Griffin, 1989).

10. Supervisors (cooperating teachers and university personnel) must recognize that a primary focus of novices is their survival as students, not as teachers. Addressing these concerns and how they might influence their engagement with teacher education assignments is a priority if teacher educators are to acquire positive leverage in shaping the views of preservice students (Graber, 1989).

11. Dodds (1989) presented the following four guidelines in the development of more effective field experiences.

   • All people associated with field experience don't necessarily share the same teaching perspectives, and thus no training program will strongly affect its students until the perspectives of all participants become broadly similar.

   • Teacher educators must design deliberately progressive, sequential, and well-timed field experiences. These experiences must support the programmatic teaching perspective and provide opportunities for trainees to compare and contrast their views of teaching with their education program and the cooperating teachers or clinical educators with whom they are working.

   • Teacher educators must explore implications of sport within field experiences by encouraging open discussion about the effects of sport when its messages are elitist, sexist, or homophobic.

   • Teacher educators must ensure that the processes of reflection and choice become interwoven and apparent in field experiences. A haphazard series of field experiences does little to ensure that trainees receive a programmatic perspective.

Acknowledgment

I would like to thank Dr. Susan Brown for assistance in retrieving literature on physical education teacher education since 1996 for this chapter. At the time Susan was a doctoral student in sport and exercise education at Ohio State University. She is now an assistant professor at the University of Vermont.

REFERENCES

Amade-Escot, C. (2000). The contribution of two research programs on teaching content: "Pedagogical Content Knowledge" and "Didactics of Physical Education." *Journal of Teaching in Physical Education, 20*, 78-101.

Arnold, P. (1988). *Education, movement and the curriculum.* London: Falmer Press.

Bain, L.L. (1990). Physical education teacher education. In W.R. Houston (Ed.), *Handbook of research on teacher education* (pp. 758-781). New York: Macmillan.

Beighle, A., Pangrazi, R., & Vincent, S. (2001). Pedometers, physical activity, and accountability. *Journal of Physical Education, Recreation and Dance, 72*(9), 16-19, 36.

Berliner, D. (1986). In pursuit of the expert pedagogue. *Educational Researcher, 15*(6), 5-13.

Bolt, B. (1998). Encouraging cognitive growth. *Journal of Teaching in Physical Education, 18*, 90-102.

Capel, S., & Katene, W. (2002). Secondary PGCE students' perceptions of their subject knowledge. *European Physical Education Review, 6*, 46-67.

Chedzoy, S. (2000). Students' perceived competence to teach physical education to children aged 7 to 11 years in England. *European Journal of Physical Education, 9*, 104-127.

Clandinin, D., & Connelly, F. (1995). *Teachers' professional knowledge landscapes.* New York: Teacher College Press.

Cochran-Smith, M. (2002). What a difference a definition makes: Highly qualified teachers, scientific research, and teacher education. *Journal of Teacher Education, 53*, 187-189.

Cochran-Smith, M., & Lytle, S. (1999). Relationships of knowledge and practice: Teacher learning in communities. *Review of Research in Education, 24*, 249-305.

Collier, C., & O'Sullivan, M. (1997). Case method in physical education higher education: A pedagogy of change? *Quest, 49*, 198-213.

Corbin, C., & Eckert, H. (1990). *The evolving undergraduate major. American Academy of Physical Education Papers, No. 23.* Champaign, IL: Human Kinetics.

Curtner-Smith, M. (1998). Influence of biography, teacher education, and entry into the workforce on the perspectives and practices of first-year elementary school physical education teachers. *European Journal of Physical Education, 3*, 75-98.

Daniel, M., & Bergman-Drewe, S. (1998). Higher-order thinking, philosophy, and teacher education in physical education. *Quest, 50*, 33-58.

Devis-Devis, J., & Sparkes, A. (1999). Burning the book: A biographical study of a pedagogically inspired identity crisis in physical education. *European Physical Education Review, 5*, 135-152.

Dewar, A. (1989). Recruitment in physical education teaching: Toward a critical approach. In T. Templin & P. Schempp (Eds.), *Socialization into physical education: Learning to teach* (pp. 39-58). Indianapolis: Benchmark Press.

Dodds, P. (1989). Trainees, field experience, and socialization into teaching. In T.J. Templin & P.G. Schempp (Eds.), *Socialization into physical education: Learning to teach* (pp. 81-104). Indianapolis: Benchmark Press.

Dodds, P. (1994). Cognitive and behavioral components of expertise in teaching physical education. *Quest, 46*, 153-163.

Doolittle, S., Dodds, P., & Placek, J. (1993). Persistence of beliefs about teaching during formal training of pre-service teachers. *Journal of Teaching in Physical Education, 12*, 355-365.

Doyle, W. (1990). Themes in teacher education. In R. Houston (Ed.), *Handbook of research on teacher education* (pp. 3-24). New York: Macmillan.

Feiman-Nemser, S. (1990). Teacher preparation: Structural and conceptual alternatives. In R. Houston (Ed.), *Handbook of research on teacher education* (pp. 212-233). New York: Macmillan.

Fernandez-Balboa, J.M. (1997a). Knowledge base in physical education teacher education: A proposal for a new era. *Quest, 49*, 161-181.

Fernandez-Balboa, J.M. (1997b). *Critical postmodernism in human movement, physical education and sport.* Albany, NY: SUNY Press.

Graber, K.C. (1989). Teaching tomorrow's teachers: Professional socialization as an agent of socialization. In T. Templin & P. Schempp (Eds.), *Socialization into physical education: Learning to teach* (pp. 59-80). Indianapolis: Benchmark Press.

Graber, K.C. (1991). Studentship in pre-service teacher education: A qualitative study of undergraduates in physical education. *Research Quarterly for Exercise and Sport, 62*, 41-51.

Graber, K.C. (1995). The influence of teacher education programs on the beliefs of student teachers: General pedagogical knowledge, pedagogical content knowledge, and teacher education coursework. *Journal of Teaching in Physical Education, 14*, 157-178.

Graham, K. (1991). The influence of teacher education on pre-service development: Beyond a custodial orientation. *Quest, 43*(1), 1-19.

Griffey, D., & Housner, L. (1991). Differences between experienced and inexperienced teachers' planning decisions, interactions, student engagement, and instructional climate. *Research Quarterly for Exercise and Sport, 62*, 196-204.

Griffin, L., Mitchell, S., & Oslin, J. (1997). *Teaching sport concepts and skills.* Champaign, IL: Human Kinetics.

Griffin, L., & Placek, J. (2001). The understanding and development of learners' domain-specific knowledge. *Journal of Teaching in Physical Education* [Monograph], *20*(4).

Griffin, P. (1989). Gender as a socializing agent in physical education. In T. Templin & P. Schempp (Eds.),

Socialization into physical education: Learning to teach (pp. 219-234). Indianapolis: Benchmark Press.

Grossman, P. (1991). Mapping the terrain: Knowledge growth in teaching. In H.C. Waxman & H.J. Walberg (Eds.), *Effective teaching: Current research* (pp. 203-215). Berkeley, CA: McCutchan.

Hardy, C. (1999). Preservice teachers' perceptions of learning to teach in a predominantly school-based teacher education program. *Journal of Teaching in Physical Education, 18,* 175-198.

Hickey, C. (2001). "I feel enlightened now, but . . ." The limits to the pedagogic translation of critical social discourses in physical education. *Journal of Teaching in Physical Education, 20,* 227-246.

Hodge, S. (1998). Prospective physical education teachers' attitudes toward teaching students with disabilities. *Physical Educator, 55,* 68-77.

Holt, N.L., Strean, W.B., & Bengoechea, E.G. (2002). Expanding the teaching games for understanding model: New avenues for future research and practice. *Journal of Teaching in Physical Education, 21,* 162-176.

Housner, L., & French, K. (1994). Expertise in learning, performance, and instruction in sport and physical activity. *Quest, 46,* 149-152.

Houston, W.R. (1990). *Handbook of research on teacher education.* New York: Macmillan.

Howey, K., & Zimpher, N. (1989). *Profiles of preservice teacher education: Inquiry into the nature of programs.* Albany, NY: SUNY Press.

Hutchinson, G. (1993). Prospective teachers' perspectives on teaching physical education: An interview study on the recruitment phase of teacher socialization. *Journal of Teaching in Physical Education, 12,* 344-354.

Hutchinson, G., & Buschner, C. (1996). Delayed-entry undergraduates in physical education: Examining life experiences and career choice. *Journal of Teaching in Physical Education, 15,* 205-223.

Jones, R. (1992). Student teachers: Incidents that lead them to confirm or question their career choice. *Physical Educator, 49,* 205-212.

Juniu, S. (2002). Implementing handheld computing technology in physical education. *Journal of Physical Education, Recreation and Dance, 73*(3), 43-48.

Kirk, D. (1997). Thinking beyond the square: The challenge to physical educators in new times. *Quest, 49,* 182-186.

Ladson-Billings, G. 1994. *The dreamkeepers. Successful teachers of African American children.* San Francisco: Jossey-Bass.

Laker, A., & Jones, K. (1998). A longitudinal study of evolving student teacher concerns. *European Journal of Physical Education, 3,* 200-211.

Lawson, H. (1983). Toward a model of teacher socialization in physical education: The subjective warrant, recruitment, and teacher education. *Journal of Teaching in Physical Education, 2,* 3-16.

Lawson, H. (1999). Education for social responsibility:

Preconditions in retrospect and in prospect. *Quest, 51,* 116-149.

Livingston, C., & Borko, H. (1989). Expert-novice: Differences in teaching: A cognitive analysis and implications for teacher education. *Journal of Teacher Education, 40,* 36-42.

Livingston, L. (1996). Re-defining the role of physical activity courses in the preparation of physical education teaching professionals. *Physical Educator, 53,* 114-121.

Lortie, D. (1975). *Schoolteacher: A sociological study.* Chicago: University of Chicago Press.

McCullick, B. (2001). Practitioners' perspectives on values, knowledge, and skills needed by PETE participants. *Journal of Teaching in Physical Education, 21,* 35-56.

Metzler, M., & Tjeerdsma, B. (1998). PETE program assessment within a development, research, and improvement framework. *Journal of Teaching in Physical Education, 17,* 468-492.

National Academy of Education. (1999). *Recommendations regarding research priorities: An advisory report presented to the National Education Research Policy and Priorities Board.* Washington, DC: Author.

National Association for Sport and Physical Education. (2002a). *Initial guidelines for physical education teacher education* (5th ed.). Reston, VA: AAHPERD.

National Association for Sport and Physical Education. (2002b). *Guidelines for advanced programs in physical education program reports.* Reston, VA: AAHPERD. www.aahperd.org (available May 1, 2002)

National Commission of Teaching for America's Future. (1996). *What matters most: Teaching for America's future.* Kutztown, PA: Author.

National Commission of Teaching for America's Future. (1997). *Doing what matters most: Investing in quality teaching.* Kutztown, PA: Author.

National Research Council. (2001). *Scientific inquiry in education.* Washington, DC: National Academy Press.

Oakes, J., & Lipton, M. (1999). *Teaching to change the world.* New York: McGraw-Hill.

O'Bryant, C., O'Sullivan, M., & Raudensky, J. (2000). Socialization of prospective physical education teachers: The story of new blood. *Sport, Education, and Society, 5,* 177-193.

O'Connor, A., & Macdonald, D. (2002). Up close and personal on physical education teachers' identity: Is conflict an issue? *Sport, Education, and Society, 7,* 37-54.

O'Sullivan, M. (1990). Physical education teacher education in the United States. *Journal of Physical Education, Recreation and Dance, 61*(2), 41-45.

O'Sullivan, M., & Doutis, P. (1994). Research on expertise: Guideposts for expertise and teacher education in physical education. *Quest, 46,* 176-185.

O'Sullivan, M., Siedentop, D., & Locke, L. (1992). Toward collegiality: Competing viewpoints among teacher educators. *Quest, 44,* 266-280.

O'Sullivan, M., & Tsangaridou, N. (1992). What undergraduate physical education majors learn during a field experience. *Research Quarterly for Exercise and Sport, 63*, 381-392.

O'Sullivan, M., & Tsangaridou, N. (2001, November). *Community awareness and community mapping.* Presentation at the AIESEP International Conference, Madeira, Portugal.

Pare, C. (Ed.). (1995). Better teaching in physical education. Think about it? *Proceedings of the international seminar on Training of Teachers in Reflective Practice in Physical Education.* Trois-Rivières, Quebec: University du Quebec à Trois-Rivières.

Placek, J. (1983). Conceptions of success in teaching: Busy, happy, and good? In T. Templin and J. Olson (Eds.), *Teaching in physical education* (pp. 46-56). Champaign, IL: Human Kinetics.

Randall, L. (1992). *Systematic supervision for physical education.* Champaign, IL: Human Kinetics.

Richardson, V. (2001). *Handbook of research on teaching.* Washington, DC: American Educational Research Association.

Rink, J. (1993). Teacher education: A focus on action. *Quest, 45*, 308-320.

Romar, J.E. (1995). Case studies of Finnish physical education teachers: Espoused and enacted theories of action. (Doctoral dissertation, Ohio State University, 1995). *Dissertation Abstracts International, 55*, 3134A.

Rovegno, I. (1991). A participant-observation study of knowledge restructuring in a field-based elementary physical education methods course. *Research Quarterly for Exercise and Sport, 62*, 205-212.

Rovegno, I. (1995). Theoretical perspectives on knowledge and learning and a student teacher's pedagogical content knowledge of dividing and sequencing subject matter. *Journal of Teaching in Physical Education, 14*, 284-304.

Rovegno, I., Nevett, M., & Babiarz, M. (2001). Learning and teaching invasion-game tactics in 4th grade. *Journal of Teaching in Physical Education, 20*, 341-351.

Sanders, W. (1998). Value-added assessment. *School Administrator, 14*, 24-27.

Schalock, M.D. (1998). Accountability, student learning, and the preparation and licensure of teachers: Oregon's teacher work sample methodology. *Journal of Personnel Evaluation in Education, 12*, 269-286.

Schempp, P., Manross, D., Tan, S., & Fincher, M. (1998). Subject expertise and teachers' knowledge. *Journal of Teaching in Physical Education, 17*, 342-356.

Schön, D. (1987). *The reflective practitioner.* New York: Basic Books.

Sebren, A. (1995). Pre-service teachers' reflection and knowledge development in a field-based elementary physical education methods course. *Journal of Teaching in Physical Education, 14*, 262-283.

Shulman, L. (1986). Those who understand: Knowledge growth in teaching. *Educational Researcher, 15*(2), 4-14.

Shulman, L. (1987). Knowledge and teaching: Foundations of the new reform. *Harvard Educational Review, 57*(1), 1-22.

Shulman, L. (2002). Truth *and* consequences? Inquiry and policy in research on teacher education. *Journal of Teacher Education, 53*, 248-253.

Siedentop, D. (1989, April). *Content knowledge for physical education.* Paper presented at the Curriculum and Instruction Academy on the Implications of the Knowledge Base for Teaching and Teacher Education, at the annual AAHPERD convention, Boston.

Siedentop, D. (1990). Undergraduate teacher preparation. In C. Corbin & H. Eckert (Eds.), *The evolving undergraduate major. American Academy of Physical Education Papers, No. 23* (pp. 28-34). Champaign, IL: Human Kinetics.

Siedentop, D. (1994). *Sport education.* Champaign, IL: Human Kinetics.

Siedentop, D. (2002). Ecological perspectives in teaching research. *Journal of Teaching in Physical Education, 21*, 427-440.

Silverman, S. (1994). Communication and motor skill learning: What we learn from research in the gymnasium. *Quest, 46*, 345-355.

Silverman, S. (1997). Technology and physical education: Present, possibilities, and potential problems. *Quest, 49*, 306-314.

Sparkes, A. (1989). Paradigmatic confusions and the evasion of critical issues in naturalistic research. *Journal of Teaching in Physical Education, 8*, 131-151.

Sparkes, A. (Ed.) (1992). *Research in physical education and sport: Exploring alternative visions.* London: Falmer Press.

Stanley, C. (1997). Pre-service physical educators' attitudes toward cultural pluralism. A preliminary analysis. *Journal of Teaching in Physical Education, 16*, 241-249.

Stroot, S., Ward, P., O'Sullivan, M., Hodge, S., & Goodway, J. (2002). *Teacher work sample in a teacher education program.* Presentation at the annual AAHPERD convention, San Diego.

Templin, T. (1979). Occupational socialization and the physical education student teacher. *Research Quarterly, 50*, 482-493.

Thomas, J.R. (1990). The body of knowledge: A common core. In C. Corbin & H. Eckert (Eds.), *The evolving undergraduate major. American Academy of Physical Education Papers, No. 23* (pp. 5-15). Champaign, IL: Human Kinetics.

Tinning, R. (1992, July). *Teacher education and the development of content knowledge for physical education teaching.* Keynote address for the conference "The Place of General and Subject Matter Specific Teaching Methods in Teacher Education," Santiago de Compestela, Spain.

Tinning, R. (1997). *Pedagogies for physical education: Pauline's story.* Geelong, Australia: Deakin University Press.

Tinning, R. (2000). Unsettling matters for physical education in higher education: Implications of "New Times." *Quest, 52,* 32-48.

Tsangaridou, N., & O'Sullivan, M. (1994). Using pedagogical reflective strategies to enhance reflection among pre-service physical education teachers. *Journal of Teaching in Physical Education, 14*(1), 13-33.

Tsangaridou, N., & O'Sullivan, M. (1997). The role of reflection in shaping physical education teachers' educational values and practices. *Journal of Teaching in Physical Education, 17,* 2-25.

Valenzuela, A. (2002). Reflections on the subtractive underpinnings of education research and policy. *Journal of Teacher Education, 53,* 235-241.

Weiner, L. (2000). Research in the 90s: Implications for urban teacher preparation. *Review of Educational Research, 70,* 369-406.

Weiner, L. (2002). Evidence and inquiry in teacher education: What's needed for urban schools. *Journal of Teacher Education, 53,* 254-261.

Wilson, S., Floden, R., & Ferrini-Mundy, J. (2001). *Teacher preparation research: Current knowledge, gaps, and recommendations. A research report prepared for the U.S. Department of Education.* Seattle: Center for the Study of Teaching and Policy.

Wilson, S., Floden, R., & Ferrini-Mundy, J. (2002). Teacher preparation research: An insider's view from the outside. *Journal of Teacher Education, 53,* 190-204.

Wright, J. (1995). A feminist poststructuralist methodology for the study of gender construction in physical education: Description of a study. *Journal of Teaching in Physical Education, 15,* 1-24.

Zeichner, K., & Liston, D. (1987). Teaching student teachers to reflect. *Harvard Educational Review, 57*(1), 1-22.

Zeichner, K., & Miller, M. (1997). Learning to teach in professional development schools. In M. Levine & R. Trachtman (Eds.), *Making professional development schools work: Politics, practice, and policy* (pp. 15-32). New York: Teachers College Press.

CHAPTER SEVENTEEN

TEACHERS' KNOWLEDGE CONSTRUCTION

Inez Rovegno

Teachers work in complex, ever-changing environments. Within these environments, their work is practical, that is, oriented toward actions—helping students learn, teaching and managing large numbers of students, reacting to unpredictable situations that arise during a school day, recognizing and solving problems, working with colleagues, and dealing with a host of other day-to-day activities. What works for one teacher in one setting will not necessarily work for another teacher in a different setting. Schools are different, and teachers are different. Teachers are not born with the knowledge to deal with this complex environment; they construct this knowledge over time and with experience. Because teachers' knowledge plays a critical role in what and how they teach, researchers have begun to study teachers' knowledge and how this knowledge grows out of and reflects practice.

Research on teachers' knowledge construction began in the 1980s for several reasons. First, researchers needed to ask questions that quantitative, behavioral research on teaching effectiveness, the predominant form of research, could not address. For example, researchers were curious about teachers' knowledge of subject matter, their curricular choices and preferences, their beliefs about teaching practices, their philosophies, and why they behaved as they did. Examining teachers' knowledge enabled researchers to have more complete understanding about what happens in classrooms.

A second reason that scholars began to study teachers' knowledge was that in the 1970s much of the research used researcher-designed, predetermined observation tools that could quantify what researchers were delineating as most effective practice. Although this was and remains an important agenda, relying solely on researchers' perspectives was too narrow for defining good teaching. To understand good teaching, we needed to hear teachers' voices and study what good teachers thought, knew, and believed. Thus, researchers began, in Shulman's (1987) terms, to codify the wisdom of practicing teachers.

Third, scholars recognized the importance of understanding how teachers learn and develop. In the same way that knowledge of how children learn and develop informs teachers, understanding how teachers learn and develop helps teacher educators and staff developers design programs that are more effective and improve professional development opportunities.

WHAT IS THE NATURE OF TEACHERS' KNOWLEDGE?

Researchers began by asking "What is the nature of teachers' knowledge?" Studies in general education and physical education identified the following characteristics of teachers' knowledge.

Teachers' Knowledge As Practical Knowledge

Elbaz (1981, 1983) and Clandinin (1986) found that teachers' knowledge is a practical form of knowledge. Oriented toward practice, practical knowledge enables teachers to know what to do, how to do it, and how to manage the dilemmas and problems that arise in specific situations.

Teachers' Knowledge As Personal Knowledge

Teachers' knowledge also was found to be personal, meaning that it reflects an individual teacher's biography, values, knowledge, and experiences in the school context. For example, in physical education McCaughtry (2001) showed how teachers' deep, personal concerns about their students' difficult life experiences and negative reactions to sports units caused the teachers to seek and acquire knowledge of project adventure units that developed a cooperative ethic and fitness units that addressed adolescent girls' concerns about their bodies and weight. Thus, the teachers' practical knowledge had personal and emotional dimensions.

Teachers' Knowledge As Complex

Because teachers use their knowledge in practice, it develops through experience and, in turn, reflects the world of practice where tacit understandings, intuition, and on-the-go appraising, adjusting, and improvising are necessary components (Schön, 1983). In practice, problems often lack clear definition, and linear, systematic problem solving cannot easily provide solutions (Schön, 1983). Practice is complex, and teachers' knowledge reflects this complexity.

Because of the complexity of practice, teachers' knowledge is not a tightly woven set of coherent ideas and principles. Rather, it can include illogical, incomplete, and contradictory elements. For example, Green (2000) studied teachers' philosophies and found that teachers held confused and sometimes contradictory views. O'Reilly, Tompkins, and Gallant (2001) described how the teachers in their study wanted students to have fun in physical education to encourage their lifelong participation in physical activities. To keep lessons enjoyable, the teachers used large group games and de-emphasized skill development, thus preventing students from being skillful enough to participate in lifelong physical activities.

Teachers' Knowledge As Situated

Finally, teachers' knowledge was found to be "situated," meaning that it functions (or is "situated") in practice, grows out of and is shaped by practice, and shapes practice (Elbaz, 1983; Rovegno, 1994).

A theoretical perspective useful for understanding teachers' knowledge is a situated perspective (Clancey, 1997; Lave, 1988; Newell, 1986; Rogoff, 1990). Situated perspectives describe how individuals think, know, and act in practical situations. One major principle of situated perspectives is that the individual, the activity in which the individual is engaged, and the environment are an inseparable unit of analysis. When conducting a study, therefore, researchers must consider, at a minimum, the individual, the activity, and the environment as a unit. Relationships and interactions of the individual teacher (including the teacher's biography, values, goals, and capabilities); the act of teaching; and the physical, social, and cultural school environment are critical and cannot be ignored because these relationships will affect the findings. For example, Barrett and Collie (1996) in their study of pedagogical content knowledge of lacrosse, described understanding how changes in the task and environment (from children running on different pathways in a random pattern about the gymnasium to a wave organizational pattern in which small groups of children all run in the same direction straight across the gymnasium) resulted in changes in the children's lacrosse cradling movements. Having more space to accelerate (a change in the environment) allowed faster speed (a change in the task) that elicited more mature movement patterns in the lacrosse cradle (a change in the individual's response). Rovegno, Nevett, Brock, and Babiarz (2001) also described learning how changes in the task and environment of game play could benefit or constrain cutting and passing in an invasion game. For example, a larger space (an environmental constraint) elicited more unsuccessful long passes. Adding a defender (a task constraint) facilitated better cutting and passing as the defender added authenticity and helped the children understand that the purpose of cutting and sending lead passes was to keep the ball away from a defender.

HOW IS TEACHERS' KNOWLEDGE CONSTRUCTED?

As researchers examined the characteristics of teachers' knowledge, they also studied how this knowledge developed, which aspects changed over time, and the factors that facilitated or constrained knowledge development. They asked "How is teachers' knowledge constructed?"

What Is the Theory Underlying the Research?

In general, constructivist theories on learning and knowledge have guided (explicitly or implicitly) the research on teachers' knowledge construction. Researchers have used two major ideas from these theories. First, based on their prior knowledge and experiences, teachers actively construct new knowledge (Fosnot, 1996; Grennon-Brooks & Brooks, 1993; Iran-Nejad, 1990; Prawat, 1992; Resnick & Williams Hall, 1998; Shuell, 1986, 1990). Teachers do not listen to or read about new information or ideas and simply absorb it into their heads exactly as it was presented. Instead, teachers (or any learners) make sense of new information in relation to what they already know and have experienced. In essence, individuals learn by starting with what they know and asking, at either a conscious or an unconscious level, "How is this new information related to what I already know?" "How is it different?" "How can I connect this new information to my previous experiences?" "How might I reconsider my previous experiences in light of this new information?" "How does my intuitive sense of the world relate to this new information?" This process is called active because the teacher engages with, or in a sense plays with, the new information. The knowledge that results from this active engagement is not the same as the information that was presented.

The second major idea from constructivist theories is that knowledge is socially constructed (Cobb, 1994; Denzin & Lincoln, 1994; Driver, Asoko, Leach, Mortimer, &

Scott, 1994; Prawat, 1992). More narrowly applied, the social construction of knowledge means that individuals learn through social interactions with other individuals. Important social interactions for teachers include other teachers, students in their classes, and school and professional personnel. More broadly applied, the social construction of knowledge means that as a profession we collectively produce and agree on what is knowledge and that this knowledge changes over time. This concept can be as simple as the fact that basketball field goals were once worth two points and are now worth two or three depending on where they were shot from or as complex as the now well-accepted idea that no group of students should be privileged and given greater access to resources based on race or gender.

What Is the Direction of Knowledge Development: Increased Connections and Details

One theoretical principle of knowledge construction is that with development, knowledge becomes more differentiated (i.e., includes increased details) and more connected. In other words, individuals understand more and finer details about each concept while at the same time understanding more connections among concepts. Werner first articulated this principle of development in 1957.

Recent studies comparing novice and expert teachers have supported this principle as viable for understanding teachers' knowledge development. Within physical education, studies found that compared with novices, experts' knowledge is more differentiated, more organized, and more connected (Chen & Rovegno, 2000; Ennis, Mueller, & Zhu, 1991; Graham, French, & Woods, 1993; Housner & Griffey, 1985; Rink, French, Lee, Solmon, & Lynn, 1994; Schempp, Manross, Tan, & Fincher, 1998; Sharpe & Hawkins, 1992; Tan, 1996). Specifically, experts know more concepts and more details about concepts. Experts make more connections among concepts and broader issues, principles, and ideas. Experts see and interpret teaching in more depth. In addition, experts' knowledge appears to be more situated in that they base teaching decisions more on contextual cues, attend to a wider range of children's needs, focus more on performance quality and helping children make connections, and more fully integrate cognitive processes into movement lessons (Byra & Sherman, 1993; Chen, 2001; Chen & Rovegno, 2000; Ennis, 1991; Graham, Hopple, Manross, & Sitzman, 1993; Hastie & Vlaisavljevic, 1999; Housner & Griffey, 1985; Sharpe & Hawkins, 1992; Tan, 1996).

Studies that looked directly at the knowledge construction process report similar findings. For example, whereas teachers initially seemed to have little sense of progression, with development they learned to break down content into progressions with smaller steps, build progressions based on broader, long-term objectives, and build more detailed progressions that include all of the critical content needed for culminating unit activities (Pissanos & Allison, 1996; Rovegno 1992a, 1992b, 1993a, 1993b, 1998; Sebran, 1995). Similarly, although teachers initially lacked detailed knowledge about content, over time they constructed more detailed knowledge that enabled them better to modify tasks, focus children's attention within an activity, observe and give relevant feedback, ask questions to facilitate children's learning, and use equipment to refine performance (Rovegno, 1992b, 1993b, 1998).

Studies examining the knowledge construction process also suggest, like the novice-expert studies, that teachers' knowledge develops from disconnected knowing and understanding the parts to connected knowing and understanding the parts in relation to a larger whole. This includes constructing knowledge about how skills connect to movement concepts, movement concepts to sport, and lesson activities to broader, long-term objectives (Rovegno, 1992a, 1993a, 1998; Sebran, 1995). Studies that have examined the observations made by preservice teachers reported that students early in their programs pay little attention to details, but as seniors they report seeing more movements and a broader range of movements (Allison, 1987; Barrett, Allison, & Bell, 1987; Bell, Barrett, & Allison, 1985).

In summary, in the beginning of the learning process teachers do not recognize details or connections. As learning continues, they recognize details and connections and understand concepts as part of a larger whole. In the next sections of this chapter, I will describe the role of experience, the role of prior knowledge, and the role of the school context in teachers' knowledge construction. I end with a summary of several studies that describe successful, large-scale knowledge development.

Role of Experience

As a practical, action form of knowledge, experience plays a critical role in teachers' knowledge construction. When teachers construct their knowledge about teaching, they construct a cognitive understanding of, for example, a particular teaching technique such as giving feedback or a new curricular approach. This idea is called knowing "that," or knowing about teaching. However, knowing "that" is not the same as knowing "how," a distinction first made by Ryle, a philosopher, in 1949. Knowing "how" means being able to do a teaching technique in practice. Through experience, teachers learn to use their knowledge about teaching in practice. Several studies have found that beginning teachers report knowing about various teaching techniques but not being able to use their knowledge in practice (Napper-Owens, 1996; Rovegno, 1992b, 1993a). They knew "that" but not "how." Experience was critical in helping them develop knowledge of how to teach.

Experience is also a critical source of knowledge for teachers (Schempp, 1993), most significantly in helping them develop their pedagogical content knowledge. Pedagogical content knowledge is knowledge of content for teaching that blends knowledge of how to teach, subject matter, and how children learn (Shulman, 1987). In regard to pedagogical content knowledge, research reports that experience helps teachers learn how students respond to the tasks teachers presented, how to observe and what to look for, how to give content specific feedback, how to change tasks on their feet to respond to student responses, how to break down tasks to enable greater student learning, how to demonstrate and present information, how the task and environment affects students' responses, and how to differentiate what is developmentally appropriate for different grade levels (Barrett & Collie, 1996; Barrett & Turner, 2000; Napper-Owen, 1996; Rovegno, 1992a, 1992b, 1998). Thus, understanding how students learn content in school contexts and the relationships among content, learning, and teaching that content are significant aspects of knowledge construction for teachers.

Finally, experience enables teachers to understand theory in practice and theory through practice. Through experience, teachers learn how curricular innovations and theoretical ideas work for them in their situation and what to modify and how to adapt theory to their particular students (Cothran, 2001; Kirk, 1988; Rovegno, 1998, Schempp, 1993). Experience requires that teachers work out the details of ideas they learn in in-service workshops and professional reading. This process can help them better understand theory or a new curricular approach in a more concrete and integrated way (Barrett & Turner, 2000; Cothran, 2001; Rovegno, 1998). In other words, teachers can refine their knowledge of theory through practice.

Role of Prior Knowledge

As constructivism predicts, researchers have consistently found that prior knowledge and experiences influence teachers' knowledge construction. Researchers examining knowledge construction have approached the role of prior knowledge broadly, discussed first, and more narrowly in relation to learning specific concepts, discussed second.

Kirk (1988) was one of the first researchers in physical education to describe the broad role of prior knowledge and experience in teachers' knowledge construction and use of an innovative curricular approach. The curricular approach was a health-related fitness program that emphasized theory lessons, lifestyle management, problem solving, various fitness activities, and the use of sport for fitness and leisure. The new fitness program was intended to replace a traditional sport program emphasizing competitive success. Kirk found that the teachers' prior knowledge and past experiences teaching the traditional approach influenced their actions and constrained how they understood the new approach. Kirk termed the impact of the traditional approach "residual ideologies." Residual ideologies influenced what teachers considered successful and not successful and resulted in their modifying the innovation in unintended ways. Ennis, Mueller, and Hooper (1990) also showed how teachers' orientation toward a traditional, disciplinary mastery approach constrained their acceptance and use of aspects of an innovative approach learned in an in-service workshop.

Experience in athletics and knowledge of typical coaching practices are common elements of physical education teachers' knowledge and prior experiences (Placek, Dodds, Doolittle, Portman, Ratliffe, & Pinkham, 1995; Wright, 2001). Because of its prominence and because athletics subscribes to an elitist ideology in which the most skilled performers are privileged with rewards, playing time, and prestige, researchers have focused on understanding the effect of teachers' experience in athletics.

Although one study reported a close correspondence between the amount of experience in athletics and the extent to which teachers were conservative toward change to a new curricular approach (Curtner-Smith, 1999), most research shows that the effect of sport experiences is not universally positive or negative. The results of three studies illustrate this point.

Hickey (2001) presented two contrasting case studies on preservice teachers' responses to learning and implementing critical pedagogy. Critical pedagogy attempts to overcome inequity and injustice in schools. Because of prior knowledge and experiences, one participant encountered critical pedagogy and found it "confirming and enlightening." She made serious attempts to implement inclusive and equitable pedagogy. The other participant tried critical pedagogy once and then went back to teaching in a more familiar, traditional style. His concern that critical pedagogy would lower standards along with his successful experiences in elitist sport settings led to his rejection of a critical orientation.

Pagnano and Langley (2001) also presented two contrasting case studies. One teacher valued an authoritarian style and control and used exercise as punishment—values and teaching behaviors that she experienced in competitive sport. The other teacher did not agree with using exercise as punishment. She valued a democratic style and the empowerment of students—values associated with the joy and positive self-esteem she experienced as a participant in exercise and sport settings. Finally, of the 11 students studied by Rovegno (1993a), 3 preservice teachers with athletic experience and 2 without athletic experience initially reacted negatively to an educationally oriented physical education curriculum, whereas 3 with athletic experience and 4 without athletic experiences reacted positively. Thus, prior knowledge and experiences sometimes constrain teachers' knowledge construction and sometimes do not.

Reconstructing Taken-for-Granted Aspects of Prior Knowledge

Several studies have shown that teachers can build new knowledge that is discrepant with their prior knowledge (Curtner-Smith, 1997; Metzler & Tjeerdsma, 2000; Rovegno, 1993a; Woods, Goc-Karp, & Escamilla, 2000). Although we often think about knowledge as information that has been made explicit and learned at a conscious level, teachers' knowledge also includes information that they have not actively considered or examined in any depth. Teachers may take ideas for granted because they seem obvious or because teachers assume them to be accurate and appropriately applied in educational settings. Research has reported that transformations of taken-for-granted knowledge can be critical in teachers' development. Two examples follow.

Cultural Templates

In a large study of one entire cohort and a portion of a second cohort, Rovegno (1993a) examined how the teacher education program at the University of South Florida helped preservice teachers overcome the taken-for-granted cultural templates of sport and stereotypes of physical education teachers. Regardless of their initial reaction, all 11 students eventually embraced and attempted to implement an educational approach in their first-year teaching. Faculty formed a united front and across courses presented a critique of elitist sport practices; roll-out-the-ball, recreational practices; and the preservice teachers' prior knowledge of and experiences in physical education and athletics. This critique helped the preservice teachers understand the political aspects of marginality and elitist sport that they had taken for granted in their understanding of physical education. This new awareness set the stage for the development of pride in a movement approach that emphasized learning movement skills, cognitive processes, social responsibility, educational goals, and equity and success for all children.

Although a concerted effort by teacher educators to present alternative conceptions to preservice teachers' prior knowledge can help, it is not enough to ensure use of that new knowledge in teaching. Brown (1999) showed how course work helped two male preservice teachers reject sexist approaches to physical education and the use of "macho" stereotypes to deal with management and control. Nevertheless, in student teaching they reacted in keeping with stereotypes, although these reactions reinforced the very stereotypes that they did not accept. Their biographies did not limit what they learned and valued, but their limited knowledge and experience with activities such as dance and gymnastics did not give them enough alternative practices to do what they wanted in their teaching.

Curriculum Scripts

Curriculum scripts are taken-for-granted ideas about the appropriate progression of tasks within a lesson or unit. A teacher talking about what she had taken for granted in her early years described an example of a curriculum script familiar to many teachers:

> *Lori:* If I taught basketball, I taught dribbling, throwing and catching, all the passes. I taught shooting. Then I just kind of shoved them [the students] into the adult game. It was very frustrating to me as a teacher because, of course, they couldn't play the adult game. (Pissanos & Allison, 1996, p. 8)

Another common curriculum script reported in research is to teach the biomechanically efficient body position of the forearm pass, set, and serve and then play volleyball games without teaching students how to use skills in gamelike ways (Rovegno, 1995).

Research has shown that teachers can critique curriculum scripts they have taken for granted and reconstruct a new understanding of progression—one that includes teaching skills as open skills and combining skills and tactics in gamelike situations (Barrett & Turner, 2000; Pissanos & Allison, 1996; Rovegno, 1993b; Rovegno & Bandhauer, 1994). For example, Barrett and Turner (2000) described the initial resistance and then successful attempts of a teacher to reconstruct her knowledge of progression from, in the teacher's words, "skills first, game second" to "game first, skills second," letting the skills and tactics emerge and develop together.

Restructuring Prior Knowledge and Initial Conceptions: The Road Is Bumpy

Research has shown that the knowledge construction process is not simple, linear, or straightforward. What teachers need to learn and know about teaching, subject matter, children, and the context of schools is complex and poorly structured, and teachers must adapt their knowledge of those aspects across a range of different situations. Acquiring this kind of knowledge is called advanced knowledge acquisition because teachers must learn about many concepts within an ill-structured domain and be able to apply those concepts flexibly (Spiro, Coulson, Feltovich, & Anderson, 1988). Because of the complexity, teachers do not simply acquire chunks of knowledge that get added on to what they already know. The process of knowledge construction includes times when teachers are confused, when they maintain conflicting ideas, when they have only partial or inaccurate understanding, and when their knowledge changes in substantial ways, almost seeming like a reversal.

One theory proposes that knowledge develops through three major processes: accretion, tuning, and restructuring (Rumelhart & Norman, 1978). In accretion, new information is added to old knowledge structures. In tuning, new information is added and knowledge structures are modified, resulting in new knowledge. Restructuring means that knowledge changes in substantial, qualitative ways. Research has reported all three forms of knowledge change. Ennis, Mueller, and Zhu (1991) found that preservice teachers early in their program appeared to take new information presented by teacher educators and fit this information in their prior, sport-oriented knowledge structures. These changes most often represented accretion although tuning occurred in some instances. Students who had completed student teaching had more knowledge that showed evidence of tuning and some restructuring. Experts, whose knowledge was compared with the preservice teachers, showed characteristics of restructuring.

Other research has identified several aspects of teachers' prior knowledge and initial conceptions that show evidence of restructuring, and teachers reported that these important qualitative changes in their knowledge helped them be better teachers. Sometimes they labeled these changes "Ah ha" moments—times when the light bulb went on.

The first example of knowledge restructuring is a shift from focusing on presenting activities and management to focusing on children's learning and on the meanings that children make. One study of four highly experienced teachers found that, over time, the teachers shifted from an authoritarian approach and concern with management to a concern about their influence on student learning and a more flexible style aimed at meeting individual student's needs (Tsangaridou & O'Sullivan, 1997). Three other studies found that teachers initially conceived of teaching as telling (i.e., simply presenting information to students) and content simply as presenting activities one right after the other (Rovegno, 1992a, 1992b, 1992c, 1998). After they restructured these conceptions, teachers understood that teaching meant getting children to learn the content within the activity and, moreover, that activities included a substantial amount of content, including movement components within skills, tactics within games, and movement quality within movement variety activities that, initially, seemed simple and devoid of content. In other words, the teachers learned to focus on what children were learning at a more detailed level. The expert-novice studies also support a similar shift from novices focused on teaching activities and experts focused on the effect on students' learning (Goc-Karp & Zakrajsek, 1987, Graham, French, & Woods, 1993; Graham, Hopple, Manross, & Sitzman, 1993)

The second example of knowledge restructuring that teachers considered important is a change from blaming students for problems to taking responsibility for problems and revising their teaching, content, and interpretations of students' responses (Cothran,

2001; McCaughtry & Rovegno, 2002; Pissanos & Allison, 1996; Rovegno, 1991). For example, preservice teachers initially thought that the children were to blame for problems with learning and claimed that the children were not listening and not trying (Rovegno, 1991). They then learned that the same children were eager, trying, and wanted to learn and that the problem was their initial, inaccurate interpretation of what they saw. In another study, preservice teachers initially blamed student attitudes for lack of learning and success and then came to realize that student problems resulted from the teachers' tasks and the ways they taught and interacted with the students (McCaughtry & Rovegno, 2002).

A third example of knowledge restructuring is a change from initially thinking that (a) constructivist-oriented teaching, (b) problem solving styles, and teaching (c) decision making, creative thinking and critical thinking meant not telling children what to do, not intervening, and accepting any and all responses the children made (Rovegno, 1992a, 1998). Teachers learned that there are times to tell children what to do, times to elicit movement responses, times to give explicit information, and times to ask questions. They learned that they need to teach thinking skills, that they could teach those skills explicitly, and that they need to intervene and guide creative thinking and decision-making tasks. Studies of novice and experienced teachers suggest that a sophisticated understanding of how to facilitate cognitive and social processes while teaching motor content is a critical part of the teacher development process (Chen, 2001; Chen & Rovegno, 2000; Ennis, 1991; Pissanos & Allison, 1996).

These three transformations in teachers' knowledge are critical in that they represent more "relational" knowledge of the teaching and learning process. By "relational" I mean that the teachers learned about the relations among the physical and social environment, the tasks they designed, and students' responses. As situated theory (Clancey, 1997; Lave, 1988; Newell, 1986; Rogoff, 1990) predicts, teachers learned that problems with children's learning are not the fault of children but occur because of the interactions among the children's capabilities and the activities and environment structured by the teacher. Teachers learned about the complex, interactive nature of the teaching learning process and learned to take responsibility for what they controlled within that process.

Role of the School Context: Does It Facilitate or Constrain Knowledge Construction?

In addition to experience and prior knowledge, the school context plays a role in teachers' knowledge construction. Research has shown that teachers' knowledge develops within the school context and is shaped by that context (Elbaz, 1983; Rovegno, 1994). The community (Pissanos & Allison, 1996; Schempp, 1993), peers and administrators, and students have all been found to have an influence on teachers' knowledge construction. The critical question is whether this influence is positive or negative. The answer, it seems, is that it depends on the teacher and the context.

Social Interactions and the Construction of Knowledge: Peers and Administrators

One major tenet of constructivist theory is that knowledge is socially constructed through social interactions (Prawat, 1992; Cobb, 1994; Driver, Asoko, Leach, Mortimer, & Scott, 1994). Research shows that teachers' knowledge can be constructed through social interactions among peers and administrators (Doutis & Ward, 1999). For example, Kirk (1988) described the process by which all members of a secondary physical education department collaborated on a new curriculum. The collaboration included conflicts, negotiations, and the development of shared ideals. Teachers' discussions and conflicts had a major effect on the teachers' understanding of the new curriculum. In another example, Howarth (2000) compared three teachers who participated in schoolwide programs aimed at integrating thinking skills in all subject areas—a difficult and complex task for the physical education teachers. The two schools supporting the most successful collaborations among the teachers best facilitated the physical education teachers' knowledge and use of teaching thinking skills in physical education.

Through social interactions, teachers and administrators create and maintain shared knowledge and cultural norms for their schools. These norms can both facilitate and constrain teachers' knowledge development. For example, Sparkes (1987) described the collaboration within one department that resulted in the construction of new ways to justify physical education within the school and provide a rationale for change. But most of the teachers did not change their practices. Teachers learned to engage in "strategic rhetoric" to justify physical education, which constrained the possibilities of change.

In contrast, Rovegno and Bandhauer (1997a) described how the administrators, classroom teachers, and the physical education teacher interacted to create a set of school norms that worked to facilitate teachers' knowledge construction. First, they collaborated and developed a set of shared visions and a school philosophy that guided the development of new ideas and approaches. Second, teachers and administrators created a norm for teacher learning and continual school improvement. Because of this norm, teachers collaborated, shared ideas, and experimented with new approaches, which in turn facilitated knowledge construction. In addition, teachers, administrators, and staff shared the belief that they could successfully identify and solve problems in their school. This "can do" norm also facilitated knowledge construction. Similarly, Dyson and O'Sullivan (1998) described two schools in which teachers and administrators collaborated to develop a shared vision and philosophy that supported the successful construction and use of an innovative curriculum.

At a more individual level, social interactions with more experienced peers can be an important way for beginning teachers to construct knowledge (Rovegno, 1998). One study showed that by observing and talking informally with more experienced peers, beginning teachers constructed more developed knowledge about how to make connections between lesson tasks and broader objectives, how to give feedback when children were learning to make decisions and solve problems, and when to ask questions and when to give information. Although social interactions with peers and administrators can be a significant way to construct new knowledge, teachers without such opportunities but with some support of administrators can create their own space (Curtner-Smith, 2001) and even their own programs (Cothran, 2001; McCaughtry, 2001) within a school in which they can build and refine knowledge.

Students

Studies show that students are a primary source of knowledge for teachers (Pissanos & Allison, 1996; Rovegno, 1998; Rovegno & Bandhauer, 1997b; Schempp, 1993; Tsangaridou & O'Sullivan, 1997; Ward & O'Sullivan, 1998; Woods, Goc-Karp, & Escamilla, 2000). Teachers observe the responses of students and construct more detailed knowledge about how to teach specific content, how students respond and learn, how to structure the learning environment and motivational climate, and how to establish objectives for their students.

On the negative side, research shows that if teachers believe that students will react in negative ways or if they experience negative reactions, they can teach within a curricular zone of safety and limit what they attempt to teach and learn (Rovegno, 1994; Schempp, 1993; Siedentop, Doutis, Tsangaridou, Ward, & Rauschenbach, 1994). As Green (2000) showed, teachers' goals for what activities they taught were based on what they perceived they could do in their contexts. They constructed their "everyday philosophies" within the limits of what they perceived to be their constraints. Research by Chen (1999), Ennis (1995), and Cothran and Ennis (1997), in which teachers describe long-term changes in their curriculum from a focus on learning to a focus on discipline as a result of changes in the student population, provides evidence that teachers' understanding of students can seriously constrain knowledge development.

On the positive side, teachers' perceptions of students can facilitate long-term and substantial change in teachers' knowledge and curriculum. I will discuss this in the next section of the chapter.

Long-Term, Substantial Knowledge Construction

Although research on the role of the context shows that some contexts constrain teachers' development, other studies report that some teachers exhibit resiliency, have the ability to solve problems, and maintain optimistic expectations and a sense of personal power (Woods & Lynn, 2001). These teachers can manage difficult situations in their school contexts.

Several studies have described teachers who have successfully developed their knowledge and made substantial changes in their teaching and programs. Five qualitative studies with remarkably similar results are discussed next. I have combined the teachers' stories and included direct quotations from the teachers. One of the goals of qualitative research is to share teachers' stories in the hope of opening possibilities of change for other teachers. Here is their collective story:

Being Dissatisfied

Teachers who describe positive, substantial knowledge development and curricular change all report the major impetus for this change was looking at the effect of their programs on their students and being dissatisfied with what they saw.

> *Karen:* It was kind of like the saying, "If it ain't broke, don't fix it." Well, it was broke. We were having kids who were not taking responsibility for their own discipline. I was really open to finding something that would really affect them in their heart, not just in their head. I was having trouble reaching what I considered a connected level with the kids on the issue of their social responsibilities in class. I was ready to try something and the something that I was fortunate to find was the Hellison Model. (Cothran, 2001, p. 72)

Thus, teachers looked at their lessons and saw lack of student learning and skill development, students with disrespectful attitudes, students who were bored and disconnected, students who argued after games, and students who felt bad about themselves after they lost. The teachers held themselves accountable for these problems and decided to change (Cothran, 2001; McCaughtry, 2001; Pissanos & Allison, 1996; Rovegno & Bandhauer, 1997b).

The Bumpy Road

For the teachers, change meant learning new curricular approaches through various professional development avenues. The knowledge development process meant taking ideas from their reading, workshops, graduate course work, or discussions with nearby university faculty and experimenting with these ideas in practice, most often over an extended period.

> *Robin:* You're always looking for that instant fix or something that is so wonderful that everybody will just say, "Yes, this is it!" But it just doesn't work that way. You know you have to adapt so many things to your situation or your personal strength. It's an evolving process to see how this works. It's a work in progress as to how it will end up. Next year maybe I'll try something different and look for the next natural step to take. (Cothran, 2001, p. 76)

Teachers described several reasons that transferring ideas to practice was not easy. Sometimes the information in the literature was not specific enough or adapted to the teachers' particular situations, or sometimes the teachers did not have enough training to be able to use what they learned (Cothran, 2001; Pissanos & Allison, 1996; Rovegno, 1998; Rovegno & Bandhauer, 1997b).

> *Elaine:* The whole lesson, every sentence was a question sentence. Can you do this and do that? And there was no meat inside the lesson, it was just questions. There was no concrete portion. I was just like, "Well do I just stand there and read these questions?" It had no structure—how you go about teaching it. How do you put these in a lesson plan? . . . I'm looking at it now, and I'm knowing what to do. I can tell you when I first read this, I was like, "How am I supposed to do this?" (Rovegno, 1998, p. 156)

Quite simply, constructing knowledge of a new curricular approach is not easy. Change takes time and a willingness to suspend judgment, experiment, and practice new ideas repeatedly. When faced with problems, the teachers did not give up on the new idea, themselves, or their students, but tried and tried again, watching the responses of their students and then modifying their practice to get the new idea working (Cothran, 2001; Pissanos & Allison, 1996; Rovegno, 1998; Rovegno & Bandhauer, 1997b).

> *Vicki:* At first you'll make a lot of mistakes and it won't be easy. It will be rough and crude the first unit you try it on. Then you refine it and go ahead and then put it in another unit. (Cothran, 2001, p. 76)

Being confused about a new content idea, teaching technique, or approach to learning was part of the knowledge construction process (Pissanos & Allison, 1996; Rovegno, 1993a, 1993b, 1998). Teachers who successfully build substantial new knowledge over time keep going despite confusion and false starts.

It's About Kids

Critical for sustaining teachers through the difficult and long-term process was their commitment to the philosophy of the new curricular approach and what it could do for students.

> *Dianna:* A lot of people see what you do and like it, but go and say, "It won't work in my school," or "My kids will never do that," because they never were instilled in the deeper meaning, I mean really, that is a real crucial thing—the deeper meaning of what all this is going to do for kids. Because I went to all those trainings with *Every Child a Winner*, I always kept thinking, "reinforcement of the philosophy." Every workshop that I went to, the books that I would read, I always kept reinforcing that. So, I had something ingrained in me and I didn't want to let that go. Those things were right for children and no matter what anybody else says, I wasn't going to get off that path, no matter how hard it was. I was going to stay on that path. Maybe that's what allowed me to keep going ahead. Maybe it's the pedigree that kept me from changing. (Rovegno & Bandhauer, 1997b, p. 145)

Although we often write about teachers' prior knowledge and experiences as a constraint to further learning and as something that must be critiqued, teachers also hold prior conceptions and beliefs about what is right and good for students that can support new knowledge construction. In these instances, knowledge construction means beginning with ideas a teacher considers theoretically sound and philosophically warranted, and then applying and reconstructing these ideas through practice.

Thus, students not only serve as an impetus for knowledge development and as critical sources of knowledge but also play a critical role in sustaining teacher development.

Lori: You know when I started to see them increase in their skillfulness in games, dance, and gymnastics . . . it changed my opinion of what I was doing. . . . What I could see was the end product, not just that they were skillful, but I could see their pleasure in being able to do it [the skill]. . . .That fostered a lot of my pleasure in being a physical educator and my feelings that my content was important, that it did have an impact on the lives of the children. (Pissanos & Allison, 1996, p. 6)

In the end, teachers' knowledge construction is about kids.

SUMMARY

Teachers' knowledge construction can have a direct effect on improving practice. Teachers construct new knowledge in relation to their prior knowledge, current experiences, and their particular school context. What works in one context for one teacher might not work in another context or with another teacher. Although some teachers work in oppressive settings that can stifle their development, others are working toward positive knowledge construction that can benefit both themselves and their students.

IMPLICATIONS FOR PRACTICE

1. Like-minded teachers can, through social interactions, create new ways of understanding teaching, content, and learning.
2. Teachers who are dissatisfied with the influence of their teaching on students can (individually or with other teachers) acquire knowledge of new curricular approaches and over time adapt and apply their new knowledge in their schools.
3. Change takes time, and the road is bumpy—confusion and false starts are part of learning.
4. The following dispositions can help knowledge construction:
   - being a continual learner;
   - going beyond blaming students and instead taking responsibility for what happens in your classes;
   - sustaining judgment of new ideas and experimenting, modifying the ideas, and practicing;
   - matching your practice to your philosophy; and
   - focusing on what students are learning, their meanings, and their experiences.
5. Teachers' knowledge is a practical, action-oriented form of knowledge. Thus, experience plays a critical role in knowledge development.
6. Observing students' responses carefully and trying to acquire a more detailed understanding of the relationships among tasks, the environment, and students' capabilities can facilitate knowledge construction.
7. Prior knowledge, prior experiences, and current experiences can constrain or facilitate further knowledge construction.
8. Understanding the big picture (i.e., connections between theory and practice; teaching for broader and integrated motor, cognitive process, social, and affective objectives; and connections between elements of practice and overarching issues and ideas) develops over time and is a sign of expertise.

REFERENCES

Allison, P.C. (1987). What and how preservice physical education teachers observe during an early field experience. *Research Quarterly for Exercise and Sport, 58,* 242-249.

Barrett, K.R., Allison, P.C., & Bell, R. (1987). What preservice physical education teachers see in an unguided field experience: A follow-up study. *Journal of Teaching in Physical Education, 7,* 12-21.

Barrett, K.R., & Collie, S. (1996). Children learning lacrosse from teachers learning to teach it: The discovery of pedagogical content by observing children's movement. *Research Quarterly for Exercise and Sport, 67,* 297-309.

Barrett, K.R., & Turner, A.P. (2000). Sandy's challenge: New game, new paradigm (a correspondence). *Journal of Teaching in Physical Education, 19,* 162-181.

Bell, R., Barrett, K.R., & Allison, P.C. (1985). What preservice physical education teachers see in an unguided, early field experience. *Journal of Teaching in Physical Education, 4,* 81-90.

Brown, S. (1999). Complicity and reproduction in teaching physical education. *Sport, Education and Society, 4,* 143-159.

Byra, M., & Sherman, M.A. (1993). Preactive and interactive decision-making tendencies of less and more experienced preservice teachers. *Research Quarterly for Exercise and Sport, 64,* 46-55.

Chen, A. (1999). The impact of social change on inner-city high school physical education: An analysis of a teacher's experiential account. *Journal of Teaching in Physical Education, 18,* 312-335.

Chen, W. (2001). Description of an expert teacher's constructivist-oriented teaching: Engaging students' critical thinking in learning creative dance. *Research Quarterly for Exercise and Sport, 72,* 366-375.

Chen, W., & Rovegno, I. (2000). Examination of expert and novice teachers' constructivist-oriented teaching practices using a movement approach to elementary physical education. *Research Quarterly for Exercise and Sport, 71,* 357-372.

Clancey, W.J. (1997). *Situated cognition: On human knowledge and computer representations.* Cambridge, UK: Cambridge University Press.

Clandinin, D.J. (1986). *Classroom practice: Teacher images in action.* London: Falmer.

Cobb, P. (1994). Constructivism in mathematics and science education. *Educational Researcher, 23*(7), 4.

Cothran, D.J. (2001). Curricular change in physical education: Success stories from the front line. *Sport, Education and Society, 6,* 67-79.

Cothran, D.J., & Ennis, C.D. (1997). Students' and teachers' perceptions of conflict and power. *Teaching and Teacher Education, 13,* 541-553.

Curtner-Smith, M.D. (1997). The impact of biography, teacher education, and organizational socialization on the perspectives and practices of first-year physical education teachers: Case studies of recruits with coaching orientations. *Sport, Education and Society, 2,* 73-94.

Curtner-Smith, M.D. (1999). The more things change the more they stay the same: Factors influencing teachers' interpretations and delivery of National Curriculum Physical Education. *Sport, Education and Society, 4,* 75-97.

Curtner-Smith, M.D. (2001). The occupational socialization of a first-year physical education teacher with a teaching orientation. *Sport, Education and Society, 6,* 81-105.

Denzin, N.K., & Lincoln, Y.S. (1994). *Handbook of qualitative research.* Thousand Oaks, CA: Sage.

Doutis, P., & Ward, P. (1999). Teachers' and administrators' perceptions of the Saber-Tooth Project reform and of their changing workplace conditions. *Journal of Teaching in Physical Education, 18,* 417-427.

Driver, R., Asoko, H., Leach, J., Mortimer, E., & Scott, P. (1994). Constructing scientific knowledge in the classroom. *Educational Researcher, 23*(7), 5-12.

Dyson, B., & O'Sullivan, M. (1998). Innovation in two alternative elementary school programs: Why it works. *Research Quarterly for Exercise and Sport, 69,* 242-253.

Elbaz, F. (1981). The teacher's "practical knowledge": A report of a case study. *Curriculum Inquiry, 11,* 43-71.

Elbaz, F. (1983). *Teacher thinking: A study of practical knowledge.* New York: Nichols.

Ennis, C.D. (1991). Discrete thinking skills in two teachers' physical education classes. *Elementary School Journal, 91,* 473-487.

Ennis, C.D. (1995). Teachers' responses to noncompliant students: The realities and consequences of a negotiated curriculum. *Teaching and Teacher Education, 11,* 445-460.

Ennis, C.D., Mueller, L.K., & Hooper, L.M. (1990). The influence of teacher value orientations on curriculum planning within the parameters of a theoretical framework. *Research Quarterly for Exercise and Sport, 61,* 360-368.

Ennis, C.D., Mueller, L.K., & Zhu, W. (1991). Description of knowledge structures within a concept-based curriculum framework. *Research Quarterly for Exercise and Sport, 62,* 309-318.

Fosnot, C.T. (1996). *Constructivism: Theory, perspectives, and practice.* New York: Teachers College Press.

Goc-Karp, G., & Zakrajsek, D.B. (1987). Planning for learning—theory into practice? *Journal of Teaching in Physical Education, 6,* 377-392.

Graham, G., Hopple, C., Manross, M., & Sitzman, T. (1993). Novice and experienced children's physical education teachers: Insights into their situational decision making. *Journal of Teaching in Physical Education, 12,* 197-214.

Graham, K.C., French, K.E., & Woods, A.M. (1993). Observing and interpreting teaching-learning processes: Novice PETE students, experienced PETE students, and expert teacher educators. *Journal of Teaching in Physical Education, 13,* 46-61.

Green, K. (2000). Exploring the everyday "philosophies" of physical education teachers from a sociological perspective. *Sport, Education and Society, 5,* 109-129.

Grennon-Brooks, J.G., & Brooks, M.G. (1993). *In search of understanding: The case for constructivist classrooms.* Alexandria, VA: Association for Supervision and Curriculum Development.

Hastie, P.A., & Vlaisavljevic, N. (1999). The relationship between subject-matter expertise and accountability in instructional tasks. *Journal of Teaching in Physical Education, 19,* 22-33.

Hickey, C. (2001). "I feel enlightened now, but . . .": The limits to the pedagogic translation of critical social discourses in physical education. *Journal of Teaching in Physical Education, 20,* 227-246.

Housner, L.D., & Griffey, D.C. (1985). Teacher cognition: Differences in planning and interactive decision making between experienced and inexperienced teachers. *Research Quarterly for Exercise and Sport, 56,* 45-53.

Howarth, K. (2000). Context as a factor in teachers' perceptions of the teaching of thinking skills in physical education. *Journal of Teaching in Physical Education, 19,* 270-286.

Iran-Nejad, A. (1990). Active and dynamic self-regulation of learning processes. *Review of Educational Research, 60,* 573-602.

Kirk, D. (1988). Ideology and school-centered innovation: A case study and a critique. *Journal of Curriculum Studies, 20,* 449-464.

Lave, J. (1988). *Cognition in practice: Mind, mathematics and culture in everyday life.* Cambridge, UK: Cambridge University Press.

McCaughtry, N.A. (2001). *An inquire into two secondary physical education teachers' pedagogical content knowledge of students' experiences.* Unpublished doctoral dissertation, University of Alabama, Tuscaloosa.

McCaughtry, N.A., & Rovegno, I. (2002, April). *The development of pedagogical content knowledge through field-based teaching experiences.* Paper presented at the meeting of the American Educational Research Association, New Orleans.

Metzler, M.W., & Tjeerdsma, B.L. (2000). The physical education teacher education assessment project [Monograph]. *Journal of Teaching in Physical Education, 19.*

Napper-Owen, G.E. (1996). Beginning teacher induction assistance: A look at the impact of involvement beyond the first year. *Journal of Teaching in Physical Education, 16,* 104-121.

Newell, K.M. (1986). Constraints on the development of coordination. In M.G. Wade & H.T.A. Whiting (Eds.), *Motor development in children: Aspects of coordination and control* (pp. 341-360). Amsterdam: Marinus Nijhoff.

O'Reilly, E., Tompkins, J., & Gallant, M. (2001). "They ought to enjoy physical activity, you know?": Struggling with fun in physical education. *Sport, Education and Society, 6,* 211-221.

Pagnano, K., & Langley, D.J. (2001). Teacher perspectives on the role of exercise as a management tool in physical education. *Journal of Teaching in Physical Education, 21,* 57-74.

Pissanos, B.W., & Allison, P.C. (1996). Continued professional learning: A topical life history. *Journal of Teaching in Physical Education, 16,* 2-19.

Placek, J.H., Dodds, P., Doolittle, S.A., Portman, P.A., Ratliffe, T.A., & Pinkham, K. (1995). Teaching recruits' physical education backgrounds and beliefs about purposes for their subject matter. *Journal of Teaching in Physical Education, 14,* 246-261.

Prawat, R.S. (1992). Teachers' beliefs about teaching and learning: A constructivist perspective. *American Journal of Education, 100,* 354-495.

Resnick, L.B., & Williams Hall, M. (1998). Learning organizations for sustainable educational reform. *Daedalus, 127*(4), 89-119.

Rink, J.E., French, K., Lee, A.M., Solmon, M.A., & Lynn, S.K. (1994). A comparison of pedagogical knowledge structures of preservice students and teacher educators in two institutions. *Journal of Teaching in Physical Education, 13,* 140-162.

Rogoff, B. (1990). *Apprenticeship in thinking: Cognitive development in social context.* New York: Oxford University Press.

Rovegno, I. (1991). A participant-observation study of knowledge restructuring in a field-based elementary physical education methods course. *Research Quarterly for Exercise and Sport, 62,* 205-212.

Rovegno, I. (1992a). Learning a new curricular approach: Mechanisms of knowledge acquisition in preservice teachers. *Teaching and Teacher Education, 8,* 253-264.

Rovegno, I. (1992b). Learning to teach in a field-based methods course: The development of pedagogical content knowledge. *Teaching and Teacher Education, 8,* 69-82.

Rovegno, I. (1992c). Learning to reflect on teaching: A case study of one preservice physical education teacher. *Elementary School Journal, 92,* 491-510.

Rovegno, I. (1993a). Content knowledge acquisition during undergraduate teacher education: Overcoming cultural templates and learning through practice. *American Educational Research Journal, 30,* 611-642.

Rovegno, I. (1993b). The development of curricular knowledge: A case study of problematic pedagogical content knowledge during advanced knowledge acquisition. *Research Quarterly for Exercise and Sport, 64,* 56-68.

Rovegno, I. (1994). Teaching within a curricular zone of safety: School culture and the situated nature of student teachers' pedagogical content knowledge. *Research Quarterly for Exercise and Sport, 65,* 269-279.

Rovegno, I. (1995). Theoretical perspectives on knowledge and learning and a student teacher's pedagogical content knowledge of dividing and sequencing subject matter. *Journal of Teaching in Physical Education, 14,* 284-304.

Rovegno, I. (1998). The development of in-service teachers' knowledge of a constructivist approach to physical education: Teaching beyond activities. *Research Quarterly for Exercise and Sport, 69,* 147-162.

Rovegno, I., & Bandhauer, D. (1994). Child-designed games—experience changes teachers' conceptions. *Journal of Physical Education, Recreation, and Dance, 65*(6), 60-63.

Rovegno, I., & Bandhauer, D. (1997a). Norms of the school culture that facilitated teacher adoption and learning of a constructivist approach to physical education. *Journal of Teaching in Physical Education, 16,* 401-425.

Rovegno, I., & Bandhauer, D. (1997b). Psychological dispositions that facilitated and sustained the development of knowledge of a constructivist approach to physical education. *Journal of Teaching in Physical Education, 16,* 136-154.

Rovegno, I., Nevett, M., Brock, S., & Babiarz, M. (2001). Teaching and learning basic invasion game tactics in fourth grade: A descriptive study from situated and constraints theoretical perspectives. *Journal of Teaching in Physical Education, 20,* 370-388.

Rumelhart, D.E., & Norman, D.A. (1978). Accretion, tuning, and restructuring: Three modes of learning. In J.W. Cotton & R.L. Klatzky (Eds.), *Semantic factors in cognition* (pp. 37-53). Hillsdale, NJ: Erlbaum.

Ryle, G. (1949). *The concept of mind.* London: Hutchinson.

Schempp, P.G., Manross, D., Tan, S.K.S., & Fincher, M.D. (1998). Subject expertise and teachers' knowledge. *Journal of Teaching in Physical Education, 17,* 342-356.

Schempp, P.J. (1993). Constructing professional knowledge: A case study of an experienced high school teacher. *Journal of Teaching in Physical Education, 13,* 2-23.

Schön, D.A. (1983). *The reflective practitioner.* New York: Basic Books.

Sebran, A. (1995). Preservice teachers' reflections and knowledge development in a field-based elementary physical education methods course. *Journal of Teaching in Physical Education, 14,* 262-283.

Sharpe, T., & Hawkins, A. (1992). Study III: Expert and novice elementary specialists: A comparative analysis. *Journal of Teaching in Physical Education, 12,* 55-75.

Shuell, T. (1986). Cognitive conceptions of learning. *Review of Educational Research, 56,* 411-436.

Shuell, T. (1990). Phases of meaningful learning. *Review of Educational Research, 60,* 531-547.

Shulman, L.S. (1987). Knowledge and teaching: Foundations of the new reform. *Harvard Educational Review, 57*(1), 1-22.

Siedentop, D., Doutis, P., Tsangaridou, N., Ward, P., & Rauschenbach, J. (1994). Don't sweat gym! An analysis of curriculum and instruction. *Journal of Teaching in Physical Education, 13,* 375-394.

Sparkes, A. (1987). Strategic rhetoric: A constraint in changing the practice of teachers. *British Journal of Sociology of Education, 8,* 37-54.

Spiro, R.J., Coulson, R.L., Feltovich, P.J., & Anderson, D.K. (1988). Cognitive flexibility theory: Advanced knowledge acquisition in ill-structured domains. In *Tenth Annual Conference of the Cognitive Science Society* (pp. 375-383). Hillsdale, NJ: Erlbaum.

Tan, S.K.S. (1996). Differences between experienced and inexperienced physical education teachers' augmented feedback and interactive teaching decisions. *Journal of Teaching in Physical Education, 15,* 151-170.

Tsangaridou, N., & O'Sullivan, M. (1997). The role of reflection in shaping physical education teachers' educational values and practices. *Journal of Teaching in Physical Education, 17,* 2-25.

Ward, P., & O'Sullivan, M. (1998). Similarities and differences in pedagogy and content: Five years later. *Journal of Teaching in Physical Education, 17,* 195-213.

Werner, H. (1957). The concept of development from a comparative and organismic point of view. In D.B. Harris, *The concept of development* (pp. 125-147). Minneapolis: University of Minnesota Press.

Woods, A.M., & Lynn, S.K. (2001). Through the years: A longitudinal study of physical education teachers from a research-based preparation program. *Research Quarterly for Exercise and Sport, 72,* 219-231.

Woods, M., Goc-Karp, G., & Escamilla, E. (2000). Preservice teachers learning about students and the teaching-learning process. *Journal of Teaching in Physical Education, 20,* 15-39.

Wright, S.C. (2001). The socialization of Singaporean physical educators. *Journal of Teaching in Physical Education, 20,* 207-226.

CHAPTER EIGHTEEN

ORGANIZATIONAL SOCIALIZATION: FACTORS AFFECTING BEGINNING TEACHERS

Sandra A. Stroot • *Christine E. Whipple*

Learning to teach is a complex endeavor, with multiple variables affecting the prospective teacher's movement toward success. Examining the potential developmental stages of a prospective teacher and the influence of the workplace on the teacher will improve understanding of the process of learning to teach. Perhaps the most important time in a teacher's career is the induction phase, described as "a transitional period in teacher education between teacher preparation and continuing professional development, during which assistance may be provided and/or assessment may be applied to beginning teachers" (Huling-Austin, Odell, Ishler, Kay, & Edelfelt, 1989, p. 3). Developmental stages, workplace conditions, and how they affect teachers during the first years of teaching will be discussed in this chapter. In addition, strategies for addressing concerns of beginning teachers as they enter the school setting will be suggested.

CAREER DEVELOPMENT OF TEACHERS

Scholars have presented several models to identify and describe developmental stages of preservice (Caruso, 1977; Fuller & Bown, 1975; Sacks & Harrington, 1982; Yarger & Mertens, 1980) and inservice teachers (Burden, 1980; Gregorc, 1973; Katz, 1972; McDonald, 1982; Peterson, 1979; Unruh & Turner, 1970; Yarger & Mertens, 1980). Most teachers are familiar with the developmental stages of children and know how to adapt tasks and activities to meet each child's needs according to these developmental stages. The same concept applies to the developmental stages of teachers. All teacher development models represent a continuum, in which teachers move from feelings of anxiety and concerns for survival to mastery of teaching. Mature teachers are fully functioning professionals who are able to address individual cognitive, social, and emotional needs of their students.

A Model of Teacher Development

Katz's (1972) model of developmental stages provides an in-depth description of teacher development. The model illustrates a developmental progression of stages experienced by teachers already in the school context rather than preservice teachers in teacher preparation programs. Katz organized a teacher's development into four stages. A brief summary of stages and assistance for inservice teachers is shown in figure 18.1.

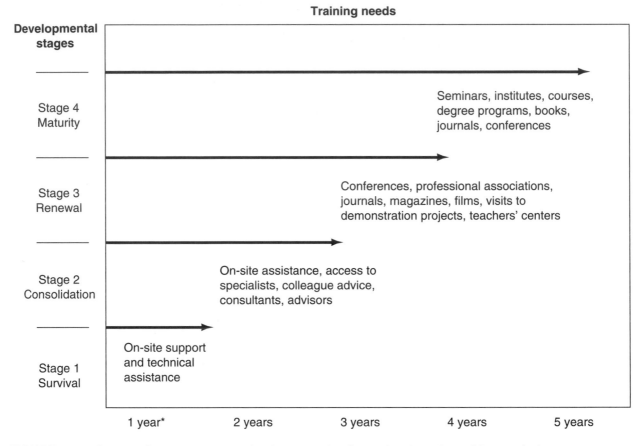

Training needs

Developmental stages

Stage 4
Maturity

Seminars, institutes, courses, degree programs, books, journals, conferences

Stage 3
Renewal

Conferences, professional associations, journals, magazines, films, visits to demonstration projects, teachers' centers

Stage 2
Consolidation

On-site assistance, access to specialists, colleague advice, consultants, advisors

Stage 1
Survival

On-site support and technical assistance

1 year*   2 years   3 years   4 years   5 years

FIGURE 18.1   Stages of development and training needs of preschool teachers. *time periods are approximate.

Reprinted, by permission, from L.G. Katz, 1972, "Developmental stages of preschool teachers," *Elementary School Journal* 73(1):51.

Survival

In the first stage of survival the main concern was merely coping on a daily basis, and teachers began to question their competence and desire to teach. Katz stated that this stage could last throughout the entire first year. On-site assistance is needed at this time to provide encouragement, reassurance, and specific skills to help teachers adapt to life in the schools.

Consolidation

By the second year most teachers have entered the consolidation stage and have begun to focus on problems and needs of individual children. Again, on-site assistance by someone thoroughly familiar with the context is helpful. Opportunities to discuss a child's characteristics and strategies to address individual needs of children are important for teachers at this stage. Experienced colleagues and other professionals who can give suggestions for successful strategies can help teachers implement new ideas in their gymnasiums.

Renewal

Teachers in the third stage, renewal, are typically in their third or fourth year of teaching and have become competent in their teaching practice. Activities and patterns previously established are now routine and boring, and teachers look for new ideas that provide variety in the teaching setting. At this stage, teachers are interested in new developments in their area of specialization and find value in attending conferences and workshops. Assistance from other teachers comes from exchanging ideas and journals. Formal or informal conversations with other teachers will result in a strong network, encouraging continued professional growth.

Maturity

In the final stage, maturity, teachers begin to ask questions of themselves and their teaching, focusing on insights, perspectives, and beliefs about teaching and children. Teachers strive to understand more subtle meanings of a complex teaching setting. Teachers may question dominant societal values and their effect on children from disadvantaged neighborhoods, or they may examine the appropriateness of state mandates in education. A broad range of reading material or conference presentations directed toward changing perspectives can assist these teachers.

Teachers should share their concerns with others at the same stage of development. Teachers need reassurance that they are not alone. Interactions with others at the same level of development can provide ideas and additional insight to help them overcome the struggles of learning to teach. Needs of teachers in various stages of development differ, and teacher educators and mentors in school settings must understand these stages if they are to provide assistance appropriate to teachers' changing developmental needs.

LEARNING THE ROPES

As we begin to understand factors that allow teachers to move through these developmental stages and become effective teachers, we must also understand the process that teachers follow as they learn about teaching and what it means to be a teacher. The most prevalent model used to study socialization into physical education has been occupational socialization. Occupational socialization was defined by Lawson (1986) as "all of the kinds of socialization that initially influence persons to enter the field of physical education and that later are responsible for their perceptions and actions as teacher educators and teachers" (p. 107). One important aspect of occupational socialization has been organizational socialization, or "the process by which one is taught and learns 'the ropes' of a particular organizational role" (Van Maanen & Schein, 1979, p. 211). These authors also identified three work orientations adopted by new teachers.

- Custodial orientation perpetuates the existing system and maintains the status quo.
- Content innovation orientation promotes change in how teachers define and implement the teaching of their own content.
- Role innovation orientation redefines the teacher's role in the school and community context.

These three descriptions reflect differing philosophical perspectives about the amount of control a teacher has over the workplace environment and the process of socialization.

Custodial orientation and role innovation orientation represent contrasting perspectives and outcomes. In the former, the teacher is passive and willing to accept the existing system, and no significant changes occur. In the latter, the teacher is proactive and empowered to make changes in a particular context, and perhaps beyond.

Van Maanen and Schein also described socialization tactics that influence how teachers learn the ropes and how the socialization process winds up. Lawson (1983) provided scenarios representing these tactics as he discussed custodial and innovative orientations. The first example provides socialization tactics representing the custodian approach, which will result in perpetuating the existing structure. The tactics in the second example represent the innovative approach, which will encourage empowerment of the teacher and promote change in the status quo.

> **Example #1.** Schools with socialization tactics that are collective, sequential, variable, serial, and involve divestiture will breed custodial orientations in new teachers.
>
> **Example #2.** Schools with socialization tactics that are individual, informal, random, disjunctive, and involve investiture, will nurture innovative orientations in new teachers. (p. 7)

Socialization into a new school setting has huge implications for beginning teachers. In one sense the existing system will shape the outcome for the beginning teacher by the socialization tactics in that particular context. The alternative view is that the beginning teacher can become empowered to change the system by choosing socialization strategies that would make these changes possible. The context in which the beginning teacher is working, particularly the workplace conditions that enhance or inhibit the teacher's ability to be effective, strongly influence her or his ability to make these choices.

WORKPLACE CONDITIONS: CREATING A QUALITY ENVIRONMENT

Louis and Smith's (1990) Quality of Work Life (QWL) indicators offer a useful framework for understanding workplace conditions as significant variables affecting teaching performance. The intent of these indicators was to "promote working conditions that tangibly contribute to the establishment of a more professional work life and career for teachers" (Louis & Smith, 1990, p. 35). Many factors inherent in the school setting affect a teacher's ability to achieve the criteria for the ideal QWL to enhance teaching performance. Based on the relationship of organizational contexts to teacher's QWL, seven criteria were identified as indicators of QWL:

- Respect from relevant adults
- Participation in decision making
- Frequent and stimulating professional interaction
- A high sense of efficacy
- Use of skills and knowledge
- Resources to carry out the job
- Goal congruence

Louis and Smith (1990) provided specific factors that may serve as reference points toward achieving the seven criteria of QWL. These factors, shown in table 18.1, were organized into three categories.

TABLE 18.1

FACTORS THAT MAY AFFECT TEACHERS' QUALITY OF WORK LIFE

Social-cultural changes	Administrative-political changes	Technical-instructional resources
Professional growth plans Expanded teacher roles Teacher-initiated problems Peer observations Retreats or other mechanisms to increase social cohesiveness	Structures promoting formal participation in making school policy Strong decentralization to departments	Restructuring the conditions for teaching and learning: • Alternate schedule • Student empowerment • Parent involvement

In addition, all of the above factors must be examined in light of the local conditions of school-based leadership, students, and the school culture.

K. S. Louis and B. Smith, *Teachers and their workplace,* © 1990 by Sage Publications. Reprinted by permission of Sage Publications, Inc.

As teachers enter a school setting, they should begin to examine their workplace conditions relative to the seven QWL indicators and other relevant environmental influences that may influence their ability to teach. Teachers may be able to exert immediate control on the variables in the category of social-cultural changes. A teacher can immediately plan a strategy for professional growth, request observations from a trusted peer, and gather information relative to retreats, conferences, and workshops available through school and professional organizations. Administrative-political changes and technical-instructional changes require a different type of intervention because institutional flexibility determines the extent to which these variables can be changed. Although we all know that change cannot be instantly implemented, with persistence, support, and an understanding of criteria that lead toward a quality of work life, even systemic change can (and does) occur.

INDUCTION INTO THE FIRST YEAR OF TEACHING

This section will identify concerns of beginning teachers in physical education and illustrate those concerns with statements and quotations from various research studies. Stories from beginning teachers who have been proactive in their induction year and emerged from it with feelings of success and accomplishment are included. The section also provides suggestions and strategies to help new teachers make a positive and successful transition into the school setting.

Reality Shock

Reality shock seemed to be a major concern of beginning teachers, including physical educators. Reality shock was described as "the collapse of the missionary ideals found during teacher training by the harsh and rude reality of classroom life" (Veenman, 1984, p. 143). Stevens-Smith (2000) argued that the realities of the profession must be addressed to prepare teachers to enter the teaching field. When previous experiences do not prepare new teachers for their work environment, overwhelming feelings of inadequacy result in reality shock. Reality shock is likely to occur when the teacher preparation program does not adequately address issues faced upon entrance into the field. A program that provides teachers with multiple field experiences and opportunities to practice their teaching strategies in diverse settings will reduce reality shock. The more similar the teaching setting of new teachers is to their previous experiences, the less inhibiting will be reality shock.

A group of beginning physical education specialists in Chicago shared some important aspects of their first year of teaching in the school setting (Williams & Williamson, 1995). Several of these teachers worked in the inner-city schools, a context very different from the reality of their own lives. Statements from several of the teachers reflect the type of reality shock they experienced working with inner-city youth. Torres stated, "One week there were two shootings outside the school. Thirteen-year-old children were carrying guns and chasing other children" (p. 66). Vince commented about a boy from Latin America who did not understand English: "I was thrown for a loop at that moment. . . . How many times have I stood there talking while the students just looked at me and didn't know what was going on" (p. 39)? Katie also commented on her surprise at the issues she had to address in schools, when she stated, "I never imagined having to deal with substance abuse in my school. I thought that occurred 'somewhere else'" (p. 67). When discussing expectations about her school setting, Jackie reflected on her critical observations of other teachers and then stated that she was not realistic about working with students in the cities. She said, "To think I went into this situation thinking it would be great and I didn't have to follow anyone else's structure or rules, it was all up to me. . . . It just wasn't like that" (p. 28). Wright (2001) reported that a group of Singaporean teachers had similar experiences in their first teaching positions. "During their PETE experiences, participants remembered rather ideal conditions," but the ideal conditions they experienced during their preservice preparation "were not the norm in the schools in which they now taught" (p. 221).

In Chicago the urban setting in which these children lived was reflected in the problems teachers faced in the school setting, and the problems were not familiar to the beginning teachers. They felt helpless and had to learn new strategies for themselves and for their students. In Singapore the teachers found the context to be much more difficult than the one in which they had completed their student teaching. In both situations, the teachers had their first teaching experiences in settings far different from that which they felt prepared to undertake. Although all these teachers had early field experiences in urban settings, their new school setting was so different that they experienced a debilitating reality shock in their new positions.

Kelley and Mike found teaching positions in school settings that were familiar to them and aligned with their personal and professional backgrounds and experiences. They graduated from a teacher preparation program with several field experiences similar to what they would experience in their first teaching positions (O'Sullivan, 1989, p. 240), and they found no surprises relative to their responsibilities and expectations. Mike felt "that everything he thought would happen has happened." Similar to Mike and Kelley, Ed was involved in extensive field experiences during his undergraduate and master's work and felt prepared for his school site (Curtner-Smith, 2001). He commented, "I think our program had a lot of experiences dealing with all sorts of kids and tons of hours in the schools" (p. 94). Because of these experiences, Ed had a good sense of what to expect during his first year.

Previous experiences in contexts similar to the teachers' first teaching position seemed to have considerable influence on the ease of entry into the first year of teaching. Teacher preparation programs with multiple field placements can provide a variety of field experiences for the preservice teachers, thereby limiting reality shock when they begin their careers.

Washout Effect

Zeichner and Tabachnick (1981) described the washout effect as the period when the effect of the teacher education program diminishes. Sometimes the reality of the school context does not support the goals and philosophies adopted by beginning teachers during the teacher preparation program. Lawson (1989) referred to this type of situation when he stated, "School practices progressively erode the effects of teacher education" (p. 148). Providing new teachers with effective strategies to implement learning objectives for students, along with support in the school context, will enhance a new teacher's ability to provide a learning-centered program.

Lisa's description of how her teaching changed over the year provides a clear picture of the washout effect:

> At the beginning of the year, I did physical fitness, then basketball. . . . By the end of the year, it came down to those kids who wanted to play basketball on one side of the gym and those kids who wanted to play volleyball on the other side of the gym. Some studied for finals while I did work I had to get done before the end of the year—and no one cared. . . . I could just see myself falling into a rut and being a roll-out-the-ball-type. (Stroot, Faucette, & Schwager, 1993, p. 381)

Kelbe also recognized changes in her teaching as she stated, "I just feel like I'm not teaching, and it really drives me nuts. I have such a phobia about PE teachers that don't teach, and I see myself slipping into that category" (Stroot et al., 1993, p. 381).

Smyth (1992) described the washout effect of another first-year teacher, Mr. Miller: "Because of lack of support for his efforts to promote skill acquisition, he sought and implemented teaching practices that modified or replaced many of the teaching methods that he had learned in his teacher education program" (p. 19). "Despite initial training, it appears that Mr. Miller's context served to reward a 'busy, happy, and good' curriculum" (p. 17).

In contrast to these teachers, Mike and Kelley (O'Sullivan, 1989) did not experience washout of the strategies they learned in their teacher preparation program. They found those strategies to be effective in meeting their managerial and instructional goals, and they were able to continue to improve on their teaching strategies as the year progressed. Both Kelley and Mike felt their teacher preparation program provided necessary skills for them to be successful, and both felt that their building principals strongly supported them. Mary (Solmon, Worthy, & Carter, 1993) also felt she was well prepared to teach. Despite having to address several hurdles during the first year, Mary felt that her ability to discipline and control the class, and the administrative support of one of her principals, helped her meet her goals for the year.

Similarly, Paul felt prepared to teach. Although he inherited a weak program and large classes, he attempted to teach much as he had been taught during his core PETE program (Curtner-Smith, 1998). Paul had been able to establish rules and routines, explore innovative teaching strategies, and modify his evaluation procedures to align better with what he had learned. Paul felt that he was able to accomplish his goals because he had the support from his administrator to "innovate the school's physical education programme" (p. 87). By the end of the year, however, Paul was becoming frustrated with some of the issues he was facing in his school context. He stated, "I am also realizing that it is quite difficult to teach . . . as I have been prepared to do. There are so many situations that make the teaching of PE a very difficult task" (Curtner-Smith, 2001, p. 97).

Even when first-year teachers have received strong preparation, they have difficulty sustaining the intense commitment necessary to ensure quality physical education programs. High-quality teacher preparation, as well as support within the school context, seemed to be extremely important to a first-year teacher's ability to transfer successful teaching strategies learned at the university to the school context.

Isolation

Physical isolation from other professional adults is a common problem faced by beginning teachers because they spend so much time interacting with children or young adults (Kurtz, 1983; Ryan, 1979). Because physical education teachers are often the only physical education specialists in the school building, especially at the elementary level, this problem is further exacerbated (Stroot, 2001). Torres commented on his need to share his frustrations and receive feedback on his teaching, but no one was available for him (Williams & Williamson, 1995).

> One day a class didn't go right. I was depressed and the kids were going bonkers. I asked myself, "Am I teaching them anything?" I felt so down and continued to question what I was doing. It made me feel very insecure. I never felt that way before, even when I was student teaching. . . . I felt so isolated and didn't have anyone to give me feedback on what was happening in my classes. . . . That would have helped a lot. (p. 12)

Kelbe experienced social isolation as she attempted to develop casual interactions with the teachers in her school (Stroot et al., 1993). Her lunchtime interactions were negative because the conversations became "half-hour bitch sessions" for the teachers as they continued to criticize students and the school. Mike also experienced this type of isolation:

> You walk in to get a cup of coffee in the teachers' lounge, or you sit down to eat lunch and there is no interest to get to know you. They have all been together years and years. . . . They look at the gym teacher, as they put it, "differently than they would a real teacher." So there is isolation. (O'Sullivan, 1989, p. 235)

Mary was attempting to build a program in two inner-city elementary schools where the previous programs used the throw-out-the-ball style (Solmon et al., 1993). She encountered resistance and began to look to others for reassurance and encouragement. Mary stated, "As the only physical educator in either school, I felt isolated without anyone to turn to for support and advice" (p. 318).

Marginalization of Physical Education

The legitimacy of physical education as a subject area is serious issue, not only for beginning physical educators but also for many members of the physical education profession. O'Sullivan (1989) highlighted this issue for beginning teachers as she described a major paradox in the settings in which Mike and Kelley worked. "The struggle for legitimacy of their subject matter was overshadowed by the collegial respect (legitimacy) both teachers received for their managerial rather than instructional abilities" (p. 240). Mike and Kelley were respected for their ability to manage students but not for their ability to teach. Ron reported a similar situation. He felt that the "majority of the classroom teachers supported him because of his ability to maintain discipline and because he gave them a 45-minute break each day . . . rather than because they valued what he taught (Curtner-Smith, 1998, p. 84). Solmon et al. (1993) described Courtney's experiences as "she encountered some difficulty in being taken seriously as a teacher. She believed other teachers perceived her as a supervisor of play rather than a specialist in physical education" (p. 324). Lisa stated, "Elementary classroom teachers seemed to value physical education only for the 'prep period' it provided them" (Stroot et al., 1993, p. 379). Similarly, Tim commented, "Classroom teachers were frequently late bringing and collecting their classes, and often gave me no notice of field trips. . . . some kept pupils out of physical education as a punishment . . . and most saw the purpose of physical education as providing them with a break during the day" (Curtner-Smith, 1997, pp. 85-86). Lisa felt that she had no parental support for physical education: "The parents supported athletics, and they supported after-school programs . . . but they didn't care what went on in the classroom" (p. 383).

When looking across contexts, issues of marginalization of the content and context of the physical education teacher seem to be consistent. Wright (2001) shared the socialization experiences of eight of Singaporean physical educators, who reported similar concerns. One female teacher stated, "Frankly . . . PE is not recognized [as legitimate] in schools. . . . Most of the schools take PE as just a play session. . . . There was a perception that 'anyone can teach PE'" (p. 220). Similarly, in Australia, physical education was seen as "a Mickey Mouse subject," and "as a break for the more educationally worthwhile 'mental,' rather than 'manual,' activity" (Macdonald, 1995, p. 132).

Education specialists and the public rarely perceive physical education as a legitimate subject area. Cartoons and television clips regularly identify physical education class as playtime for students and portray physical education teachers as stereotypical dumb jocks who bumble their way through life. Everyone in the physical education profession, not just beginning teachers, needs to take this issue seriously.

Workload and Role Conflict

Most teachers have six to nine classes per day as well as an additional duty. A number of elementary teachers travel because they have assignments in two schools. In some cases, teachers have a supplementary contract for other responsibilities, especially coaching at the secondary level. Although Kurtz (1983) reported that, in general education, beginners received the most difficult courses and experienced teachers chose the best class assignments, no real evidence suggests that this is a problem for beginning physical educators. Several beginning teachers, however, mentioned workload as an area of concern. Reed reflected a concern for the number of classes he would teach as well as other variables that would affect his ability to organize time (Solmon et al., 1993). Reed knew that he would have large classes, increased in size by mainstreamed special-education students. He was also concerned about the number of classes he would have to teach and the pace he would have to maintain to allow 30 minutes of instructional time for each class (p. 321).

Most teachers were not concerned about the number of classes that they would teach, but they were anxious about scheduling and time available for organization and instruction. Mr. Miller stated, "The number of classes that I have aren't [sic] really a big problem, but they're really congested" (Smyth, 1992, p. 10). His complaint was that he was unable to have time between classes to organize for the upcoming grade level and activity. Many concerns focused on the extra duties assigned to the beginning teachers. Kelbe assumed the position of department chair during her first year, and the administrative duties were overwhelming. Besides ordering equipment, writing the physical education curriculum, and observing and evaluating the teaching of her peer, she faced daily interruptions that inhibited her ability to teach.

> I feel scattered in so many directions. . . . It's so outrageous. Thirty to 40% of my time . . . is spent trying to find stolen clothes, misplaced things, shoving kids out of the locker room. . . . It's a never-ending, constant battle. . . . I'm expected to be full-time PE teacher, full-time locker-room attendant, retail clerk, lost-and-found clerk. I can't teach effectively under these circumstances. (Stroot et al., 1993, pp. 379-380)

Although Ed always felt confident about teaching abilities, he stated, "The additional responsibilities that are a part of the job are staggering" (Curtner-Smith, 2001, p. 91). Similarly, Barbara stated, "There are so many other things that you have to do other than teaching. . . administrative type things that you have to do all the time that take your mind away from the actual teaching job itself" (Macdonald, 1995, p. 134).

Some teachers who had supplemental coaching contracts felt the pressures of role conflict and found coaching responsibilities to be time consuming. Kelbe and Lisa

(Stroot et al., 1993) struggled as they realized that the rewards for being a good coach were sometimes greater than the rewards for being a good teacher. They also realized that their teaching suffered. Lisa reinforced this with comments regarding the type of support she received.

> I didn't have any support for my teaching. They supported me as a coach, but as a teacher, I could do anything or nothing at all. [To] sit on the bleachers and roll out the ball would have been fine. (p. 279)

Cathy was one of a few teachers who found limited benefits related to teaching from her supplemental coaching contract (Napper-Owen & Phillips, 1995). Cathy felt that what she learned about giving feedback during her coaching experiences transferred to her teaching experience but that she had little time or energy to implement changes in her teaching suggested by her mentor. Most of the Singaporean teachers were involved in multiple extracurricular activities as well (Wright, 2001). One teacher commented, "I find I cannot really teach and coach well at the same time" (p. 219). But many of the Singaporean teachers seemed to be gaining some benefits because 44% of them were overwhelmingly positive about their involvement in extracurricular activities and 32% had mixed feelings about the positive contribution of their involvement in these programs. When discussing this issue in Australia, Macdonald (1995) found that the "responsibilities frequently associated with sport organization and coaching were a source of challenge and reward for those teachers who had them" (p. 134). Ben felt it was during the extracurricular activities "where you spend quality time . . . and the kids are there to learn." He felt the extracurricular activities were the "stuff that makes the time worthwhile, because the opportunities associated directly with teaching are sometimes monotonous" (p. 134). Similarly, Ed commented that he "enjoyed working with the highly skilled and motivated teachers and pupils." By spring, however, Ed admitted that coaching was "tiring" and "stressful" and "makes for a quite busy workload for a first-year teacher" (Curtner-Smith, 2001, p. 91).

Management and Instruction Concerns

Concerns about management of students, time, and facilities differed according to perceptions of preparation for the context and factors within the school setting. If the prior experiences of teachers provided strategies and skills necessary to work in the setting they found in their first teaching position, the transition was much smoother.

Management Concerns

The most difficult scenarios were those in which teachers familiar with the concerns of middle-class students were working in inner-city schools where student problems were more severe than anything they had experienced or anticipated. These scenarios produced the examples of reality shock reported previously. Students in those environments did not seem to care about disciplinary options available to teachers, such as time-outs or detentions.

First-year teachers found that they were not always able to cope with students' lack of respect, and teachers' expectations were challenged on a regular basis. Katie stated, "The students did not seem responsible for their behavior. They'd just say, 'I have a detention, oh well,' and probably skip it. The school had no attendance policy" (Williams & Williamson, 1995, p. 52). These situations were frustrating, and without assistance, some teachers struggled through the entire year. The fact that the school administration did not establish or uphold such policies left few options for the beginning teachers—they found it virtually impossible to find success.

Kelley and Mike experienced almost the opposite situation (O'Sullivan, 1989). Both felt that the strategies taught in the teacher preparation program were useful in the school setting, and school administrators supported their efforts as disciplinarians. Their management concerns revolved around getting everything accomplished within limited time rather than disciplining students.

Instructional Concerns

The most common instructional concern reported by teachers was grading. With several hundred students to grade each quarter, teachers struggled with providing fair evaluations. Several new teachers entered settings where all students received A's. When attempting to implement a differential grading procedure, they encountered resistance by students, administrators, and parents. In some cases, behavior rather than student learning had been the basis of grades, another indication of the lack of recognition for physical education as a legitimate content area. In Ron's school, he was required only to "pass or fail pupils based on how well they had behaved during the classes," and although he talked with the principal, members of the parent-teacher associations, and the physical education coordinator about evaluating pupils on "what they had learned," he received little support. In other situations, parents objected to the grading procedure. A parent in Jackie's school commented, "How could my kid fail gym. Look, A's and B's all across this report card, and then an F in gym." Jackie stated, "That was the most frustrating thing throughout the whole year" (Williams & Williamson, 1995, p. 25). In Tamara's school, the physical education grade was not averaged into the students' grade point average, providing perceptions of limited importance for parents and causing lack of respect for the subject matter (Williams & Williamson, 1998). Mike's expectations for student learning also resulted in parent complaints. Mike wrote, "There has been a lot of flack from parents of students who earned a U—unsatisfactory—for the third six weeks of the year. 'Failing gym is like failing lunch or recess,' one parent told me" (O'Sullivan, 1989, p. 235).

Not all efforts went unnoticed. With the support of the principal, Paul was able to make changes in the grading system during his first year of teaching (Curtner-Smith, 1998, p. 90). The "previous physical education teacher had graded the pupils . . . on the basis of how well they behaved during lessons." Paul changed the evaluation to inform parents about "what their children had learned . . . based on a combination of their performance on skills tests, his observations of their skill level during classes, and their performance on written tests."

Mike identified an instructional issue pertaining to individualizing activities to meet specific needs of students in classes. He stated that his major concern was "greater individualization of instruction by matching class activities more closely to student competencies" (O'Sullivan, 1989, p. 233). The teacher can address goals such as these only after classroom management is no longer an issue. Because Mike had already addressed this issue, he was better able to focus on individual student concerns. Paul's situation was similar because he was able to focus on "establishing rules, routines, and expectations" within the first three weeks and then "his instructions clearly focused on pupil learning. . . . He chose challenging and progressive content which appeared to be developmentally appropriate for each class" (Curtner-Smith, 2001, p. 89). This ability to focus on individual students reflected a more advanced stage of development for Mike and Paul as they continued to become more effective teachers.

Interactions With Colleagues

Recently, collegial interaction has been shown to be one of the most powerful contextual variables in the beginning teachers' ability to be successful in elementary or secondary settings. Four of the teachers in Williams and Williamson's (1995) text struggled with their coworkers. Vince stated, "The hardest thing for me this year was getting along with the other physical educator. Working with Connie has been her way or no way. That made team teaching extremely difficult, since she would not accept any of my ideas" (p. 38). Kelbe (Stroot et al., 1993) also had differing perceptions and "saw herself and her primary colleague at opposite ends of a continuum regarding expectations for student learning" (p. 378). Jessie stated that "her teacher education preparation did not prepare her for how to deal with uncooperative colleagues" (p. 382). Ed worked in a department with five other teachers and was frustrated with the "lack of collaboration among members of the department." He commented that his department was "a group of individuals rather than a team," without much "professional interaction or exchange of ideas" (Wright, 2001, p. 92). In spite of Ed's frustration, however, the support of two of the five colleagues encouraged him in his efforts to teach effectively.

Katie was one of the fortunate teachers. She worked with committed and supportive coworkers who had a positive influence on her first year as a physical education teacher. She described her coworkers:

> Jane developed a new worksheet for weight training and she shared it with the staff. If I asked her any questions she would tell me whatever I needed to know. . . . We also had a really dynamic male teacher. . . .We worked together for about a month and I benefited from observing and teaching with him. . . . It was inspirational to work with a person who was innovative and truly cared about the outcome of his efforts. (Williams & Williamson, 1995, p. 50)

Support for Beginning Teachers

Mike and Kelley were both successful in gaining the respect and support of their administrators. Administrators seemed to have great respect for physical education teachers' ability to manage students, but they had little respect or understanding for their ability to teach (O'Sullivan, 1989). Lisa, too, commented that her principal liked her because of her personality, not because she was a good teacher (Stroot et al., 1993).

Kurtz (1983) stated that supervision of beginning teachers usually consists of "one to three formal visits, a few incidental contacts, and a number of group contacts" (p. 44). Needed support, reassurance, and assistance during the first year tend to be inadequate to meet the needs of novice teachers. Beginning teachers in Williams and Williamson's group (1995, 1998) received limited administrative assistance. The number of evaluations ranged from zero to two for the entire year. Tamara's comment is typical of those that beginning teachers make about their principals, who seem to be supportive but can offer little substantive assistance to these teachers.

> The principal would come over and talk to me when the children were playing a game. She gave positive feedback to the kids, but she never gave me any feedback on my teaching. . . . She formally observed me once and left without saying a word to me, and even when I saw her later she didn't mention the evaluation. (p. 34)

Mentoring for most of these teachers was virtually nonexistent. Courtney was left entirely on her own. "Prior to the start of the school year, the principal informed Courtney that she knew nothing about physical education and would leave everything in her hands" (Solmon et al., 1993, p. 323). At the school where Courtney taught

> inservice provided for new teachers by the administration was somewhat lacking and a source of some concern. She [Courtney] regretted that she was not apprised of the details needed for complete success at the beginning of the year. "They have a good assertive discipline program, but nobody bothered to go over the procedures. I have a homeroom and nobody told me what to do during homeroom. I just had to feel my way through it." (p. 324)

Of the 70 Singaporean participants described in Wright's (2001) study, only 17 were offered any assistance, 9 were assigned a mentor from their school, but only 5 felt that the induction program helped them. One of those without assistance stated, "It was hell because I was just left alone. Nobody guided me. There was no mentor" (p. 221).

In Williams and Williamson's text (1995), Heather reported that she was supposed to work with a mentor in her building, but the reality was quite the opposite. She stated, "The administration told us at the beginning of the year to find somebody to be a mentor teacher." She commented, "There are no PE teachers around this building. Who is going to be my mentor?" (p. 2). Heather was put in an impossible situation—she was told to find a mentor, yet who could provide encouragement and expertise to the only physical education specialist in the school?

Ed was assigned a mentor who was described as "a good-hearted man" and "a weak teacher" who was "not taken seriously." The mentor's "knowledge of content and teaching methodology is not as strong as it should be" (Curtner-Smith, 2001, p. 92). Although he had an official mentor, Ed turned to Joanne, the department head, when he needed assistance. Joanne was a teacher for whom Ed had "a great deal of respect" (p. 91). Ed stated that Joanne helped him tremendously, because "her door is always open to me and I go to her with a lot of questions" (p. 91).

Mentors positively influenced several teachers. As Jessie moved into her first year of teaching, she called on her university student-teaching supervisor for assistance, and an informal mentoring relationship developed (Stroot et al., 1993). The mentoring relationship continued as Jessie moved into another teaching position during her second year, and the association proved valuable as she continued to learn to teach. Lisa also found support as she moved to a new school system during her second year. In the new setting she was involved in a formal mentoring program instituted by the school district, and she found support through the district's coordinator of health and physical education. Lisa was observed approximately once per week, and she received feedback and suggestions. Lisa felt encouragement and support in her efforts to be effective and was able to move toward that goal as the year progressed. Katie (Williams & Williamson, 1995) not only had a mentor who "was always available to answer questions and help with difficult situations" (p. 50) but also had, as mentioned previously, coworkers who were willing to help her get through her first year in any way possible. Peter and Cathy (Napper-Owen & Phillips, 1995) both felt that the induction program provided a positive influence.

Peter believed that the feedback he received throughout his first year enabled him to teach more effectively and to apply his undergraduate training. He believed that the supervision and assistance encouraged him to explore new methods of instruction and to vary instructional activities. The induction assistance encouraged Cathy to think about her teaching and determine ways to make her teaching more effective (p. 323).

Summary of Induction Into the First Year of Teaching

The scenarios of these beginning teachers reflected several deep concerns that influenced their successful transition from the university to the schools. Workplace factors greatly influenced their perceptions of their success and their roles as physical education professionals. We must begin to take an assertive role to modify these conditions and help all teachers, not just the lucky ones, have a positive experience during their first year of teaching. Mentor programs have been successful in many schools, providing guidance for first-year teachers by pairing them with an experienced teacher. Stevens-Smith (2000) suggested exploring the Faculty Center for Learning and Teaching Web site (www.mrs.umn.edu/academic/fclt/mentor.shtml) to find resources that can provide information on implementing a successful mentoring program. As stated by Sparkes, Templin, and Schempp

(1993), "At best [the workplace] should promote a positive socialization process whereby all teachers are made to feel welcome, secure, enriched, empowered, and valued in terms of their actual and potential contributions to school life" (p. 386).

SUGGESTED STRATEGIES FOR BEGINNING TEACHERS

These scenarios demonstrate that mentors were beneficial in helping beginning teachers through the transition from the university to the school setting. Lisa, Katie, Jessie, and Cathy spoke of the positive influence of the emotional and instructional support they had during their first year of teaching. In these settings, both the formal and informal mentoring models seemed to enhance entry into the schools for these teachers. The scenarios also showed that beginning teachers who had a clear perspective of what they wanted to do and how they wanted to do it eventually found support within their settings and success in accomplishing their goals. These teachers were empowered to be proactive. Workplace conditions, however, vary considerably, and the beginning teacher must often be assertive to create a positive work environment.

Seek Out Mentors

The first approach teachers can use to begin to empower themselves is to ask about the availability of mentoring opportunities. Many states provide support to beginning teachers throughout the year, with some programs offering feedback based on observations and conferences that take place in the teachers' own classroom (Stroot, 2001). In addition, beginners could ask questions about the availability of a mentoring program within the school context. Beginning teachers might ask questions like these: What type of mentoring is available? Does this include evaluation? Who chooses my mentor? How often will I see my mentor? What is the expectation of me? What is the expectation of my mentor?

Besides gathering information about the mentoring program, new teachers could ask about opportunities to meet other specialists in a similar content area—both beginners who will be facing the same struggles and veterans who have moved positively and productively through their career paths. These people will provide a supportive network to share struggles and ideas to enhance the first years of teaching. Observing peers and having peers observe others will assist and benefit all involved as teachers share ideas and strategies. These relationships will continue throughout a teacher's career and provide valuable professional interactions to help each individual continue to grow.

New teachers should not limit interactions to other beginning teachers. Experienced teachers are eager to work collaboratively as well. Tannehill and Coffin (1996) offer suggestions for peer mentoring, which can be applied across levels of experience. Beginning teachers may wish to maintain interactions with their cooperating teachers. They have already established professional relationships, and technological communication options offer a way to continue to debate perspectives and share resources, no matter where teachers may relocate. Collaborative projects or involvement in professional development schools offers opportunities to focus energies on similar interests and outcomes while meeting new colleagues.

Take Advantage of Published Resources

Current journals and books can provide useful ideas and suggestions to beginning teachers. Journals that provide ideas specific to the classroom include the *Journal of Physical*

Education, Recreation and Dance and *Strategies* (both published through the American Alliance for Health, Physical Education, Recreation & Dance, Reston, VA) and *Teaching Elementary Physical Education* (published by Human Kinetics). Articles such as Ratliffe's (1987) paper "Overcoming Obstacles Beginning Teachers Encounter" or Fernandez-Balboa's (1990) article "Helping Novice Teachers Handle Discipline Problems" provide practical suggestions for beginning teachers. A book suggested for beginning teachers is *Positive Behavior Management Strategies for Physical Educators* (1997) by Lavay, French, and Henderson. This book offers helpful suggestions for classroom management and focuses on promoting appropriate student behavior and enhancing student performance

As teachers become members of their state and national professional organizations, many of these journals become available as a part of the membership. Also valuable are programs to improve teaching for physical educators, like the American Master Teacher Program (see the PE Central Web site, http://pe.central.vt.edu/), where teachers can take workshops and gather resources designed for practical implementation. Stevens-Smith (2000) also suggested becoming involved in professional organizations and activities at the state, district, or national level. Stevens-Smith suggested that teachers subscribe to professional journals and use journals and college textbooks because they are valuable materials. Stroot (2001) provided several suggestions to reduce professional isolation, including using on-line opportunities, such as PE Central or PELINKS4U (www.pelinks4u.org/), and becoming involved in graduate courses and workshops. Another suggestion for beginning teachers is to find vignettes of beginning teachers such as those presented earlier in this chapter and read about experiences of teachers in situations similar to their own. All the suggestions mentioned here are in the reference section of this chapter.

Be Reflective

Having a method to reflect and act on the struggles and successes encountered throughout a teaching career is helpful. An observing teacher can gather information to help establish goals for teaching. Using systematic observation instruments to code the feedback provided to students, the amount of time children are spending in appropriate practice, or other aspects of teaching is a way to get baseline information to begin designing goals. Journal writing is another way to devote time to thinking about strategies that worked and those that did not. Teachers can identify concerns and begin to think about how they can modify their teaching to reduce the problem and enhance the learning environment. Using these suggestions, teachers can begin to create a plan like the following one to address some of the struggles:

1. What is the first issue or concern that you would like to address in your learning environment?
2. How would you like to address this issue or concern?
3. How would you measure whether your effort was successful?
4. Implement the project.
5. What were the results of your project?
6. Modify the project or identify a new project.

Network

Some concerns identified by beginning teachers are systemic concerns that the teacher cannot overcome alone. In these settings, the teacher must again ask questions to find out what networking has already occurred and how to become socially and politically active in these networks. Responsibilities for these issues should be with the veterans, who are already established in the existing setting. In many cases, however, these veterans have already compromised, so the beginner must be proactive. One of the more recent movements that are outcomes of educational reform is the increased collaboration between universities and public schools. A collaborative project including university faculty could help teachers as they continue to learn to teach. A collaborative action research project "brings together teachers, staff developers, and university faculty with the goals of improving practice, contributing to educational theory, and providing staff development" (Oja & Smulyan, 1989, p. 24). Closer interaction between school and university personnel would further ease the transition to the school setting for beginning teachers. Perhaps collaborative groups such as these would also assist in addressing the more difficult systemic concerns that have an overwhelming influence on beginning and veteran teachers alike.

For a beginning teacher who is willing to be proactive in requesting assistance, multiple options are available. Teachers entering a new school setting need not learn the ropes in isolation. But the new teacher must usually take the initiative because the system often encourages the perpetuation of the workplace conditions that are themselves the concerns of beginning teachers.

SUMMARY

Implications relative to the socialization process for teacher education programs and school districts are great. During professional preparation, novice teachers must be provided with the knowledge, opportunity, assistance, and support to practice their teaching skills in a variety of settings, including some of the tough urban settings in which beginners are likely to find their first teaching positions. In addition, as teachers work in the school setting they should receive the continued assistance and support suggested by Katz (1972) throughout their careers. Collaborative efforts between university and school faculties would help make the transition from the university to the school setting smooth and successful for each teacher.

IMPLICATIONS FOR PRACTICE

1. One of the most important times in a teacher's career is during the induction phase, described as "a transitional period in teacher education between teacher preparation and continuing professional development" (Huling-Austin, Odell, Ishler, Kay, & Edelfelt, 1989, p. 3).

2. The workplace conditions at the site will greatly influence a teacher's induction into the school context and the teacher's quality of work life (QWL). Although the beginning teacher can become empowered to initiate change in these sites, effecting administrative and political changes requires more time and greater effort than making technical and instruction changes.

3. When beginning the school year, new teachers seem to experience similar concerns of reality shock, isolation, washout effect, and workload and role conflict. Physical educators also find that administrators and colleagues tend to marginalize their subject matter.

4. Within the classroom, many teachers identify concerns about management of students, specifically their irresponsible behavior and lack of respect for others.

5. Instructional concerns revolve around issues of grading and individualizing instruction to meet the needs of each student.

6. The extent to which teachers struggle with these concerns seems to relate closely to prior experiences. If teachers' prior experiences provided strategies and skills necessary to work in

their new settings, the transition is much smoother than it is for teachers whose prior experiences occurred in a setting different from the new one.

7. Good mentors make a difference, whether they are a part of a formal or informal mentoring system. New teachers should actively seek mentors in their school and school district and should not hesitate to ask for help when necessary. Experienced teachers have a great deal of knowledge, specific to the context in which new teachers teach. In most cases, experienced teachers are eager to share their expertise. New teachers should take advantage of this valuable resource to ease their transition into teaching.

8. Beginning teachers should seek additional professional growth opportunities. They can network with colleagues, read journals, explore professional sites on the Internet, take graduate course work, and go to conferences. These professional growth experiences will keep them excited about the profession and help them stay abreast of current knowledge and practices.

9. New teachers should allow time to reflect on their teaching practice, because good teachers never stop learning. Changes occur quickly in the teaching profession, and children will continue to come to teachers with diverse needs and abilities. Continued reflection and professional growth opportunities will help teachers remain effective throughout their careers.

REFERENCES

Burden, P.R. (1980). *Teachers' perceptions of the characteristics and influences on their personal and professional development.* Manhattan, KS: Author. (ERIC Documentation Reproduction Service No. ED 198 087)

Caruso, J.J. (1977). Phases in student teaching. *Young Children, 33*(1), 57-63.

Curtner-Smith, M.D. (1997). The impact of biography, teacher education, and organizational socialization on the perspectives of first-year physical education teachers: Case studies of recruits with coaching orientations. *Sport, Education and Society, 2,* 73-94.

Curtner Smith, M.D. (1998). Influence of biography, teacher education, and entry into the workforce on the perspectives and practices of first-year elementary school physical education teachers. *European Journal of Physical Education, 3,* 75-98.

Curtner-Smith, M.D. (2001). The occupational socialization of a first-year physical education teacher with a teaching orientation. *Sport, Education and Society, 6*(1), 81-105.

Fernandez-Balboa, J.M. (1990). Helping novice teachers handle discipline problems. *Journal of Physical Education, Recreation and Dance, 66* (7), 50-54.

Fuller, F.F., & Bown, O.H. (1975). Becoming a teacher. In K. Ryan (Ed.), *Teacher education 74th yearbook of the National Society for the Study of Education, Part II* (pp. 25-52). Chicago: University of Chicago Press.

Gregorc, A.F. (1973). Developing plans for professional growth. *NASSP Bulletin, 57,* 1-8.

Huling-Austin, L., Odell, S.J., Ishler, P., Kay, R.S., & Edelfelt, R.A. (Eds.). (1989). *Assisting the beginning teacher.* Reston, VA: Association of Teacher Educators.

Katz, L.G. (1972). Developmental stages of preschool teachers. *Elementary School Journal, 73*(1), 50-54.

Kurtz, W.H. (1983). Identifying their needs: How the principal can help beginning teachers. *NASSP Bulletin, 67,* 42-45.

Lavay, B., French, R., & Henderson, H. (1997). *Positive behavior management strategies for physical educators.* Champaign, IL: Human Kinetics.

Lawson, H.A. (1983). Toward a model of teacher socialization in physical education: Entry into schools, teachers' role orientations, and longevity in teaching. *Journal of Teaching in Physical Education, 3*(1), 3-15.

Lawson, H.A. (1986). Occupational socialization and the design of teacher education programs. *Journal of Teaching in Physical Education, 5,* 107-116.

Lawson, H.A. (1989). From rookie to veteran: Workplace conditions in physical education and induction into the profession. In T. Templin & P. Schempp (Eds.), *Socialization into physical education: Learning to teach* (pp. 145-164). Indianapolis: Benchmark Press.

Louis, K.S., & Smith, B. (1990). Teacher working conditions. In P. Reyes (Ed.), *Teachers and their workplace* (pp. 23-47). Newbury Park, CA: Sage.

Macdonald, D. (1995). The role of proletarianization in physical education teacher attrition. *Research Quarterly for Exercise and Sport, 66*(2), 129-141.

McDonald, F.J. (1982, March). *A theory of the professional development of teachers.* Paper presented at the meeting of the American Educational Research Association, New York.

Napper-Owen, G.E., & Phillips, D.A. (1995). A qualitative analysis of the impact of induction assistance on first-year physical educators. *Journal of Teaching in Physical Education, 14,* 305-327.

Oja, S.N., & Smulyan, L. (1989). *Collaborative action research: A developmental approach.* New York: Falmer Press.

O'Sullivan, M. (1989). Failing gym is like failing lunch or recess: Two beginning teachers' struggle for legitimacy. *Journal of Teaching in Physical Education, 8,* 227-242.

Peterson, A.R. (1979). Career patterns of secondary school teachers: An exploratory interview study of retired teachers (Doctoral dissertation, Ohio State University, 1978). *Dissertation Abstracts International, 39*, 4888A.

Ratliffe, T. (1987). Overcoming obstacles beginning teachers encounter. *Journal of Physical Education, Recreation and Dance, 58*(4), 18-23.

Ryan, K. (1979). Toward understanding the problem: At the threshold of the profession. In K.R. Howey & R.H. Bents (Eds.), *Toward meeting the needs of the beginning teacher* (pp. 35-52). Lansing, MI: Midwest Teacher Corps Network; St. Paul: University of Minnesota Press.

Sacks, S.R., & Harrington, G.N. (1982, March). *Student to teacher: The process of role transition.* Paper presented at the meeting of the American Educational Research Association, New York.

Smyth, D. (1992, April). *"The kids just love him": A first-year teacher's perceptions of how the workplace has affected his teaching.* Paper presented at the annual meeting of the American Educational Research Association, San Francisco.

Solmon, M.A., Worthy, T., & Carter, J.A. (1993). The interaction of school context and role identity of first-year teachers. *Journal of Teaching in Physical Education, 12*, 313-328.

Sparkes, A.C., Templin, T.J., & Schempp, P.G. (1993). Exploring dimensions of marginality: Reflecting on the life histories of physical education teachers. In S. Stroot (Ed.), Socialization into physical education [Monograph]. *Journal of Teaching in Physical Education, 12*, 386-398.

Stevens-Smith, D.A. (2000). Help! It's my first year of teaching, and I don't know where to start! *Journal of Physical Education, Recreation and Dance, 71*(4), 50-54.

Stroot, S.A. (2001). When I graduate, am I an expert? *Teaching Elementary Physical Education, 12*(2), 18-20.

Stroot, S.A., Faucette, N., & Schwager, S. (1993). In the beginning: The induction of physical educators. In S. Stroot (Ed.), Socialization into physical education [Monograph]. *Journal of Teaching in Physical Education, 12*, 375-385.

Tannehill, D., & Coffin, D.G. (1996). Mentoring within physical education teacher education in the USA: Research trends and developments. In M. Mawer (Ed.), *Mentoring in physical education: Issues and insights* (pp. 217-238). London: Falmer Press.

Unruh, A., & Turner, H.E. (1970). *Supervision for change and innovation.* Boston: Houghton Mifflin.

Van Maanen, J., & Schein, E. (1979). Toward a theory of organizational socialization. In B. Staw (Ed.), *Research in organizational behavior* (Vol. 1, pp. 209-261). Greenwich, CT: JAI Press.

Veenman, S. (1984). Perceived problems of beginning teachers. *Review of Educational Research, 54*, 143-178.

Williams, J., & Williamson, K.M. (1995). *Beginning to teach physical education: The inside stories.* Dubuque, IA: Kendall/Hunt.

Williams, J., & Williamson, K.M. (1998). The socialization strategies for first-year physical education teachers: Conflict and concessions. *Physical Educator, 55*(2), 78-88.

Wright, S.C. (2001) The socialization of Singaporean physical educators. *Journal of Teaching in Physical Education, 20*, 207-226.

Yarger, S.J., & Mertens, S.K. (1980). Testing the waters of school-based teacher education. In D.C. Corrigan & K.R. Howey (Eds.), *Concepts to guide the education of experienced teachers.* Reston, VA: Council for Exceptional Children.

Zeichner, K., & Tabachnick, R. (1981). Are the effects of university teacher education "washed-out" by school experience? *Journal of Teacher Education, 32*(3), 7-11.

CHAPTER NINETEEN

ENHANCING LEARNING: AN EPILOGUE

Catherine D. Ennis • *Stephen J. Silverman*

This project began one evening while we were having dinner in Washington, DC. What started as a social occasion turned into business and an in-depth discussion about physical education. We believed that a collection of the accumulated research in our field was needed. As physical education researchers, we knew that a vast reservoir of published work was out there. But we also knew that it was not summarized and collected for easy access. As we indicated in the first chapter, we realized that the field had become specialized. Many of the chapters we envisioned would be valuable not only for teachers, teacher educators, and beginning graduate students but also for researchers in sport pedagogy who wanted to keep up with other subareas.

As we discussed the need for the first edition of this volume, we were mindful that some scholars in other areas (most notably Wade, 1991) did not believe that there was an accumulated body of literature in physical education. We hope you'll agree, after reading this text, that the body of literature has grown considerably in the last decade. We think that the strong ties we previewed in chapter 1, showing the relationships between teaching, curriculum, and teacher education (figure 1.1), are increasingly influential and important in physical education practice.

The preceding chapters make it clear that schools and physical education classes are complex places and that no one research result will provide the silver bullet for improvement. Each of us must use the research on physical education to inform our professional judgment, considering our workplace and the contextual factors that would interact with any changes we make. The way informed professionals use the knowledge base in teaching physical education, in curriculum development, and for preparing future teachers will affect the growth of the field. As many of the contributors noted, the perceived problems with school physical education are remediable. We should be optimistic because research results suggest alternatives to some of the problems of current practice. As Berliner (1987) has noted, the knowledge base of teaching can help transform the teaching profession.

Many issues—for example, content standards, the teacher's role, assessment, context, and instructional effectiveness—were discussed both in chapters specifically dedicated to that purpose and as threads woven through other chapters. This overlap demonstrates the complex, connected, and diverse nature of physical education teaching and the need for professionals to be both deeply and widely informed. Although, as we discussed previously, research often is conducted on discrete subareas, teaching physical education is the intersection of these subareas. We have tried to make connections among the chapters in this book, but many more are desirable and possible.

As you can see from these chapters a large number of elements, issues, and factors coexist and interact to maintain current physical education practices. Some of these are the structure of schools, the philosophy and beliefs of teachers, and the expectations of students. Our ability to stimulate relevant and lasting change depends first on understanding what is occurring and why and how it has come to be this way. As we begin to grasp the complexity of the teaching setting, we are better able to envision, design, and implement more effective programs.

Although dealing with complexity sometimes can be overwhelming, anticipating and responding to complexity can lead to more focused efforts to describe and track connections or relationships that are inherent in the physical education classroom. For example, as Judy Placek noted in chapter 15, once we accept that our body of knowledge shares many natural connections with other subject areas, we begin looking for opportunities to emphasize these connections in our teaching. Likewise, once we expect both teachers and students to cognitively mediate their understanding of performance and ability to perform, we can reinforce opportunities for reflection and mindfulness in physical activity and physical education. Connections are everywhere in these chapters and in physical education. Once you know where and when to look, you can use them strategically to influence both teaching and learning. Shuell (1986) reminds us that nothing is learned in isolation. For knowledge to be learned and remembered it must be connected to previously learned information that is meaningful and relevant. When teachers help students build strong connections between current and new knowledge, students gain knowledge about physical activity and come to value and respect it.

As we learn more about the complexity and connections that define practice in physical education, we are struck by the diversity of philosophy, place, and people that coexist and thrive in effective programs. With diversity comes the flexibility to weave together many perspectives, allowing us to meet more effectively the future needs of individuals who will seek the benefits of physical activity and use it for many purposes. Nothing can be more important to the continued growth of our profession than to position it to meet future expectations for quality educational, social, and health-related practice.

Likewise, we hope the diversity of our field, evidenced both in the topics addressed by researchers and the methods they employ, will continue to grow. Without ongoing, focused work by researchers in a variety of areas and with a variety of methods, we will not continue the progress shown throughout this new edition. We hope that those contemplating a research career will see opportunities in sport pedagogy and that teachers and teacher educators will look for opportunities to apply what they've read here. The vitality of physical education necessitates that we continue to grow by using what we've learned and attempting to learn more. As a field, we have grown greatly, but we still have much to learn. Important research questions will continually evolve. If physical education and sport pedagogy are to grow, we must continue to expand our knowledge—and use it effectively to inform practice.

REFERENCES

Berliner, D.C. (1987). Knowledge is power: A talk to teachers about a revolution in the teaching profession. In D.C. Berliner & B.V. Rosenshine (Eds.), *Talks to teachers* (pp. 3-33). New York: Random House.

Shuell, T. J. (1986). Cognitive conceptions of learning. *Review of Educational Research, 56,* 411-436.

Wade, M.G. (1991). Unraveling the Larry and Daryl magical mystery tour. *Quest, 43,* 207-213.

AUTHOR INDEX

A

Abrutyn, L. 190
Ahonen, T.P. 90
Aikin, W.M. 256
Ajzen, I. 149, 151
Alcaraz J.E. 152, 153, 209, 214, 216
Aldrich, J.E. 49, 50
Alexander, D. 46, 49
Alexander, K. 235
Allard, R. 178
Allen, J. 181
Allen, L.D. 96
Allen, V.L. 266
Allensworth, D. 207
Allison, P. 16, 111, 298-299, 301, 303-307
Allison, S. 232
Almond, L. 231
Alpert, B.S. 210
Alvestad, K.A. 199
Amade-Escot, C. 277, 284
American Academy of Pediatrics 213
American College of Sports Medicine 213
Amstutz, D. 54
Anderson, D. 200
Anderson, M. 59
Anderson, W.G. 12, 15, 34, 167-168
Angoff, W.H. 197
Apple, M. 134
Applebee, A.N. 266
Arnold, P. 283
Arter, J. 191-192
Ashworth, S. 19, 35, 95, 248
Associated Press 50, 56
Aufderheide, S. 12, 90
Aufsesser, P.M. 91
Ayers, W. 249

B

Babcock, G. 83
Babiarz, M. 155, 237, 283, 297
Bacharach, N. 49
Bailey, D.A. 210, 259
Bailey, L. 230-231
Bailey, T. 50
Bain, L.L. 10, 11, 14, 19, 111, 132, 155
Baker, E.T. 92
Bandhauer, D. 15, 61, 117, 301, 304-306
Bandura, A. 158
Banks, J.A. 113, 115
Baron, M.A. 196

Barrett, K.R. 11, 16, 18, 297, 299, 301
Barrette, G.T. 12, 34
Barton, G. 188
Bartz, D. 190
Battig, W.F. 99
Bauman, K.J. 47, 48
Beane, J. 122-123, 257
Beckett, L. 76
Bedward, J. 75, 78-79
Beers, M.K. 95
Beighle, A. 259, 287
Bell, R. 16, 299
Ben-Ezra, V. 96
Bengoechea, E.G. 285
Bennett, B. 228
Bennett, F. 96
Bennett, J.P. 208, 217
Bennett, R.G. 234
Benson, P.L. 241
Berger, G.G. 90
Bergman-Drewe, S. 282
Berliner, D. 165-166, 169, 178, 285, 329
Berman, P. 47
Beuter, A. 93
Beveridge, S. 16
Biddle, B.J. 87
Biddle, S.J.H. 158
Bielick, S. 47
Bilard, J. 90
Bird, P.J. 89
Bishop, P. 95, 96
Blair, S.N. 213, 216
Block, B.A. 263
Block, M.E. 83, 84, 86, 90, 91, 93, 94, 96
Bloom, B.S. 13, 139
Bobbit, F. 139
Bockoven, J. 261
Bolt, B.R. 59, 278
Boone, J. 18
Booth, F.W. 207, 213
Booth, K. 231
Bouchard, C. 117, 209-210
Bouffard, M. 90
Brake, N.L. 48, 50
Brenzel, B. 116
Britwistle, G.E. 153
Brock, S. 297
Brodie, D.A. 153
Bronson, J. 262
Brooker, R. 58, 59, 61
Brophy, J.E. 10, 13, 43, 52, 165-166, 172, 178, 266

Broudy, H.S. 109
Brown, S. 301
Bruce, T. 33
Bruner, J. 135
Bryce G.R. 14, 168
Bryson, L. 70, 72, 73
Buchanan, A.M. 236
Buck, M. 14, 68, 180
Buell, C. 263
Buell, C.M. 263
Bunker, D. 177, 230-231
Burden, P.R. 311
Burger, S.E. 196
Burgeson, C.R. 54, 57, 59, 61
Burgess-Limerick, R. 112, 14, 257
Burnelle, J. 12, 13, 14, 68
Burton, A.W. 99
Burwitz, L. 176
Bushner, C. 290
Butler, L.F. 261
Butler, S. 262
Bycura, D. 259
Byra, M. 16, 36, 188, 298

C

Calfas, K.J. 210
California State Postsecondary Education Commission (CSPEC) 46
Callahan, R.E. 133, 135
Campbell, D.T. 35
Cantell, M.H. 90
Capel, S. 281
Carlisle, C. 13
Carlson, T. B. 58, 121, 152, 153, 229, 34, 265
Carnegie Council on Adolescent Development 241
Carpenter, W.A. 50, 51
Carroll, J.B. 13
Carter, J.A. 15, 17, 111, 118, 152, 153, 154, 155, 317-319, 322
Caruso, J.J. 311
Centers of Disease Control and Prevention (CDCP) 45
Chadsey-Rusch, J. 92
Chakravarth, M.V. 207
Chandler, T. 58, 61, 181
Chase, M.A. 158
Chedzoy, S. 281
Cheffers, J. 12
Chen, A. 17, 18, 114, 117, 120, 121, 157, 181, 304
Chen, W. 19, 298, 303
Chi, M. 16
Children's Defense Fund 55

Chiogioji, E. 229
Churton, M. 89
Cizek, G.J. 193, 197
Clancey, W.J. 296, 303
Clandinin, D. 277, 296
Clark, C. 15, 16
Cleland, F. 19
Coates, T.J. 213, 259
Cobb, P. 297, 303
Cochran-Smith, M. 276-279, 288
Coelho, J.D. 44, 59
Coffin, D.G. 324
Coleman, M. 90, 99
Collie, S. 18, 297, 299
Collier, C. 58, 59, 60, 277-278, 285
Collins, A. 190
Compagnone, N. 251
Cone, S.L. 257, 263, 265
Cone, T.P. 257, 263, 265
Conner-Kuntz, F.J. 264
Connell, R.W. 69, 72, 73, 76, 79-80
Conway, T.L. 19
Cook, T.D. 251
Cook, T.H. 35
Cooper Institute for Aerobics Research 91
Corbin, C.B. 112, 208-209, 212, 282
Costello, J. 168
Cothran, D.J. 18, 19, 58, 109, 116, 117, 123, 157, 267, 299, 302, 304-306
Cremin, L. 132
Cresanta, J.L. 210
Cress, P.J. 96
Creswell, J.W. 33, 36, 37
Crowe, P. 178
Crull, G. 35, 74
C-Span 54
Cuban, L. 131
Cummings, T.K. 251
Curtner-Smith, M. 277, 300, 304, 316-321, 323
Cusimano, B.E. 13, 90, 93, 97, 67
Cutforth, N. 113, 123, 190, 42, 246-248, 250-251

D
Dana, T.M. 190
Daniel, M. 282
Danielson, C. 190
Darden, G.F. 59
Darst, P. 12, 18, 90, 93, 97, 259
Das, J. 97
Davidson, K.S. (Stockin-Davidson) 18, 19, 116, 121, 149
Davis, K.T. 89
Davis, W.E. 99
Dawkins, M. 188
Deal, L.O. 259
Deal, T.B. 188, 259
Deam, R. 75-76
DeBusk, M. 251
Deci, E.L. 157
Delignieres, D. 90
Dempsey, S.D. 89

Denzin, N. 29, 36, 297
DePaepe, J. 83, 93, 167
DePauw, K.P. 83
Des Dixon, R.G. 241
Desimone, L. 48, 49
Devillier, R. 167
Devis-Devis, J. 281
Dewar, A. 266, 290
Dewey, J. 134-135, 256
Dewitt Wallace – *Reader's Digest* Fund 250
Diamond, J. 136
Dishman, R.K. 215-216
Dodds, P. 12, 15, 16, 77, 90, 93, 155, 258, 267, 281, 285-286, 290, 300
Doll-Temper, G. 83
Donahoo, S. 47
Donnelly, F.C. 112
Doolittle, S. 15, 188, 199, 231, 267, 281, 300
Doutis, P. 43, 46, 50, 57, 58, 59, 60, 61, 200, 283, 303-304
Doyle, W. 13, 30, 147, 151, 171-172, 181, 285
Dreeban, R. 43, 52
Driver, R. 297, 303
Duchanne, K.A. 95
Duda, J. 181
Dugas, D.M. 14
Dummer, G.M. 89, 264
Dunaway, D. 259
Dunbar, S.B. 196
Dunkin, M.J. 87
Dunn, J.L.C. 90
Dunn J.M. 95, 96
Dweck, C.S. 157-158
Dyson, B. 57, 59, 261-262, 265, 304

E
Earls, N. 180
Ebbeck, V. 261-262
Ebbinghouse, H. 133
Eccles, J.S. 116, 117, 118, 156-157
Eckert, H. 282
Eddy, M. 251
Education Commission of the States (ECS) 50
Eisenman, P. 96
Eisner, E.W. 111, 130
Elbaz, F. 296, 303
Elbourn, J. 259
Ellis, D.N. 96
Emmer, E. 171-172
England, K. 58, 59, 60, 117, 119, 152, 157
Ennis, C.D. 5, 10, 11, 16, 17, 18, 53, 58, 79, 109, 111, 112, 113, 114, 116, 117, 119, 120, 121, 122, 123, 132, 149, 152, 157, 166, 172, 229-230, 236, 267, 298, 300, 302-304
Epstein, L.H. 216
Erickson, F. 121
Erickson, H.L. 257
Ericson, J. 47
Ermler, K.L. 113, 229, 258

Escamilla, E. 300, 304
Espiritu, J.E. 269
Evans, J. 75
Evans, S.A. 43, 57
Everhart, B. 259
Evertson, C. 165, 171-172

F
Falls, H.B. 210
Faucette, N. 17, 20, 37, 59, 60, 212, 317-320, 322-323
Fay, T. 199
Federal Register 85, 87, 89
Feiman-Nemser, S. 43, 52, 53, 276, 279, 281
Fejgin, N. 59, 60
Feltz, D.L. 98
Fernandez, T.R. 116, 119
Fernandez-Balboa, J.M.. 19, 278, 282-283
Fernhall, B. 90
Ferrer-Caja, E. 157
Fersch, E. 262
Feuer, M.J. 190
Figley, G.E. 152
Fincher, M. 283, 298
Finkenberg, M.E. 28
Finley, S.J. 46, 49, 50, 51
Fisher, C.W. 13
Fisher, S. 259, 261
Fitts, P.M. 170
Fitzclarence, L. 58, 73, 76
Flintoff, A. 75, 78
Floden, R.E. 43, 52, 53
Fogarty, R. 256-257
Fosnot, C.T. 297
Freiberg, H.J. 166, 172
French, K.E. 16, 169-170, 176, 180-181, 232, 237, 283, 298, 302
French, R.F. 83, 90, 95, 96, 97, 325
Fry, F. 112
Fry, M.D. 157
Fullan, M. 46
Fuller, F.F. 311
Furst, N. 34

G
Gage, N. L. 6, 30, 32, 147, 165-166
Gagnon, J. 90
Gail, K. 94
Galanter, E. 135
Gall, M.D. 29, 34, 36
Gallant, 296
Gallego, M.A. 46, 49, 50, 54
Gallop, A. 47, 48, 51, 53
Galvan, C. 251
Gangstead, S. 16
Gansneder, B.M. 89
Garbarino, J. 241
Gard, M. 73, 76
Gardner, H. 132, 134
Garrison, J.W. 30
Gates, W.E. 188
Gelinas, J.E. 99-100
George, P.S. 256

Georgiadis, N. 251
Gerald, D.E. 52
Gerney, P. 35, 167
Gibbons, S.L. 261-262
Gills, H.J. 262
Gilroy, S. 75-76
Glasgow, N.A. 257
Glatthorn, A.A. 193-194, 196
Glover, D.R. 259, 262
Goc Karp, G. 36, 300, 302, 304
Godbout, P. 12, 13, 14, 168, 285
Goldberger, M. 35, 167
Gomez, R.L. 16
Good, S. 171
Good, T.L. 10, 13, 43, 52, 165-166, 172
Goodman, J. 90
Goodway, J. 285
Goodwin, D.L. 90, 93
Gottlieb, J. 92
Gough, R.W. 261
Gould, D. 176
Graber, K.C. 15, 113, 155, 288, 290
Graham, G. 3, 13, 28, 111, 123, 147, 152, 298, 302
Graham, K.C. 174, 232, 237, 280, 298, 302
Graham, P. 44
Grant, B. 59
Green, J.C. 36
Green, K. 296, 304
Greendorfer, S.L. 33
Greenockle, K. 17, 181
Gregorc, A.F. 311
Grehaigne 285
Grennon Brooks, J.G. 297
Griffey, D.C. 16, 284-285, 298
Griffin, L.L. 111, 112, 123, 147, 155, 232, 277, 285
Griffin, P.S. 18, 19, 166, 196, 229, 290
Griffith, J.B. 113, 117, 119
Grineski, S. 259, 261
Grossman, P. 256, 265-266, 284
Guba, E.G. 33
Guskey, T.R. 194-195
Gusthart, J. L. 174, 176

H

Haan, J. 12
Hackman, D.G. 48
Halas, J. 116
Hall, M.A. 68
Halliday, N. 261
Hambleton, R.K. 197
Hanke, U. 17
Hansen, J.M. 48, 54
Hardy, C. 281, 285
Hare, M.K. 155
Hargreaves, J. 71
Harold, R.D. 116, 118
Harris, J. 259
Harrison, J.M. 14, 168, 180
Harrison, L. Jr. 159
Harter, S. 153, 157

Hastie, P. 5, 19, 79, 112, 114, 121, 168, 177, 196, 234-236, 277, 298
Hawkins, A. 13, 16, 298
Health Education Authority 212
Heath, S.B. 241, 251
Hebert, E. 15, 157, 158
Heikinaro-Johansson, P. 93, 95
Helion, J. 112
Hellison, D. 5, 37, 112, 123, 172, 195, 236, 242, 245-251, 260-261
Henderson, H. 96, 325
Henderson, S.E. 90
Hennessy, B. 259-260
Henry, F.M. 11
Hetherington, C. 228
Hewitt, P. 188
Hickey, C. 73, 76, 229, 278, 285, 300
Hill, J. 44, 45, 59,
Hill, P. 47
Hodge, S. 281, 285
Hoffman, H.A. 258
Hohn, R.C. 188, 208
Holdsworth, R. 238
Holt, N.L. 285
Holyoak, C. 259
Hood, P. 44
Hooper, L.M. 17, 300
Hopper, C. 90, 98
Hopple, C. 111, 123, 298, 302
Horwood, B. 264
Housner, L.D. 16, 113, 170, 176, 257, 263, 283-285, 298
Houston, W.R. 277
Houston-Wilson, C. 95
Howard, B. 90
Howarth, K. 43, 50, 303
Howey, K. 279-280
Hsu, P.Y. 96
Hudson, S.D. 250
Hughes, D.M. 250
Hughley, C. 12
Huling-Austin, L. 311, 326
Humberstone, B. 78
Hussey, K. 174
Hutchinson, G. 281, 290
Huuhka, H. 95

I

Ianni, F.A.J. 242
Iran-Nejad, A. 297
Iwata, B.A. 96

J

Jacobs, H. 196, 256, 265
Jackson, S. 230-231
Jaeger, R.M.. 197
James, A. 155
James, P.T. 210
Jankowski, C.M. 90
Janney, R.F. 95
Jansma, P. 93, 96
Jeltma, K. 90, 96
Jenkins, J. 188
Jewett, A.E. 10, 11, 111, 113-114, 133

Johnson, D. 251
Jones, D. 99, 230
Jones, K. 281
Jones, M.G. 46
Jones, R. 286
Journal of School Health 218
Joyner, A.B. 192, 196
Juniu, S. 59, 287

K

Kahne, J. 250
Kallusky, J. 113, 123, 242, 246-251, 261
Kalverboer, A.F. 90
Kane, M.T. 192-193
Kanfer, F.H. 221
Kannapel, P.J. 50
Kantor, H. 116
Karper, W.B. 90, 93
Katene, W. 281
Katz, L.G. 311-313
Kay, T. 75
Keating, S.D. 17, 117
Keh, N. 13
Kelly, E. 266
Kelly, I. 174, 176
Kelly, L.E. 89, 90
Kendall, J.S. 189
Kennedy, J. 173
Keramidis, K. 251
Kerlinger, F.N. 29
Kinchin, G.D. 90, 94, 260
Kingston, N.M. 197
Kinnison, L. 96
Kirk, D. 19, 38, 70, 74, 76, 112, 114, 139, 190, 231-232, 251, 257, 283, 299-300, 303
Kiss, M. 112, 114, 257
Klein, T.J. 255
Klesius, S.T. 258
Kliebard, H.M. 110, 251
Kneer, M. 258, 266
Kohn, A. 132
Kolody, B. 20
Koranda, P. 90, 94
Kovar, S.K. 113, 229, 258
Kowalski, E.M. 98
Krampitz, J. 13, 35, 178
Kudlacek, M. 83
Kulinna, P.H. 17, 35, 117, 174
Kurtz, W.H. 318-319, 322
Kwak, C. 174, 176

L

Ladson-Billings, G. 287, 290
Lahey, J. 112, 114, 257
Laker, A. 281
Lalik, R. 69, 79
Lambdin, D. 59, 60, 263
Lambdin, D.V. 263
Lambert, L. 5, 45, 54, 59, 61, 112, 131, 134, 140, 141, 187-189
Land, M. 173
Landin, D.K. 13, 14, 17, 155, 156, 58, 168, 176

Landrieu-Seiter, M. 96
Landry, J. 159
Langley, D.J. 155, 300
LaPorte, W.R. 228
Larkin, D. 90
Lavay, B. 96, 325
Lave, J. 296, 303
Law, D.R. 111
Lawson, H.A. 14, 15, 43, 57, 58, 60, 116, 242, 250, 258, 266-267, 277-278, 281, 313-314, 316
Lee, A. 13, 14, 16, 17, 18, 147, 151, 153, 54, 155, 156, 158, 159, 166, 168, 170-171, 176, 181, 298
Lee, M. 228
Leipe, M.R. 153
Leitch, S. 267
LeMaster, K. 94
Lesko, N. 116, 119
Levin, S. 212
Li, W. 159
Lifka, R. 251
Light, R. 76
Lincoln, Y.S. 29, 36, 297
Lindholm, J.A. 60, 61
Lindsay, C. 266
Lindsey, R. 112, 208
Lippman, L. 43, 53
Livingston, C. 285
Livingston, L. 283
Locke, L.F. 3, 10, 11, 28, 29, 31, 32, 33, 34, 36, 57, 58, 278
Lomax, R. 17, 181
Loovis, E.M. 89
Lortie, D. 14, 281
Louis, K.S. 314-315
Lowy, S. 17
Luckman, J. 235
Luke, M.D. 152, 153, 167
Lund, J. 187, 190, 191
Lynn, S. 16, 169, 180-181, 298, 305

M

McBride, R. 17, 19
McCarthy, M.M. 47, 48
McCaslin, M. 172
McCaughtry, N.A. 296, 303-305
McCauley, M.T. 116, 120, 121
McCubbin, J. 95
McCullagh, P. 98, 176
McCullick, B. 281, 283
Macdonald, D. 15, 57, 58, 59, 61, 229, 266-267, 281, 319-320
McDonald, E. 165,
McDonald, F.J. 311
McDonald, J.P. 244, 251
McGowan, C. 177
McHugh, E. 261
McIntosh, P.C. 71
McKenzie, T. 5, 12, 19, 20, 37, 152, 153, 208-209, 212-216, 218, 260
McLaughlin, M.W. 43, 111, 116, 241-242, 248, 250-251
McManis, B.G. 192, 196
MacPhail, A. 112
McTighe, J. 132, 134, 142

Madden, N.M. 92, 94
Madigan, R. 176-177
Magill, R. 13, 98, 99, 168-169, 171, 176, 178-179
Mahut 285
Malen, B. 43, 46, 52, 53
Malina, R.M. 117, 209
Mancini, V. 12
Mand, C. 258
Mangan, L.A. 71, 74
Manross, D. 200, 283, 302
Manross, M. 111, 123, 298
Marcoux, M.F. 214, 217
Marcus, B.H. 213
Marshall, C. 37
Marshall, S. 19
Martel, D. 91
Martens, R. 176
Martin, A.D. 210
Martin, L.T. (Tyson) 13, 14, 35, 152, 153, 171, 178, 229
Martinek, T.J. 17, 19, 83, 90, 93, 113, 117, 119, 123, 154, 178, 232, 242, 246-251
Marzano, R.J. 189, 194, 196
Maslow, A.H. 112
Masser, L. 176, 180
Maxwell, N.L. 47
May, D.S. 90
Mays, A. 169, 180-181
Meadows, S. 46
Medley, D. 10
Megginson, N. 89
Mehrhof, J.H. 113, 229, 258
Melagano, V.J. 89, 189, 190, 193-194, 196, 200
Mendon, K. 59
Mensch, J. 116, 121
Messner, M.A. 76
Metheny, E. 230
Metzler, M.W. 12, 167-168, 288, 300
Meyenn, R. 73, 76
Meyer, C.A. 190
Midgley, C. 116, 117
Midura, D.W. 259, 262
Miller, G.A. 135
Mitchell, M. 188
Mitchell, S. 112, 123, 181, 187, 232, 285
Mohnson, B. 59, 112, 114, 257, 259
Monti, W.H. 259-260
Morford, L.M. 14, 35, 229
Morton, P. 16
Mosston, M. 19, 35, 95, 248
Mueller, L.K. 16, 17, 298, 300, 302
Mullan, M.R. 114
Murata, N.M. 93

N

Nader, P.R. 12, 210, 212-214, 217
Napper-Owens, G.E. 113, 229, 258, 299, 320, 323
Nasser-McMillan, S.C. 262
National Academy of Education 288
National Association for Sport and Physical Education (NASPE) 45,

57, 58, 59, 129, 132, 140-141, 166, 87-190, 196, 220, 258-259, 261, 265, 283
National Center for Educational Statistics (NCES) 44, 45, 51, 52, 53, 55, 56, 57
National Clearinghouse on Families and Youth 242, 250
National Commission on Teaching for America's Future (NCTAF) 275
National Consortium for Physical Education and Recreation for Individuals with Disability 89
National Council for the Accreditation of Teacher Education (NCATE) 83, 287-288
National Education Goals Panel 52, 54
National Institute of Child Health and Human Development (NICHD) 212, 216
National Research Council 289
National School Boards Association 116
Nelso, J. 48, 49
Nelson, B. 47
Nelson, J.K. 29, 34,
Nevett, M. 155, 237, 283, 297
Newell, K.M. 296, 303
Nichols, J.G. 158
Nilges, L. 75, 113, 117, 263
Ninot, G. 90
Nixon, J.E. 10, 11, 34
Noddings, N. 112
Norman, D.A. 7, 302
Nugent, P. 37

O

O'Brien, D.G. 267
O'Brien, T. 96
O'Bryant, C. 288
O'Conner, A. 281
O'Connor, J. 83
O'Donnell, M.D. 262
O'Sullivan, M. 4, 15, 33, 57, 58, 59, 60, 61, 117, 119, 152, 157, 180, 260, 277-278, 280, 283, 285-286, 288, 302, 304, 316-318, 321-322
Oakes, J. 43, 50, 54, 117, 287
Oja, S.N. 327
Oliver, K.L. 12, 37, 69, 79
Oregon Department of Education 189
Orlich, D.C. 46
Ormell, C. 110
Ornstein, A.C. 166, 190
Oslin, J. 112, 123, 187, 232, 285
Östman, L. 112, 114
Owens, L.M. 18, 116, 121, 149
Owens, N. 264

P

Pagnano, K. 300
Paige, R. 46, 49
Pajares, M.F. 117
Paling, D. 261
Pangrazi, R.B. 209, 212, 259, 287

Panicucci, J. 262
Parcel, G.S. 212-213
Pare, C. 277
Park, R.J. 74
Parker, M. 12, 113, 123, 180, 190, 242, 246-251, 261
Pate, R.R. 208-210, 212, 216
Patterson, B. 264
Patterson, P. 212
Pawlas, G.E. 47, 48
Peck, C.A. 92
Penney, D. 58, 61, 112, 114, 257
Pennington, T.R. 200
Peshkin, A. 117
Peterson, A.R. 311
Peterson, D.W. 48
Peterson, P.L. 15, 147, 150, 182
Phillips, D. 13
Phillips, S.E. 198
Physical Best 259
Piaget, J. 135
Piéron, M. 3, 12
Pinheiro, V. 16
Pinkham, K.M. 15, 52, 57, 60, 267, 300
Pissanos, B.W. 15, 111, 298, 301, 303-307
Placek, J. 5, 12, 15, 16, 18, 58, 60, 90, 93, 111, 147, 155, 166, 257-258, 260, 264-265, 267, 277, 281, 285-286, 300, 330
Plakc, B.S. 197
Podgursky, M. 47
Poetter, T.S. 46, 47, 48
Politino, V. 90
Polman, J.L. 112, 114
Poole, J. 200
Portman, P. 15, 153, 267, 300
Posner, M.I. 170
Powell, K.E. 213
Prawat, R.S. 297-298, 303
Pribram, K.L. 135
Puckett, K. 251

R

Ramírez, T. 167
Randall, L. 286
Ratliffe, T.A. 15, 267, 300, 325
Raudensky, J. 288
Rauschenbach, J. 304
Raymond, C. 155
Raymond, M.R. 197-198
Raynes, M. 95
Reckase, M.D. 197
Reed, C.J. 49, 50
Reich, W. 69
Reid, G. 99-100
Reif, G. 167
Rejeski, W. 178
Renyi, J. 256
Resnick, L.B. 297
Rice, P.L. 153
Richardson, V. 120, 147, 277
Richmond, M. 259
Rickard, L. 169, 178, 181
Riddoch, C. 209-210

Rife, F. 12, 90, 93
Rimmer, J.H. 90
Rink, J. 5, 12, 16, 18, 19, 58, 84, 87-88, 96, 97, 99, 152, 167-171, 174, 176-181, 188, 232, 237, 258, 278, 298
Rizzo, T.L. 93, 95
Roberts, D.A. 112, 114
Roberts, G.C. 116, 150, 154, 157, 158, 176
Robinson, N.M. 92
Roby, J. 20,
Rocchini, A.P. 210
Rogers-Wallgren, J.L. 96
Rogoff, B. 296, 303
Rohnke, K. 262
Rolider, A. 13,
Romance, T.J. 90, 94, 261
Romanow, S.K.E. 90
Romar, J.E. 117, 118, 152, 157, 277
Rønholt, H. 117
Rose, B. 90
Rose, L. 47, 48, 51, 53
Rosenberg, D. 117, 119, 152, 157
Rosenshine, B. 34, 165-167, 173
Ross, D. 98
Ross, J. 17
Ross, J.G. 216
Rossman, G.B. 37
Rothman, R. 188
Rovegno, I. 4, 7, 15, 59, 61, 117, 155, 237, 277, 283, 285, 288, 296-306
Rowan, B. 111, 116
Rowland, C. 51
Rowland, R.S. 112, 196
Rukavina, P.B. 19, 159
Rumelhart, D.E. 7, 302
Rutter, R.A. 116, 119,
Ryan, K. 318
Ryan, R.M. 157
Ryan, S. 59

S

Sabo, D.F. 76
Sacks, S.R. 311
Saffici, C. 12, 58
Safrit, M.J. 191, 197
Sallis, J. F. 12, 19, 20, 37, 152, 153, 208-210, 212-217, 219
Salter, W.B. 13
Sanders, S. 152, 153
Sanders, S.W. 112, 196
Sanders, W. 275
Sanholtz, J.H. 43, 52, 53
Sarkin, J.A. 212
Satina, B. 19, 53, 116, 121
Schalock, M.D. 285
Schempp, P.G. 15, 33, 57, 59, 283, 298-299, 303-304
Schevrich, J.J. 46
Schiemer, S. 196
Schnorr, R.F. 92
Schoemaker, M.M. 90
Schön, D.A. 251, 277, 280, 296
Schrag, F. 111
Schubert, W.H. 109, 118

Schuldheisz, J.M. 36
Schwager, S. 59, 60, 317-320, 322-323
Scranton, S. 75, 78
Seaman, J.A. 90
Searle, M.S. 251
Sebren, A. 280, 298
Semmel, M.J. 92
Serrien, D. 170-171, 176
Shabazz, B. 251
Sharpe, T. 16, 59, 60, 61, 235, 298
Shea, J.B. 99
Shephard, R.J. 209, 213-214
Sherman M.A. 16, 298
Sherrill, C. 83, 84, 89, 90, 91, 95, 96, 98
Shilling, C. 70
Shilling, T. 251
Short, F.X. 90, 91
Short, P.M. 47, 50
Shuell, T.J. 133, 135, 136, 297, 330
Shulman, L. 13, 17, 18, 148, 151, 277, 282, 284, 287-289, 295, 299
Shultz, B. 96
Shultz, J. 121
Shute, S. 12, 90, 93
Siedentop, D. 12, 13, 14, 33, 57, 58, 59, 73, 79, 94, 119, 121, 123, 157, 217, 228-229, 233-234, 238, 258, 277-278, 282, 304
Silliman, L.M. 96,
Silverman, S. 6, 11, 12, 13, 14, 17, 28, 29, 31, 32, 33, 34, 35, 36, 45, 47, 59, 91, 93, 117, 149, 151, 152, 153, 154, 156, 167-168, 171, 174-175, 178, 229, 285, 287
Simon, H. 16,
Simons-Morton, B. 209-210, 212-213, 215
Sinclair, G.D. 152, 153
Siskin, L.S. 266
Sitzman, T. 111, 123, 298, 302
Sizer, T.R. 136, 243
Skaggs, S. 98
Skelton, C. 73, 76
Skinner, B.F. 99
Skonie, R. 11
Skrla, L. 43
Slavin, R.E. 92, 94
Slininger, D. 90
Smith, G.A. 116, 119
Smith, J.K. 194, 196
Smith, M.D. 232
Smith, S.L. 90
Smyth, D.M. 15, 52, 57, 59, 60, 61, 317, 319
Smyth, M.M. 90
Snell, M.E. 95
Soar, R. 171-172
Soar, R.M. 171-172
Sokolowski, M. 90
Solmon, M. 5, 15, 16, 17, 19, 28, 35, 53, 57, 59, 61, 111, 116, 118, 121, 148, 151, 152, 153, 154, 155, 156, 157, 159, 170, 181, 261, 298, 317-319, 322

Spackman, L. 231
Sparkes, A.C. 15, 57, 59, 279, 281, 304
Spellman, C.R. 96
Spindt, G.B. 259-260
Spirduso W.W. 28, 29, 31, 32, 33, 36
Spiro, R.J. 302
Sprigings, E. 176
Stader, D.L. 48, 50
Stainback, S. 85, 93
Stainback, W. 85, 93
Stallings, J. 165
Stanley, J.C. 35, 281
Staub, D. 92
Stevens, R. 166-167, 173
Stevens, T. 209
Stevens-Smith, D.A. 315, 323, 325
Stewart, C.C. 90
Stiehl, J. 113, 123, 176, 242, 246-251
Stiggins, R.J. 194, 200
Stinson, S.W. 119
Stockin-Davidson, K. *See* Davidson, K.S.
Stone, E.J. 213
Strean, W.B. 285
Stroot, S. 4, 15, 16, 58, 59, 60, 61, 285, 317-320, 322-325
Subramaniam, P.R. 6, 17, 149, 151, 152, 153, 154
Sullivan, D. 99
Swanson, L. 18, 116, 121, 149
Sweeting, T. 18, 170, 177
Swinnen, S. 170-171, 176

T

Taggert, A.C. 217, 258
Taggert, G.L. 191
Taggert, J. 217
Talbert, J.E. 43, 111, 116
Tan, S. 283, 298
Tannehill, D. 57, 58, 59, 117, 119, 152, 157, 324
Tanner, D. 256, 265
Tashakkori, A. 251
Taylor, F. 133, 135
Taylor, J. 96, 229
Taylor, J.L. 12
Taylor, K. 174
Taylor, W.C. 210
Temple, V.A. 90, 93
Templeton, J. 188
Templin, T. 14, 15, 57, 59, 60, 61, 286
Theberge, N. 71
Thomas, G. 180
Thomas, J.R. 29, 34, 36, 97, 283
Thompson, L.P. 90
Thorpe, J. 99
Thorpe, R.A. 177, 230-232, 235
Tichenor, S. 50
Tinning, R. 58, 229, 266-267, 277-278, 282-284, 286
Tjeerdsma, B.L. 152, 288, 300
Toby, C. 178

Tom, A.R. 244, 251
Tomlinson, C.A. 137
Tousignant, M. 11, 12, 13, 14, 90, 157, 168, 229
Travers, R.M.W. 147
Treanor, L. 113
Treasure, D.C. 116
Tremino, F. 155
Trilling, B. 44, 45, 50, 54
Troisi, A. 263
Trudeau, F. 213
Tsangaridou, N. 277-278, 280, 285-286, 302, 304
Turner, A.P. 19, 111, 232, 299, 301
Twardy, B.M. 12, 14, 16
Tyack, D. 131
Tyler, R.W. 139
Tymeson, G.T. 90
Tynan, D. 96
Tyson, L. *See* Martin, L.T.

U

Umney, M. 90
United States Department of Health and Human Services (USDHHS) 207, 210, 213, 216
Unruh, A. 311
Usnick, V. 263

V

Valenzuela, A. 290
Vallerand, R.J. 157
van der Mars, H. 13, 36, 90, 93, 95, 97, 179
Van Houten, R. 13
Van Maanen, J. 313-314
Van Oteghen, S.L. 260
Vars, G.F. 256
Veal, M.L. 17
Veenman, S. 315
Vertinsky, P. 75, 79-80
Vickers, J.N. 258
Vincent, S.D. 259, 287
Visher, M.G. 48, 49, 50
Vlaisavljevic, N. 298
Vogler, W. 61, 83, 90, 93, 94, 95, 96, 97, 99
Von Glasersfeld, E. 151

W

Wade, M.G. 329
Walberg, H.J. 92, 241
Walker, H.M. 96, 97
Walkley, J.W. 90, 93
Walkwitz, E. 16
Walsh, D. 250-251
Walter, H.J. 214
Wang, M.C. 92
Ward, B. 259
Ward, P. 43, 46, 50, 57, 58, 59, 60, 61, 200, 285, 303-304
Watkinson, E.J. 90, 93
Weber, R.C. 99
Webster, G.E. 90, 94
Wehlage, G.G. 116, 119

Weinberg, H. 259
Weiner, L. 241, 287, 290
Weiss, M.R. 98, 157
Weiss, S. 51, 54, 176, 261
Welk, G.J. 213, 218, 259
Wentzel, K. 118, 119
Werner, P. 12, 168-170, 174, 180-181, 232, 257, 263, 265-266, 298
Whilden, P. 11
Whipple, C. 4, 61
White, C.J. 117
Whitehead, A.N. 256
Whittaker, A. 263
Wiegand, R. 13, 113
Wigfield, A. 156-157
Wiggins, G. 132, 134, 142
Wiggins, G.P. 193
Wilkerson, S. 181
Williams, A. 75, 78-79
Williams, J. 316, 318, 320-323
Williamson, K.M. 316, 318, 320-323
Williamson, L. 18
Williamson, T. 230
Wilmore, J.H. 210
Wilson, E.O. 135, 141
Wilson, S. 276, 282
Wineburg, S. 265-266
Winnick, J. 90, 91, 98
Winther, K. 97
Wirt, J. 48, 49, 53, 56
Wiseman, T. 83
Wittrock, M.C. 15, 147, 150, 154, 173
Wood, K. 259
Wood, T. 61, 190, 191, 197, 200
Woods, A.M. 6, 257, 263, 265, 297, 302, 304
Woods, L.A. 44
Woods, M. 300, 304
Worthy, T. 15, 111, 118, 317-319, 322
Wright, J. 19, 75, 77, 229, 282
Wright, P.M. 251
Wright, R. 135
Wright, R.G. 95
Wright, S.C. 300, 319-320, 322-323

X

Xiang, P. 17, 18, 158

Y

Yarger, S.J. 311
Yerg, B.J. 12, 14, 16, 178
Yoder, J. 264
Young, J. 270

Z

Zakrajsek, D. 12, 119, 302
Zeichner, K. 280, 289, 316
Zeman, R. 90, 93
Zhu, W. 16, 17, 298, 302
Zimbardo, P.G. 153
Zimny, S.T. 99
Zuckerman, J. 176

SUBJECT INDEX

Note: The italicized *f* and *t* following page numbers refer to figures and table, respectively.

A

ability 157-158
Academic-Learning Time-Physical Education (ALT-PE) 12, 13, 94, 168
academic achievement 214, 275
access 74
   equal 75
   information 47
accommodation 44, 45
accordion principle 249
accountability 3, 46, 51, 58, 60-61, 62, 145, 172, 194, 235, 239
accretion 302 303
achievement 10, 17, 18. *See also* academic achievement; motor skill achievement; skill acquisition; student achievement
achievement goal theory 158-159
action research 278
adapted physical education pedagogy 83
administrator's
   beliefs 118
   control 133
   support 118, 317
adolescents 212
adventure education 262
advocacy 78, 80
affective domain 235, 242. *See also* student attitude
agency 113
agents 151
aggressive behavior 116, 229
American Alliance for Health, Physical Education, Recreation and Dance (AAHPERD) 28, 288
American Master Teacher Program 325
antisexist pedagogy 75
applied behavior analysis 13, 33, 35
analysis tools 19
androgynous 74
appropriate level of difficulty 168. *See also* practice appropriate; task difficulty
assessment. *See also* evaluation; grading; testing
   alternative 189-193
   as learning goal 142
   authentic 188, 189-193
   for children with disabilities 85, 86, 88-91

formative 238
high-stakes 187, 193
in teaching personal and social responsibility 248-249
performance 189-193, 198, 200
performance-based 193
personal 141
physical activity 218-219
physical fitness 208, 217-218
staff development opportunities 61
student 59, 60, 62, 112, 130, 131,139, 235.
systems 194
teachers' beliefs about 17
validity and reliability 196-198, 201
assessment-based education 187
assimilation 44, 45, 53
athletic programs 217
at-risk kids 242
attitude 149, 159, 244. *See also* student attitude; teacher attitude
attribution theory 182
avoidance behaviors 149
avoiding challenge 158
autonomy 157
awareness strategies 247-248
awareness talk 246

B

back-to-basics movement 256
backward design 140
barriers to change 116
baseline data 36
Basic Stuff series 259
Beginning Teacher Evaluation Study (BTES) 13
beginning teacher standards 288
behavioral
   paradigm 141
   theory 133-135
behavioral interventions 97
behavior modification 36, 98
behavior problems 47
beliefs 117-118, 244. *See also* student beliefs; teacher beliefs
benchmarks 142, 189, 189*f*, 193, 196
biography 14, 15, 36, 281, 296
biological
   characteristics 69
   differences 68
biomechanics 260
block approach 228
block scheduling 48

bone health 210
Boston Conference of 1889 228
boy's experiences in sport 76
Brockport Physical Fitness Test 91
Brown versus Board of Education (Topeka, KS) 84
bureaucracy 133-134
busy, happy, and good 286

C

cardiovascular fitness 213. *See also* fitness
career academies 47
case-based teaching 277, 285
case study 36, 300
change agent 278
charter schools 47
character development 242, 261
checks for understanding 159, 177
Cheffers Adaptation of Flanders Interaction Analysis System (CAFIAS) 12
Child and Adolescent Trial for Cardiovascular health (CATCH) 212-213, 214
class
   climate 117, 120, 171
   control 118, 156, 172
   meetings 195
   size 10, 58, 59, 111, 195, 196, 201, 244, 250, 319
coaching 60, 319-320
coaching clubs 250
coeducation 75
cognition 149-150
cognitive
   approach 154
   functioning 133
   mapping techniques 16
   mediation 148, 181, 330
   process 156, 301
   processing 170
   psychology 16
   theory 135
   understanding 299
cohorts 289, 301
collaboration 49, 50, 61, 303-304, 326
colleagues 60, 61
communicating student learning 194-195, 201
community 51, 62, 199, 242
   agencies 241
   mapping 285
competence 157, 158, 168
   pedagogical 281

competence *(continued)*
    perceived 158, 181
competence motivation theory 153,
    157
competent performance 231
competition 159, 161, 220, 229, 235,
    236
complexity
    curricular 256-257.
    of context 43, 115
    of interactions 117-118
    of learning 143
    of motivation 159
    of professional practice 296
    of relationships 15, 21
    of research 17, 151
    of schools 277, 295, 302
    of sport 168
    of teaching setting 313
    physical education 329
    reducing level of task 169, 179
computerized indices 38. *See also*
    electronic retrieval systems
conceptual framework 138
conceptual understanding 19
conflict resolution 54, 116
connectedness 113, 122-123
connections between teaching and
    learning 20
consilence 136, 141
consolidation stage 312*f*, 312-313
constructivist
    approach 18, 21, 151
    oriented teaching 303
    theories 297-298, 303-304
content
    development 99, 130, 152, 167
    dissatisfaction with 152
    innovation orientation 313-314
    knowledge 267, 282, 289. *See also*
        subject matter
    maps 284
    mastery 229
    meaningful 131
    ownership 111
    presenting more holistically 19
    relevant 229-230
    scope 100
    specific feedback 299
    standards. *See* national standards
context
    and skill learning 137-138
    complexity of 43, 115
    cultural 50, 137
    disciplinary 140
    educational 124, 134
    intellectual 277
    of practice 99
    political 50
    social 9, 121, 137, 321-322
    specific 19, 166, 314
contextual factors 43, 111, 113, 148,
    152
contrasting groups method 197

cooperating teachers 12, 280, 285-
    286, 324
cooperation 120, 234, 260-261
cooperative ethic 296
cooperative learning 92, 94, 261
coordinated school health program
    207
correlational research design 12
correlation and prediction 33, 35
counseling time 246, 247
creative thinking 120, 303
cross-age teaching 250
criterion-referenced 160, 193, 194
critical approach to pedagogy 280,
    300
critical theory 33, 37
critical thinking 19, 50, 112, 303
cues 12, 176-177, 183
cultural
    diversity 44, 56. *See also* diversity
    messages 79
    norms 304
    phenomena 37
    pluralism 281
    templates 301
    understanding 54
curricular
    approach 300, 305-307
    coherence 121-124
    complexity 256-257
    decision making 114,119, 183
    generic models 11
    goals in teaching personal and
        social responsibility 243-246
    models 123, 230, 238, 242-246,
        249, 257-264
    plans 120
    purpose 252
    relevance 122, 256
    scope and sequence 109, 121, 122,
        124
    worth 124
curriculum
    aligning 46, 62, 196
    as a factory 110, 133
    as a garden 110
    as a journey 110
    as a subarea of physical education
        pedagogy 4
    concept driven 257
    content 152, 160, 219.
    definition 109
    design 134, 139. *See also* instruc-
        tional design; program design
        developers 268
    evolving 9-11
    functional 68, 77
    hidden 19, 76-78
    implementation 4
    mapping 196
    metaphors 110,124
    multiactivity 79, 228-230, 237,
        258
    philosophy 124

scripts 301
selection 4
standards-based 193
custodial orientation 286, 313-314
cutoff score 193, 197-198, 200

D

daily physical education 57
decision making 5 ,16, 231. *See also*
    student decisions; teacher deci-
    sions
    group 248
    process 156
decontextualized lessons 232
demonstrations 177
descriptive-analytic research 11
descriptions
    of teachers and classes 12
    research 12, 33, 34
developmentally appropriate 230, 234
developmental stages of teaching
    312*f*, 312-313
Dewey, John 134-135
didactics 277
difficulty level 13
direct instruction 182-183
disabilities
    mild 84, 92-93
    severe 84, 92-95
disability
    children with 84-85
    diverse nature of 89
disengagement 111, 230
dispositions 14, 150, 275, 287, 288,
    290, 307
diverse
    nature of physical education 329
    roles 234
    settings 234, 315
diversity
    cultural 44, 56
    schools 43. *See also* school
    students 45, 49, 110, 113, 198. *See*
        also students'
dropout rates 52
drug use 56
due process 87, 88*t*

E

early research efforts 9-11
eating disorders 217
ecological integration value orienta-
    tion 113-114
educaring 55
educational
    beliefs 111
    environment 114, 121
    model 133
    program design 138-140, 145
    philosophy 109
    reform 3, 46, 49, 50, 58, 61, 62,
        135-136, 188, 193, 194, 200,
        276
    research 147

standards movement 129
Educational Resources Information Clearing House (ERIC) 28
Education for Handicapped Children Act (PL 94-142) 85
Education Index 28
education through the physical 10, 228
effort 158, 159.
ego-oriented goal perspective 158-159
electronic retrieval systems 28. *See also* computerized indices
empowering girls 75
empowering sport 236, 237
empowerment 37, 113, 235, 251
    of students 243, 247, 248, 300
    of teachers 314
energy expenditure 12
engaged time. *See* student engaged time; time engaged
engagement. *See* student engagement
enjoyment 157, 219, 261-262. *See also* student enjoyment
enthusiasm 13, 233
equity 75, 79, 113-114, 178, 301
    approach 19
equality of opportunity 45, 74
ethical behavior 260-261
ethnicity 19, 48, 79
ethnic
    group 119
    heritage 117
    identity 69
ethnography-like interpretive research 33, 36
evaluation 50, 87, 167, 190. *See also* assessment; grading; testing
examinee centered methods 197
expectancy value theory 156
expectations 115, 117, 118, 119
experimental and quasi-experimental research 33, 35
expert-novice studies 16, 302
expert teachers 298
extended-day programs 250, 252
external interdisciplinary curriculum 258t, 263-264, 265, 268. *See also* interdisciplinary curriculum

F

facts 137
families 54-56, 116-117, 209, 217, 221
Faculty Center for Learning and Teaching 323
fair play 236
father's participation 48
feminist
    theoretical perspectives 19
    liberal 74
    radical 74
femininity 67, 71, 75, 77
    heterosexual 70
femininities 67-72
    biological characteristics 69
    social construction of 68, 69

field experiences 285-287, 290, 315-316
field systems analysis 16
fitness 259-260
    programs 10
    tests 132
    units 296
FitnessGRAM 91, 209
FITT principle 219
flexibility 210
frequency counts 17

G

games 232
gamelike conditions 169
games ethic 71
gender 67-80
    appropriate activities 77
    discrimination 19
    equality 79
    fluidity 69
    groups based on 19
    inequity 72, 75
    issues 67
    neutral 68
    power relationships 9
    social construction of 68, 70, 72, 79, 80
    student attitude and 153; *See also* student attitude
gendered
    body 69-70
    history 68
    identities 69, 79
girls'
    participation in physical activity 19
    satisfaction 236
goal congruence 314
goals and objectives 86, 139, 173t, 288
goals and outcomes 137
goal-setting 46
Good Behavior Game 97
grading 194, 218, 321. *See also* assessment; evaluation; testing
grounded theory 36
group
    challenges 114
    meeting 246-247
gymnastics 228

H

healthy lifestyle 20, 121, 222
Healthy People 2000 210, 213, 219
Healthy People 2010 210, 211f, 215, 222
health-related
    physical activity interventions 213-214
    physical education 208, 210, 220, 223
    physical fitness 209
Hellison Model 305. *See also* Teaching Personal and Social Responsibility

heredity 218
hidden curriculum 19, 76-78
higher level thinking 190f
higher standards 46
high-inference scales 12
high-intensity exercise 216
high school drop out 251
holistic development 243
home schooling 47
homophobia 76
hypothesis 32

I

inclusion 83, 86-87, 92-96. *See also* least restrictive environment; mainstreaming
ideologies 75
implementing change 7
incentive systems 46
individual
    decision making 248
    development 10
    differences 166
    improvement 158
    interpretations 154
Individual Education Program (IEP) 84, 85, 88t
Individual Family Service Plan (IFSP) 86
individualized instruction 85, 94, 116, 321
Individuals with Disabilities Education Act (IDEA, PL 105-17) 85-87, 95, 100
Individual Transition Plan (ITP) 86
induction program 323
induction phase 311, 315-324, 326
inferior players 72
influences
    classroom 14
    cultural 9, 10, 114
    economic 10, 11
    political 9, 10, 11
    social 9, 10, 11, 114
    student 14
information processing 176
inform practice 330
inquiry approach to teaching 280
instruction 139. *See also* teaching
    assessment-drive 193-194
    quality 20
instructional. *See also* curriculum; teaching
    design 142; *See also* curriculum design; program design
    effectiveness. *See* teaching effectiveness
    goals 317. *See also* curriculum goals
    methods. *See* teaching methods
    strategies. *See* teaching methods
    time 62, 118, 229. *See also* student engaged time; student engagement; time engaged
    units 229

integrated curriculum 255-257, 268
intelligent performance 230, 231
interactive decisions 167
interdisciplinary curriculum 255, 256-257, 258t, 268. *See also* external interdisciplinary curriculum; internal interdisciplinary curriculum
interdisciplinary understanding 136
interest 159. *See also* student interest
internal interdisciplinary curriculum 257-263, 258t, 268; *See also* interdisciplinary curriculum
Internet resources 28, 327
interpretive research 33, 36; *See also* qualitative research
intervention programs to change teacher behavior 15
interrater reliability 196
interviews 36
intrinsic reward system 113
intrinsic value 157
invasion games 231, 232

J

Journal of Physical Education, Recreation and Dance (JOPERD) 259, 261
Journal of Teaching in Physical Education 232
journals 324-325, 327
journal writing 277, 289

K

knowledge base 11
    for professional practice 7
knowledge. *See also* student knowledge; teacher knowledge
    base 112
    basic 116
    body of 3, 11, 330
    differentiated 298
    domain-specific 18
    fitness 216-217
    for practice 276-277
    in practice 277
    isolation and fragmentation of 265
    progressions for 298-299
    of most worth 124
    of practice 277-278
    prior 159, 299-303, 307
    relational 303
    resist 17
    scientific 11
    structures 16

L

leadership 113, 120, 234, 247
learner. *See also* student; students
    attention 170
    characteristics 169
learning
    environment 151, 155, 167, 172, 224
    experiences 170
    process value orientation 111-112
    objectives 317

outcomes 14, 131, 134, 137, 140, 143, 145, 229, 285
    targets 189, 200
least restrictive environment 86-87, 88t, 88-89, 91, 95, 100. *See also* inclusion; mainstreaming
lesson
    plans 16
    number 233, 235
life history approach 15
life story 36
lifetime activities 213
listening to students 160, 161
list server 28
locus of control 182

M

magnet schools 47
mainstreaming 84, 92-93, 319. *See also* inclusion; least restrictive environment
management
    classroom 96, 171, 183, 317-318, 321, 322
    concerns 320-321, 326
    instructional setting 121
    system 235, 239
managerial goals 317
marginalization
    of girls 75, 76
    of physical education 58, 60-61, 265, 318-319
masculinity 67, 76, 77
masculinities 67-72
    biological characteristics 68, 69
    characteristics of 71
    dominant form 70, 72, 76
    hegemonic 72, 73, 79, 80
    social construction of 68, 69
maturity stage 312f, 313
mediating factor 151
mental processes 15, 135
mentoring 322-324, 327
Middle School Physical activity and Nutrition (M-SPAN) 212-213, 215
Mills versus Washington, D.C. 84
minimal competency testing 193
missionary ideals 315
modeling 98, 176
modifications and adaptations 84, 244
monitoring student progress 121, 172
moral development 261
mothers' educational levels 55
motivation 150, 156-159, 171-172
    extrinsic 157
    intrinsic 157
motivational climate 304
motor plan 171
motor skill
    achievement 12. *See also* achievement; student achievement
    acquisition 10, 180. *See also* skill acquisition
    learning 10, 11
movement approach 11, 301

movement concepts and principles 259-260
movement education. *See* movement approach
multidisciplinary approach to providing services to individuals with disabilities 86
multidisciplinary curriculum 256, 268
muscular strength 210

N

National Association for Sport and Physical Education 3, 28, 111, 129, 132, 134, 140-141, 187, 258-259, 288
National Commission on Teaching for America's Future 275
National Consortium for Physical Education and Recreation for Individuals with Disabilities 89
National Council for the Accreditation of Teacher Education (NCATE) 282, 288
national standards 11, 58, 132-133, 140-141, 141f, 142, 187-189, 196, 200, 259-262, 265-267
naturalistic view 70
net games 231
networking 313, 324, 325-326, 327
norm-referenced 161, 194
novice teachers 298

O

obese children 45
obesity 210
objectives
    based approach 134, 139-140
    learning 317
observation. *See also* systematic observation
    intense 37
    of teacher student behavior 34
    skill 16
    of teacher 315
observation instruments 12
obstacles 15
occupational socialization 15, 313-314
Olympic games 138, 227
on-site assistance 312
organizational skills 171
organizing centers 257
osteoporosis 210
OSU Teacher Behavior Instrument 12

P

parents
    educating 199
    engaging 48
    expectations 118
    involvement 48-49, 61, 321
    partnership with 117
    perceptions 118
    support 318
patriarchal
    consciousness 19

oppression 19
practices 75
partnerships 49, 62, 117
PE Central 28, 259, 325
pedagogical content knowledge 267, 282, 283-285, 299
pedagogical knowledge 282, 283-285, 297
peer 94
    coach 234, 235
    group beliefs 119
PELINKS4U 259, 325
Pennsylvania Association for Retarded Citizens (PARC) 84
performance-based standards 287-288
performance cutoffs 192
performance standards 192, 196-198
persistence 158
personal
    confidence 262
    improvement 159, 161
    knowledge 296
    meaning 37, 149, 159
    responsibility 113, 234
personal and social development 242-243
personal and social-moral decisions 242-243
personal and social responsibility 236. *See also* teaching personal and social responsibility
perspective of those being studied 36
phenomenology 36, 37
phenomenology-like interpretive research 33, 37
physical
    contact 73
    violence and aggression 73
    well-being 10
physical activity 207, 209, 210, 222-223, 260
    adult 212
    and gender 212
    health benefits of 19
    in physical education 212-213, 214, 215, 216
    in teaching personal and social responsibility 243
    intensity 215-216
    moderate to vigorous 20, 212, 215, 223
    motivation to engage in 213
    out-of school 209, 214
    promotion 222, 223
    versus fitness 215
physical education
    benign neglect of 278
    change 17
    context 15
    daily 57
    early programs 228
    history of 10
    marginalization of 58, 60-61, 265, 318-319
    objectives 216, 223

participation in 119
program design 127 *See also* curricular; curriculum
programs 58, 217
requirements 57-58
research in 29
single-sex 75
status of 57-59, 318-319
theoretical bases 30
value of 159
physical education pedagogy 4-5, 329. *See also* sport pedagogy
    history of 9
    research specialists 11
    specialization of field 4, 329
physical educators'. *See also* teacher; teachers'
    beliefs 118
    coaching responsibilities 60
    elementary 196
    isolation 69
    job satisfaction 60
    work 57
    workload 58
    workplace 60
physical fitness 207, 208, 209, 210
    textbooks 208-209, 215
physically active lifestyle 166
Piaget 135
placheck 218
planning 91, 167
Plato 255
portfolios 61
postactive decisions 167
posttest 35
poverty 44, 51, 241, 242, 313
power
    inequities 37, 38
    relationships 9
    sharing of 246
practical knowledge 284, 296
practice
    appropriate 180; *See also* appropriate level of difficulty; task difficulty
    design 183
    focused 179
    level of 169
    quality of 168, 170, 183
    task 10
    transfer of 168
Praxis tests 281-281
preactive decision 167
presage variable 10
preservice
    teachers 265, 298-299, 300, 301, 302, 303, 311
    training 89, 316. *See also* teacher training
pretest 35
principal. *See* administrator's
prior experience 151, 159, 299-300, 307, 326
prior knowledge 159, 299-303, 307
problem-focused core curriculum 256

problem solving 19, 113, 303-305
    and discovery 19
    teachers 277, 300
process
    criteria 194
    data 35
    variable 13, 14
process-product
    paradigm 148, 151
    research 17, 20, 168, 182
    research programs 11, 13, 14, 165, 287
product
    criteria 194
    variable 10
professional
    associations 28. *See also* American Alliance for Health, Physical Education, Recreation and Dance; National Association for Sport and Physical Education
    judgment 329
    practice 5
professional development schools (PDS) 49, 61
program
    design 130. *See also* curriculum design; instructional design
    development 130
programmatic architecture 133
progress criteria 194
progressions
    in teaching personal and social responsibility 243-246
    skill 100, 169, 174, 301
    teaching 230
progressive era 135, 228
ProQuest 28
Project SPARK (Sports, Play, and Active recreation for Kids) 37, 214-215, 220-221
prospective teachers' skills 283
public health objectives 210
pupil-teacher ratios 52

Q

qualitative research 33, 34*f*, 36-38
Qualitative Measures of Teaching Performance Scale (QMTPS) 12, 174, 175*f*
Quality of Work Life (QWL) 314-315, 315*t*, 326
quasi-experimental research. *See* experimental and quasi-experimental research
quantitative
    data 11
    research 33-36, 34*f*
    measure 13

R

race 9
racism 241, 242
random assignment 35
reality shock 315-316, 320, 326

reciprocal coaching 248
reflection time 247, 248, 249
reflective
    inquiry 286
    of personal and social behavior
        113, 242
    orientation 20
    practitioner 277
    process 77
relationships
    among teaching aspects 307
    among teaching, curriculum, and
        teacher education 329
    in ecological integration 114
    in research 12, 17
renewal stage 312f, 313
reporting formats 195
research
    as situation specific 5
    career 330
    collaborative 20
    conceptual 20
    database 6
    efforts 10
    focused program 30
    formal and informal 30
    integrated approach to 20
    interpretation 6, 30
    methods 33-38, 34f
    models 32
    papers 31. *See also* research reports
    paradigms 32, 33
    problem 32
    programmatic 34
    progress 12-14
    quality 5
    question 5, 30, 32-33
    reading 32
    replication 6
    reports 28, 38. *See also* research
        papers
    reviews 28, 38
    theory in 11, 20
    trade-offs 6
    variables 6. *See also* process vari-
        able; product variable; quant-
        tative measure
    why do 29
research-based actions 20
researchers 30
researchers' caveats 5
resources allocations 118
responsibility. *See also* personal re-
        sponsibility; teaching personal
        and social responsibility
    for learning 303
    shared 236
    student 246
    teaching 243
responsible personal and social be-
        havior 260-261. *See also* XXXXX\
restructuring 302-303
role conflict 319-320, 326
role innovation orientation 313-314
roll out the ball 238

rubric 191, 248-249; *See also* scoring
        guide
rules and routines 317

S

scaffolding 142
schedule patterns 10
school
    academic mission 121
    budgets 60
    change 275
    choice 46
    climate 116
    community 54
    context 15, 57, 296, 299, 302,
        303, 305, 316, 317
    culture 15, 52, 54, 315t
    discipline 53
    enrollment 51, 53
    environment 14,116, 215, 223, 330
    irrelevance of 265
    norms 304
    overcrowding 53
    resources 53
    schedules 47-48, 60
    size 116
    support 53
    violence 53
school-based leadership 315t
schools
    inequity in 300
    primary function of 16
    urban 53, 287, 316, 320
scoring 191
scoring guide 191-193, 200. *See also*
        rubric
self-actualization value orientation
        112-113
self-control 113, 248
self-determination theory 157
self-efficacy 158
self-management 214, 221, 223
self-monitoring 235
self-reflection 243, 277
self-reports 218
sequencing 176
service-bonded inquiry 251
sex 68; *See also* gender
sexist approaches 301
sex-segregated model 74
showering 216
single-sex physical education 75
single subject research 36
site-based management 60, 116
situated knowledge 296-296
situated theory 303
skill
    acquisition 169-170, 317; *See also*
        achievement; motor skill achieve-
        ment; motor skill acquisition
skill *(continued)*
    competence 236
    fitness 209
    isolated 137
    level 153, 156, 229, 231, 234, 236

mastery 160
    progressions 138, 143. *See also*
        progressions
    related activities 152
    retention 169-170, 230
    tests 59
skillfulness 232
social
    change 283
    class 19, 69, 79
    comparison 153, 158, 160
    controls 116
    development 5
    interactions 260-261, 303, 304, 307
    practice 70
    justice 9, 93, 113-114, 278
    responsibility 301. *See also* Teach-
        ing Personal and Social Re-
        sponsibility
    responsibility and justice value
        orientation 113
    responsibilities 305
    support structure 116
    system 234-235
social and cognitive mediational con-
        structs 18
social cognitive paradigm 148
social-cultural changes 315
socialization process 15, 314
socializing agent 14
sport 10, 227, 228, 238, 301
    authentic 233
    competitive 300
    modern 71
    team 229
sport and society 260
sport education 79, 168, 230, 232-
        236, 238-239, 282
    culminating event 233
    reward system 233
    roles in 235
    seasons in 233
sport for peace 79, 236
sport pedagogy 3, 329. *See also* physi-
        cal education pedagogy
sport person 233
sport psychology 260
Standards 110, 120, 129-133, 143,
        145, 187-188, 193, 196-198. *See
        also* national standards
standards-based program design 130-
        133, 136, 138, 140, 141-144, 145
state mandates 313
steroids 217
Strategies 259
strategy clusters 247-248
strength training 209, 219
striking or fielding games 231
structural barriers 67
student
    achievement 12,14, 56, 134, 146,
        156; *See also* achievement; mo-
        tor skills achievement; motor
        skill acquisition; skill acquisi-
        tion

affiliation 237
as participant 18,21, 234
attention 155
attitude 9, 20, 151-154, 156, 160, 238, 244, 247
backgrounds 116
behaviors 5, 247
beliefs 19
challenge 156
characteristics 166
cognition 154-156
comfort level 119
competence 6, 17
compliance 235
concentration 155
conceptions 18
confidence 262
conflict 121
decisions 112, 237, 238, 247, 304
developmental stages 311
disruptive behavior 116, 119, 172
drug use 56
efficacy 113, 161, 236
effort 21, 151, 156, 161, 170, 181, 247-248
engaged time 13, 14; *See also* instructional time; time engaged
engagement 21, 136, 137f, 138, 156, 169, 171, 181,183, 235
enjoyment 144, 152
entry characteristics 17, 231
expectations 9, 267, 330
feelings 9, 17, 20
goal perspective 17
goals 9, 20
independence 172
influence 6, 177
interest 17, 157, 160
knowledge 20,134. *See also* knowledge
learning 121, 130, 134,137, 138, 142, 286, 302
learning goals 131
mastery 193, 197, 200
meaning 155, 302
mediation 17, 154
motivation 17, 21, 131, 160, 161
misunderstanding 284
off-task behaviors 286
opinions 57
outcomes 148
participation 243
perception of teacher behavior 17
persistence 156
perspectives 5
practice 14. *See also* task practice
prior experience 119, 151, 154, 159, 160
prior knowledge 151, 154, 159, 160
past performance 117
resources 53
responses120, 299, 321
responsibility 137, 242-243, 247. *See also* Teaching Personal and Social Responsibility

responsive behavior 121
role 17
self-direction 248
self-esteem 113, 118, 300
success 6
thinking 17, 154.
thought processes 155
thoughts 9, 17
understanding 131, 173f, 181
use of learning strategies 17
value of physical education 119, 121, 123, 156
variables 12
student-mediating paradigm 13, 17, 21
students
 African-American 52
 alienated 234
 challenging 112, 156
 ethnic minority 56
 Hispanic 52
 lower-income 46, 53
 motivating and engaging 62
 of color 46
 self-directed 247
 special needs 47, 59, 61
 transient 53
student teachers 12, 33, 285-286, 301
student-teacher ratios 47
subdisciplines 257
success 157-159, 167, 181, 183, 220, 234, 237
 rate 169-170, 180, 231
subjective warrant 281
subject matter
 knowledge 282-283, 284. *See also* content knowledge; knowledge; teacher knowledge
 expertise 283
supervisor of play 318
supervisors 287, 290
support for beginning teachers 322-323
survival stage 312, 312f
symbolic properties 73
systematic observation 11, 48, 212-213, 216, 218-219, 325. *See also* observation
System for Observing Fitness Instruction Time (SOFIT) 12
system language 31

T

tacit knowing 277
tacit understanding 296
task-oriented goal perspective 158-159, 160
tactical
 awareness 231
 knowledge 232
 solutions 231
task
 analysis systems 99
 application 235

appropriate 168, 169, 180
 clarity 97
 constraints18
 difficulty 14, 170. *See also* appropriate level of difficulty; practice appropriate
 explicitness 174
 extending 179, 235
 mastery 162
 meaningful 190f
 modeling 98, 176
 presentation 12, 96, 167, 174, 177
 progressions 158, 159, 170, 179, 180
 refining 179, 180, 235
 structure 160
 value 156
taxonomy 142
teacher. *See also* physical educators'; teachers'
 actions 9, 13, 14
 as a subfield of physical education pedagogy 5
 as curriculum creator 278
 as facilitator 18, 21, 137, 237, 245
 as problem solver 277, 278
 as school leader 278
 attention 178
 attitude 9, 281
 behavior 5, 12,13, 15, 148
 behavior research 12
 candidates 281-290
 caring 244, 275
 certification 27, 53
 challenges 235
 characteristics 10, 21
 clarity 173-175
 colleagues 321-322
 communication 173-179
 competence 283, 313
 decisions 17, 21, 278, 303, 314
 demonstration 12
 development 14-15, 49, 276, 303, 305, 306, 311, 312-313
 disillusion 118
 dissatisfaction 305, 307
 dispositions14
 effectiveness 165. *See also* teaching effectiveness
 efficacy 119, 314
 empowerment 61, 314
 evaluation criteria 315
 expectations 119, 154, 172, 305, 316, 320, 322
 expertise 167
 feedback 12-13, 116, 154, 178-179, 183, 304
 feedback from administrators 61, 317, 318, 322, 323. *See also* administrator's
 feelings 9
 goals 9, 304
 improvement of practice 27

inadequacy 315
in-service training 19, 61, 322-323
isolation 61, 267, 317-318, 326
knowledge 15, 267, 276-277, 282-285, 288, 295-307. *See also* knowledge
learning 276-277
perceptions 43
personal traits 10
perspectives 5, 313
problem solving 277, 300
professional development 49, 59, 198-199, 278, 327
professional growth 62, 313
rating 10
reassurance 313
recruitment 15
reflection 325, 327
resiliency 305
rewards 53, 61, 320
role conflict 319-320, 326
roles 278
sense of personal power 305
sensitivity to students 120
shortage 275
skills 287-289
socialization 14, 326
subject matter knowledge 282-283, 284. *See also* content knowledge
success 315, 323
thoughts 9
training 4, 5, 266. *See also* pre-service training; teacher inservice training
transition 315, 323
values 4, 296
variables 12
workload 319-320
workplace 52, 314, 323, 326, 329
work sample 285
teacher education 266-267, 276-285
as a subfield of physical education pedagogy 4-5
conceptual orientations 279
programs 266-267, 275, 279-280, 287-289, 321
research 278, 287-289
teacher educators 9, 286, 290
teachers'; *See also* physical educators'; teacher
beliefs 16, 17, 21, 114, 118-119, 244, 281, 289, 295, 304, 306, 313, 330

caring 243, 288, 289
developmental stages 312-313
educational experiences 14
ethics code 27
influence 6, 117
instructional concerns 321, 326
role models
voices 295
work life 313-314
teacher-student relationship 243
teaching
art of 176
as complex endeavor 15
as a subarea of physical education pedagogy 4, 5
decision making 232
effectiveness 5, 9, 10, 12,130, 329
expertise 16, 176
explicit 182
feedback about 319
methods 5, 121,131-132, 171, 231
comparison of 13
direct 19, 182-183
indirect 19, 171
quality 49
rewards 320
routines 16, 317
situation 6
Teaching Elementary Physical Education 259, 325
Teaching Games for Understanding 19, 230-232, 238, 277
teaching-learning process 281
Teaching Personal and Social Responsibility 242-252
assessment 248-249
cumulative levels 244-245, 245f, 249
five responsibilities 246-247
goals 244f
integrating content in 243, 252
lesson format 246-249
transferring responsibilities in 252
transfer to other settings 243
Team Building Through Physical Challenge 262
team size 237
teamwork 234, 260
technological orientation 20
technology 44, 47, 49, 50, 51, 59, 61, 62
technique 14
test-centered methods 197
testing. *See also* assessment; evaluation; grading
fitness 209, 217

high-stakes 48, 132, 136
mandatory 208
standardized 48, 132
therapeutic exercises 10
therapy 84
think aloud techniques 16
thinking skills 303-304
thought processes 16, 21, 154
time
active 168
allocated 167
constraints 195
engaged 12, 167, 168, 237; *See also* instructional time; student engaged time; student engagement
for change 307
for learning 6
for physic activity and fitness 216-217
limited 321
physically active 20
planning 319
practice 229
Title IX 74-75
traditional sport and fitness emphasis 11
transitions 97, 124
trail and error 30
tuning 302-303
Tyler, John 139

U

uniform 75
unit approach 228
university supervisor 280, 286, 290.

V

value orientations 111-114,124
value profile 114
values-context model 114-121
variability of practice 99
videotape 35
violence 76, 242
voluntary participation 250

W

washout effect 316-317, 326
Web of Science 28
wellness 209
what if questions 31
What's Going on in Gym 12
written tests 59

Y

youth development programs 250

ABOUT THE EDITORS

Stephen J. Silverman has spent over 20 years studying the teaching process in physical education. He is a professor of education and coordinator of a large grant to enhance the training of educational researchers at Teacher College, Columbia University. Steve has made over 125 presentations to national and international groups, has published numerous papers and chapters, and has coauthored 10 books related to teaching and research methods. He is an active fellow in the American Academy of Kinesiology and Physical Education and a fellow in the Research Consortium American Alliance for Health Physical Education, Recreation and Dance (AAHPERD). Steve has served as chair of the AAHPERD Curriculum and Instruction Academy and president of the Research Consortium. In addition, he served as co-chair of the American Academy of Pediatrics expert panel on physical education and physical activity and as a member of National Board of Professional Teaching Standards physical education committee. He is a past editor of the *Journal of Teaching in Physical Education* and currently is serving as editor-in-chief of the *Research Quarterly for Exercise and Sport*. Steve received his doctorate in education from the University of Massachusetts at Amherst. He and his wife, Patricia Moran, reside on the Upper West Side of Manhattan, where Steve enjoys running, aquatic sports, and following politics.

Catherine D. Ennis has established a strong program of research that focuses on curriculum theory and development in physical education with specific applications to urban school settings. Cathy has published over 50 refereed research articles in journals in education and physical education; has made over 100 presentations to international, national, and regional audiences; and has coauthored two books. She is an active fellow in the American Academy of Kinesiology and Physical Education and a fellow in the AAHPERD Research Consortium. Cathy served as chair of the AAHPERD Curriculum and Instruction Academy and, in 2002, received its Honor Award. She also served as chair of the American Educational Research Association (AERA) Special Interest Group on Research on Learning and Instruction in Physical Education. Cathy was the pedagogy section editor for *Research Quarterly for Exercise and Sport* and is a member of the Editorial Board for the *Journal of Teaching in Physical Education; Sport, Education, and Society;* and *The European Physical Education Review.* She received the University of Maryland, College of Health and Human Performance, Muriel Sloan Communitarian Award for her service to public schools in 1997 and the Celebration of Teaching Award from the University of Maryland, Center for Teaching Excellence. A resident of Silver Spring, MD, Cathy enjoys gardening, hiking, and touring the country in her RV.

ABOUT THE CONTRIBUTORS

Peter A. Hastie is an associate professor in the Department of Health and Human Performance at Auburn University. He has been on faculty there since 1994, having previously taught at the University of Queensland and in public schools in Australia. His research interests focus on the analysis of the ecology of physical education settings (interrelationships between teacher instruction, the academic tasks of the class, and the student responses), as well as sport education. Peter has authored or coauthored five books and published over 60 research papers. His most recent book is a secondary methods and curriculum text, *Teaching for Lifetime Physical Activity Through Quality High School Physical Education*, for use in the preparation of high school physical educators. Peter currently serves as a pedagogy section editor for the *Research Quarterly for Exercise and Sport*.

Don Hellison is professor of social work and education at the University of Illinois at Chicago. He is most well known for his work with underserved youth and the development of affective approaches to teaching physical education. He has been the recipient of several awards, including the 2000 Curriculum and Instruction Academy Honor Award, the 1999 National Association of Sport and Physical Education Hall of Fame Award, the 1995 International Olympic Committee President's Prize, and the 1995 University of Illinois Excellence in Teaching Award. He is the author or coauthor of five books, including *Teaching Responsibility Through Physical Activity* (Human Kinetics, 1995 and under revision) and is a past editor of *Quest*.

David Kirk joined Loughborough University in November 1998, where he is professor of physical education and youth sport. He formerly held academic appointments at the University of Queensland and Deakin University, Australia. David studied at the Scottish School of Physical Education and the University of Glasgow and completed a doctorate at Loughborough University. He has made numerous presentations around the world and published widely on school physical education and, more recently, on young people's experiences of community-based sport. He currently is European editor of the *Journal of Curriculum Studies* and a member of the advisory board of *Sport, Education and Society*. In 2001 David was awarded the International Olympic Committee's President's Prize for his contribution to research in physical and sport education.

Leslie T. Lambert has been a teacher, scholar, and educational leader for the past 25 years. Currently, she is professor and director of the Center for Education and Innovation in the Liberal Arts at Roanoke College in Salem, Virginia, where she has also served as chair of the Department of Education, Health and Human Performance since 1993. Leslie was interim vice president of academic affairs in 2001–2002. An experienced physical education teacher, Leslie also was a curriculum and instruction leader in public school central administration. She has worked with numerous boards of education, colleges and universities, and state departments of education across the United States and Canada to implement effective physical education instruction. A frequent contributor at professional conferences and to the professional and scholarly literatures, Leslie specializes in innovation and reform in education, curriculum theory, and assessment.

Amelia M. Lee is Mary E. Baxter Lipscomb Professor and chair of the Department of Kinesiology at Louisiana State University. Her research focuses primarily on teacher and pupil thinking about physical education instruction and learning. Amelia has written widely on these topics and has coauthored four books on physical education for children. For seven years she was an elementary physical education teacher. Two of Amelia's doctoral students have received the AERA SIG Group's Award for Outstanding Dissertations. Amelia is a fellow in the American Academy of Kinesiology and Physical Education and is a past president of the AAHPERD Research Consortium. She was a member of the Task Force for Revision of the NASPE/NCATE Advanced Guidelines for Physical Education Teacher Education. Amelia was editor of *Quest* and served as member of the editorial boards of the *Journal of Teaching in Physical Education* and the *Research Quarterly for Exercise and Sport*.

LeaAnn Tyson Martin is an associate professor of physical education at Western Washington University where she teaches courses in elementary physical education and physical education pedagogy. Her scholarly interests focus on teacher effectiveness. LeaAnn is currently serving on the National Association for Sport and Physical Education (NASPE) Public Relations Committee, has served on the American Academy of Pediatrics physical activity and physical education expert panel, and has assisted in the development of school physical education curriculum in a number of school districts. She has taught elementary physical education and was a physical education–health coordinator for a school district in Texas. LeaAnn is a member of the board of directors of the United States Handball Association and serves as its women's commissioner and as the national schools program coordinator. Besides winning more than 15 national and world championships in handball, she has a second-degree black belt in Goju Ryu karate. LeaAnn lives in Bellingham, Washington with her husband, Joel.

Thomas L. McKenzie is a transplanted Canadian who has been a physical education and health teacher, coach, athletic director, school administrator, director of summer residential programs for obese adolescents, researcher, and teacher educator. Since 1988 Thom has served as a major investigator on four long-term, multidisciplinary school intervention projects funded by the National Institutes of Health—Sports, Play, and Active Recreation for Kids (SPARK), Child and Adolescent Trial for Cardiovascular Health (CATCH), Middle School Physical Activity and Nutrition (M-SPAN), and Trial of Activity for Adolescent Girls (TAAG). His expertise in behavior analysis and program development and assessment is widely recognized, and he is a fellow in the American Academy of Kinesiology and Physical Education, the American College of Sports Medicine, and the AAHPERD Research Consortium. Thom has published extensively in the area of health-related physical education and was the 2002 AAHPERD Alliance Scholar.

Mary O'Sullivan is professor of sport and exercise education and associate dean of the College of Education at Ohio State University. She is a fellow in the American Academy of Kinesiology and Physical Education and serves on the board of governors of the International Association for Physical Education in Higher Education (AIESEP). Mary was a member of the National Association for Sport and Physical Education's task force for the 2002 Advanced NCATE Guidelines for Graduate Programs in Physical Education. A former editor of the *Journal of Teaching in Physical Education*, Mary currently serves on the editorial board of *Sport, Education and Society*. She has published widely on teachers, teaching, and teacher education in physical education. Mary's current research focuses on professional development for urban physical education teachers. She has advised several students who now hold faculty positions in Europe, New Zealand, and North America.

Judith H. Placek is a professor and director of teacher education in the School of Education at the University of Massachusetts Amherst. Judy's interest in integrated curricula began when she developed and taught an integrated curriculum for four years at a Seattle high school. The book based on this experience, *Physical Education in the Secondary Schools: Curricular Alternatives*, coauthored with Hal Lawson, is considered a seminal work on integrating conceptual material into physical education. She has continued her work in this area through articles, presentations, and workshops. Her other scholarly interests include qualitative research, teacher education, and teacher socialization. A widely published author in physical education, Judy was chair of the AAHPERD Curriculum and Instruction Academy and, in 2002, was the AERA Special Interest Group on Research on Learning and Instruction in Physical Education Scholar.

Judith E. Rink is a professor in the Department of Physical Education at the University of South Carolina. She has authored many books, book chapters, and research articles on teaching. Judy has been the coeditor of the *Journal of Teaching in Physical Education* and section editor for pedagogy for the *Research Quarterly for Exercise and Sport*. She was the chairperson of the National Association for Physical Education and Sport committee that developed *Moving Into the Future: National Standards for Physical Education* (NASPE, 1995). Judy also has received the NASPE Hall of Fame Award and the Curriculum and Instruction Academy Honor Award. She has presented many keynote addresses and was the AERA Special Interest Group on Research on Learning and Instruction in Physical Education Scholar. Judy is currently the program director for the South Carolina Physical Education Assessment Program. She enjoys gardening and spending the day on the water in her boat.

Inez Rovegno is a professor in the Department of Kinesiology at the University of Alabama where she teaches undergraduate courses in elementary physical education curriculum and instruction, gymnastics, dance, and graduate courses on curriculum and research on teacher education. Inez has published research in a range of journals including the *Journal of Teaching in Physical Education, Research Quarterly for Exercise and Sport, American Educational Research Journal,* and *Teaching and Teacher Education.* She also published elementary physical education curricular work in the *Journal of Physical Education, Recreation and Dance* and *Teaching Elementary Physical Education.* A recipient of the Exemplary Research Paper Award and the Scholar Award from the AERA Special Interest Group on Research on Learning and Instruction in Physical Education, Inez has a scholarly focus on teachers' and preservice teachers' pedagogical content knowledge and how that knowledge develops, constructivist and situated approaches, creative dance, child-designed games, and basic game tactics. Her hobbies are gardening, sewing, and walking.

Melinda A. Solmon is the Roy Paul Daniels Endowed Professor in the Department of Kinesiology at Louisiana State University, where she serves as the coordinator of the graduate pedagogy concentration. Her research interests focus on factors that influence motivation in a broad range of physical activity settings, with the goal of learning to structure environments that facilitate active engagement. Melinda has served as the NASPE representative for NCATE's New Professional Teacher Standards Development Project, program chair for the AERA Special Interest Group on Research on Learning and Instruction in Physical Education, secretary of the AAHPERD Research Consortium, and section editor for pedagogy for *Research Quarterly for Exercise and Sport.* She is on the editorial board for the *Journal of Teaching in Physical Education.* Melinda enjoys tennis, golf, and running.

Sandra A. Stroot has been at The Ohio State University for the past 16 years, where she is professor of sport and exercise education and the director of the Office of Outreach and Engagement in the College of Education. Sandy's work initially focused on the socialization processes of entry-year teachers in physical education, and her interest in collaborative partnerships has offered extensive involvement in a variety of innovative programs and practices in school settings. She has been examining the effect of various reform efforts in Ohio, including a Peer Assistance and Review (PAR) program in Columbus. One of Sandy's specific interests as is to understand the underlying policies and practices that have allowed programs such as PAR to be successful and to connect the policies and practices with teacher change and student achievement. Sandy has been a member of the *Journal of Teaching in Physical Education* editorial board and is a pedagogy section editor for the *Research Quarterly for Exercise and Sport*.

E. William Vogler is a professor in the School of Kinesiology and Recreation at Illinois State University, where he teaches courses in adapted physical education, has served as graduate program director, and is currently chair of the university Institutional Review Board. Professionally, Bill has served on the editorial board for *Adapted Physical Activity Quarterly* and has been a reviewer for many journals in physical education and education. He has published numerous papers on adapted physical education. Bill has been an officer in a number of professional organizations, served as vice president of the National Consortium for Physical Education and Recreation for Individuals with Disability (NCPERID), and is the current president of the North American Federation of Adapted Physical Activity, a group of international scholars devoted to research in the field of individuals with disabilities. Bill is an accomplished sailor and a masters swimmer.

Christine E. Whipple is an assistant professor at William Paterson University in Wayne, New Jersey. Her research interests focus on knowledge development of novice teachers, and she is expanding this to include long-term investigations at both the elementary and secondary school levels. Christine spent four years teaching physical education in the public schools in Florida before earning a masters degree in sport administration and coaching from the University of Southern Mississippi and a PhD in sport and exercise education from The Ohio State University. An avid fan of the Red Sox, Christine enjoys jogging, biking, and reading.

Terry M. Wood is an associate professor in the Department of Exercise and Sport Science at Oregon State University. Specializing in measurement and evaluation, statistics, and research methods, he earned BA, BPE, and MPE degrees from the University of British Columbia and a PhD from the University of Wisconsin-Madison. Terry coauthored the NASPE *National Content Standards for Physical Education* and is currently involved with developing and implementing physical education content standards and benchmarks in Oregon. He has published manuscripts and presented scholarly papers at the state, national, and international levels, has served as measurement and evaluation section editor for the *Research Quarterly for Exercise and Sport,* and has coauthored two measurement and evaluation textbooks.